All inquiries should be addressed to: Frank Amato Publications,
P.O. Box 82112, Portland, Oregon 97282.

Printed in the U.S.A.

Book Design: Kathy Johnson
Fish Illustrations: J. L. Hart
Illustrations: Jeff Poirier and Todd Hardman
Map Illustration: Tony Amato
Typesetting: Charlie Clifford

ISBN: 0-936608-99-4

Northwest Coastal Fishing Guide

By Doug Olander

Frank Amato Publications
Portland, Oregon

Vancouver Island
Nootka
Nootka Sound
Ucluelet
Port Alberni
Clayoquot Sound
Barkley Sound
Bamfield
Western Strait of Juan De Fuca
Victoria
San Juan Islands
Vancouver
CANADA
UNITED STATES
Neah Bay
Eastern Strait of Juan De Fuca
Northern Puget Sound
Port Angeles
Central Puget Sound
La Push
Seattle
Hood Canal
Southern Puget Sound
WASHINGTON
Westport
Ilwaco
Nehalem Bay
Astoria
Tillamook Bay
Tillamook
Portland
Lower Nestucca/Siletz River
Depoe Bay
Newport
Yaquina Bay
Lower Siuslaw River
Florence
Eugene
Lower Umpqua River/Winchester Bay
Reedsport
OREGON
Coos Bay
Coos Bay
Lower Rogue River
Gold Beach
Lower Chetco River
Medford
Lower Smith River
Crescent City
Lower Klamath River
Trinidad Harbor
Humbolt Bay
Eureka
CALIFORNIA
San Francisco
PACIFIC OCEAN

Table Of Contents

PREFACE

THE UNIQUE, RUGGED COASTLINE OF THE Northwest—for our purposes, northern California, Oregon, Washington and British Columbia—offers a wealth of opportunities for many different angling interests, whether offshore, in protected sounds and straits, around rocky headlands, from jetties and sandy beaches, in bays and lower rivers, and more.

For many years, I fished this coast while wishing for a reliable and comprehensive guide to its diverse sport fisheries. It became obvious that the only way I'd have such a reference would be to write it myself, so in the early 1980s I did. The result was the first *Northwest Coastal Fishing Guide,* the only book of its kind then—and now.

This second edition is almost completely rewritten. And while the first book was hailed as unusually thorough and detailed, this guide is yet much, much more exhaustive. That reflects further development of sportfisheries in the Northwest (in many cases of new fisheries, nonexistent in 1980) and an increase in my own knowledge in and experience of all the things that go into sportfishing in well over 1,000 miles of coastline.

The size of this book also reflects still more area covered, with the inclusion of the three major, lower sounds of Vancouver Island (Nootka, Clayoquot and Barkley).

It is my hope that, within these many pages, any angler who may fish anywhere along the Northwest coast for any species will find all the critical information necessary for success. If this guide serves that purpose, then all the effort that went into it will prove justified.

Acknowledgements

IN SETTING OUT TO PRODUCE A SINGLE, TRULY comprehensive and accurate guide for all Northwest coast fishermen, I recognized the necessity to consult local authorities. To the many experts, listed as consultants below, I owe much gratitude for their candor and the time they spent with me reviewing my copy and perusing charts.

I am also grateful to several individuals for their nontechnical support, particularly my family. As with the writing of the first book, once again they seldom saw me for many months, as I remained tied to the word processor in my office by the umbilical of The Deadline. Yet once again, I received only encouragement rather than complaint from my wife Jackie, daughter Rachel and son Gabriel.

Thanks also: to my capable research assistant, Kirsten M.L. Ritter, who spent over 100 hours on the phone updating the book's "Facilities" listings; to Sissy once again for her company and proofreading; to Todd Hardman for adding new line drawings to those done by Jeff Poirier in the first guide—both extremely talented young artists; to Dave and Jitka for the word processor without which I'd *still* be writing this; and to publisher Frank Amato for his interest in this project and permitting me complete freedom in all decisions.

Consultants

I have fished just about every area described in this guide, some of them many times over the years. But the degree of detail I have offered here would have been impossible without adding the combined knowledge of many of the most experienced, reliable local authorities. These experts hail from all professional areas: guides, charter skippers, biologists, tackle dealers, outdoor writers, lure manufacturers, resort owners and sometimes "just fishermen." If this guide merits commendation, a good part of that belongs to the people below.

San Juan Islands

Tony Floor, Chief of Information for Washington Department of Fisheries in Olympia and tireless angler of the islands; **Jeff Lingbloom**, skipper/owner of Sea King Charters in Bellingham; **Pete Nelsen**, guide on Shaw Island and one of the most highly respected authorities on fishing these waters.

Northern Puget Sound

Mike Chamberlain, outdoor writer, lecturer and owner of Ted's Sport Center in Lynnwood—perhaps no one knows the state's fisheries better; **Russ Orrell**, fisheries biologist in Mt. Vernon and angler extraordinaire in north sound area for 30 years; **George Stevens**, longtime skipper of Northsound Charters in Everett.

Central Puget Sound

Greg Bargmann, fisheries biologist in Seattle specializing in Puget Sound marine recreational fisheries; **Mike Chamberlain**, as above; **Dave Nelson**, owner of Seacrest Boathouse in Elliott Bay for many years.

Southern Puget Sound And Hood Canal

Bruce N. Ferguson in Gig Harbor, co-author of *Flyfishing for Pacific Salmon* and pioneer of light-tackle fly fishing techniques for south sound and Hood Canal salmon and searun cutthroat; **Dick Geist**, fisheries biologist in Olympia and an expert on south sound recreational salmon fisheries; **Frank Haw** of Olympia, co-author of venerable *Saltwater Fishing in Washington*, a lecturer and renowned light-tackle south sound salmon expert; **Dave Hurd** at Tacoma Narrows Marina.

Eastern Strait Of Juan De Fuca

Paul Ingham, "Hi-Catch" charter skipper in Port Angeles and **Mike Schmidt**, fisheries patrol officer in Sequim, ceaseless angler of eastern strait bank and developer of the "Terminator" salmon jig.

Western Strait Of Juan De Fuca

Pete Hanson, owner of Farwest Fishing Resort in Neah Bay, charter skipper and past president of the Washington State Charter Boat Association; **Al Seda**, owner of Big Salmon Resort in Neah Bay with a degree in fisheries biology; **John Truex**, skipper and owner of Woodie's Charters in Sekiu.

Westport

Mark Cedargreen, owner of Westport Charter Service, past president of the Westport Charter Boat Association, has served on southern panel of Pacific Salmon Commission and as groundfish advisor on Pacific Fishery Management Council; **Tom Hampton**, owner and skipper of the charter *Outlaw*. **Phil Westrick**, charter skipper.

Ilwaco

Chuck Elliott, co-owner of Pacific Salmon Charters and one of the most experienced Ilwaco charter skippers around for salmon, sturgeon, bottomfish and albacore; **Ed Johnson**, owner of Ed's Bait and Tackle in Ilwaco and jetty fishing pioneer/authority.

Nehalem Bay

Sherry Lyster Newman, owner of Lyster's Bait and Tackle in Rockaway and ardent angling enthusiast and **Ed Lyster**, former owner of Jetty Fishery and retired north coastal river guide (one of the best).

Tillamook Bay

Joe Gierga, owner of *Siggi-G* Charters in Garibaldi and a top offshore skipper; **Sherry Lyster Newman** and **Ed Lyster** (as above).

Nestucca River/Siletz Bay

Dorothy Gunness, lifelong resident and tireless angler of the lower Nestucca; **Jim Brunette**, former owner of Siletz Moorage.

Depoe Bay

Rich Allyn, owner and skipper, *Tradewinds* charters.

Yaquina Bay

John Crowe, former owner of Deep Sea John's (now Newport Waters sports), jetty fishing authority; **Russ Sisley**, owner of South Beach Charters; **Burt Waddell**, owner and lifelong skipper, Newport *Tradwinds*.

Siuslaw River

Jerry Macleod, fisheries biologist for many years at Florence; **Bill** and **Warner Pinkney**, owners of The Sportsman in Florence.

Umpqua River/Winchester Bay

Terry Jarmain, lower Umpqua River guide in Reedsport; **John Johnson**, for many years the local fisheries biologist; and **Ed Kiste**, veteran skipper and owner of the Winchester Bay charter *Becky Lynn.*

Coos Bay

Reese Bender, assistant district fisheries biologist in Charleston and a great striped bass enthusiast; **Bob Pullen**, Charleston charter skipper retired after 25 years.

Rogue River

Lou Giottonini, owner of Jot's Resort, former commissioner of Port of Gold Beach with 30 years' experience fishing the lower Rogue and area.

Chetco River

Dee Shurtleff, former owner of the Sporthaven Marina in Harbor where he produced a daily radio fishing show.

Smith, Klamath River

Chuck Overson, owner and guide, Six Rivers Guide Service in Crescent City; **Lenny Fike**, former owner of Western Rivers Guide Service and Saxton's Tackle in Smith River; **Chub Morris**, former owner of Klamath Beach camp and river guide.

Crescent City

Mark Fleck, manager of Englund Marine in Crescent City.

Trinidad Harbor

Richard Allen, owner of Salty's Sporting Goods in Trinidad; **George Collins**, owner of charter *New Corregidor* and charter skipper for nearly a half-century.

Humboldt Bay

Greg Rice, owner of Bucksport Sporting Goods in Eureka.

Barkley Sound

Bill Otway, Sportfishing Ombudsman for the Department of Fisheries and Oceans in Vancouver; **Norm Reite**, owner of Island West Resort in Barkley Sound.

Marilyn Murphy, Port Alberni Sportfishing Centre & Marina in Port Alberni.

Mike Hicks, Tyee Lodge in Bamfield, longtime Barkley Sound Guide and sport fisherman.

Clayoquot Sound

Dick Close, manager, Weigh West Resort in Tofino.

Nootka Sound

Tim Cyr, co-owner of Nootka Island Fishing Camp and a guide there; **Ray Williams**, fishing guide and lifetime resident of Nootka Sound.

General

Scott Clendenin, Chief, U.S. Coast Guard and instructor in the National Motor Lifeboat School at Cape Disappointment.

USING THIS GUIDE

LEAVING NO STONE UNTURNED IS PRETTY DIFFICULT when the "beach" extends from Humboldt Bay, California to Nootka Sound, British Columbia. But hopefully not too many of those stones remain untouched in this guide.

The reader should keep in mind that this is a *coastal* guide, including several marine habitats—*pelagic* (open ocean), *nearshore* (waters just off/along the coast), *inshore* (protected bays, sounds) and *tidewater* (estuarial waters of lower rivers). Steelhead, a major northwest game fish, are mentioned here and there in this guide, but are not of primary interest since most fishing for them occurs in fresh water above tidewater (except in northern Puget Sound), beyond the realm of this guide.

Part of the joy of fishing is knowing what you're catching. The great variety of game fishes along this coast as well as a hodgepodge of misleading local names often make difficult the correct identification of fish. The chapter "Marine Game Fish of the Northwest" should help you avoid some of the confusion with its precise line drawings from the authoritative text *Pacific Fishes of Canada* by J. L. Hart, reproduced with permission of the Minister of Supply and Services Canada. In addition, capsule summaries describe each species in some detail.

The chapter "Fishing Northwest Salt Waters" could really stand as a book in itself. In it you'll find all the basic information as well as many specialized tips and suggestions for fishing nearly any area and species from perch around piers to giant halibut over deep, offshore banks.

Most of the remainder of the *Northwest Coastal Fishing Guide* is divided geographically into four chapters: Washington (10 separate, major fishing areas), Oregon (10 areas), northern California (5 areas) and western Vancouver Island in British Columbia (3 areas).

Each of these 28 separate sections (fishing areas) offers all the details in the how, when and where of fishing there. Highlights of each section you may find useful include:

A "Sport Fish and Seasons" chart shows at a glance all major sport fish taken and the months of availability;

Reprinted sections of nautical charts for the area with shaded areas show best fishing spots for various species and launch ramps;

A "Crossing the Bar" or "Small Boat Safety" sidebar summarizes the unique hazards each area poses for boaters and lists phone numbers for Coast Guard information and weather conditions;

A "Facilities" listing at the end of each section emphasizes selected facilities offering services for sport fishermen—charters, guides, marinas, launch sites, marine resorts, bait and tackle shops, campgrounds, chambers of commerce and so on.

FOREWORD

ALTHOUGH THE COPYRIGHT ON THIS BOOK is dated 1991 and the actual writing has taken place over the past few months, I think it's safe to say that Doug Olander has been researching this coastal fishing guide, in one way or another, as long as I've known him.

Doug was a serious saltwater angler and a solid outdoor writer when he and I met back in 1976, and I guess it was inevitable that his love for saltwater fishing and his ability as a communicator would culminate in a book such as this.

I can't think of anyone better qualified to write a fishing guide of this scope and magnitude. Doug has fished and thoroughly investigated every marine area that I know of from central California to the northern tip of Vancouver Island and beyond, and readers can rest assured that he has "lived" the fishing spots he writes about. Never content to do his research from a desk, he has fished these waters with local guides, charter captains, resort owners and other experts, and if he wasn't yet satisfied that he knew everything he needed to know, he'd fish those spots again from his own boat, often discovering things that even the locals had overlooked.

He has brought to this volume the same eye for detail and painstaking accuracy that has marked the columns and articles he has written for nearly every major national and regional angling publication over the past decade. That in itself would be enough to make this fishing guide a "must" for any serious angler's bookshelf. But Doug is also an innovator, and it's nearly impossible to read his material without picking up something new or discovering a twist that you've never thought of or were hesitant to try. When it comes to fishing new places or experimenting with new techniques, he's ready and willing, and many of us more "traditional" West Coast saltwater anglers have learned a lot from what he has written over the years.

This fishing guide offers more of that fresh, insightful approach that has always set Doug's articles apart from the standard where-to and how-to fishing material we read so much of these days. If you're expecting just another salmon book, you'll be pleasantly surprised. Sure, Doug loves to catch (and write about) salmon, but he also loves to catch halibut, lingcod, albacore, rockfish, flounder, sole, perch and all the other species so readily available along the Pacific Coast, and I have no doubt that all are discussed with equal enthusiasm on the following pages.

If there's a marine fish worth catching, or a spot along the coast of northern California, Oregon, Washington or British Columbia worth fishing, Doug Olander probably knows about it, and much of what he knows on the subject he shares here with his readers.

I'm proud to have this opportunity to recommend Doug's *Northwest Coastal Fishing Guide* to every serious angler in this part of the country, and even prouder to say that he once invited me to be its co-author. When I turned down that opportunity, I told Doug that I was saying no because I was re-starting my career as a full-time magazine freelancer and couldn't afford to commit the time and effort to a major book project. I'll confess here that there was a second reason why I didn't agree to co-author this guide: my knowledge of Northwest fish, fishing spots and fishing techniques are woefully inadequate when compared to those of Doug Olander, and I knew my half of the final product would be noticeably inferior. Nobody wants to look bad, so I let the real expert write this book.

Readers will no doubt benefit from my decision!

Terry Rudnick
Outdoor writer, photographer
Olympia, Washington

Marine Game Fish Of The Northwest

Salmon

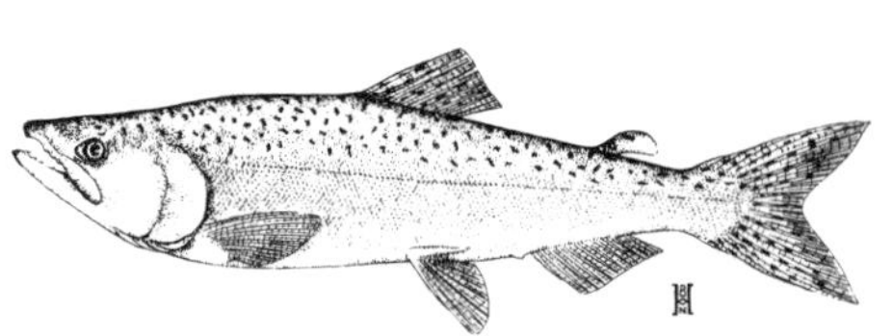

Chinook ***(Oncorhynchus tsawytscha).*** Also: *blackmouth* (Washington), *king* (central California through Washington and Alaska), *feeder, tyee, spring* or *springer* (British Columbia). Major game fish from central California through Alaska. Bluish black above to silver below; black gum line, heavy spotting extends down entire tail. To 126 pounds (International Game Fish Association (IGFA) record: 97 pounds, 4 ounces in 1985). Commonly 5 to 40 pounds. Spends three to eight years at sea, from nearshore waters to over 1,000 miles out, feeding from surface to great depths. Most often taken along steep points/ledges or over reefs. June-August or early September is approximate legal ocean sport season in most Northwest waters, but longer season off southwest Vancouver Island and legal all or most of the year in Washington-B.C. inland marine waters. Readily takes deep-trolled herring or anchovies, plugs or plastic squid as well as mooched plug-cut herring or metal jigs from drifting boats. Most prized of all Pacific salmon. Esteemed as food fish (flesh may vary from deep red to orange-pink to nearly white).

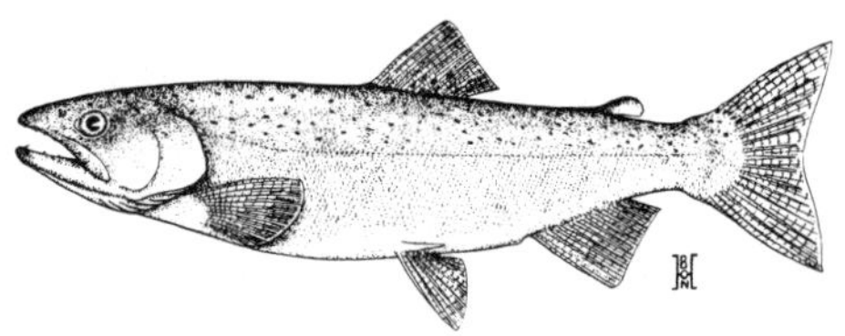

Coho ***(Oncorhynchus kisutch).*** Also: *silver.* Similar in color to chinook but white gum line, spotting only on upper half of tail. Major game fish from northern California through Alaska. Can exceed 30 pounds (IGFA record: 33 pounds, 4 ounces in 1989). Commonly 2 to 8 pounds (through midsummer) and 8 to 15 pounds (late summer). Wide-ranging salmon of upper layers in nearshore and offshore waters. Typically caught wherever riplines concentrate baitfish, often far offshore, in upper 60 feet of water. Sport fishing seasons similar to those listed for chinook. Taken on trolled herring or anchovies, plastic squid, flies or spoons often at or near the surface, as well as on metal jigs (particularly in B.C. waters). Like chinook, fight may be wild and unpredictable, but tends to leap more often. Superb light tackle targets. Outstanding as food fish; deep red flesh.

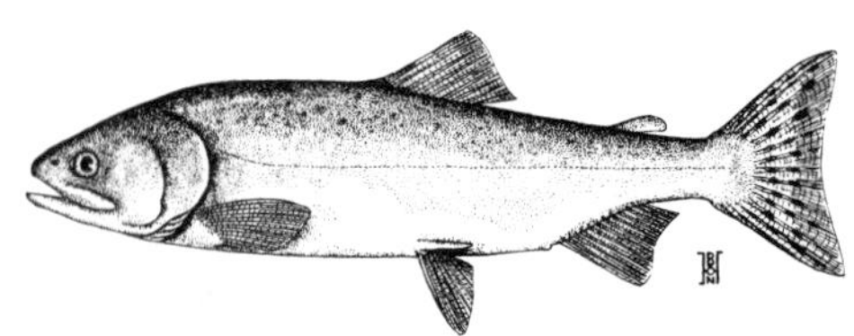

Pink ***(Oncorhynchus gorbuscha).*** Also: *humpy* (northern Washington). Significant locally as game fish in northern Washington and southern British Columbia, less valued though common north through Alaska. Similar to chinook in color and in spotting pattern (with spots on entire tail), but spots oval, larger, bolder; very fine scales. Male develops characteristic hump at spawning. IGFA world record: 12 pounds, 9 ounces in 1974; the smallest of Pacific salmons, commonly 3 to 6 pounds. Main runs in northern Washington/southern B.C. from Fraser, Skagit and several smaller rivers with fish showing every other year on odd-numbered years. Fishery essentially limited to July-early September. Like coho, pinks feed in offshore/nearshore riplines near the surface. Aggressively strikes trolled baits and lures as well as jigs or mooched herring. Lively, persistent battler and frequent jumper on appropriately light tackle. Fine eating, though meat of pinks held in considerably less esteem than the richer flesh of chinook or coho.

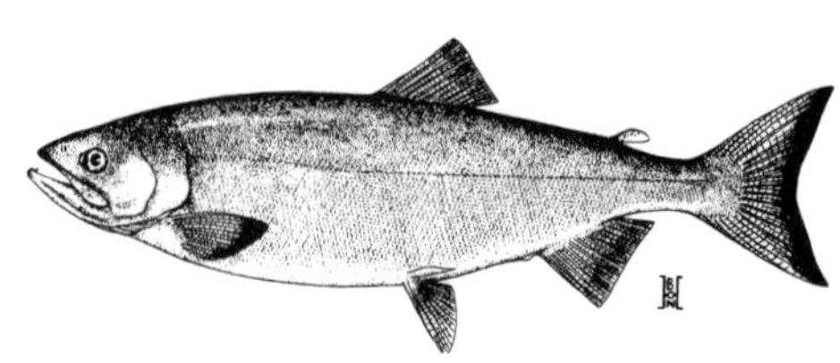

Chum ***(Oncorhynchus keta).*** Also: dog salmon. A major commercial species, of limited local interest as game fish—primarily in Hood Canal and Puget Sound in October-November (chum are late spawners). Unlike chinook, coho or pinks, chum lack distinct spots; distinguished from sockeye by tail edged with black. IGFA world record: 32 pounds in 1985; common to 15 pounds. Mostly an incidental catch. Chums strike *small* herring lures or flies (green flies most popular in major Hood Canal fishery). Very dogged fighters, offering a good challenge on any gear. Edibility generally considered inferior to other salmon—often dark when caught—but favored for smokers.

Sockeye ***(Oncorhynchus nerka).*** Also: red salmon (Alaska). Like chum, more important as commercial species. Caught in salt water from northern Washington through Alaska, but seldom targeted. Like chums, bright

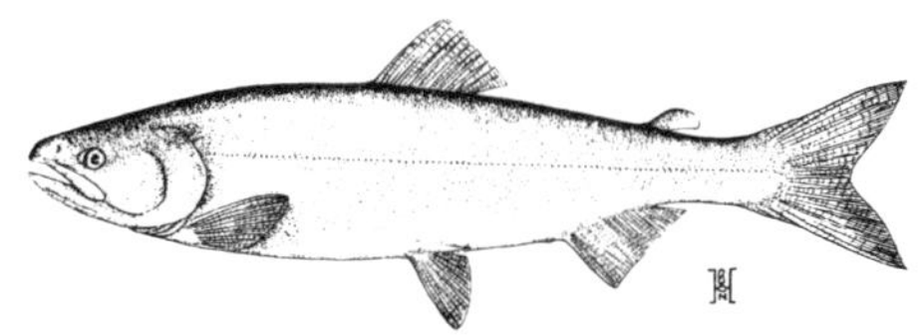

silver without spots, but lack black tail edging of chums. IGFA world record: 15 pounds, 3 ounces, in 1987. Also taken incidentally, often by anglers after coho or pinks. Most inclined to strike small, bright hoochys (plastic squid) or spoons/jigs. Fight similar to coho. Superb as food; one of the richest, most deeply red-meated of salmon.

Bottomfish

Halibut

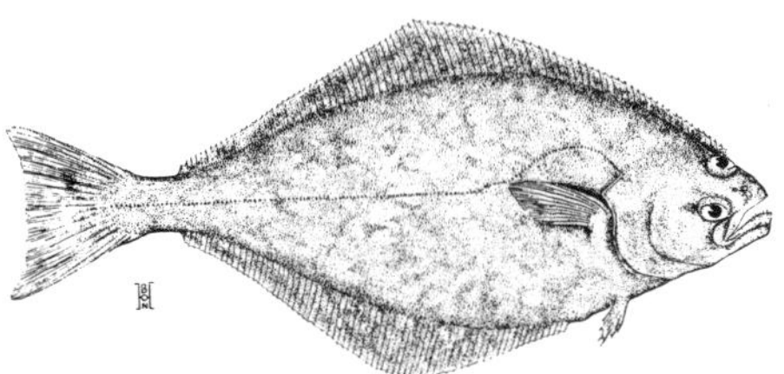

Pacific halibut *(Hippoglossus stenolepis).* Locally very important game fish from central Oregon to northern Washington—particularly the Swiftsure Bank grounds off Neah Bay (of more widespread importance, B.C. and Alaska coasts). Dark brown to greyish-black on eyed side; white on blind side. As the northern Pacific's largest game fish, size is also a distinguishing characteristic. Common 5 to 50 pounds, occasionally over 100. IGFA world record: 350 pounds in 1982; grows to over 500. Prefers gravelly shoals where large numbers may congregate in site-specific "beds." Most Oregon and Washington halibut are taken in 200 to 400 feet of water. Sportfishing seasons in the Lower 48 have been generally short and varied in recent years, widely during the late spring and summer, as the International Pacific Halibut Commission has begun tightening restrictions through catch quotas. Halibut will strike nearly any large bait or lure; large herring and jigs or spoons account for most deepwater catches, often with heavy tackle filled with dacron line. These are extremely powerful fighters, never tiring easily, using large, flat sides to their advantage. They are customarily landed with harpoons, flying gaffs and sometimes shotguns; big halibut pulled into small boats can be very dangerous. Not only are halibut good eating, in the opinion of many (including me), they are one of the very finest eating of the world's fish.

Greenlings

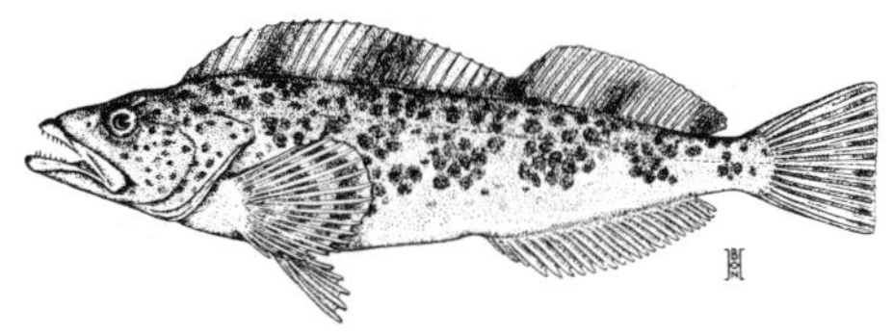

Lingcod *(Ophiodon elongatus).* Important game fish from southern California through Alaska. Color varies: generally shades of gray, brown and white, blotched and spotted on sides and dorsal surface; large, irregular, dagger-like teeth. IGFA record: 64 pounds, in 1988, but known to reach over 80 pounds. Commonly to 30-40 pounds (fish this large are always female) in northern part of range (seldom over 20 in southern California). Prefers deep, steep, current-swept rocky terrain—ledges, reefs, pinnacles, banks and the like. Smaller lings widely available around jetties and off kelp beds near rocky headlands. Generally available and open season year-round, except in Puget Sound waters; weather is typically the limiting factor in winter-spring. Greatest number of large females become available in relatively shallow water in winter and early spring spawning season. Readily strikes any bait or lure; one of the best bets for big lings is a live bait—a kelp greenling or rockfish of a pound or so rigged with large hooks and fished near bottom. Lingcod often try to swallow smaller hooked fish, frequently holding on right to the boat where they can be netted or gaffed. Occasionally powerful when hooked, but not generally a spectacular fighter except on light lines (8- to 12-pound is ideal for bona fide *sport* with lingcod). First-rate as a food fish, particularly fish under 15 to 20 pounds (larger fish tend to get coarse).

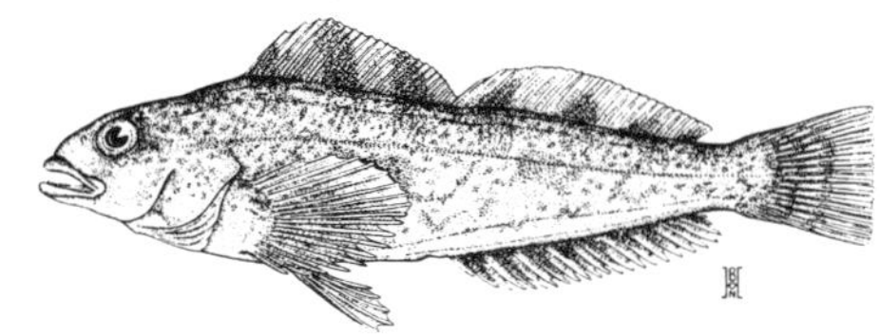

Kelp greenling *(Hexagrammos decagrammus).* Also: *sea trout, kelp trout, kelp cod.* Occasional catch from central California through Alaska. Females with orange-brown sides, orange-gold fins and belly; males are a deep blue with bright blue spots on front half of body. IGFA record: 2 pounds, 2 ounces in 1988, but may exceed 4 pounds. Common 2 or 3 pounds. Generally abundant around kelp, jetties, headlands, shallow reefs and often into lower stretches of large bays. Available year-round. Most are taken on shrimp, marine worms or cut bait; will also take small lures or jigs. Great sport on light tackle. Delicious eating.

Red Rockfishes—"Red Snappers"

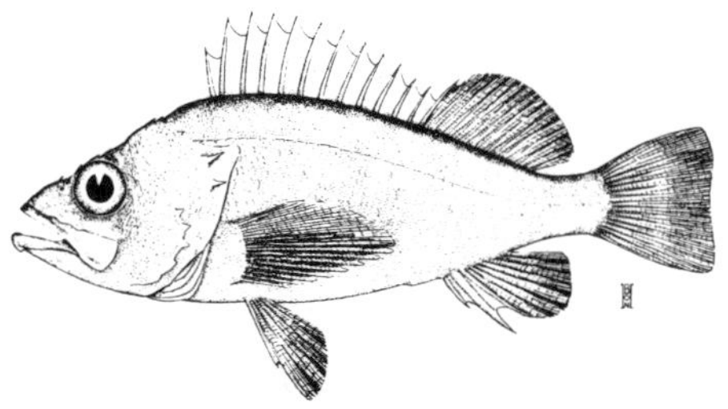

Yelloweye rockfish *(Sebastes ruberrimus).* Also: *red snapper.* Significant game fish from southern California through Alaska. Uniformly rose-orange red with black fin edges and bright yellow eyes. IGFA world record: 21 pounds, 4 ounces, but exceeds 30 pounds. Common 5 to 15 pounds, occasionally over 20. Slow-growing, long-lived, site-specific yelloweye show strong preference for deep, very rugged terrain in areas of fast current. Seldom caught in less than 150 feet of water. No closed season. Baits such as herring or squid are effective, as are metal jigs or leadhead jigs with plastic tails and, particularly, large spoons. Often taken on heavy lines, but lighter lines (8- to 15-pound test) not only make reaching bottom easier but offer a real fight with big yelloweye. Otherwise, after very strong initial strike/run, their resistance is minimal thanks to gases trapped in an air bladder that expand as yelloweye are pulled to surface, debilitating the fish. Very good as a food fish.

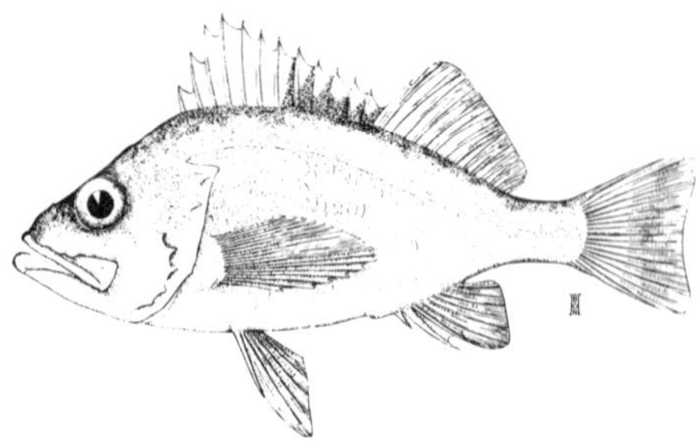

Canary rockfish *(Sebastes pinniger).* Also: *red snapper.* Significant game fish from central California through Alaska. Orange mottled with gray, may be tinged with yellow, usually with three orange stripes discernible on each side of head. IGFA world record: 10 pounds in 1986; grows somewhat larger. Commonly 2 to 7 pounds. Prefers moderately rocky or smooth, hard bottomed areas, usually in over 100 feet of water and often much deeper. Available all year. Typically caught with cut bait, shrimp flies or jigs on heavy bottomfish gear. Minimal fight unless taken on very light line. Excellent eating.

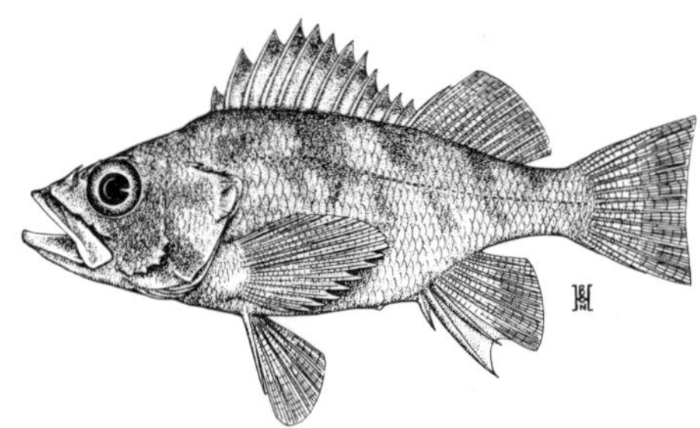

Vermilion rockfish *(Sebastes miniatus).* Also: *red snapper.* Common in southern California; increasingly less so northward, though taken as far up as the central B.C. coast. Vermilion shades under dusky black blotches and mottling on sides; fins may be edged in black. IGFA world record: 9 pounds in 1988, but reaches at least 15 pounds; common 3 to 10. Vermilion inhabit rugged, rocky areas in 150 to 1,000 feet. Available year-round. They readily strike bait, jigs, spoons, shrimp flies. Fight can be impressive when taken in fairly shallow water on light lines; expect it to rush stubbornly downward toward the rocks. Excellent eating.

Midwater Schooling Rockfishes—"Sea Basses"

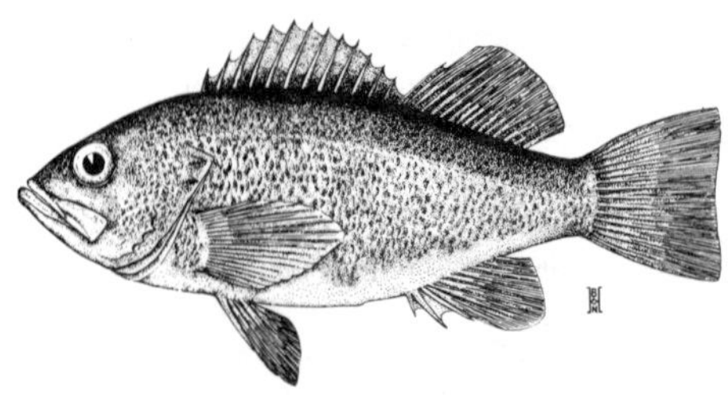

Black rockfish *(Sebastes melanops).* Also: *sea bass.* Important coastal game fish from northern California through Alaska. Catch data show this abundant species is easily the most important Northwest rockfish for sport fishermen. Black along back, lightening to mottled grey-white on sides to white on belly. IGFA world record: 10 pounds in 1986. Wide-ranging, from jetties and headlands rocks (especially at night) to offshore banks. Black rockfish are often found in vast schools at middepths or even at the surface, especially over submerged pinnacles or reefs. Available year-round, when weather provides access. Blacks aggressively strike any bait or lure, often those trolled for salmon. They offer outstanding sport, particularly when schooled and boiling at the surface, when they'll strike small jigs, spoons or even surface plugs cast with "trout gear" or "bass tackle" as well as streamers cast by fly fishermen. Good eating (some find the flavor noticeably stronger than in other rockfish).

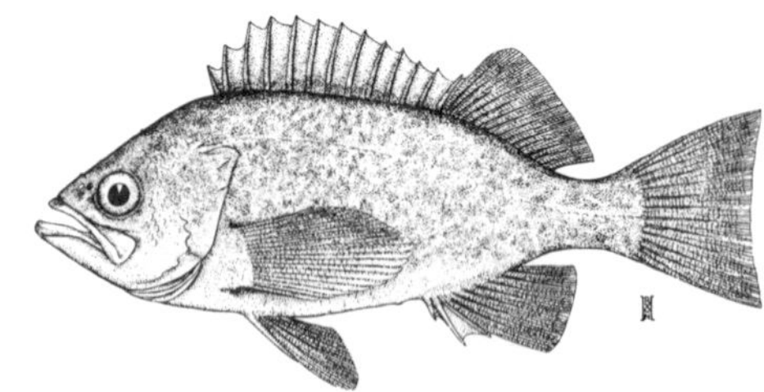

Blue rockfish *(Sebastes mystinus).* Also: *sea bass.* Important game fish from central California through Alaska. Less common in the Northwest than is the black rockfish, but in any case many anglers find them indistinguishable. Still, the blue has a noticeably more bluish color, a smaller mouth and often vague streaks down the side of its head. No IGFA world record established yet. Maximum size probably similar to black. Midwater species similar in most respects to—and often found mixed in with—black rockfish.

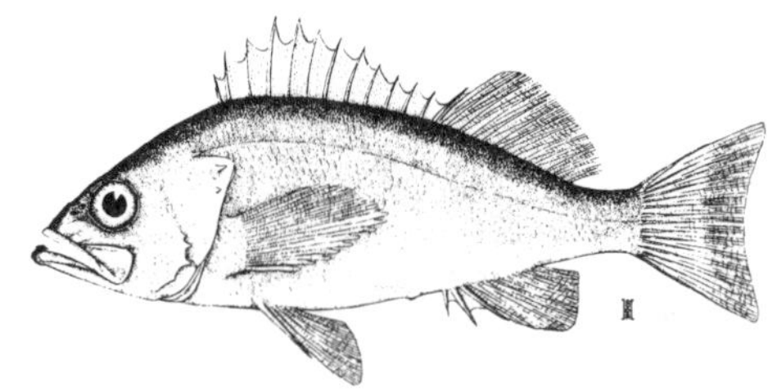

Yellowtail rockfish *(Sebastes flavidus).* Also: *sea bass.* Frequent game fish from central California through Alaska. Olive to brownish grey along back, whitening on belly; fins often greenish-yellow. IGFA world record: 5 1/2 pounds in 1988, but approaches or exceeds 10 pounds. Found in dense schools over offshore banks; may occur at any depth. Available year-round. Small but active fighters, especially on ultra-light tackle. Excellent as a food fish.

Shallow-Water Rockfishes—"Rockcod"

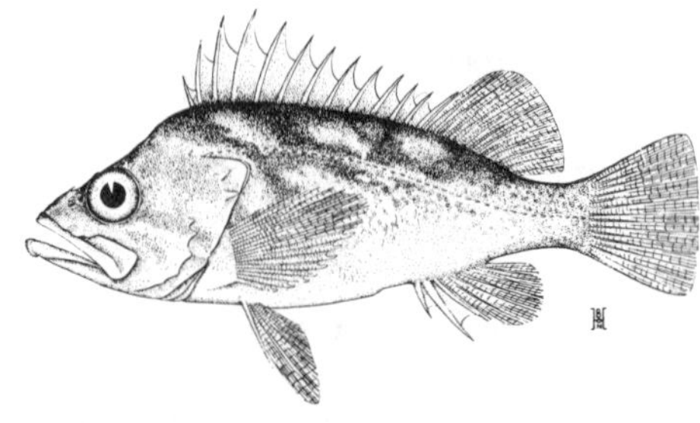

Copper rockfish *(Sebastes caurinus)* and **brown rockfish *(S. auriculatus).*** Also: *rockcod.* Important inshore game fish from northern California through Alaska. Considerable variation in color but generally dark brown to olive brown, lightening along sides and belly; copper rockfish have a clear (whitish) strip along the back half of the lateral line; brown rockfish nearly identical but with a dark spot on gill cover and no clear strip along the lateral line. No IGFA world record established. Exceeds 8 pounds, common 1 to 6. Prefers rocky areas, often very shallow around kelp, rocks, pilings and at times over eelgrass or gravelly areas, but may be taken in water up to 300 feet deep. No closed season. Copper and brown rockfish aggressively strike baits, jigs and other lures. They are surprisingly strong, dogged fighters when taken in shallow water.

Quillback rockfish *(Sebastes maliger).* Also: *rockcod.* Occasional catch from Oregon through Alaska, but particularly important in northern Washington. Cream colored, especially front third of body, often with freckles in throat area, usually becoming more mottled with darker orange-brown in middle and darkening toward the tail. IGFA world record: 5 pounds, 11 ounces in 1988, but may exceed 8 pounds. Common 1 to 5. Unlike many bottom-dwelling rockfishes, the quillback is less specific to rocky areas and more frequent over current-swept, smooth, hard-bottomed reef plateaus, usually in 50 or more feet. One of the most common rockfishes in Washington and southern B.C. Available all year. Strikes any bait or lure, including some surprisingly large jigs. Usually caught on lines far too heavy to permit any sport whatsoever. In fact, pound-for-pound, the quillback is one of the hardest-striking of all rockfish, but it tends to give up almost at once. The quillback merits the author's top rating among rockfishes for its sweet, mild flavor.

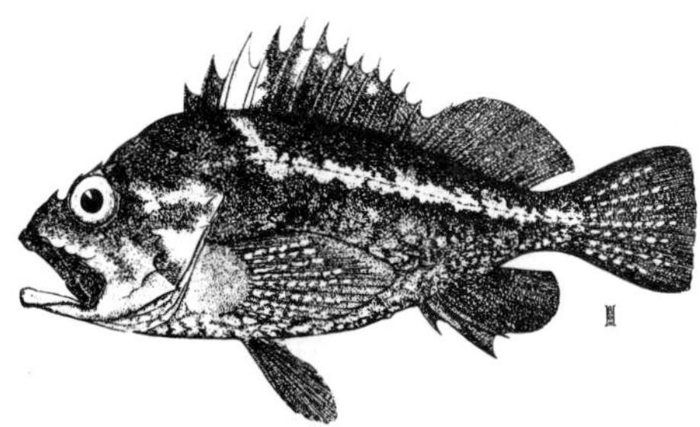

China rockfish *(Sebastes nebulosus).* Also: *China cod.* Occasional game fish from northern California to southeast Alaska. One of the Northwest's more interesting rockfishes in color, black with irregular white to yellow spotting and a light strip running from the third dorsal spine down to and along the lateral line to the tail. No IGFA record established; probably doesn't exceed 4 or 5 pounds and usually just a pound or two. Inhabits shallow water (50-200 feet) rugged nearshore reefs along the open coast. No closed season. A small, bright, incidental catch, Chinas will readily strike small jigs or baits. They offer little fight and little meat (though that is of fine quality).

Other Rockfishes

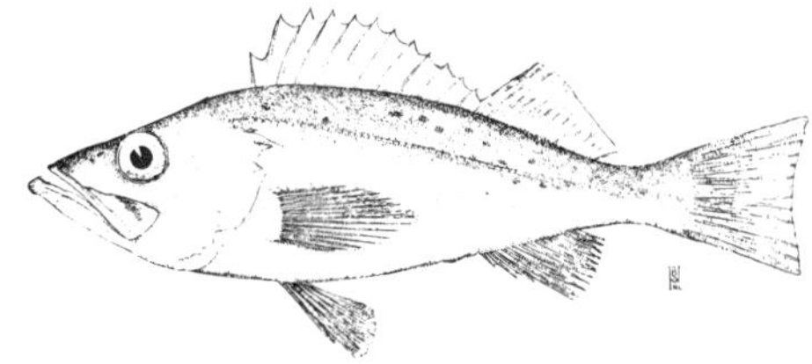

Bocaccio rockfish *(Sebastes paucispinus).* Also: *snapper* (or, in California—*salmon grouper*). Rare but locally common in Northwest waters; a major part of the bottomfish catch in southern and central California. Dusky-red to brick-red on back, lightening on sides to pinkish below. I have seen a uniformly intense scarlet-red variation taken occasionally over Swiftsure Bank off Neah Bay. Bocaccio are very elongate, almost streamlined rockfish, with a very large mouth and jutting lower jaw. IGFA world record: 21 pounds, 4 ounces; exceeds 25. Common to 15 pounds in northern part of range. Prefers deepwater offshore banks (typically over 300 feet) but I have encountered isolated populations of smaller fish in Puget Sound and Nootka Sound (west coast of Vancouver Island). No closed season. Readily strikes heavy jigs, shrimp flies, baits. Usually caught on heavy bottomfish gear precluding much fight. Excellent eating, especially smaller fish.

Tiger rockfish *(Sebastes nigrocintus).* Infrequent game fish apparently ranging south into northern California but probably more often caught from northern Washington through British Columbia. No IGFA record established. One of the most strikingly colored Northwest game fish, the base color varying from pink to light red with five bold black bars ranging from black to dark red down each side. There are also two dark bars extending diagonally down gill cover behind each eye. Upper limits of size probably approach 10 pounds, more often 2 to 5. This is a solitary species, rarely taken by sportfishermen in fairly shallow water but commercially much deeper, preferring very rocky areas. Indiscriminately strike baits or lures, offering fair resistance but no distinctive fight. They are probably excellent food fish, though I've always found those I caught too rare and beautiful to justify keeping, so I can offer no personal opinion.

Codfishes

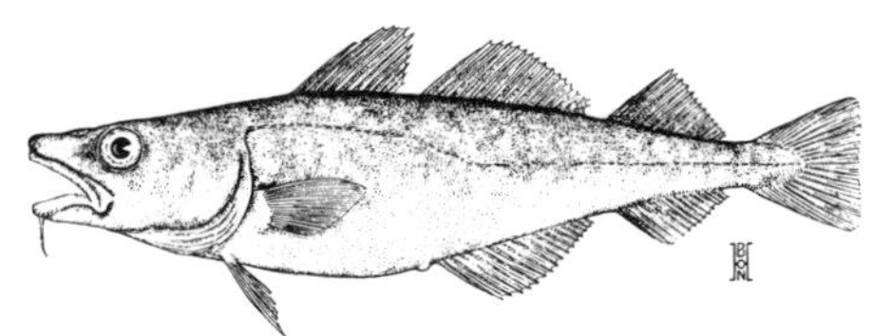

Pacific cod *(Gadus macrocephalus).* Also: *true cod.* In the 1970s and early 1980s, an important game fish of

Puget Sound; may be taken off Oregon and increasingly abundant north, off British Columbia and Alaska. In recent years, the thriving recreational cod fishery in Puget Sound has declined markedly. Some suggest a cyclical decline in abundance; others blame commercial draggers. Long, narrow body with three separate dorsal fins; brown to gray above, lighter below; irregular brown-gold spots on upper body; a distinctive barbel (whisker) on chin. IGFA world record: 30 pounds in 1984. Apparently exceeds 40 pounds in northern part of range, though 20-pounders are unusual. In Washington waters, cod weighing over 12-15 pounds are seldom caught. Typically caught over sandy or hard bottoms in 30 to 300 feet (and much deeper in commercial trawls). No closed season; traditionally available in large numbers in central and south Puget Sound during December-March. Fertile, fast-growing "true cod" are fine light-tackle sport fish, eagerly striking any bait or lure. Fine eating (best if cleaned immediately and kept cool)—also valued by many for the roe.

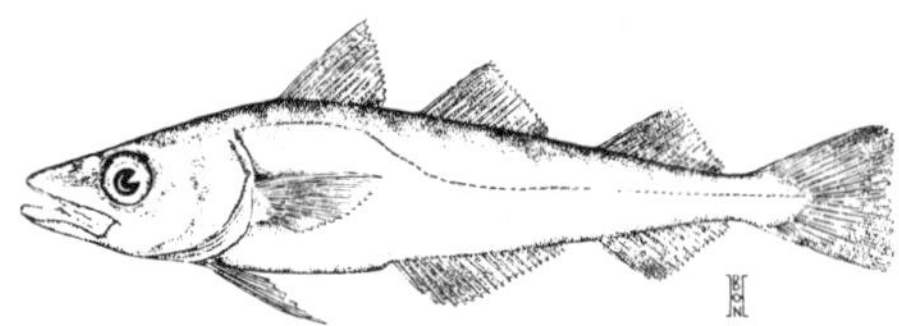

Walleye pollock *(Theragra chalcogramma).* The pollock is similar to the Pacific cod in range and in declining abundance in Puget Sound—the only area in the Northwest of any significant interest and effort for pollock. In the 1970s, consistently available most of the year in Puget Sound, especially south part. Similar in appearance to Pacific cod, but darker on sides with gold-brown markings less distinctive and lacks barbel under chin. No IGFA record established, but apparently exceeds 10 pounds though unusual over 5 to 6. Similar in habits and habitat to cod, with which it is often caught. No closed season. Hits jigs readily, but is especially fond of bait. Meager fight when hooked. Flesh is tasty but softens quickly: cleaning or at least bleeding immediately and keeping cold retains firmness.

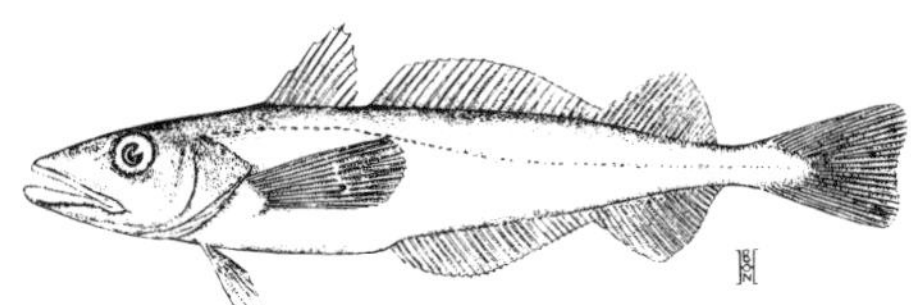

Pacific hake *(Merluccius productus).* Also: *whiting* (commerically). Occasional game fish but very abundant Pacific species from Baja California to the Gulf of Alaska. Typical codfish shape; metallic grey above, bright silver below (no mottling); large mouth rimmed with fine, sharp teeth. IGFA world record: 2 pounds, 2 ounces in 1988 but may exceed 10 pounds; 1-4 is average. Often found in large midwater schools in deep, muddy areas but may move into nearshore shallows to feed at night, especially in summer when it is caught from piers in Puget Sound. No closed season. Caught occasionally along the Northwest coast and more often in Puget Sound by bottomfishermen using cut bait—though it will aggressively strike jigs as well. Minimal fight on any gear. Comments regarding flesh of pollock apply even more emphatically to hake.

Pacific tomcod *(Microgadus proximus).* Range from northern California through Alaska. Olive green above, white below; small barbel on chin; lacks pattern on sides.

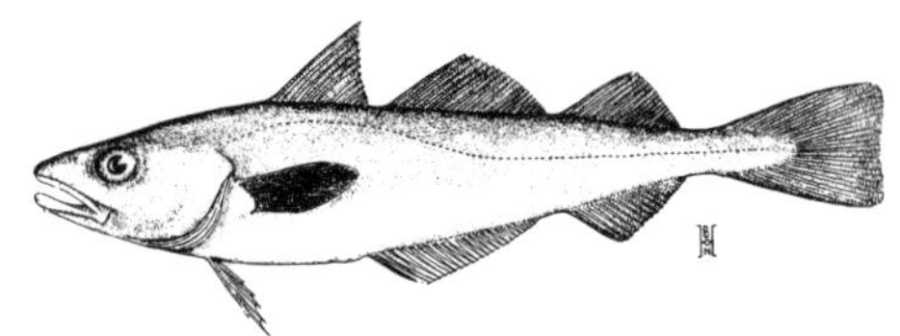

Small—no IGFA record established, but in any case a true Northwest marine panfish of a half-pound or so (though may reach a pound or 2). Found in schools but capriciously—some summers nonexistent yet others swarming abundantly near shore. No closed season. Most are caught in bays by small boaters or from docks on tiny hooks baited with squid, marine worms or shrimp (and often caught by small anglers—children without too much pride to enjoy the action for little tomcod). Thanks to small size and occasional availability, tomcod are often overlooked as a food fish but in my opinion, are one of the tastiest treats the Northwest coast has to offer.

Flatfishes (Flounder, Sole)

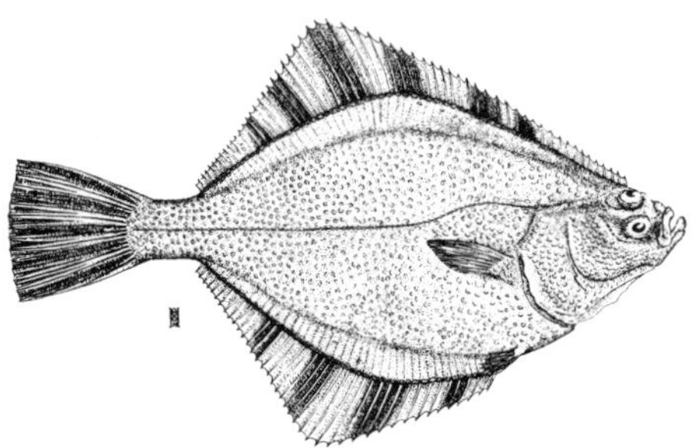

Starry flounder *(Platichthys stellatus).* Important inshore, shallow-water game fish of bays and estuaries for shore fishermen and small boaters from central California to Alaska. Dark brown on eyed side, with raised, rough warts on skin resembling sandpaper; white on blind side; distinctive orange and black bars on fins. No IGFA world record established, apparently reaches 20 pounds though commonly 1 to 5. Prefers sandy, gravelly or muddy bottoms often around river mouths. No closed season. Best baits are shrimp and marine worms; will also hit small jigs. Fun on ultralight tackle. Edibility is good, though flesh, in some areas, is heavily parasitized.

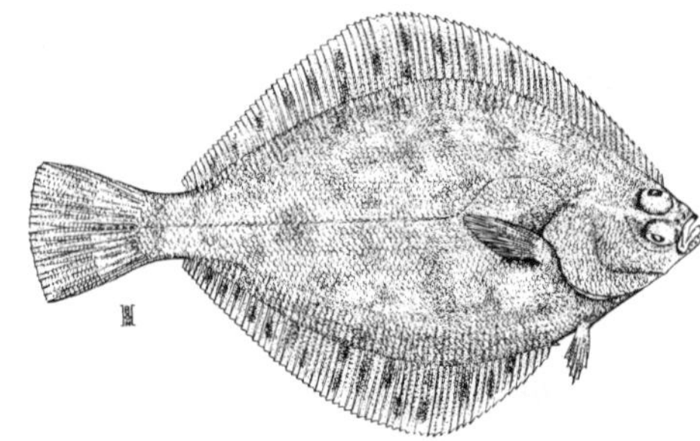

Rock sole *(Lepidopsetta bilineata).* Abundant flatfish throughout the north Pacific, common catch for inshore anglers using small hooks. Brownish-grey on eyed side with irregular, light spotting; eyed side white. Rough, slightly raised scales on eyed side very evident to the touch. No IGFA world record established, but seldom over 3 or 4 pounds. Abundant in most smooth, shallow areas of nearly all nearshore marine waters. No closed season. Accepts any small baits or jigs. Edibility is excellent.

sportfishermen throughout its range. Uniformly … eyed side, white on blind side; large mouth. IGFA world record not established; grows to at least 7 pounds. Along open coast and in inland marine waters over sand/mud bottoms, in water 100 feet and much deeper. No closed season. Will strike nearly any bait or lure it can get its large mouth around. A superb food fish (highly regarded commercially).

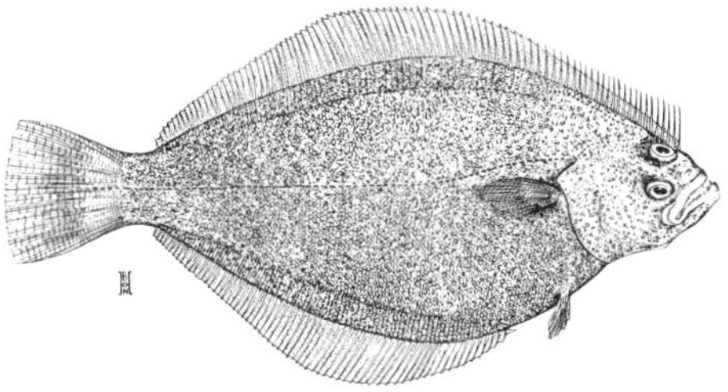

Sand sole *(Psettichthys melanostictus).* Similar in most respects to rock sole. Brown to grey on eyed side with many fine, dark specks; large mouth. Frequents shallow sandy areas.

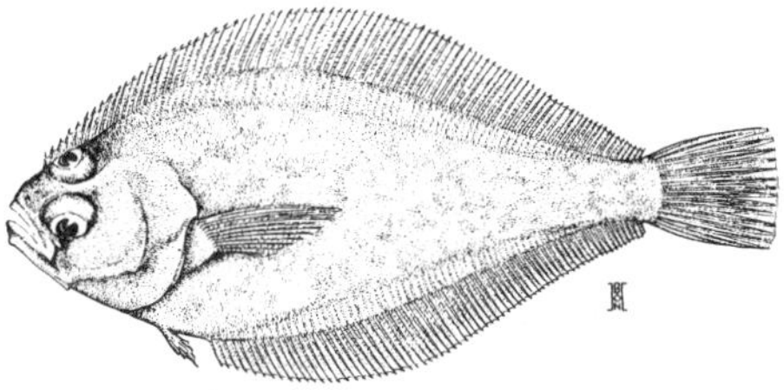

Pacific sanddab *(Citharichthys sordidus).* An abundant shallow-water flounder from Baja through Alaska. Light brown with yellowish mottling on eyed side, white on blind side. IGFA world record not established, typically a pound or less, though it may reach 2 or 3. One of the most common small fish of shallow inshore smooth areas. No closed season. Takes any small bait or lure. Fine eating.

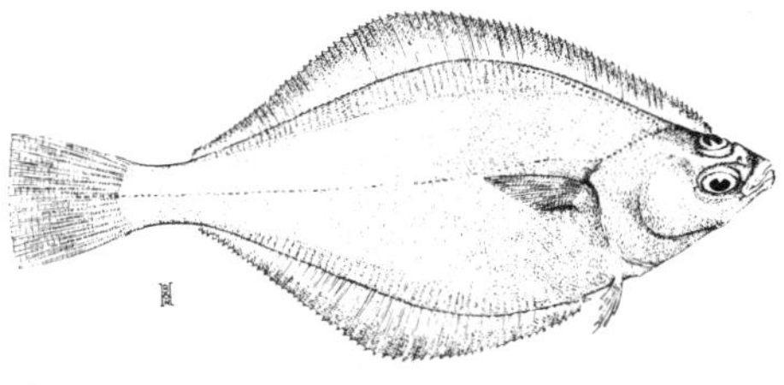

English sole *(Parophrys vetulus).* Abundant from Baja through Alaska. Uniformly brown on eyed side, white on blind side; small mouth, slender shape. IGFA world record not established, though grows to at least 5 pounds; common 1-3. Habitat similar to that of starry flounder (though …up into estuaries); common over subtidal eelgrass …d. No closed season. Takes any small …mall hooks. Not caught by anglers in … with their abundance in shallow water, …baits/hooks used are too large for their

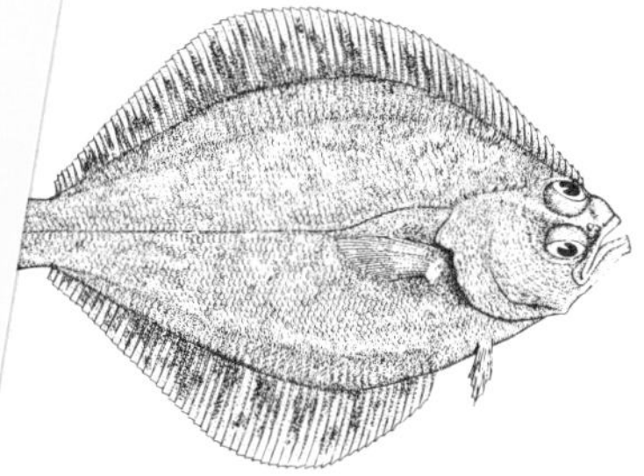

Flathead sole *(Hippoglossoides elassodon).* Common from northern California through Alaska; on occasional catch among anglers. Uniformly brownish to gray on eyed side, blind side white; large mouth. IGFA world record not established, commonly just 2 or 3 pounds. Smooth bottoms from shallow to deep water. No closed season. Will strike any bait or lure it can handle.

Sculpins

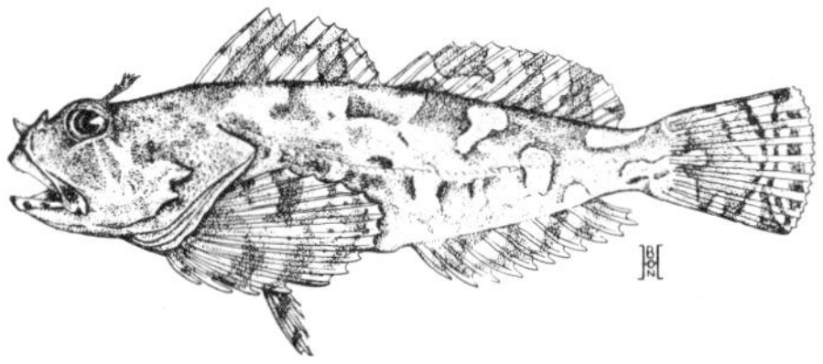

Cabezon *(Scorpaenichthys marmoratus).* Also: *bullhead.* A common game fish from southern California to southeast Alaska. Varies from brown to green to reddish with light mottling, often with a marbled effect. IGFA world record: 23 pounds in 1990, but grows much larger. Commonly 2-10. Abundant off rocky coastal headlands and submerged pinnacles as well as over gravel or eelgrass flats and around kelp beds, generally in shallow water. No closed season. Will strike herring, shrimp and, particularly, 1/2- to 2-ounce leadhead jigs with plastic skirts and tails. Considerable populations in Puget Sound seem curiously unaggressive, while those along the open coast seem more prone to strike. One of the hardest-fighting, most stubborn of all bottomfish and a real handful on light tackle. Flesh has an excellent flavor, which some claim to be like crab (the cabezon's main diet). Its meat is unusually dense—some find it tough, while others appreciate its almost lobstertail-like consistency.

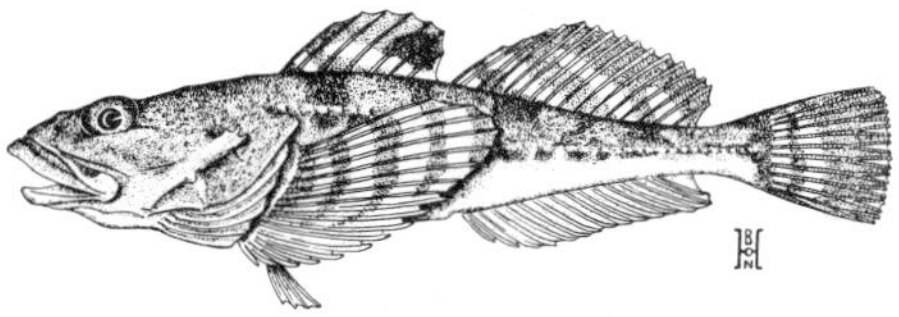

Pacific staghorn sculpin *(Leptocottus armatus).* Also: *bullhead.* Ubiquitous little fish of estuaries and all inshore habitats from southern California through Alaska. Greenish-brown above, white below; body lacks scales; long, sharp spine on each gill cover. IGFA world record not established. May reach 2 pounds; more commonly 3-8 inches. Actively forages over bottom in most shallow waters. No closed season. Mostly despised by jetty and bay fishermen as a bait-stealing nuisance. Edible but an awfully tiny tidbit. Popular live bait for striped bass in Oregon. Important forage fish for many species.

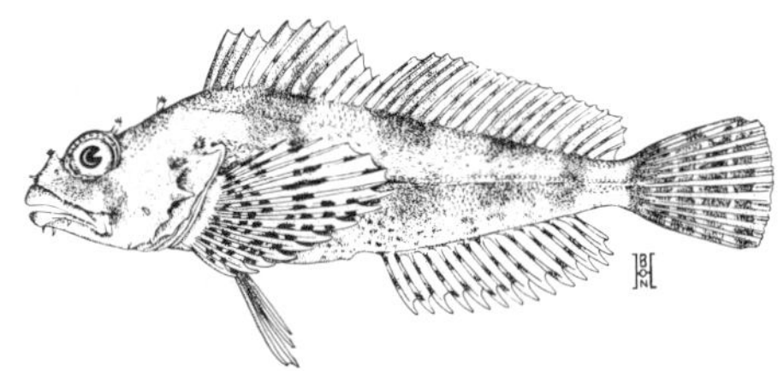

Red Irish Lord *(Hemilepidotus hemilepidotus).* Also: *bullhead.* An infrequent sport catch but common from northern California through central Alaska. Shades of brick red and rose above, lightening below; mottled with black spots. IGFA world record not established; reaches at least 3 pounds. Inhabits gravelly/rocky areas. No closed season. Readily strikes small baits; occasionally hits small lures as well. Marginally worth cleaning for the very small filets, though their quality is excellent.

Sablefish

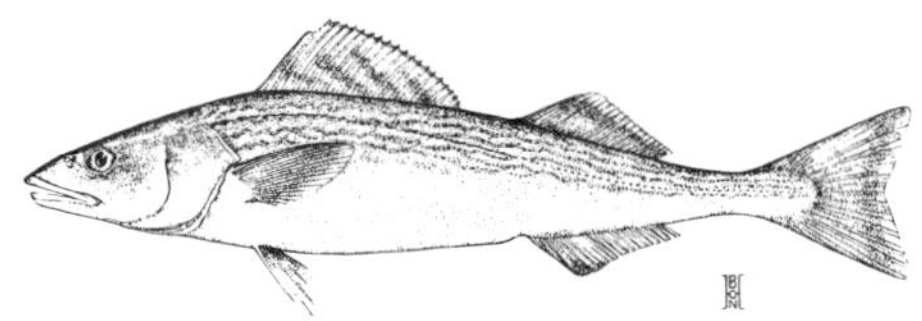

Sablefish *(Anaplopoma fimbria).* Also: *black cod* (commercially). Taken from southern California through Alaska, where it supports major commercial trawl and trap (but not sport) fisheries. Varying shades of black and grey above, lightening on sides and becoming white on the bottom. IGFA world record not established. Apparently recorded to 126 pounds in Alaska, not common in commercial catches over 40 pounds; most sport catches are juveniles of 1 to 4 pounds. Adults are generally very much a deepwater fish, taken from 200 to 500 fathoms (1,200 to 3,000 feet) offshore. Young fish are sometimes found in much shallower areas in Washington's and B.C.'s inland marine waters. No closed sport season and roam at varying depths. Often hooked by salmon anglers, readily taking herring as well as jigs. Sablefish offer a lively fight on light lines. Edibility perhaps best described as fair to excellent, depending upon taste. The flesh is rather dark and oily in young; it has proved a popular smoked item, but can also be fine for the grill.

Pelagic (Open Ocean) Game Fish

Tunas

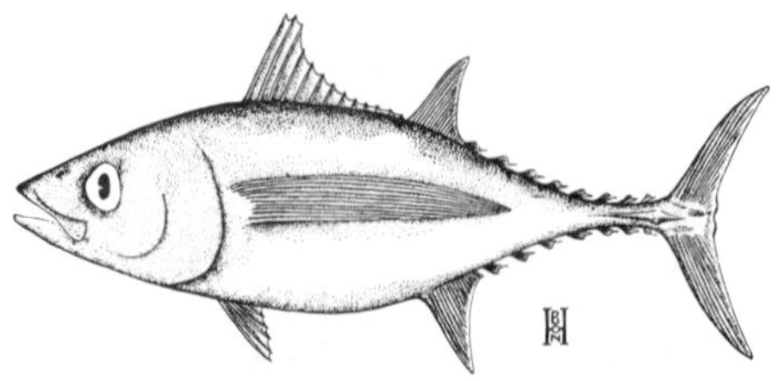

Albacore *(Thunnus alalunga).* Major game fish when seasonally present from San Diego to Washington. Steely blue-black on dorsal surface, silvery grey below; very long pectoral fin. IGFA world record: 88 pounds, 2 ounces in 1977. Commonly 15 to 30 pounds. These fast-moving schooling tunas roam near the surface of blue waters of 58-61 degrees F. They show up 30 to 200 miles offshore along the Northwest coast as early as July or as late as September, *if* they show at all. The late 1970s were excellent years for close-in albacore fishing in the Northwest, then after a long dry spell, the late 1980s offered several more productive summers particularly for southwest Washington boats. No closed season; no limit. Caught by fast trolling feather jigs or, when schools are located and the boat is equipped, by drifting and chumming/fishing live anchovies. Tremendously powerful, enduring fight on medium tackle. Outstanding as food, raw (sashimi) or cooked; to many, the finest eating of all the tunas.

Sharks

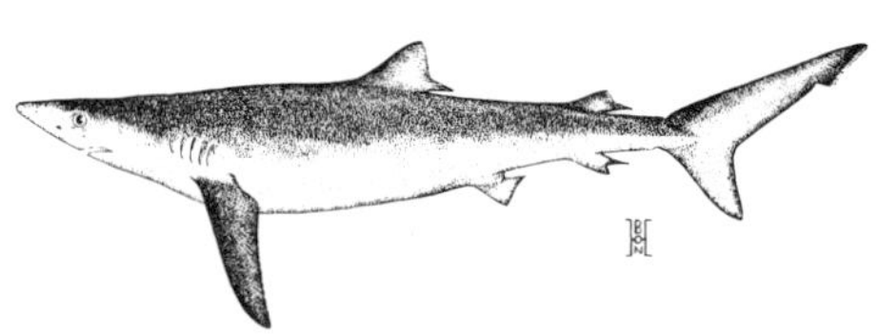

Blue shark *(Prionace glauca).* An abundant species in nearly all the world's warm temperate, subtropical and tropical oceans, certainly including the entire U.S. Pacific Coast as far north as southeast Alaska in the summer. Cobalt blue back, white below. To at least 12 feet; IGFA world record: 437 pounds in 1976. Commonly 4 to 8 feet. An active swimmer in offshore waters of 58 to 60 degrees F. No closed season. May be encountered by albacore and occasionally salmon fishermen; considered a bait- and fish-stealing nuisance, but can be great sport on light tackle. Fair eating if cleaned (bled) and iced immediately.

Thresher shark *(Alopias vulpinus).* Widespread from Baja to southern B.C. (in summer), though infrequent north of Oregon. Grey to brown above, shading to white below; tail as long as body. IGFA world record: 802 pounds in 1981. No closed season. Hits baits or trolled lures. An unpredictable, hard-fighting game fish. Edibility is superb; thresher shark is one of the finest sharks and in fact one my favorite fishes for the table.

Salmon shark *(Lamna ditropis).* Along the Pacific coast, this common shark ranges from southern California to the Gulf of Alaska. Dark grey on upper half, white on lower half. IGFA world record not established, but reportedly reaches 10 feet. Apparently moves near shore at times, probably in summer. I have no information on the salmon shark as a game fish, though it is known to be an aggressive, active species which does indeed include salmon in its diet.

larger and thought to reach at least 20 feet. Always a possibility along our coast from far offshore to near the surfline, but always a great rarity. An awesome and dangerous animal, whites have attacked divers, surfers and small boats—along the Northwest coast as elsewhere in their range. Clearly a formidable opponent if hooked, though of course specialized shark or, at least, big game tackle would be needed for any serious effort.

Other Anadromous Game Fish

Trouts And Chars

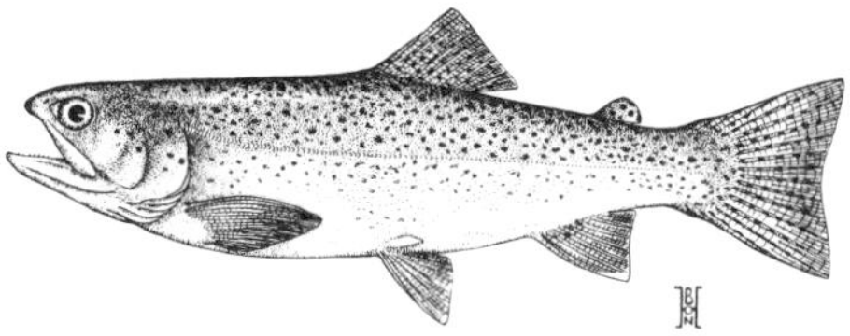

Steelhead *(Oncorhynchus mykiss*—A sea-run rainbow trout). Also: *half-pounder* (southern Oregon/northern California). Common, major game fish from the central California coast to the central Alaska coast. Metallic blue on top, silver sides with black spots, white below; square tail. IGFA world record: 42 pounds, two ounces in 1970. Caught in coastal rivers and streams, some in tide waters but most above that in fresh water. Also caught in a specialized beach fishery from Whidbey Island in Puget Sound, using bright pink/orange Hoochy skirts behind pencil lead. Tough, exciting fight. Excellent eating.

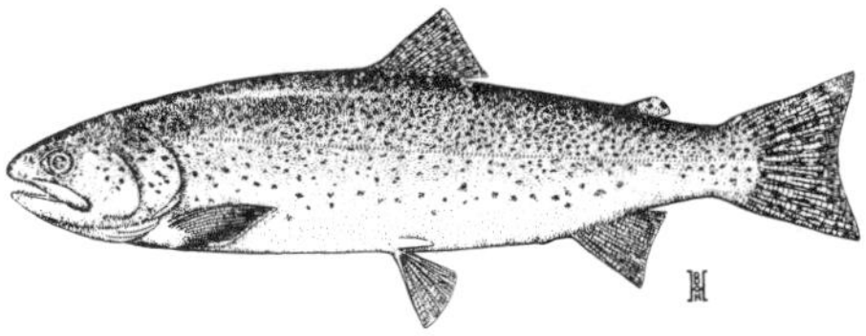

Sea-run cutthroat trout *(Oncorhynchus clarki).* Also: *blueback* (Oregon). Common, important game fish from northern California to the central Alaska coast. Similar in coloration to steelhead, but more heavily spotted and greenish dorsally. Also with red/orange streaks inside lower jaw. No IGFA world record for sea-run cutthroat (held by much larger landlocked fish). To at least 4 pounds, though averages much less. Available in shallow tidewater of nearly all coastal streams. Also caught consistently off gravelly shorelines around Puget Sound and Hood Canal. No closed season though most available summer and fall. Most sea-run cutts are taken on trolled nightcrawlers behind multiple spinning attractor blades, but also takes streamer flies, especially in upper tidewater. Spirited fight on appropriately light line. Excellent eating.

Strikes trolled lures or baits or drifted live baits. Both the fight and meat have been described as inferior—but there are Northwest anglers who enjoy fishing for the species who'd differ.

Striped Bass

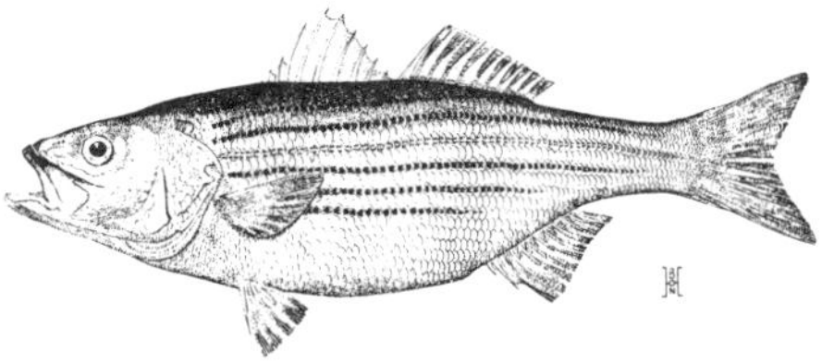

Striped bass *(Morone saxatilis).* On the Pacific Coast, enhanced populations occur in Southern California; major populations are found in San Francisco Bay-Sacramento Delta; and in the Northwest, the Umpqua and to a lesser extent Coos River systems. Dark olive along back, silver sides with distinctive stripes, white belly. IGFA world record: 78 pounds, 8 ounces in 1982, though commercial Atlantic record apparently 125 pounds. Common 5 to 30+. (Oregon has produced fish well over 50 pounds, years ago.) Oregon populations are taken from river mouths to well up above tidewater (but not out in the surf as off San Francisco Bay or in the Atlantic) where it feeds on whatever is available (including salmon/steelhead smolts at times thus incurring the hostility of many local anglers). Check for locally closed seasons in Oregon, though most striper waters in the state are open year-round. Taken on trolled plugs, jigs, plastic eels, live baitfish and large flies. A fierce, powerful, unpredictable fighter and an esteemed food fish.

Sturgeon

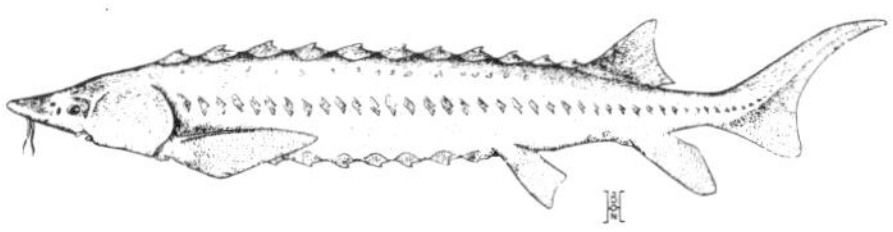

White sturgeon *(Acipenser transmontanus).* A locally significant game fish, ranging from central California to the Gulf of Alaska. Grayish, light below. IGFA world record: 468 pounds in 1983, though documented to nearly 1,400 pounds (sturgeon are the largest of any freshwater fish). Common in Oregon—legal range 40-72 inches. Inhabits the ocean (where seldom caught) and coastal rivers, particularly the Fraser, Columbia, Tillamook, Umpqua, Coos and Rogue. Generally no closed season. Caught with fresh smelt or shrimp as well as commercially prepared sturgeon bait from anchored boats and in some areas from shore. Strong fighter—may leap clear of the water when hooked, particularly if shallow. Flesh and roe both prized as food.

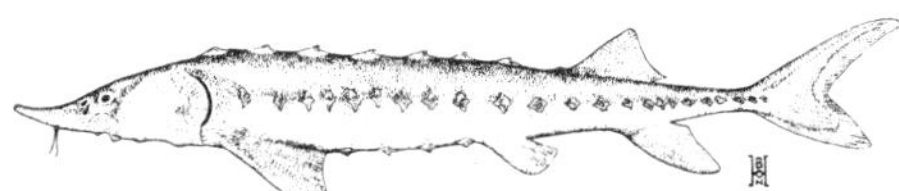

Green sturgeon *(Acipenser medirostris).* An occasional game fish ranging from Southern California to the Gulf of Alaska. Olive green to bronze, white below. No IGFA record established; grows to at least 7 feet and 300 pounds. Inhabits areas similar to those of white sturgeon, but apparently spends more time in salt water. No closed season. Caught in the general sturgeon sport fishery along with whites. Also a strong fighter, but considered inferior in edibility due to strong flavored meat (though small greens are considered excellent smoked).

Shad

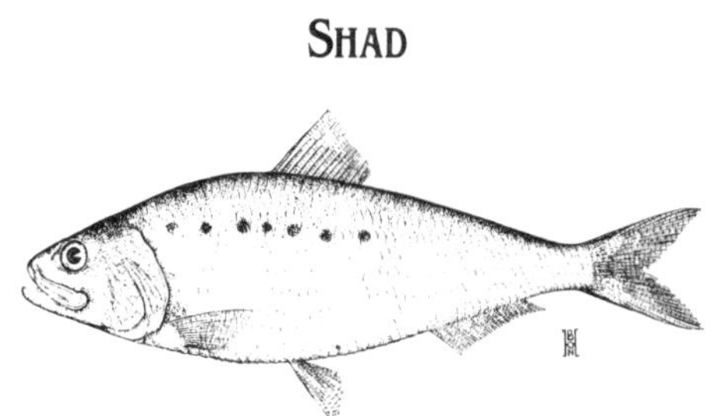

American shad *(Alosa sapidissima).* A seasonally important game fish from southern California to Alaska. Dark blue above, shading to silver-white on sides and bottom; a series of spots along upper front body. IGFA world record: 11 pounds, 4 ounces in 1986. Commonly 2 to 4 pounds. Most of the anadromous shad's life is apparently spent in the ocean feeding on plankton and small fish. No closed season but typically available in spring and early summer when they move through lower coastal rivers (notably the Columbia, Siuslaw, Umpqua, Coos and Rogue) to spawn. Shad strike small jigs as well as lures or hardware. They're a wonderful game fish on suitably light lines, displaying sizzling runs and leaps when hooked. Flesh is actually reported to be quite tasty, but few anglers bother keeping the meat of this bony fish. The roe, however, is recognized as a delicacy.

Panfishes Of The Bay And Surf

Surfperches

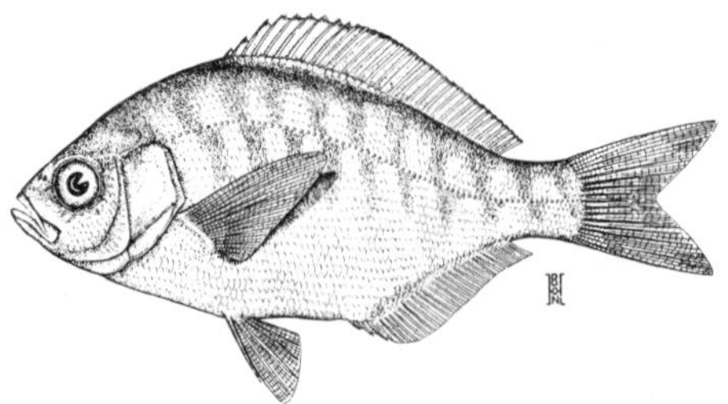

Redtail surfperch *(Amphistichus rhodoterus).* Also: *pinkfin* (Oregon). A common and important game fish of the surf from the coast of northern California to central Washington. Silver with olive green bars irregularly spaced on either side of lateral line; fins—especially tail—are pink to purple. IGFA world record not established; average 1-3 pounds, probably exceeds 4. Inhabitants of surf zone along almost all Northwest sandy beaches. No closed season; spring is a prime period. Surfcasters use sand crabs, ghost shrimp, marine worms, mussel or clam meat. Fine eating.

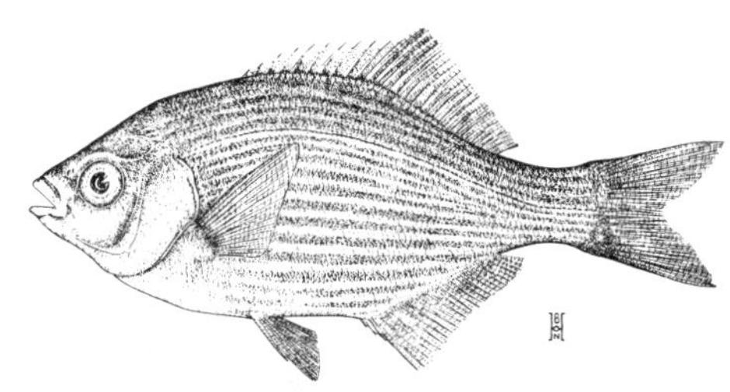

Striped surfperch *(Embiotoca lateralis).* A common and significant game fish for shore anglers in much of its range from northern Baja to southern Alaska. Bright blue, red and yellow stripes over coppery sides. IGFA world record not established; average a pound or 2, growing only a bit larger. Inhabits inshore areas around rocks, pilings, bridges and other obstructions as well as kelp, often in large schools. Valuable target species for jetty and pier anglers who use very small hooks and live or fresh marine worms or ghost shrimp (and sometimes earthworms as well). Put up a lively fight on light line. Edibility is good.

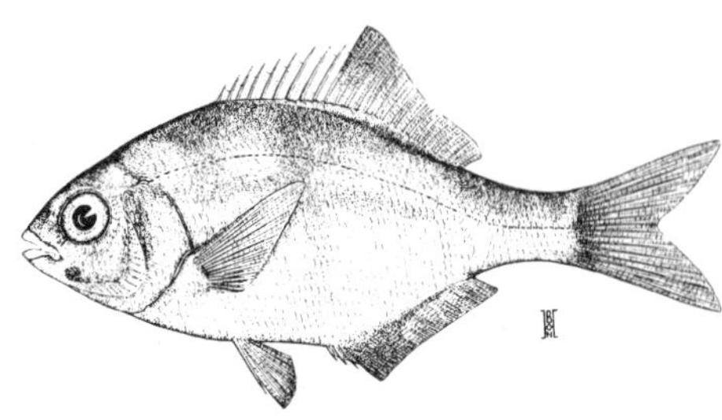

Pile surfperch *(Rhacochilus vacca).* Also: *pile perch*. Range and value as sport fish similar to that of striped surfperch. Bright to dusky silver sides, darker on top, often with dark bar on midbody; tail longer, more forked than on striped or redtail surfperch. IGFA world record not established. Averages 1-3 pounds, exceeds 4. Habitat and sport fishing approaches generally same as for striped surfperch.

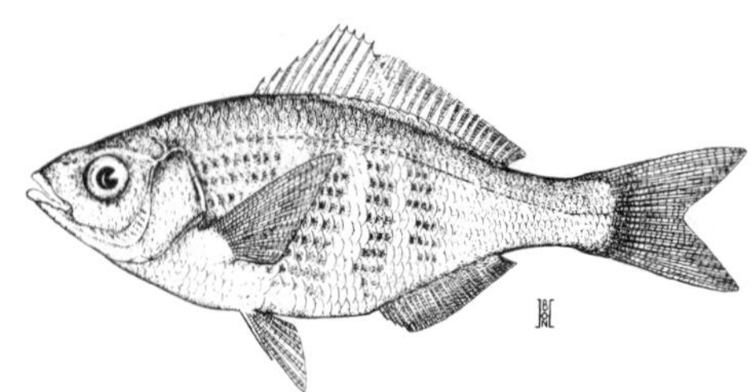

Shiner perch *(Cymatogaster aggregata).* Also: *pogey*. Range similar to that of striped surfperch. Greenish- or greyish-silver above, lighter below with three vague yellowish bars on each side. Grows to at least 7 inches. Ubiquitous little forage species of nearshore and inshore areas (look down from any pier). Easily caught on small hooks and pieces of bait. Edible but too small for most to keep; caught by kids for fun or occasionally by anglers for bait.

Other surfperches not pictured: **Walleye *(Hyperprosopon argentum)*,** **Silver *(Hyperprosopon ellipticum)*** and **White *(Phanerodon furcatus)*.** All are common in the Northwest, generally in sandy or rocky surf, around jetties and sometimes in lower bays. None are taken much over 12 inches.

for anglers. Reaches 18 inches, common to 10. Schooling fish throughout Northwest marine waters which may range throughout the water column. May form thick "herring balls" at or near the surface and can be dipnetted or jigged on multiple small-hook rigs by small boaters and, when in close, pier fishermen. Eight to 12-inch "horse herring" could offer fast sport for fly fishermen or ultralight anglers when herring are feeding at the surface on calm days. But most herring are jigged to freeze for bait or to make pickled herring, a delicacy to many.

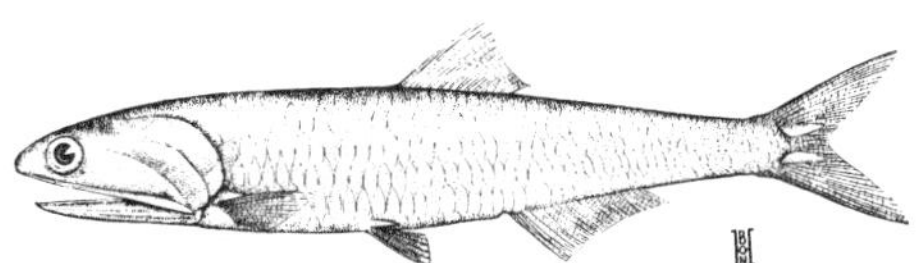

Northern anchovy *(Engraulis mordax).* One of the most abundant baitfish from southern Baja California to northern California and, seasonally (summer) north to Washington and British Columbia. Similar in color to herring; scales rub off easily. Usually 3-6 inches; may be slightly larger. Often moves into harbors in schools that some summers form dense black clouds and other summers remain few and far between. When thick, easily snagged from docks with treble hooks or jigged with tiny, shiny hooks. Generally sought for bait, but fair eating when fried like smelt.

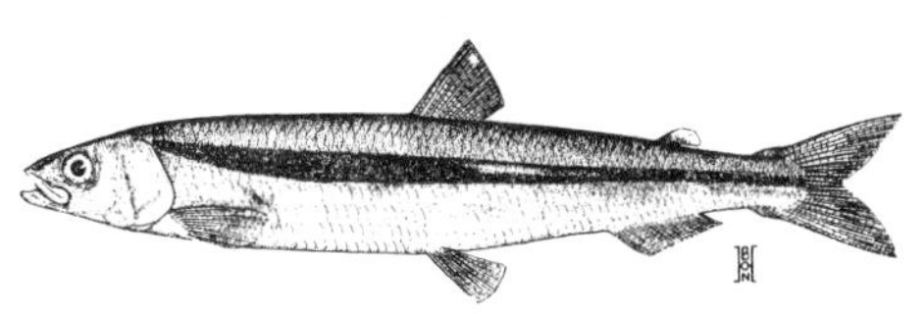

Surf smelt *(Hypomesus pretiosus).* Also: *day fish* (northern California beaches). Eastern subspecies common from southern California to Oregon; increasingly less so north to Alaska coast. Light green dorsally, silver sides with purple sheen. To 12 inches in California but smaller farther into the smelt's northern range. Moves into breakers (especially around high tides) at several different periods during year to spawn. Netted along southern Oregon and northern California sandy beaches with A-frame surf nets, spring and summer and with long-handled dip nets along northern Oregon and Washington coasts. Also jigged with hooks in some bays and northern Puget Sound. A fresh fried treat. (Also occuring similarly, but moving into breakers at night to spawn—and there be netted, is the smaller **night smelt** *(Spirinchus starksi).*

Eulachon *(Thaleichthys pacificus).* Also: *candlefish.* This important forage fish ranges from northern California into the Bering Sea. Bluish-brown above with silver sides.

spawn when a high tide returns, though [illegible] the possibility. Excellent baitfish, candlefish are also said to be fine eating. Along with herring, the major forage fish for salmon in Washington, B.C. and Alaska. "Candlefish" were so named for a high oil content supposedly permitting drying and, when fitted with a wick, using as a candle.

Sharks And Skates Of Bay And Sound

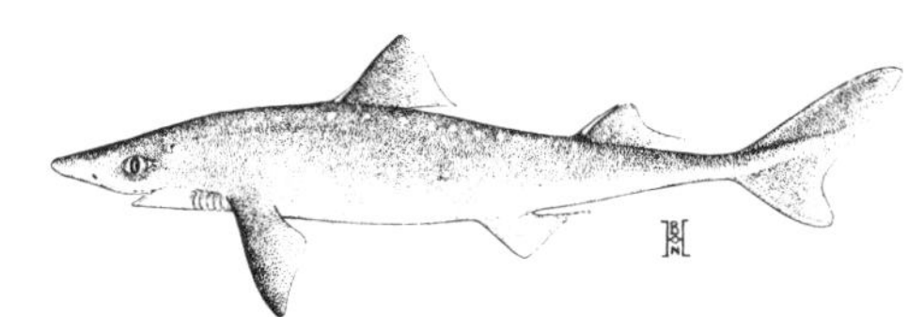

Spiny dogfish *(Squalus acanthius).* Common in temperate and tropical waters of both Pacific and Atlantic oceans. Grey or brownish grey shading to dirty white on bottom (younger fish have white spotting along back); one sharp spine before each dorsal fin. IGFA world record: 14 pounds, 1 ounce in 1988 (Ireland), but reported to at least 20 pounds. Common along Northwest coast, especially in Washington and B.C. inland marine waters, where at just about any depth they may shred herring and leaders of frustrated salmon moochers. Definitely no closed season. Unimpressive fight when hooked. Good, mild meat if properly cared for, but seldom eaten in Northwest (though a major food species in Europe).

Sixgill shark *(Hexanchus griseus).* Also: *cow shark.* Common in most of the world's temperate oceans. Similar in color to dogfish. IGFA world record: 1,027 pounds in 1987. I have seen photos of a 13-footer taken from Hood Canal on hook-and-line; much larger sixgills probably swim the depths of Northwest waters. Inhabits deep waters of ocean, straits, sounds and bays. No closed season. Will take large, whole or cut fish (apparently fond of live dogfish); usually hooked unintentionally on herring fished deep—but that is rare and landing them is rarer still unless the angler is using rugged gear or is very lucky. Reportedly good eating (if, like all sharks, bled at once and perhaps soaked overnight in a mild lemon juice or vinegar solution). A commercial sixgill fishery decades ago in Puget Sound used drums, rope, cable and whole dogfish as bait.

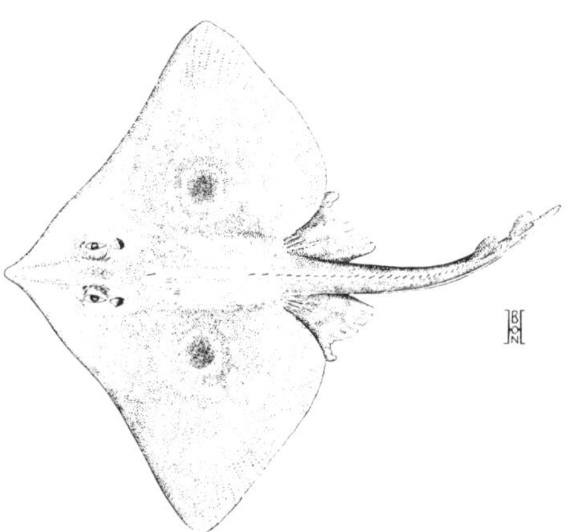

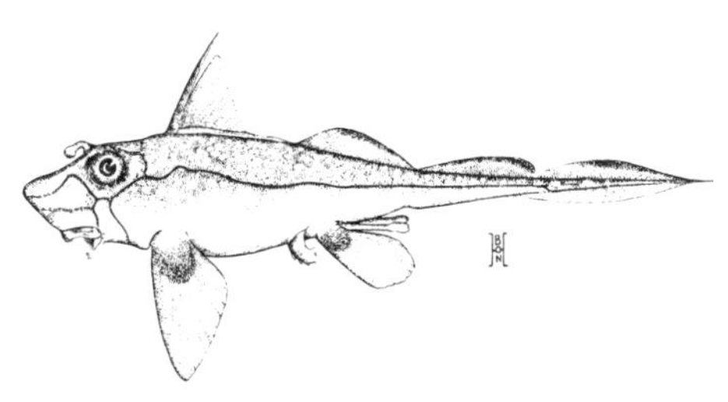

Illustrations by J.L. Hart, Pacific Flishes of Canada. Reproduced by permission of the ministry of Supply & Services, Canada.

Big skate *(Raja binoculata).* Common from central California to southeastern Alaska, where it is a very occasional catch of anglers. Brown to blackish grey on dorsal surface, white below, round "eye" spot atop each pectoral fin. IGFA world record not established, but reaches about eight feet and documented to about 200 pounds. Commonly 10 to 80 or so. Common in shallow near-shore and inshore waters of Northwest over smooth bottoms. No directed sport fisheries for skate and no closed seasons, but hooked incidentally. Feeds heavily on invertebrates but will pick up herring baits. Powerful runs with large pectoral fins ("wings") present quite a challenge on salmon tackle. Meat in pectorals is excellent eating; round muscle segments may be cut and cooked to resemble scallops.

Ratfish *(Hydrolagus collei).* This common scavenger from Baja to southeastern Alaska is neither truly a shark nor a more evolutionarily advanced bony fish. Bronze hues on upper body, silvery below, with white spotting on sides; unmistakable shape and features including large emerald green eyes, rodent-like teeth, pointed snout. Note long, reportedly venomous dorsal spine. IGFA record not established. Exceeds 3 feet in length. May inhabit water over 1,000 feet especially in the southern part of its range but often caught in Washington and B.C. inland waters in water less than 100 feet, usually on herring. Bizarre, soft-bodied, unloved and unwanted incidental catch, usually over muddy bottoms where currents are light. Offers no real fight. Edible—and, from personal experimentation, bland—but seldom eaten. Valued for copious liver oil as a lubricant before synthetics.

DESPITE INCREASINGLY REGULATED RECREATIONAL fisheries on the Northwest coast, bountiful marine resources continue to draw anglers by the thousands to one of the world's most beautiful saltwater settings. But the blessings of beauty and abundance come with a price, that of cantankerous ocean, often inclement weather and steep topography.

So anyone serious about catching salmon and other species from this ocean and these straits, sounds, bays and tidewaters must be aware of certain realities.

For one thing, many exceptions notwithstanding, a *boat* of some sort is generally a necessity. Shore fishing is limited by lack of access, by hook-sticky rocks and kelp, and by game fish which tend to live/feed beyond casting range.

Then the Pacific, despite its name, is *not* the most peaceful of oceans. The traditional popularity of cabin boats over center consoles here is testimony to the realities of heavy currents and riplines and commonly brisk winds. Fortunately, the seas *do* lay down now and again (especially late summer). Of course, seaworthy boats help and, for smaller boats, semi-protected marine waters offer a chance to fish year-round.

Luckily, one needn't *have* a boat to *fish* from a boat thanks to a considerable fleet of charter boats from southern Oregon to Vancouver Island.

NORTHWEST CHARTER BOAT FISHING

You should find charter boats just about anywhere you find a port or harbor in the Northwest. Actually, the term "charter boat" needs explanation. The Northwest charter is a synthesis of the true charter boat and the larger "partyboat," "headboat" or "driftboat" of the Atlantic, Gulf and southern California coasts.

Partyboats are typically 50- to 100-foot, 25- to 35-passenger offshore vessels that target bottomfish and schooling surface species. They generally take out a mixed-group of walk-on passengers. Charterboats are usually 24-to 50-foot, fast offshore boats chartered by one group of 4 to 6 anglers for the day, typically to pursue big game fish.

Northwest charterboats tend to be 30 to 60 feet in length and carry 6 to 16 passengers, occasionally more, normally walkons. Their traditional target is salmon but over the past 2 decades bottomfishing trips have become a regular alternative and late summer offshore albacore trips are an annual possibility.

Most salmon charters from northern California to Ilwaco (southwestern Washington) troll. From Westport norththward, most salmon charters driftmooch herring. Charters out of Ucluelet on Vancouver Island's Barkley Sound strictly driftjig with metal salmon jigs and enjoy consistent success.

Over the past decade, specialized charter operations for halibut have sprung up in several areas, notably out of Newport and Neah Bay. These trips entail longer runs to rugged offshore banks to drift deep water, typically using heavy dacron line on 4/0 reels to drop heavily weighted spreader rigs baited with large whole herring or squid to bottom.

In recent years, particularly from several northern Washington ports, a number of smaller charters have begun operation. These 2 to 4-person boats are typically 18 to 24 feet in length. They are characteristically fast, planing hulls, often center consoles or walk-around cuddies, and emphasize quality light-tackle fishing, either jigging or downrigger trolling. In many respects, these operations fit

HOPE FOR THE SEASICK?

There may be a feeling worse than being stuck on a rolling, pitching and (you should pardon the expression) heaving boat all day when you're seasick—but I can't imagine it and don't want to try.

Mal de mer, the bane of some ocean fishing wannabe's, afflicts people differently—many people not at all. Those who do suffer are victims of motion-induced irritation of the inner ear nerve fibers that normally help maintain balance. (Perhaps that knowledge explains why, when seasick, I've felt like a pinball machine on "tilt.") Theories and remedies abound. Most seem worthless.

Northeast Pacific seas are often lumpy, with swells particularly prone to keeping boats rocking and rolling in a way that can challenge those with even the sturdiest constitution.

Still, there is hope for at least some potential victims. In the '80s, along came the Transderm (scopolamine) skin patch, a thin adhesive disc worn behind the ear. Developed by NASA for use in space, the anti-motion sickness drug is dispersed through the skin over a three-day period. But these have not proven a panacea: some anglers swear by Transderms, but I've also seen plenty of them stuck on heads hung low over the railing all day. Trial and error is about the only way to know if they may work for you.

Some still prefer the traditional remedies, pills such as Dramamine, Marazine, Bonine and the like. In fact, one authority recommends a combination of two remedies. Cathy Cedargreen, who with her husband Mark has owned and operated Westport Charter Service for years, says 1 dosage of Marazine and 1 of a newer product, Triptone, seem by far the most effective way to stave off seasickness when taken together, well *before* the boat's departure.

One alternative to medication which may appeal to the naturopathic angler is ginger root, perhaps chewed (if you can stand the heat) or just cut small and swallowed. I've never been able to verify the effectiveness of this, but I continue to hear it mentioned over the years.

Other recurrent suggestions which may be reasonble include advice to keep your eyes on the horizon (the lone unmoving reference point) and to stay out of the pitching, deadair wheelhouse. If seasickness strikes and won't let up, relief is usually a matter of lying down and staying down—for some, flat on their stomach seems to work best.

Finally, to those immune from motion sickness, a plea for compassion. As if feeling like something the cat disgorged weren't bad enough, it's tough being the butt of jokes from other anglers who are fortunate enough to feel just fine. If others are seasick around you, save the jokes. And for crying out loud, *don't* keep telling them, "C'mon now, it's all in your head!"

That's not what they need to hear—nor it is true.

A particularly successful bottomfishing trip meant full boat limits on this Westport charter—though some anglers "helped out" the less fortunate to fill their limit.

the concept of saltwater "guide boats" which operate along the Gulf Coast.

Costs vary widely, but within a harbor rates tend to be fairly uniform as do the size and quality of boats and the length of trips they take. In Westport, for example, figure on $55 to 60 or so for a salmon trip lasting from a few hours (when limits come quickly) to a full day, aboard large, sleek, very modern boats. I've been on salmon charters out of southern Oregon and northern California, on the other hand, that cost only $30 to 35 for 4-hour trips aboard smaller boats, some fairly new and some old and ramshackle.

Albacore trips will last 12 hours or longer at a cost of $125 or more. Bottomfishing can be as simple as a halfday trip to fish nearshore reefs from several Oregon ports or more serious outings that require a run of 20 to 30 miles (e.g. out of Neah Bay, Tillamook or Newport). The latter will cost you in the vicinity of $100.

If you're new to an area and planning to hop aboard a charter, check around the docks, particularly in the afternoon when the boats return. Check out and compare catches, note size and condition of boats and if feasible chat with some skippers. The skipper makes the difference: a few are out there just putting in their time; many others combine experience, knowledge and persistence with genuine concern for their passengers.

Think about making advance reservations, particularly when salmon (or albacore) fishing is hot; boats may become booked up several days in advance.

When you throw your gear together for a day on a Northwest charter, figure on plenty of clothing in layers that are warm and, on top, waterproof (you can always take it off). You'll want a lunch and tackle if you're bringing your own. Most charters provide hot coffee, tea and water throughout the day.

Sometimes tackle is included in the trip cost; otherwise, you can rent boat gear for a few bucks. However, boat tackle is generally pretty heavy and may be much more functional than sporting. (Though few more coastal charters have begun to stock lighter rods, primarily for schools of black rockfish.)

I've had great success aboard charters fishing my own light tackle (spinning and "miniature big game" reels) with 8- to 12-pound line while staying out of others' lines—but it takes experience, skill and a bit of luck. Still, I can't imagine using heavier gear for most charter salmon or bottomfish angling. If you have quality light tackle, try it. Two suggestions: first, let the skipper know before booking a trip that you'll be using your own light gear and be sure he has no objections. Second, work from the bow. It's usually the least crowded and gives you—with your gear's better casting ability—the chance to cast within a 180-degree radius from the boat and keep well away from others' lines.

One additional suggestion for anyone with even a slight inclination to queasiness: Do your best to get a good night's sleep, since it may well be true that weary fishermen are more prone to seasickness than those who are well-rested. And by all means avoid partying down—crossing the bar at 6 a.m. to the fishing grounds on a few hours of sleep with a hangover may make you wistful for hell.

Tips for Charter Boat Fishermen

Board early. Avoid last-minute rushing and, depending upon charter operation, assure yourself a stern or corner position if you want that.

Follow instructions! Different boats may use different systems. Each works for that skipper.People who fail to follow directions given by the skipper or deckhand tend to catch fewer fish and cause problems for other fishermen.

Ask questions. When uncertain, don't hesitate to ask for help or advice.

Fight fish wisely. Don't overtighten the drag; novices tend to lose many fish this way—or by loosening it so much a backlash results. Don't try to lift a good fish into the boat. Leave it in the water, with at least 6 feet of line out, and call for a net.

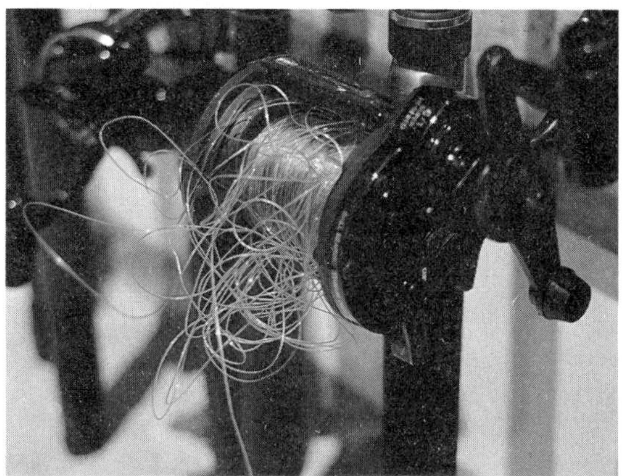

Few deckhands haven't seen this, many times—the result of anglers hooked on bottom or into fish taking it upon themselves to try loosening the star drag.

By law you're allowed to keep only *your* fish. As those are caught, they are usually marked with numbered pins, with a specified pattern of cuts in the head, throat or tail, or by putting fish into bags, each with an angler's designated number. By law, you must stop fishing if you catch your limit. In reality, however, the practice of most boats is to allow you to keep fishing even after catching your limit as long as there are other anglers who haven't yet reached their limits. Thus you'd give away your overlimit fish, but keep the largest of your total catch. It is this custom that accounts for the frequent phenomenon of full boat limits—sometimes by midmorning.

When in doubt aboard any charter, ask. When answered, listen. Most deckhands and skippers are very proficient at helping people hook and land their fish.

Charterboats involve a fair number of people fishing together in a rather confined space. A certain etiquette becomes essential in ensuring the harmony and proficiency of all aboard. (After all, 1 line can tangle 15 others in a moment.) Simply listening to and following instructions of the deckhand and skipper will eliminate most problems. In general, keep in mind that when fishing from a drifting boat you want to stay with a hooked fish. Slip over or under lines as you move up or down the railing to keep a good fish as directly straight out from you as possible. This helps minimize tangles (and lost fish). One other small suggestion: if you need to leave the rail mid-drift, *secure* your rod. Too often I've seen anglers simply set a rod against the railing and walk away, so it inevitably crashes to the deck—or into a nearby fisherman.

Tipping the deckhand at the end of a trip is common practice, whether that's just a couple bucks or considerably more—or nothing at all if you felt slighted or turned off by indifferent service. Some anglers who win the "pool" or "jackpot" will split it with a good deckhand. (The jackpot is an optional lottery, often just a dollar or two collected by a passenger. The winner—the largest fish, of course—takes all.)

Fishing The Ocean From Small Boats

What's a "small boat"? A 30-footer may seem small when traversing a rough ocean bar or climbing steep swells. Yet much smaller boats regularly fish the northeastern Pacific. Factors in determining how safely one can fish the ocean from a smaller boat include the size, design and condition of the boat and the knowledge and experience of its skipper (and maybe his condition, too). As a rule of thumb, even on calm summer days, anything less than a seaworthy 17-footer is probably too small.

Crossing the Bar. The "bar" is that general area at a river mouth where the outflow of fresh water meets the incoming ocean swells. By nature, bars tend to be shallow areas of sand buildup, forever shifting, and often made impassable by crashing breakers.

At most major Northwest coast river mouths, human development has altered the picture. Long rock jetties run from river mouths out into the ocean. Between them, a channel is dredged to make the river navigable to and from the ocean.

However, each of these bars is different, some more "crossable" than others and even the better entrances in poor conditions and worse entrances in good conditions can be tricky. (See box.) Make no mistake: lives are lost on Northwest bars each year.

Photo courtesy Portland District U.S. Army Corps of Engineers.

Some general recommendations for private boaters traversing these bars:

1. *Check with local Coast Guard officials before attempting to cross any bar with which you're not familiar.* There is a Coast Guard station either at most entrances or at least no farther than an adjacent entrance. Often you can obtain a copy of a printed bar guide. (This book lists those stations in each section.) Check conditions; ask questions. Remember that the configuration of these harbor entrances often changes seasonally with the shifting sands. Ask what areas to avoid.

2. *Do not fish or stop ON (over) the bar!* Fish either well inside the bar (where large waves have already broken leaving only the "suds") or well outside, beyond the bar (where large waves may begin to crest but won't yet be curling over). Don't be lulled into false security by nice weather and a calm bar: they're never guarantees of safety in this icy, unpredictable ocean where "sleeper" waves can sweep a bar without warning (see Tillamook Bay section).

3. *Be alert to the tides.* Many bars easily crossed during slack or flood tide become treacherous during the ebb, when outrushing water challenges the incoming surf.

4. *Scoot back in if conditions become questionable* (no matter how good fishing may be!). Remember that returning in following seas may be trickier than running out against them. Try to keep the boat's stern square to the seas to avoid broaching and ride in on the back of a swell. And, of course, make sure everyone aboard is wearing a life preserver.

A very useful publication available free to the public from the Oregon State Marine Board (3000 Market St. NE, #505, Salem, OR 97310) is "Boating in Coastal Waters" which offers general advice to boaters and covers each of Oregon's bar crossings separately.

A Small Boater's Comparison Of Bar Crossings At Northwest Coastal Rivers And Bays

(Derived with assistance from U.S. Coast Guard 13th District officials)

RATING SCALE:

0 = not crossable
1 = cross at considerable risk
2 = cross with caution
3 = cross with relative ease

CROSSABILITY

LOCATION	CONDITIONS GOOD	CONDITIONS POOR	COMMENTS
La Push	1 1/2	0	faces south; enter ocean behind island, abeam troughs
Grays Harbor	3	1 1/2	stay in main channel
Columbia River (Ilwaco/Astoria)	2	1	watch currents—check tides; one of last bars to close in bad weather
Nehalem River	1 1/2	0	shallow; beware "horse collar" where sand piles up out front
Tillamook Bay	2	0	shallow; current may be heavy; avoid ranges—better to the south
Depoe Bay	2	1 1/2	watch cross-swell (surge); ok west/southwest or northwest sea, bad from west
Yaquina Bay (Newport)	3	2	Deep water entrance; '89 rebuilt north jetty, redredged
Siuslaw River (Florence)	2	0	shallow, not regularly dredged
Winchester Bay	1 1/2	0	training jetty, rocky areas present hazards
Coos Bay	3	1	wide and deep; watch freighter traffic
Coquille River (Bandon)	1 1/2	0	shallow; rock-filled wrecked freighter has extended north jetty
Rogue River (Gold Beach)	1 1/2	0	shallow, shifting
Chetco River	3	1 1/2	north-south bar, small boater friendly; somewhat narrow
Humbolt Bay (Eurkea, CA)	2	1/2	beware a treacherous ebb tide

Even a portable LCD fishfinder can offer the difference between "fishing blind" or knowing what's beneath you—which in the Northwest could be 50 feet of water or 500.

Northwest Salmon Fishing

Finding Salmon on the Ocean. Being at the right place at the right time means knowing when and where to find salmon. In the big picture, "when" means knowing the seasons. Ah, but there are two ocean seasons along the Northwest coast. One is the natural season that runs from about May through September. Weather conditions begin permitting boaters to fish along the open coast in May, about the time when chinook are moving in to feed. By September, the last month of bankable good weather, big coho are still swarming toward coastal streams.

The other season is that dictated by the Pacific Fishery Management Council and state management agencies. It is shorter, more variable and less dependable than the natural season. Salmon are one of the most difficult, environmentally-sensitive, politically-governed species in the world to manage, as reflected in sportfishing seasons.

For many years in the 1980s, Washington and Oregon coastal salmon seasons opened in late June (or even early July) and closed in early to late August. In recent years, thanks to an international treaty, better ocean conditions and successful enhancement programs, seasons have been longer, often from Memorial Day through Labor Day. But seasons are not set until spring each year and even then may change during the summer according to the rate at which catch quotas fill. So *always check local regulations before fishing when unsure.*

On a daily basis, when to fish varies but early morning and evening remain times of great feeding activity. Still, "the bite" can occur at any time throughout the day.

It's a big ocean, especially when you're looking for salmon. But of course that's the key to success. There are no simple answers. But there are certainly clues to locating fish. Perhaps the best clue is a concentration of boats in one area—either seen or heard on VHF. That may mean that only a few fish were taken on a slow day and the word spread or it may mean a wide-open bite, but it's always worth checking out. Then there are those other, full-time fishermen: schools of birds, wheeling and diving on bait, will often point the way to salmon below. In any case, at least a good LCD depthsounder these days is essential on a fishing boat to detect schools of baits and/or salmon and note their depth. If all else fails, drop over the gear and start trolling, initially trying different depths (between 30 feet and 150).

Often a seamount or other sharp rise from the bottom will tend to concentrate baitfish and of course predators such as salmon hang around. For coho and pinks, working riplines near or far from shore is almost always a good way to locate fish. Again, these rips—converging walls of current—hold schools of bait that attract foraging salmon.

Opting for her own spinning gear with six-pound line and a metal jig on this Westport charter, Jackie Olander enjoyed a particularly exciting and challenging fight from this stubborn chinook.

Finding Salmon in Inland Marine Waters. Northwest "inland marine waters" could include all the countless deep straits, sounds, passes, channels and bays that begin at the Strait of Juan de Fuca along the northern Washington coast, including Puget Sound and southern B.C.'s Strait of Georgia, and continue on up to central Alaska.

Given the geographical scope of this guide, only the Strait of Juan de Fuca and adjacent waters of Puget Sound and the San Juan Islands will be specifically included when describing inland marine waters. (However, information such as that in this section is certainly valid for inside waters north to Alaska.)

Perhaps one of the most noteworthy differences between the ocean and inland waters is the fishing season. In a natural sense year-round fishing is very feasible, both because of the opportunity to fish in protected, lee areas and because there are salmon available year-round. Specifically, these salmon are known in Washington as winter blackmouth—in fact, immature chinook of a few pounds to 15 or 20 (but commonly 5 to 8). Actually, winter blackmouth fishing is most popular from November into late winter in some areas and midspring in others.

Also making this year-round salmon fishing in these waters feasible are sport fishing regulations which allow fishing all year in most areas.

But interest typically turns toward the bigger, mature, returning kings (mature chinook of 20 to 50+ pounds) from June into August. In addition, mature coho move in during August and, particularly, September. They may be joined by pink salmon, though only during odd-numbered years and, at that, run size varies tremendously.

It seems particularly important when fishing salmon in inland waters to get out on the water early (or fish late) for mature salmon. Perhaps that prime feeding period means more for these bigger fish which are feeding evermore selectively as they catch the scent of fresh water. The traditional rule of thumb is simply, "If you can cut bait without a flashlight, you're out on the water too late." For blackmouth, the bite is often early, but not necessarily at daybreak.

Locating salmon here is less tricky since anglers are faced not with a wide-open ocean but a limited body of water with well-known fishing spots (marked clearly on charts in this guide). As a very general rule, trollers work along steep ledges that often run for miles. Moochers and jiggers are more likely to fish sharp, jutting points where the depth drops away quickly. Large bars or banks (underwater plateaus) attract all types of salmon anglers.

Sekiu, Wash. skipper John Truex owes many of the big summer-run kings he catches each year to downrigger trolling.

Trolling for Salmon. Coastwide, trolling remains by far the most popular method for catching salmon. For chinook and often for coho as well, getting baits or lures deep is required and is accomplished either with plastic diving planes and/or weights or with downriggers.

For fishing diving planes or weights, reasonably stout tackle is needed. This usually means a large levelwind or thumbguided open reel with 20- to 30-pound line on an 8-to 9-foot medium-action rod. Terminal rigs typically use a large plastic diving plane (such as Deep Six or Pink Lady) or a very heavy sinker to keep lines down a good 30 or 40 feet. Unfortunately such gear means the line will never be free from a considerable amount of resistance. (Some fishermen, who presumably have a cheap lead supply, use lead balls weighing a pound or more designed to drop off when a fish strikes and hooks are set. I've seen northern California/southern Oregon charters do this—and charge customers a buck per ball.) Some charters still use very heavy gear with one-pound balls fixed to the leader, typically known as meatlines: coho can offer little fight as they're simply cranked in.

Many trollers off Oregon and almost all off Washington favor herring for bait. It is variously used whole, plugcut or stripped (fileted). More often off Oregon and northern California, anchovies are the bait of choice. Lures most often mean Hoochys (plastic squid)—often with a herring strip—or plugs such as Silver Hordes, J-Plugs, Tomics and the like. Spoons are effective, particularly for coho. When swivels are used on trolling setups, at least one should be a ball-bearing swivel. Costly but well worth it in preventing line twist.

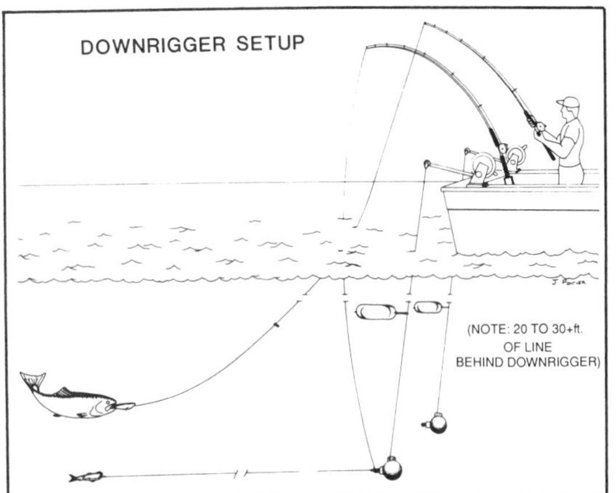

The uppper 20 to 40 feet is typically coho country; chinook may be mixed in with them (particularly early and late in the day). But larger chinook tend to feed deeper than coho. Downriggers make getting down to them even in very deep water absolutely feasible. And you can do so without having to drag a lot of additional weight on your line. Another big plus: you can use lighter rods and lighter lines. I favor medium levelwinds or thumb-guided open reels with 12- to 20-pound line. As the illustration shows, the bait or lure is simply clipped to the downrigger line by an adjustable-tension trip release so it works 20 to 30 or more feet in back of the boat. The line derives all the benefit of having up to 10 pounds of weight that's on the down-rigger cable but, when tripped, is free of all resistance.

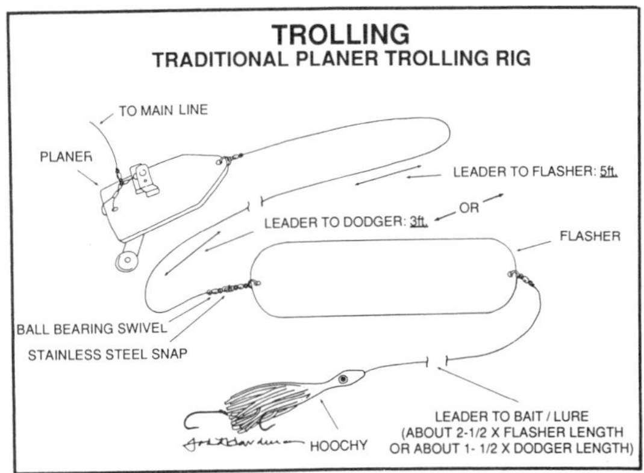

At times, salmon are in the upper 20 or so feet of water—most often coho but sometimes chinook as well. Then, for those lacking downriggers, simply trolling herring and/or a Hoochy on a 6- or 7-foot leader behind a 2- to 6-ounce trolling (kidney) sinker may be all that's necessary. And ordinary mooching tackle is heavy enough. For coho, many anglers swear by a faster trolling speed, often pulling the bait or lure—or a coho fly—at or near the surface. I've also caught trophy-size chinook in British Columbia simply trolling a few ounces of lead ahead of a plugged herring, with 30 to 50 pulls of line out. But the key to success, as it often is with chinook, is s-l-o-w trolling—with a small outboard throttled all the way down. That allows the herring to rotate in large, lazy circles (see illustration of plug-cutting).

One trolling variation that's brought me considerable pleasure is worth keeping in mind when small coho are the main opportunity. I rig up an ultralight baitcast or spinning outfit filled with 4-pound line simply as follows. Tie the main line to a small ball-bearing swivel and to that tie 6 to 8 feet of 10-pound leader. (This shock leader gives your wispy main line a bit of protection.) On the end of this leader should be a traditional mooching rig with two 1/0 or 2/0 beak hooks. Rig a small plugcut herring with the lower hook swinging free. Finally, on the main line ahead of the swivel, attach a 1/2- to 2-ounce *sliding* trolling sinker. Troll with a considerable amount of line out. You'll find that small coho are amazing fighters on such light gear.

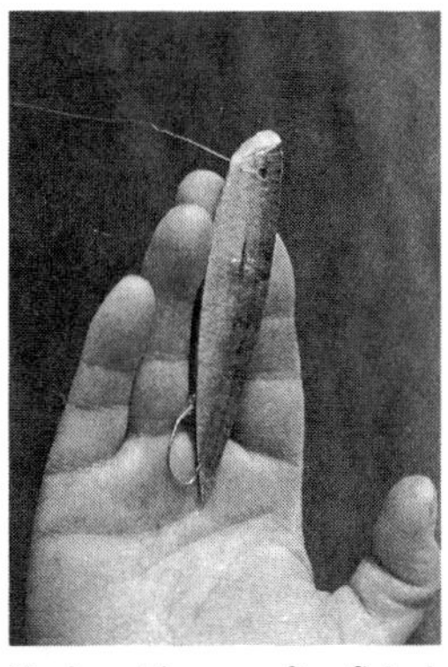

Herring strips are often fished behind a flasher this way or with a plastic squid (Hoochy) just above the strip.

Drift-Mooching for Salmon. Mooching, I once began an article on the subject, has about as much to do with "dunkin' a minny" as a wine cooler has to do with a Chateau Lafite-Rothschild. This unique method of fishing for Northwest salmon is so steeped in tradition that it can seem almost ritualistic. But like many traditions, it is based on the soundest of principles. It is a method that has endured because *it works.* Of course it works best when done correctly.

"Correctly" may be a loaded term, depending upon the individual moocher and how he may have fine-tuned his own variations upon the basic theme. But there are fundamentals worth keeping in mind.

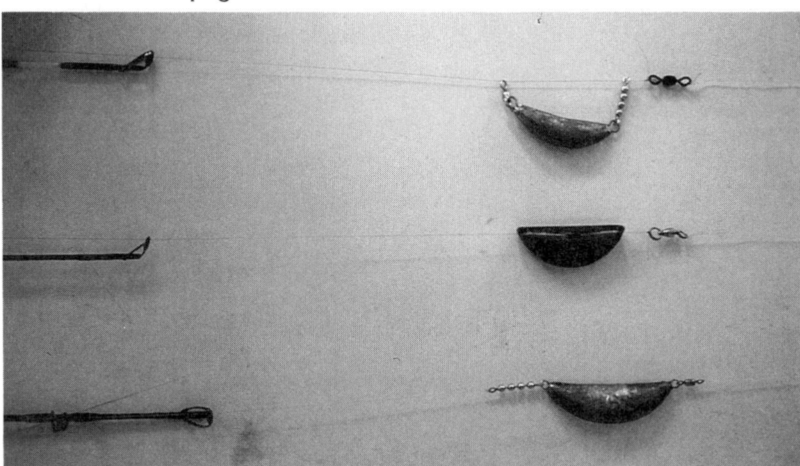

Traditional mooching setup at bottom has kidney sinker connecting main line and leader. Better are top two sliding sinker rigs, particularly that in the middle since it uses a ball bearing swivel to connect line and leader.

That begins with having the "correct" tackle. Traditionally that means a medium levelwind reel with a direct drive retrieve allowing immediate response filled with 12- to 20-pound line. (I've used 8-pound line very successfully.) Mooching rods are long and limber, generally eight to nine feet or so.

You'll see somewhat different tackle used customarily in Canadian waters. There, a big single-action "knucklebuster" reel with 15- to 25-pound line is set at the base of an even longer mooching rod—often 10 feet or so.

Terminal rigging is simple: a leader nearly as long as your rod, usually 2 to 4 pounds lighter than the main line (though using the same weight may work out just fine). The end of the main line is tied to one end of a mooching sinker (kidney or banana sinker) of 1 to 6 or 8 ounces and the other to the leader. At the business end of the leader is a 2-hook mooching rig: 2/0 to 5/0 short shanked beak hooks.

However, consider this variation on the traditional rig. Connect main line to leader with a ball-bearing swivel. Then above the swivel on the main line clip on a sliding mooching sinker. If a slider is unavailable, before tying on the main line, run the end of it through the ends of the traditional kidney sinker (or through the swivel eyes if it has swivels attached) so it slides freely on the main line to

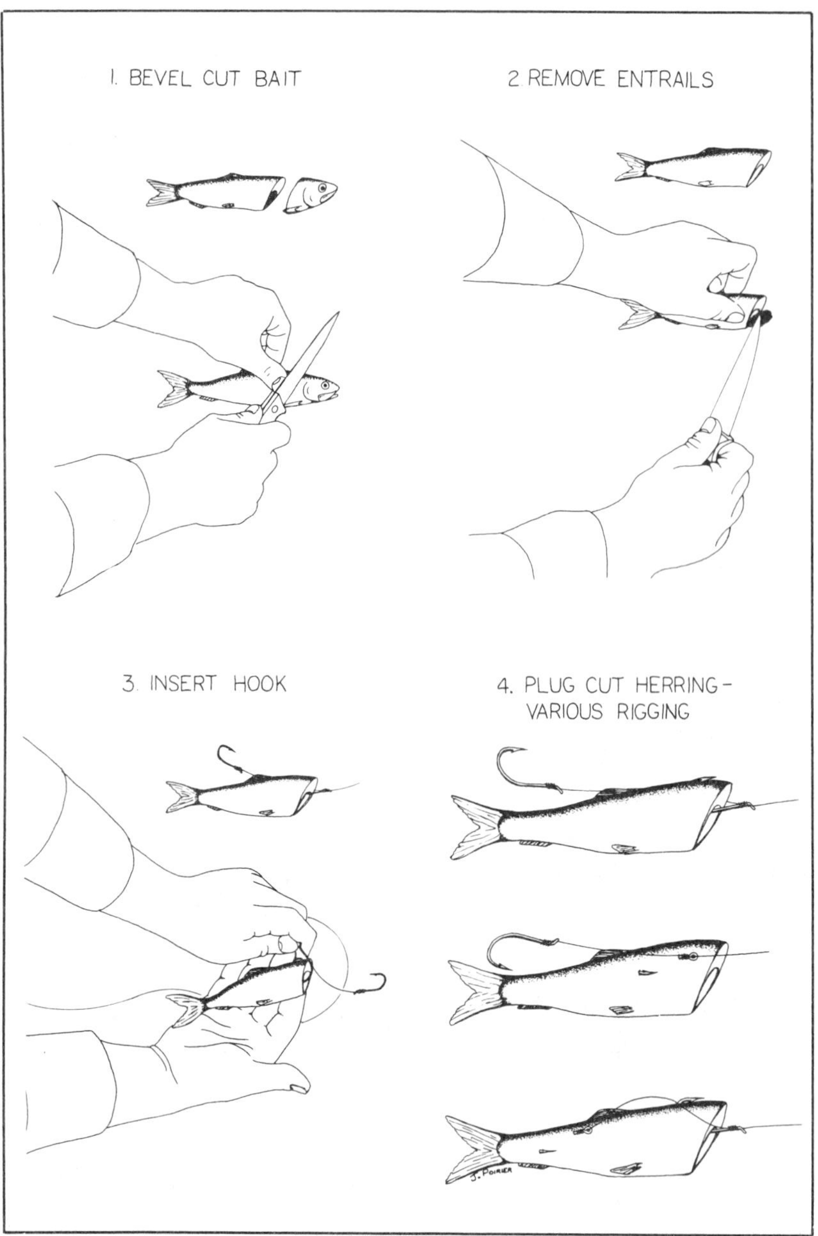

the swivel. This rig uses a ball bearing swivel which helps keep down frustrating line twist. The sliding sinker certainly permits the angler to better feel the fish while helping to keep the fish from feeling the angler or his gear.

The two major steps to baiting up are cutting and hooking herring—"plug-cutting" the bait. Cutting is accomplished as per the illustration. Besides those basic steps, there are many "little things" that the productive moocher must keep in mind.

Is it really worth all the hassle of plugcutting herring? The answer certainly seems to be yes. Herring, at least when fresh, are a shiny, flashy baitfish. Visual predators, like salmon, are clearly tuned to the flashes a wounded fish makes. An effectively fished plugcut herring is always rotating, and flashing from all angles.

There are 2 different types of movement the experienced plugcutter/rigger can accomplish. I suspect either works well for both chinook and coho when the bite is on. Still, you may want to be aware of each and their differences.

First, there is a tight, quick spin or roll. This is traditionally used for coho with a faster motor-mooch (slow troll). (I do know expert guides who swear by this cut for trophy sized chinook.) Generally, the longer, more obtuse the angle of the cut at the front of the body (where the head is removed), the quicker the spin.

The alternative cut is a sharp, acute angle which, when hooked properly, causes the herring to rotate slowly in wide circles. In addition to the cut, placement of the front hook can make quite a difference in the bait's action. Experiment a bit to get the action you want.

The actual process of "mooching" involves letting the bait sink to a desired depth and slowly jigging it. The "desired depth" may be determined by what shows up on a depthsounder screen or by trial and error. Often, if there's no indication of activity at the surface or middepths, moochers will let the bait to bottom and mooch a few turns above that.

Let the line out slowly or the herring, on a long leader, will inevitably become a twisted mess around the main line. Many let line out with "pulls," counting the number of times they pull an arm's length of line from the reel. Others use their direct drive reels (with no anti-reverse on) to turn backwards, spooling the line down a few feet at a time. Be

How To Make The Most Of Mooching

1. *Start with good herring and keep it cool.* Fresh herring is generally good herring. It feels, looks and smells... well, fresh. Frozen can be fine when fish are hungry. But *don't* toss the packages in a bucket on deck and leave them there. In no time, oily herring will turn soft, foul-smelling and sheenless. Keep them on ice. You may want to plug cut the baits before getting out on the water.

2. *Keep hooks "sticky sharp"* (see box on hooks in light tackle section). Points should be filed so they are like fine needles. Salmon bite lightly and sometimes only once.

3. *Snip line ends close to knots* so when you pull the hook through a herring while rigging, the soft flesh is not torn.

4. *Always check the action of a rigged herring before fishing it.* It takes only a moment to toss a bait over the side, let out a bit of line and watch how it moves. It should spin or rotate enticingly, but sometimes a bait has no spin. A slight rehooking with the top hook can make all the difference.

5. *Check baits frequently* so you can answer that age old question: Do you know what *your* plugcut herring is doing right now? Oily and soft by nature, a herring's thin gut cavity walls soften and begin to flare out after a while and it will end up dragging through the water. Or if struck once, the bait may be off one hook, dragging backwards. Any weeds that end up on your line will hamper the action as well. So check frequently and don't hesitate to put on a new bait often.

BLAINE FREER'S SECRET "TOOTHPICK SPINNER"

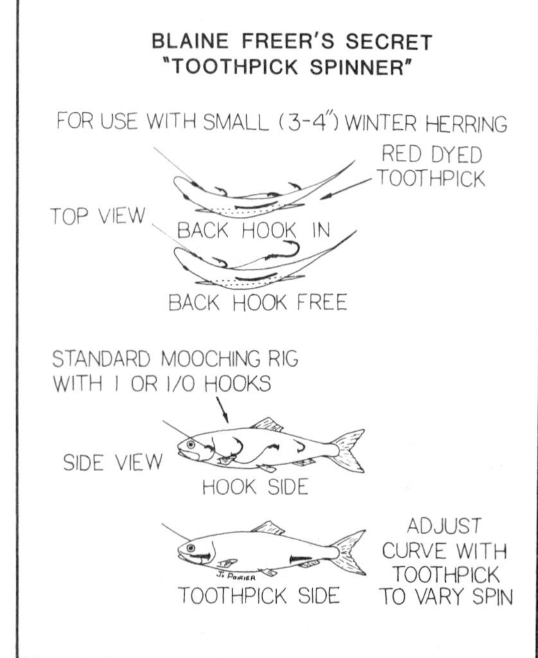

This 30-pound tyee (chinook) was taken on a plug cut herring rigged like that shown.

alert for taps as you lower the bait: the herring should be spinning as a struggling, dying bait might and salmon often pick it up in descent.

When mooching, lift and lower the rod tip slowly in long sweeps. When you feel a strike, respond according to the strike. That is, sometimes salmon will make like a freight train running away with the bait, pretty much hooking themselves if you tighten up and set quickly. But often, salmon tap and mouth a bait a while before taking it (or before darting away—particularly if they sense anything "strange"—leaving a tense and frustrated angler above). I've had 40-pound chinook bite as gently as 1-pound blackmouth.

With that typically light bite, it is best to *wait* before setting the hooks or you'll only pull the bait from the fish. Start by lowering the rod tip slowly to the water. Then if the pull is solid, set. If not, be ready to wait and if necessary give the fish some line until there is a pull solid enough to set against. Patience is indeed a virtue.

Patience can be an insufficient virtue when measured against the seething hordes of dogfish sharks that can infest an otherwise hot spot for salmon. Dogfish are enough to drive a dedicated moocher to drink, since they'll chew up carefully-crafted baits and shred your best leaders right and left. Mooching is surely one of the most intricate, satisfying and effective methods of fishing for salmon. But *not* when dogfish are about. However, you needn't stop fishing. Just break out the jigs.

Drift-Jigging for Salmon. Jigging from a drifting boat, like mooching, offers certain advantages over trolling that some anglers (like this one) really enjoy. Perhaps the first that comes to mind is that it is *quiet.* Without the droning of an outboard, you can hear the splash of a coho, the cry of an eagle or the growl of your stomach because you need a break. Secondly, it is *active fishing.* It isn't rod-in-holder-beer-in-hand fishing; it's you feeling the bite, setting the hook and holding the rod when a salmon has the line sizzling out.

Those who prefer trolling cite, as a major disadvantage of drifting, that boats doing so cover much less ground. And that may be, but often salmon are concentrated in an area—which is why mooching/jigging enjoys particular popularity in small, specific spots like Point No Point and Point Wilson in Puget Sound where salmon congregate.

That may also explain why driftjigging is not particularly popular on the ocean off Oregon and Washington. Yet that is the *only* method used—with great success—by the several big Canadian Princess charters off Barkley Sound for chinook, coho and halibut.

In the 1970s, a small revolution in salmon fishing occurred. The first shots were fired in southern British Columbia where Rex and Doug Field came up with something called the "Buzz Bomb." Shortly after that, Rock D'Acquisto in Port Townsend, Washington patented his "Point Wilson Dart Candlefish" jig.

Today, seemingly countless manufacturers large and small throughout the Northwest have jumped on the jig bandwagon. The 2 mentioned remain abidingly popular with jig fishermen, though many other styles work well. Look through the jig section of a well-stocked tackle shop and you'll see names like Point Wilson Dart Candlefish and Anchovy, Buzz Bomb, Zzinger, Nordic, Mooch-a-jig, Crippled Herring, Stingsilda and many others. Spoons deserve mention here since they may be effectively jigged for salmon. I've caught chinook as large as 37 pounds while jigging Krocodile spoons.

All these various types and brands operate on pretty much the same principle—a falling, fluttering, thin slab of shiny metal makes salmon strike. It works. Frankly, I still can't agree with jiggers who say jigs are more effective than herring. But I *can* say that dogfish rarely strike the odorless pieces of metal and that's a blessing, and I can also say that it's quicker and easier to tie on a jig than worry about keeping, cutting and rigging bait all day. And my hands don't stink. I *do* like jigging.

Jigs and spoons are generally available from less than an ounce to 8 or more ounces. For most applications, salmon fishermen choose jigs of 1 to 1 1/2 ounces up to 4-to 6-ounces with the 2- to 3-ounce range most useful. (Generally, go no heavier than possible. And remember: the lighter your line the easier it is to fish a jig at any depth desired.)

Jigging tackle need be nothing more than a light mooching outfit. However, the soft action of the typical mooching rod can slow the quick, sharp hookset the jig fishermen must often make, particularly when using a heavy jig that keeps the rod constantly bent. My preference is for something a bit shorter, with a bit more backbone. What is known along the Gulf Coast as a "popping rod" is ideal. These are typically 6 1/2 to 7 1/2 feet long, with a long butt section and thick lower end for leverage and a fast-action, narrow tip for sensitivity and casting. These can be found in well-stocked tackle shops in the Northwest, or you may choose to special order.

Reels described for mooching work well enough, but I've found levelwinds of the sort used for bass or walleye with 8- to 12-pound line a lot of fun. High quality spinning gear is hard to beat for jigging. There is generally an aversion among many Northwest saltwater anglers to spinning gear, but in some areas inside Vancouver Island where folks do more jigging than anything else spinning reels have become preferred. Doug Field, the manufacturer of Buzz Bombs and Zzingers, told me he finds he can respond more quickly to strikes when jigging with spinning gear. I have probably caught more fish jigging with a small spinning reel filled with 6-pound (4-kg) line than with any other outfit. Whatever reel you choose, be sure you have at least 200-250 yards of high-quality line.

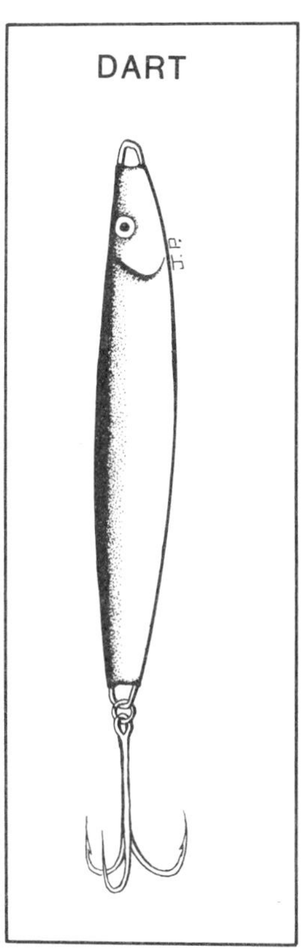

This is going a bit overboard, so to speak, but most Northwest coast fishermen these days carry at least a few jigs and spoons in their tackle boxes.

Many tidewater chinook remain bright until they've ascended well past tidewater. (Photo courtesy Buzz Ramsey, Luhr-Jensen and Sons, Inc.)

It is possible to tie a jig directly to the main line, but with lines as light as I recommend, a shock leader of three or four feet is advisable. To such a length of 20- to 30-pound monofilament, tie a small barrel or ball-bearing swivel to connect leader to main line.

The process of "jigging" is not terribly complex. I've seen many novices take good fish by simply dropping a jig to bottom, reeling up a bit and just working the rod up and down, rather mindlessly in fact.

I prefer to put a bit more "mind" into it—though I'm not really sure that makes a difference. Still, being aware how salmon strike jigs can help work them most effectively, I think.

Once you lower a jig it is always moving in one of two ways: either coming up with little action as you reel or fluttering erratically downward when line is released. Logically, more strikes come on the downward flutter. But a jig isn't a herring: it doesn't feel or smell like anything very tempting. So you can't expect a salmon to hang onto a jig for long. That means hooks must be kept perfectly sharp and set quickly when a jig is picked up.

The need to set hooks quickly can present a problem. A salmon can easily pick up a jig fluttering downward and drop it before the angler has a chance to set hooks—often before he even knows he's been "struck." So limit your jigging motions. Don't jig in huge sweeps of the rod but in shorter pulls of 18 inches or so. Let the rod drop that distance quickly so the jig can flutter freely downward. Be ready.

Also, when letting a jig out, to bottom for example, try to be conscious of the lure's progress. You're bound to run into "slack liners." What happens is this: you're freespooling (or open-bailing) a jig out and it's fluttering merrily toward bottom when it suddenly stops. But you know bottom is 90 feet or 140 or whatever and your jig can't be more than 50 feet down.

At that point beginning jig fishermen often scratch their heads and mumble something about how "the bottom came up." Often, while they're pondering, a salmon will burst from the surface trying to rid itself of the jig which as far as the angler knows is still "on the bottom," having felt nothing. After having that happen a time or two, jiggers learn whenever their line is suddenly slack to start reeling like crazy and catch up to the salmon before it can spit the jig.

Usually, if jigging for chinook, unless the fish are known to be at a certain depth, it's best to let the jig hit bottom. That's where chinook most often feed, over sand where they'll pursue candlefish that bury themselves in the bottom. (Inspect chinook you've just caught along bottom: sometimes you can actually see fresh scrape marks along their gill covers from digging after candlefish.) Work the jig within 10 feet or so of bottom, frequently letting the jig flutter all the way back to bottom. Expect to hook into species other than salmon rather often. Lots of halibut, lingcod and rockfish are taken this way. Such surprises add to the excitement of jigging.

If salmon are suspended at a particular depth, as coho are particularly likely to be, lower the jig to approximately that depth and work it there.

If salmon (again, most likely coho) are near the surface, cast and retrieve fishing at an angle (rather than straight up and down below the boat) may be most effective. Anglers casting from piers or jetties often use this technique successfully. Sliding Buzz Bombs seem particularly productive fished this way.

Many jigs, by the way, can be bent so they form a curve or an S-shape. But they are packaged straight and some of the most ardent jig fishermen use them just that way. That includes Rock D'acquisto, manufacturer of Pt. Wilson Dart jigs. (White is his favorite color, incidentally, though he admits it may matter much more to him than to the fish.)

Coastal Weather In The Northwest

The coastal climate from northernmost California through southern British Columbia follows much the same patterns, a general understanding of which will facilitate planning fishing types and times.

Fishermen, particularly boaters, are concerned with wind velocity. Much of the year, the Northwest coast gives them reason for concern since it is by most standards a windy place.

During the late spring and through the summer, northwesterlies prevail over the ocean. From about midway along the Oregon coast south to Cape Mendocino (California) lies a "wind belt" in which these typically stiff northwest winds create rough seas (and, in bays, a chop) for many days in a row. These winds, however, also help produce ecologically necessary upwellings, as waters from nutrient-rich depths are drawn upward.

From middle to late summer and sometimes into late autumn there is a lull in the winds and the ocean may be mill-pond flat. Any such lull may be prevalent during late summer some years but minimal others. Often there is a daily pattern much of the summer, particularly along more northerly waters during high-pressure systems, when mornings will be calm—often with fogs hanging in thick for hours—but giving way to brisk afternoon northwesterlies.

Winter storms occur from about November into the spring and can be both frequent and severe; they come roaring in from the southwest, often packing 30- to 50-knot winds. There can be a day or two between such low pressure systems when light, variable winds offer a welcome chance to fish. January, February and much of March can be particularly nasty months. In any case, ocean fishing along the Washington coast shuts down from about midautumn through late spring. On calm days most Oregon harbors offer bottomfish trips to nearshore reefs right through the winter when demand warrants.

Weather patterns in Puget Sound are less severe than along the open coast, allowing small boaters to fish protected areas year-round.

No matter the time of year, serious Northwest coast anglers are never far from their rain slickers, deck boots and warm clothing. (A bright yellow Sou'wester hat can be a blessing, too.)Rain, drizzle, mist and fog are facts of life along this coast. Even during midsummer when it's hot and sunny all day 10 miles inland, a bone-chilling solid-grey dampness often hangs over marine waters all day.

Catching Tidewater Salmon. For the purposes of this guide, "tidewater" is generally that part of a river mouth from "the jaws" (jetties) on upstream to include the estuarine waters where tidal inflow and freshet runoff mix regularly with fresh and salt waters.

Major tidewater fisheries along the Northwest coast occur mostly in Oregon, its coastline frequently split by rivers pushing to the Pacific's edge. In some lower rivers, tidewaters extend for many miles, forming large fertile bays such as shallow, meandering Coos Bay. On the other hand, the swift rushing waters of steep rivers like the Rogue flood into the river entrance at a volume that precludes much estuarine mixing of waters.

Just about every coastal river in the Northwest has runs of salmon, wild or hatchery fish, and often both. Major runs occur in the fall, both chinook and coho. Some rivers have productive spring chinook runs as well.

"Springers" move into rivers during April and May. Most of these chinook are caught in the upper reaches of tidewater and beyond, since spring-run kings are *not* prone to linger in lower tidewater but generally move right upriver.

Fall kings and coho, on the other hand, take their time, feeding and awaiting freshets. Good fishing just outside and between jetties can be found up and down the coast starting in August. The action continues, gradually shifting farther up into tidewater during September and into October. In recent years, lower Tillamook Bay has had a particularly strong run of trophy-sized chinook each August-September.

There are two basic approaches to fishing tidewater salmon, depending upon where (how saline) are the waters fished. In the mostly salt waters in and around river mouths, trolling is the method of choice, much as done in offshore waters. In some bays, particularly on a strong ebb tide, with the heavy weights necessary in such powerful currents, a wire spreader is often used. A downrigger, of course, makes all that unnecessary. Whole herring or anchovies are preferred baits, with or without a flasher ahead. Some anglers use large spinners, trolling or casting them from shore. Spinners are particularly popular in certain rivers such as the Nestucca and up into the Umpqua, as well as in Puget Sound's lower Skagit River.

In upper tidewater, most boaters anchor rather than troll, fishing sand shrimp or spinners on spreader rigs or on weighted, straight leaders below large styrofoam floats (see illustrations in the Tillamook Bay and Nestucca River sections). They may also do this near river mouths, especially where there is "hog lining"—boats anchoring in a row across part of a river, with floats on anchor ropes rigged for quick release when a good fish is hooked.

Tackle for fishing tidewater salmon is typically heavy mooching-type tackle, though some use heavy spinning gear which, for bank fishermen, may cast more easily. In any case, light lines can be a problem in this situation, since rivers crowded with salmon are almost always crowded with fishermen as well.

If small lines are a problem, small boats are not. Even cartoppers can safely take advantage of tidewater fishing, given a dose of common sense. Fishing near a river mouth during a strong ebb tide can be hazardous. Trollers who work the jaws at ebb tide should have plenty of confidence in their engines—those with two engines have an advantage.

Northwest Bottomfishing

Northwest salt waters are replete with many species of "bottomfish"—many of which actually do live and feed on the bottom, and some of which do not. Besides a range of sizes at maturity varying from a pound or two to several hundred, these species offer something else salmon don't: a great variety of shapes and colors. Nearly all are excellent eating and most, when taken on tackle appropriate for their size, are combative game fish.

Yet, historically for decades, Northwest residents tended to feel that "If it ain't a salmon, it ain't a fish." That attitude really began to change in the late 1970s as salmon sport fishing went into a tailspin, seasons growing short and catches small. Interest in and appreciation of non-salmonids picked up proportionately.

Today, most Northwest charter offices offer regular bottom-fishing trips and many private boaters not only no longer disdain these species but actively pursue them.

What's In A Name?

"A snapper and a rockcod" would sum up this double-header for many Northwesterners. In fact, the fish at left is a canary rockfish and the other is a copper rockfish. Neither is a snapper nor a cod.

The historical status of bottomfish species as second class citizens among Northwest anglers shows up in the many names—and misnames—bestowed arbitrarily upon them over the years. Many of these names remain in use, making things confusing as ever.

There are advantages to knowing what kinds of fish you're *actually* catching. For one thing, understanding more about all game fish by understanding their relationships helps make you a better angler in the long run. Also, knowing what's really what helps keep your catch legal in these days of increasing regulations.

As a general rule, you'll be 'way ahead if you can simply remember that in fact ***THERE ARE NO SNAPPER, ROCK COD OR SEA BASS IN THE NORTHWEST.*** Those almost universally applied names on this coast are given to various species of *rockfish.* Specifically:

Red snapper: yelloweye rockfish, canary rockfish, vermilion rockfish.

Rock cod: quillback rockfish, copper rockfish, brown rockfish.

Sea bass: black rockfish, blue rockfish, yellowtail rockfish.

You'll also hear the names "kelp trout" and "kelp cod" variously applied to kelp greenling. (As a matter of fact, lingcod are actually the largest member of the greenling family.)

Finding Bottomfish In Northwest Waters

Rocky areas for lingcod and rockfish

Habitat is usually linked closely with success for bottomfish anglers. Knowing what habitat factors to look for and being able to find them are critical.

The great majority of non-salmonid game fish will be found over rocky areas. In general, you'll find bottomfish wherever you locate rocky reefs, ledges, shelves and pinnacles which rise abruptly from the bottom. Even relatively small areas of rock-strewn bottom in midst of smooth, rather barren ground can hold surprising numbers of fish.

Many reefs and pinnacles rise to the surface, often marked with buoys, lights or post markers, while some continue above the surface as small rocky islands. But often the most productive spots (perhaps because they're less easily located and so less easily fished) are those pinnacles and reefs which rise abruptly from deep water but to within not more than a few fathoms of the surface. Along the steep sides of such areas you'll find big lingcod and yelloweye rockfish; on and above the top you'll find cabezon, copper rockfish and schooling species such as black, yellowtail and blue rockfish.

Although not the only example of this habitat, one of the very best, most productive areas of light tackle "pinnacle hopping" the Northwest has offered me is off (outside

Halibut charters rely on substantial gear with dacron line for fishing deep, swift water with heavy weights for big fish.

of) Barkley Sound's Broken Islands. There, the bottom is riddled with huge stalagmites of rocky reefs; depth changes constantly, and fish are everywhere.

Far offshore are often-huge seamounts—great plateaus that rise gradually from the ocean floor. These are generally labeled as "banks" (such as Stonewall, Heceta and Swiftsure banks), but many smaller seamounts are not named. These may lie 15 to 30 miles offshore and even at their *shallowest* points may be over 300 deep. When currents and winds permit fishing them, bottomfishermen inevitably find some of the biggest lingcod, yelloweye, canary rockfish and where, gravelly, halibut.

How you go about finding rocky bottomfish habitat wherever you want to bottomfish depends upon your gear. At the least, a good nautical chart of the area and a compass are essential. So is a depth sounder or recorder of some sort. These days very effective LCD depthsounders are available for $200 or so; no serious salt water angler should be without one. (For those who bottomfish, a minimum of a 60-fathom range is desirable.)

Then look for two key ingredients: "rky" for rocky areas and sudden depth changes. You can chart a course using your compass figuring distance traveled over time and come close, but locating deep spots is still hit and miss. Removing much of the initial and all of the subsequent guesswork is Loran and any angler who has it should be able to begin filling a logbook with Loran numbers for productive bottomfish habitat.

Far removed from the sophistication of electronics is the occasional or visiting angler in a cartopper or rental skiff with no electronics—perhaps no chart as well. Even so, some excellent bottomfishing may be available, depending upon area and how accomodating the water conditions are. Look for steep shorelines, particularly points of land, where the bottom drops precipitously away from the kelp hugging the rocks and where there is a good current flow. Expect to lose plenty of gear, but I've caught many good fish in such areas. Along the coast or strait, long "blind" drifts along (just off) kelp beds in 30 to 60 or more feet will inevitably produce action from various rockfish and smaller lings.

Poor Man's Instant "Vacuum Sealer"

In these days of increasingly regulated catches, those fish that are kept to eat deserve to be properly cared for. Most fishermen realize that means keeping their catches cool—on ice if possible—and cleaning them or at least bleeding them soon after capture.

But even fish treated carefully may not last long in the freezer where they often end up. The oil-laden, rich flesh of salmon, of course, is particularly prone to freezer burn and acquiring a strong, bitter taste after a few weeks at best. Salmon to be frozen are best left whole or at least in large steaks, skin on. Still, be prepared to cut away any exposed flesh which will have turned a whitish or yellowish color until you reach the deep red flesh beneath. That should still taste almost fresh.

White-meated fish such as lingcod and halibut will keep much longer. I've eaten tightly-packaged halibut filets after they sat in my freezer for a year, cutting away very little, and enjoying meat almost as good as fresh.

But no matter what you plan to freeze, you can benefit from a wonderfully simple trick I learned in the Caribbean. All you need are a deep bucket (you could also use an ice chest) and plenty of 1-gallon heavy Ziploc-type plastic bags.

Cut the fish into steak or chunks to fit into the bags. Fill the bucket with water. Into each bag, place enough fish for a meal and pour a bit of water over it, into the bag. (Cool fresh water is fine, though I prefer saltwater *IF* offshore or far away from any harbor or busy area.) Then, *without sealing the bag,* gradually immerse it in the bucket while kneading it slightly so all the air is forced up and out the top. Then with the bag underwater, seal it tightly. When you pull it out, your filets or steaks should be in a virtual airtight package, with a bit of water around them to form a light glaze as well.

Smooth areas for halibut, smaller flatfish, codfishes

There are two good reasons to *not* seek rocky areas. First, if the fish you seek include flatfishes of any type, they will seldom be taken there. Secondly, such rocky habitat is simply not to be found at all in some areas.

The Northwest's most awesome trophy bottomfish, the Pacific halibut, prefers a hard, gravelly bottom. Even though seamounts may offer hundreds of square acres of just such habitat, halibut are typically site-specific. That is, they seem to congregate and feed in tight areas which anglers often term "halibut beds."

Here again, Loran is invaluable, not only in finding the seamount but in then pinpointing the often surprisingly small areas of specific "beds" of halibut.

However, many anglers catch many halibut with no fancy gear. Some simply hop aboard a charter and utilize *its* fancy gear. But in areas where halibut do occur, blind drifting over smooth gravelly bottoms (which can be roughly determined with a nautical chart—or by spotting drifting charters) can produce halibut. This is particularly true where good numbers of halibut are normally found.

In other areas, occasional halibut are picked up incidentally, often by salmon fishermen. But here, too, it is usually while trolling deep over a smooth bottom.

In general, the farther south one goes (and Oregon is about as far south as Pacific halibut go), the deeper you'll find halibut. So off the Oregon and Washington coasts, most halibut fishing is in 200 to 400 feet. But off the B.C. and Alaska coasts, halibut are often taken nearer shore in shallow waters. (Alaskans often hook huge halibut in 20 or 30 feet of water. For instance, I once interviewed a 72-year-old Ninilchik, Alaska angler who dropped her herring bait over in 38 feet not far from shore—and ended up with a halibut that bottomed out a 300-pound scale. State biologists with whom I spoke had measured it and estimated it to weigh 466 pounds.)

Certainly not all areas of smooth bottom harbor halibut. For example, they are a rarity inside Puget Sound, but smooth bottom is omnipresent. What you *will* catch over inside or nearshore sandy bottoms, deep and shallow, includes many species of flounder and sole. These saltwater panfish may be taken in great abundance; in most areas they are underfished. Generally, sandy/grassy areas are best; soft mud attracts fewer species—but you are likely to run into dogfish over muddy bottoms.

Also over shallower sandy/gravelly bottoms you'll find sculpins—sometimes including good-sized cabezon—and, at least during years they're available—Pacific cod, as well as pollock and hake.

Catching Bottomfish In Northwest Waters

Catching Halibut

Halibut aren't like most fish. Besides the fact that they have two eyes on side of their head, I mean. When an anglers sets the hooks on a halibut, he has no way of knowing whether the fish is a 10-pounder or a 100 pounder—or if it is a really *big* one.

Over the past decade or so, interest in catching halibut in Northwest waters has surged. Conveniently, so did halibut populations in the late 1980s, most probably a natural cycle. With that increase in interest, tackle specifically designed for halibut has also become more prevalent. That tackle reflects the fact that halibut are not a fish to be taken lightly.

These giant flounder combine their often large size with immense, brute power to prove dogged, difficult adversaries on a line. Most often, rods are heavy fiberglass, graphites or composite with fast-retrieve 4/0-sized reels filled with 40- to 80-pound line. Often this line in Washington and Oregon waters is Dacron, since its minimal stretch helps fish deep water and its thin diameter offers less resistance in swift currents. But it is less durable than monofilament and not universally preferred.

On the other hand, "chicken" halibut of 10 to 50 pounds can be landed on lines of 8- to 14-pound test. Fishing such lines when currents were light, I've caught many halibut to 50 pounds and, in fact, have landed three or four 60- to 90-pounders. The chances of hooking chicken halibut is infinitely greater than hooking a barndoor, and playing smaller fish on lighter lines is great fun. (For details on light tackle and techniques, see the Light Tackle section.) There is some risk however. After all, you could "play" a 200-pounder all day on light line that never even knew it had been hooked.

Pacific halibut are taken on a variety of baits and lures, reflecting the fact that they're highly opportunistic and aggressive predators. Perhaps herring still account for the majority of those caught, as it is so widely used. Squid or small octopus are also effective and unlike soft herring do offer the advantage of great tenacity on the hook. Some halibut enthusiasts insist on small live baits such as true cod or greenling; others—particularly in Alaska—favor the oily heads or belly strips of fresh pink salmon.

Whatever the bait, it should be fished on or near the bottom. Often, in the current-swept waters that halibut favor, that means a considerable amount of weight. When depths aren't too great or currents not too severe, a simple short leader of heavy (60- to 80-pound) monofilament with single or double 5/0 or larger hooks will do. A sinker of 3 to 12 ounces can be attached to the main line on a plastic sliding sleeve which prevents fraying.

To keep the baited leader from tangling around the main line when fishing very deep water and/or a hard-running tide, often a wire spreader like that in the illustration is employed, commonly with 1 to 2 pounds of lead. This requires reasonably stout tackle.

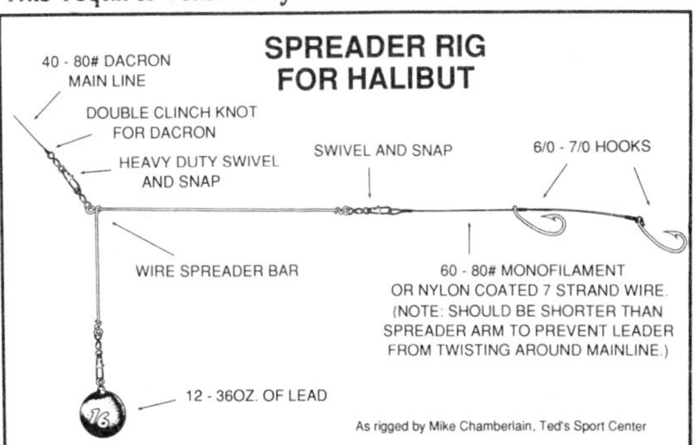

Any heavy, shiny jig or spoon, or a leadhead jig with a large, ostentatious plastic tail will readily take halibut. Many anglers make their own pipe jigs simply by pouring melted lead into a 10- to 12-inch length of copper or chrome pipe with one end crimped or otherwise sealed. Then after drilling through, a heavy cotter pin holding a large treble hook (often with a hoochy skirt on it) is slid through and the ends bent securely. Although more expensive, I've had good success—especially when fishing lines testing 20 pounds or less—using larger metal jigs such as Pt. Wilsons and big Krocodile spoons.

I've also found that the biggest, foot-long plastic curlicue or twin-tail plastic lures are excellent. To liven up their action even more, try customizing them by adding "legs." Smaller curlycue tails of the size a freshwater bass angler might use can be permanently and easily attached with a lighter or candle. Heat the tops (heads) to melting point and secure three or four along each side of the body (which may also have to be heated). Rather than bother with a jighead, I often rig these by sliding a single, long-shank 10/0 hook down through the body so the eye just sticks out the top (front). When driftfished on a six- to 10-foot heavy monofilament leader, well behind a heavy sinker, these move about with an action understandably hard for any halibut to pass up.

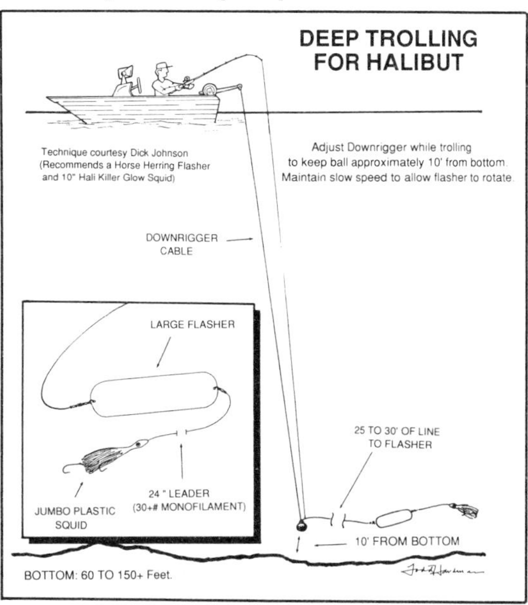

Certainly, the place to fish any bait or lure for halibut is on the bottom since they do spend most of their time resting there waiting to pick off anything edible. Still, halibut will and do rise far off the bottom at times—perhaps to gorge themselves on herring suspended at middepths. In any case, lots of halibut are hooked (and many lost) by surprised fishermen trolling for salmon every year, particularly in more northern waters.

Turn Of The Management Screw

Sport fishing regulations for Pacific halibut have long been the domain of the International Pacific Halibut Commission (IPHC) which manages this enormously valuable resource.

For many years, sport seasons generally ran from late winter through fall with a standard limit of two halibut (daily/possession), any size.

There certainly seemed no reason for concern during most of the 1980s, when halibut abundance seemed to peak. The Washington sportcatch alone exceeded a half-million pounds by 1987. But numbers and sizes seemed to decrease in the last part of the decade and, since 1989, the IPHC has tightened regulations off Washington and Oregon.

Now, annual catch quotas guide authorities in determining seasons which can vary considerably from year to year and area to area. Typically, sportfishing begins in early spring and runs into early autumn or until quotas are met. However, to stretch out seasons, daily limits are but a single fish in some areas and sportfishing may be limited to certain days of the week. Also, there have been minimum size limits imposed off southern Oregon and that may spread.

The bottom line with such increasing restriction means that anyone interested in fishing for halibut anywhere in the Northwest would be well advised to be familiar with current regulations.

The author's backup "halibut insurance" isn't as effective as a harpoon or flying gaff—but a whole lot better than nothing (or a net) for a big barndoor.

Be Prepared To Boat Big Barndoors!

Pulling any large, "green" fish into a small boat is asking for trouble. But halibut are a different story—they're often much larger and not likely to be so tired they can't flail their muscular bodies with great power. And those bodies can do real damage to your tackle and even your arms or legs.

The danger these fish present is evidenced in the tradition among serious Northwest halibut anglers of carrying a pistol or shotgun. Usually a shot or two (or three) in the head will be enough to tame an angry halibut.

But many fishermen prefer not to carry firearms aboard—and shooting a fish precludes any chance of it being accepted for a world record by the International Game Fish Association (IGFA).

The best prepared halibut fishermen carry a harpoon; the detachable head is thrust through the fish so it is then secured on a rope. Another good alternative is a flying gaff, also with a detachable, barbed head on a rope. (Such a harpoon, however, also disqualifies a fish under IGFA rules—keep that in mind with any potential record halibut.)

Often, anglers are anything but prepared, and end up trying to net halibut. A good net can handle a 20- or 30-pounder. But in fact, "halibut insurance" need be neither large nor expensive. Even on fly-in fishing trips to the northern coast, I carry in my tackle box a big, barbed shark hook with about 20 feet of nylon cord tied to the eye and wrapped around the shank. This, along with a good, simple hand gaff and a heavy fish billy can be a godsend with a big halibut.

Even without any of these things, it is quite possible to land a big flattie—given a lot of luck. Two of us in a 13-foot skiff well off the northwest Washington coast managed to boat a 90-pounder by wearing it down over two hours (on 15-pound line), then slashing its gills until loss of blood finally did it in.

One more suggestion: be prepared to "hogtie" any good-sized halibut you'll leave on deck. Before a clubbed halibut can come around, tie a length of rope from through its mouth and gills then back to and around its caudal peduncle—the small area ahead of the tail—so the halibut remains bent in a tight head-to-tail "U." Even the largest halibut can thus be rendered immobile.

1. A cut is made through the flesh to the backbone. Follow the lateral line.

2. Work away from the cut toward the dorsal fin, sliding the knife blade along the bones and pulling away the filet as it is cut free. Do the same on the other (ventral) side.

3. You should have two filets as shown. Then turn halibut over and repeat the same process.

4. You should end up with four filets as shown and then need only skin them. (However, it is best to leave the skin on any meat that will remain in the freezer any length of time.)

Catching Lingcod And Yelloweye Rockfish

So you want to catch some big bottomfish (other than halibut)? That means lings or yelloweye. The biggest lingcod (females of 25 to 50+ pounds) have a decided preference for live baits. Just about any small, live fish you can put down into ling territory is likely to draw a strike.

"Small," of course, is a relative term—particularly considering how cavernous is the mouth of a lingcod. In my first such experience with lings, in the San Juan Islands, I

Keep The Net Ready For Lings!

"I think it went in bottom!" My fishing partner, not very experienced in these matters, strains to hold up the rod suddenly bent in a tight arc, after beginning to reel up a feisty little fish of some sort. It doesn't move, but then it seems to; I see a telltale throbbing.

"Baloney! There's a fish on there. Keep reeling—don't jerk the thing, but keep pumping it toward the surface, gently."

Anyone who's done much bottomfishing in ling territory should be familiar with variations on this conversation. Sure enough, up will come a rockfish of a few pounds—with 20 or 30 or 40 pounds of lingcod hanging onto it. Often they'll hang on right to the boat where, if you're quick with net or gaff, you can end up with both fish. Sometimes they'll decide to let go right at the boat, often lingering for a moment, before darting back toward bottom.

One of the most surprising moments in my experience with lings came one May morning in northern Puget Sound when a buddy and I, jigging leadheads 180 feet down using identical tackle, enjoyed simultaneous strikes. It became immediately clear that our fish were good-sized, especially for the six-pound line we used.

About 20 minutes later at almost the same instant, we pulled four lingcod to the boat. When all were in, we took stock and found, amazingly, what had happened: At the same moment, two little lingcod weighing a couple pounds had been hooked on our two jigs. But even before we could tell we had hooked such small fish, they were in the mouths of nearly identical lings of about 23 pounds each, both of which hung on to the boat.

So after several hours of fruitless jigging, we had what was then our combined daily limit of four lings, in 20 minutes and on one cast each!

The evidence of this 44-pound lingcod's fatal misjudgment is the rockfish's tail still sticking out of its mouth. Just about anyone who spends much time bottomfishing in the Northwest is likely to land such "bonus lingcod."

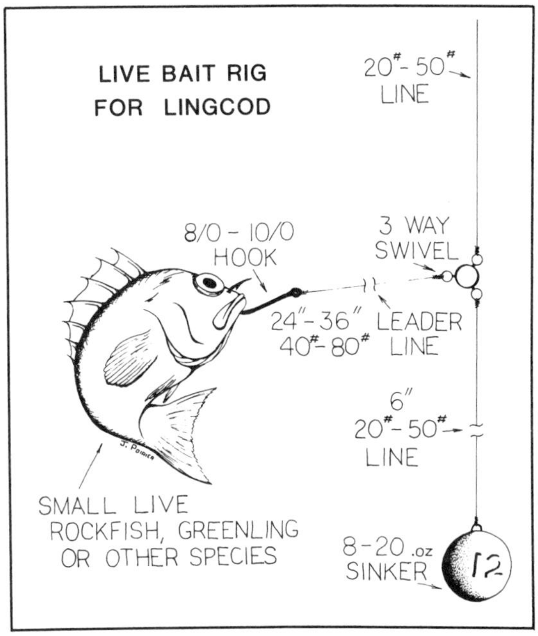

LIVE BAIT RIG FOR LINGCOD

20#-50# LINE

8/0 - 10/0 HOOK

3 WAY SWIVEL

24"-36" LEADER LINE 40#-80#

6" 20#-50# LINE

SMALL LIVE ROCKFISH, GREENLING OR OTHER SPECIES

8-20 oz SINKER

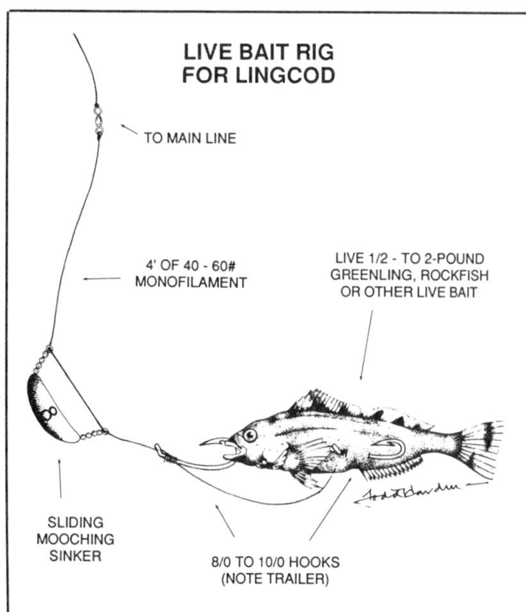

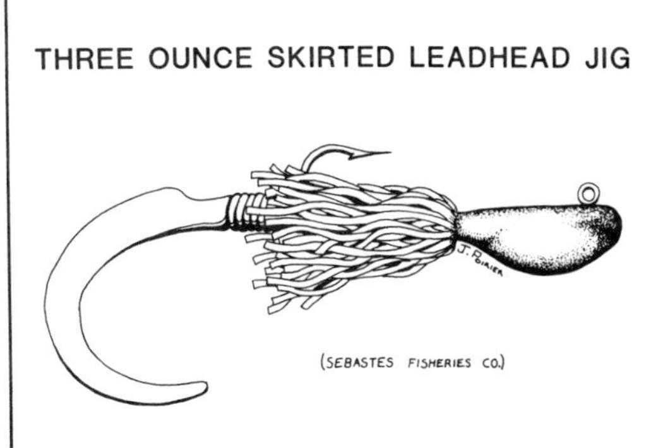

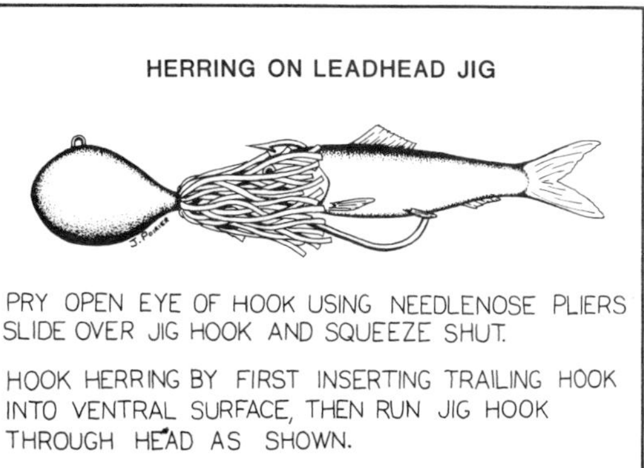

hooked up a quillback rockfish that weighed 2 to 3 pounds. That's a big live bait. Yet I caught what I was after: a 38-pounder on one drift and, using the same battered-but-alive rockfish, a 43-pounder on the next drift.

Still, I prefer a live bait of about a pound. Rockfish are easiest to come by and lings like 'em. But lings like best of all their cousins, little greenling (perhaps because they lack spines and are less ornery morsels than rockfish).

At times I am shamefully lazy and simply rig such live baits on a 10/0 hook through the lips. Trouble is, particularly if the live bait is large and the ling less so, the bait may not be swallowed in a hurry. Best bet: rigging a 10/0 through the lips but with a trailer hook tied from that front hook. Whether using a treble or a single hook, run it just through the skin near the tail so the point faces forward.

Lingcod will of course strike just about anything that moves, but they can be selective. Still, I've always done well

Jigging deep water with a Krocodile spoon on 8-pound line produced this big yelloweye rockfish.

with leadhead jigs with plastic tails or pork strips. Big jigs or spoons also work. When fishing's slow, try this: Rig a 2/0 to 4/0 "teaser" hook on a six-inch loop at the upper end of your heavy monofilament leader and slide onto it a long, scintillating pork strip (such as Uncle Josh's Ripple Rind). Then tie a jig or spoon at the bottom of the leader (at least three or four feet below the pork rind) and fish normally. I've had good-sized lingcod pass up the jig and go for the Ripple Rind.

Whatever terminal gear you opt for, keep in mind that lingcod are heavy-duty critters with spiny heads and sharp teeth and that they live in rocky areas. Surprising numbers of fishermen still seem prone to rig for bottomfish as they might, traditionally, for salmon: with a leader lighter than the main line. Unless you're using gear far too heavy, this is a bad idea. A three- to six-foot shock leader of 30- to 60-pound monofilament will save you both fish and lures.

Net It Or Gaff It?

Around most of the coastal U.S. anglers gaff bottomfish. Visitors to the Northwest coast may be surprised to see that many big bottomfish are still netted. That, I suspect, is part of the legacy left by anglers traditionally equipped to land salmon.

Nets can work effectively for bottomfish also, provided they are large enough and hung with tough nylon or poly material. But nets are seldom as quick as a good gaff. Worst of all may be the aftermath of a thrashing bottomfish in a net: the tedious process of extricating fish, hooks and line may take up many minutes of valuable fishing time during a hot drift.

A gaff is quick, sure and clean (albeit there may be some blood to contend with—though an experienced gaffer can hit home in the head almost every time). However, often gaffs used in these waters are *not* designed for sportfishing, but are the thick, very short-handled gaffs with long, barely angled hooks that commercial fishermen have used for years.

An ideal sport gaff for these waters uses a four-foot aluminum handle with a gaff hook measuring three inches (gap, point to shank). The hook should have a sharp angle like that of a fish hook (but lack a barb, of course). With this sort of gaff and some experience, nearly any fish can be in the boat in one motion.

One case in point (pardon the expression) is a 60-pound chinook salmon that I fought for about a half-hour on 8-pound (spool strength; 6-kg actual strength) line to the side of the boat where I gaffed it myself. With that big a fish on such a light line in a small skiff, a long awkward net would have made the job a whole lot trickier; I was glad I had my gaff aboard.

It's natural to want to catch *big* fish. But many lings you'll land in Northwest waters will run a relatively modest 5 to 15 or 20 pounds. And that may be just as well, since these are by far the best eating. Unlike chinook salmon or halibut, lingcod do tend to become coarse as they grow larger—at least to many palates, mine included. It makes sense to release the older, larger, more reproductively valuable lings lacking a specific reason to keep them.

Yelloweye rockfish can be taken on much the same gear as one would fish for lingcod, and often are. Live baits are not necessarily the bait of choice, though small offerings work well. Leadhead jigs, metal jigs and spoons produce consistently when fished in the right areas.

I've had the best success with 5- and even 7-ounce Krocodile spoons, which yelloweye seem particularly fond of. Leadhead jigs with plastic tails—particularly in blue, it seems—also attract yelloweye.

Perhaps the single most worthwhile rule of thumb for really enjoying bottomfishing is simply to *use light tackle.* Lines testing as light as 4 pounds can be adequate, and in fact can make yelloweye rockfish a real challenge.

Lingcod, lacking an air bladder, can fight all the way to the surface—and some do, while others (particularly when their mouth is open, around a hooked fish) are lethargic. Rockfish, on the other hand, quickly "blow up" or inflate as they are pulled upward from the depths since the gases trapped in their air bladders expand with decreasing pressure. This prevents them from fighting much; indeed, they may pop to the surface like an inert red balloons. On the other hand, on 4-pound line with tiny spinning or bait-casting outfits, I've caught many 12- to 17-pound yelloweye that intermittently sizzled out line and fought me all the way up. The long, drawnout fight inevitable with wispy lines means they "inflate" less quickly. In any case, 20-pound line is about as heavy as anyone ever needs to fish for lingcod or yelloweye.

One of the biggest challenges in using light lines for deepwater bottomfish is a heavily-running tide. Consult a tide calendar: look for periods of tide changes to fish and light tides—when runoff velocity won't greatly exceed one foot of vertical rise/fall per hour.

Catching Small Rockfish And Other Nearshore "Bottomfish"

There are over a dozen species of rockfish taken by sport fishing along the Northwest coast that commonly run from a pound or 2 to 6 or 7. Some are deepwater; others strictly shallow (less than 100 feet or so). Some fight with surprising strength; others are as fierce as an old boot. All of them are fine eating.

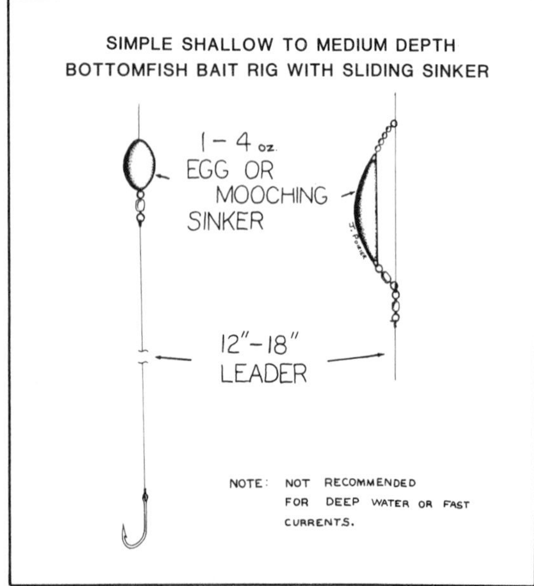

Nothing fancier than a chunk of herring is needed to catch rockfish. But they readily hit artificials and I prefer and recommend combining jigs or lures with light tackle to enjoy the genuine sport these fish can offer.

Several species of rockfish are likely in deep waters, particularly quillback. These 2- to 4-pound, freckled

"FISHFINDER"
MEDIUM TO DEEPWATER
BOTTOMFISH RIG
4'-6' LEADER
NOTE: MAY USE THREE HOOKS IF LOCAL REGULATIONS PERMIT.
TRY ANY VARIETY OF BAIT LURES — SEE WHICH WORK BEST.
(MAY BE MOOCHING OR OTHER SINKER TYPE)
2-20oz. DEPENDING ON DEPTH AND CURRENT

rockfish can be one of the most ubiquitous sport fish, particularly over hard, smooth-bottomed banks and reefs. They take small jigs and spoons without a second thought. I've also caught them by drifting large, floating minnow plugs (Rebels and the like) on a 20-foot leader behind a weight of a few ounces. In fact, I've taken some doubleheaders this way: one quillback on the front treble hook and one on the rear—further evidence that they do congregate in areas where food is plentiful. That food is most often clouds of tiny euphasiid shrimp but, clearly, they'll eat anything they can ingest.

Watch Those Poisonous Spines!

Rockfishes all belong to the family Scorpaenidae—the family of scorpionfishes that include fish that carry some of the most deadly toxins in the world: tropical stonefish and turkey/lion fish.

Fortunately, Northwest rockfish don't have hollow spines filled with deadly fluid like their tropical cousins. Rather, their dorsal and ventral/anal (bottom) spines are grooved. In the grooves is a slimy toxin that is not deadly but can sure hurt like hell.

Some people seem to react more to the pain than others, but most anglers who have gotten a deep puncture from a rockfish spine know the throbbing discomfort that may result.

The best bet is to know where these spines are on rockfish and avoid them. Handle with care. Rockfish can be picked up by their lower jaw—abrasive but without real teeth—like freshwater bass.

However, a careless slip is always possible—as I realized one day years ago while fileting a big quill-back rockfish and ended up with a dorsal spine a good quarter-inch in my thumb. Soon after I'd pulled it out, the throbbing grew intense. And icing it down only seemed to worsen it.

Turns out, ice is indeed exactly the wrong thing to do. If you get "stung" by a rockfish spine, remember: *heat*. Stick the affected member into very hot water and quickly the toxin will be neutralized, relieving most of the pain.

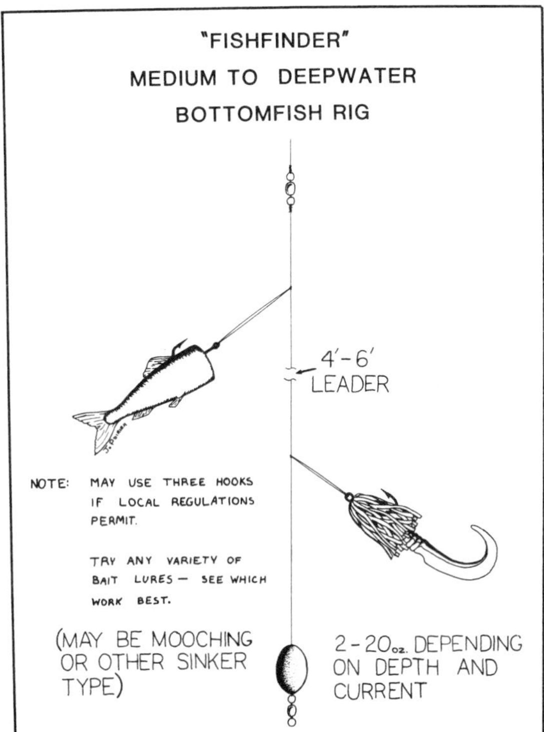

Jigging Deep Water In Current Using Light Tackle

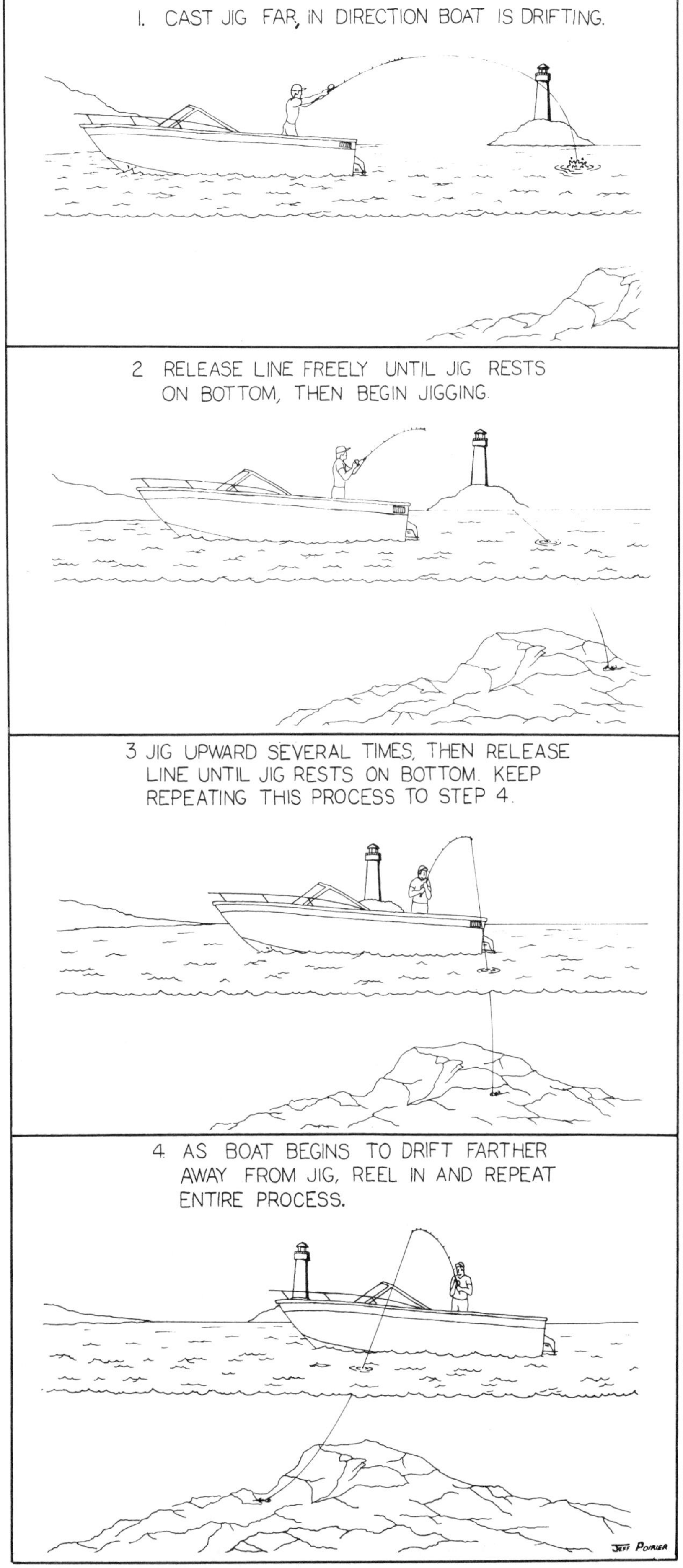

1. CAST JIG FAR, IN DIRECTION BOAT IS DRIFTING.
2 RELEASE LINE FREELY UNTIL JIG RESTS ON BOTTOM, THEN BEGIN JIGGING.
3 JIG UPWARD SEVERAL TIMES, THEN RELEASE LINE UNTIL JIG RESTS ON BOTTOM. KEEP REPEATING THIS PROCESS TO STEP 4.
4 AS BOAT BEGINS TO DRIFT FARTHER AWAY FROM JIG, REEL IN AND REPEAT ENTIRE PROCESS.
JEFF POIRIER

Oregon's bays offer great perch fishing, particularly spring and early summer. At anchor in a few feet of water on a rising tide, this spot in lower Coos Bay produced several species of perch for guide Darrel Gabel on a day off.

At times, particularly along or near kelp beds that rim the open ocean and outer Strait of Juan de Fuca, huge schools of black rockfish will be feeding at the surface or just under. Sometimes their noisy splashing will alert you. In any case, when you find blacks in such abundance, plan on catch-and-release fishing because even with ultralight tackle it is often possible to catch many more rockfish than one limit in a morning of fishing.

This situation is one reason I carry surface and subsurface plugs in my tackle box (plugs such as Mirrolures, Rapalas and various needlefish-type "jumpers" and cupfaced chuggers). Casting surface plugs to feeding rockfish and watching them strike is particularly exciting. Flyfishing enthusiasts can effectively fish streamers at such times, as well. I've also enjoyed drifting outside kelp beds on calm, quiet mornings—when no feeding fish were evident—casting subsurface plugs to take a variety of fish.

In more shallow waters, from the 15- to 20-feet of water around kelp beds to 100 feet or so, look for coppers, browns, more quillback at times and occasionally blacks and yellowtails, among others. Also mixed in with them are likely to be kelp greenling and cabezon, as well as small lingcod.

In fact, one of the most productive *simple* methods of fishing the Northwest coast involves starting a drift just off the kelp and working plugs or jigs over the bottom for any of the species mentioned above. After the boat has drifted into deep water, reel up, run back and continue to make drifts working up or down a shoreline or around a rocky shoal edge.

For this, keep your gear very light—ultralight for real sport. In fact, this may be one of the Northwest coast's most enjoyable and most overlooked recreational fisheries. A tiny spinning outfit is great. The reel should hold at least 200 yards of 4- to 6-pound line. The rod should be 5 to 6 feet with a fair amount of backbone—definitely *not* a whippy little "trout pole."

It's hard to beat 1/2- to 2-ounce leadhead jigs with bucktail or plastic skirts and bright plastic tails for shallow-water bottomfishing. Whites, yellows, chartreuse and hot pink are among the most effective colors. Cast up and down (parallel to) the edge of the kelp and work the jig back toward the boat—avoiding as best possible both kelp and rocks. (But take plenty of jigs in any case.) As the drift gets deeper, continue to cast far out and work the jig back after it hits bottom. Be ready for strikes as the jig sinks toward bottom and particularly just after it has landed and you make initial sweeps of the rod.

Catching Perch

A very different sort of fishing is required to take a very different sort of "bottom fish," surfperches. Redtail surfperch are indeed fishes of the open coastal surf zone, taken in the breakers on sandy beaches. Certain areas are known to be particularly productive, often around river mouths or next to rocky headlands.

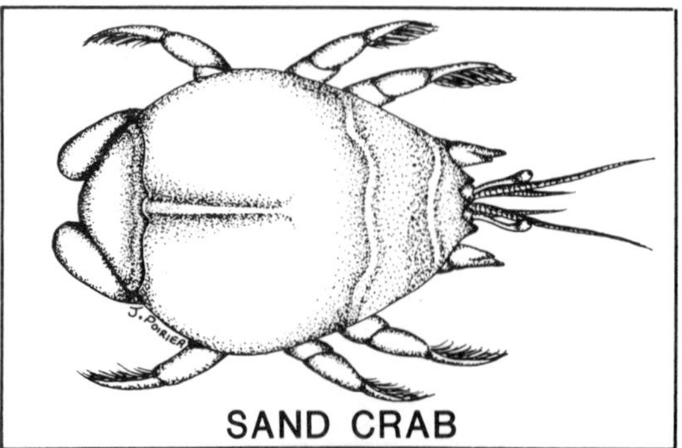

SAND CRAB

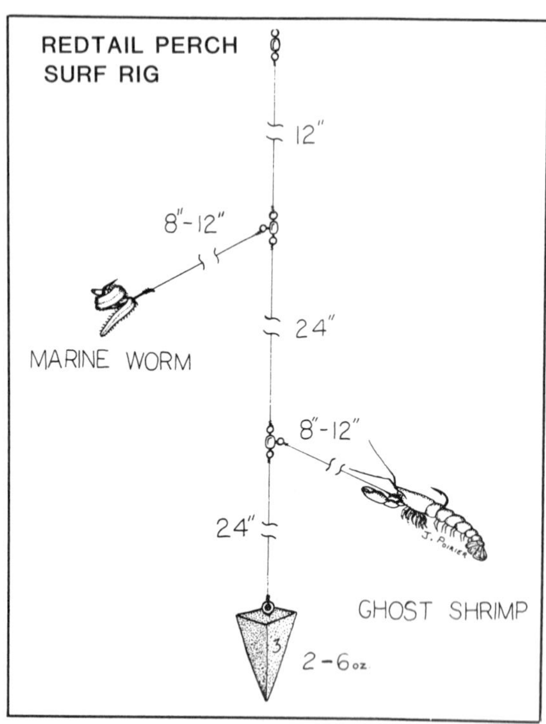

For redtails, traditional surfcasting tackle, as light as possible, is used: spinning gear most often on very long (10- to 12-foot) rods. A pyramid sinker of 2 or 3 ounces and often more helps cast to the outer breakers and anchors the terminal rig. Sand (mole) crabs, which make tough, enticing perch baits, are very popular in southern Oregon and northern California. So are segmented intertidal polychaete ("sand," "piling" or "mud") worms.

Pinpointing a spot to fish can be difficult when mile upon mile of sandy beach stretch before you. Look for pockets made by slight sandbar-like buildups of sand just out from the beach. And have patience: these fish tend to feed in schools that come and go. In between schools, many anglers prop rods on the beach with forked stakes stuck into the sand. They pull up a log or bucket and have a seat. In any case, as a rule by far the best time to fish for perch is during the incoming or slack tides.

Hip or chest waders are essential most of the year, though the thick-skinned can manage with jeans and sneakers on warm summer days.

Most other species of surfperch caught in the Northwest, notably the striped and pile perch, are actually taken not in the surf but in bays and sounds around pilings, bridge abutments, jetties or other obstructions and often off river mouths. In the spring they invade lower rivers up and down Oregon in great numbers. In fact, spring is prime time everywhere for perch.

But their abundance cannot necessarily be equated with fast fishing. Many anglers have been frustrated to look down around a dock and see legions of plate-sized perch finning lazily past their juiciest offerings without a sniff. These fish can be frustratingly finnicky feeders, with a discerning eye and sensitive, small mouth. But at times they will strike readily, particularly fresh shrimp, polychaete worms or fresh mussels on hooks no larger than a no. 2.

Ultralight tackle is great when perch are located around jetties or eelgrass but more often, around pilings, heavier line is essential to keep the headstrong panfish from passing monofilament over razor sharp mussel and barnacle shells.

Another panfish available during the summer in various bays and sounds, often around docks, is the tomcod. These appear only occasionally and irregularly some summers, but can be abundant. The 1/2-pounders (or less) are much less fussy than perch. When large schools move into a harbor, and kids have access to the docks, tomcod will be filling buckets right and left.

Though many fishermen more sophisticated than such kids will turn up their noses at little tomcod, I have found them to be one of the tastiest, sweetest of Northwest fish when headed and gutted, then rolled in flour and fried. Tomcod are best taken on multiple, small hook rigs baited with nearly anything—but squid is great and tough enough to last.

Catching Pacific Cod, Pollock And Hake

As described earlier in this book, Pacific (true) cod fishing in Puget Sound and the eastern Strait of Juan de Fuca has had its ups and downs—and recent years have been all down. Still, it's probably just a matter of time until the cycle changes and the fast-growing, fertile cod return.

When they do, anglers will find a gold mine of schooling fish which readily strike baits or artificials. Jigging with metal jigs and spoons or leadheads is by far the best way to go, working the lure on or very near bottom. The use of heavy tackle or lines heavier than 12-pound is absolutely unnecessary for these 2- to 12-pounders that feed over sandy (snag-free) bottoms, and will account for no more fish but much less joy in catching them.

Walleye pollock are often mixed in with true cod—or vice-versa, since in fact pollock can be by far the more common. This smaller cousin weighs only a couple pounds, but has saved the day for many fishermen—though their numbers have also declined in recent years. Pollock are taken much as are true cod, though lures or baits need not be so large. They are weak fighters to begin with, so the only chance to eke any excitement out of pollock is with ultralight gear and lines of 4- or 6- pound test.

There has never been much of a directed fishery for hake. Their tendency to remain well above bottom in very deep water during daylight hours makes them less available to sport fishermen. But occasionally they are encountered early or late in the day as they make diurnal migrations into shallower water where they feed at night. For the same reason, pier fishermen have found that on summer nights hake can be caught in good numbers using small baited hooks.

Pollock and hake, by the way, are very mild, white-meated fish. Though not as esteemed as many other Northwest game fish, they should be acceptable on any table. However, the texture may become rather undesirable, since the flesh of both species softens quickly unless taken care of. That means cleaning and icing them right after they're caught.

Catching Smelt And Herring

As with perch, there are two categories of Northwest smelt fishing—in the surf and in bays and sounds. Each offers a very different sort of sport.

Surf fishing is really surf *netting.* Smelt occur in the surf all along the Northwest coast but are actively sought by netters primarily in southern Oregon and northern California. Two species are netted: the surf smelt ("day fish") and the smaller night smelt (popularly called by that name). These delectable morsels are most available spring and summer. The locations of schools in the surf are given away by seagulls hopping on the beach and diving in the breakers.

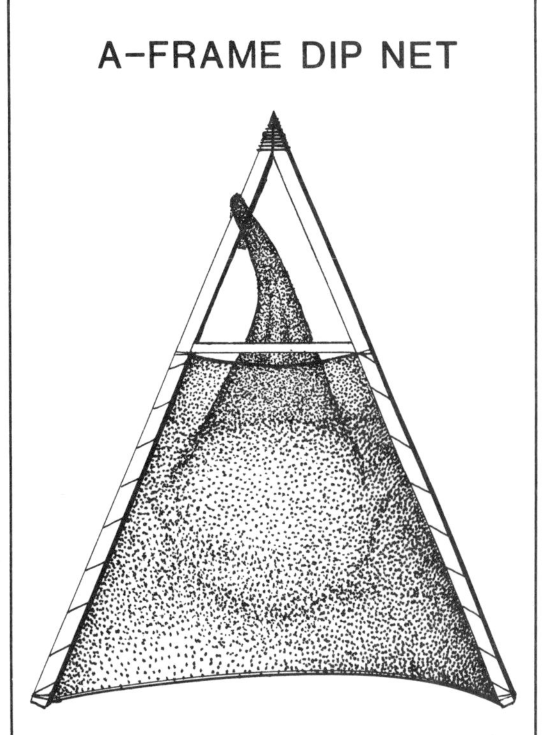

Serious smelters use A-frame nets. These are planted, wide end down, in the breakers, then lifted up and outward in one motion to scoop up the smelt. (At times, the fish may be thick enough to pick up with bare hands, grabbing the living silver flashes as they flop agilely on the sand.)

Apparently a locally popular fishery for surf smelt has developed around Yachats, Oregon (as described in the Siuslaw River section) where long-handled, fine-mesh round nets are used.

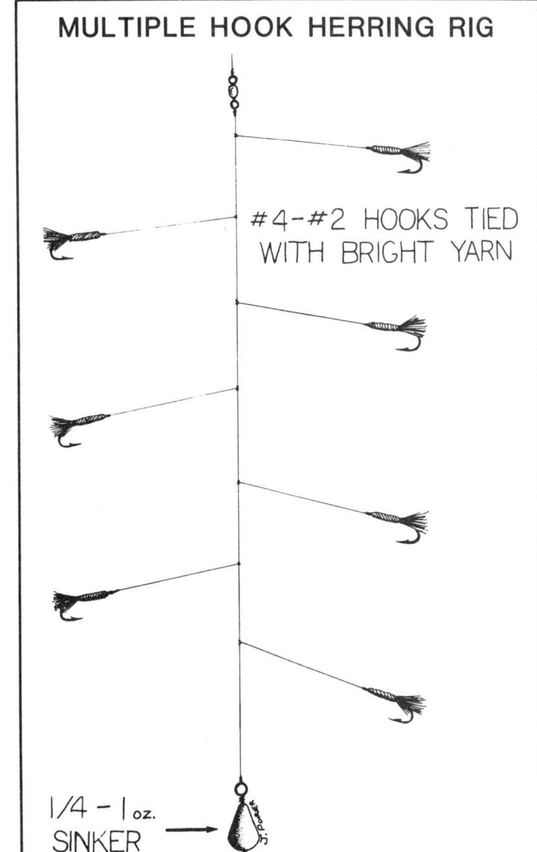

Striper populations in Oregon's Umpqua River are tenacious, holding their own despite conditions often unfavorable to spawning.

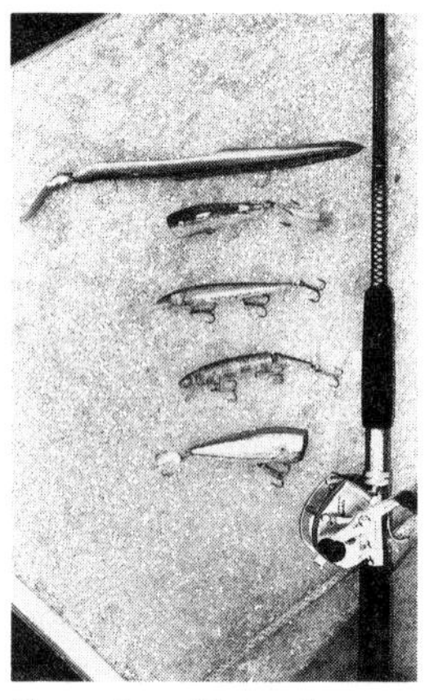

Beno eels and large plugs can be found in the tackle boxes of most striper fishermen.

Smelt and herring can be successfully jigged from jetties, docks and small boats in bays and lower rivers. Late winter and early spring seem to be the most popular periods. The two species may be mixed together, as they often are in northern Puget Sound.

Multiple hook herring rigs with tiny plastic "wings" or yarn on the hooks and with small weights on the bottom are jigged vertically, gently. The same rig will take anchovies when they move into harbors in the summer.

It is also eminently advisable to carry such rigs—already tied onto a light spinning outfit and stowed *if* there's room—aboard a boat. Often herring balls or schools may be located at the surface or, with electronics, at middepths. It is then possible to jig up a dozen or even several dozen big, fresh herring for live or fresh bait in a short time.

Fishing Northwest Tidewaters And Blue Water

The section earlier in this book, "Catching Tidewater Salmon," effectively describes what is meant by tidewater. Most game fish of Northwest estuaries other than salmon are also anadromous, typically available at certain periods of the year when they move up into rivers to feed or spawn. The Oregon coast, with its relative abundance of rivers, offers the bulk of Northwest tidewater fishing. There are, however, lower rivers in southwest Washington and northern California that offer coastal tidewater fishing.

Tidewater Guides

Guides are widely available for river fishing well above tidewater (most often for steelhead) but tend to be less in demand for fishing lower rivers —perhaps because most bays can be fairly easily fished from small private or rented skiffs.

Still, guides for tidewater fishing are available to show you how and where to fish for some of tidewater's more prized or tricky game fish such as striped bass, sturgeon, and chinook.

Several guides are listed in these pages; others may be found through local tackle dealers and resorts. Guides are not inexpensive—you are likely to pay $100 or more for a seat in a topnotch guide's boat (with tackle, bait and lunch thrown in), but if you intend to fish a river on your own in the future, the cost may be well worth it. No one usually fishes an area as much as a guide or knows it so well.

Catching Striped Bass

The major fishery for striped bass on the Pacific Coast has long been the waters of San Francisco Bay and the Sacramento Delta. In fact, there has been but a single area north of this central California striper stronghold that has provided real, consistent striped bass fishing: southern Oregon's lower Umpqua-Smith river system and Coos Bay.

Stripers apparently wandered northward decades ago and in the 1960s and 1970s offered fishermen some of the best big striper fishing anywhere. (The local fishing population by and large tended to view stripers not as the tough, intelligent, aggressive game fish they are, but rather as a predacious threat to trout and salmon smolts. Studies showing that other fish and invertebrates comprised a much larger share of stripers' diets were never popularly accepted.)

But by the 1980s, the reality of an environment *not* naturally conducive to the growth and development of young striped bass showed in greatly reduced availablility of striped bass. Most of the very large fish from earlier years of unusual spawning success have been caught and fewer young fish have been showing up to take their place.

Nevertheless, viable fishing opportunities remain, particularly in the Umpqua system—and may yet be looking up in the Coos *if* the Oregon Department of Fish and Wildlife's sputtering, shoestring commitment to enhance striper populations through stocking of penreared juveniles eventually pays off.

Striped bass can be taken year-round. Fishing does tend to slow considerably as cold weather sets in. Most bass are taken from small boats on trolled lures or live baits (including herring, sculpins, shiner perch or pileworms). In some areas, bait fishermen or plugcasters do connect from shore.

Success in catching wary and wily big stripers requires skill and knowledge of the area. Read the Umpqua River-Winchester Bay and Coos Bay sections carefully.

Catching "Bluebacks" And Jacks

During summer months, tidewater fishermen are increasingly psyched for the fall run of big chinook. Until that time arrives, there are alternatives to stay in shape. One is trolling for sea-run cutthroat. These anadromous trout, widely known as "bluebacks," are available from Puget Sound south into California and are generally underfished. In fact, in some Oregon estuaries, such as the Siuslaw and Alsea, bluebacks are among the most important game fish.

Most sea-runs are taken by small boaters trolling near the bank or log booms, pulling a string of trolling blades (Ford Fenders or Doc Sheltons or the like) in front of a nightcrawler or small lure. In some areas, such as Puget Sound or the lower Rogue River, a strip of baitfish or small whole herring is trolled. Incoming tide is almost universally recognized as the time to take sea-run cutts.

Precocious, immature salmon returning to rivers of their birth a year early are known as jacks all along the Northwest coast. They arrive earlier than mature, fall-run fish and can be quite numerous during the summer. They often provide a bonus catch for blueback fishermen.

Catching Shad

Tarpon in the Northwest? Not exactly, but the the American shad does resemble the mighty tropical tarpon both in appearance and in its wild runs and leaps clear of the water. These fish, however, seldom exceed four or five pounds, and their fighting spirit is best challenged with ultralight tackle. Many fishermen use fly tackle or tiny spinning rods with 4-pound line. Anything heavier than 6- to 8-pound test makes the battle too one-sided to be much fun. Red or white shad darts (essentially large, bevel-faced crappie jigs) are standard, though shad will take flies and small lures. Unlike most fish, they seem to hit most actively toward midday.

Shad move into several Northwest river estuaries in May and June. The Siuslaw, Umpqua, Coos and Rogue offer shad fishing, but the largest of all Northwest runs occurs in the Columbia and its tributaries far above tidewater.

Shad are widely considered inedible by Northwest anglers. In fact, they are delicious smoked and can be prepared in a variety of ways. The roe is a delicacy widely appeciated on both Pacific and Atlantic coasts.

Catching Sturgeon

Perhaps one of the least heralded developments in Northwest coastal sport fisheries has been that of sturgeon fishing. Anglers limited their interest to just a few river systems only a decade ago. Today these prehistoric monsters are taken from most of Oregon's bays and lower rivers. The lower Columbia and Umpqua rivers still account for the lion's share of effort and catch, but recently Tillamook Bay has come on strong.

Sportfishing regulations for sturgeon seem to grow increasingly complex and variable each year, so check locally before fishing. Keep in mind that not only are catches limited by minimum size (at press time 40 inches but likely to increase) but by a traditional 72-inch maximum as well.

Two species of sturgeon, green and white, are found in most coastal rivers. Both are often caught in the legal size range, but the more common and more coveted white sturgeon are often over the six-foot maximum and must be released. They are known to exceed 10 feet—several hundred pounds plus. Whites are considered a delicacy while greens are more coarse and, if not released, generally kept for smoking.

As much tail as body, the unique thresher shark offers some of the finest eating in the Pacific and, as this Westport charter angler discovered, a very tough opponent on sportfishing gear. (Photo by Terry Rudnick).

In most areas, sturgeon fishing can be good as early as midwinter and as late as midautumn. But catching sturgeon is not always easy. It takes good fresh bait—live or very fresh smelt, herring or ghost shrimp are favored—though some anglers do well on prepared sturgeon bait. This is fished on extremely sharp hooks beneath a heavy sliding sinker. Some use a short length of dacron tied to the hook since it has a less unnatural feel than does monofilament. Unfortunately, these large fish often give baits the third degree with their tough, tubular mouths, so a patient, light touch is requisite. So is a hard, no-nonsense hook-set when the time is right (which is an experience-based decision)—and lots of luck. Sturgeon fishing is, most often, a waiting game.

Tackle need not be fancy. It is often heavy, with many anglers fishing 30- to 60-pound line. It is true that an eight- or nine-footer on much lighter lines may consume hours to bring to the boat only to be released. Still, I prefer 20-pound line. (Lighter monofilament makes sensing strikes easier.)

One valuable item for sturgeon fishermen ought to be a working camera at the ready. That is one way an angler can prove he or she actually caught that 300-pounder released by law next to the boat.

Catching Albacore

If albacore fishing in Northwest offshore waters could best be described by a single word, that would be *unpredictable.* These long-finned tuna migrate thousands of miles annually, showing up along the U.S. Pacific coast during the summer. Two stocks frequent the coast, one occurring roughly north of central California and the other south.

The recent history of albacore sport fishing shows some excellent years for anglers off the Washington and northern Oregon coasts in the late 1970s. Then, for the most part, there was no albacore fishing for over a decade. (One exception was in 1983 when schools of albacore swung in to within 15 miles of the southern/central Oregon coast.) Anyone who wanted consistently good albacore fishing had to travel to the southern half of California's coast.

Then late 1980s saw a shift again, so southern California could scarcely buy an albacore, but the Northwest had several consecutively excellent seasons. What is in store for albacore enthusiasts in years ahead is anyone's guess.

In fact, these tuna generally show up off the coast *every* year. Problem is, they may remain 200 or more miles offshore—far too distant for sport boats. Some charters will run out 80 miles or so, but most anglers don't get excited until the fish are within 50 to 60 miles at most. Much of that movement is dictated by water temperatures. Albacore prefer a warmish 58 to 60 degrees.

Clearly, a seaworthy, properly equipped boat is needed to pursue albacore offshore. The majority of fishermen who chase albacore do so from charter boats, which offer trips lasting at least 12 hours and costing $125 or more. Catches on a good trip can average several tuna per person, with the fish weighing 12 to at least 30 pounds.

Most Northwest charters troll metalhead feather jigs just behind the boat at 5 knots or faster. In recent years, more have offered the *real* sporting opportunity to take albacore—from drifting boats, chumming and fishing live anchovies with little or no weight. Much lighter tackle can be used this way. Of course charter boats furnish this, but anyone fishing his own should figure 15- to 20-pound line for live bait fishing.

No one can predict the movements of albacore, but when fishing's good it can be great and charters have been known to return with catches of up to 10 to 20 tuna per angler.

Catching Sharks

Although popular in some areas of coastal U.S., shark fishing has never developed much of a following in the Northwest. Still, there are sharks, large and small, to be caught.

Ocean shark fishing has never developed as a sport here as it has in the Atlantic states. But during the summer months, you can find blues and salmon sharks as well as occasional other species. They will run from several feet to over 10, offer exciting and rugged sport, and if bled at once can be very good eating.

However, getting out to shark fish is a different story. Few charters offer regular shark fishing trips, and these can require a considerable run for private boats which should be equipped to set up a chum line.

On the other hand, it is not unlikely that anyone fishing offshore whether 'way out for albacore or close in for salmon may encounter a shark (most often a blue), quite possibly at the end of his or her line. If the monofilament leader holds, you'll have a dogged if not spectacular battle on your hands.

Encounter With a Thresher Shark

It was a warm late summer day—and the ocean water was even warmer, coming off an El Nino year. (That's the phenomenon of unusually warm ocean waters off the coast.) The ocean off Westport was full of visitors strange to these waters—first, numerous mackerel that had been caught that morning, and then the bonito that I landed (a small tuna unusual north of central California).

Then, in the stern of the boat, a fellow hooked up with what might have been a big chinook. But after 45 minutes around and around the charter, it looked more and more like something else—but what?

Only when the strange grey shape came into sight was the catch evident: a six-foot thresher shark, three feet of it body and the rest tail. For a fish weighing perhaps 30 pounds, it had put up a tremendous fight. I quickly came to the conclusion that I'd like to hook into a thresher someday.

At day's end, the fellow who caught it decided he didn't want to drag a shark home, cleaned or otherwise. So it was left at the dock. I'd always heard that thresher meat is one of the best, so even though it had not been properly cared for I cleaned it. The result: quite a few subsequent meals that left me with another conclusion: thresher shark is one of the ocean's finer fishes on the table.

Unfortunately, the species will never be common along the Northwest coast. But they are one of several species which do frequent these waters in the summer, even in non-El Nino years.

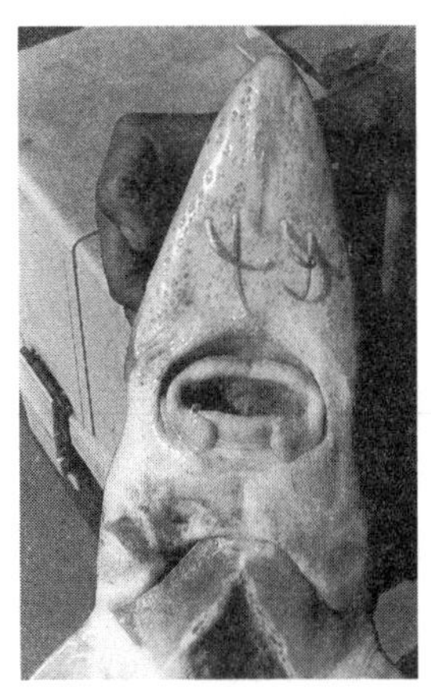

Sensitive pores, barbels and an inquisitive tubular mouth often means a long wait as a sturgeon checks out a bait. But once swallowed, hooks must be set firmly since there is little soft flesh a hook can easily penetrate.

Fortunately, most dogfish encountered in Washington and British Columbia waters are not as large as this dandy, taken east of Port Townsend, Washington.

Catching—Or Avoiding—Dogfish

The dogfish (*Squalus acanthius*) is hardly a bluewater shark, but it is a shark—albeit not exactly a maneater. And it is practically an inevitable catch for anyone fishing bait in the inland marine waters of Washington and British Columbia.

Dogfish seldom grow larger than three or four feet. They don't offer much fight. And they tend to be a detested nuisance among sport fishermen because they shred lovingly prepared mooching baits and, once hooked, roll in line and leader until the monofilament is worthless. Then they have to be removed—most often anglers just cut the line since the rig is ruined.

In any case, beware when handling a dogfish or you may discover the two very long, very sharp spines ahead of each of the two dorsal spines. They're very adept at twisting and turning in such a way to thrust a spine into a careless arm. I can tell you that—and tell you that the common belief that these spines are toxic is false—but they can draw plenty of blood.

Do these nondescript, rather sluggish, small grey sharks have any redeeming features? I suppose they're fun on light tackle and they're certainly plentiful enough. But it's hard to get excited about fishing for dogfish.

Dogfish are edible. In fact, great numbers of them are consumed outside the U.S. (In Britain, called "greyfish," they're a common part of the omnipresent fish and chips.)

As with most sharks, the key requirement for making them palatable is *immediate* cleaning, to get rid of uric acid, and icing. I have found them easy to eat, but too bland to get very enthused about. (As one veteran Northwest angler has told me, "No matter how I fix dogfish, it always tastes like the batter.")

Fishing Light Tackle For All Northwest Salt Water Game Fish!

Humming like an angry mosquito, my tiny reel broke the almost unearthly stillness surrounding us. Something over 200 feet below the boat seemed determined to keep the reel singing. It was a misty-white, gentle July morning, far back in one of the countless mazes of inlets and passes that make up the British Columbia coast.

Most anglers who fish Northwest waters would reasonably assume from hearing such hard, sustained runs that I had to be struggling with either a halibut or a chinook.

What I finally managed to coax to the boat was neither of those, but a fiery red 15-pound yelloweye rockfish. These deep-water dwellers look impressive, but their fight has been justifiably compared to a chunk of driftwood. And that's with good reason: when hauled quickly upward, gases in their swim bladders incapacitate them.

So had I hooked the Superfish of yelloweye? It had taken off on several scorching runs at intervals and kept arguing with me from bottom to top.

In fact, this yelloweye was no different from thousands of others caught up and down the Northwest coast. No, the difference was that which connects angler to fish. In my case that was a wispy thread of monofilament testing 2 pounds (that's stated spool strength; actual strength is about 4 pounds).

There is really little reason to fish these salt waters with lines testing over 8 to 12 pounds (again, stated spool strength; actual strength will be 12 to 16 pounds).

Yet heavier lines, typically twice that weight, have prevailed traditionally for decades. Why have Northwesterners been slow to gain the interest shown in light lines by anglers in much of the Atlantic, Gulf and southern California coasts?

For one thing, marine fishing grounds in the north Pacific are typically deep and driven by hard, powerful tides. Then, too, the use of relatively heavy lines is traditional and fishing traditions in the Northwest have always seemed to die a slow, lingering death.

Yet probably 90% of all my Northwest saltwater fishing since the early 1970s has been with lines actually testing 4 to 12 pounds (and occasionally to 16). Using such light lines I've caught yelloweye well over 20, many lingcod in the 30s and halibut in the 50- to 90-pound range, as well as chinook to 60 pounds. It's been great fun; I can't imagine fishing heavier gear and suspect that most anglers who go light will be hooked as well.

Believe it or not—line testing no more than 8 pounds is plenty for big yelloweye rockfish like this one the author caught in southern British Columbia, jigging a Krocodile Spoon in deep water. A prolonged, more exciting, trickier fight is guaranteed.

Some Tips On Hooks

In any fishing, the hook you use is important. In fishing light lines it becomes critical because driving a hook home with line testing a few pounds is a whole lot trickier than doing so with 15- or 25-pound line. But there are a few things you can and should do to give yourself slightly better odds.

Choose narrow diameter hooks. Using the narrowest diameter you can get by with is smart with any line. Thin hooks, simply, sink in much easier than thick ones and that's important given that just about all Northwest game fish have tough mouths.

Keep a hook file in your pocket and use it. Check the sharpness of your hooks when you first tie them on and again occasionally as you fish. The test is to simply prick a finger slightly: the hook should be "sticky sharp" so it grabs with no effort. It takes only a few moments to keep them that sharp. When sharpening, don't try for a rounded point. File from three sides, so three triangular wedge faces result.

Consider fishing barbless. In some areas (such as Washington waters) barbless hooks are required by law, so there's not much to consider. Even where barbless hooks are not requisite, you might try filing down at least most of the barb if you're having trouble setting hooks. A long barb can be a real sticking point, so to speak, when trying to set the point into a fish's mouth. The less the barb, the more easily the hook slides in. Barb or no barb, it's then a matter of keeping a tight line on the fish.

However, having the right gear and knowing how to use it is essential for catching salmon and bottomfish on light lines. By the numbers, then, practical advice for staying light:

1. Reels. Spinning reels in the Northwest have yet to gain widespread acceptance for any saltwater application. Yet high-quality spinning reels are a pleasure for fishing light lines. Levelwinds are okay, but I can much more enthusiastically recommend the new generation of miniature "big game" or trolling reels such as Daiwa's SL20SH. This model, like any small reel ideal for deep water use, holds many hundreds of yards of light line, offers better than a 6:1 retrieve ratio and a supersmooth oversized drag.

2. Rods. Fishing deep water means fishing fairly heavy jigs or spoons. Typically, the length of salmon rods is too great and the action too spongy to be ideal. Better is a popping rod action—a fiberglass, graphite or composite stick of 6- to 7-feet with a fast action (sensitive tip, powerful lower end) and a long butt section for leverage. (In essence, a compromise between a long, light salmon rod and a short, powerful stand-up rod.)

3. Line. Buy *quality* monfilament and buy lots of it in large spools. Not only will you use and lose more line when you go lighter, but you should be changing or adding fresh line frequently. Small nicks can be devastating with small threads. If actual strength is a concern, look for IGFA-class ratings in pounds/kilograms. (Typically, stated spool strength is underrated considerably.)

4. Terminal rigging. Use a heavy monofilament shock leader. This concept is standard practice around most of coastal U.S., but not in the Northwest. Nevertheless, it is essential. Tying directly to a jig with the main line simply won't do with very light lines. The rough, scaly heads of bottomfish as well as rocks or even the bottom of a boat can quickly abrade through narrow diameter lines. Two or three feet of 40-pound monofilament, connected to the main line with a tiny black barrel swivel will do the trick.

Light line fishing in big waters for big fish demands high-quality gear with super-smooth drags and plenty of line capacity. The author has found that a regular, liberal spraying down of such reels with a good Teflon-based lubricant spray (there are several brands available) and subsequent wiping with a soft rag keeps reels looking and working like new.

Light tackle and artificials go together naturally. Long, slender metal salmon jigs are great—easily fished with light gear and effective for both bottomfish and salmon, as are 3-to 7-ounce spoons such as Krocodiles.

In any case, remember that light lines allow you to get by with much lighter jigs and still reach bottom easier. Increasing line diameter produces geometric increases in water resistance. So the 8-ounce jig necessary to take 20-pound line with it down to 300+ feet can be put aside in favor of a 2- or 3-ouncer when put down with 8-pound line.

Downriggers can be a marvelous way to fish light lines for salmon. But fishing ultralight tackle may be too tricky when trying to set releases reliably down to, say, 4 or 6 pounds of pull.

5. Technique. Remember just how easily parted are wispy lines. Tactics used with traditional gear must be modified. A particularly critical moment when working a lure in deep water is the initial strike when solid rod sets must be coupled with quick cranking to compensate for significant line stretch and any slack "belly." It's a balancing act with light line: too slow or gentle at this point may mean hooks never driven home and fish lost; sets too emphatic once the line is tight will surely snap it. Practice helps develop the right touch. Keeping hooks needle sharp also helps set them.

6. Timing. One other crucial consideration for any light line enthusiast headed to deep North Pacific waters is *tidal flow.* Many productive pinnacles, reefs, ledges and gravel banks are swept by currents with a velocity of several knots. At such times, put up the light gear. But be ready to break it out in a hurry during slack tides or light tides when a vertical rise or fall of only a few feet mean light line time.

Another fact of light line fishing is that fish show a marked tendency to jump more often. Light tackle expert LaGrande Long hangs on here as an angry chinook clears the surface repeatedly.

No line-class world record, but a lot to handle—that's what this 20-pound halibut proved to be when hooked on 4-pound line.

Light Line World Records (And The IGFA)

Anyone who doubts that some frighteningly large fish can be and are taken on some very light lines need only glance over line-class world records kept by the International Game Fish Association (IGFA). At press time, world records in lighter line classes for three major species of Northwest marine game fish[1] were as follows:

Chinook salmon:[2] 2#=34 lb., 10 oz., 4#=59 lb., 12 oz., 8#=62 lb., 8 oz, 12#=67 lb. 4oz, 16#=77 lb., 8oz.

Pacific halibut, men's division: 2#=10 lb., 13 oz., 4#=39 lb., 8#=244 lb., 12#=127 lb., 16#=150 lb. Women's division: 2#=20 lb., 1 oz., 4#=26 lb., 15 oz., 8#=123 lb., 12#=142 lb., 16#=131 lb.

Lingcod, men's division: 2#=10 lb., 13oz., 4#=16lb., 13oz., 8#=27 lb. 8 oz., 12#=38 oz., 6 oz., 16#=44 lb. Women's division: 2#=vacant, 4#=4 lb., 2 oz., 8#=16 lb. 13 oz., 12#=30 lb., 8 oz., 16#=46 lb.

For more immediately current or additional information about world records as well as about the IGFA itself, write the association at 3000 Las Olas Boulevard, Ft. Lauderdale, FL 33316 or call 305-467-0161. A modest annual membership fee supports this nonprofit organization dedicated to keeping records of game fish and enhancing recreational fisheries around the world. Also members receive bimonthly newsletters which include world record updates and the impressive, informative annual *World Record Game Fishes* book.

[1]Yelloweye rockfish are so far not part of the IGFA's line-class record-keeping system, but is recognized with one all-tackle world record—the largest caught and entered on sport gear (probably not with light line)—at press time, 21 pounds, 4 ounces.

[2]Salmon are considered by the IGFA to be a freshwater species; therefore, there are no separate men's and women's divisions as there are for strictly saltwater game fish.

WASHINGTON

WASHINGTON OFFERS TWO WORLDS FOR SALT water fishermen. The open coast concentrates intense angling interest among larger private boats and charters in a single summer season. A very different world in many respects, the vast inside marine waters of Puget Sound are a small boater's delight much of the year.

The Evergreen State provides opportunities not generally available elsewhere for coastal U.S. anglers south of Alaska. Besides year-round protected fishing, it offers blackmouth—smaller "resident" chinook that remain in the sound and strait rather than going to sea. And there's the biannual run of pink salmon to spice up the action. Only Washington offers the incomparable San Juan Islands—with fishing often matching the backdrop of their dramatic scenery. And Washington boasts the two largest coastal sportfishing centers north of San Francisco, Ilwaco and Westport.

Those centers of fishing activity are in an area of modest development along a generally unspoiled and largely inaccessible state coastline. The ocean fishing season begins in a limited way in May when bottomfishing charters start sneaking out over the bar to load up on black rockfish and lingcod. Though bottomfishing charters continue to be available into September, the salmon fishing dominates all other activities when it begins, as early as the latter part of May or as late as early July. Unforunately, in recent years annual opening dates have varied considerably. Season closings are at least as variable, determined by quotas; some years filled quotas have ended ocean seasons as soon as early August; traditionally and in recent years, they have lasted into September.

Sandy beaches and, beyond them, a shallow, smooth, gradually sloping bottom characterize the state's coast south of Kalaloch. The northern two-thirds of Washington's coast is dominated by rocky headlands and nearshore rocky reefs, interrupted by only one small port, La Push, used by a few charters and private boats.

At Cape Flattery, the most northwesterly point of land in the contiguous United States, the Pacific meets the Strait of Juan de Fuca. This 20-mile wide channel links the ocean to Puget Sound and the Strait of Georgia. The western end of the strait affords some protection from the ocean, while at the same time its coastal environment offers richly rewarding angling for salmon, halibut and other bottomfish out of Neah Bay, Sekiu and Pillar Point. RV parks and marinas dot these harbors, offering launch and moorage facilities and skiff rentals as well as charters. Their season runs from early spring through early autumn.

For the eastern Strait of Juan de Fuca, Port Angeles is a center of sportfishing activity. This scenic seaport, at the northern foot of the Olympic Mountains, offers some of the state's best fishing for winter blackmouth salmon, spring halibut and summer kings. Well offshore in the eastern strait are a series of banks or seamounts which can be as productive for salmon and halibut as they can be hard to locate without Loran.

Still farther east, where the strait floods into/out of Puget Sound is Port Townsend, with its Midchannel Bank in the 1980s proving, year in, year out, to be one of the state's most consistent small boat salmon fishing areas. Metal jigs, particularly the locally-manufactured Pt. Wilson Dart, account for the majority of salmon taken here.

The Puget Sound region has been divided into five separate areas in this guide: San Juan Islands, Northern Puget Sound, Central Puget Sound, Southern Puget Sound and Hood Canal. Generally these waters offer salmon angling all year, varying from dreadfully slow (fish checks commonly showing well under a fish per boat) to marvelously fast. Some years, hungry winter blackmouth, November-January and beyond, can be thick enough to account for red-hot action, as was the case in the late 1980s when the fish were small but oh, so plentiful. Trolling with downriggers has become very popular, but the tradition of mooching hasn't died, especially at crowded areas like Point No Point and Point Defiance.

The once thriving Puget Sound bottomfishery for Pacific cod dwindled to nothing by 1990, but tight regulations on lingcod has put that species clearly on the rebound wherever habitat provides it shelter—though the season is only a few weeks each spring and the limit just one fish per day. Small rockfish are still locally abundant, though larger fish are increasingly scarce. Flounder and perch populations remain plentiful and underfished.

Sport fishermen in Washington are pinning high hopes for a return to the fishing success enjoyed many years ago

In recent Novembers, throngs of waders, float-tubers and small boaters have flocked to Western Hood Canal to capitalize on great runs of hard-fighting hatchery-bound chum (dog) salmon.

The protected waters of Puget Sound offer year-round salmon action for small boat angling.

on an ambitious, $1 million, Recreational Fishery Enhancement Plan, published in late 1989. The major goal is certainly set high enough: "...to make Washington the recreational fishing capital of the nation." Among the specific goals are a return to a Memorial Day-Labor Day ocean salmon season, improved fishing in Puget Sound and more stable regulations, as well as particular projects including more artificial reefs, public beach access points, fishing piers and launch ramps.

Most recreational angling in these waters takes place from private boats, but there are a number of well-established, year-round charters fishing all areas of the sound (except Hood Canal). A few modest fishing piers offer limited angling possibilities. Shore angling possibilities are extremely limited.

Anyone planning to fish Washington's salt waters is advised to thoroughly study current sportfishing regulations. For many years, sport salmon regulations have become increasingly complex. The state's marine waters have been divided into several management areas and within those areas there are different seasons and size restrictions for the various species and different gear restrictions. Bottomfishing, once wide open, is also increasingly regulated. There are several lingcod season for different areas and varying bag limits. Halibut regulations are more variable than ever now that the managing agency, the International Pacific Halibut Commission, has gone to an annual quota system which is broken down into allotments for different areas.

Overlooked by many, surfperch are always available along Washington Beaches and jetties. This fish was caught on the Columbia River Jetty.

For More Information

All telephone numbers in western Washington are in the 206 area code.

Washington State Department of Fisheries, 115 General Administration Building, Olympia, WA 98504, 753-6600 (main number), 753-6583 (information office), 976-3200 (toll-call recorded information hotline). Write for free regulations pamphlets *(Salmon, Shellfish, Bottomfish Sport Fishing Guide)* if unavailable at local outlets.

U.S. Coast Guard, 13th District, 915 Second Avenue, Seattle, WA 98174, 442-5295 (or Public Affairs, 442-5896). (Also see local stations listed in each separate area in this guide.) Free annual publication "Special Local Notice to Mariners" is a must for private boaters fishing off the Washington Coast. To request one, write the Aids to Navigation Office (at above address) or call 442-5864.

Pacific Marine Center, 1801 Fairview Avenue East, Seattle, WA 98102, 442-7657. Free index to Pacific coast nautical charts, including list of authorized agents around the state.

Washington Public Ports Association, P.O. Box 1518, Olympia, WA 98507, 943-0760. Free pamphlet, "Recreational Boating Facilties" with map showing all 34 major public port marinas around the state, also describes faclities and rates for each.

National Park Service, Fourth and Pike Building, Seattle, WA 98109, 442-0170. For information on fishing and camping in the Olympic National Seashore as well as in Olympic National Park.

Washington State Parks and Recreation Commission, 7150 Clearwater Lane, Olympia, WA 98504, 753-2027 or toll-free, in-state, summer only: (800) 562-0990. Free pamphlets, "Washington State Parks Guide" and "Saltwater Marine Facilties." The former lists all state park areas, describes rates and facilities and explains the reservations system. The marine guide describes 44 separate marine parks (most accessible only by boat) around the state's inland marine waters.

Washington Department of Natural Resources, Public Lands Building, QW-21, Olympia, WA 98504, 753-5330. Write or call for information about DNR public lands and beaches. For free pamphlet, "Your Public Lands" or "Washington Marine Atlas, Volume III, North Coast" and "Volume IV, South Coast," each $4.31 with tax, write the DNR Photo and Map Sales Office, 1065 South Capitol Way, A-11, Olympia, WA 98504 or call 753-5338.

Washington State Ferries, Colman Dock, Seattle, WA 98104, 464-6400 or in-state toll-free, (800) 542-7052. Free schedule/fare pamphlets; call for specific schedule information.

Washington Department of Commerce and Economic Development, Travel Development Division, General Administration Building, Olympia, WA 98504, 753-5630. Maps and general information of interest to visitors.

Pacific Salmon Sportfishing Council, 1023 South Adams, Suite G-52-A, Olympia, WA 98501, 268-9134. Information from major saltwater sportfishermen's lobby on how to help ensure a fair share of the game fish resource for recreational use. Quarterly tabloid "The Pacific Salmon Monitor" with subscribing contribution ($25+).

Also a very valuable reference for small boat fishermen and shorebound anglers alike, is the 348-page book ***Washington Public Shore Guide, Marine Waters*** by James W. Scott and Melly A. Reuling, published by University of Washington Press, Seattle, Washington.

San Juan Islands

In many respects, the San Juan Islands are Washington's Bahamas. These serene—but increasingly busy—islands are reached only by water or air, an attraction for those wanting to leave things behind for a while. And, like the Bahamas, they offer some of the best fishing in their region.

In physical respects, the San Juans differ completely from the low, sandy, tropical islands of the Caribbean. These are high, steep and craggy, cold-water islands. Yet they are accessible, served by the state's extensive ferry system. Boaters travel to and through the islands each summer in outboards and inboards, sailboats and motoryachts. There is also regular air service from and to Sea-Tac International.

While sport fishing is hardly the only attraction that draws thousands of visitors to these islands each year, it is certainly one major factor. And with good reason. Mile after mile of steep, rocky shoreline hints of similar habitat below the surface. These waters are characterized by current-swept points, precipices, pinnacles, shelves and ledges.

Teeming baitfish beckon to salmon to feed and fatten here, year-round. The San Juans are known for excellent fishing for some of the Northwest's largest winter blackmouth. Trophy-sized kings start showing in spring as early Fraser River and then Skagit River chinook move in. Late summer coho and pink fishing is often red-hot along the western reaches.

And salmon fishermen have a wealth of spots in which to pursue their quarry: the islands abound with jutting, rocky points of land and deep passes, around and through which currents sweep and drift-moochers score. Downrigger trollers take salmon consistently, working the length of long stretches of steep cliffs.

The endless rugged, rocky marine habitat throughout these islands offers drift-fishermen a great variety of bottom-dwelling game fish. That includes some very large lingcod (I've seen them over 60 pounds here) and yelloweye rockfish (I've caught a number between 20 and 24 pounds) as well as black rockfish to 10 pounds. Logically, the inevitable increase in fishing pressure has meant a decrease in the number of big fish available, but plenty of trophies remain to be caught.

Despite a multitude of resorts and marinas, there is hardly a room, campsite or boat slip to be found for love or money in June, July and August. Summer rates reflect that demand, too. Yet the other nine months a year find the islands nearly deserted by visitors. There is less competition for facilities and rates are down, yet fishing can be quite pleasant and rewarding through the winter.

Fishing, boating and camping can be uniquely combined in the San Juans. Many of the smaller islands are state owned. Several offer natural, protected harbors, and state parks provide buoys or docks, pit toilets, tables, campsites and footpaths. (Few provide drinking water, however.)

Steep Points And Ledges Harbor Big Salmon

There isn't any period in the year when salmon *can't* be caught in the islands. Two methods account for chinook (blackmouth and kings): deep-trolling along mile after mile of steep shoreline and mooching plugcut herring off points of land around which the sides drop off steeply into the depths. In the force of heavy currents, huge back-eddies form around such points, providing natural holding areas for baitfish—and salmon. A limited number of drift-jigging enthusiasts "work the metal" instead of soaking herring.

From midspring through August, most salmon anglers have one thing on their minds: the big kings that cruise through the islands. Many of the early fish are Canada-bound (for the Fraser River). Some of these chunky brights are known as "white kings" for their exquisitely-flavored flesh which is indeed nearly white, rather than the usual pink-red. Early kings over 30 pounds are not unusual, with those in the 40s and 50s increasingly likely as the season progresses. But keep in mind that recent regulations have required throwing back all salmon *over* 30 inches in the spring.

Steep ledges like this one along the northern shore of Orcas Island continue just as steeply below the surface, and along their length baitfish collect, salmon feed and anglers troll.

Required Catch-And-Release For Trophy Chinook—No Picnic For Fishermen

The western sky over the Olympic Mountains had begun to glow red as the northerlies of a clear May evening pushed our 17-foot Wellcraft center console out against a hard-running tide. My fishing partner and wife, Jackie, had already freespooled to the bottom a fluttering Pt. Wilson Dart jig. And before our host, Rock D'Acquisto of Port Townsend, or I could get in gear, her rod danced from the pull of the evening's first salmon.

With her spinning reel singing, Rock and I reeled in to stay out of the way while the chinook stripped off 12-pound line.

"That's got to be a good one!" I said.

"Yeah—too good," Rock responded glumly.

And so it was: about 15 minutes later, a silver prize between 20 and 30 pounds thrashed alongside the boat as I slipped the jig's hooks—barbless by law—from the chinook's jaw.

A few expletives were bandied about. But curse as we might, and as we did, and as anglers here have for years, releasing big and even trophy-sized chinook became an acknowledged anomaly of fishing much of northern Washington from April 16 to June 15—when many of the year's biggest, hungry spring-run chinook are taken—since the early 1980s.

That's been perhaps the single most unpopular regulation to ever face salmon fishermen, who are understandably less than eager to throw back what for many may be the trophy of the year or even a lifetime. One charter skipper admitted giving up his south San Juans spring fishing, depressed at seeing his clients continually forced to release prize kings.

The Department of Fisheries insists that it hopes rebuilding spring chinook stocks will keep this regulation off the books in the future, and a promising start at least was the lifting of that law from northern Puget Sound in 1990. But at press time that closure remained through the San Juan Island and the straits.

In any case, with any salmon sport fisheries, when not absolutely positive what the latest regulations are it is always advisable to check before fishing. Things change.

Cattle Pass is one of the islands' most productive areas for big chinook.

Beware The Raging Rips

It is not unusual to be fishing the islands on a calm summer day, drifting along quietly, only to hear the sound of breakers and look out to see an area of waves cresting as upon a beach—into which your boat is drifting. Yet you know you're far from shore over deep water.

That is a "tide rip" or "ripline." And it is an omnipresent phenomenon in these waters. In calm weather, such riplines can be an annoyance since they'll have a boat of drift fishermen spinning and twisting about madly and may splash water over a low transom, but they can also be a blessing since they can concentrate bait and salmon. When driven by winds, such riplines can become deadly to the small boater.

Enormous volumes of water pour through the San Juans with each tide change. The waters here are full of constricted passageways and sharp points of land, changing water mass, forcing it in new directions. The result is an infinitely varied, ever-changing pattern of water movements.

Currents are constantly meeting, but at various angles with various velocities. Where these planes of water meet, a convergence line is formed. While they may meet at an angle, when they hit head-on, the result can be quite turbulent. Classically, this phenomenon is most dramatically evident at bar crossings on a flood tide where river outflow meets the ocean.

Riplines often build up miles-long "junk lines" where all debris caught in two converging currents collects. (This includes drifting boats, eventually.) This can vary from styrofoam cups to whole logs. Only foolish boaters fail to slow a bit to work their way through junk lines.

On calm days, the junk can be seen; in rough conditions it is hidden by the seas. And, from my experience, riplines become one of the greatest threats to small boaters in rough weather. It is often difficult to discern these areas until you're in them. Then, you must negotiate conditions much nastier than the surrounding seas—steeper, very close-set, cresting waves.

Although a stiff windchop on the water will tend to obscure areas of riplines, the best advice in rough conditions is to watch for them and try to avoid them by going well around them when possible, even if it takes you a mile out of your way.

Riplines are a river-like torrent far from shore—good fishing in calm weather like this, but a difficult hazard to small boaters when the water grows rough.

Among a number of areas most favored for kings, Point Lawrence, at the easternmost tip of Orcas Island, must rank near the top. From Point Lawrence west, the long, steep northeast shoreline of Orcas is an ever popular trolling route—and a thankfully protected one on days when strong southerlies or southwesterlies kick up. Trollers work the 20-fathom line most often.

Driftmoochers work the point on an ebb tide, typically motoring nearly up to the rocky tongue to drift out through the backwash and beyond into deep water, to return to the point and repeat the drift. (But beware of invasions of the dreaded dogfish. At times, tiny dogfish in maddening hordes can make bait fishermen prematurely gray. Then, remember the jigs!)

At the southernmost end of the islands is another premiere spot for motor mooching (kicking the motor in and out of gear to guide the pace and/or direction of the drift). A steep shelf begins just at the edge of Goose Island in Cattle Pass (between the southern tips of San Juan and Lopez Island). Start the drift very close to the south end of the island, until you're over deep water (which may not take long given the ferocious currents through this narrow slot), then repeat the drift. Also, nearby Pile Point and Lime Kiln Point on the southwest side of San Juan Island are great spots not only for chinook but for coho and pinks later in the summer, as well as bottomfish.

The area below Lime Kiln and down to Pile Point holds a resident herring population throughout the year. Often these are quite large, 6- to 9-inchers known as "horse herring." They make great bait, fresh or, if possible, alive—not only for chinook but halibut, lingcod and yelloweye as well. Jigging them is easy once they're located. For that, electronics are a great help; otherwise, huge schools below the surface may go undetected.

The ledge along western Cypress Island, from Tide Point to Strawberry Rock, is a good bet in June for prized Fraser River white kings. Downrigger fishermen work bait or plugs in 100 to 150 feet of water, trolling from the rock to the near the point, always careful to avoid motoring *too* near since the bottom at Tide Point rises sharply.

Alden Point at Patos Island is a first-class driftmooching area. Start the drift at the edge of the kelp, in 40 or 50 feet of water, mooching along bottom until out around 150 feet, then repeat. Peak activity typically occurs about an hour after a tide change.

Even as fishermen enjoy the last few weeks of San Juan kings, late-summer silvers and (in odd-numbered years) pink salmon are heading into the islands from the ocean. They are encountered in many of the king hot spots described above. Pile Point and Lime Kiln points, again, pay off, as do the areas from Tide Point to Strawberry Rock, Point Lawrence and Point Doughty (northwest Orcas Island). Open Bay, at the northwest corner of San Juan Island, is also a reliable silver/pink fishing hole. Patos Island's Alden Point and Toe Point are usually productive, especially in a good pink year.

The run of silvers may last well into October, as it did during 1989 for example, when the few anglers out then found great numbers of big silvers (into the upper teens) all along the west side of San Juan Island.

Trolling accounts for most silvers and pinks, though mooching can be effective. Small herring are good baits for trollers and moochers alike.

Ironically, some of the islands' very best salmon fishing occurs when the fewest anglers are around to take advantage of it. Tony Floor, for many years the Washington Department of Fisheries information chief and one of the best veteran San Juan Islands anglers, puts it this way: "The islands' blackmouth offer clearly the most underutilized winter chinook fishery with the most potential in Washington State."

Blackmouth are both plentiful much of the time and *big*, with many over 20 pounds taken each winter. Also, many of these fine winter fish are taken from protected coves and bays, in fact often around marinas and even from docks, making unnecessary long, cold runs into more open waters. Large concentrations of herring winter in the islands and blackmouth stay with them. Often vast schools of herring will fill bays such as Eastsound at Rosario or invade public docks at Friday Harbor. Local fishermen often snag or jig herring, quickly rigging one on a no. 1 hook and casting out with little or no weight. The bait will struggle just below the pack where chinook wait to pick off such injured herring. Others cast out Buzz Bombs or other metal jigs and do quite well. There can be good winter salmon fishing for those who hike to steep rocky points, particularly when baitfish are showing.

Trolling is popular, in part probably because it allows anglers to duck inside a cabin and warm their hands while fishing. It is also highly productive. A dodger-and-squid or dodger-and-herring are popular rigs. Some trollers still rely on plastic diving planes to get gear deep enough, but downriggers are *de rigeur* nowadays for most anglers.

But dedicated moochers who endure numb fingers on cold winter days consistently take their share of blackmouth. And happily, the hordes of dogfish that often make summer mooching impossible tend to be more scarce when the weather turns cold.

One of the most successful moochers, Tony Floor, notes that during the winter the herring that so abound are young-of-the-year fish. To "match the hatch," Floor plugcuts the little herring, typically 4 inches or so, and rigs them with a single no. 1 hook. Fished on light line, "This has worked fantastically for me," he says.

Most spots popular with summer king fishermen also produce lots of winter blackmouth, such as Point Lawrence, Tide Point, Pile Point, Iceberg Point (keep an eye to the rips and winds, here), Lovers Cove, Salmon Bank off the south tip of San Juan Island and Patos Island. For one of the islands' best guides, Jeff Lingbloom of Bellingham, both sides of Waldron Island and both sides of adjacent President Channel have proven among the most consistent areas of all for blackmouth.

Topnotch salmon action is also found in areas offering protection from the winter winds common during the November-February blackmouth peak. These include Obstruction Pass, Humphrey Head, around the Orcas Ferry Landing and East Sound. The latter frequently offers some of the fastest action in the winter when hordes of herring are stacked up in the long watery arm.

While there are frequently glassy-calm periods during winter months, winds do indeed whip up, and can be sudden and intense. Among the islands the winds, waves and riplines are smaller and more manageable than on the outside. If you venture out, as onto Rosario or Haro straits, remember to watch the weather closely. The return trip may prove tricky.

Small boaters can usually find protected shorelines among the islands, but the run over from Anacortes across Rosario Strait can be tricky.

Small Boat Safety

When winds are light, small boaters can travel throughout the islands with relative ease. It's always a good idea to keep an eye out for riplines, since these shifting walls of converging currents can grow quite large. When tides run strong, these form areas of roaring, steep, cresting waves—even in only moderate winds.

Waters south and west of the islands offer some excellent fishing over vast underwater banks but these easternmost fringes of the Strait of Juan de Fuca can also be treacherous. If you fish from a small boat, only venture far out on calm days between frontal systems, or during high pressure systems that generate light to moderate northerlies in the afternoons.

Fortunately, such a run to open water isn't essential since there are always lee shorelines to fish, no matter what the wind direction.

One other area for caution which deserves mention is the western half of Guemes Channel. Many boaters launch at Anacortes or nearby Washington Park and cross this channel en route to the islands. In good weather it is a benign enough stretch, but any sort of fresh west or southwest wind—particularly against an ebb tide—can fill this channel with 4- to 6-foot, close-set swells that make returning to the launch area a nasty business.

U.S. Coast Guard Station San Juan Island Area

Patrol Boat, Bellingham (24-hour) (206) 734-1692 Cutter *Point Richmond*, Anacortes (24-hour) . . . (206) 293-9555 or 396-9619.

Bottomfish—A Rich Resource In Rugged Waters

In the past two decades, the sportfishing interest and pressure on San Juan Islands' bottomfish have increased dramatically. But some of the state's best bottomfishing remains in these rocky, bait-filled waters.

A glance into the fish boxes of anglers returning from a day of successful bottomfishing here should reveal how good the sport can be. It is often possible to catch a limit of 10 rockfish including four or five species, as well as a lingcod or two.

Fortunately, many sport fishermen who could keep limits are satisfied to come in with just a few fish for dinner. In fact, extending catch-and-release fishing to include bottomfish is a timely concept that may help maintain a high level of quality sport for the San Juan Islands in the future.

Despite these waters' productivity, bottomfishermen may still return with barely enough fish for a meal. More than likely, they were fishing the wrong area, the wrong tide, or both. To ensure success, bottomfish anglers should use nautical charts with a compass (plus, of course, Loran if one is aboard) to locate steep, rocky habitats, and tide tables to determine periods of tidal flow light enough to make serious bottomfishing possible without using enough lead to sink a ship.

Virtually all species of bottomfish listed in this guide can be taken in the San Juans. A synopsis of some of the better areas by major species:

Halibut are caught mainly in the spring. They frequent large, hard, smooth-bottomed banks in open water, notably

Big yelloweye rockfish like these taken over Middle Bank are less common than in years past but are still taken over deep, rugged, rocky areas.

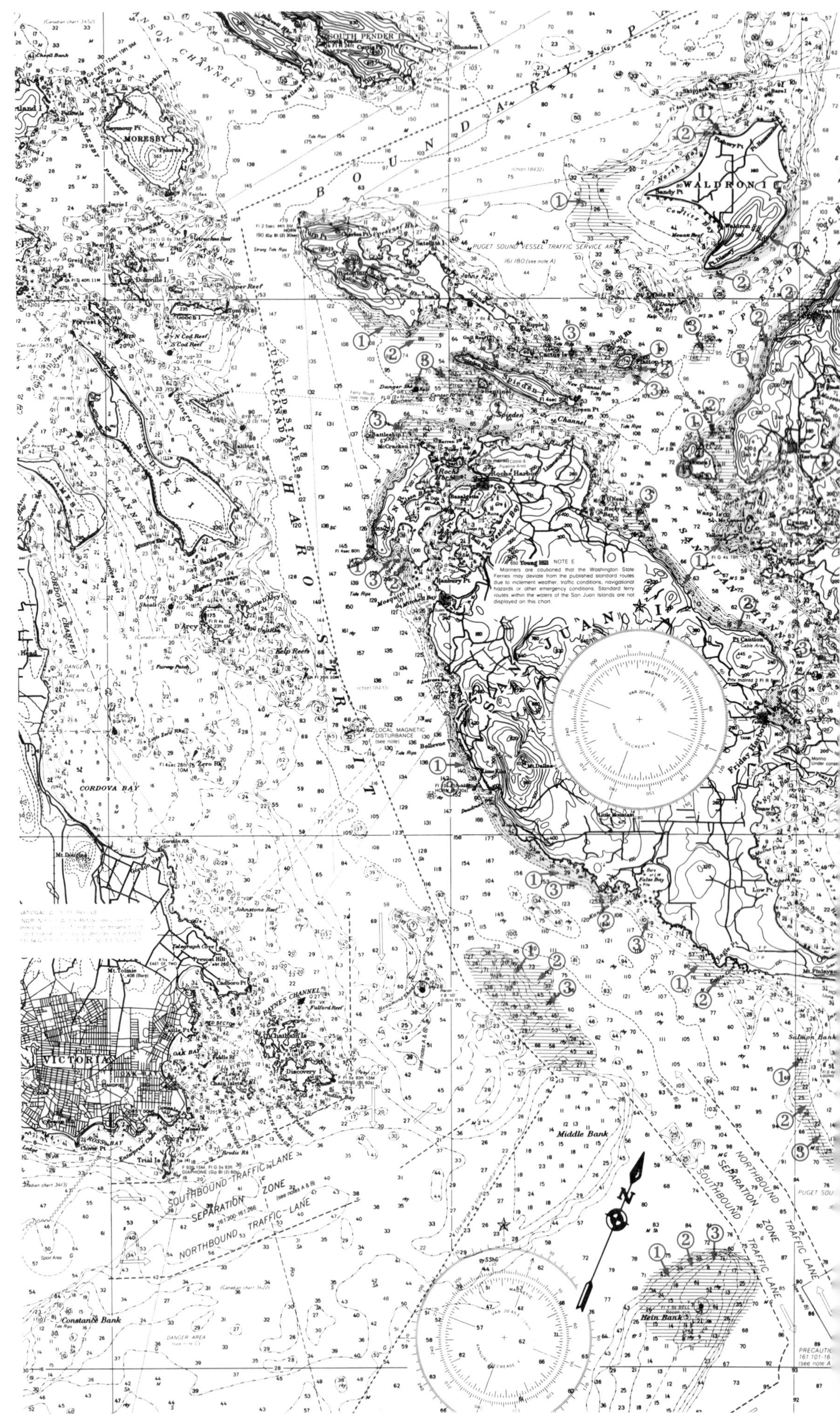

San Juan Islands

Legend
1. Salmon—trolling.
2. Salmon—mooching.
3. Bottomfish.
M Moorage, state park.
■ Launch Site
Scale: 3/8'' = 1 nautical mile

Chart #18421

Not for navigational purposes.

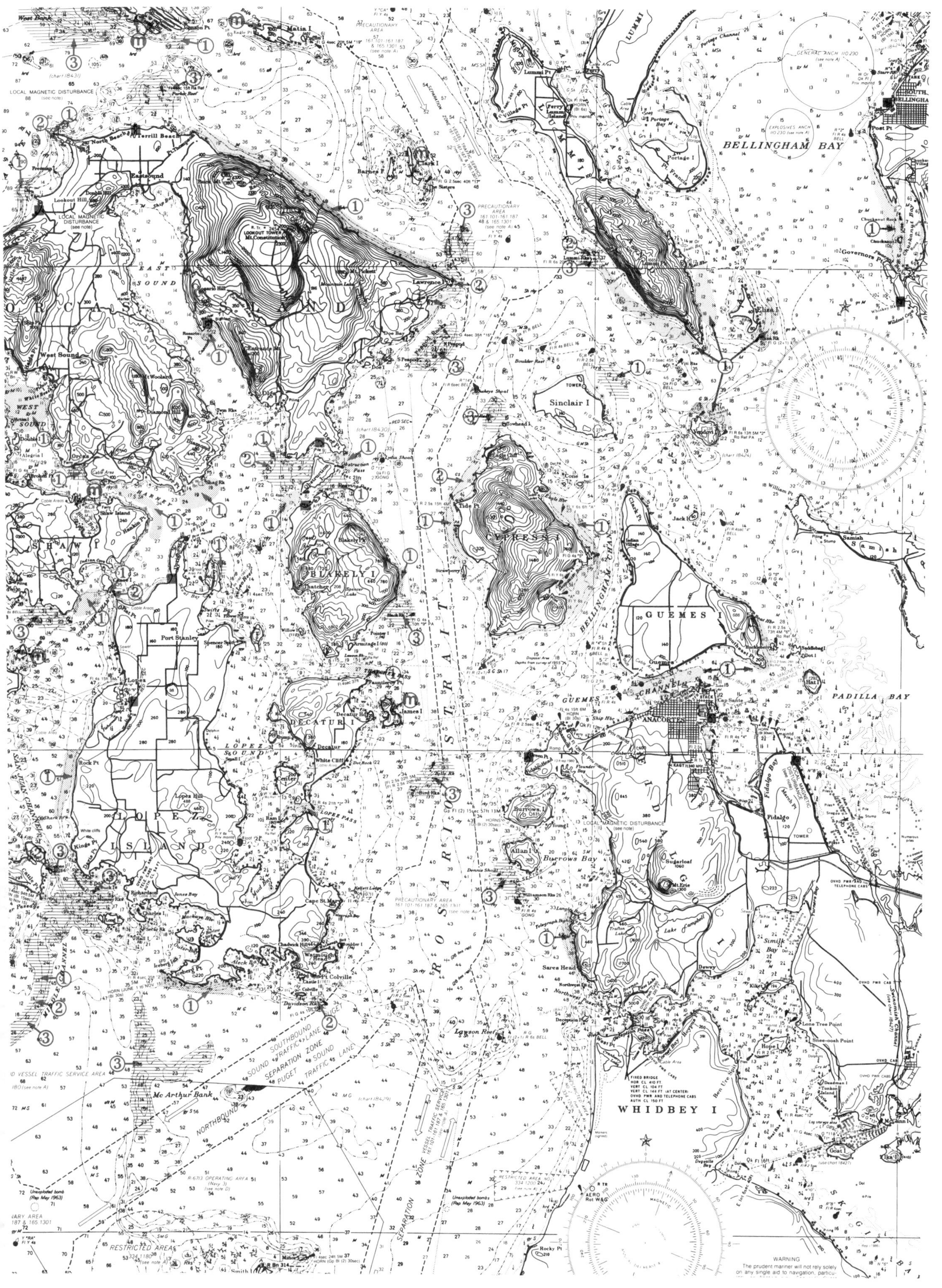

West Bank
Matia I
PRECAUTIONARY AREA
LOCAL MAGNETIC DISTURBANCE
(see note)
Terrill Beach
North Beach
Eastsound
Lookout Hill
Barnes I
Clark I
LOOKOUT TOWER
Mt.Constitution
EAST SOUND
ORCAS ISLAND
Lawrence Pt
Lummi Pt
Village Pt
Portage I
Portage Bay
LUMMI
Lummi I
GENERAL ANCH
EXPLOSIVES ANCH
BELLINGHAM BAY
SOUTH BELLINGHAM
Post Pt
Chuckanut Rock
Governors Pt
Eliza I
Vendovi I
Sinclair I
Boulder Reef
Cone Is
Obstruction Pass
Peapod
Doe I
Olga
Rosario
West Sound
WEST SOUND
Mt Woolard
Diamond Hill
Orcas
Shaw Island
SHAW I
BLAKELY I
CYPRESS I
Strawberry
Tide Pt
Jack I
William Pt
Samish
Clark Pt
Indian Village
GUEMES I
BELLINGHAM CHANNEL
Port Stanley
Spencer Spit
Thatcher
Armitage I
Guemes
GUEMES CHANNEL
Cap Sante
ANACORTES
Hat I
PADILLA BAY
Saddlebag I
Dot I
DECATUR I
Decatur
James I
White Cliff
LOPEZ SOUND
ROSARIO STRAIT
Lopez
Rock Pt
Lopez Hill
LOPEZ ISLAND
LOPEZ PASS
Bird Rks
Burrows I
Burrows Bay
Allan I
Young I
Flounder Bay
Fidalgo Bay
March Pt
Fidalgo
TOWER
Sugarloaf
Mt.Erie
Lake Campbell
Similk Bay
Williamson Rks
Telegraph Bight
Richardson
Jones Bay
Mackaye Hbr
Iceberg Pt
Watmough Bay
Cape St. Mary
Pt Colville
Colville
Castle I
Davidson Rk
Kellett Ledge
Sares Head
Northwest Pass
Deception Pass
Lawson Reef
Dewey
Kiket I
Hope I
Lone Tree Point
Snee-oosh Point
Swinomish Channel
Goat I
WHIDBEY I
SAN JUAN CHANNEL
Cattle Pt
Kings Pt
Mc Arthur Bank
SOUTHBOUND TRAFFIC LANE
SEPARATION ZONE
PUGET SOUND
NORTHBOUND TRAFFIC LANE
PRECAUTIONARY AREA
R-6713 OPERATING AREA (Navy 3) (see note D)
Unexploded bomb (Rep May 1963)
RESTRICTED AREA
Smith I
Minor I
Rocky Pt
AERO Rot W&G
MAGNETIC
FIXED BRIDGE
Deadman I
Dugualla Bay
SKAGIT BAY
WARNING
The prudent mariner will not rely solely on any single aid to navigation, particu-

Critical Variables Of Bottomfishing Where And When

The better one can determine where among the islands to fish, the greater the chance for success. For bottomfishermen, that translates into two key words: rocky and irregular.

An essential accessory and a relatively inexpensive one is a National Oceanographic and Atmospheric Administration (NOAA) nautical chart (often two or three) for an area. Those charts are of course used as base maps for this book.

For the most part, it is best to avoid "M" or "S," where it is muddy or sandy, respectively. Such areas will give up lots of dogfish and ratfish, and if you're lucky, flounder. But for rockfish and lingcod, you'll want to find areas marked "Rky" for rocky.

In addition to the type of bottom, depth and contour are important. Depth is shown at a glance by 10-fathom contour lines and more specifically by individual sounding numbers of actual depths at given spots. Look for areas where the contour lines nearly merge—either in long, straight stretches showing underwater cliffs/ledges, or perhaps best of all in circles indicating underwater pinnacles. It is this irregular, vertical change that tends to collect bait and provide innumerable hiding spots for large and small predators in the face of currents that bring food.

The other essential ingredient to finding the best underwater "fishing holes" is a fishfinder—an LCD, chart recorder or video sounder. That, with the aid of a compass and "eyeballing" nearby landmarks will enable the angler to pinpoint the spots he sees on a chart. Try triangulation, first on the chart, then on the water. For example, with a straightedge, line up on paper two objects—such as a buoy and a point behind it—so the line crosses the pinnacle you want to find, then do the same with another pair of landmarks. Then line up the same objects on the water. But remember: fog and low clouds or haze obscure distant landmarks.

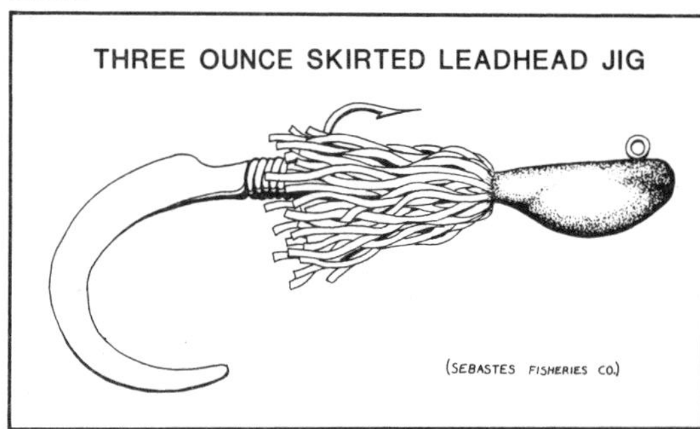

Of course, as long as steep topography of surrounding islands doesn't hamper its use, Loran is an invaluable tool to locating and relocating hotspots.

But finding the right habitat is only part of the successful bottomfishing game. Fishing at the right *time* is important; much of the time severe currents rip through the islands, the fast drift making it almost impossible to fish bottom. And even using heavy gear to fish very heavy weights, you'll find that hanging up in the rocks over and over and losing gear become inevitable. Such times are better spent in endeavors other than bottom fishing.

To determine the times when you *should* plan to fish, consult a tide table or, better, tide calendar. The latter shows at a glance periods when tides are light—that is, when there isn't much difference between the low and high tides. (That difference may be as little as a few feet or as much as 13 or more.)

A light tide period helped this angler sink a leadhead jig to about 240 feet of water near Point George to take this 22-pound yelloweye rockfish on 10-pound-test line from his sailboat.

Partridge, Hein and Middle banks. But other areas with similar habitat throughout the islands may surprise fishermen on occasion with a halibut. Deepwater Bay on the east side of Cypress Island, for example, gives up a few halibut many years. Drifting large herring or working heavy metal jigs is most likely to produce.

Lingcod are one of the most sought species among island bottomfishermen's catches. They're available throughout the open season, in recent years April 16 through November 30. The closed season helps protect the large spawning females—but also discourages anglers from catching the 30- to 60-pound lunkers particularly available at this time in shallow waters.

Catch-and-release light tackle angling for huge lings can be an exciting winter sport, well worth a try (take a camera). Probably the best time to catch and keep a lunker ling is the latter part of April before they've dispersed into the depths until late fall. But remember: smaller lings are much better eating, so why keep the big ones? Lings are hardy and easily released alive, a particularly good investment in future fishing when one considers the many thousands of eggs a big female produces each year.

Deepwater banks and pinnacles are again best bets, especially where they are rocky. Such areas may be found north of Orcas and off the southwest and south sides of San Juan Island. Examples of good ling habitat include any steep reefs such as those near Peapod Rocks off Orcas, north of Waldron Island, around Spieden Island or Middle Bank off southwest San Juan Island. Any area where you can make long drifts over a rugged, constantly changing bottom is worth a try.

Leadhead jigs of 2 to 8 ounces with big plastic tails or strips of pork rind are excellent for ling. There is little reason to use line testing heavier that 20 pounds, if that. Particularly effective for enticing really big ling is any small live fish, a pound or so—greenling or rockfish are most often used—rigged as shown in the chapter on "Fishing Northwest Salt Waters."

Very light or ultralight spinning or baitcasting gear is perfect for lings of 2 to 10 pounds in shallower waters. Cast a variety of plugs around and off kelp beds, sometimes deep divers but also floaters or shallow-runners on a six-foot leader behind a mooching sinker. Retrieved at a moderate pace, this is a very effective, sporting way to catch lings. Such gear *can* take much larger lings: the 38-pound, six-ounce ling I caught south of Spieden Island on 12-pound line in 1982 held the line-class world record for many, many years.

Yelloweye rockfish are never really common but are always prized. Their brilliant red hue and large size make them the most desirable rockfish. Some island fishermen are able to make a yelloweye or two a regular part of their catches by fishing the deeper waters (usually 150 to 400 feet), around the most rugged and rocky reefs or pinnacles when moderate tides permit. In particular look for dramatic changes in bottom structure—very steep shelves. Tony Floor attributes his consistent success for yelloweye to doing just that, fishing the "downhill side." Middle Bank probably offers the most extensive stretch of yellow-eye country—but getting out there can be tricky unless the winds are particularly light. And the slow-growing yelloweye are nowhere near as abundant as they were even a decade ago, with this area hit hard on a regular basis these days by private boaters and charters as well.

Some good yelloweye await in more accessible areas. In fact, I've caught yelloweye to 24 pounds drifting over the rocky peaks and valleys in San Juan Channel across from Friday Harbor. I've had great success with plastic tails or, particularly, big Krocodile spoons.

Quillback rockfish are the ubiquitous "rock cod" of the islands, 2 to 6 pounds, freckled, cream-colored and seldom shy about grabbing a bait or lure. They often congregate in great numbers throughout the island around

This small ling was taken on the eastern edge of Lopez Island on "bass type" gear, by casting a bright yellow Mirrolure along the edge of kelp and working in slowly back.

SAN JUAN ISLANDS / Sport Fish and Seasons

Species	J	F	M	A	M	J	J	A	S	O	N	D
	BEST MONTHS											
Kings (Chinook)	poor	poor	poor	fair	fair	best	best	best	fair/poor	poor	poor	poor
Silvers, pinks	poor	poor	poor	poor	poor	poor	poor	best	best	fair/poor	poor	poor
Blackmouth	best	best/fair	poor	poor	poor	poor	poor	poor	poor	poor	best	best
Lingcod[1]	poor	poor	poor	poor/best	best	best	best	best	best	best	best	poor
Halibut[2]	poor	poor	poor	fair/best	best	fair/poor	poor	poor	poor	poor	poor	poor
Other bottomfish	fair	fair	fair	best	best	best	best	best	best	best	best	fair

[1]Legal season for many years has been April 16 - November 31.
[2]Halibut seasons vary annually according to quotas set each winter.

LEGEND: best (shaded) / fair (hatched) / poor (blank)

Almost anytime fishermen can make drifts over the reefs of Middle Bank when currents and winds are light, chances are they'll catch lingcod.

Getting There Isn't Always Half The Fun

Most people visiting the San Juan Islands must rely on the state's extensive ferry system to get them there and back. These huge, multilevel ships make several runs daily, stopping at the islands of Lopez (Upright Head), Shaw, Orcas (Orcas Landing) and San Juan (Friday Harbor), with some runs going on to Victoria, Vancouver Island.

There is a certain charm and pleasure in the scenic ride—once you're aboard. This overtaxed fleet moves great numbers of visitors into and out of the islands, but during the summer there are often long lines and long waits—of up to several hours.

It is possible to make reservations and doing so well in advance, when possible, will help avoid hours spent in line. Otherwise, arriving at least an hour or two before scheduled departure time will increase the odds of catching the ferry you want.

Remember that all this applies to in-season travel only (late May-early September); colder weather means little or no waiting as winter ferries often sail with light loads.

For the most current schedule of sailing times or for reservation information, call the state ferry system's toll-free (in state) numbers: (800) 542-7052 (recorded information) or (800) 542-0810. (Again: be prepared for a recorded message and, in season, a long wait on hold to actually talk to anyone.) The direct line to the main offices in Seattle: 464-6400. The Anacortes Terminal number is 293-8166. You can also write for information and copies of schedules: Washington State Ferries, Colman Dock, Seattle, WA 98104.

Kelp greenling are common, tasty panfish. This one hit a small jointed Mirrolure plug near Patos Island.

reefs and hard, smooth-bottomed plateaus in 60 to 300 feet, especially in the summer. Then, the habitat itself may be less a factor than their food: clouds of krill (tiny shrimp-like crustacea) on which quillbacks gorge. Don't look for much of a fight after a walloping strike (which is likely to convince you at first that you've hooked a much larger fish), but they are fun to catch and superb eating.

Cabezon are the largest of the sculpins, reaching well over 15 pounds. This crab-eating "bullhead" will take baits, but seems most likely to strike skirted leadhead jigs. "Cabs" inhabit fairly shallow waters as a rule (under 150 feet) and prefer gravelly or rubble-covered bottoms. They're among the hardest-fighting of bottomfish, making determined rushes that strip line off the spool again and again, all the way to the boat. Some folks may consider them ugly, but their meat is unusually firm and flavorful.

Copper rockfish are the most prevalent shallow-water rockfish, particularly caught around kelp and nearby dropoffs, in 20 to 120 feet. I've caught them as large as 7 pounds while drifting over eelgrass beds in 12-15 feet of clear, still, herring-filled water on thick-fog mornings. Coppers are one of the hardest fighting rockfishes and offer some unbeatable sport on appropriately light tackle.

Black rockfish are seldom caught in the large numbers taken by open coast fishermen, but are common in the islands. At times these "sea bass" are as likely to be picked up by salmon trollers and moochers as by bottomfishermen. I've caught 1- to 2-pounders consistently by casting small jigs-and-worms from the rocks on the steep western shoreline of San Juan Island. I've seen 10-pounders taken over deep reefs south of Lopez Island.

Kelp greenling may be abundant in fairly shallow water, often around kelp beds. Small-mouthed but aggressive, these 1- to 3-pound fish strike baits and lures readily. They're one of the best live baits for big lingcod.

Fish Or No Fish...

Fish or no fish, spending a pleasant day cruising and drifting the waters that rush around these unspoiled, craggy islands is a reward in itself. They are indeed a natural treasure. Besides almost inevitable sightings of eagles and seals, I've seen several different species of cetaceans in these waters. Most likely among those are killer whales and Dall porpoise, the latter sharing the black-and-white colors of killers, but much smaller and zippier. In fact, they are one of the smallest and fastest of the cetaceans—and often speed around a moving boat to everyone's delight.

An encounter with a pod of killer whales is not simply delightful but breathtaking. Large enough to dwarf most private boats, orcas frequent these islands. It was once thought that these magnificent animals ruined the sportfishing in an area, scattering salmon far and wide. But the experience of many anglers has shown that to be a wives' tale.

Facilities

Area code for all listings is 206.

Because this area relies so heavily on tourism, visiting anglers have a wealth of facilities from which to choose. They do fill up in the summer, though. For lodging and/or moorage during the season, it is best to call for reservations weeks or, better, months in advance. (Some resorts accept reservations up to 1 year ahead.) Costs tend to be up during summer as well.

Charters

Most charters that fish the San Juans are "six-pack" boats—smaller charters that take up to 6 anglers but will go out with just 2 or 3. At press time, inclusive rates for a day of fishing varied from $60 to $100 per person. Call around for prices.

Anacortes Salmon Charters, P.O. Box 194, Anacortes 98221, 293-4071. 30-foot boat carries up to 6 anglers. Year-round operation, skipper/owner Dean Brazas emphasizes winter blackmouth, concentrating on eastern San Juans. Offers both mooching and trolling. Brazas is an Anacortes native who's fished here for 3 decades. Anacortes Salmon Charters began operation in 1987 and docks at Skyline Marina.

Buffalo Works Charters, P.O. Box 478, Friday Harbor 98250, 378-4612. 30-foot boat carries up to 6 anglers. Year-round operation. Skipper/owner Bob Brittain concentrates on bottomfish unless salmon are in thick. For about $30 over the usual cost, he'll take you out for halibut in season.

Captain Clyde's Charters, K-Dock, Port of Friday Harbor 98250, 378-3404. 28-foot boat carries 4 anglers for half-day trip to catch either salmon or bottomfish. Skipper/owner: Clyde Rice.

Grayline Charters, 9600 Semiahmoo Parkway, Blaine 98230, 371-5222. Both bottomfish and salmon charters available through Semiahmoo Resort.

Jim's Charter and Marine Sales, 65 Marine Drive, Blaine 98230, 332-6724. 24-foot boat—skipper Jim Jorgensen fishes various species of salmon year-round.

"Moby Max" Charters, Route 1, Box 1065, Eastsound 98245, 376-2970. New 22-foot Seasport boat with heated cabin fishes 2 to 4 anglers comfortably. Owner/skipper Max Schwald operates out of Westsound Marine and fishes year round for salmon, mostly chinook, particularly winter blackmouth. He fishes primarily around Orcas Island.

Pete Nelsen, P.O. Box 394, Shaw Island 98286, 468-2314. One of the most respected salmon guides in the islands, Nelsen fishes up to six anglers in his 25-foot walk-around console Aquasport, year-round.

San Juan Charters, 1806 22nd Street, Anacortes 98221, 293-0584. This 42-footer fishes both salmon and bottomfish, year-round. Also books through Rosario Resort.

Sea King Salmon Charters, 2818 McLeod Road, Bellingham 98225, 671-7570. Jeff Lingbloom is an enthusiastic skipper who enjoys taking up to 4 anglers out on his 23-foot charter year-round, concentrating on salmon for the most part.

Marinas

The list below shows full-service marinas. However, many resorts incorporate marinas as well. Those that are part of a larger resort are listed under "Resorts," below.

Blaine Harbour, P.O. Box 1245, Blaine 98240, 332-8037. 243 slips for pleasure craft. Fuel, engine repair, bait and tackle. Excellent, new 2-lane launch ramp good on minus tides. In business since 1935.

Blakely Island Marina, 1 Marine Drive, Blakely Island

98222, 375-6121. Open year-round except January. 70 slips, at least 1/2 available for transient moorage. Gas and diesel fuel and limited engine repair. Good selection of bait and tackle. Store with food, clothing, gifts. Blakely Island is private property; when on shore, don't plan to leave Marina premises. In business since the 1950s.

Cap Sante Boat Haven, P.O. Box 297, Anacortes 98221, 293-3134. 1,100 slips for boats up to 65 feet. Fuel, engine repair, bait and tackle. Boat hoist on premises. In business since 1926.

Fisherman's Cove Marina, 2575 Lummi View, Bellingham 98226, 758-2444. 220 slips, fuel, engine repair, some bait and tackle. Hoist for boats to 32 feet. In business since 1945.

Islands Marine Center, Fisherman's Bay Road, Lopez Island 98261, 468-3377. Open all year, 7 days/week, with 25 slips. Reservations accepted. Engine repair on premises—large inventory of marine parts; fuel available next door. Bait and tackle. Paved ramp good except on minus tides. Lift launch good for boats to 13 tons.

Point Roberts Marina, 713 Simundson Drive, Point Roberts 98281, 945-2255. Open all year, 7 days/week. Over 1,000 slips, about 40 of those kept for transients. Reservations not accepted. Fuel (diesel and gas), engine repair (full-service shop) and a good selection of bait and tackle. Sling launch for boats to 20 feet and a traveling lift hoist for boats to 30 tons. At press time, the marina was working on development into a full-scale resort with condominiums and overnight accomodations.

Port of Friday Harbor, 204 Front Street, Friday Harbor 98250, 378-2688. Transient moorage available, reservations accepted. Fuel and engine repair available. Bait and tackle. No launch on facilities, but ramp located at Jackson Beach.

Semiahmoo Marina, 9550 Semiahmoo Parkway, Blaine 98230, 371-5200. 294 slips, fuel, engine repair, bait and tackle and boat rentals. Lift launch for boats up to 50 feet.

Skyline Marina, Flounder Bay, Anacortes, WA 98221, 293-5134. No overnight/transient moorage, but fuel, engine repair and bait and tackle available. Two sling launches for boats to 24 feet.

West Sound Marina, P.O. Box 19, Orcas 98280, 376-2314. Located midsound on eastern shore with 100 slips (a limited number for transients). Fuel, engine repair, tackle (no bait). 30-ton hoist launch.

Resorts

Beach Haven Resort, Route 1, Box 12, Eastsound 98245, 376-4420. A year-round resort on the rugged northwest side of Orcas Island with 13 beach cabins (7-day minimum stay in summer). No facilities for boaters here except moorage buoys. Launch, moorage, fuel at nearby West Beach Resort.

Deer Harbor Resort and Marina, Box 176, Deer Harbor 982243, 376-4420. Open year-round, 25 ''bungalows,'' cottages, villas. 64 slips, most for transient use in season; reservations wise, especially for larger boats. Gas and diesel on site; boat repair in vicinity. Launch ramp not here, but just across the bay at Carpenter's Marina (good paved ramp except on minus tides). Rents 14- and 15-foot Lund aluminum skiffs with power hourly or daily. Bait and fair tackle selection. Also rents kayaks, charters sailboats.

Guemes Island Fishing Resort, 325 Guemes Island, Anacortes 98221, 293-6643. Located at northeast tip of island, just north of Youngs Park. Open year-round, 7 days/week summer, 5 days/week winter. 6 cabins and several tentsites. No docks but 7 buoys (dinghies available on shore). Gas available from 100-foot hose on shore. Rents 14- or 16-foot Smokercraft with or without outboards. Limited selection of bait and tackle.

Mar-Vista Resort, 2005 False Bay Drive, Friday Harbor 98250, 378-4448. Offers strictly lodging (no moorage or launch facilities).

Roche Harbor Resort, P.O. Box 4001, Roche Harbor 98250, 378-2155. A year-round resort built around historic 20-room hotel built in 1880s. Offers about 30 condominium units and 9 housekeeping cottages. 250 moorage slips—reservations needed in season. Single-lane paved launch ramp (no float) good to about a zero tide—free to guests, a moderate charge otherwise. Gas and diesel available, island mechanics on call. Rents 13-foot Whalers with small outboards. Bait and tackle in store—fair selection of terminal gear.

Rosario Resort, One Rosario Way, Eastsound 98245, 376-2222 or toll-free, 800-562-8820. The island's largest and most famous resort—and a virtual community unto itself, offering everything including a restaurant with famous buffets, lounge, sauna and whirlpool, 3 swimming pools, tennis courts, golf and various lodging from premiere suites to cabins. Don't look for economy rates. Guests who trailer up a boat can use a paved ramp at no charge. Moorage is available, as is fuel, engine repair, boat rentals and bait and tackle.

Smuggler's Villa Resort, P.O. Box 79, Eastsound 98245. 376-2297. Very nice condominium villas. Limited moorage just behind villas is available. Reservations are needed in season for a villa or dock space. Private gravel launch ramp adjacent. Fuel and engine repair at nearby West Beach Resort.

Snug Harbor Marina Resort, 2371 Mitchell By Road, Friday Harbor 98250, 378-4762. Year-round resort tucked into Mitchell Bay on the northwest side of San Juan Island with 6 cabins and 4 RV sites on the water with additional RV/tent space on the hill above. 72 slips to 40 feet—reservations needed. Fuel and engine repair available. Single lane paved ramp on site, good shape but not functional on low tides. Rents 14-foot aluminum skiffs with power. Bait and tackle.

West Beach Resort, Route 1, Box 510, Eastsound 98245, 376-2240. Open all year with 13 cabins on the water (available only by the week in summer), 36 RV spaces (some full, some partial hookups) and 28 tent sites. Moorage buoys and dock space. Gas available. Paved single-lane launch ramp good to about a +4 tide. Rents Whaler-type fiberglass skiffs with power hourly (4-hour minumum) or daily. Also rents large boats and canoes.

Anglers still debate whether the presence of killer whales is a good or bad sign for salmon fishermen, but few deny the impression left by an encounter with a passing pod.

Bait/tackle Shops

Friday Harbor Hardware and Marine, 270 Spring Street West, Friday Harbor 98250, 378-4622. Open 7 days/week, stocks complete line of tackle and books trips on charters.

H&H Outdoor Sports, 814 Dupont, Bellingham 98225, 733-2050. Open 7 days/week, stocks all tackle, with plenty of gear for flyfishermen.

Norm's Bait and Tackle, 1801 Roeder, Bellingham 98225, 671-3373. Open 7 days/week. Emphasis on saltwater gear. Books trips on charters.

Yeager's Sporting Goods and Marine, 3101 Northwest, Bellingham 98225, 384-1212. Open 7 days/week. Very large tackle shop, all types of gear.

San Juan ferries offer a relaxing, scenic ride—once you're aboard.

Public Campgrounds

Bayview State Park (Recreation Area), 7 miles west of Burlington off Highway 20, 757-0227. 90 tent sites and 9 sites with hookups for RVs (to 32 feet). On Padilla Bay with beach access.

Birch Bay State Park (Recreation Area), 8 miles south of Blaine, 371-2800. 147 tent sites, 20 sites with hookups for RVs (to 70 feet). Mile-long beachfront on bay. Facilities for handicapped.

Larrabee State Park, 7 miles south of Bellingham on Chuckanut Drive, 676-2093. 61 tent sites, 26 sites with hookups for RVs (to 60 feet). On Samish Bay with footpath trails and tidal flats. Boat launch but no moorage.

Moran State Park on Orcas Island, 6 miles past Eastsound on Horseshoe Highway, 376-2326. 136 tent sites, 45 sites with hookups for RVs (to 45 feet) and 12 primitive sites. Far inland on island (not near saltwater) but lovely, large park with fabulous 360° view atop Mt. Constitution. Trout fishing in lake.

Spencer Spit State Park (Recreation Area) on the northeast side of Lopez Island, 468-2251. 30 tent sites, no hookups. Great waterfront, extensive sandy spit, good clamming.

Washington Park, southwest of Anacortes ferry terminal on Fidalgo Head's Sunset Beach. A city of Anacortes facility. 62 campsites, 22 with hookups. Excellent 2-lane launch ramp with floats.

Marine Parks

The marine parks listed below are maintained by the Washington Parks and Recreation Commission specifically for private boaters' use—and are accessible only by boat. Some offer extensive harbors with docks and buoys, and with well-developed camping areas. Others are little more than tiny rocks with 2 or 3 primitive tentsites and perhaps a moorage buoy. Like the rest of the San Juans, these parks can become crowded during the summer. But between Labor Day and Memorial Day, most offer nothing but solitude and space. By the way, moorage where available is limited to three consecutive days. In most cases, bring your own drinking water, also. The designation "Natural Area" means that use of these parks should not leave them altered in any way. Rather, leave them as you find them—and unless cans are provided, pack your garbage out.

Blind Island State Park (Natural Area), north end of Shaw Island. 4 primitive tentsites on 3 acres on, literally, an unforested rock. Moorage buoys (no floats).

Clark Island State Park (Natural Area), northeast of Orcas Island, 8 tentsites on 55 acres. Moorage buoys. Lovely beaches for beachcombing or sunbathing.

Doe Island State Park (Natural Area), a tiny secluded island (6 acres) a stone's throw from Doe Bay, southeast Orcas Island. 5 tentsites and 60 feet of moorage space on float.

James Island State Park (Natural Area), east of Decatur Island on the western edge of Rosario Strait. 13 tentsites on 114 acres. 3 buoys and over 100 feet of moorage on floats.

Jones Island State Park, 1 mile off the southwest tip of Orcas Island. 21 tentsites on 177 acres. 3 moorage buoys and 276 feet of moorage on floats. Campground near beach, convenient for small boaters.

Matia Island State Park (Natural Area), 2.5 miles north of northeast Orcas Island. 6 primitive tentsites. 2 moorage buoys, 90 feet of moorage space on floats.

Patos Island State Park (Natural Area), 4 miles northwest of Sucia Island. 4 primitive tentsites on 207 acres. One moorage buoy.

Posey Island State Park (Natural Area), north of Roche Harbor with a single primitive tentsite. No buoys or floats; very close to San Juan Island and recommended for those in canoes, kayaks or light cartop boats.

Saddlebag Island State Park (Recreation Area), east of Guemes Island and north of Anacortes. 5 tentsites on 23 acres. No buoys or floats. Very popular crabbing area.

Stuart Island State Park (Recreation Area), northwest of San Juan Island. A large island offering 19 tentsites on 85 acres. Excellent harbors—15 moorage buoys and 219 feet of moorage space on floats in Reid Harbor; 7 buoys and 539 feet of moorage space on floats in Prevost Harbor.

Sucia Island State Park, 2.5 miles north of Orcas Island, this relatively large island offers long, narrow protected bays. 51 tentsites on 562 acres. 48 moorage buoys and 720 feet of float space in a total of 6 separate bays around the island. Very lovely and often very crowded.

Turn Island State Park (Recreation Area), a 35-acre island just east of Friday Harbor. 10 primitive tentsites. 3 moorage buoys.

Motels, RV Parks

The list of motels and RV parks is long. Most are centered in and around Bellingham and Anacortes. Check with local chambers of commerce (below) for more information.

For More Information

Whatcom County Visitors and Convention Bureau, 904 Potter, Bellingham 98225, 671-3990.

San Juan Island Chamber of Commerce, P.O. Box 98, Friday Harbor 98250, 378-5240.

Orcas Island Chamber of Commerce, P.O. Box 252, Eastsound 98245, 376-2273.

Anacortes Chamber of Commerce, 1319 Commercial Avenue, Anacortes 98221, 293-3832.

NORTHERN PUGET SOUND

THE SECOND LONGEST ISLAND IN THE UNITED States; the dramatically scenic and sheer Deception Pass, flushed by monstrous currents where it splits sheer rock cliffs; a unique saltwater surf fishery for steelhead; some of the best fishing for pink salmon in the state; and arguably *the* most reliably productive *protected* spot for chinook year-round at Midchannel Bank—all this and more are part of northern Puget Sound.

Whidbey Island dominates the geography of this area. Compared to southern and central Puget Sound, areas of heavy population are few. The vast percentage of fish caught in the north sound are taken from private boats. Shore fishing opportunities are limited and few facilities rent boats. Some charter service is available out of Everett and Anacortes.

Salmon are the primary target throughout northern Puget Sound and in some areas are the only species actively sought. Bottomfishing varies greatly from one side of the island to the other. The west side's Admiralty Inlet is frequently rocky and the bottom firm; currents are heavy. The waters of the east side are more protected, less current-swept and the bottom mostly mud. Conditions favor flatfish, dogfish and, in areas where gravel bottom or rocky structure occurs cabezon and greenling. The main feature at the northern end of this region is Deception Pass, where waters rushing through its constricted reaches resemble a powerful river. Fishing it can be tricky—and rewarding.

Know the regulations well before you fish. Always good advice for Washington salmon enthusiasts, but particularly for this area which some years has suffered through the imposition of a 30-inch maximum limit on spring-run chinook and Friday salmon fishing closures.

WEST OF WHIDBEY: ALL KINDS OF SALMON

The waters of Admiralty Inlet and the easternmost reaches of the Strait of Juan de Fuca have a feeling distinctly more wild than that of the central sound. Perhaps that's because of the sparse population lining distant shores or perhaps it's the swift tumultuous currents that give these waters a big feel. In any case, the quality of salmon fishing most of the year contributes to that feeling in north sound waters. And it's the quantity of salmon that help account for that quality: one way or the other—whether down the east or west side of Whidbey Island—all salmon returning to spawn in every river in north, central and southern Puget Sound *must* traverse these long, north-south stretches of water.

Several spots in the southern reaches of this region are particularly popular for their winter blackmouth fishing. Double Bluff, between Mutiny and Useless bays, is reliable with moochers working it regularly between Thanksgiving and late February. They start their drifts in close to the buoy, particularly on ebb tide, and fish along the edge of the shelf. Summer and fall fishing can also be excellent—look for kings, silvers and—in odd years—pinks.

Foulweather Bluff, just across the sound from Double Bluff and at the entrance to Hood Canal, is also popular with both moochers and trollers for chinook.

The "Windmill Hole," located roughly halfway between Double Bluff and Bush Point, is another area long popular with winter fishermen. It has also produced good numbers of large early-summer kings. Traditionally, moochers work somewhat shallower here than many areas, 50 to 60 feet considered optimum. Effort here seems to have declined in recent years, perhaps with the demise of western Whidbey boathouses offering skiff rentals, since this spot is a long way from almost anything.

One of the most famous spots, and justifiably so, is Bush Point. Around this prominent spit, about halfway down the island's west shore, the shoreline plummets and the tide rushes past with great force.

Teamwork helps this pair of anglers land a steelhead in the surf at Lagoon Point. (Photo by Terry Rudnick.)

It is difficult for salmon fishermen to find fault with Bush Point. It is a top producer of each of four major sport species. The point and the rips extending out from it shine particularly when silvers and pinks move into the north sound, generally July into October. Bush Point is widely considered one of the top spots in the state for catching pinks when runs are in. Chum fishing in October and November has gained popularity here, also. Although the early morning and late evening are always good periods to fish, tide changes can bring on a bite at any time of day.

Bush Point is one of those rare spots where shorecasters have a genuine shot at salmon. Try casting Buzz Bombs, particularly for silvers as they move south at the start of a flood tide.

Lagoon Point, the next prominent point of land north, shares many similarities with Bush Point in terms of topography and fisheries, though it may be less heavily fished.

Fishing the rips off Fort Casey means keeping one eye out for ship traffic.

Steelhead In The Surf: A Unique Fishery

Of the many hundreds of steelhead that will be caught in Washington this year, the great majority will be taken well up in rivers. But a tiny fraction of steelheaders will have the unique experience of hooking these magnificent sea-run rainbow from a saltwater beach. Just about all of them will do it from the west-central shore of Whidbey Island.

This fishery traditionally occurs mainly in December, January and February at Bush and Lagoon points and at Fort Casey.

Steelheading here is actually less tricky than angling for steelies in swift rivers, subject to rapidly varying water conditions and often filled with submerged snags. In fact, given the right tackle, one need only good timing (that is, flood tide or a tide change) and some luck. The rig shown here, when used with standard steelhead tackle, is a time-honored producer. It's easy enough, requiring only a bright orange Spin-N-Glo and Hoochy with a bit of pencil lead ahead of that. Most surf steelheaders prefer a high incoming tide though some claim the end of the outgoing is also a good time.

Anglers will quickly give away their novice status to their exasperated neighbors by wading knee deep in order to cast out farther. *Stay on shore and keep casts short.* Steelhead feed near shore in very shallow water (they'll sometimes follow a lure almost to water's edge) and spook easily.

The sort of gravelly beaches that steelhead roam are widespread along the island's west-central shore. However, most of these beaches are off limits to sport fishermen, locked up in private hands. Access has grown more limited as surf steelheading's fame and attendant problems for waterfront landowners have grown. Fishermen can utilize the area of public access northeast of Bush Point and around the boathouse, as well as at Lagoon Point. Fort Casey, of course, is the least problematical since it is all publicly accessible. Some landowners still permit access by request—if they haven't been burned by thoughtless anglers leaving trash or worse.

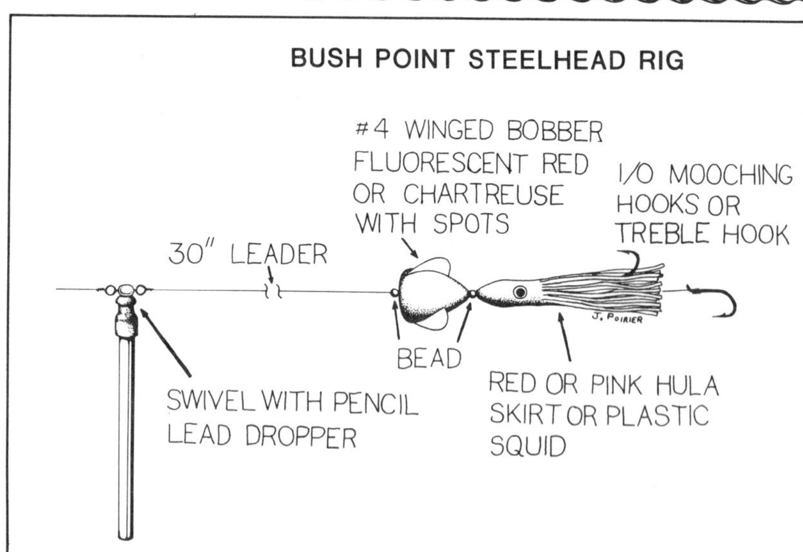

Less fished but well worth a try, particularly in late summer and early fall for big silvers are the tide rips off Lake Hancock. To find this area once on the water, watch for a break in the cliffs or high hills where the shoreline slopes gently down to the water along the west side of Whidbey, about a third of the way north from Lagoon Point to Fort Casey (across Admiralty Inlet from Marrowstone Point). Trolling squid or flies on or near the surface about 200 yards off the kelp in about 90 feet of water is the best way to connect with silvers, which include fair numbers of hooknose (large spawners) to 15 pounds, particularly early or late in the day.

This young angler aboard a Puget Sound charter is bemused at the sight of one of the Northwest's most bizarre and comical fishes is the ratfish, with its huge emerald eyes, pug nose and rat's tail.

North of Lake Hancock is Fort Casey, at Admiralty Head. It is a natural feeding grounds for salmon, but winter blackmouth fishing is less popular than at many north sound areas—perhaps in part because of the unsettled weather in this region (exposed to the whims of the eastern strait) and violent rips that form off the head.

The blackmouth fishing at Casey seems to come on strong in March to peak during April and May and again in November and December when conditions happen to be fishable. Drift moochers work just off the point in the ripline, starting their drifts close to shore. There seems to be a greater tendency for blackmouth here to bite throughout the day than in many fishing spots. The kings that move in during May and June are best fished on a flood tide. Here, too, silvers and pinks in season offer fast fishing. The pinks are often concentrated in the rips around the north side of the head; try casting and retrieving a red-and-white or pink Buzz Bomb rather than trolling. Shore fishermen casting jigs from Admiralty Head itself occasionally connect with salmon.

Still farther north is Partridge Point, which looks west not to land but directly out the strait to the Pacific. Obviously it is often rough, but it also may offer some fair salmon fishing. Unfortunately, dogfish also find the area attractive and may be abundant.

Partridge Bank, about three miles northeast, is even more exposed. But when calm enough to fish, this extensive, shallow plateau at times each spring attracts great numbers of large blackmouth. The area can also be a good bet in the summer for chinook moving though the strait. Most who fish the bank troll near bottom in water 90 to 120 feet deep.

At a similar depth, blackmouth are also a good possibility along the ledge off Rocky Point, north of Point Partridge. West Beach, just south of Deception Pass, is a favorite area for silvers and pinks. Trollers with downriggers may take fish throughout the day, but the hot bite here is generally after the sun has descended to touch the

Olympic Mountains. Then, trolling with only two or three ounces of lead will often suffice. In past summers, West Beach was also a hot spot for big summer chinook. And it still can be at times, though the decline of Skagit River chinook runs have impacted this fishery. Still, it can be worth a try: stay in relatively shallow waters when trolling.

Midchannel Bank: North Sound's Premiere Salmon Spot

Midchannel Bank looks rather unassuming on a nautical chart, a gently sloping extension of the north end of Marrowstone Island that drops off rather sharply once it reaches 12 to 15 fathoms. Yet it has gained a reputation as one of the very best spots, if not the best spot, for consistent salmon fishing all year. Granted, Midchannel has its dog days when hardly a salmon can be found. But overall, it's hard to beat this fising hole.

Located in northern Admiralty Inlet, about 35 or 40 miles northwest of Seattle, Puget Sound here meets the waters of the Strait of Juan de Fuca and the inlet is a natural bottleneck. Huge volumes of water are constantly funneled into and out of the inlet.

These conditions create a naturally productive area for migrating and resident salmon to linger, feed and fatten. Forage fish, both herring and candlefish, form great tide-oriented shoals where currents are thrust over Midchannel Bank.

October often marks the first month of good blackmouth fishing here, though pressure tends to remain light until later in the year. In fact, January sees the real surge in effort, and catches seem to increase steadily through the spring.

One of the most experienced Midchannel anglers, with hundreds of hours on the water, is Rock D'Acquisto who lives in Port Townsend where he designed and manufactures the famed Point Wilson Dart salmon jigs. May is his favorite Midchannel month. Then, blackmouth are often still in good supply and early kings are moving in as well.

D'Acquisto advises fishing where the bottom is 60 to 130 feet, with 90 just right, on the ledge of the bank's outer lip. Keep drifts short, where fish are found, since they are typically *not* spread out over the bank. The jig must be worked along and just off the bottom, since that's where most chinook feed (but be alert for strikes on the way down or up—including "slack-liners" that will hit a jig and come straight up leaving the angler with a slack like and puzzled expression).

D'Acquisto, of course, strictly drift-jigs. But he's not alone; that is the method of choice, here, though jiggers are always joined by moochers. Of course, jiggers have a particular edge when dogfish come to town. Some Midchannel anglers do troll, but as any area where salmon tend to concentrate, drifting-fishing is ideal and keeps weekend crowds of boats out of each other's hair.

Tidal movement here may be quite light but is often a virtual river. A moderate tide is best—plenty of water to move the baitfish around and keep salmon feeding, but not so fast that working a jig near bottom becomes nearly impossible. Morning is often a hot time, but locals prefer evenings.

Private boaters can easily cruise up to Midchannel from Seattle on nice days in an hour or so. But many trailer up Whidbey Island (taking the ferry from Mukilteo) to Fort Casey which is a run of only 10 minutes or so and offers a fine multilane ramp, good in all conditions. There are also launching facilities in Port Townsend and at the north end of Marrowstone. And nonboaters can find charters in Port Townsend.

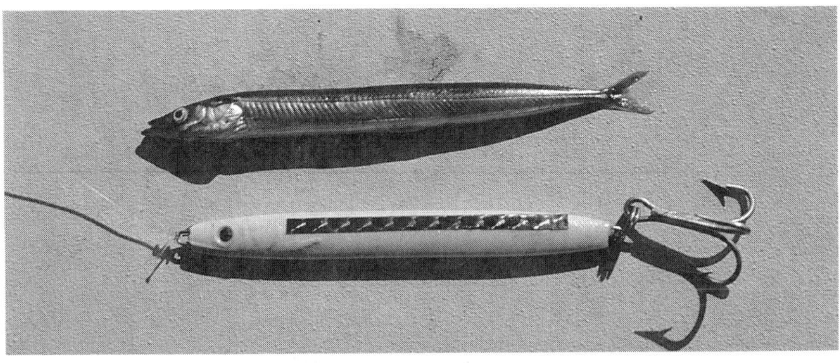

Seen side by side, it is easy to see how carefully patterned after its namesake is the Pt. Wilson Dart Candlefish jig made in Port Townsend.

Candlefish: The "Other" Baitfish

In truth, the correct common name for *Thaleichthys pacificus* is eulachon. Origins for the term "candlefish" supposedly go back to coastal Indians who dried these oily little fish and used them as candles. But to most Northwest saltwater anglers, they'll remain "candlefish."

By any name, they are a forage fish of major importance. Huge schools form in the sound, often in deep water, where they may be large black shadows on depth sounders. (In northern British Columbia and Alaska, it's common to see them feeding on plankton at the surface, so thick that on calm summer days you'd swear a hard rain was falling all about.)

Fishermen seldom offer candlefish as bait, though they are certainly excellent as such. They're small, long and narrow, and not as easily rigged as herring. Moreover, they're much less readily available from bait shops nor so easily jigged out on the water as herring. But they can be a great bait (logically, "matching the hatch" in the north sound and eastern strait, particularly in spring).

In fact, candlefish can be collected rather easily at the right places and times. In the spring, they'll collect in great numbers in shallow sandy/muddy bays at low tides to spawn. (Just one spot is, among the acres of such habitat in Cultus Bay, at the south end of Whidbey Island.) Then, they can be raked, netted or literally picked up by hand. Candlefish are characterized by their habit of burying themselves tailfirst in the loose sand to spawn and escape predators. As the tide goes out, they stay put in the moist sand.

Candlefish bury themselves not only in intertidal situations, but in deep water. Proof of this can be seen at times on the freshly scratched gill covers of chinook, caught where they are feeding on candlefish on the bottom. They'll turn on their sides and dig nosefirst into the sand to root out candlefish.

This may further explain the appeal to chinook of jigs like the Pt. Wilson Dart Candlefish (not only the first such candlefish imitator, but a nearly perfect replica in size and shape, down to the scales). These jigs are most effectively fished in sandy areas such as Midchannel Bank when allowed to flutter over and over to bottom and immediately jigged up over and over—much as a candlefish darting from the sand, no doubt.

Candlefish are easily rigged as shown with a single small (no. 1 or 2) snelled hook.

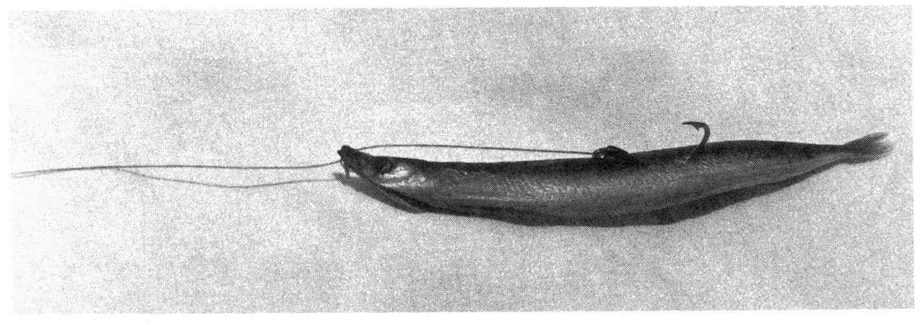

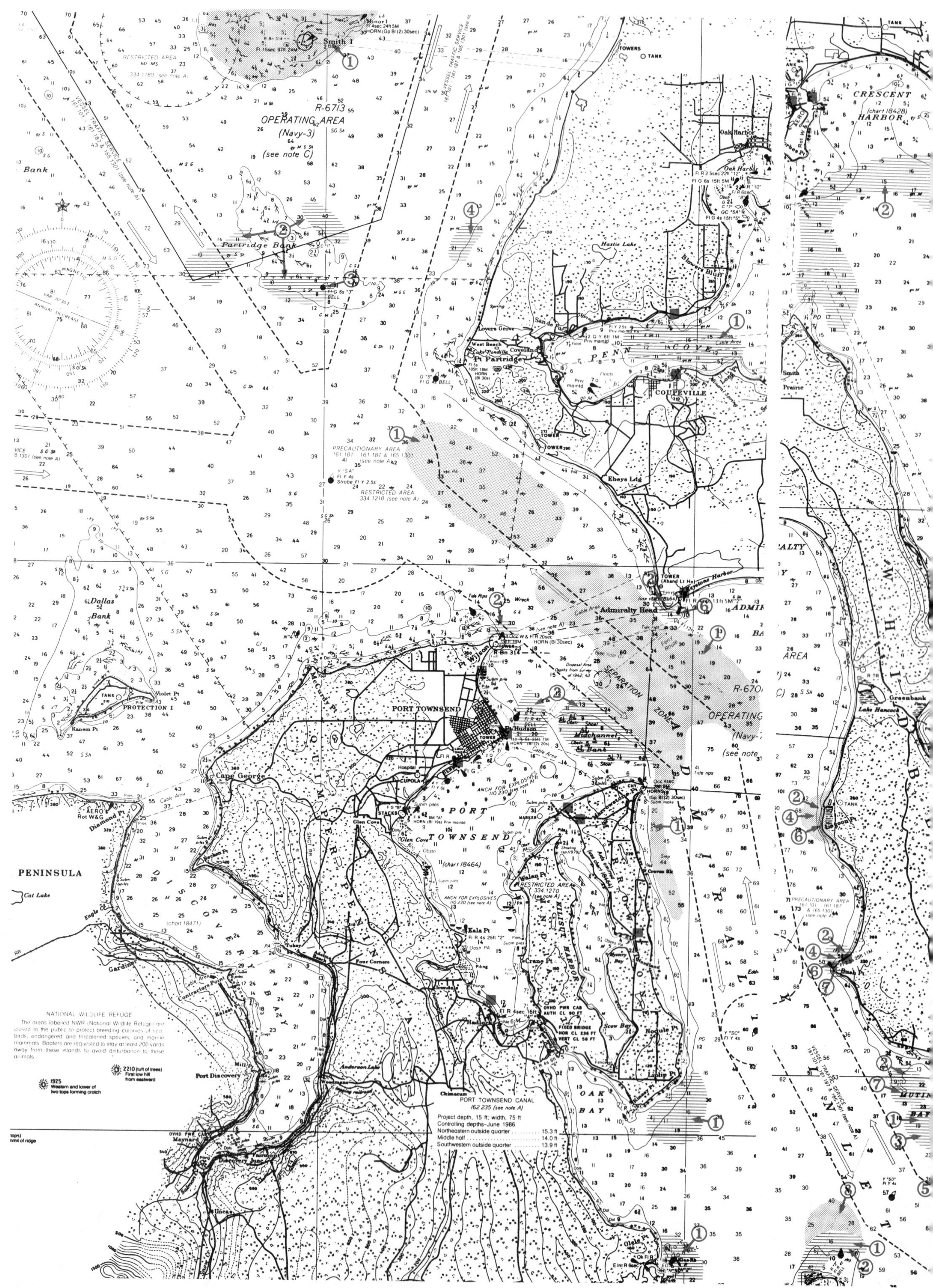

Smith I
R-6713
OPERATING AREA
(Navy-3)
(see note C)
RESTRICTED AREA
Partridge Bank
Bank
Dallas Bank
PROTECTION I
Violet Pt
Kanem Pt
PENINSULA
Cat Lake
Cape George
Diamond Pt
DISCOVERY BAY
Gardiner
Contractors Point
Port Discovery
Mill Pt
NATIONAL WILDLIFE REFUGE
The areas labelled NWR (National Wildlife Refuge) are closed to the public to protect breeding colonies of sea birds, endangered and threatened species, and marine mammals. Boaters are requested to stay at least 200 yards away from these islands to avoid disturbance to these animals.
PRECAUTIONARY AREA
PORT TOWNSEND
Pt Wilson
Pt Hudson
Midchannel Bank
Admiralty Head
Keystone Harbor
SEPARATION ZONE
QUIMPER PENINSULA
PORT TOWNSEND
Glen Cove
Kala Pt
Irondale
Hadlock
Chimacum
Anderson Lake
Four Corners
PORT TOWNSEND CANAL
162.235 (see note A)
Project depth, 15 ft; width, 75 ft
Controlling depths–June 1986
Northeastern outside quarter .... 15.3 ft
Middle half .... 14.0 ft
Southwestern outside quarter .... 13.9 ft
OAK BAY
Crane Pt
Scow Bay
KILISUT HARBOR
Nodule Pt
Liplip Pt
Maynard
Uncas
Oak Harbor
Hastie Lake
Blowers Bluff
PENN COVE
COUPEVILLE
Pt Partridge
West Beach
Lake Pondilla
Coveland
Ebeys Ldg
CRESCENT HARBOR
Smith Prairie
Lake Hancock
Greenbank

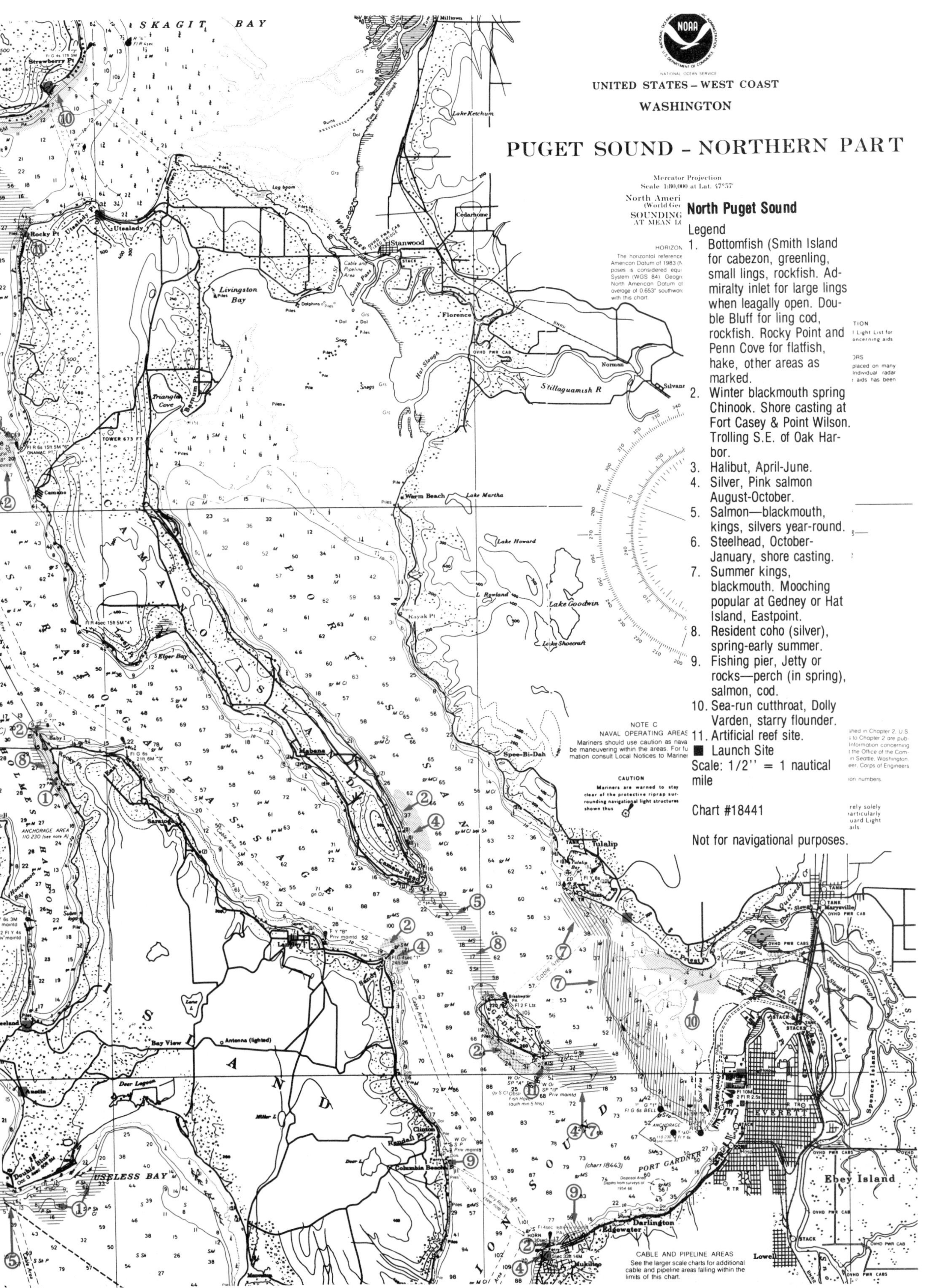

UNITED STATES – WEST COAST
WASHINGTON
PUGET SOUND - NORTHERN PART
Mercator Projection
North Puget Sound
Legend
1. Bottomfish (Smith Island for cabezon, greenling, small lings, rockfish. Admiralty inlet for large lings when leagally open. Double Bluff for ling cod, rockfish. Rocky Point and Penn Cove for flatfish, hake, other areas as marked.
2. Winter blackmouth spring Chinook. Shore casting at Fort Casey & Point Wilson. Trolling S.E. of Oak Harbor.
3. Halibut, April-June.
4. Silver, Pink salmon August-October.
5. Salmon—blackmouth, kings, silvers year-round.
6. Steelhead, October-January, shore casting.
7. Summer kings, blackmouth. Mooching popular at Gedney or Hat Island, Eastpoint.
8. Resident coho (silver), spring-early summer.
9. Fishing pier, Jetty or rocks—perch (in spring), salmon, cod.
10. Sea-run cutthroat, Dolly Varden, starry flounder.
11. Artificial reef site.
■ Launch Site
Scale: 1/2'' = 1 nautical mile
Chart #18441
Not for navigational purposes.
NOTE C
NAVAL OPERATING AREAS
CAUTION
CABLE AND PIPELINE AREAS
See the larger scale charts for additional cable and pipeline areas falling within the limits of this chart.
SKAGIT BAY
Strawberry Pt
Utsalady
Rocky Pt
Stanwood
Cedarhome
Livingston Bay
Florence
Norman
Silvana
Stillaguamish R
Hat Slough
Triangle Cove
Camano
Warm Beach
Lake Martha
Lake Howard
Lake Goodwin
Lake Shoecraft
Kayak Pt
Elger Bay
Mabana
Spee-Bi-Dah
Camano Head
Saratoga
Langley
Sandy Pt
Tulalip
Priest Pt
Marysville
Smith Island
Spencer Island
EVERETT
Ebey Island
Lowell
PORT GARDNER
Darlington
Edgewater
Mukilteo
Clinton
Columbia Beach
Glendale
Bay View
Deer Lagoon
Double Bluff
USELESS BAY
HOLMES HARBOR
SARATOGA PASSAGE
CAMANO ISLAND
WHIDBEY ISLAND
POSSESSION SOUND
GEDNEY I
Lake Ketchum
Log boom
Milltown

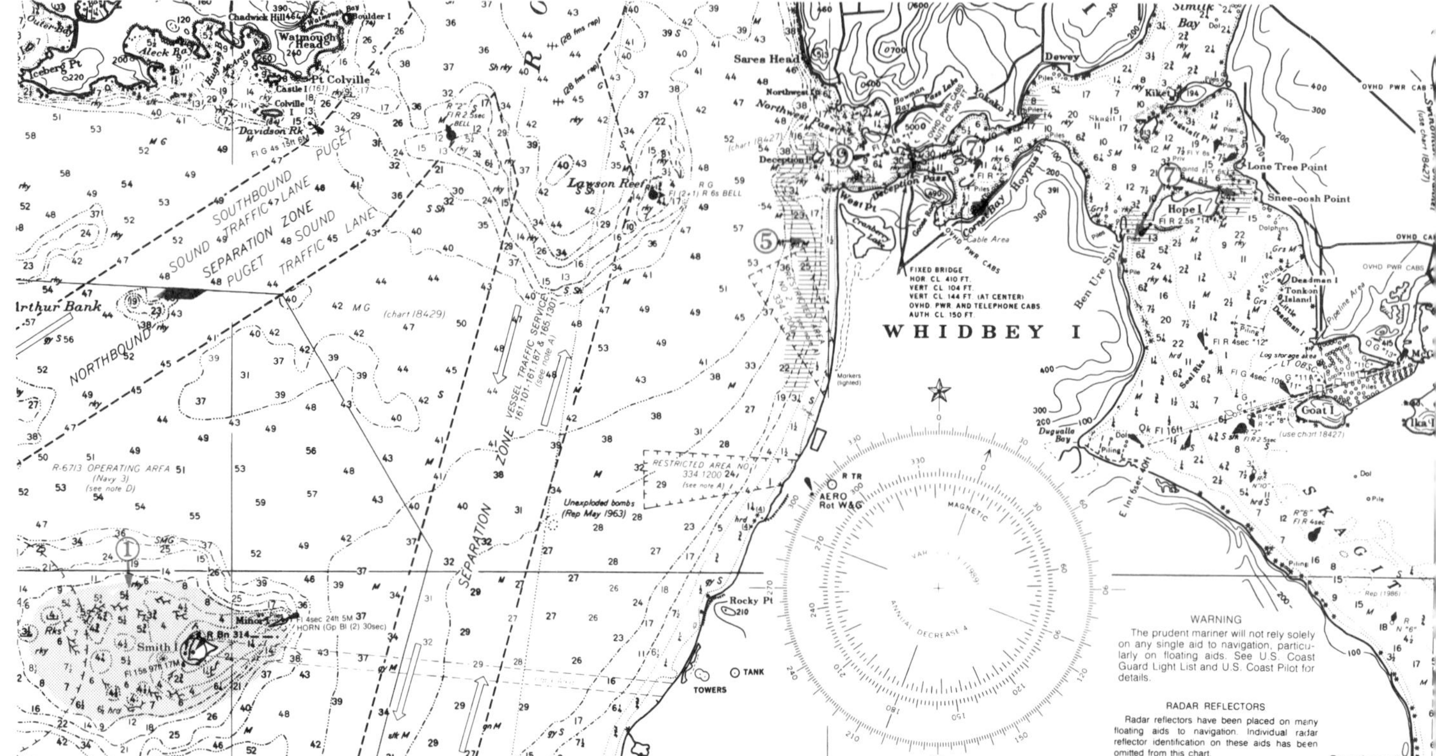

North Puget Sound

Legend

1. Bottom Smith Island for cabezon, greenling, small lings, rockfish. Admiralty inlet for large lings when legally open. Double Bluff for ling cod, rockfish. Rocky Point and Penn Cove for flatfish, hake.
5. Salmon—blackmouth, kings, silvers year-round.
7. Summer kings, blackmouth. Mooching popular at Gedney or Hat Island, Eastpoint.
9. Fishing pier, Jetty or rocks—perch (in spring), salmon, cod.

☐ Launch Site

Scale: 1/2'' = 1 nautical mile

Chart #18421

Not for navigational purposes.

...And Then There Were Four

We'd gone for hours without a strike. The fishing was downright tough, though the weather wasn't. The early May morning was calm, sunny and warm. And conditions made for easy fishing, with currents light. Todd George and I jigged leadheads with identical spinning outfits loaded with six-pound line.

Toward midday it appeared we might go in without a single fish. Then suddenly something grabbed my jig. I was about to announce a small fish when it started running out line—clearly not so small after all.

But on the other stern corner, Todd's rod was bent as double as mine. Our lines seemed determined to make a ''V'' and surely one was tangled in the other's fish.

Fifteen minutes later the lines were well apart and, clearly, we each fought our own separate fish. But the real surprise came at the boat, when skipper Brock Gilman had to do some fast gaffing. Almost simultaneously we each had big lings within sight. Once they were in the boat it became clear that:

(1) the two lings we'd gaffed were practically identical 23 1/2-pounders that had struck at the same moment; and

(2) neither was hooked since both had swallowed identical 2-pound lingcod that had grabbed our leadhead jigs at the same moment; and

(3) that the two big lings must have gobbled up the two little lings immediately after the small ones took our jigs since neither of us really felt anything but the big lings; and

(4) that with one cast each, we had our combined daily limit (at that time) of four lings in the boat!

West Side Bottomfishing: Fast Water, Rocky Terrain

The mostly smooth bottom of central Puget Sound becomes increasingly hard and rocky as one moves north into Admiralty Inlet, where the rugged, irregular bottom swept by powerful currents is just what lingcod like. The reefs extending far to the south of Admiralty Head and north of Midchannel Bank offer prime habitat and, when tidal flow is reasonably light, still give up good catches of lingcod during the six-week open season.

It isn't likely that lingcod will ever reach the levels the inlet offered in the 1970s. I can recall winter days (the area's now closed to ling fishing during the winter) of three-lingcod limits (it's now one) with every fish over 30 pounds—and catching and releasing still others.

The key to catching lings here during the open season is the same now as in that heyday: working the deep, rocky—tackle-grabbing—reefs. These can be located with a nautical chart (#18441), a compass and depthsounder, or Loran if your boat is so equipped.

But these reefs are fishable only during periods of light tidal runoff or during slack water at tide change. With much current at all, the bottom here will inevitably gobble up all the tackle you can throw at it. Sometimes it seems that *too* little water movement may put the lings off the bite for a while. And, believe me, lingcod in an area like this *do* go ''on a bite'' much like salmon. Fishing may be dead for some time, then suddenly the same drifts will pay off with strikes and fish for an hour or two until the bite slows and only a sporadic catch is made.

Charters here have fished large whole herring with great success. Some of my best catches have been on leadhead jigs and plastic worms or large pork rind strips (such as Uncle Josh Ripple Rinds). The largest lings are most likely to be taken early in the spring season before they head out to deeper areas, and of course are particularly likely to go for live baits.

Besides the occasional yelloweye rockfish, black rockfish are taken now and then. Although I've never caught great numbers, in the spring I've caught several blacks of 6 to 8 pounds. Whenever the drift takes you off the big rocks and over somewhat less bumpy terrain, figure on quillback rockfish.

Sandy areas produce fair numbers of halibut in the spring, some years much more than others. Most of these are chicken halibut of 10 to 40 pounds.

Although not heavily fished, the expansive, shallow bank mainly west of Smith Island, north of Partridge Bank, can be a hotbed of activity for shallow-water bottomfish anglers who want to give it a try. Cast skirted leadhead jigs for copper rockfish, greenling, small lings and cabezon. The latter may be particularly available around kelp beds in late April and May. (However, this is often a breezy time of year and no matter from which directon a breeze blows, Smith Island is in the center of things.)

Deception Pass: Tricky Fishing In An Awesome Setting

High vertical rock walls loom over this dramatic slot separating Whidbey and Fidalgo islands. These walls continue to drop nearly vertically below the water's surface. Currents rush in and out with velocity of 5 to 7 knots.

Some of the state's most impressive king salmon (to at least 50 pounds) are pulled from waters under the southwest corner of the Deception Pass Bridge, from a spot known as "the hole." June and July are hot months for kings, but they'll continue to be caught even into September, here. Silvers are also available later in the summer, and on odd years so are pinks: try the rips that form across the mouth (west of the bridge, where the waters from the pass meet Rosario Strait).

Fishing "the hole" is strictly an ebb-tide show. Small boats fish in tight to the sheer rock wall, where a large backeddy will help them stay in place. Trolling is obviously not very feasible in so small and swift an area, so anglers mooch herring, fishing with as few as a dozen pulls of line out.

Beginners would be smart to watch others fishing the hole, noting where they start the drift and where the eddy takes them. Also, consult fishing regulations closely since this area has been affected by spring closures in the past.

Once the tide begins flooding, salmon fishermen leave "the hole," and head through the pass to the inside (east side), where a spot known as "Marlin II" offers more salmon. This is along the northern bank near Yokeko Point, just east of the "convict slide."

Still further east, at the eastern edge of the pass, is Hope Island, a famed big king spot. The shallows here are swept by severe currents but, unlike Deception Pass, offer open water where more anglers troll than drift-mooch. Large spoons or plugs are kept deep enough, whatever the current, with downriggers. A 5-inch white Silver Horde lure can be a hot item and a no. 6 Canadian Wonder also works well. Troll the west side of the island on an incoming tide and the east side on the ebb. Plugs or spoons should be kept near bottom, generally 25 to 50 feet deep.

The rocky channel in and around the pass is home to consistent populations of lingcod and rockfish. Bottomfishing is generally limited to the very brief period between fierce tides, when it's possible to present a bait or lure near the bottom. Evening flood tides during the summer can produce good action for black rockfish on white jigs.

An inexpensive, uncomplicated and fun fishery for striped and pile perch can be enjoyed from the rocks at the southwesternmost entrance to the pass (northwest of the state park). These 1- to 3-pound scrappers will hit sand shrimp or mussel meat readily. The best baits, though, are marine pileworms which can be gathered ahead of time at low tide. Incoming tide is the best bet for those who cast from the rocks. Rig with the weight at the bottom of the line and one or two No. 6 hooks above.

NORTHERN PUGET SOUND /Sport Fish and Seasons

Species	J	F	M	A	M	J	J	A	S	O	N	D
	BEST MONTHS											
Blackmouth[1]	best	best	best	best	best	fair	poor	poor	poor	poor	fair	best
King salmon[1, 2]	poor	poor	poor	poor	fair	best	best	poor	poor	poor	poor	poor
Silver salmon[2]	poor	poor	poor	poor	poor	poor	poor	best	best	fair	poor	poor
Pink salmon[2]	poor	poor	poor	poor	poor	poor	poor	poor	best	fair	poor	poor
Lingcod[3]	poor	poor	poor	best	best	best	fair	fair	fair	best	best	poor
Halibut[4]	poor	poor	fair	best	best	fair	poor	poor	poor	poor	poor	poor
True cod, pollock	best	best	best	best/fair	fair	poor	poor	poor	poor	poor	poor	poor
Other bottomfish	best	best	best	best	best	best	best	best	best	best	best	best
Dolly Varden,cutthroat	poor	fair	best	best	fair	fair	fair	fair	poor	poor	poor	poor
Steelhead (salt water)	best	fair	poor	poor	poor	poor	poor	poor	poor	poor	poor	best

[1]Check regulations carefully for closed areas and special size restrictions.

[2]Special or emergency closures or other regulations changes may be in effect in lower Skagit River.

[3]Where not closed year-round (consult regulations) a December 1 - April 15 seasonal closure may apply.

[4]Seasonally closed, November 1 - February 28 (or 29)in recent years -- check regulations.

LEGEND: best fair poor

Small Boat Safety

The most dangerous areas in northern Puget Sound for boaters will be found from northern Admiralty Inlet north through Deception Pass. This entire area west of central and northern Whidbey Island can be dangerous. A long south fetch up from Puget Sound hits an even longer west fetch where marine winds are often funneled in from the western Strait of Juan de Fuca. These waters can and often do get downright nasty in a hurry. Nor are there safe ports along the northern Whidbey shoreline into which one can duck. Obviously, small boaters should venture forth here only as far as their craft's size, power and radio capabilities and their own experience permit.

Special mention should be made of the rips that form off Admiralty Head. They can be treacherous and trying to get through them may seem like crossing an ocean bar on a rough day. Wait for the current to slow or try to avoid them by motoring far south if necessary.

Most seaworthy small boats with a reasonable power-to-weight ratio should have little difficulty negotiating the swift currents of Deception Pass. But put a stiff westerly behind a strong ebb tide and the area from the bridge on out can be a mess. When the waters are calm, anglers fish from very small boats but they must stay alert to the many big commercial fishing vessels that may be passing in and out since they often leave behind steep swells. There is little room to run and gain distance from these swells to allow them to smooth out a bit.

U.S. Coast Guard Stations North Sound

Port Townsend
Cutter *Point Bennett* 385-3070
Everett
Cutter *Point Durand* 252-5281

"Piling worms" can be gathered along beaches in the Deception Pass area during low tide—and fished for perch on the flood.

Lowering a leadhead jig to 350 feet of water north of Lagoon Point on a slow summer day with a slow current produced this 30-pound lingcod for the author.

The Protected East Side

The waters off the eastern shore of Whidbey Island afford small-boat fishermen protection from the prevailing southwesterlies and plenty of good fishing at times.

Oak Harbor Bay can be great for blackmouth fishing, January through March. (An annual February derby usually sees plenty of nice blackmouth weighed in.) Most fishermen here troll over a large area, generally with their gear in the 90-foot range, from Snakelum Point north across Penn Cove and northeast across Crescent Harbor, then southeast to Camano Island's Polnell Point. Some of the best winter fishing occurs mid-channel in Saratoga Passage off Oak Harbor.

Shore casters and small boat trollers vie for Dolly Varden (March-April) and sea-run cutthroat (March-August) along the beach from Polnell Point to Strawberry Point. Small herring strips or a McMahon no. 4 1/2 spoon are trolled in water shallow enough to see the bottom. Shore fishermen cast out Wonder Lures or similar hardware. Best fishing is usually about an hour either side of low slack or at high slack tide.

These fertile flats are also home to good numbers of starry flounder. For something different, try flycasting a shrimp pattern fly to flatfish during low tides.

Farther south, more good salmon trolling occurs southward around Onamac and Lowell points on the west side of Camano Island and Rocky Point on Baby Island and East Point on Whidbey. There can be some excellent bottomfishing around Onamac as well, with natural populations of starry flounder and sole. Also, the state's artificial reef (1,000 feet north of the navigational light at the point in 45 to 100 feet of water) attracts various species.

Sandy Point, south of Langley, is often overlooked for blackmouth and a few summer kings, as well as resident coho. To the east is a long underwater shelf extending south from Camano Head to Gedney ("hat") Island where salmon trolling is productive just about all year. Ardent moochers can fish herring in close to the head. Along the steep drop-off beneath the bluffs northeast of Camano Head, trollers pick up blackmouth, silvers and pinks. The majority of fishing is trolling plugs or squid, often with herring strip teasers.

When smelt are running at LaConner, anglers crowd the waterfront in hopes of filling buckets with limits of the delectable silver fish.

This sole appears healthy, but closer to Everett it is not unusual to see tumors on and around fins and tail.

The south side of Hat Island and Mission Bar (the sharp north-south dropoff at the western edge of the Snohomish River mouth delta) are both popular with trollers who pull plugs or herring deep for kings and blackmouth. Spoons work well just off the mouth of the river for chinook of all sizes. Pull flies or plastic squid somewhat shallower for both silver and pinks, when runs are in. The steep shore southwest of Hat Island can be worth drift-mooching much of the year.

Sea-run cutthroat and Dolly Varden are particularly available throughout this area. Gravelly beaches along Camano Head and in fact almost anywhere along Saratoga Passage and Skagit Bay up to and including the Swinomish Channel should produce cutts and dollies. The shallows southwest of Priest Point (Mission Beach) have been a standout area for many years. A yellow-bodied spider pattern fished on outgoing tides has been a good producer here. Most sea-runs will be taken near shore, where they tend to feed heavily on juvenile salmon early in the spring and later on candlefish. Very small plugcut herring, slow-trolled, are excellent; plugs such as Rebels or 3/8-ounce Krocodile spoons are also effective. Look for the parr (rainbow trout) color in the early spring when fish are feeding actively on juvenile salmonids. Expect a second and often peak period from midAugust into October.

Some of the best fishing for pink salmon in the state is enjoyed in the Everett area in August of odd-numbered years. The favored spots include Camano Head, Hat Island and Mission Bar. Another top spot, appropriately enough nicknamed "Humpy Hollow," is a 1-mile stretch of shoreline just south of the Mukilteo Lighthouse.

Much of the time during midwinter herring ball up in great numbers around Saratoga Passage. Those lucky enough to have long-handled, small-meshed nets may catch the 20-pound daily limit in a few swipes. But others lacking a net or a boat from which to use it can still catch plenty of herring most years right in and around the Port of Everett by jigging with standard rigs of six or so tiny gold hooks. At times smelt may be as numerous as herring. Access to the best jigging can be a problem, since often the shiny little silver fish fill the waters around docks that are off limits to those not boat owners holding moorage slips. (A little cartopper or canoe immediately opens up new worlds to jiggers.) These herring can be frozen for bait or pickled for some of the sound's tastiest eating.

In late summer, schools of huge horse herring often appear splashing and leaping along the calm surface early in the morning, looking more like small coho. Mission Bar is one of the areas where they tend to school up. These 10- to 14-inch herring will strike tiny lures, flies and even small Buzz Bombs—and the angler who has flycasting or ultralight tackle will find them great fighters. They're well worth a stop when spotted.

The tiny town of LaConner on the Swinomish Slough, north of the Skagit River mouth, is perhaps best known for its popular February fishery for surf smelt (with herring usually getting into the act as well). Fishermen jig strings of tiny gold hooks from docks and when the run is really in, often take home 20-pound limits of the firm smelt.

Bottomfishing in the waters east of Whidbey Island is usually less than spectacular. Not surprising, with the bottom almost everywhere soft and muddy. Major species available here include flatfish (English, rock and sand soles, sanddabs and starry flounder), hake and—in past years and hopefully again— cod and pollock, sculpins, a few rockfish and plenty of dogfish as well as the odd ratfish here and there. Hake, incidentally, were profuse enough in lower Saratoga Passage and off Port Susan in early winter as recently as the late 1980s to support a considerable commercial otter trawl fishery.

In this same area—lower Saratoga/Port Susan—are sixgill cow sharks, though no one knows how many. These sharks to 15 feet prowl the bottom in waters too deep for most sport fishermen. Decades ago, commercial fishermen sought them for their huge livers using 50-gallon drums as floats, rope and chain for leader, and huge hooks baited with whole dogfish.

At least a few rockfish and the occasional ling (illegal to keep most of the year) should be available around the artificial reef site constructed of concrete rubble in the 1970s by the Department of Fisheries. It's located 1,000 yards south of the southern tip of Gedney (Hat) Island in 45 to 70 feet of water and should be clearly marked.

Flatfish are found just about everywhere in these waters and can be lots of fun on ultralight gear. Drift and cast tiny leadhead jigs in 10 to 50 feet of water for great sport. Of course, drifting small pieces of cut bait, shrimp or pileworms should also provide fast action. Some species may be taken in much deeper water.

Priest Point and the entire Snohomish River bar area are loaded with starry flounder much of the year and offer an almost untouched fishery. They average 3 pounds or so, feeding most actively during the late flood and high slack tide. They'll strike spoons or plastic worms rigged as one might for freshwater bass fishing as well as small baits. Ultralight tackle is a must for these fish and the great sport they can provide. (Given concerns about the safety of eating resident bottomfish from this area—see "Drink the Water—But Don't Eat the Fish?"—you may want to release the majority of starries you catch here.)

Shorebound anglers can enjoy some fast perch action, particularly from February through May, when these livebearing panfish move in during their spawning season. Good bait, small hooks and a light touch are necessities for these finnicky sight-feeders. Most successful anglers use pileworms or sand shrimp. Almost anywhere one can find access to pilings, riprap or any sort of subtidal structure, perch are likely. A few small piers offer additional opportunities, such as that at Mukilteo next to the ferry terminal and fishing piers at Langley and Clinton on Whidbey.

These piers also offer a shot at salmon early in the morning and late in the evening, most often taken on Buzz Bombs or other metal jigs.

How To Pickle A Peck (Or Less) Of Herring

Probably no one is indifferent about pickled herring. Either you love it or you hate it. Those who love it may not have it often, since those little jars in the supermarket cost plenty and are quickly emptied.

But a few anglers jigging together in winter may find themselves with a bucketful of herring in a hurry. If you're willing to take some time and trouble, you can end up with several quarts of homemade pickled herring.

This recipe, which has worked well for me, comes from the father of Tony Floor who is the longtime information chief for the state Department of Fisheries (and one of this guide's consultants).

Salt fresh-caught herring well with medium coarse rock salt for no less than two weeks.

Prepare a brine with the following proportions (amounts given will accomodate only a few large herring so you may want to increase the amounts considerably):

1 cup of vinegar
1 cup of water
4 tablespoons of sugar
1 tablespoon of whole black peppercorns
3 bay leaves

(I've found it preferable to use 1 1/2 cups vinegar to 1/2 cup of water, but that is undoubtedly a matter of taste: experiment.)

Boil the brine for several minutes, then cool, strain and put aside.

Clean the herring, cutting off tail and head. Rinse well in cold water. Put herring in a 50:50 mixture of milk and water, enough to completely cover, and let stand in a cool place for six hours. Remove and drain. Make a shallow cut in the skin along the backbone and peel off the skin by pulling towards the tail. You can filet to avoid the small bones, but most people don't bother. Cut the fish in one-inch pieces. Slice onions (preferably red) and put layers of herring and onion slices alternately in clean, glass jars. Pour the brine solution over the herring and let stand 36 to 48 hours in the refrigerator before sampling.

Certainly, the bigger the herring, the better the pickling since you get much more fish for much less work (cleaning, skinning, cutting).

Common in mixed catches of those jigging during winter from docks and shore in northern Puget Sound are surf smelt (top) and herring.

Smelt are on hand in this area much of the year to be jigged and/or raked, for the relative few who take advantage of them, according to Dan Pentilla, the Department of Fisheries smelt expert. Jigging of course is popular in LaConner during midwinter, but smelt are likely to be around on and off from October through March. To the north, Fidalgo Bay at March Point is a good spot to rake spawning smelt from November through March. Try east of the Shell Oil pier and north of the railroad bridge. One of the famous "classic" smelt raking areas at Utsalady on north Camano Island is not easily reached now, with access limited, but smelt should be on hand from June through October. Look for a similar situation at Cavelero's Beach near the county park and at Penn Cove on Whidbey Island.

Smelt rakers wait and watch for signs of their quarry moving in along the shore east of the Shell Oil pier east of Anacortes.(Dan Penttila photo, Wash. Dept. of Fisheries)

Drink The Water—But Don't Eat The Fish?

Diseased fish and polluted waters once seemed a problem distant from Puget Sound's cold, clean waters. That bubble was broken in the late 1970s. Bottom sediments from Commencement Bay near Tacoma and the Duwamish Waterway in south Seattle were found to contain significantly high levels of pollutants, and many bottomfish from the areas proved to be diseased.

The problem hit home hard in the Everett area in 1982 when 84% of the English sole from the waters of Port Gardner off Everett's industrial waterfront checked by the National Marine Fisheries Service were found to have diseased livers. That generally indicates pollution from hydrocarbons, chlorinated compounds, or other complex mixtures. Besides the diseased livers, nearly a third of the sole had fin deformities.

It is difficult to say how much fish from this area would be harmful for a person to eat. It would, at the least, seem prudent to avoid eating many bottomfish from Port Gardner (as well as the Duwamish Waterway or Commencement Bay) on a regular basis.

Fortunately, there's been little evidence to suggest that the rest of Puget Sound's bottomfish have been affected by the ingestion of toxins. And salmon, wherever they're caught, are not benthic (bottom-dwelling) or site-specific resident fish, and are eminently safe to eat.

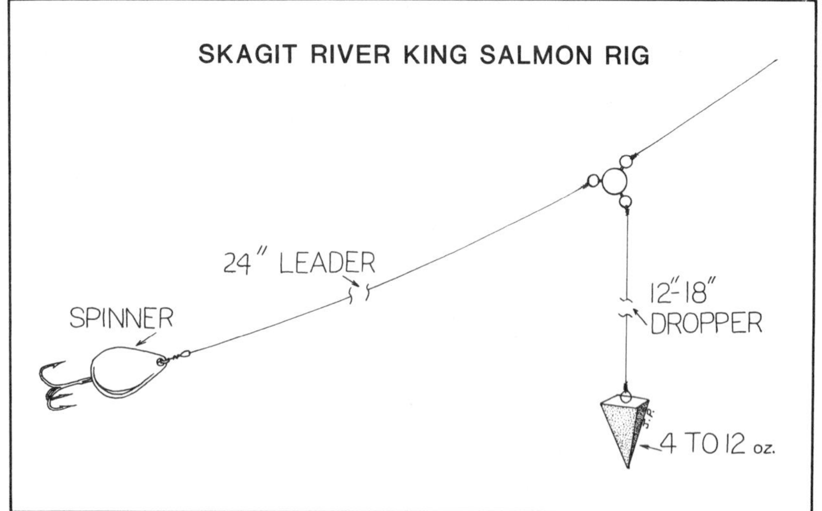

Skagit River Tidewater—An Anadromous Smorgasbord

Just about 60 miles north of Seattle, the wide north fork of the Skagit River, from Bald Island up to Mt. Vernon, remains one of the best tidewater fisheries in Puget Sound for a variety of upstream trout and salmon.

The Skagit is particularly famous for the monstrous chinook it once produced in great numbers each summer. Fish well over 50 pounds are still possible, though the runs are not as strong as in years past. The last hour or two of the ebb tide and the first couple hours of the flood are the prime periods for these fish. (Water clarity should be at least a couple feet or so; snowmelt early in the summer may put the river out of shape.) Big spinners such as Bear Valleys or Winners are still-fished from anchored boats, using a pyramid or teardrop sinker to keep the spinner fluttering just above the bottom.

Jacks (small precocious salmon that return to rivers a year or two early) may be in the river during this same time and can be great fun. They'll hit all sorts of lures as well as drifted salmon eggs.

Silvers offer prime sport in August and September when they are taken on trolled Hot Shots, Dick Nites, Canadian Wonders and the like. About the same time during odd-numbered years, pinks invade the river, some years in a trickle, some years in a veritable flood. When profuse, they become the only show in town for fishermen trolling or casting from anchored boats or fishing from the Skagit's shore. Small spoons and spinners, flatfish, and where still available fireglow Guppys have proven themselves best bets for 3- to 5-pound humpies.

Interest has increased somewhat in the Skagit's Dolly Varden spring fishing. Dollies to at least 5 pounds are taken on trolled spoons or stillfished worms and eggs.

The smaller south fork is a good bet for sea-run cutts. These 12- to 17-inch trout are in best condition from late August through early November. Most troll, but this is a great area for flyfishing.

Small boaters pursuing large summer salmon in the Skagit should consider rigging a quick release on their anchor lines where those attach to the boat, using a float as a marker. Then, if a big fish is hooked, it can be followed instantly (without losing one's anchor!)

Facilities

Except as noted, all phone numbers listed are within 206 area code.

Charters

Only a few charters operate in the waters covered within the "North Puget Sound" section. At press time, the going rates varied from $65 to 80 per day, including bait, tackle, tax and often license. Most of these charters troll. However, Northsound in Everett offers drift fishing trips at substantially less money.

For charter operations based in Port Townsend, see the "Eastern Strait" section; for charters in the Anacortes area, see the "San Juan Islands" section.

Deception Pass Charters 565 West Cornet Bay Road, Oak Harbor 98277, 675-9597 or 679-1043. Owner Ken Quinn skippers the 34-foot *Irish Mist* for salmon and bottomfish (including spring halibut in the eastern strait) year-round, leaving from Cornet Bay Marina.

Island Charters, P.O. Box 231, Langley 98260, 321-5945. Ben Reams has been skippering charters around Whidbey and the San Juan Islands for many years and knows his stuff. He takes 2 to 4 anglers on his 25-footer, operating year-round and concentrating on chinook. Island Charters departs from Langley and fishes primarily the Saratoga Passage area.

North Sound Charters, 2815 West Marine View Drive, Everett 98201, 339-1275. Several boats from 28 to 40 feet in length for both trolling and driftmooching trips, the latter for a combination of salmon and bottomfish. Driftboats generally work Possesson Bar.

Marinas, Launch Sites

Bush Point Marina, 326 South Main Street, Freeland 98249, 321-1824. No moorage here, but fuel (gas), engine repair and bait and tackle. A rail launch will accomodate boats up to 4,000 pounds. Rents 14- to 16-foot boats on hourly basis (4-hour minimum) or all day with or without power. Open summer through midautumn. Winter steelheading here. Camping and grocery store nearby.

Cornet Bay Marina, 265 West Cornet Bay Road, Oak Harbor 98277, 675-5411. Overnight moorage, fuel, engine repair, bait and tackle all available. Launching via a 5-ton hoist lift; free ramp at adjacent Deception Pass State Park.

Deception Pass State Park launch ramp, just east of Deception Pass bridge on south side—a superb, multi-lane paved ramp with floats good at most tides. Lots of parking. And it's free.

Port of Everett, 720 West Marine View Drive, Everett 98201, 259-6601. Open year-round. Some 2,000 moorage slips, but only a fraction of those for transients. Reservations recommended. Multi-lane paved public ramp with floats is an outstanding facility, good on almost any tide. Also a travel-lift for larger boats. Fuel, engine repair, bait and tackle and groceries nearby. Restrooms, showers, laundromat.

La Conner Marina, Port of Skagit County, 613 North 2nd, La Conner 98257, 466-3118. Open year-round, 8 am-5 pm, 7 days/week. 2,000 feet of moorage for transients; reservations generally not needed. Fuel, engine repair, bait and tackle. Two travel lifts for boats to 27 feet. Rents 16-foot boats with or without power.

Langley Boat Harbor, Langley 98260. A relatively new facility with 17 transient slips for boats up to 50 feet. Reservations not taken. Restrooms but no showers.

Langley Marina, P.O. Box 353, Langley 98260, 321-1771. Open year-round but on a more limited schedule during off-season. Gas (no diesel) available, along with engine repair, bait and tackle and a grocery store. Sling launch accomodates boats up to 20 feet. In business since the 1950s.

McConnell's Boat House, 718 Front Street, Mukilteo 98275, 355-3411. Open spring-fall, 7 days/week. No general moorage. Fuel, engine repair, great selection of bait and tackle. Closest launch is ramp at adjacent state park, to the southwest—but use with great caution.

Mukilteo State Park launch ramp, at Mukilteo just southwest of the ferry terminal. This wide, double-lane ramp is the only public ramp (free; lots of parking) between Seattle and Everett. Unfortunately, it is notoriously difficult with any sort of wind since it's completely exposed to winds from southwest to north. The swells often cause migraines for returning boaters trying to load their trailers, especially with heavy craft. In calm water, of course, no problem.

Mutiny Bay Island County launch ramp is located right in Mutiny Bay with limited parking. The paved ramp (no floats) is free and functional on most tides. There used to be a problem with sanding over during the winter months, but the county has been cleaning it weekly.

Oak Harbor Marina, 8075 Catalina Drive, Oak Harbor 98277, 679-2628. Open 7 days/week. Moorage, fuel, engine repair. No bait, tackle. Big ramp and a monorail-hoist launch.

Tulalip Marina, 3515 Totem Beach Road, Marysville, 659-7999. Open all year. Gas, bait and tackle available. Paved launch ramp in fair shape but not good at lower tides.

Resorts

Mutiny Bay Resort, 5856 S. Mutiny Bay Road, Freeland 98249, 321-4500. Open year-round. Located on southwest Whidbey Island, rents cabins, offers moorage buoys (no docks), bait and tackle.

Blake's Skagit Resort and Marina, 1171-A Rawlins Road, Mount Vernon, WA 98273, 455-6533. On lower Skagit River, open 7 days/week. Rents cabins, offers RV space with hookups and tent sites. Restrooms and showers. Moorage, fuel, bait and tackle. Excellent launch ramp, always usable. Rents 14- to 16-foot boats with or without power.

Bait And Tackle

Big 5 Sporting Goods, 1201 Everett Mall Way, Everett 98201, 353-9100, 7 days/week.

Bud's Bait, Port of Edmonds, Edmonds 98020, 774-1921, 7 days/week (opens at 4 am in summer, but later in winter). Sell herring—live.

Bush Point Rod and Reel, 4888 South 1st Street, Freeland 98249, open "Whenever owner Larry Scheider is not fishing." Emphasis is on salmon and bottomfish gear. Repairs reels, builds custom salmon rods, books trips for salmon guide.

Camano Marine and Rental, 909 East Highway 532, Camano Island 98292, 629-4507. Open 9-6 daily in the summer. Sells variety of tackle. Also: boat storage, inside or outside.

Coast to Coast Hardware, 1298 West Pioneer Way, Oak Harbor 98277, 679-3533. Open 7 days/week all year. Carries basic gear.

Ed's Sporting Goods, 307 Main Street, Mount Vernon 98273, 336-3232. Open year-round Monday-Saturday. Old, established shop, carries a wide selection of tackle, fresh and salt.

Everett Boat House General Store, 1001 14th Street, Everett 98201. Open 7 days/week year-round. Emphasis on saltwater gear, fresh herring on summer weekends.

Jerry's Surplus, 2031 Broadway, Everett 98201, 252-1176. Open 7 days/week, all year.

John's Sporting Goods, 1913 Broadway, Everett 98201, 259-3056. Closed Sundays. Owner John Martinez Jr. keeps a complete stock of all types of saltwater gear used in Washington fishing and is a good source of fishing information and advice. Carries a wide range of rod and reel parts; expert reel repair, all makes.

La Conner Landing, 101 North First, La Conner 98257, 466-4478. Open 7 days/week, carries mostly saltwater tackle.

Mutiny Bay Company, Tara Village, Freeland 98249, 221-2313. Open 7 days/week.

Northsound Charters Tackle Shop, 2815 West Marine View Drive, Everett 98201, 339-1275. Open 7 days/week, with lots of salmon and bottomfish gear.

Possession Point Bait Company, 8311 South Franklin Road, Clinton, 321-4704. Open 7 days/week, May-October. Fresh or live herring. This is right on the water; many fishermen in small boats cruise up for bait. On southeastern tip of the island, just north of Possession Point.

Public Camping Areas

Camano Island State Park (Recreation Area), at Lowell Point, west-central shore of Camano Island (exit 211 off Interstate-5). 89 campsites on 134 acres. Launch ramp though no buoys or floats. Very pleasant, quiet camping area. Some beach fishing for flounder and cutthroat.

Deception Pass State Park, at the pass along Highway 20 (10 miles north of Oak Harbor). 251 tent sites on almost 2,500 acres. Excellent boat launch, moorage buoys and floats. This large park is set in one of the most scenic and striking areas in the state. Not surprisingly, it often fills up quickly on Friday evenings in summer.

Fort Casey State Park, 3 miles south of Coupeville off Highway 20, at Admiralty Head (adjacent to Keystone ferry terminal). 38 tentsites looking west across Admiralty Inlet. Excellent public double-lane paved ramp with floats; plenty of parking, free. Winter steelheading.

Fort Ebey State Park (Recreation Area), 8 miles south of Oak Harbor off Highway 120. 53 tent sites on 220 acres. No facilities for boaters, but good fishing points (and ramp) just south at Fort Casey.

Fort Flagler State Park, 8 miles northeast of Hadlock on Marrowstone Island. 118 tentsites on 793 acres/ This large park in Kilisut Harbor is a great spot for boaters, with 7 moorage buoys and 256 feet of moorage float space, as well as a launch ramp.

Kayak Point County Park, due east from Lowell Point, across Port Susan. 32 tent or RV sites, most with hookups on 60 acres.

Mystery Bay State Park, on the east side of Marrowstone Island at Nordland. Day use only but boaters can utilize the launch ramp, moorage buoys and floats.

South Whidbey State Park (Recreation Area), southwest shore of Whidbey Island—watch for signs on highway 525 just north of Freeland. 60 tentsites (6 primitive) on 85 acres. No facilities for boaters. Nearby launch facilities at Bush Point and Mutiny Bay.

For More Information

Greater Oak Harbor Chamber of Commerce, P.O. Box 883, Oak Harbor 98277, 675-3535.

Central Whidbey Chamber of Commerce, Coupeville, 678-5434.

Freeland Chamber of Commerce, P.O. Box 361, Freeland 98249, 321-1980.

Langley Chamber of Commerce, 220 1st Street, Langley 98260, 321-6765.

Clinton Chamber of Commerce, 6256 South Central, Clinton, 321-4545.

Everett Chamber of Commerce, 1710 West Marine View Drive, Everett 98201, 252-5181.

Port of Everett ramp at Norton Street is one of the biggest and best around.

Central Puget Sound

There's a certain unique satisfaction to catching salmon in the central sound, often in the shadow of this growing urban skyline. Perhaps that feeling involves the endurance of the natural world that salmon represent and enjoying a token part of that world's bounty in the face of man's progress.

No other protected marine area in the Northwest draws as many year-round fishermen as does central Puget Sound. From Seattle and its suburbs come thousands of fishermen seeking fish in the waters at their doorstep.

Gone, of course, are the days when Puget Sound salmon were as plentiful as dogfish. And gone are the days when lingcod and rockfish were plentiful, but scorned as trash fish.

Now, more and more boats haunt everyone's favorite spots, competing for legal salmon. Salmon regulations tightened inexorably during the '70s and '80s. Fishermen had to struggle to keep up with new rules in terms of areas, seasons, sizes and gear. Lingcod were nearly depleted by the late 1970s, when a complete lingcod closure was slapped on the entire sound for years—and populations have rebounded. In response to intensive fishing of slow-growing rockfish populations, bag limits have come down from 15 to 10 to 5. Yet sport fishing endures in the central sound and, while few anglers try to fill or succeed in filling ice chests, fishermen still bring home fish for dinner.

If this area's claims to the nation's highest per-capita boat ownership are valid, you couldn't tell it by the number of public launch sites. As the map shows, launches—especially public ramps—are few and far between. That's a fact small boaters learn to consider when deciding where to fish. It is particularly astonishing that in the entire stretch of shoreline from Seattle's Shilshole Bay ramp to Everett's Norton Street ramp, there isn't another major ramp, protected and reliable in all conditions. There are still a few boathouses, with rentals available, at West Seattle, Brownsville, Mukilteo and Point No Point.

A number of charters operate year-round. Those out of Edmonds generally fish Possession Bar south to Jefferson Head. Several out of Shilshole fish any number of areas within 10 or so miles but focus considerable effort on Jefferson Head much of the time. Some smaller charters strictly troll; others (particularly larger boats) only drift-mooch. Some concentrate on salmon while others target on bottomfish as well. Rates vary, but figure on $40 to 50 for a day of fishing. Most charter fishermen do return with fish; their catch rates tend to be higher than those of private boat anglers.

Fishing Central Puget Sound—An Overview

Like the rest of the Puget Sound basin, the waters here are characterized mostly by muddy or sandy bottoms and shorelines that drop away steeply below the surface to great depths. Most fishing occurs near points of land and extensive underwater shelves such as Possession Bar and off Jefferson Head.

Blackmouth (immature chinook) are available most of the year, peaking to provide what is often an outstanding winter fishery from November through at least January. Just *when*, in the winter, fishing will heat up, and when it will cool off (which may not happen until as late as April, as in 1990 for example) varies from year to year. So, too, do numbers of blackmouth available. Some years they're everywhere; other years they remain few and far between. Some years they'll run well over the legal 22-inch minimum but many winters fish of 18 to 20 inches seem to outnumber the legal individuals 20 to 1. In other words, the certainty of central sound blackmouth fishing each winter is its uncertainty.

Summer Kings average 12 to 18 pounds in the central sound.

Blackmouth tend be be active feeders, particularly during the first couple hours of the day and around tide changes. They are taken by all methods—trolling, mooching herring or working metal jigs. Increasingly, smart fishermen are learning to gear down; very light lines will catch the same fish with more sport than traditional 15- to 20-pound test.

The fishing for large kings returning from two or three years at sea is more brief and intensive, traditionally beginning about the third week of June and tapering off late in August. This run, also, varies considerably. Recent years have been making many Puget Sound anglers very happy. For example, the 1989 run of summer kings was one of the best in years.

These kings will average 12 to 18 pounds, but may occasionally exceed 40. Most are taken on mooched herring or on plugs trolled deep with downriggers.

Inbound mature silvers begin to show in late August and may be available through early October. Most average about 5 pounds, only occasionally exceeding 10 (though late "hooknose" fish can top 15). Most silvers are taken by trollers, except in very specific spots such as Point No Point where mooching is favored. Silvers tend to be found around riplines, often. They are likely to be within a couple fathoms of the surface early and late in the day but otherwise downriggers are often set much deeper—as deep as 100 feet.

Pink salmon provide a major fishery in the northern part of this area during odd-numbered years when runs are strong. Many of the Skagit River fish cruise down the west shore of Whidbey Island and then around Possession Bar, which can be hot for pinks.

Recreational fisheries for bottomfish continue to change in the central sound. Once-great fishing for Pacific cod and its smaller relative, the walleye pollock, began fading in the 1980s and by the end of the decade there was barely a cod or pollock to be found in the sound.

Rockfish became increasingly popular in the 1970s as salmon grew more scarce and regulations more strict. But

Cove. Years back, large schools of young, hungry sablefish swarmed Possession and other areas. You certainly never know what you may catch in the sound.

Where Have All The True Cod Gone

Pacific ("true") cod all but disappeared from Puget Sound since the 1980s. Sampling efforts of Department of Fisheries biologists in late winter of 1990 produced virtually no cod in the Agate Pass area (west of Seattle, across the sound). Only a decade earlier, all manner of small boats would crowd into this protected slot between Bainbridge Island and the mainland in February and March, often bringing in 3- to 10-pound true cod hand-over-fist. Nearly any simple jigging rig, even traditional handlines, caught cod.

True cod offered fast winter and spring sport when they were abundant in the sound, eagerly striking artificial lures.

So what happened to such great numbers of these prolific, relatively fast-growing game fish? It's a question without a satisfactory answer. Many sport fishermen lay the blame on commercial draggers and on the spiraling population of seals and sea lions in the sound. Greg Bargmann, the state Department of Fisheries resource manager for marine fish, leans toward a theory of a natural, cyclical decline in abundance.

"It seems an effect of the warm water in the early 1980s (years of El Nino, the abnormal warming of the eastern Pacific), particularly since Puget Sound is in the southern extreme of the Pacific cod's natural range," Bargmann says.

"But," he adds, "true cod do have the ability to come back quickly." Cooling water temperatures could make a noticeable difference, he feels.

For the near term, at least, Puget Sound anglers aren't likely to find many true cod on their lines. But those who can remember the fast fishing, drifting over schools of hungry cod almost anyplace around the central sound from midwinter through early summer, are bound to hope for a return of the true cod.

Rachel Olander discusses a pollock taken off Point Monroe with her dad. These fish, like the related true cod, have largely disappeared from the sound.

they are very slow-growing and territorial, and rockfish of more than a few pounds aren't easy to come by anymore. Lingcod are still taken in central Puget Sound, primarily over Possession Bar. (A 1978-1982 moratorium on the keeping of any Puget Sound lingcod and, since then, an open season of a mere 6 weeks each spring for a single fish per day have helped the species reestablish itself.)

Bottomfish anglers in the central sound enjoy occasional surprises, such as a 5-pound petrale sole or a 15-pound yelloweye rockfish or a bright orange canary rockfish. In past years, I've located large schools of yellowtail rockfish on the northeastern slopes of Possession Bar, and for several consecutive summers, a population of 2- to 5-pound bocaccio rockfish set up shop in Appletree

Point No Point—Fishing A Legend (And The Area Around It)

Point No Point means *salmon fishing* and has to thousands of sport fishermen for decades. The topography around this steep, jutting point of land creates broad back-eddies that hold baitfish and attract salmon, year-round.

The point's popularity derives not only from the quality of its fishing, but from its convenience for small boaters. Skiffs can be rented right at the point and a sling/rail launch will accomodate private boats. There is little reason to travel more than a few hundred yards from the point, which offers protection from prevailing southwest winds.

Although the fishing action is near No Point, No Point isn't near anything else. Many boaters cruise over from Everett or Edmonds and some from Seattle (not a bad run in calm waters, but it can be a long one if the wind kicks up). Most traveling by car take the Edmonds-Kingston ferry, though on summer weekends that may require some waiting.

Point No Point and mooching are synonymous. For one thing, a steep point of land that concentrates salmon in a limited area lends itself to mooching. For another, drift- or motor-mooching allows crowds of boats to fish a small area—and, on many weekends, crowds do so. Those who would try to troll near the point are less likely to pick up salmon than lines—and shouted obscenities.

All 5 species of salmon are caught at the point at various times of the year. The largest of these are summer-run kings that linger around the point from late June through August. In odd-numbered years, pinks may be abundant in August. Close on the heels of kings are ocean-run silvers through September. By mid-October and well into November, chums move in. Then, blackmouth fishing often starts to sizzle by November (sometimes in October), continuing at a healthy pace into late winter on and off into the spring.

Most No Point moochers favor traditional plugcut herring rigs. Less than first light, tide changes are considered prime time at No Point, from about 2 hours before slack water to about an hour after. Some veteran No Pointers do well during the entire ebb tide where there's at least six feet of runoff.

A few shore fishermen take advantage of the fact that the smooth bottom drops steeply at the point, and when salmon are in good supply, some anglers do manage to connect by casting from shore, using Buzz Bombs and other metal jigs.

Occasionally bottomfish are picked up at the point, but the odds for them are better to the north, in Skunk Bay. There, a combination of habitats attract cabezon, various rockfish, greenling and—in past years—true cod.

An area that's become increasingly popular in recent years is *Pilot Point* just to the south of Point No Point. While Pilot actually lacks so pronounced a point, kings often seem to spill over from No Point to feed along this steep shoreline. This is particularly true as the tide reaches high slack, when the salmon seem to move south from No Point. And while No Point belongs to the moocher, Pilot Point is a downrigger trollers' show. July and August are good months to pull a Hotspot Flasher and glow-in-the-dark plastic squid.

Possession Bar—Central Sound's Grand Central Station

This enormous shelf stretching one-and-one-half miles into the sound south of Whidbey Island is one of the few areas in central Puget Sound where just about every type of habitat can be found. It is a natural holding area for baitfish and most types of fishes found in these waters. Besides three species of salmon, I have caught or seen caught lingcod, several species of rockfish (copper, yelloweye, black, yellowtail, quillback), halibut and several species of flatfish, greenling, sablefish, Pacific cod, pollock and hake, and cabezon—all on Possession Bar.

The great majority of anglers are there, of course, for salmon. Many different runs bound for rivers in southern and northern Puget Sound cross Possession. And of course resident fish feed here much of the year. Those who abide by two basic Possession rules greatly increase their chances for success: fish early and (except for resident silvers) fish deep.

Many charters fish Possession Bar regularly, some strictly trolling but others (particularly larger boats) commonly drift-mooching.

The worn maxim about being on the water too late if you can cut bait without a flashlight is not wasted on Possession fishermen. Knowing from experience that the hot bite here is most likely to occur around daybreak, launch ramps get busy as early as 3:30 on summer mornings with anglers headed to Possession Bar.

People don't stop fishing after dawn, of course; they do it deeper. In fact, the vast percentage of those who fish the bar for salmon deep-troll plugs with downriggers in 60 to 150 feet of water.

As Mike Chamberlain, a long-time well-known authority on Possession Bar fishing says, "Downrigger trolling is an effective method, and people are able to keep their gear deep and fishing." Moreover, trolling keeps the angler trying new territory when the fish may be scattered over so large an area as Possession.

Trolling lures also helps avoid close encounters with dogfish, which at times can be thicker than fleas on an old hound. One of the most popular lures for many years has been a white or pearl Silver Horde lure, but trollers also use the usual variety of plastic squid, flies and herring or some combination (with squid and herring strip always popular).

Several charter skippers rely on Possession Bar much of the year to keep holes in their clients' punchcards. Most have found that it's best to leave a generous amount of line between downrigger release clip and bait or lure—30 to 50 feet or so, sometimes even more.

The widespread use of downriggers has reduced the number of moochers on the bar, but mooching can be very productive and retains a dedicated following. After the early morning peak, the next period when moochers are most likely to score is the first hour after slack tide: work along the bar's dropoff (the perimeter).

Metal jigs such as Point Wilson Darts are popular with some Possession anglers. They are effective, but like mooching involve drift-fishing and the area covered is not so great as when trolling. Also, tidal runoff at times can be horrendous enough to make getting a jig (or herring) to bottom from a drifting boat difficult at best.

Predicting where one will find salmon on this vast plateau is impossible. One very general rule of thumb by which some trollers operate is: fish the east side on the incoming tide and the west side on the ebb.

At least some salmon are available here most of the year, on a schedule similar to that of Point No Point. Winter blackmouth are equally unpredictable and may slow down by midwinter. Some years they'll offer good fishing in the spring and are often joined in late April and May by spring chinook fresh from the ocean. During the summer, the big kings take center stage. Look for fall chinook to move in early in August and silvers from the ocean to begin mingling with them on the bar later in the month.

Often in the spring, 2- to 5-pound resident silvers may be available at the surface in tide rips, and on very light lines provide fast sport. I've had some fine times trolling nothing more than a tiny plugcut herring on an eight-foot leader) tied to my main line with a ball bearing swivel and above the swivel a *sliding* weight of an ounce or perhaps two. Not much weight, but then these fish are feeding at the surface and I'm using "trout tackle" with 4-pound line—which is the key to lots of action and sport.

Pinks show in August of odd years and remain well into September. Troll a 2 1/2-inch cerise or hot pink squid or no. 4 1/2 Martin Radiant behind a no. 0 or 1 dodger. Casting small pink Buzz Bombs ought to work, also, though for some reason that approach has never caught on here as in the San Juans.

During the six-week open season for lingcod, fair numbers of the toothy predators are taken from rocky slopes along the western slopes of the bar. Less plentiful than in years past, rockfish are still taken in fair numbers. Coppers, quillbacks and blacks are the most common species.

Boating a legal salmon in the shadow of Seattle skyscrapers offers a unique sensation of mixing enduring wilderness and expanding civilization.

Halibut roam the bar in the mid to late spring. Catching one this far inside the sound was a very rare event until something of a north Pacific halibut population explosion (and in interest in catching them) during the 1980s, when fair numbers of the prized flatfish from Possession were boated. Few are barn-door-sized but a 10- to 25-pound halibut in central Puget Sound is generally a welcome catch. Once in a while a halibut over 50 pounds is picked up.

Occasional yelloweye are caught, usually in deep water (180 to 300 feet) around the southernmost tongue of the

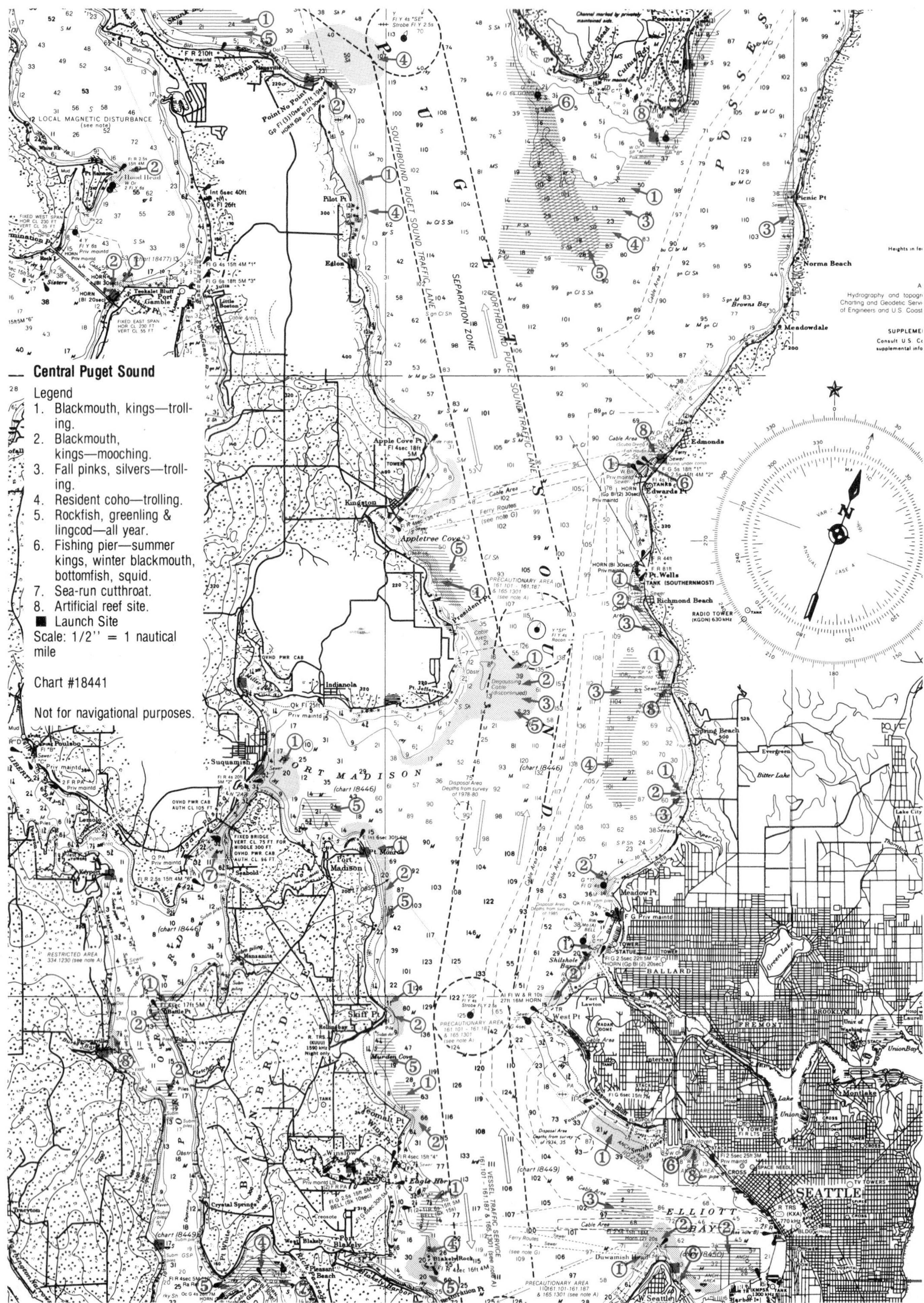

Central Puget Sound
Legend
1. Blackmouth, kings—trolling.
2. Blackmouth, kings—mooching.
3. Fall pinks, silvers—trolling.
4. Resident coho—trolling.
5. Rockfish, greenling & lingcod—all year.
6. Fishing pier—summer kings, winter blackmouth, bottomfish, squid.
7. Sea-run cutthroat.
8. Artificial reef site.
Launch Site
Scale: 1/2'' = 1 nautical mile
Chart #18441
Not for navigational purposes.
PUGET SOUND
PORT MADISON
BAINBRIDGE ISLAND
PORT ORCHARD
ELLIOTT BAY
SEATTLE
BALLARD
Point No Point
Norwegian Pt
Hood Head
Port Gamble
Pilot Pt
Eglon
Apple Cove Pt
Kingston
Appletree Cove
President Pt
Indianola
Pt Jefferson
Suquamish
Poulsbo
Lemolo
Keyport
Seabold
Manzanita
Pt Monroe
Port Madison
Skiff Pt
Murden Cove
Yeomalt Pt
Wing Pt
Winslow
Eagle Hbr
Crystal Springs
Creosote
West Blakely
Port Blakely
Blakely Rock
Restoration Pt
Battle Pt
Brownsville
Possession
Cultus Bay
Picnic Pt
Norma Beach
Browns Bay
Meadowdale
Edmonds
Edwards Pt
Pt Wells
Richmond Beach
Spring Beach
Bitter Lake
Meadow Pt
Shilshole Bay
West Pt
Fort Lawton
Interbay
Smith Cove
Duwamish Head
W Seattle
Green Lake
Fremont
Lake Union
Montlake
Union Bay
Brooklyn
SOUTHBOUND PUGET SOUND TRAFFIC LANE
SEPARATION ZONE
NORTHBOUND PUGET SOUND TRAFFIC LANE
PRECAUTIONARY AREA
Ferry Routes
Cable Area
LOCAL MAGNETIC DISTURBANCE

Small Boat Safety

The problem for most small boaters fishing central Puget Sound waters arises from their residency—on eastern shores. Windy days are more the rule than exception during much of the period from November through April. The frequent, brisk winds borne of low pressure systems crossing the state nearly always come from south, west or between. That means most protected, lee shores are located *across* Puget Sound—as are some of the most productive fishing areas.

Small boaters may make the run to the west side to fish such popular spots as Jefferson Head or Blake Island, but with a run of 4 or 5 miles over open water only the foolish forget to keep a sharp eye on the weather. Otherwise they may face a sloppy and possibly hazardous trip back across. Some regulars tell me they've managed to find fairly smooth waters when crossing in nasty seas by returning just behind a ferry.

There are anglers who elect to trailer a boat across the sound on a ferry (out of Mukilteo, Edmonds or Seattle) and drive to a launch on south Whidbey or the west side, but many prefer to avoid the hassle and expense.

Possession Bar, exposed as it is to winds from just about all directions and beset with heavy rips that form from currents around and over it, has gained a well-earned reputation as one the Puget Sound's roughest, least predictable areas on windy days. But there are many calm weekends in any year when 13- and 14-foot boats will be out, fishing the bar. If the weather starts to change, however, few of those linger.

During the summer and early fall, prevailing weather brings high pressure systems that may last for days. These offer calm mornings when the bar is most fishable—though they may bring heavy, persistent fogs—with afternoon breezes of 5 to 15 or even 20 knots from the north. Weak high pressure systems may occur throughout the year; when they move in during the winter, plan to fish the bar, since for a day or at least a few hours only very light, variable winds are likely.

U.S. Coast Guard—Seattle

Recorded information.................. 442-5295
24-hour operations/emergencies.......... 442-5886

Photo by Doug Wilson

bar. I have heard of some bocaccio from the same area. However, deep water along Possession can be effectively fished only during slack tides or during tides of light runoff. Otherwise, the current is far too fast to permit bottomfishing in deep water.

But there are opportunities to find fish in closer and shallower. One spot worth a try is the Department of Fisheries' artificial reef south of Possession Point. Specifically, it's located 600 feet west of the navigation buoy just south of the point in 55 to 100 feet of water. Much of the Possession Bar teems with small flatfish—sanddabs and sole (rock, sand, English) which are all vastly underutilized as light-tackle sport fish.

Jefferson Head—Seattle's Favorite Fishing Hole

If granted but a single spot to fish, many central Sound anglers would pick "Jeff Head." On just about any nice weekend throughout the year, one can find a substantial flotilla of sportfishing boats—from cartoppers and runabouts to yachts and charters—drifting and trolling the head.

What draws them here is some of the sound's most consistent year-round fishing for salmon within five miles of downtown Seattle.

Central Puget Sound

Legend
1. Blackmouth, kings—trolling.
2. Blackmouth, kings—mooching.
3. Fall pinks, silvers—trolling.
4. Resident coho—trolling.
5. Rockfish, greenling & lingcod—all year.
8. Present or proposed artificial reef site.

■ Launch Site

Scale: 1/2'' = 1 nautical mile

Chart #18448

Not for navigational purposes.

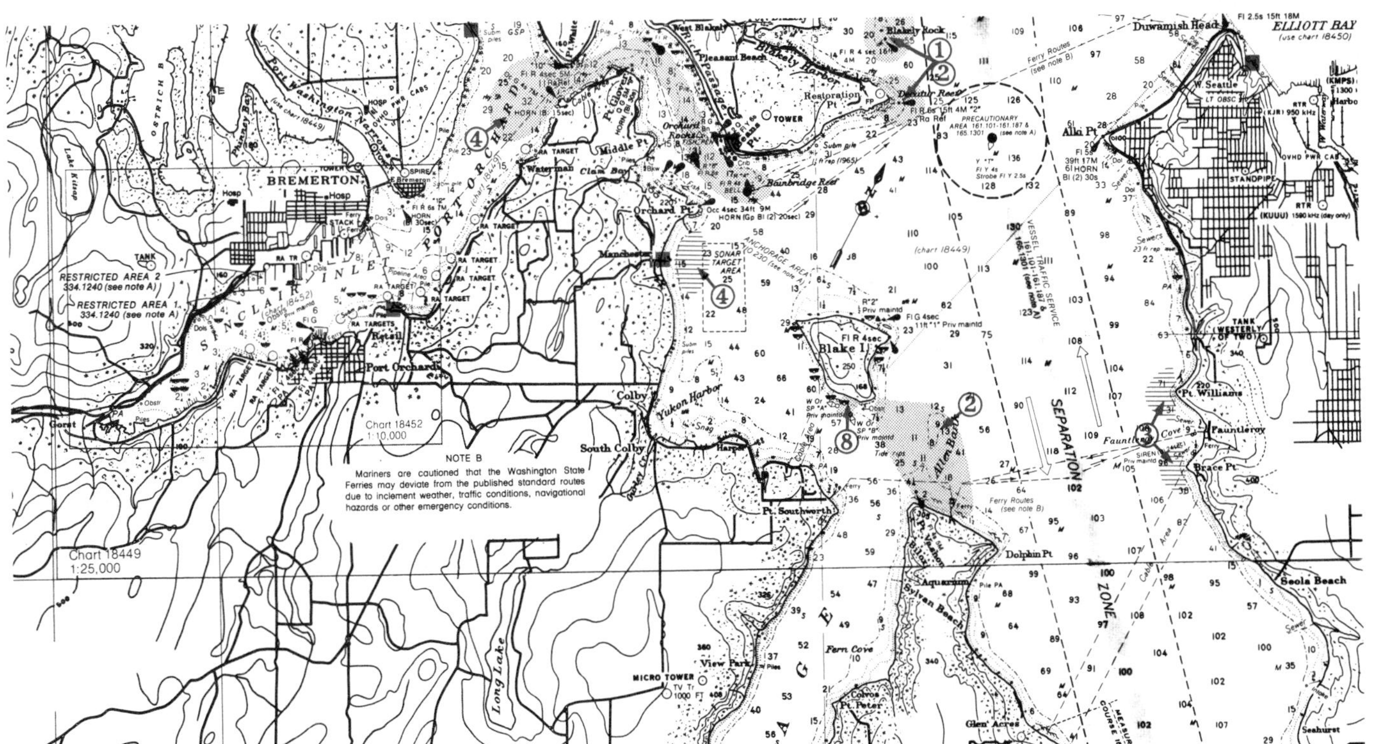

An ice cold, but calm and crystal clear winter morning brings this motor moocher to Jefferson Head. The famed "white house" is evident in the background.

Jefferson Head is, particularly, a top spot for winter blackmouth, November through February. Mooching is the most popular method, early in the day, though fair numbers of metal jig fishermen also drift here. Jeff Head blackmouth tend to "go on the bite" early, anytime between 7 a.m. (that is about daybreak in midwinter) and about 9 or 10 a.m. After that, it's pick-and-scratch fishing, though on some days the salmon will explode into activity in the afternoon, particularly during the last of an ebb tide.

One productive area is just off and somewhat south of the famed, big "white house" on the shore. Fish 90 to 140 feet of water. Another good drift starts at the old dock at the south corner of the head and into water about 180 feet deep, before a run back to repeat the drift. Also worth a try: the 90-foot area out from the yellow house.

Pinch Or Get Pinched

A Washington Dept. of Fisheries Patrol officer pulls up to a small boater to check his gear.

Puget Sound was certainly a harbinger of things to come when, in the mid1970s, barbless hooks were required among salmon fishermen in an effort to facilitate the unharmed release of salmon too small—or large—to keep. Those who fished the central sound felt the rule was unfairly restrictive to them and would make salmon fishing unreasonably difficult.

Time has proven them wrong on both counts. For one, the law requiring barbless hooks for salmon has spread to include the rest of the state. Secondly, most fishermen have learned that barbless hooks don't necessarily mean more fish lost than with barbed hooks. The key, of course, to landing fish on barbless hooks is to keep a tight line. That is basic and essential to playing a fish with any hooks, barbed or not, but becomes particularly critical with barbless hooks. As long as that is done, there is little reason to lose salmon because a hook has no barb.

Indeed, some moochers and jiggers have come to the conclusion that they are actually better off without the barb. One of the trickiest moments in salmon fishing is getting the hook set in a tough jaw during what may be a delicate bite. A hook will slip into that jaw much easier without the added thickness that a barb presents.

In any case, whether an angler agrees with the law or detests it, it is the law. Although the penalty for violating the barbed hook rule has been downgraded to a misdemeanor, most anglers these days accept and comply. It takes only a moment to pinch down the barbs with a pair of pliers before fishing, which immediately makes a barbed hook barbless.

Just remember: keep that line tight!

Moochers shouldn't hesitate to go from drift-mooching to motor-mooching if the drift is slow. The fish are likely to be in pockets and must be located. Many fishermen prefer trolling to find fish. Often, they'll work the entire shore from south of Jeff Head north to Apple Cove Point.

Blackmouth caught off Jefferson Head average 4 or 5 pounds (19 to 24 inches) in early winter. Keep in mind the 22-inch legal minimum. (That may change, but has been in effect for many years.) By summer these fish will run closer to 7 or 8 pounds.

Even though Jefferson Head is not the sound's prime spot for big summer-run kings, some big kings are always boated here during late July and August. Similarly, some 10- to 12-pound ocean silvers are taken here in September and early October, but they seem less inclined to stack up and linger here as they do around Shilshole and Elliott bays on the eastern side of the sound.

There may be good numbers of resident silvers at Jeff Head during the summer. These 3- to 4-pounders are commonly picked up by trollers and seem more likely than chinook to bite throughout the day. They are of course most fond of riplines, and one productive area is the rip that forms where the water deepens to 140 feet off the south corner of the head, out from the old dock and out from the white house.

The generally smooth, sandy bottom that forms a plateau extending out from the western edge of the head attracts species other than salmon. Quillback rockfish and various species of flatfish are common here. Petrale sole—some as large as 7 pounds—seem more common around Jeff Head than much of the sound. In past years, true cod, pollock and sablefish have been abundant here; hopefully, they'll return again soon.

Elliott Bay—Salmon In The Shadow Of Seattle's Skyline

Many of central Puget Sound's most productive salmon fishing holes are right at Seattle's doorstep; a long run to the west side is not essential to find fish. And there are plenty of windy days when fishermen in skiffs could do without such a rough, cold, wet run. Fortunately, Elliott Bay offers some protection from south or southwest winds. And while the backdrop may not be the pristine wilderness of the San Juan Islands or western strait, it is a unique experience to fight a big fish in the midst of Seattle's vibrant and dynamic urban waterfront.

Although there is some good winter fishing here, Elliott Bay really shines in the summer and early fall when the biggest prizes move in from the ocean. For most summers in the late 1980s, the bay was closed to chinook fishing during much of the summer. But that closure was lifted in 1990 as stocks strengthened and once again fishermen could get excited when the first of the big kings moved in during late May. Through June and into July, many 20- to 40-pound salmon are taken here; they are more inclined to feed actively than are kings showing up later in the summer.

Best bet for a big Elliott Bay chinook: be on the water before sunup. Serious anglers will have their baits preplugged and of course all mooching leaders rigged and ready. The great majority of anglers here drift- or motor-mooch. Not only is this an effective method, but as at Point No Point allows more intensive fishing of a smaller area than would be possible for trollers.

More kings generally move in during late July, through August and into early September. These kings tend to be smaller than the earlier run and more finnicky. There is no steady flow; a day or two of hot fishing is likely to be followed by a lull, between runs. Good timing and good luck are everything.

The natural avoidance of competition among salmon species returning to spawn works to the angler's advantage. Just about the time the last of the kings have moved through in September, silvers, fresh in from the ocean, are hitting Elliott Bay. These three-year-olds will run 6 to 12 pounds. Like coho everywhere, they like the rips and that's where anglers troll most often—generally *not* in close, as with chinook. You may see visual signs of feeding coho—birds, bait and silvers themselves, jumping. That's particularly true early in the morning, but soon after daylight coho move deeper and trollers fish their baits/lures 30 to 50 feet or more, often well out in open water.

Winter blackmouth fishing heats up in late November—though some years offer action much earlier. By January it begins to taper off, and many blackmouth fishermen head west to spots across the sound for the duration of winter's fishing. Although Elliott Bay is not the central sound's premier hotspot for winter blackmouth, at times fishing is chaotic—but often for sublegal shakers. Then, the (light-tackle) fishing is great, but the keeping isn't. Blackmouth beating the 22-inch minimum may be much more the exception than the rule.

Most Elliott Bay anglers favor the traditional approach of mooching for winter blackmouth, though trollers certainly do well.

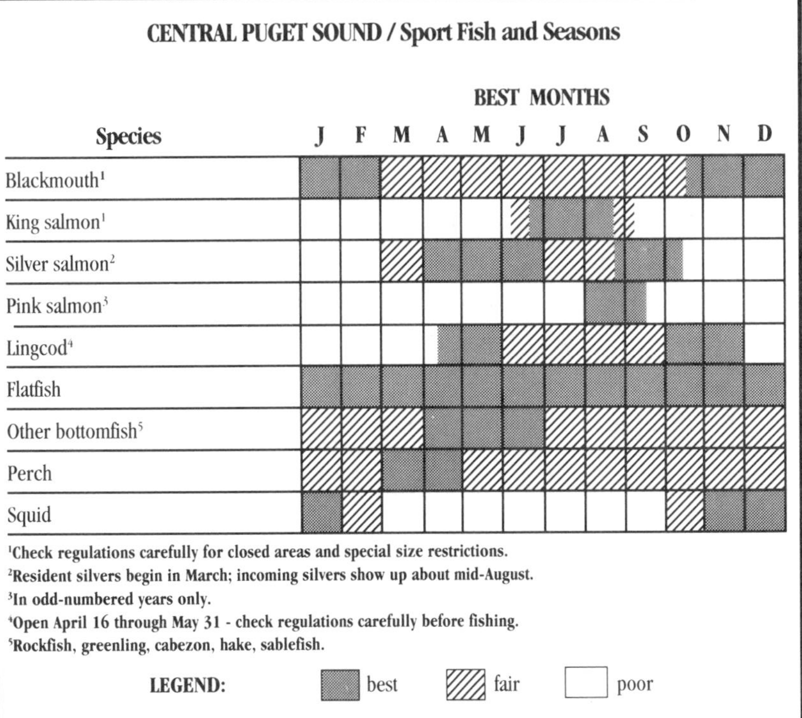

CENTRAL PUGET SOUND / Sport Fish and Seasons

BEST MONTHS

Species	J	F	M	A	M	J	J	A	S	O	N	D
Blackmouth[1]	best	best	fair	fair	fair	fair	fair	fair	fair	fair/best	best	best
King salmon[1]	poor	poor	poor	poor	poor	fair/best	best	best/fair	poor	poor	poor	poor
Silver salmon[2]	poor	poor	fair	best	best	best	fair	fair/best	best	best/poor	poor	poor
Pink salmon[3]	poor	poor	poor	poor	poor	poor	poor	best	best/poor	poor	poor	poor
Lingcod[4]	poor	poor	poor	poor/best	best	fair	fair	fair	fair	best	best	poor
Flatfish	best	best	best	best	best	best	best	best	best	best	best	best
Other bottomfish[5]	fair	fair	fair	best	best	best	fair	fair	fair	fair	fair	fair
Perch	fair	fair	best	best	fair	fair	fair	fair	fair	fair	fair	fair
Squid	best	fair	poor	poor	poor	poor	poor	poor	poor	fair	best	best

[1]Check regulations carefully for closed areas and special size restrictions.
[2]Resident silvers begin in March; incoming silvers show up about mid-August.
[3]In odd-numbered years only.
[4]Open April 16 through May 31 - check regulations carefully before fishing.
[5]Rockfish, greenling, cabezon, hake, sablefish.

LEGEND: best fair poor

Most serious Elliott Bay king fishermen have a pile of fresh herring preplugged before they hit the water by daybreak.

Although Elliott Bay is not exactly a bottomfishing paradise, its soft, structureless substrate apparently offers what some species want. In past years, cod, pollock and even the once bothersome hake all offered fair fishing. But they'd all but vanished here, as they had around the rest of the sound, by 1990.

One species that seems wont to remain is the sablefish. Once common about the sound, Elliott Bay is one of the few spots where sablefish are still taken with any regularity. Although fair numbers of the 1- to 3-pound juveniles are on hand, they are rarely targeted and usually taken incidentally. But they are tasty and fun to catch on light gear. Early in the day, look for schools of the little "black cod" just off the mouth of the Duwamish. The rest of the day, they'll usually be in at least 200 feet of water, typically between the grain terminal and Duwamish Head.

Many flatfish make Elliott Bay their home. Small hooks and small baits will produce. Starry flounder in good numbers can be taken from Alki Point to Duwamish Head in fairly shallow water during the summer months. There have been profound concerns about the edibility of such benthic resident species in these waters where the bottom is infused with industrial and urban wastes; many people are justifiably reluctant to eat flatfish from this area—particularly following warnings from the National Marine Fisheries Service. (Active and/or nonresident species such as salmon and sablefish should be quite safe to eat.)

Any sort of dock or rocky outcropping on a late incoming tide ought to offer shorebound fishermen a shot at perch, which have always been in good supply. Polychaete ("piling") worms, which can be gathered from under rocks during low tides, on small hooks are tough, effective baits, though shrimp, mussel meat and even nightcrawlers will work.

Resident coho offer fine sport in and around Elliott Bay, particularly during midspring. These aggressive little silvers typically feed at the surface where they'll eagerly attack small trolled spoons, tiny plastic squid or flies. Only very light lines should be used, for more hits and fun when silvers are hooked.

In years past (and perhaps yet again), small sablefish were common around the central sound, apparently using these waters as a nursery area. Today, Elliott Bay is one of the few places where small "black cod" can still be caught.

Shilshole To Richmond Beach On The East And Islands To The West

Shilshole Bay, site of the sound's major marina, often provides fishing similar to that of Elliott Bay, immediately

SQUID JIG

Central Puget Sound's Fishing Piers

Sport fishing in Puget Sound has been almost exclusively the domain of boaters, but not entirely. There are a few piers offering at least some fishing opportunities to nonboaters. The fishing is seldom fast or furious but it is cheap and hassle-free.

Among the public piers are several built by the Washington Department of Fisheries. One is located at Edmonds (just south of the ferry landing), another is on the Seattle waterfront (Pier 86, just west of the grain terminal) and a third at the Des Moines Marina. The naturally smooth, featureless bottoms which surround these piers have been enhanced with artificial reefs—concrete debris or tires placed nearby.

A newer pier is one operated by the City of Seattle at the site of the Seacrest (formerly Seacrest Marina).

The Des Moines Marina, located in water somewhat shallower than that off the Seattle and Edmonds marinas, attracts mostly flatfish. There is also some good spring and summer perch fishing from the breakwater rocks, here.

A number of species are taken from the piers at Seattle and Edmonds, depending mostly on time of day. During most of the day, pier fishing is slow; the many sightseeing strollers catch nearly as many fish as fishermen. But at night, things happen.

During the summer, hake move in if they are generally present in the sound. (In recent years, they've been scarce.) They can be taken simply on herring chunks with one or two hooks rigged above the sinker.

Soon after these piers were built, in the early 1980s, fishermen discovered squid. They move into the area during late fall and through the winter and congregate in masses under the lights at night. Oriental squid jigs—often with Cyalume glow sticks—catch them quickly, their sticky tentacles easily entangled in the many sharp points around the base of the jig.

Squid fishing is generally a chilly business—best in the wee hours of calm, clear, cold, dark winter nights. But it can be productive—many fishermen manage to put limits (10 pounds per day) in their buckets in short order when the squid are in—and the railings not too crowded with competition. But squid populations are highly variable from year to year and seemed to thin out markedly in the late '80s, with sport catches from piers slowing somewhat.

Piers provide ample opportunity for fishermen to tangle with salmon. On the one hand, it is absolutely true that considerably more hours on the average must be spent for each salmon caught by pier anglers than by boaters, it is also true that many good salmon are taken from these piers—including kings in the 20s and even 30s every year.

It is essential to fish early and late; that's when salmon most actively feed, particularly in waters so close to shore. Two approaches used for salmon are casting Buzz Bombs and floating herring out.

Herring is plugcut and rigged on a mooching leader with a small (1/2-ounce or so) kidney sinker, then set as much as 20 to 25 feet below a styrofoam float. (Anglers tie a tiny piece of thin monofilament onto their lines as a stop for the float.) Others prefer tossing Buzz Bombs which is easy and offers good distance from the pier.

Good-sized salmon can be tricky to land from piers, which are as much as 10 to 20 feet above the water (depending on tide). Dedicated pier fishermen come equipped with a pier net—a frame and rope with which to lower and raise it.

Salmon can be taken from all these piers. The newest of the lot, at Seacrest, seems likely to yield some impressive summer kings when they move into Elliott Bay.

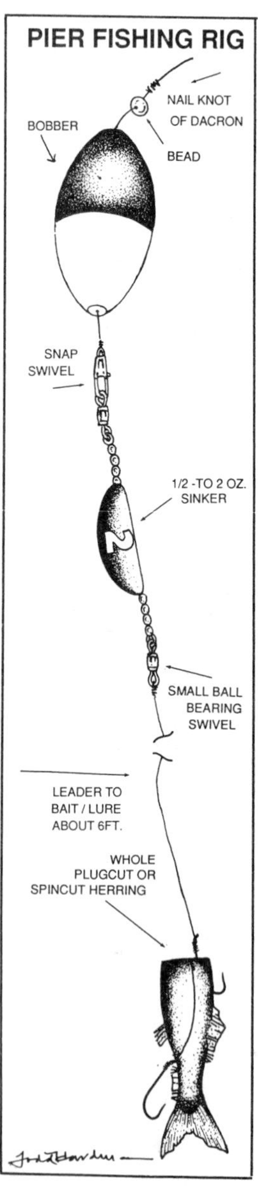

to the south. Try just north of West Point when the big kings are in. The 90- to 120-foot contour in this same area can be good for winter blackmouth, trolling a flasher and squid.

North of Shilshole are a number of areas traditionally popular with salmon fishermen. One is "The Trees," so named for four poplar trees that once stood near the railroad tracks at the point between Spring Beach and Richmond Beach. It can be another fine winter blackmouth producer. And in August-September, the rips from Shilshole to the trees may harbor pinks and silvers.

Across the sound, northern Vashon, Blake and Bainbridge islands offer protected salmon fishing. After blackmouth action has slowed in the vicinity of Elliott Bay, it is just heating up here. In fact this whole area can offer topnotch blackmouth action through the spring. Small boaters leaving Elliott Bay may find this area further appealing since the 2 1/2 miles or so from Alki Point to due west to Restoration Point at the southeast corner of Bainbridge is a relatively easy crossing.

The broad, shallow reef running from the north end of Vashon northwest to the southeast tip of Blake Island provides good fishing for late-winter blackmouth (and some bottomfish).

On the central eastern shore of Vashon is another of the Department of Fisheries artificial reef sites. Any number of species may be taken here. It's located 1,000 feet southeast of Pt. Heyer (site of the KVI radio tower) in 45 to 100 feet of water.

To the north, several points along the eastern side of Bainbridge Island offer good mooching and trolling. The rips and eddies around Blakely Rock and the mouth of Blakely Harbor are worth a try. At the far northeast corner of Bainbridge is Point Monroe which can be very good for blackmouth at times—and is more protected from southwest winds.

Some of Puget Sound's very best action for resident coho is available around Manchester, northwest of Blake Island, and through Rich Passage at the south end of Bainbridge. Spring is prime time for these small coho. Most are taken by trolling, but they can offer excellent sport for flycasters, especially when found feeding at the surface. (For more specific suggestions from an expert about flyfishing for resident coho, see the South Sound Section.)

Around the inside of the north tip of Bainbridge is famed Agate Passage. Its fame derives from its former status as home to amazing numbers of big, hungry true (Pacific) cod in the late winter each year. I can recall paddling my 17-foot canoe around on nice winter days in this very protected spot among a fleet of boats of all sizes to jig for cod and easily ending up with over 100 pounds of cod in a few hours, even though fishing very light lines. As noted elsewhere in this section, those days ended by the early 1980s. But blackmouth are available here still, though few anglers try for them.

FACILITIES

All phone numbers listed are within the 206 area code unless otherwise noted.

CHARTERS

Light "bass-size" levelwinds with 6-pound line is one of the author's favorite rigs for jigging winter blackmouth in central Puget Sound. Photo by Jackie Olander.

Two types of charters fish the sound. Generally the smaller "six-pack" boats troll using downriggers and charge a bit more—at press time, $60 to 90 for a day of fishing. Larger boats driftmooch/jig and at press time their rates were $45-50. Many of these charter offices have been around for decades; many offer both types of fishing. These charters definitely operate year-round, often less busy in winter but only for lack of passengers, not for lack of fish since winter blackmouth (and when they're in the area true cod) offer fast fishing. Summer trips leave the docks early, typically around 5 a.m., but in winter departure—like daybreak—is considerably later.

All Season Charter Service, 300 Admiral Way, Edmonds 98020, 743-9590/672-1195/771-3277. 8 boats, 28 to 50 feet. Fishes throughout Puget Sound, often around Possession Bar and Point No Point. Fishes salmon all year and bottomfish when available/open.

Ballard Salmon Charters, 2620 NW 63rd #4, Seattle 98107, 789-6202. 2 boats, 36 feet (up to 12 anglers), driftfishes.

Captain Coley's Charters, 1053 B Avenue, Edmonds 98020, 778-4110. Two boats, 43′ and 45′ concentrate on salmon and miscellaneous bottomfish. Driftmooching the central sound.

Major Marine Tours, 1415 Western Avenue, Suite 503, Seattle 98101, 292-0595. One boat, at 100 feet long easily the largest charter around. Fishes salmon and bottomfish all year.

Sea Charters, 115 W. Dayton, Edmonds 98020, 776-5611. Several boats 24′ to 27′ that specialize in trolling Possession Bar; larger boats to 43 feet that driftfish Possession, Point No Point and other areas occasionally.

Sound Charters, 3616 NE 123rd, Seattle 981215, 363-5896. Operates 1 36′ boat out of Shilshole Marina, books the entire boat only (no individual walk-ons) at an hourly rate (4-hour minimum). "We cater to families and business groups" says skipper Jim Smart. Primarily driftmooching with plugcut herring year-round.

MARINAS

Bay Marine, P.O. Box 36, Suquamish 98392, 598-4900. Open year-round. Located on Miller Bay (Miller Bay Road), there are 40 slips here; transient moorage is most assured with reservation. No fuel, but engine repair and bait and tackle. Launch ramp and hoist will accomodate boats up to 23 feet.

Port of Brownsville Marina, 9790 Ogle Road Northeast, Bremerton 98310 (Highway 30 north to Brownsville), 692-5498. Open 7/days week all year. Moorage available. Fuel, bait and tackle. Excellent 2-lane ramp, not free but cost very modest. Also a hoist launch. Restrooms, showers, laundromat, picnic area, pump-out station, deli. Here since the 1920s.

Des Moines Marina, 22307 Dock Avenue South, Des Moines 98198, 824-5700. Open 7 days/week, year-round. Guest moorage, reservations unnecessary. Fuel and launching via a sling.

Port of Edmonds Marina, 338 Admiral Way, Edmonds 98020, 774-0549. 7 days/week, year-round. Guest moorage available. No tackle; bait available at nearby Bud's Bait. Fuel dock. Sling launch accomodates boats to at least 26 feet. Also showers, restuarants, shops, charter offices, engine repair all nearby.

Port of Kingston Marina, 25864 Washington Boulevard Northeast, Kingston 98346, 297-3545. 7 days/week, year-round. Guest moorage, fuel, engine repair, bait and tackle. Hoist launch for boats of nearly any size. Showers, laundromat, restuarants. Boat rentals with power available at Kingston Rentals: 297-8320.

Meadowdale Marine, 16111 76th Place West, Edmonds 98020, 743-2211. Open all year, moorage monthly. Fuel, engine repair, bait and tackle. Elevator/travel-lift launch for baots to 18 feet. Rents 15-foot aluminum boats (only) without power. In business here since the 1930s.

Point No Point Beach Resort, 8708 NE Point No Point Road, Hansville 98340, 638-2233. Open 7/days week, June-October and weekends November-May. No moorage or fuel, but located at one of state's premiere salmon spots with a rail launch for boats to 16 feet long. Also rents boats (no outboards). Bait and tackle. Also offers 5 rental cabins, 38 RV spaces with hookups and 12 spaces without hookups. Resort has been here nearly a half-century.

Port Orchard Marina, (Port of Bremerton), 8850 State Highway 3, Port Orchard, 98366, 876-5535. In addition to 44 slips, 1500 feet of breakwater also utilized for moorage. Fuel, restrooms and showers. Closest launch is City of Port Orchard ramp.

Port Orchard (City of) public launch ramp, 1 block from Port Orchard marina. Two lanes, paved with center float. Excellent condition, good on most tides. Free.

Port of Poulsbo Marina, P.O. Box 732, Poulsbo 98370 (3 miles north of Keyport at the end of Liberty Bay), 779-3505. 7 days/week, year-round. 130 moorage slips, fuel. Bait and tackle available nearby. Free paved launch ramp in good shape down to at least a zero tide. Scenic central sound harbor fills up on nice summer weekends with boats from Seattle and area.

Seacrest Marina, 1660 Harbor Southwest, Seattle 98126, 932-1050. Located just northeast of Alki Point, open 7 days/week year-round. Excellent free public launch ramp nearby. Rents 16-foot Lund skiffs with or without power. Good bait and tackle selection.

Shilshole Bay Marina, 7001 Seaview Avenue Northwest, Seattle 98117, 728-3385. Open all the time, all year, a major facility with 1,200 slips. Gas and diesel fuel, some bait. Restaurants, showers, laundromat. Hoist launch and at north end of marina (at Golden Gardens), is a free, huge multi-lane ramp with floats at each end, good at all but lowest tides. Lots of parking (but in summer you may have to park off street somewhere).

Suldan Boat Works, 1343 Southwest State Highway 160, Port Orchard 98366 (2 miles south of Port Orchard), 876-4435. Open year-round, Monday-Saturday. 100 slips, monthly only. 3 rail launches for boats up to 55 feet. Engine repair available.

Smart Bait and Boat Rentals, 6049 Seaview Avenue Northwest, Seattle 98107, 782-8322. Open May-October, dawn-dusk. Located at site of old Ray's Boathouse on Shilshole Bay, rentals of 14-foot aluminum skiffs available with or without power. Also sells *live herring* when available and limited tackle (mostly for mooching).

Big pile perch remain a largely underutilized sport species around the sound.

Bait And Tackle Shops

Avid Angler, 11714 15th Avenue Northeast, Seattle, 362-4030. Closed Sundays. Flyfishing gear only; owner Tom Darling carries everything for flyfishing northwest salt waters.

Ballard Bait and Tackle, 5517 Seaview Avenue Northwest, 784-3016. Open 7 days/week all year. The Relei family carries only saltwater gear and offer something different: vaccuum-packed frozen herring.

Bud's Bait, P.O. Box 21, Edmonds 98020 (Port of Edmonds, A-dock), 774-1921. Open 7 days/week (noon-6 pm in winter). Sells herring, live and fresh.

Ed's Surplus and Outdoor Store, 5911 19th Street Southwest, Lynnwood 98036, 778-1441. Open 7 days/week with a good selection of tackle.

The Fishing Corner, 14604 Pacific Highway, Seattle, 246-8653. Open 7 days/week. Carries all sorts of fishing gear.

The Fishing Tackle Store, 16811 Redmond Way, Redmond 869-5117. Wide selection of tackle.

Flip's Tackle and Sport, 19800 Highway 99, Lynnwood 98036, 771-6577. Open Tuesday-Saturday.

Happy Hooker Bait and Tackle, 955 Alaskan Way West, Seattle, 284-0441. Located at Pier 86, the Seattle public fishing pier, downtown waterfront with bait and tackle for pier fishermen. Access for handicapped. Different management likely at press time.

Kaufmann's Streamborn Flies, 1918 4th Avenue, Seattle 98101, 448-0601 (also a Bellevue store). Closed Sundays. Saltwater flyfishing tackle.

Kingston Tackle and Marine, 27027 Miller Bay Road Northeast, Kingston 98346, 297-2521. Open 7 days/week. Owner Dick Johnson is an increasingly-known expert on salmon fishing and carries salmon and bottomfish gear including a line of his own products.

Kitsap Bait Sales, 1595 Southwest State Highway 160, Port Orchard 98366, 876-1189. Closed Sundays. Herring—no tackle.

Kitsap Sports Shop, 10516 Silverdale Way Northwest, Silverdale, WA 98383, 698-4808 (Clear Creek Center). Open 7 days/week. Carries a fine selection of tackle.

Kitsap Sports Shop, 630 Cale Avenue North, Bremerton 98312, 373-9589. Closed Sundays.

Stoneway Hardware and Supply, 4318 Stoneway Avenue North, Seattle, 545-6910. Open 7 days/week. Carries freshwater and saltwater gear.

Ted's Sport Center, 156th SW and Highway 99 North, Lynnwood 98036, 743-9505. Open 7 days/week in-season; closed Sundays October-March. One of best saltwater bait and tackle selections for Northwest (and tropical) saltwater fishing. Run by writer/lecturer/fishing authority Mike Chamberlain.

Viking Marine Center, 11264 State Highway 104, Kingston 98346, 297-3838. Open 7 days/week. Carries mainly saltwater tackle.

Viking Marine Center, P.O. Box 1028, Poulsbo 98370 (at Poulsbo Marina), 779-4656, Open 7 days/week. Excellent selection of saltwater tackle.

Warshal's Sporting Goods, 1000 1st Avenue South, Seattle 98104, 624-7300. Excellent selectoin of tackle for all purposes. This store, located in downtown Seattle, is a venerable outdoor equipment institution.

Resorts

Captain's Landing, P.O. Box 113, Hansville 98340, 638-2257. Open year-round, closed Mondays. 5 cabins, 22 RV spaces with hookups, 10 tentsites. Restrooms and showers. Hoist and rail launch for boats to 18 feet. No moorage but fuel, engine repair, bait and tackle (including live herring when available). Rents 14-foot kickerboats with or without power. Waterfront restaurant with pub.

Public Campgrounds

Blake Island State Park, 3 miles west of Seattle, south of Bainbridge Island. Accessible by boat only. 30 standard tentsites and 11 primitive sites on 476 acres. Facilities on the island area well-developed and boaters can tie up to one of 22 moorage buoys or 1,018 feet of moorage float space. (Nevertheless, things get crowded here on nice summer weekends.) Underwater park and artificial reef nearby.

Fay Bainbridge State Park (Recreation Area), northeast end of Bainbridge Island, off Highway 305, 5 miles west of Seattle. 26 RV sites (30' long), 10 primitive tent sites on 17 acres. Offers fishermen a boat launch and two moorage buoys. Also an excellent location for Jefferson Head salmon and bottomfish. Facilities for handicapped.

Illahee State Park (Recreation Area), 3 miles northeast of Bremerton off Highway 306. 25 standard tent sites and 8 primitive sites on 75 acres. Launching via a paved ramp; 5 moorage buoys and 311 feet of moorage float space.

Manchester State Park (Recreation Area), on Rich Passage, southwest of Bainbridge Island, .6 mile east of Port Orchard. 50 standard tent sites and 3 primitive sites on 111 acres. No small boat facilities here, but available in nearby Manchester.

For More Information

Bremerton Area Chamber of Commerce, 245 Fourth, Bremerton, 479-3579.

Edmonds Chamber of Commerce, 120 5th Avenue, Edmonds 98020, 776-6711.

Kingston Chamber of Commerce, P.O. Box 78, Kingston 98346, 297-3813

Poulsbo Chamber of Commerce, P.O. Box 1063, Poulsbo 98370, 779-4848.

Queen Anne Chamber of Commerce, P.O. Box 19386, Seattle, 283-6876.

Seattle Chamber of Commerce, 215 Columbia, Seattle, 389-7200.

Silverdale Chamber of Commerce, 9729 Silverdale Way, Silverdale, 692-6800.

South Snohomish County, 344 188th Street #102, Lynnwood 98037, 774-0507.

West Seattle Chamber of Commerce, 1510 Palm Southwest, Seattle, 932-5685.

Southern Puget Sound

MANY PROTECTED SHORES AND AN ABUNDANCE of herring most of the year are among the features of south Puget Sound that appeal to sport fishermen.

Unhappily, the mid- and late 1980s saw a measure of deterioration in some major recreational south sound sport fisheries. The decline in Pacific cod and pollock fishing that was felt in central Puget Sound hit harder here, where these fish enjoyed a particularly enthusiastic, dedicated following. At the same time, excellent fishing for resident chinook and coho, as well as sea-run cutthroat, hit the skids to a considerable extent.

But happily, there have always been times and places where fishermen find it worth their while to wet their lines in south Puget Sound. Recently, winter blackmouth fishing has shown signs of improvement and the Department of Fisheries began producing record levels of delayed-release chinook in south Puget Sound in the late 1980s. Then, too, the ambitious restoration of salmon fishing proposed in state Department of Fisheries' ambitious Recreational Fishery Enhancement Plan (1989) offers considerable hope for a return to the fine south sound fishing of years past. Continued work with delayed-release programs for pen-reared salmon holds hope.

Those who do fish these waters can find protection from the southwest winds that prevail much of the year. The popular area just south of Point Defiance tends to be less afflicted with brisk winds and when those do occur there are plenty of scenic cliffs, points and passes to provide protection.

Bottomfishing, particularly with the decline of cod and pollock populations, draws less interest than in the past. Beyond the disappearance of cod and pollock, there is the scarcity of rocky habitat that many species of bottomfish prefer; much of this area is covered by muddy bottom with light tidal flow. These conditions seem to attract herring, but also at times great numbers of dogfish. Small rockfish are available and during the brief spring season anglers take some bragging-sized lingcod around the wreckage of the old bridge in the deep, rocky, rushing waters of the Tacoma Narrows.

Launch sites are scattered about southern Puget Sound. Boat rentals are still available at boathouses. Some charter services are available.

Year-round Fishing For Resident And Returning Chinook And Coho

For years, south sound salmon fishing relied on resident fish. Blackmouth remain a major catch of south sound anglers. While spring fishing for small resident coho has declined in recent years, it has improved considerably for mature, returning coho. This is apparently the result of increased south sound hatchery/pen production.

December and January are peak blackmouth months, but good action may continue from mid-March into summer (though some areas in past years were seasonally closed to spring salmon angling in recent years). The annual catch of blackmouth in the south sound sportcatch has been as high as 80,000 some years. In more recent years, that has averaged about 40,000 per year. Summer attention is often focused on mature chinook—kings—returning to south sound streams such as the Puyallup and Nisqually rivers.

Although the majority of south sound chinook are taken on plug-cut herring, metal jigs also maintain a following among anglers.

A number of south sound spots are well-known, traditionally fished and annually productive. Some of these are listed here.

Anderson Island is certainly one of the most popular of south sound fishing holes, particularly for drift-mooching, most of which occurs off the extreme southern tip of *Lyle Point.* The ebb tide is the most popular winter fishing period; flood tide seems best during the spring. Some big chum salmon wind up on the lines of a few Lyle Point fishermen early in the winter. (Casting small Buzz Bombs from DuPont Wharf on the Nisqually Flats may yield more chums, which may be seen rolling there in December.) Some small resident coho may be available here during the spring, particularly off the south end of the island, as well as Johnson Point and Devils Head.

In waters off the old *"Concrete Dock"* at the northeast corner of Fox Island, drift moochers and trollers are able to

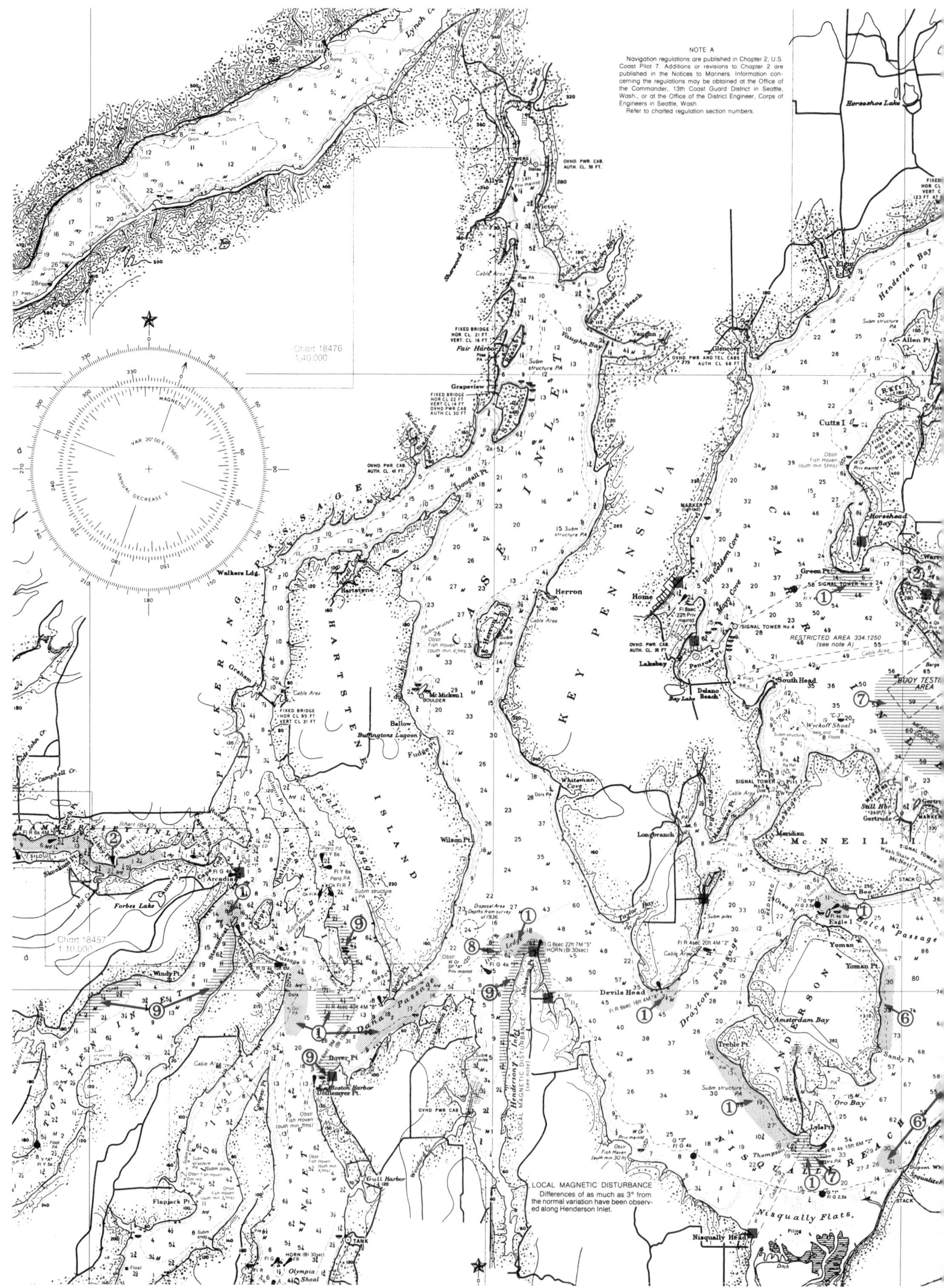
NOTE A
Navigation regulations are published in Chapter 2, U.S. Coast Pilot 7. Additions or revisions to Chapter 2 are published in the Notices to Mariners. Information concerning the regulations may be obtained at the Office of the Commander, 13th Coast Guard District in Seattle, Wash., or at the Office of the District Engineer, Corps of Engineers in Seattle, Wash.
Refer to charted regulation section numbers.
LOCAL MAGNETIC DISTURBANCE
Differences of as much as 3° from the normal variation have been observed along Henderson Inlet.
RESTRICTED AREA 334.1250 (see note A)
Chart 18476 1:40,000
Chart 18457 1:10,000
VAR 20°00'E (1989) ANNUAL DECREASE 3'
MAGNETIC
Allyn
Victor
Vaughn Bay
Vaughn
Glencove
Grapeview
Fair Harbor
Walkers Ldg.
Hartstene
Herron
Home
Von Geldern Cove
Lakebay
Penrose Pt.
Delano Beach
Bay Lake
South Head
Longbranch
Whiteman Cove
Taylor Bay
Devils Head
Drayton Passage
Ballow
Buffingtons Lagoon
Fudge Pt.
Wilson Pt.
McMicken I
Dougall Pt.
Arcadia
Forbes Lake
Windy Pt.
Dover Pt.
Boston Harbor
Dofflemeyer Pt.
Gull Harbor
Olympia Shoal
Flapjack Pt.
Nisqually Head
Nisqually Flats
Cutts I
Raft I
Allen Pt
Henderson Bay
Horseshoe Lake
Horsehead Bay
Green Pt.
Wyckoff Shoal
BUOY TESTING AREA
Still Hbr
Gertrude
Meridian
McNEIL I.
Wash State Penitentiary McNeil I.
Eagle I
Balch Passage
Yoman
Yoman Pt.
Amsterdam Bay
Treble Pt.
Oro Bay
Lyle Pt.
Thompson
Sandy Pt
ANDERSON I.
NISQUALLY REACH
PICKERING PASSAGE
CASE INLET
KEY PENINSULA
CARR INLET
HARTSTENE ISLAND
Peale Passage
Squaxin Passage
Dana Passage
TOTTEN INLET
HAMMERSLEY INLET
Skookum Pt.
Henderson Inlet
Johnson Pt.
EDDY INLET
BUDD INLET
Sherwood Cr.
Lynch Cove
Campbell Cr.
Graham Pt.
Mill Cr.
Hungerford Pt.
Squaxin I.
Hope I.
Stretch I.
Herron I.
Pitt I.
Pitt Passage
Mayo Cove
SIGNAL TOWER No 4
SIGNAL TOWER
Cable Area
Subm structure PA
Obstr Fish Haven
FIXED BRIDGE HOR CL 21 FT VERT CL 16 FT
FIXED BRIDGE HOR CL 95 FT VERT CL 31 FT
OVHD PWR AND TEL CABS AUTH CL 68 FT
Disposal Area Depths from survey of 1936
Fl R 6sec 16ft 4M "6"
Fl R 4sec 20ft 4M "2"
Fl G 6sec 22ft 7M "5" HORN (Bl 30sec)
Fl R 4sec 40ft 4M "8"
Fl R 4s 15ft 6M "2"
Fl G 4s
STACK
TANK

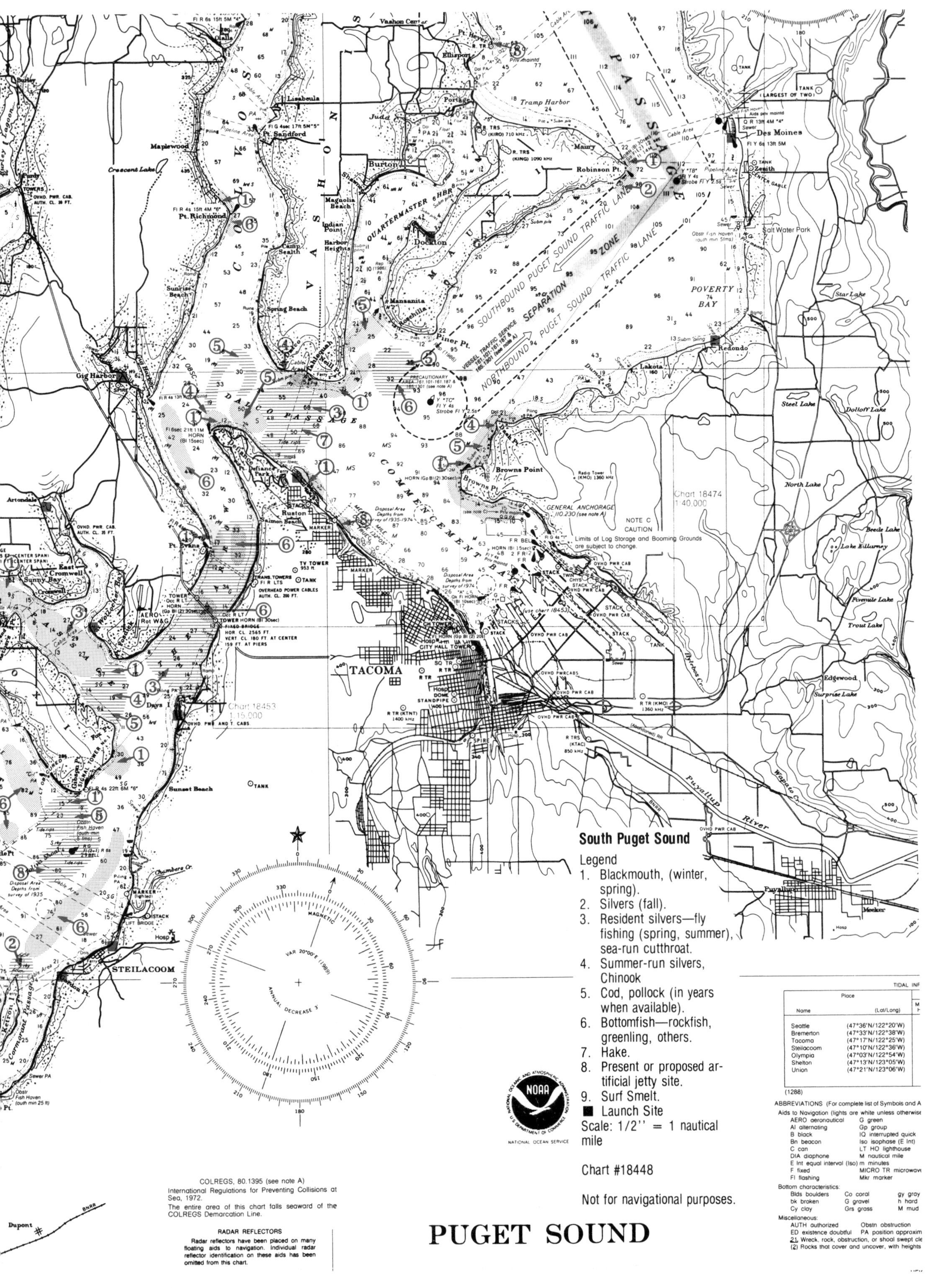
South Puget Sound
Legend
1. Blackmouth, (winter, spring).
2. Silvers (fall).
3. Resident silvers—fly fishing (spring, summer), sea-run cutthroat.
4. Summer-run silvers, Chinook
5. Cod, pollock (in years when available).
6. Bottomfish—rockfish, greenling, others.
7. Hake.
8. Present or proposed artificial jetty site.
9. Surf Smelt.
■ Launch Site
Scale: 1/2'' = 1 nautical mile
Chart #18448
Not for navigational purposes.
PUGET SOUND
NOAA
NATIONAL OCEAN SERVICE
COLREGS, 80.1395 (see note A)
International Regulations for Preventing Collisions at Sea, 1972.
The entire area of this chart falls seaward of the COLREGS Demarcation Line.
RADAR REFLECTORS
Radar reflectors have been placed on many floating aids to navigation. Individual radar reflector identification on these aids has been omitted from this chart.
TIDAL INF
Place
Name (Lat/Long)
Seattle (47°36'N/122°20'W)
Bremerton (47°33'N/122°38'W)
Tacoma (47°17'N/122°25'W)
Steilacoom (47°10'N/122°36'W)
Olympia (47°03'N/122°54'W)
Shelton (47°13'N/123°05'W)
Union (47°21'N/123°06'W)
(1288)
ABBREVIATIONS (For complete list of Symbols and A
Aids to Navigation (lights are white unless otherwise
AERO aeronautical G green
Al alternating Gp group
B black IQ interrupted quick
Bn beacon Iso isophase (E Int)
C can LT HO lighthouse
DIA diaphone M nautical mile
E Int equal interval (Iso) m minutes
F fixed MICRO TR microwave
Fl flashing Mkr marker
Bottom characteristics:
Blds boulders Co coral gy gray
bk broken G gravel h hard
Cy clay Grs grass M mud
Miscellaneous:
AUTH authorized Obstn obstruction
ED existence doubtful PA position approxim
Wreck, rock, obstruction, or shoal swept cle
(2) Rocks that cover and uncover, with heights
NOTE C
CAUTION
Limits of Log Storage and Booming Grounds are subject to change.
Chart 18474 1:40,000
Chart 18453 1:15,000
GENERAL ANCHORAGE 110.230 (see note A)
SOUTHBOUND PUGET SOUND TRAFFIC LANE
SEPARATION ZONE
NORTHBOUND PUGET SOUND TRAFFIC LANE
DALCO PASSAGE
COMMENCEMENT BAY
COLVOS PASSAGE
VASHON ISLAND
MAURY I
QUARTERMASTER HBR
POVERTY BAY
Tramp Harbor
TACOMA
STEILACOOM
Gig Harbor
Ruston
Browns Point
Des Moines
Redondo
Puyallup River
Dupont
VAR 20°00'E (1989)
ANNUAL DECREASE 3'
MAGNETIC

find salmon most of the year. Bad news for shorebound anglers was the demise of the dock, actually an old ferry landing, in the late 1980s (condemned as unsafe). From this very popular spot, surprising numbers of salmon were taken by fishermen casting Buzz Bombs and other metal jigs. The good news is that the Department of Fisheries purchased the dock and plans to maintain it for use by fishermen.

Perhaps no name in the area is more synonymous with south sound salmon fishing than *Point Defiance.* Around its steep shoreline rush waters into and out of the Tacoma Narrows. Powerful rips and strong back eddies form here, concentrating bait-fish—and salmon. Defiance is a famous gathering place for driftmoochers who most successfully work the point around a tide change or during periods of light to moderate tidal runoff. You should start the drift near the lighthouse, almost at the shore, so steep is the dropoff here.

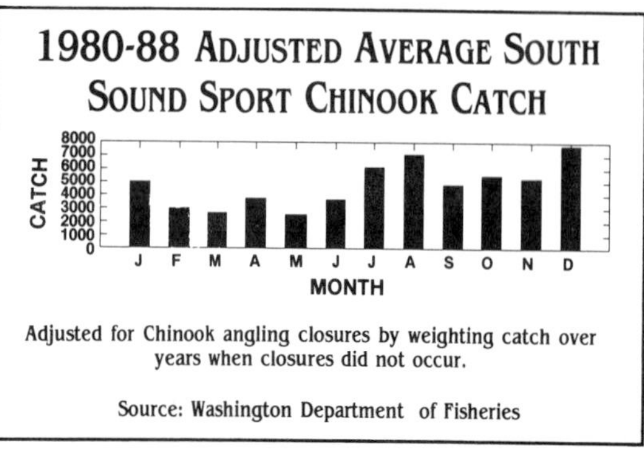

Adjusted for Chinook angling closures by weighting catch over years when closures did not occur.

Source: Washington Department of Fisheries

Typically, early winter provides some of the fastest action of the year, when winter blackmouth are in good supply. Returning mature summer kings become the the target late spring through early summer along the point.

Jutting into the northern end of Commencement Bay is *Brown's Point,* where anglers gather in late summer, trolling for mature, returning silvers.

North of Olympia, those not fishing Anderson Island are likely to be mooching off *Devils Head* or *Johnson Point.* The point is one of the very best places in southernmost Puget Sound to tangle with good-sized spring blackmouth.

Some good mature coho fishing in recent late summers has taken place in *Boston Harbor* near Olympia, apparently from hatchery/net pen production.

A south sound sport fishery around which built a very dedicated following during the 1970s and early '80s focused on resident coho. These young, delayed-release salmon spend much of their time feeding at the surface. Light-tackle and, particularly, fly fishing enthusiasts developed a superb fishery for them.

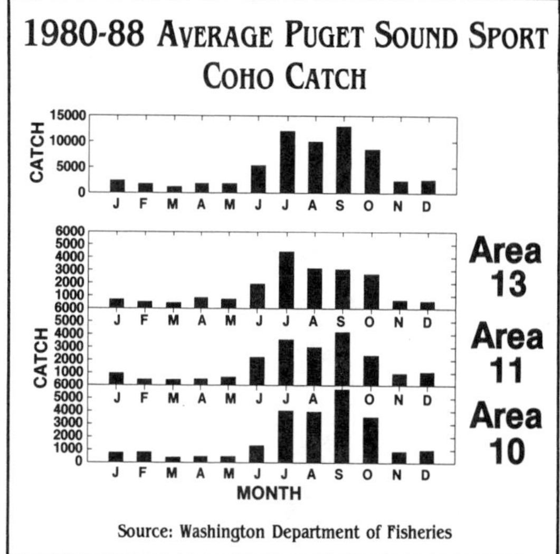

Source: Washington Department of Fisheries

Unfortunately, this was yet another fishery that saw a real decline in the late 1980s. This, despite an increase in delayed coho releases in the south sound by one-third starting in 1984. In fact, a leading authority who pioneered this specialized fishery, Bruce Ferguson, thinks *too many* delayed-release coho "may be the crux of the problem—more released fish than the available food supply....As a result, although overall survival has been good, the coho no longer remain resident south of the Tacoma Narrows Bridge as was originally the case."

However, the Department of Fisheries, anxious to see this fishery rebuilt, is experimenting with different release delay periods. Hopefully, a formula will be found so light-line resident coho fishing will again be available on the scale of years past. "But in the meantime," says Ferguson, "it's still a matter of looking hard for widely scattered pods of fish after February."

Sea-run cutthroat roam the gravelly beaches near shore in many areas of the south sound and can be taken from shore or small boats, particularly summer and fall, in areas such as under the Purdy or Fox Island bridges. The last part of the flood tide is typically a peak period for sea-runs. Small spoons and spinners are effective; some anglers fish nightcrawlers while others troll tiny plugged herring or filets of "bullhead" (sculpins).

South Sound Artificial Reefs Are Worth A Try

Of several artificial reefs that the state Department of Fisheries constructed around the sound in the late 1970s, two are located in south Puget Sound. Both provide the sort of habitat not widely available, thereby acting as magnets for structure-loving sport fishes such as rockfish, lingcod and greenling. They are marked with department signs.

One is located at Toliva Shoal, 1,300 feet northest of the Toliva Shoal navigational buoy in 60 to 90 feet of water. The other is at Itsami Ledge, 1,100 feet northwest of the South Bay navigational light in 50 to 70 feet of water.

Fly Fishing For Resident Silvers

Although there are fewer small silvers available in the late winter and early spring than in years past, there are still coho to be caught. And with any luck, a return to more bountiful fishing awaits in coming years.

The small, very active coho make exciting targets for fly fishermen who cast from small boats. The most popular areas in years past include the rips in Dalco Passage, Quartermaster Harbor and the Narrows; off points Fosdick and Gibson; and in Hale Passage, Drayton Passage and Hammersley inlets. However, they may be hard to find in some of those more southerly locations.

In January and February those who want to sharpen their fly fishing skills can do so on coho half-pounders (of 13 or 14 inches). Early in the year coho are small but relatively easy to catch. Bruce Ferguson was one of the first to really take advantage of these fish. He pioneered the fishery and has coauthored books on the subject.

Ferguson emphasizes the need for small patterns sparsley tied to a no. 6 or 8 hook (up to a no. 2 at the largest). A white wing with a fluorescent green or chartreuse body has been very effective for Ferguson.

Fluorescent pink and fluorescent white have also proven themselves effective colors. Ferguson suggests a 10- or 20-foot sink tip or the very slow sinking, intermediate fly lines. The fly is presented just under the surface, best retrieved fast in short, rapid jerks.

Look for the small silvers feeding at the surface when waters are calm. They can often be spotted jumping or line-feeding (with their noses or fins just breaking the surface). It may take a keen eye to spot them, an eye that fishermen like Ferguson develop from long experience.

Connecting with resident silvers requires the angler to lead a sighted fish much as a shotgunner leads a duck, casting a good 10 feet in front of the moving fish.

Fly fishing for these coho from a small boat requires as much as a 300-foot radius from other boats to permit free casting in all directions and enough distance to avoid spooking these often-spooky silvers.

Bottomfishing: Catch As Catch Can Until The Cod Return

Most of the south sound's submarine topography is smooth, varying from muddy to sandy. The bottom tends to be devoid of rocky areas. Decades ago, the few areas with rocky bottoms provided some good lingcod and respectable catches of rockfish and greenling. But the constant pressure in these areas took its toll and these large lings and rockfish are much fewer and farther between these days. On a hopeful note, some south sound veteran anglers note that numbers of small rockfish seem to be increasing.

There is a fair population of lingcod—some 30- to 40-pound fish—living under the Tacoma Narrows Bridge and around the wreckage of the old "Galloping Gertie" sunken in the narrows. It's a tough place to fish, but it is fished during the short open lingcod season each spring. Any bait or lure that takes lings will work, but large live herring—often available in the area by jigging—are hard to beat. Look for periods of light tidal flow—and bring plenty of terminal gear in any case. The Itsamni Ledge Reef is another good bet for south sound lings.

The outstanding fly and ultralight fishery for resident silvers in south Puget Sound hit the skids in the late 1980s but hopefully changing management techniques will bring this back.

The few piers from which south sound anglers can fish do offer a shot at pile and striped perch, particularly in the spring. Those that are lighted provide winter squid jigging at night.

In the 1970s and early 1980s, there were Pacific (true) cod and its relatives, pollock and hake, to keep sportfishermen busy—often hand-over-fist busy, so bountiful were numbers of these species. The true cod fishing bordered on sensational in the mid-1970s, when I recall multiple hookups of 10- to 15-pounders on some December drifts south of the Narrows.

Pollock seemed to be so thick they must have hidden the bottom in many areas, notably Point Defiance. The 1- to 4-pound panfish could be a nuisance to salmon fishermen but a delight to light-tackle enthusiasts looking for nonstop action. Some idea of how important they were: in the early 1970s, pollock accounted for about 5 percent of the south sound recreational catch. By the end of the '70s, that figure had soared to 70 percent.

Unfortunately, by the early 1990s there was scarcely a cod or pollock to be found in the south sound. Some put the blame squarely on commercial draggers and fisheries management policies permitting that, including Dewey Crocker, whose once-thriving Dogfish Charters operated several busy bottomfish charters but at press time was down to a single boat.

Others, such as Department of Fisheries bottomfish expert Greg Bargmann, are convinced that some natural phenomenon—perhaps a natural cycle or slight increase in water temperature—has made the difference.

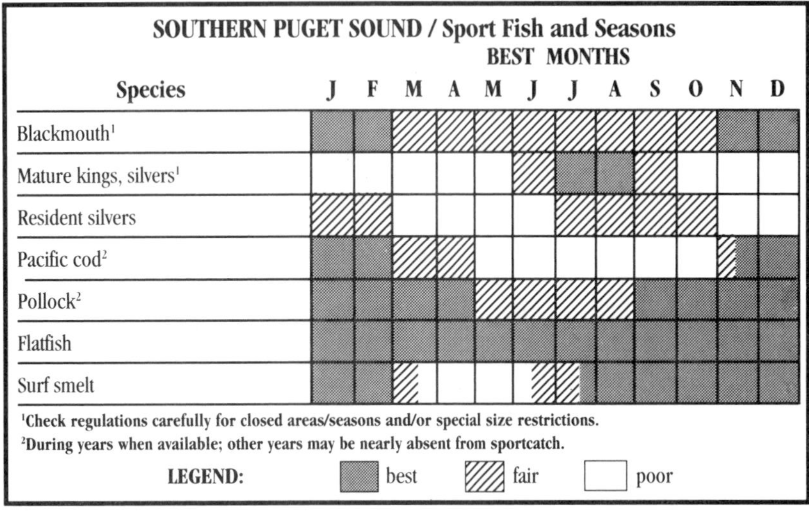

SOUTHERN PUGET SOUND / Sport Fish and Seasons

Species	J	F	M	A	M	J	J	A	S	O	N	D
	BEST MONTHS											
Blackmouth[1]	best	best	fair	fair	fair	fair	fair	fair	fair	fair	best	best
Mature kings, silvers[1]	poor	poor	poor	poor	poor	fair	best	best	fair	poor	poor	poor
Resident silvers	fair	fair	poor	poor	poor	poor	fair	fair	fair	fair	poor	poor
Pacific cod[2]	best	best	fair	fair	poor	poor	poor	poor	poor	poor	fair/best	best
Pollock[2]	best	best	best	best	fair	fair	fair	fair	best	best	best	best
Flatfish	best	best	best	best	best	best	best	best	best	best	best	best
Surf smelt	best	best	fair/poor	poor	poor	poor/fair	fair/best	best	best	best	best	best

[1]Check regulations carefully for closed areas/seasons and/or special size restrictions.

[2]During years when available; other years may be nearly absent from sportcatch.

LEGEND: best / fair / poor

Either way, the cod and pollock remain largely absent. But these are very fertile, fast-growing species and they are likely to come back strong.

When they do, break out the light gear. Lines testing 4-to 8-pound test are ideal for both cod and pollock and will give you a real battle out of these otherwise unimpressive fighters. Certainly any bait or lure will work for these. If you're not dunking herring, rely on jigs—1- to 4-ounce leadheads with plastic tails or metal jigs and spoons of similar size. They should be fished on bottom in 50 to 250 feet of water.

The most humble member of this codfish triad is the hake. They're small (not generally much over a couple pounds) and weak, but they can be remarkably abundant and easy to catch. And these toothy, bright-silver fish can be fine to eat if properly prepared.

The flesh of hake (known as "whiting" commercially) contains an enzyme that promotes a rapid softening after death. This can be minimized by immediate cleaning and icing. Some fishermen "butterfly" hake, removing not only head, gills and guts, but the entire backbone as well which can be pulled right out.

In shallow water, flatfish will readily strike artificials. This sole couldn't resist a Rapala minnow.

Unlike cod and pollock, which tend to remain very near bottom, hake migrate daily. Toward dusk they move upward in large schools to feed on small organisms that drift up toward the surface after dark. This explains why salmon fishermen often pick up hake early or late in the day. Many

Smelt By The Score

Long stretches of gravelly intertidal beaches of southern Puget Sound offer extensive spawning habitat for the surf smelt. Much of these beaches remain undeveloped and sufficiently undisturbed for smelt spawning.

Fishermen at these beaches at the right times can enjoy the fun of raking or dipping surf smelt. Those "right times" are early or late in the day during high slack water when smelt move to the water's edge to spawn, leaving eggs in the gravel. (Much spawning goes on after dark, also, if smelt can be located.) The high slack should be a tide of +7.0 feet to 11.0 feet, according to Washington Department of Fisheries research, since that is the tidal elevation at which smelt prefer to spawn.

Generally, smelt seek gravel of a certain size, typically known as "pea gravel" or very coarse sand. Avoid beaches that are composed mainly of fine sand or of larger, coarse gravel.

In calm waters, smelt can fairly readily be seen. A smelt "rake" is used—a rigid-frame dip net with a 5- to 6-foot handle attached at about a 45-degree angle to the mouth. Hardware cloth or netting with a mesh size not to exceed 1/2-inch is used for the net bag. By law, the bag frame can be not more than 36 inches across. (Mesh too fine slows the netting process from water resistance and collects too much gravel.)

The netting procedure is simple enough: the net is plunged into the water beyond a school of spawning smelt, then swept in toward the beach.

If raking is yielding dozens of smelt, keep in mind the daily limit is 20 pounds (and that the taking of smelt has been restricted to certain days of the week traditionally—check the regulations). That's 20 pounds of succulent little fish. Most seafood lovers, this one included, find true surf smelt decidedly preferable to the soft-bodied, freshwater Columbia river smelt (eulachon) so available in the spring.

Small Boat Safety

Most waters in southern Puget Sound are protected, with the area a maze of narrow, curving channels separated by islands and peninsulas. Less open than central or northern Puget Sound, the southern region is also less subject to rugged, wind-driven seas. Also, much of the area around Tacoma lies in a convergence zone that keeps it calm when waters to the north are breezy. However, sizeable rips and turbulent, swirling currents are a particular feature of the Tacoma Narrows and waters just north and south of that; small boaters with minimal power should use particular caution.

are caught from lighted piers at night. During the day they are likely to be in very deep water, at times well up off bottom (often showing as dark clouds on fishfinder screens).

One of the bright spots for anglers wanting something with white flesh is the many flatfish that live in the south sound's ideal habitat. Species such as rock sole and sand dabs are "just about everywhere," in the words of Greg Bargmann. Lyle Point (Anderson Island) is one of many outstanding areas—where much of the catch will be sand sole. The mouth of the Nisqually River may harbor good numbers of starry flounder.

Flatfish are very common in Commencement Bay—and a frequent catch of many pier fishermen there. However, these flatfish have been found to contain high levels of chemical contaminants. In fact, the bay has had the dubious distinction of being rated by the Environmental Protection Agency as one of the 10 worst hazardous waste sites in the U.S. (In the 1950s and '60s, Commencement Bay served as a depository for hundreds of thousands of tons of hazardous waste.) Most people who fish the bay these days are heeding the warning of state and federal agencies to avoid eating bottomfish. (Salmon caught in areas like Commencement Bay do not live and grow just in the bay and are thus not around long enough to concentrate metal and chemical compounds as do bottomfish.)

A species that south sound fishermen occasionally hook but don't always hang onto long enough to see is the

Occasionally hooked by south sound sportfishermen, big skates use their considerable surface area to put up tough resistance.

big skate. Dogfish Charters, which fishes heavy gear, has taken many of these 20- to 100-pound tacklebusters. They frequent sandy areas such as those around Point Defiance and Toliva Shoal, in 140 to 200 feet of water. Most are taken on herring.

Many skates that are brought to a boat are cut off by anglers who don't know what to do with them. That's a shame, since they are superb eating. In fact, they have at times been cut in large circular chunks and sold as "sea scallops." While the flesh may not taste exactly like fresh scallop, it *is* distinctively reminiscent of that mild delicacy. When cleaning the flat "wings," be prepared for nary a bone, but for sheets of soft cartilage enclosing layers of the large, round muscle segments.

As big as skates grow, they pale beside the enormous sixgill sharks that ply the deepest areas of the south sound. Rarely do people get a chance to see these resident sixgills up to 15 feet long, but they are around. Headlines were made in 1983 when a commercial netter pulled in 13 of these monsters one morning, north of the Nisqually area.

They generally live too deep for sport fishermen, which is just as well since only heavy-duty gear has much chance of raising one. Again, Dogfish Charters in past years as brought up several sixgills of at least 200 pounds each (and those were small individuals). They are reported to be very palatable.

By comparison, their cousin the spiny dogfish is a guppy. It can, of course, be a most annoying "guppy." A successful commercial fishery since 1975 has removed many of them from the south sound, but they are not exactly in short supply.

This sixgill shark was caught in South Puget Sound, to large to fit within the camera's frame.

Facilities

All phone numbers listed are within the 206 area code unless otherwise noted.

Charters

There have never been many charters in the protected, small-boat friendly waters of the south sound. But at least a couple were in operation at press time, charging $35 to 40 for a day of fishing.

Captain Jerry's Charters, 1100 Dock Street, (Totem Marina) Tacoma, 752-1100. Skipper Jerry Skeen fishes south sound salmon and bottomfish year-round aboard his 30-foot boat. He'll take up to 6 anglers.

Dogfish Charters, 8115 35th Street West, Tacoma, 564-6609. Skipper Dewey Crocker operates a 40-footer that will carry up to 18 anglers bottomfishing, which is what Dogfish Charters has always specialized in. Rockfish make up bulk of catches at press time, though surprises such as skates and sixgill sharks are always possible. Will target on cod and pollock when populations are healthy.

Marinas

Boston Harbor Marina, 312 73rd Avenue Northeast, Olympia (Budd Inlet near Dofflemeyer Point), 357-5670. Open year-round, 7 days week in summer, Wednesday-Sunday in winter. 6 slips for guest moorage. Fuel, bait and tackle available. Launching via a free paved ramp (not good on low tides).

Breakwater Marina, 5603 North Waterfront Drive, Tacoma (near Point Defiance Park), 752-6663. Open all year, 7 days/week. 200 moorage slips, reservations needed in season. Fuel available, also showers. Launch ramp at adjacent Pt. Defiance Park.

City of Des Moines Marina, 22307 Dock Avenue South, Des Moines 98198, 824-5700. 50 moorage slips, reservations not necessary but a 7-day limit on stay. Fuel, engine repair, bait and tackle available at marina. Hoist launch for boats to 26 feet long.

East Bay Marina, 1022 Marine View Drive Northeast, Olympia (east of Budd Inlet) 98501, 786-1256. Open year-round, 7 days/week. 754-1650. 75 moorage slips. No fuel here but available nearby. Good 2-lane paved launch ramp usable most tides. Showers, laundromat.

Fair Harbor Marina, Grapeview, 426-4028. Open year-round, 7 days/week. 60 moorage slips. Fuel, bait and tackle. Free launch ramp in good condition, functional on most tides. RV spaces.

Jarrell's Cove Marina, East 220 Wilson Road, Shelton (at the top of Harstene Island), 426-8823. Open year-round, daily in summer, closed Sundays in winter. 1,200 linear feet of tie-up transient moorage space. Fuel, bait and tackle, as well as laundromat, grocery, propane. Closest boat launch at Lattimer's Landing, next to Harstene Island bridge. Rents rowboats (no power). Also camping area with 24 RV spaces, half with hookups and half without.

Lakebay Marina, 15 Lorenz Road, KPS, Lakebay 98349 (across from Pemrose State Park), 884-3350. Open 7 days/week March 1st-December 1st. 6 moorage slips; reservations recommended. Fuel available by appointment. Bait and tackle, groceries. Paved ramp usable on most tides.

Narrows Marina, 9007 South 19th Street, Tacoma (just southwest of Narrows Bridge), 564-4222. Open 7 days/week, year-round. No moorage, though public buoys nearby. Fuel (no premix), engine repair. Great selection of bait and tackle in a complete tackle shop offering reel repair, saltwater downriggers, electronics and more. Launch ramp in pretty good shape, modest charge. Rents 14' aluminum skiffs with outboards.

Oly and Charley's Marina, 4224 Marine View Drive, Tacoma, 272-1173. Open year-round. 10 moorage slips; reservations recommended. No fuel, but engine repair available. Bait and tackle sold at the store. Hoist launch for boats to 26 feet.

Point Defiance Boathouse, 5912 North Waterfront, Tacoma (right at Point Defiance Park), 591-5325. Open year-round, 7 days/week. 10 moorage slips, fuel, bait and tackle, groceries. Public launch ramp a couple blocks away good on most tides. Rents 14' fiberglass skiffs with or without outboard. In business here for over a half-century.

Puget Marina, 8141 Walnut Northeast, Olympia (on Johnson's Point), 491-7388. Open year-round, 7 days/week. No overnight moorage. Fuel, engine repair, bait and tackle. Launch ramp in excellent condition, modest charge. Rents 14' boats with power.

Quartermaster Marina, 23824 Vashon Island Highway Southwest, Vashon Island 98070, 463-3624. Year-round, 7 days/week. Limited guest moorage available. No fuel or engine repair; limited supply of bait, tackle in nearby grocery store. Haul-out travel-lift launch will accomodate boats up to 10 tons.

Steilacoom Marina, 1st and Champion, Steilacoom, 582-2600. Open year-round, 7 days/week. 5 moorage slips; reservations requested. No fuel, engine repair. Bait and tackle. No launch facility here, but ramp 1/2-mile north. Rents 14-foot skiffs without power.

West Bay Marina, 2100 West Bay Drive, Olympia, 352-4863. Year-round, 7 days/week. 430 moorage slips. Fuel (including propane) and engine repair. Bait and tackle, small grocery, marine supply, restaurant nearby. Nearest boat launch is across at East Bay Marina.

Zittel's Marina, 9144 Gallea Street Northeast, Olympia (at Johnson Point), 459-1950. Year-round, 7 days/week. Guest moorage available. Fuel, engine repair, good selection of bait and tackle. Grocery store. Launch ramp in pretty good shape but not for very low tides, modest fee. Also sling launch for boats to 25 feet. Rents 14- to 24-foot boats with or without power. In business here since mid1950s.

Bait And Tackle Shops

This is a partial listing of bait and tackle outlets in the south sound area.

Agate Store, East 3841 Agate Road, Shelton (12 and 1/2 miles north on Highway 3, Hammersley Inlet), 426-4016. Open 7 days/week. Lots of gear for trout and salmon fishing.

B & I Sporting Goods, 8012 South Tacoma Way, Tacoma 98499, 584-3207. Open 7 days/week. Wide selection of tackle.

Bill's Boat House, 8409 Spruce Way Southwest, Tacoma 98498, 588-2594. Open 7 days/week, dawn to dark. Salmon trolling and steelhead fishing gear.

Northwest Fisherman, 10917 Canon Road East, Puyallup 98373, 536-8756. Open Tuesday-Saturday. Flyfishing equipment—including full line of saltwater gear.

Puget Sound Herring Sales, P.O. Box 275, Gig Harbor 98335, 265-2372. Open 7 days/week for herring.

The Reel Thing, 31211 Pacific Highway South, Federal Way, 941-0920. Open 7 days/week.

Totem B&T, 821 Dock Street, Tacoma 98402, 627-8055. Open 7 days/week during main fishing season.

Public Campgrounds

Cutts (Deadmans) Island State Park, 1/2-mile west of Kopachuk. Accessible by boat only. Primitive camping (no sites) on 6 acres, pit toilets only. Mooring buoys and underwater park for divers.

Dash Point State Park (Recreation Area), 5 miles northeast of Tacoma on Highway 509. 108 standard tent sites, 28 RV sites with hookups (to 35') and 2 primitive sites on 399 acres. No facilities for small boaters.

Eagle Island State Park (Natural Area), between Anderson and McNeil islands. Day use only; accessible by boat only. Mooring buoys. Watch that poison oak!

Jarrell Cove State Park (Recreation Area), at the northwest end of Harstene Island. 20 standard tentsites. Both buoys and excellent moorage floats in this protected cove. Private marina and grocery across the cove.

Kopachuk State Park (Recreation Area), 12 miles northwest of Tacoma off Highway 16 (watch for signs). 41 standard tent sites, 2 primitive. On Henderson Bay, mooring buoys, clamming year-round, boat launch nearby.

Penrose Point Recreation Area, 3 miles north of Longbranch on Highway 302. 83 standard tent sites, 2 primitive on 145 acres. Located on Carr Inlet; provides boaters with mooring buoys and floats. Good beaches for clams and oysters. Public boat launch.

Saltwater State Park (Recreation Area), 2 miles south of Des Moines on Highway 509. 52 standard tent sites on 88 acres. Below Kent Smith Canyon, moorage buoys, clamming.

Squaxin Island State Park (Recreation Area), between Shelton and Harstene Island, accessible by boat only. 20 primitive tent sites, no showers but offers boaters both buoys and moorage floats.

Stretch Point State Park (Recreation Area), 12 miles north of Shelton on Stretch Island, accessible by boat only. No campsites (day use only). Moorage buoys. One of nicest sandy beaches in south Puget Sound.

For More Information

Gig Harbor/Peninsula Chamber of Commerce, P.O. Box 1245, Gig Harbor 98335, 851-6865.

Olympia/Thurston County Chamber of Commerce, 1000 Plum Street, Olympia 98501, 357-3362.

Shelton/Mason County Chamber of Commerce, P.O. Box 666, Shelton 98584, 426-2821.

Tacoma Area Chamber of Commerce, P.O. Box 1933, 725 Broadway, Tacoma 98401, 627-2175.

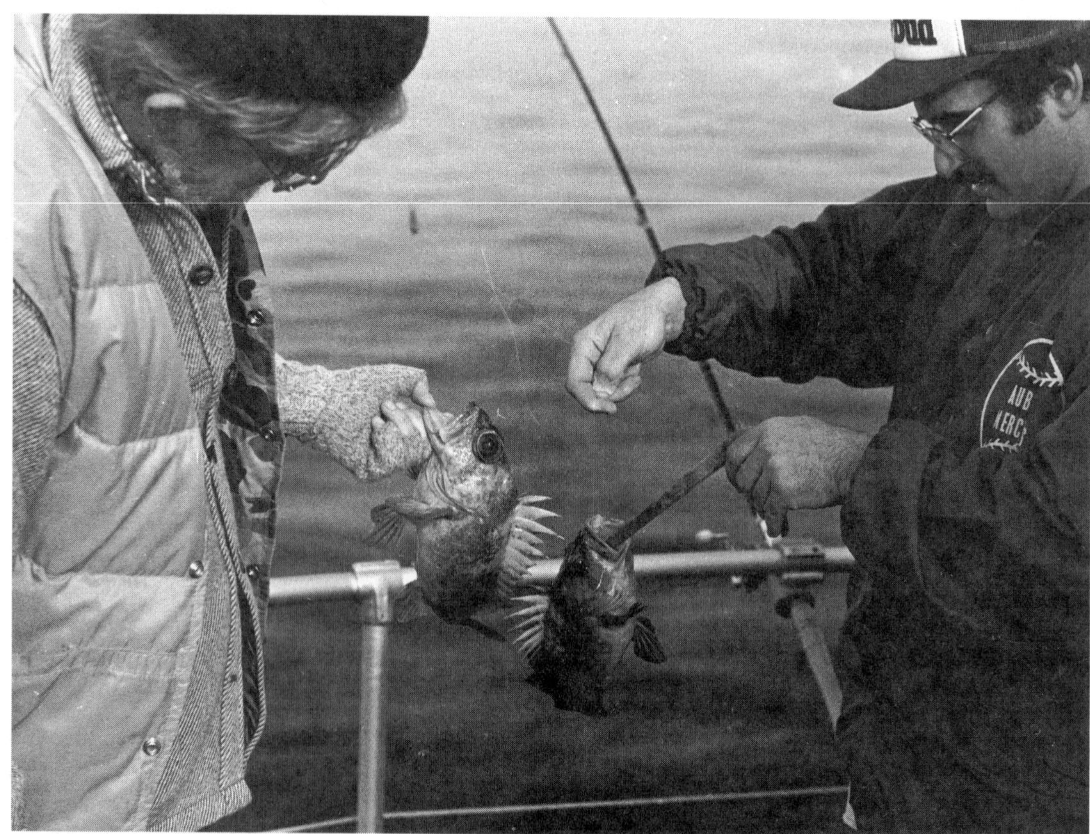

Rockfish can still be taken in fair numbers in south Puget Sound, but their average size has decreased over the years.

HOOD CANAL

A VERY DEEP, NARROW HOOKED FINGER THAT cuts into the base of the Olympic Mountains, Hood Canal has not offered great fishing for many years, but there are opportunities to catch fish and do so in a particularly unspoiled, scenic setting. Steep, fir-covered slopes of the Olympic foothills flank the canal.

The waters here are more often tranquil than in the expanses of Puget Sound. But they can get rough: in 1979, the floating bridge that spans northern Hood Canal—one of the world's longest floating bridges—actually broke apart and sank during a vicious storm that sent winds up to 100 miles per hour barreling down the canal. The middle third floated north a short distance before sinking to the bottom.

In the summer of 1982, the mouth of the canal became the scene of confrontations between federal officials and activists protesting placement of a Trident nuclear submarine base in the canal. Nevertheless, Bangor has since remained home and service port for Trident subs on the Pacific.

Facilities for anglers around the canal are decidedly limited. There are a few boat rental outlets and launch ramps but no year-round charters. Moreover, public shore access is generally quite limited in many areas, though the Department of Fisheries hopes to provide anglers more access in coming years.

Compared to Puget Sound, the smaller canal is much less varied in types of habitat. In only a very few areas do hard bottoms or rocky reefs add a signficant element of irregularity to the otherwise soft mud or sandy sides of the canal, which drop sharply to depths over 600 feet.

In the variety of fish species, too, the canal is less diverse. Blackmouth still offer sport but not as in years past. Sea-run cutthroat trout fishing, once a marvelous sport in the canal, dwindled considerably in the 1980s but management efforts may turn that around. Bottomfish tend to be mostly small rockfish and flatfish and, in past years, hake, though fishermen have shown no great interest in taking these species.

A considerable fall chum salmon fishery has developed in recent years. That—along with the hope of improved sea-run fishing and the good pink salmon fishing in many odd-numbered years—and better state shore access around streams and hatcheries has the potential to make Hood Canal one of the Northwest's prime spots for fly fishing and light tackle anglers.

SALMON FISHING: SOME BLACKMOUTH AND SEA-RUNS AND PLENTY OF CHUMS

Blackmouth are available in Hood Canal, but in limited supply. Those who hit it right, particularly during peak months of February and March, can limit out but that isn't a common event. Some years, blackmouth fishing can be good as early as November and remain good into May. Returning, mature chinook and silvers are occasional catches in late summer.

A glance at the map will show that most of the points jutting into the canal are favored salmon spots. Steep shorelines off bays and around peninsulas also harbor feeding blackmouth. Perenially popular spots include Misery Point, just north of Seabeck, and Hazel Point on the northeast corner of of the Toandos Peninsula. In the Great Bend area, much of the effort is concentrated around Ayres (''Bald'') Point.

Trolling seems more popular than mooching or jigging, perhaps because it allows anglers to cover more ground in search of salmon and because trolled lures don't appeal to dogfish which can be abundant. Some anglers still use diving planes or heavy sinkers (with a release) to get their offerings deep enough. But downriggers are increasingly popular, particularly with a mother-of-pearl or white Silver Horde plug trolled in 50 to 150 or more feet.

Late fall chum salmon fishing has seen a great surge in interest in recent years along the western shores of Hood Canal.

Any veteran Hood Canal chinook fisherman will tell you to be on the water before sunrise. It's an early morning show, here. Couple that time with a tide change, and expecting a hot bite becomes fairly realistic.

Resident silvers, once in great abundance, have largely forsaken the canal. At times they can be found, especially in spring, but don't expect much size—two-pounders are about it.

Pink salmon can provide Hood Canal anglers some consistent fishing during August and September of odd-numbered years. The strength of pink runs can vary greatly from odd-year to the next.

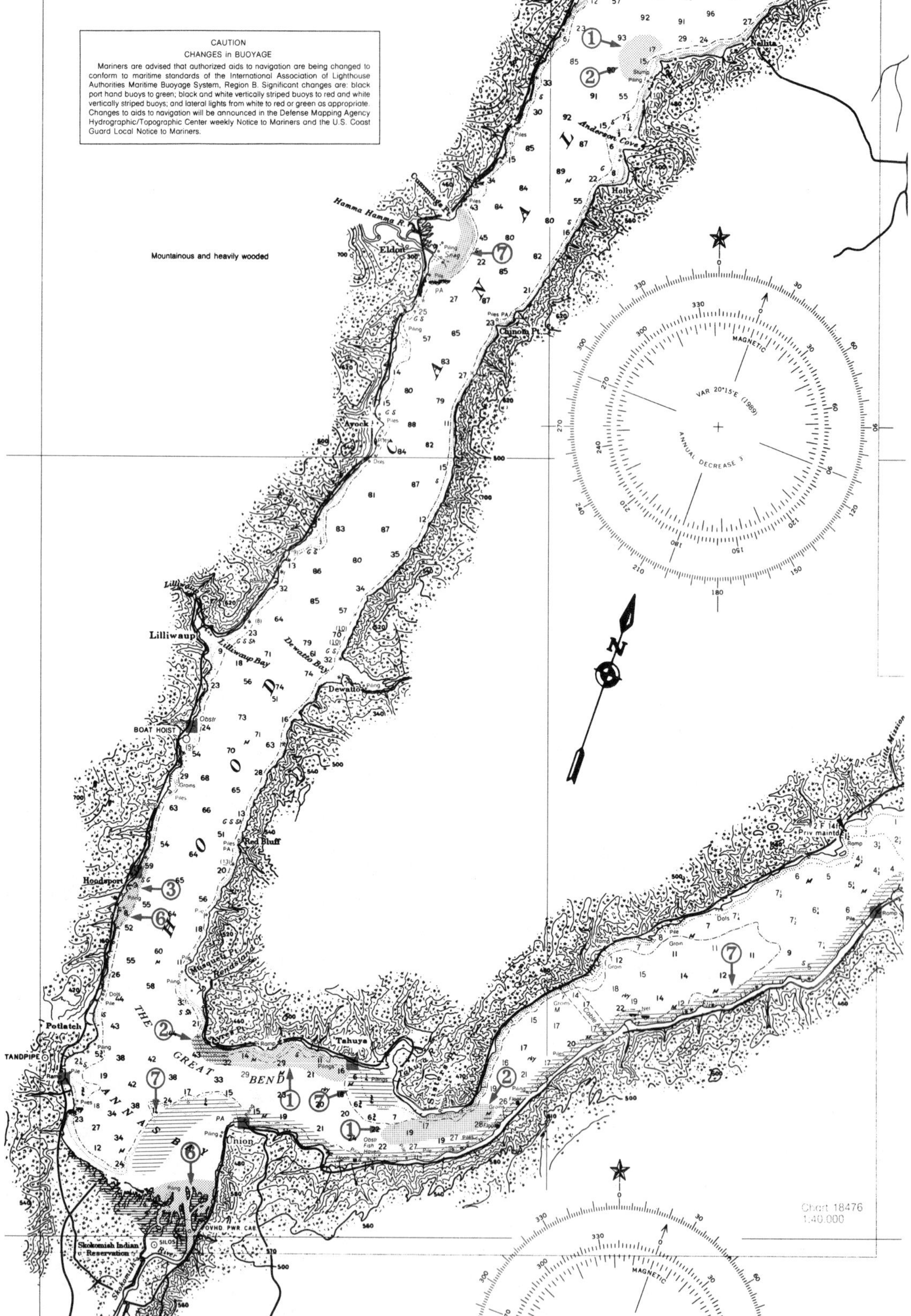

Hood Canal

Legend
1. Blackmouth, (winter, spring).
2. Silvers (fall).
3. Fall pinks—trolling, casting jigs.
6. Chums—casting flies.
7. Sea-run cutthroat.
■ Launch Site

Scale: 1/2'' = 1 nautical mile

Chart #18448

Not for navigational purposes.

One hotspot that produces particularly well is Pleasant Harbor on the west side of the northern canal, between the Dosewallips and Duckabush rivers. Try around Misery Point, also, and around the Hoodsport Hatchery. Many anglers troll a dodger and fly, squid or herring. Others cast metal jigs such as Buzz Bombs for the 3- to 7-pound "humpies," particularly when schooled in shallow water in September.

Pinks can also be a good target for fly fishermen. Fly fishing expert Bruce Ferguson suggests a small fluorescent pink or orange zooplankton fly (sizes no. 8 to no. 2). Retrieve in short strips (1/2- to 1-foot).

Traditionally, one of Hood Canal's finest fisheries—though utilized by limited numbers of anglers—has been its sea-run cutthroat trout. The gravelly beaches and river deltas that rim the canal are ideal habitat for sea runs which like to forage in such shallow subtidal waters.

Unfortunately, this is another fishery which saw a considerable decline in the 1980s. A reduction in population is blamed in part on the loss of areas of the ideal habitat described above. However, a tighter management response—a 14-inch size limit at press time and a two-fish

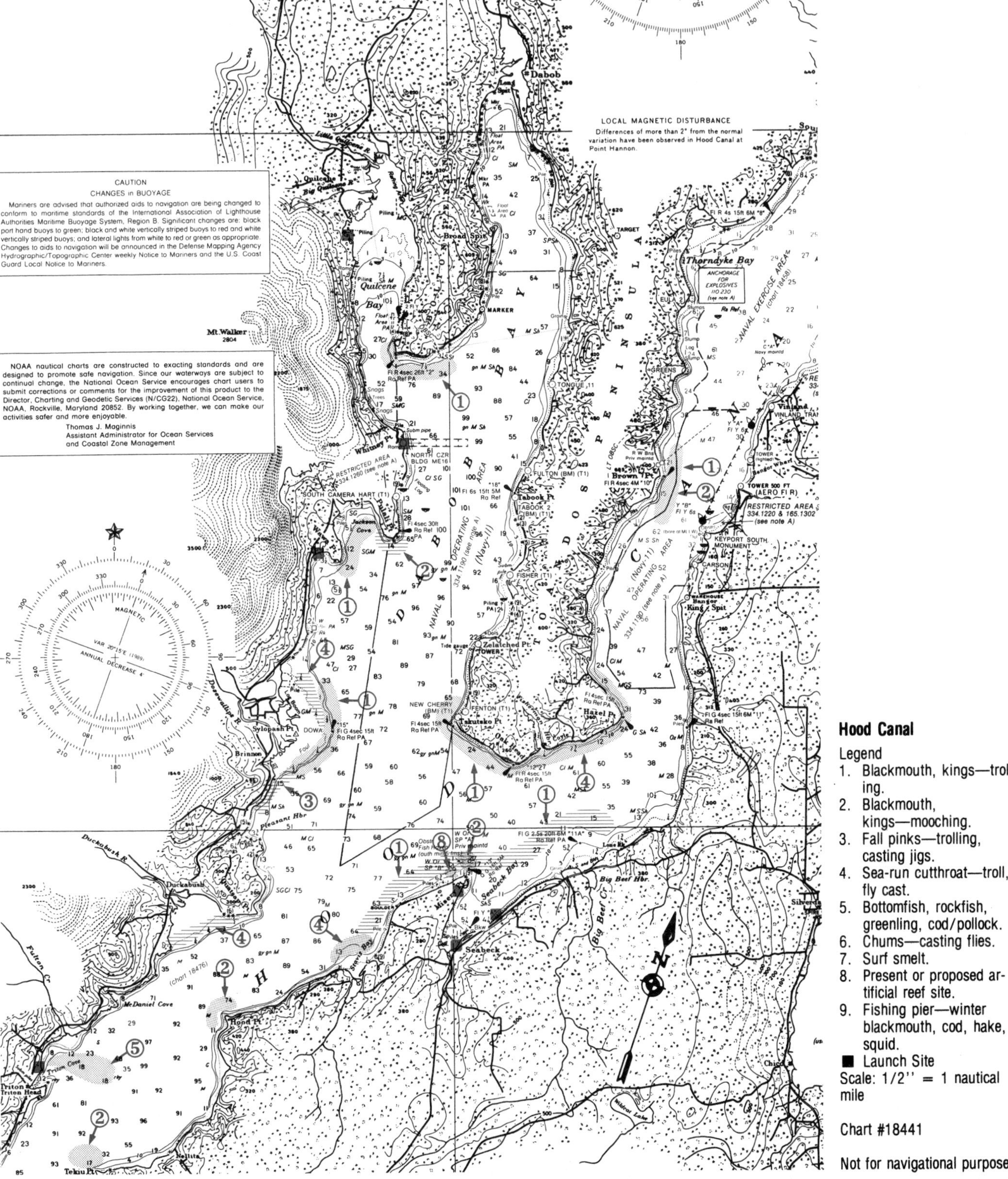

daily limit—may be putting new life back into populations of these valuable trout.

Sea-runs can be taken up and down the canal throughout the year, but best from late summer through late fall. Traditionally, the greatest effort has been in the Great Bend area, the canal's 90-degree elbow, particularly in areas such as the Tahuya River mouth (and west to Ayres Point) and the Skokomish River delta.

Most sea-runs are taken by trollers (in any manner of small boats, including canoes, kayaks and float-tubes). They follow a standard rule of thumb in sea-run fishing: If you can't see the bottom, you're fishing too deep. That translates into 10 feet or less. A lake troll spinner rig such as Pop Geer fished with a worm or a fly is popular. Also popular are small Dick Nites, Canadian Wonders, Triple Teazers; and a Martin No. 2CL spoon (white with red spots).

Fly fishing along beaches is a very effective technique for sea-runs. Fish flies in sizes from no. 8 to no. 4. Fluorescent colors with white wings are productive, as is a minnow imitation, fished on floating, sink-tip or intermediate fly lines.

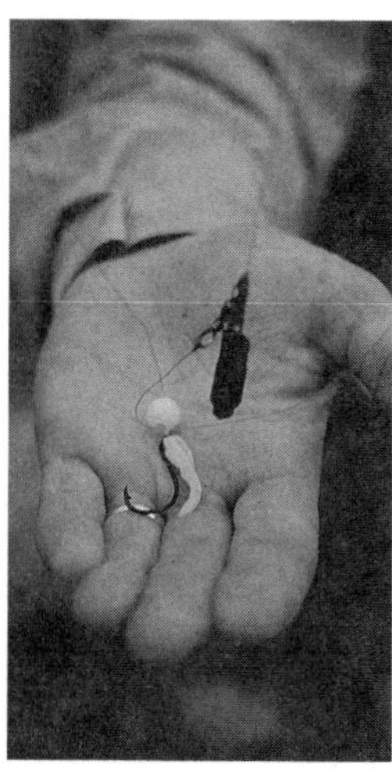

This simple rig—bright yellow bobber and chartreuse yarn on a black Gamakatsu hook behind a bit of pencil lead produced a limit of chums in short order. Tackle need not be fancy, but it should be fished slowly.

Some shore anglers report success for cutthroat stillfishing worms.

In the face of declines in some Hood Canal sport fisheries, chum salmon have offered a bright spot in recent years. Chums have always been the most abundant mature fall salmon in Hood Canal, with over a half-million spawners entering the canal many autumns. But until the 1980s, few anglers bothered trying to catch them. For one thing, their silvery shine is replaced with dark olive shading soon after entering the canal. Then, too, chums feed on very small fish and planktonic organisms; their relative disinterest in larger baits and lures has made them more valuable commercially than as a recreational fish.

But anglers have learned to utilize chums. Some take fair numbers each fall in north Puget Sound and upper Hood Canal by slow-trolling very small plugcut herring on a no. 1 or 1/0 hook.

Particularly exciting for Hood Canal fishermen has been the realization that amidst the hordes of chums milling outside Finch Creek at the Hoodsport Hatchery in October and November are fish that *will* strike properly presented flies.

Chums are very strong fighters, combining responses characteristic of both chinook and coho when hooked. They are great opponents on fly or ultralight tackle, particularly stubborn, slugging it out to the very end. Chums aren't exactly lightweight fish, either, running 5 to 18 pounds.

Most of the effort, from about midOctober through late November, is concentrated at the Hoodsport Hatchery, though there are other hatchery and wild runs (such as the Skokomish River's) that collect at other areas offering chums in somewhat less awesome numbers (but also in less crowded conditions).

The dramatic increase in popularity of chum fishing at Hoodsport strained the limited access, though in 1990 the Washington Department of Fisheries was working to improve that. Best fishing is on a rising tide, but that also poses a dilemma: The small intertidal spit in front of the hatchery lined with fishermen casting to salmon shrinks as the water rises, crowding anglers (and fish) and creating something of a circus. Weekday fishermen are much better off. Also, chest waders are an advantage at high tide, particularly. And float-tubes are increasingly popular here, permitting fishermen to get out past the mob. The smart anglers are careful not to spook these cautious fish.

In general, anglers have learned that small, bright flies fished s-l-o-w-l-y will attract strikes from chum. Bright green has been the most popular color. A bit of yarn on a no. 2 or 4 hook behind a bit of pencil lead or a split shot suffices for many anglers. But fly fishing purists may find something like "Dickson's Chum Candy" will work particularly well. The pattern is the invention of long-time guide Dennis Dickson, one of the pioneers of Hood Canal chum fishing. This is a lime-green fly on a no. 6 or 8 hook with 3 or 4 strands of misty-blue crystal flash fished on a floating fly line or a very slow sinking line. The retrieve should be in a 1- to 2-foot strip at medium speed. The same set-up behind a clear plastic bubble can be very effectively fished on light spinning or levelwind tackle.

These two chums (see photo, lower left) were caught within minutes of each other and typify the situation here in October as anglers hook not only dark bucks but bright fish, often hens, as well.

Some chums at the hatchery mouth will still be bright silver even well into November. Most, however, will be in dark fall colors, but not all such chums are soft-meated. Some are still firm and good eating. Even dark fish can be smoked successfully. But many fish are caught for the sport and released.

Take A Long Walk On A Short Floating Bridge

The Hood Canal floating bridge's misfortune during the great Columbus Day storm in 1979 ultimately became Hood Canal fishermen's fortune. In the mid-1980s, the Washington Department of Fisheries completed work to make the remaining east end of the bridge into a fishing pier. This offers a point of access to deep water for shore-bound anglers who generally find access to the canal tough up and down its length.

Anglers will find parking near the old toll booth and from there will find a walkway down to the bridge and a staircase to the pontoon atop which are catwalks with railings on both sides, extending out about 360 feet. Near shore the water depth below is about 50 feet; at the end it is at least 150.

The bridge is open year-round. Use is generally light, though a fair crowd gathers at times. All the canal's game fish species are hauled over the railings, including salmon. Catch rates are seldom high, but the price is right and the scenery is hard to beat at any cost.

Limited Bottomfish, Smelt-Dipping

Like southern Puget Sound, the floor of Hood Canal tends to be more mud than rock. The few areas that have at one time been productive for lingcod, rockfish and greenling tend to be fairly well picked over.

Some years hake can be numerous. Although these 1-to 3-pounders are hardly coveted game fish, they can be fun to catch and, if cleaned and iced immediately, fine eating. If they are around at all, hake are likely to be in good supply during late winter in Seabeck Bay, off Big Beef Creek and northwest of Hazel Point.

The few reefs extending upward from the depths may offer some rock-loving bottomfish. For example, directly out from Triton Cove is the largest such reef in the canal. Schools of black rockfish (''sea bass'') may be found in the canal and copper rockfish and greenling can be taken around kelp beds.

Anyone lowering lines into the depths could hook into a sixgill shark. One of the largest taken on rod and reel in the Northwest that I know of came from Hood Canal, a 13-footer.

Flatfish populations are still substantial. Several types are available in various soft/flat bottoms, particularly off river mouths. Some Hood Canal anglers have reported anchoring or drifting from skiffs and using light gear filling a bucket with small flatfish.

Small bottomfish like this cabezon are available wherever gravelly/rocky bottoms can be found as well as around the old floating bridge.

Perch can be found around rocky outcroppings and may be somewhat plentiful around docks with many pilings.

Hood Canal fishermen also have a shot at various bottomfish over the artificial reef created by the Department of Fisheries, located 600 feet north of the Misery Point navigation light in 45-100 feet of water.

And along the eastern end of the floating bridge, the department in 1983 completed construction of a catwalk on the lower pontoon level, extending out over 300 feet from shore.

A substantial population of surf smelt finds the beaches of southern Hood Canal to its liking. This includes most of the shoreline between Union and Belfair, particularly on the south shore of the canal, shading of trees and bluffs making this optimal spawning habitat.

Smelt can be gathered at high slack tides, much as described in the southern Puget Sound section, with nothing more than a pair of waders and a smelt ''rake.''

However, smelting may become increasingly difficult in the future. Shoreline development of the prime recreational property in this area has on the one hand severely limited access for smelt dippers and now threatens smelt spawning habitat itself. Hopefully this won't become another Hood Canal fish population in decline in coming years.

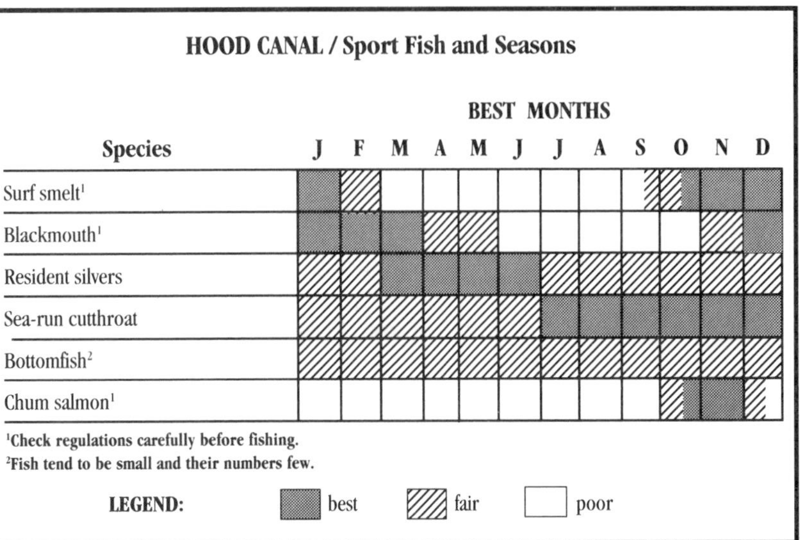

HOOD CANAL / Sport Fish and Seasons

Species	BEST MONTHS											
	J	F	M	A	M	J	J	A	S	O	N	D
Surf smelt[1]	best	fair	poor	poor	poor	poor	poor	poor	poor/fair	fair/best	best	best
Blackmouth[1]	best	best	best	fair	fair	poor	poor	poor	poor	poor	fair	best
Resident silvers	fair	fair	best	best	best	best	fair	fair	fair	fair	fair	fair
Sea-run cutthroat	fair	fair	fair	fair	fair	fair	best	best	best	best	best	best
Bottomfish[2]	fair	fair	fair	fair	fair	fair	fair	fair	fair	fair	fair	fair
Chum salmon[1]	poor	poor	poor	poor	poor	poor	poor	poor	poor	fair/best	best	fair/poor

[1]Check regulations carefully before fishing.
[2]Fish tend to be small and their numbers few.

LEGEND: best (shaded) · fair (hatched) · poor (blank)

Small Boat Safety

As serene as Hood Canal is much of the time, residents of the area know how quickly its surface can whip up into a raging chop when stiff southwest winds whistle up the canal's long fetch.

As one Seattle Coast Guard officer told me, ''The canal is not a good place to be in bad weather.'' He pointed out that its steep sides and long, straight southwest-northeast alignment provide a natural funnel. Sheltered areas along the shore can be hard to come by for considerable stretches.

All this simply requires common sense and some caution on the part of small boaters who fish the canal, especially in the popular, exposed areas around and south of the Toandos Peninsula.

There are no Coast Guard stations or ships on the canal. Rather, it is served by the cutter *Point Bennett* in Port Townsend (385-3070) and by the Seattle Coast Guard headquarters (442-5295 for recorded information or 442-5886 for a 24-hour operations line). Also, in emergencies, help may be available from U.S. Navy sources, which are a major feature of northern Hood Canal.

Its huge green eye in its eternal ghostly stare, this 13-foot sixgill shark hangs from a crane on a Hood Canal beach where an angler fishing alone in a small boat managed to noose it and tow it in.

FACILITIES

All phone numbers listed are within the 206 area code unless otherwise noted.

RESORTS

Mike's Beach Resort, N. 38470 Highway 101, Lilliwaup 98555, 877-5324. Open March-November, 7 days/week. 8 small cabins. Moorage on floats. Fuel but no bait and tackle. Excellent launch ramp for boats to 20 feet or so at a rather steep cost. A family operation, here since 1950.

Summertide Resort, Drawer E, Tahuya, 275-2268. Open year-round. 1 cottage plus RV spaces. 6 moorage slips; reservations requested. Fuel nearby. Bait and tackle available. Launch ramp at moderate cost, generally okay but not on low tides. Rental boats with power. Also laundromat, propane, great view of Olympics. Under fairly recent ownership, resort has been here since 1923.

MARINAS

Hjelvick's Store, 251 Hjelvicks Road, Brinnon 98320, 796-4720. Open year-round, 7 days/week. No moorage, but fuel, bait and tackle. Paved launch ramp good to a zero tide at very modest fee. This family-owned business has been here since before 1900.

Hood Canal Marina, P.O. Box 186 (on Highway 106), Union 98592, 898-2252. Open year-round, 7 days/week in the summer, Tuesday-Saturday in the winter. 100 moorage slips; reservation preferred. Fuel, engine repair, bait and tackle. Paved launch ramp okay but not on low tides. Also hoist launch for boats to 4,000 pounds.

Pleasant Harbor Marina, P.O. Box 116 (Highway 101), Brinnon 98320, 796-4611. Year-round, 7 days/week. 170 moorage slips; suggest reservations on holidays. Fuel, lots of bait and tackle. No launch facilities.

Seabeck Marina, P.O. Box 310, Seabeck 98380, 830-5179. Year-round, 7 days/week. 200 moorage slips, reservations recommended in season. Fuel, engine repair, plenty of bait and tackle. Hoist launch for boats to 21 feet (not on low tides). Rents 14' Highlaker boats without power. The major marina on east side of canal.

BAIT AND TACKLE

Belfair Hardware, P.O. Box 278, Belfair 98528, 275-2031. Open daily, year-round, selection of gear for trout and salmon.

Cove Park Grocery, 28453 Highway 0101 (about 3 miles north of Brinnon on Highway 101), 796-4723. Open daily, year-round. Wide selection of tackle.

PUBLIC CAMPGROUNDS

Belfair State Park (Recreation Area), 3 miles west of Belfair on Highway 300. 133 standard tentsites, 4 primitive and 47 RV sites (to 60') with hookups. No launch/moorage facilities, but on the water.

Dosewallips State Park (Recreation Area), 1 mile south of Brinnon on Highway 101. 87 standard tentsites, 2 primitive and 40 RV sites (60') with hookups on 425 acres. Good clamming and oystering.

Pleasant Harbor State Park (Recreation Area), 2 miles south of Brinnon on Highway 101. Primitive area—no numbered sites or showers, pit toilets. One acre. In sheltered bay, adjacent to private, full-service marina.

Potlatch State Park (Recreation Area), 12 miles north of Shelton on Highway 101. 17 standard tentsites, 2 primitive, 18 RV spaces with hookups on 57 acres. Moorage buoys.

Scenic Beach State Park (Recreation Area), 12 miles northwest of Bremerton on Hood Canal. 50 standard tentsites, 2 primitive. No moorage buoys or floats, but public launch ramp at Misery Point, 1 mile north. Oysters in season.

Tolmie State Park (Recreation Area), 8 miles northeast of Olympia. No campsites (day use only), but offers moorage buoy, access to underwater reefs for divers.

Twanoh State Park (Recreation Area), 30 standard tent sites, 8 primitive, 9 RV sites (to 35') with hookups on 182 acres. Launch ramp, moorage buoys and floats.

GUIDES

Dickson Fly Fishing Expeditions, 25122 115th Avenue Northeast, Arlington 98223, 435-5980. Dennis Dickson offers flyfishing expeditions from Mexico to Alaska—including fall chum salmon fishing action in Hood Canal.

FOR MORE INFORMATION

Shelton/Mason County Chamber of Commerce, P.O. Box 666, Shelton 98584, 426-2021.

Eastern Strait Of Juan De Fuca

The eastern strait of Juan De Fuca from Port Angeles to Port Townsend offers northwest sport fishermen a world unto itself. The area bridges the truly protected waters of the San Juan Islands and Puget Sound to the northeast and southeast, respectively, with the open ocean that enters the mouth of the strait to the west. The eastern strait is, in part, both of those areas and in part neither.

Boaters find few lee shores to fish but also find days calm enough to make long runs to the many offshore banks that account for much of the interest among sport fishermen in this area. Trophy sized chinook and some barndoor halibut have become a trademark feature of eastern strait waters.

Another trademark is the widespread use of metal jigs for salmon, a technique with its U.S. origins primarily in Port Townsend and Port Angeles beginning in the late 1970s.

Thanks to good year-round salmon fishing, a sizeable fleet of charters operates out of Port Angeles, Sequim and Port Townsend. Private boaters can find excellent public and private launch and moorage facilities in each of those areas.

Blackmouth, Halibut And Lingcod Fishing You Can Bank On, Winter And Spring

"The Garbage Dump," Coyote and Hein banks, Mid-channel Bank (actually just around the corner from the strait)—all name spots which have become synonymous with good and often sensational fishing from December into May for blackmouth. Often when Puget Sound winter blackmouth fishing languishes, anglers in the eastern strait still take limits.

Although blackmouth fishing can be good at times throughout the fall months, things really heat up here in the cold of winter. Several areas within a brief boat ride of Port Angeles ("PA" locally) can usually be counted on to produce chinook. One is "the Garbage Dump" (so named from its location off an old dump site high on a hill) a few miles west of PA. Baitfish concentrate in the protection of lee shelves along submarine ridges that rise from the surrounding, smooth bottom. The "Winter Hole" off the hook (look south to the Crown Zellerbach stacks) is always also popular for blackmouth. Farther out are three rises in the bottom known, respectively, as the "First, Second and Third Humps." Each is likely to harbor feeding blackmouth. These can be readily seen on a nautical chart (no. 18465).

As blackmouth remain active through the winter and into spring, the attention of many anglers shifts eastward and outward—to 10 or so nearshore and offshore banks.

These seamounts scattered about the eastern strait start coming alive with bait, both candlefish and herring, in February or so. Candlefish at times become so thick that fishermen jigging for salmon may repeatedly find two or three of them impaled on the lure's hooks.

Eastern strait blackmouth of 5 to 15 pounds are generally eager biters. Conditions here are conducive to any sort of fishing and all three major methods are in common use: jigging, mooching and trolling.

Drift-fishermen jig or mooch in from 60 to 200 feet of water. The list of metal jig brands is too long to warrant inclusion here. In the late 1970s only a few types were available but the method has proven itself so irrevocably that many manufacturers, large and small, local and far away, now market metal jigs. Still, many favor the locally-designed and produced jigs such as Point Wilson Darts and Terminators. The technique here is standard: jig the bottom for blackmouth, usually in upward lifts (not jerks) of 18 inches or so, dropping the rod tip fairly quickly so the jig flutters. Set the hooks the instant a fish is felt as there is seldom a second chance.

Many private boaters jig or mooch. Trolling is the method offered by most winter charter skippers, who have, over the years, provided a remarkably consistent record of limit catches. But at least one highly-regarded operation, Hi-Catch Charters, specializes in light-tackle drift mooching (year-round).

In April, "grand slam" catches become possible: chinook, halibut and lingcod. Spring is the best time of the year to find all three species over these banks and it is also the only *legal* time, since lingcod season has for many years opened on April 16 (through November). Halibut traditionally opened in February with first significant catches made in March, but the much tighter restrictions nowadays typically has the opening sometime in April (with a closure as early as June): this annually-assessed, quota-driven management approach can mean considerable variation from year to year, so find out each spring what the Pacific Halibut Commission's plan boils down to for sport anglers in the coming months.

All three species can be—and are—taken on metal jigs and mooched herring, often with salmon tackle. Big barndoors can spool a light salmon outfit in short order. But following a hooked fish and keeping on the pressure *can* wear down a halibut.

Baitfish move into the eastern Strait in great numbers during the winter. It's a welcome sign when candlefish and herring are thick enough to snag on lures jigged for salmon.

Some years ago, for example, one local salmon moocher headed out for a few hours of casual salmon mooching and came home with a 160-pound halibut. In 1988, a fisherman mooching a three-ounce white Pt. Wilson Dart in Freshwater Bay with 15-pound line brought home a 187-pounder. In fact, stories of that sort are not terribly unusual. Still, serious halibut fishermen tend to go with large Dacron-filled reels to lower stiff wire spreaders baited with large, whole herring. And, equally important, they go equipped to deal with a big halibut once it's at the boat.

How To Boat A Big Barndoor

Landing the typical "chicken halibut" of 20 or 30 pounds can be accomplished, as it often is, with a sturdy salmon net. Still, I prefer a gaff with a small (three-inch gap) hook on a four-foot handle (like those used in southern California). They're quick and sure.

The real trick for the halibut fisherman comes when a fish weighing in the three digit range is next to the boat. Simply dragging such a fish into a small boat is not a suggested option. These are very powerful fish, almost always showing plenty of reserve strength to thrash about once hauled right out of the water. Since most of their body is muscle, the thrashing of a halibut nearly as big as a man can do serious damage. In fact, halibut have been known to smash tackle and even human limbs. (In one celebrated case, an older commercial fisherman was found dead on his boat, along with a huge halibut he'd caught and gotten aboard.)

Noosing and dragging a subdued halibut may be safer than bringing it aboard a small boat.

Many anglers who regularly fish the strait, east and west, carry a gun (unfortunately often a pistol; a shotgun is less hazardous, of course) which can be marvelously persuasive when subduing an angry halibut. The other increasingly omnipresent piece of gear is a flying harpoon. This is a harpoon on a long pole with a detachable head. This is thrust downward into *and through* the fish (preferably its head), so the pole can be tossed back into the boat, leaving the halibut connected to a buoy line with a length of cable and rope.

"Hog-tied" halibut (lure still in mouth) cannot suddenly come to life and wreak havoc.

Small boaters may not want to devote space to a flying harpoon. An excellent alternative is a flying gaff, much the same but on a short gaff pole is a detachable, barbed gaff hook, onto which a rope is tied (which is held separately when the hook is driven home). One advantage of this method is that it is in compliance with rules of the International Game Fish Association for landing fish—just in case a halibut should happen to be a potential line-class world record.

At the very least, carry a big shark hook wrapped with 50 feet of 1/4-inch nylon or poly cord. Not as effective as a harpoon, but a whole lot better than nothing.

Lacking a gun, one may be able to slash the gills of a halibut and allow the loss of blood to sap its strength. Another sure approach is to noose a big halibut, having a partner slip a noose over the rod, down the line and around the halibut to the caudal peduncle (small area ahead of the tail) before cinching tight. It can then be dragged into port.

Finally, a suggestion for any good-sized halibut that is brought into a boat and hasn't been shot. They generally do "wake up" at some point and, boy, are they mad! Hogtie a halibut when it's first brought aboard and you'll have no worries. Simply run a piece of thin rope through its mouth and gills, tying it tightly. Then tie the other end around the caudal peduncle, pulled tight so the fish's tail is only a few inches from its mouth—that is, so its body forms a U or almost a circle. Then it will be impossible for the halibut to thrash about, wherever it is stored.

Although some lingcod are taken over smooth plateaus along with salmon and halibut, most dwell in the rockier sections of these banks. Occasional yelloweye rockfish are caught, as well. And, while anglers are generally after bigger targets, sometimes fair numbers of 3- to 5-pound quillback rockfish are there for the taking.

Serious Eastern Strait anglers know its banks as well as a Zurich businessman knows his. Some productive spots are but mere pimples protruding from the depths, while others are vast plateaus. Loran works wonders, but some bigger banks can be fairly easily located with a bit of skill and luck (by heading to small clusters of boats seemingly adrift in the middle of nowhere—or by hopping aboard and charter).

Despite their relative proximity, each bank differs in shape, substrata, current patterns and other factors that can mean hot fishing over one yet barely a sign of life on a bank just a few miles away. The following is an angler's bank-by-bank synopsis of the eastern strait, starting from the west. (Loran TD numbers are at the end of each description in parentheses.)

"**The Rockpile**"—Longtime favorite P.A. bottom fishing hole, lingcod are still taken here, along with quillback and some yelloweye rockfish, but fewer than in years gone by. But still, the greatest numbers of real monster barndoor halibut seem to come from The Rockpile each spring. (Several from 100 to 200 pounds are hauled up here in the spring of many years.) But halibut action in early spring may be nil until Indian longline quotas reached and the gear pulled. (28525.0, 42176.0)

"**31-36**"—The simple term used locally to describe this lump rising to 31 fathoms, about five miles north of Green Point. Good bet for big flatties, if you're willing to put in time. Many accounts of monsters hooked, never landed. Lings here and there are likely when bait is thick. (28500.0, 42180.0)

"**Green Point Bank**"—is actually the edge of a shore-abutting dropoff. Nevertheless, it consistently produces blackmouth and, by May, spring-run kings (though these may be illegal to keep over 30 inches—check the regs). Halibut frequently get into the act. The proximity to P.A. makes this a favorite area for those in small private boats and slower charters. Some troll the 17-fathom line. The 28-fathom circle is often productive (line up house on shore with notch in stand of large poplar trees forming a "gunsight"). Dogfish can be a killer here for moochers. (28470.0, 42185.0)

"**Coyote Bank**"—Until recent years, this remained a well-kept secret of locals, reached by Loran-C or spotting other boats already on the bank. Among these banks, Coyote has proven one of best early producers of big blackmouth, with bait and the bite building by February. It's oriented such that long tide drifts across it are possible. Some prefer the northern half for salmon, others the southwest corner. Halibut are taken on the smoother south half. Know where you're fishing on Coyote. The Canadian authorities will know; they own half the bank split by international boundary and fishing the "other" side without Canadian sport license not recommended. (28535.0, 42205.0)

Middle Bank—This enormous plateau at the lower end of Haro Strait offers a variety of habitat and a shot at anything that swims these waters. This is also covered in the San Juans Islands section but is so extensive that it really is part of both the islands and the eastern strait. Notably, no other eastern bank offers so much ideal irregular, rocky habitat as northern Middle Bank, with its substantial lingcod and rockfish populations. But it's in an area often tough to fish unless tides are reasonably light. The huge smooth south part, more fishable even with a fair current, accounts for halibut and spring salmon. Middle Bank is a considerable run from anywhere except San Juan Island or Victoria, B.C. (28575.0, 42245.0)

Hein Bank—Another huge bank, this one sits about as much in the middle of everything as possible. Hein has justifiably gained a reputation as a blackmouth hotspot, with March starting a peak period when it may teem with candlefish for many weeks. One formula for success: fish the southwest corner during ebb tide in 22 to 28 fathoms. In summer, concentrations of bait may attract kings, but few boats fish it for salmon. In April and more in May expect many halibut to come from predominantly gravel/cobble bottom. (28505.0, 48238.0)

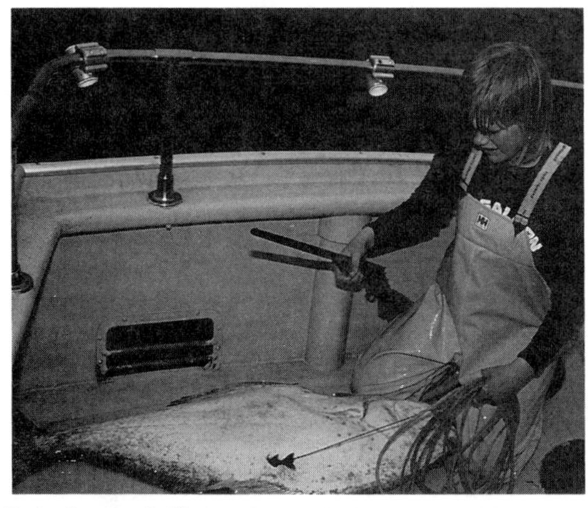

Tools of serious halibut anglers' trade. Deckhand pulls flying harpoon head from fish, still holding shotgun with which she lobotomized the fiesty fish.

Eastern Bank—Although it attracts less attention than many areas, Eastern can offer a bit of everything. Some years it proves to be one of the top producers for eastern strait halibut. Lings can be taken around the edges. Blackmouth fishing may peak by March. Dogfish at times will prove annoying. (28480.0, 42200.0)

"Dungeness Bar"—This relatively shallow plateau takes up a large area just northeast of Dungeness Spit. Part of this spot called the "target area" can offer great action for summer kings. Dungeness is practically in the backyard for those launching/mooring at Sequim. Where the northern edge drops into deep water of the strait look for both blackmouth and halibut in spring and all summer for big, mature chinook. Its east-west orientation offers pleasantly long drifts. (28455.0, 42230.0)

Dallas Bank—A shallow bank stretching far north of Protection Island. Fish the northernmost flat plateau of 20 to 30 fathoms and you're likely to find halibut. They often lay atop the edges. Dallas has been downright poor for salmon the last two/three years (but has offered no shortage of dogfish). Still, it may be worth a look now and then. Things change.... (28435.0, 42255.0)

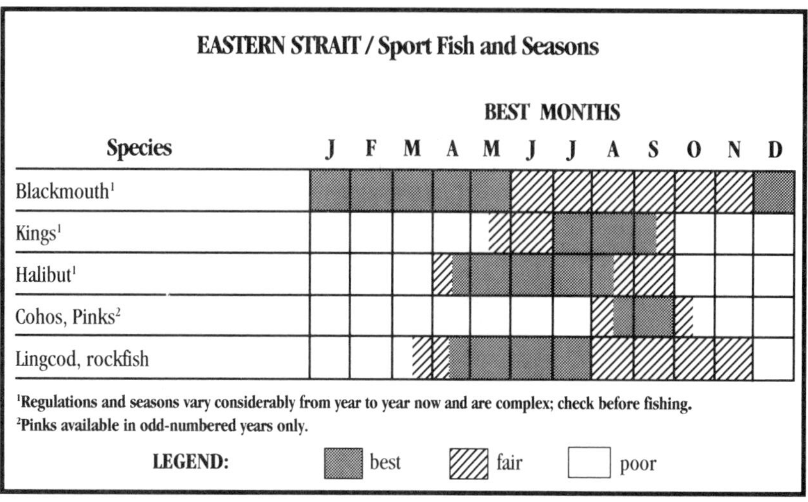

EASTERN STRAIT / Sport Fish and Seasons

BEST MONTHS

Species	J	F	M	A	M	J	J	A	S	O	N	D
Blackmouth[1]	best	best	best	best	best	fair	fair	fair	fair	fair	fair	best
Kings[1]	poor	poor	poor	poor	poor/fair	fair	best	best	best/fair	poor	poor	poor
Halibut[1]	poor	poor	poor	fair/best	best	best	best	best/fair	fair	poor	poor	poor
Cohos, Pinks[2]	poor	poor	poor	poor	poor	poor	poor	fair/best	best	fair/poor	poor	poor
Lingcod, rockfish	poor	poor	poor/fair	fair/best	best	best	best	fair	fair	fair	fair	poor

[1]Regulations and seasons vary considerably from year to year now and are complex; check before fishing.
[2]Pinks available in odd-numbered years only.

LEGEND: best fair poor

Partridge Bank—In the strait's very easternmost reaches, another vast plateau. Partridge is reached pretty readily from Port Townsend or Deception Pass in decent weather. Line up the two buoys and head south to the dropoff in about 110 feet and you may find salmon. It's no secret—but it works. Jigging ebb tide is a good way to hit blackmouth and avoid doggies. Then head west and drift in 20 to 22 fathoms for halibut, all along the southwest tongue. (28440.0, 42285.0)

Beware The Perilous Open Strait!

Stiff winds are hardly unexpected on the Strait of Juan de Fuca. It is a natural funnel for west or east winds which can come up quickly. For that reason, even in calm weather, no one should venture out to fish midstrait banks—however hot the bite may be—in a boat that isn't large or seaworthy enough to make the same run back in big seas.

On Saturday, May 5, 1990, the fishing was pretty good and the weather was fantastic. The entire strait was a millpond—calm enough to paddle across it in a canoe, it seemed.

According to reliable reports—for one, from Mike Schmidt, a Department of Fisheries patrol officer and veteran strait angler—no more than a slight breeze had rippled the surface by 12:30 pm. Schmidt reported his experience to Brad O'Connor, who in turn published the account in his "Fish and Wildlife Notebook" column in the May 13 **Seattle Times.** The horizon had held no hint of anything bigger to come, he told O'Connor.

Yet within only 20 minutes the west wind had hit 25 knots, Schmidt said and shortly it was up to 50 knots. Amazingly, most of the boats out fishing that day made it back through the 10-foot troughs that quickly replaced the glassy-smooth surface. At least five anglers did perish that day, however, a deadly reminder to never take calm seas for granted on the Strait of Juan de Fuca.

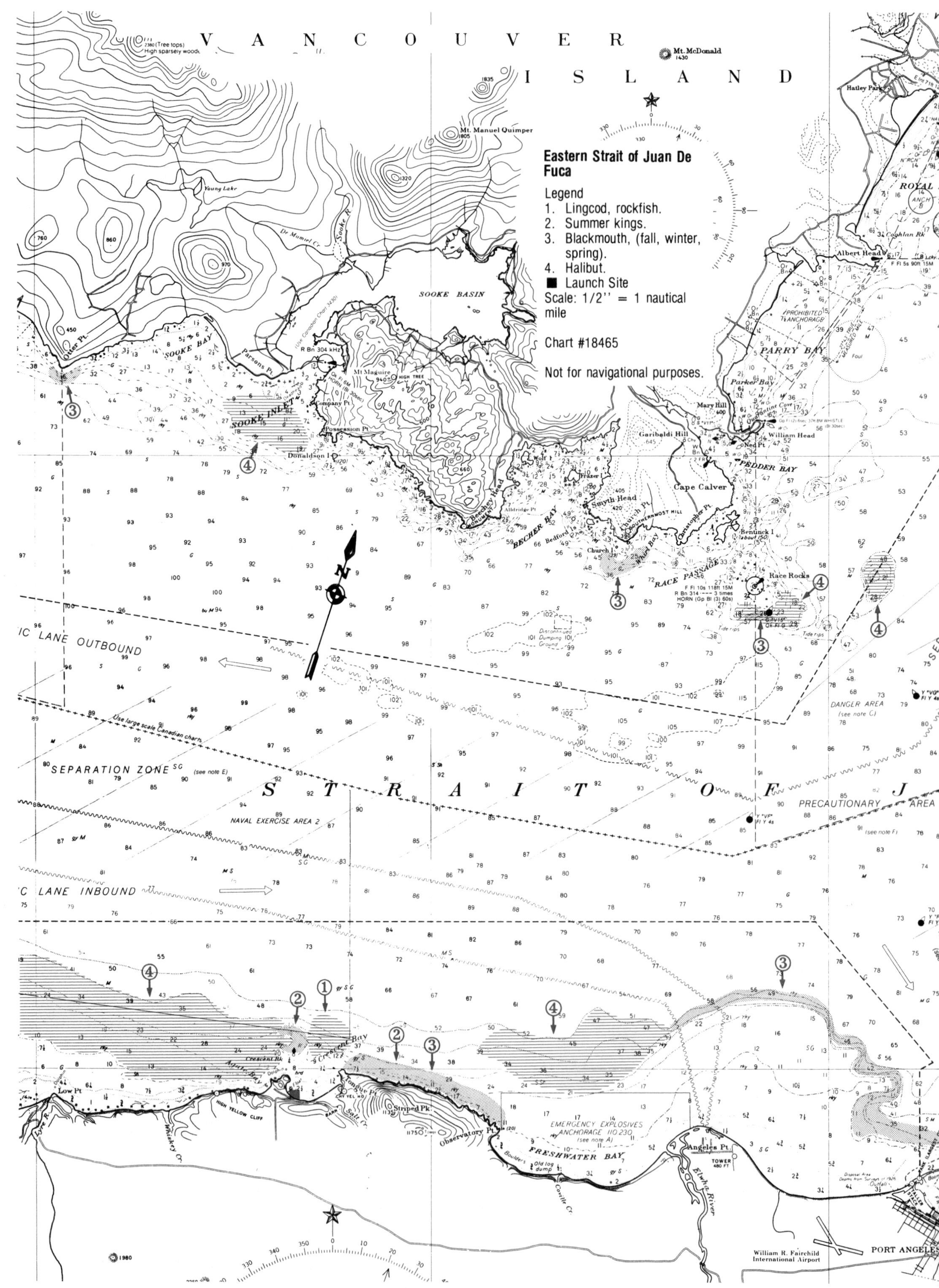
Eastern Strait of Juan De Fuca
Legend
1. Lingcod, rockfish.
2. Summer kings.
3. Blackmouth, (fall, winter, spring).
4. Halibut.
■ Launch Site
Scale: 1/2'' = 1 nautical mile
Chart #18465
Not for navigational purposes.
VANCOUVER ISLAND
Mt. McDonald
Mt. Manuel Quimper
Young Lake
SOOKE BASIN
Sooke R.
SOOKE BAY
Otter Pt.
Parsons Pt.
SOOKE INLET
Company Pt.
Possession Pt.
Donaldson I.
Mt Maguire
Beechey Head
BECHER BAY
Bedford
Church
Whirl Bay
Smyth Head
Frazer
Wolf I.
Garibaldi Hill
Mary Hill
Cape Calver
Christopher Pt.
Bentinck I.
RACE PASSAGE
Race Rocks
William Head
Ned Pt.
PEDDER BAY
PARRY BAY
Parker Bay
Albert Head
Coghlan Rk
ROYAL
Hatley Park
PROHIBITED ANCHORAGE
Discontinued Dumping Ground
TRAFFIC LANE OUTBOUND
SEPARATION ZONE
NAVAL EXERCISE AREA 2
STRAIT OF J
PRECAUTIONARY AREA
DANGER AREA
TRAFFIC LANE INBOUND
Low Pt
Lyre R.
Whiskey Cr.
HIGH YELLOW CLIFF
Crescent Rk
Crescent Bay
Agate Bay
Tongue Pt.
Salt Cr.
Striped Pk.
Observatory Pt.
EMERGENCY EXPLOSIVES ANCHORAGE 110.230
FRESHWATER BAY
Old log dump
Colville Cr.
Elwha River
Angeles Pt.
TOWER
William R. Fairchild International Airport
PORT ANGELES

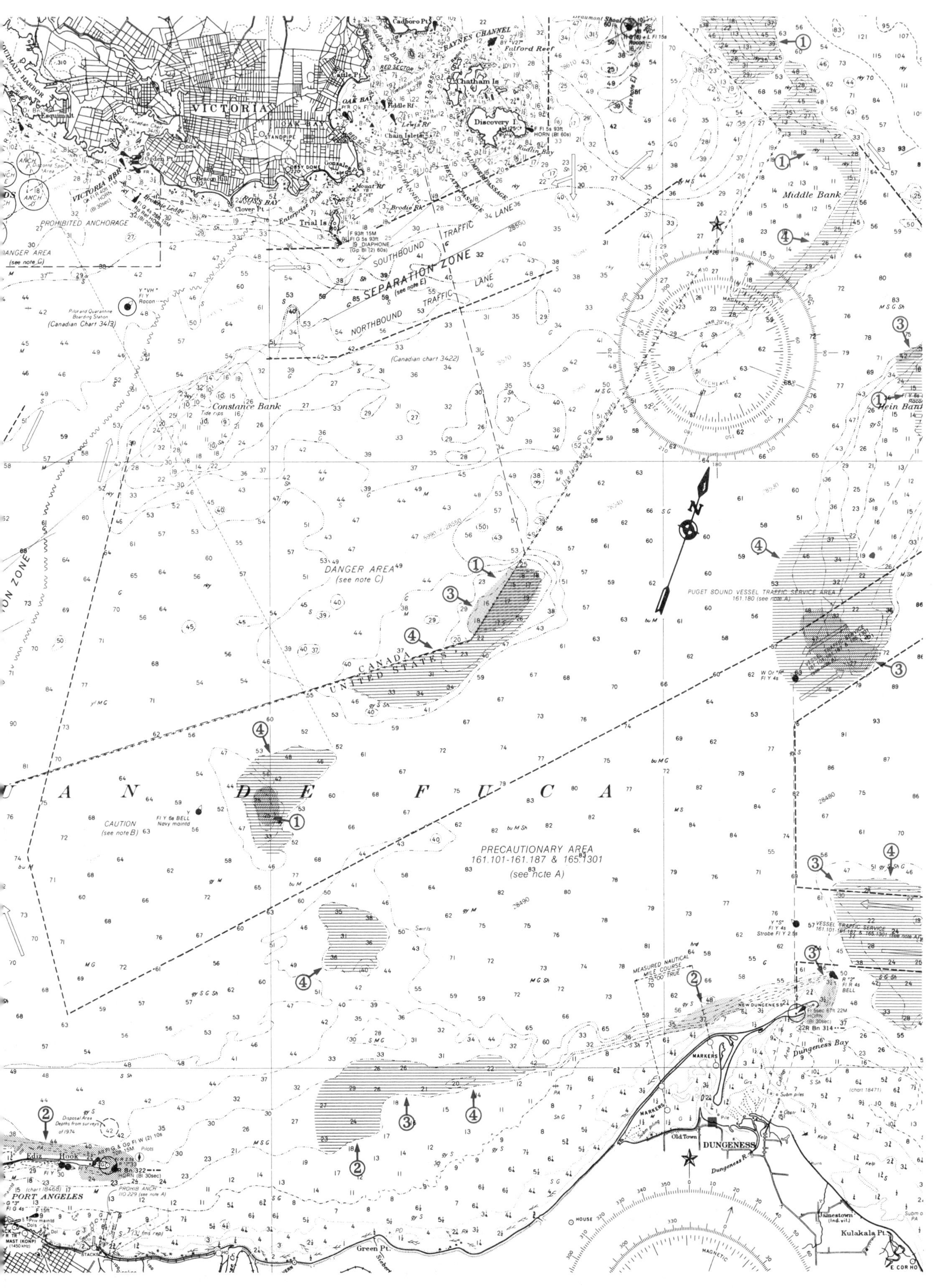

VICTORIA
OAK BAY
Cadboro Pt.
BAYNES CHANNEL
Fulford Reef
Chatham Is
Discovery I.
Oak Bay
Chain Islets
Lewis Rf
Fiddle Rf
Gonzales Pt
Trial Is
Enterprise Chan
Clover Pt
ROSS BAY
Brodie Rk
Beacon Hill
Ogden Pt
Esquimalt
ESQUIMALT HARBOR
VICTORIA HBR
PROHIBITED ANCHORAGE
DANGER AREA (see note C)
SOUTHBOUND TRAFFIC LANE
SEPARATION ZONE (see note E)
NORTHBOUND TRAFFIC LANE
Pilot and Quarantine Boarding Station
(Canadian Chart 3413)
(Canadian chart 3422)
Constance Bank
Tide rips
Middle Bank
Hein Bank
DANGER AREA (see note C)
CANADA
UNITED STATES
PUGET SOUND VESSEL TRAFFIC SERVICE AREA 161.180 (see note A)
J U A N D E F U C A
CAUTION (see note B)
Fl Y 6s BELL Navy maintd
PRECAUTIONARY AREA 161.101-161.187 & 165.1301 (see note A)
VESSEL TRAFFIC SERVICE 161.101-161.187 & 165.1301
MEASURED NAUTICAL MILE COURSE 75°00' TRUE
NEW DUNGENESS
Dungeness Bay
MARKERS
Old Town
DUNGENESS
Dungeness R.
Jamestown (Ind. vil.)
Kulakala Pt.
Disposal Area Depths from surveys of 1974
Ediz Hook
PORT ANGELES
(chart 18468)
PROHIB ANCH 110.229 (see note A)
Green Pt.
MAGNETIC

To a considerable extent, metal jigging for salmon in the U.S. began in Port Angeles and Port Townsend. Today a wealth of jig makes and styles are available.

Summer Crowds Hammer The Hook And Hit The Spit For Big Kings

Good king fishing areas stretch up the strait along the shore from Freshwater Bay past Port Angeles all the way to Point Wilson, the southeasternmost point of land in the strait. The big ocean fish begin cruising through this area in May and increase in number until a June-midSeptember peak.

Years back, the presence of big kings was all anyone here needed as an excuse to head for the hook. But it ain't necessarily so any more. Kings are tightly regulated, and waiting to determine the year's various size and seasonal restriction schemes have become an annual winter event. When uncertain, check regulations carefully and make no assumptions: some summers, the area may closed to all salmon sportfishing at least one day each week in addition to the possibility of a 30-inch maximum for many weeks.

Years ago, true (Pacific) cod offered a very busy, viable winter sportfishery in the strait around Port Angeles. That faded in the 1980s, but could return at any time.

The long-standing interest in big kings among PA residents is evident in the city's annual salmon derby, typically on Labor Day weekend, offering thousands of dollars worth of prizes.

Many trollers work the area of Freshwater Bay and the Garbage Dump west of PA. But probably no area attracts more effort than Ediz Hook itself, right at the mouth of the PA harbor. "The hook" has some strong assets to attract salmon anglers. It's just around the corner from a fine, protected multilane public launch ramp inside the harbor so on calm mornings even cartoppers can fish secure in the knowledge that freshening breezes will find them literally five minutes from protection. And the fishing is close in—no long offshore run. But best of all is the hook's productivity. It offers consistently good fishing for big kings.

Most who fish the hook in the summer driftjig or driftmooch. Things tend to get rather crowded along the hook for trolling. Effort is concentrated early in morning and late in the evening. The catch rate may drop off markedly during the main part of the day but very experienced skippers like Paul Ingham insist that "the bite" happens unpredictably at any time of the day, particularly around tide changes whenever they occur.

A reliable rule of thumb is to fish the 20-fathom line along the hook. Since along the outer side of the hook the depth plummets sharply away from the bank, most effort here occurs very near shore. Usually the tightly-packed line of boats indicates where this line is, in case your boat lacks a depthsounder. Later in the day the salmon may be more scattered, evident from the fishing boats, fewer in number and more scattered also. The kings may be much deeper as the sun reaches higher into the summer sky. If fishing's still slow, consider trying the Winter Hole or the humps beyond.

More king spots lie to the east, with Green Point Bank a favorite. Fish the dropoff in 20 to 30 fathoms. Dogfish may deter moochers at times, but king fishing can be excellent. Dungeness Spit, the shore along the Miller Peninsula and the south edge of Dallas Bank are all good king fishing.

Point Wilson at Port Townsend is a natural place for kings to congregate as they migrate, turning the corner south into Puget Sound. A substantial back-eddy forms inside the sandy, very steep point and at times a sizable flotilla of boats from kayaks to motor yachts stacks up to jig or mooch. Drifts are started in close to the point, nearly up on the beach. Best time to fish here is around a tide change; later, a hard-running tide may make driftfishing tough.

But trollers can keep plying the area, provided they stay away from drift-fishermen at the point. Most work the ledge just north of the point, along the buoy.

That the drifts begin so close to shore, that the dropoff is very steep and and that public access is easy since the point is part of Fort Worden State Park add up to this reality: Point Wilson is one of the better spots from which to connect with salmon while casting from shore. Any variety of metal jigs works when salmon are feeding near the point.

Silvers and pinks are taken when they're in, later in the summer. And Pt. Wilson can offer good winter blackmouth fishing.

Coho And Pinks In The Rips, Smaller Bottomfish Near Shore

During the late 1970s and early 1980s, interest in eastern strait silver fishing waned, but since then it has

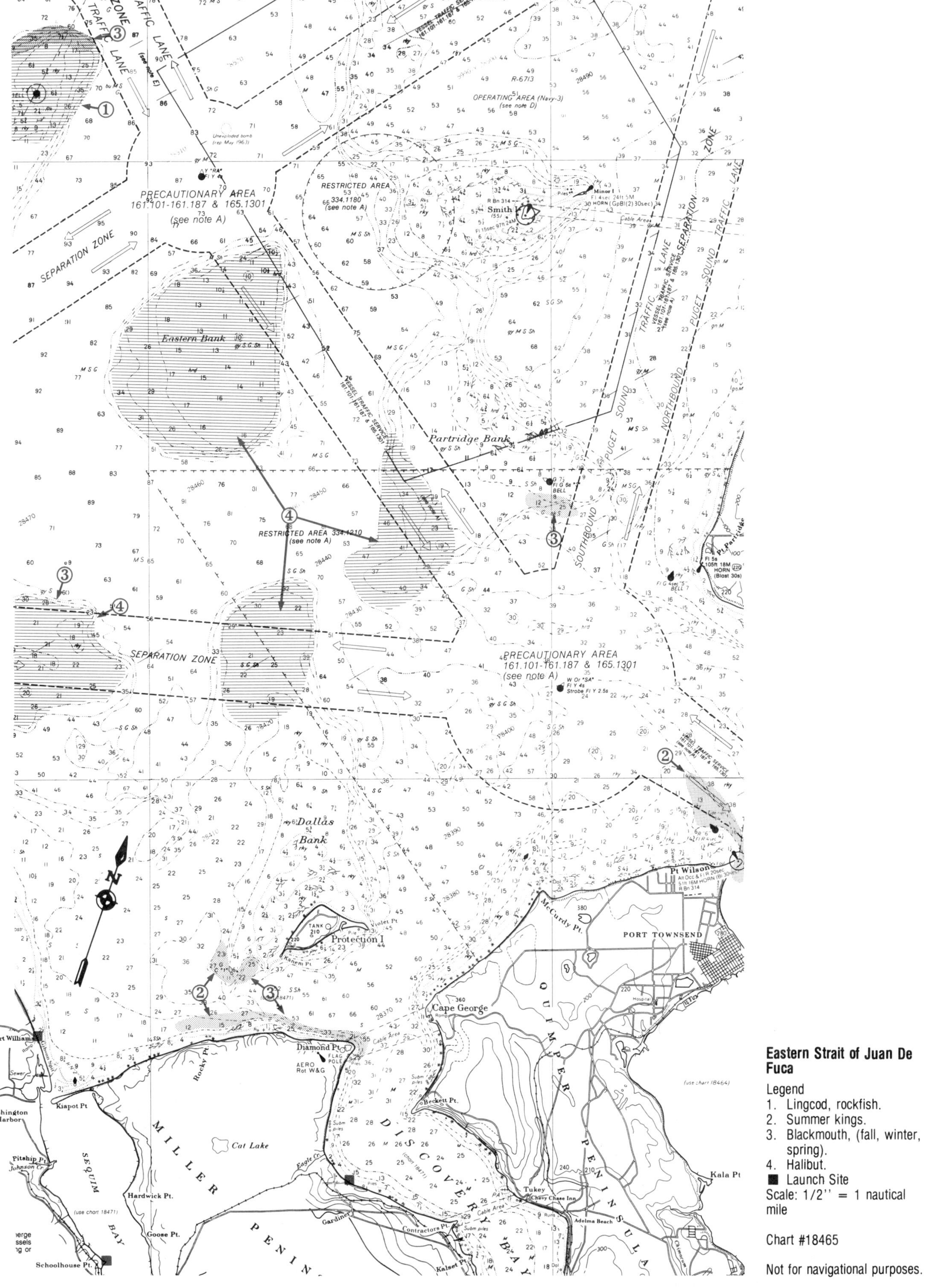

Eastern Strait of Juan De Fuca

Legend
1. Lingcod, rockfish.
2. Summer kings.
3. Blackmouth, (fall, winter, spring).
4. Halibut.

■ Launch Site

Scale: 1/2'' = 1 nautical mile

Chart #18465

Not for navigational purposes.

Many summer mornings in the eastern strait are so calm that even kayakers can troll for salmon—but wisely close to shore.

Small Boat Safety

For small boaters, the eastern strait is a tough place to figure. While many days throughout the year prove to be delightfully calm, the strait is often windy—much windier than Puget Sound or often the adjacent ocean. This long, straight east-west channel acts as a giant funnel for west winds drawn inland. Marine forecasts frequently miss the mark by a wide margin. Locals put more stock in the what the smoke's doing as it billows from huge industrial stacks, staying home (or heading in) when it starts running horizontally.

Particularly during summer, the most popular fishing time—early morning—tends to be the most cooperative for small boats to venture out of the harbor. Mornings are generally calm, often foggy, but followed by brisk westerlies in the afternoons. Late fall is often characterized by long periods of strong, storm-driven northeasterlies. By December, the calm periods may increase. Right on through the winter (conveniently during some of the very best blackmouth fishing), fishermen take advantage of many days of cold, grey and dreary but calm weather. Early spring can be particularly nasty, with April a good month for catching but often the worst for fishing.

One other potential hazard can be the oil tankers, container ships and other gargantuan vessels heading up the strait. Keep an eye out for them and, if close, for their roller-coaster wakes.

U.S. Coast Guard—Port Angeles

Weather forecast (24-hr. recording) 457-6533
Station, 24-hour general information 457-4401
Station, operations (8 am-10 pm) 457-2226

seen a resurgence. And with good reason. Trollers who work the riplines a mile or more offshore very late in the summer have been finding great action from good-sized ocean coho. The six-mile buoy off PA has been a consistent area for both silvers and pinks, particularly during the second week of September when the action peaks.

Although there is no reason driftjigging wouldn't work well when the coho are in schools, few anglers work at this. But it may be worth a try. Once coho are located, simply work jigs at about the proper depth (which could vary from 10 or 20 feet down to 50 or 60). Most, of course, troll herring, plastic squid or squid and a herring strip, spoons or flies.

Nearshore bottomfishing lacks the habitat and therefore the potential of Neah Bay to the west or the San Juans to the northeast. There are still opportunities to take mixed catches of lings, rockfish, greenling and cabezon at "the rockpile," though it has been heavily fished over the years and big fish are rare. Closer in, the occasional ling may still be picked up from the ledges off Green Point and at the shelf around the outside of the Garbage Dump region. Fair numbers of smaller lings and other species may be picked up along the rocky ledges at and east of Tongue Point, just east of Crescent Bay. Particularly abundant here are the ling's smaller relatives, kelp greening of 2 or 3 pounds.

Occasionally, black rockfish may be found in the harbor around the inside of the hook during the summer. When they school up, they are likely to be feeding at the surface, when they'll readily strike topwater or shallow-running plugs, spoons and particularly white feather jigs. Years ago feeding blacks were a regular sight in the harbor, but that's not so common today.

Another fishery that has dried up, as in Puget Sound, is the opportunity to take Pacific cod in the winter. If they return in the near future, look for good catches of big (5- to 12-pound) cod to come from Green Point and the second buoy toward the Garbage Dump and end of the hook.

Squid can be taken here, as in Puget Sound, but earlier in the year, as they make their way inland. Some summer nights beneath the lights, at the city pier for example, ample catches are made. Squid jigs are about all that's needed for a bucket of squid when they're in.

Smelt are available for raking at a few beaches, notably in Dungeness Harbor, October through January, around launch ramps and the south shore around Cline Spit. Jiggers do well right in the Port Angeles Boat Haven and in the John Wayne Marina during the winter.

Jigging is a popular method among anglers out of Port Angeles for catching winter blackmouth like this one taken in February on Coyote Bank.

The public boat launch just inside Ediz Hook is large to accomodate the fleet of private boats that arrive here during calm summer mornings.

Facilities

All phone numbers listed are within the 206 area code unless otherwise noted.

Charters

Two categories of charters operate out of Port Angeles, Sequim and Port Townsend: larger boats licensed to carry 10 to 12 or more anglers and, increasingly, small planing hull boats (often center consoles or walk-around cuddy cabins) that carry 2 to 5 (some to 6) anglers. Some troll, but the majority here drift-fish, some mooching herring but many jigging. Prices are highly variable, at press time from $55 or so per person for a day's fishing to as much as $125. Most of the more expensive charters are, logically, the smaller, faster outboards.

Admiralty Charters, John Wayne Marina, Sequim 98382, 683-1097. Year-round fishing aboard Roger Benson's 34-footer for salmon, halibut and other bottomfish. Will take up to 10-12 anglers.

Angeles Charters, 555 Highway 112, Port Angeles 98362, 928-3333. Skipper Randy Adams takes up to 6 anglers on his 32-footer for salmon and, in the spring, for halibut.

Blue Dolphin Charters, 711 East 6th Street, Port Angeles 98362, 928-3709. During October through April, Art King fishes the eastern strait from his 32-footer with up to 6 anglers. (May-September King fishes Neah Bay.) He offers trips for salmon or halibut.

Captain Tuna Charters, 2609-B Masters Road, Port Angeles 98362, 457-5995. Operating out of the Port Angeles Boat Haven, skipper Ron Marino fishes up to 6 anglers for salmon, halibut and other bottomfish aboard his 30-footer.

Doug's Charters, 25613 75th Avenue Southwest, Vashon 98070, 457-1663 or 463-2497. Doug Rickerson fishes year-round aboard his 34′ Trojan, taking up to 6 anglers for salmon and, in spring, halibut.

Dungeness Charters, c/o **Bosun's Locker**, 615 West Sequim Bay Road, Sequim 98382, 683-6521. Fishing from a 21-footer, Don Mills takes 2 to 4 anglers for salmon or bottomfish.

Great Northwest Charters, P.O. Box 1114, John Wayne Marina, Sequim 98382, 683-4023. Skipper Ray Cotter drift-jigs for salmon, halibut and other bottomfish aboard his 21-foot Chris-Craft Scorpion, year-round. He'll take 2 to 4 people.

Hi-Catch Charters, P.O. Box 841, Port Angeles 98362, 457-9046. Paul Ingham has gained a considerable reputation as a light-tackle mooching expert. He fishes most of the year out of Port Angeles, blackmouth November-April and halibut as well, April through June 15. From June 15 into September, Ingham concentrates on kings and after that, coho. Ingham takes 2 or 3 fishermen aboard his 19′ Whaler.

Kingfisher Charters, 133 Ridgeview Drive, Port Angeles 98362, 457-1935. Skipper Alan Underle fishes all species aboard his 34-footer. He takes up to 6 anglers out of Port Angeles in the winter and out of Sequim in the summer.

Little Beaver Charters, P.O. Box 22, Joyce 98343, 928-3708. Year-round driftfishing aboard Joe Schmitt's 38-foot charter with up to 12 anglers.

Lucky Strike Charters, Bosun's Locker, 615 West Sequim Bay Road, Sequim 98382, 683-2416. Operates out of John Wayne Marina. Skipper Greg Mottis knows eastern strait water well, carries 4 to 12 anglers aboard his 40-foot charter to drift for salmon, halibut and lingcod.

Marauder Charter, Bosun's Locker, 615 Sequim Bay Road, Sequim 98382, 683-2565. Operates out of John Wayne Marina. Skipper Neil Bell takes 3 to 6 anglers on his 33-foot Tiara for all species, year-round.

Port Angeles Charters, 1216 Marine Drive, Port Angeles 98362, 457-7629. Don Frizzell has been skippering charters in the eastern strait for many years. P.A. Charters operates several charters from 34 to 45 feet, carrying 6 to 16 anglers, respectively.

Satin Doll Charters, P.O. Box 2108, Port Angeles 98362, 457-6585 (summer: 645-2374). It's all in the family for Gaylord and wife Mars Jones, both skippers who've had decades of experience putting people on salmon and halibut. The 43′ *Satin Doll* fishes 10 to 12 anglers off Port Angeles in the winter (and Neah Bay during the summer).

Seasport Charters, P.O. Box 805, Port Townsend 98368, 385-3575. This 42-footer takes up to 16 anglers (if all in one party; otherwise 10 maximum). Fishes salmon and bottomfish from midApril through midNovember.

Thunderbird Charters, P.O. Box 787, Port Angeles 98362, 457-4274 or 385-3595. Operates several charters, 30′ to 44′ carrying 6 to 16 anglers, respectively. Fishes all species, year-round.

Marinas

John Wayne Marina, 615 West Sequim Bay Road, Sequim 98382 (1 miles south of the entrance to Sequim Bay on western shore), 683-9898. Open all-year, every day. 50 guest moorage slips. Fuel (8:30-4:30 daily), bait and tackle. Also showers, restaurant, laundromat, picnic area, charters. Two-lane public launch ramp is fairly new and one of the best around, good on all tides.

Point Hudson Marina, Port Townsend 98368 (1 block east of Port Townsend), 385-2828. Open daily, year-round. 23 slips and 600 lineal feet of dock spaces available. Bait and tackle, no fuel. Launch ramp but very steep. Also a 26-unit motel and a 58-site RV park.

Port Angeles Marina, 832 Boathaven Drive, Port Angeles 98362, 457-4505. 7—foot long dock with lots of moorage. Open year-round, 7 days/week. Fuel, engine repair, bait and tackle. Double lane launch ramp good to about a zero tide.

Port of Port Townsend, P.O. Box 1180, Port Townsend 98368, 385-2355. Open daily, year-round, launch ramp good on most tides, also travel-lift. Guest moorage available but may be limited. Fuel but no bait and tackle.

Thunderbird Boathouse, Port Angeles (Ediz Hook, next to Coast Guard Station), 457-3595. Open April-December. Guest moorage available. Adjacent to Ediz Hook free public launch ramp, a multi-lane ramp in excellent shape and good at low tides. Fuel, fair bait and tackle selection. Also groceries, charters. Rents 14- to 16-foot boats with or without power.

Also, the **Crescent Bay Public Ramp**, in Crescent Bay—turn off Highway 112 about 7 miles west of Port Angeles (watch for sign), then 2 1/2 miles north toward strait. One-lane ramp, paved but in only fair condition and not recommended for large boats. Still—the only public ramp for miles around.

Bait And Tackle

Bosun's Locker, 615 West Sequim Bay Road, Sequim 98382, 683-6521. Open 7 days/week, year-round. Lots of salmon, bottomfish gear. Books trips for several local charterboats.

Discovery Bay Grocery, 7760 Highway 101, Port Townsend 98368, 385-3608. Open 7 days/week all year, mainly stocks salmon gear. Fresh herring when available (suggest reserving 24 hours in advance) and up-to-date fishing information.

Fisherman's Wharf, P.O. Box 787, Port Angeles 98362, 457-4274. Open daily, year-round. Carries a good selection of saltwater gear.

Port Angeles Charters and Tackle, 1213 Marine Drive, Port Angeles 98362, 457-7629. Open daily, early, all year. Carries lots of saltwater gear. Books charter trips for several boats.

R&R Marine Supply, 1222 East Front Street, Port Angeles 98362, 452-7062. Closed Sundays. This small shop has every nook and cranny filled with tackle, including a great selection of metal jigs.

Swain's General Store, 602 East 1st, Port Angeles 98362, 452-2357. Open every day. Stocks salmon and freshwater tackle.

Motels

In Sequim, Port Townsend and Port Angeles are a wealth of motels and RV parks along Highway 101. For a complete listing of these or specific information about lodging, contact one of the efficient chambers of commerce in each of this community, listed below.

Public Campgrounds

Ford Worden State Park, northern edge of Port Townsend. No standard tentsites but 50 RV sites (to 50') with hookups and 3 primitive tentsites. Boaters will find a good launch ramp, moorage buoys and floats. Popular, busy park with historic 1900-era buildings.

Old Fort Townsend State Park (Recreation Area), 3 miles south of Port Townsend, east off Highway 20. 40 standard and 3 primitive tentsites. Moorage buoys, clamming beach.

Sequim Bay State Park (Recreation Area), 4 miles east of Sequim on Highway 101. 60 standard and 3 primitive tentsites, 26 RV sites with hookups. Launch ramp, moorage buoys, floats.

For More Information

Port Angeles Chamber of Commerce, 1217 1st Street, Port Angeles 98362, 452-2363.

Port Townsend Chamber of Commerce, Port Townsend 98368, 385-2722.

Sequim Chamber of Commerce, 1192 East Washington Street, Sequim 98382, 683-6197.

Western Strait Of Juan De Fuca

THERE IS NO AREA ON THE NORTHWEST COAST that can offer more varied, exciting sportfishing opportunities to small boaters than this corner of land, northwesternmost in the contiguous U.S.

Fishermen are blessed with a multitude of choices, here. You can mooch for a trophy king off dramatic rock pinnacles along the ocean south of Cape Flattery, or inside the strait along jagged ledges that plummet steeply along the contour of the shoreline. The next day, you can troll offshore riplines in the ocean for silvers—and, often, be back with a limit in time for a 9 a.m. breakfast. On the third day, you might elect to head out to Swiftsure Bank where the odds are good you'll tangle with a halibut. You'll probably have a big ling or two as well, but if not, you can always hit a few pinnacles or reefs west and south of Cape Flattery for lings, yelloweye rockfish and a host of smaller bottomfishes.

From good, protected harbors without any tricky bar crossings to contend with, even 15-foot kicker boats venture out into the strait from Sekiu or to the edge of the ocean from Neah Bay on calm days. The miles of shoreline inside the strait offer some protection from ocean swells and can be as productive as the adjacent Pacific.

Since the early 1980s, a one-two management punch of stingy seasonal/catch restrictions on king salmon and more recently on halibut has left the area reeling somewhat. Length of seasons, minimum sizes, closures of certain days each week, bag limits—all these are now up for grabs each winter and remain question marks until early spring when federal and state fishery management agencies announce regulations. Even then, closing dates for salmon and halibut may remain undetermined until later in the summer, depending upon quotas. All this means: anyone who plans a trip to Neah Bay or Sekiu without being certain what's open to sport fishermen is foolish.

And, considering how far this undeveloped area is from population centers, most anglers do plan trips to the western strait well in advance, staying for at least a couple days and often a week.

Summer Giants—Kings Along The Shoreline

If sport fishermen travel miles to congregate here, it's only because such great numbers of salmon do the same. By early summer, good-sized chinook have arrived to feed and fatten just outside the strait entrance. Many of these are Columbia River fish, and strengthening runs since the early 1980s have helped make for some memorably good June king fishing many years off Neah Bay and, in fact, off southwest Vancouver Island as well. They are joined by chinook bound for the Fraser and other rivers far inside the strait, as well.

King fishing for these early fish really picks up in late June and lasts through late July, with an early July peak. They'll average a respectable 12 to 25 pounds. But much larger fish begin to move in during late July—the real trophy kings of 40+ pounds. These are most prevalent until the third week of August—in a typical year.

One of the best areas for kings in the summer is just north of Umatilla Reef and inside of that, working herring near bottom in water 40 to 50 feet deep. Skagway Rocks is another consistent producer, when the ocean isn't too rough to make the run to them, out through the slot between Tatoosh and the cape into the open ocean. Moochers work in quite close to the rocks again in just 40 to 50 feet of water, when ocean swells don't make that too risky.

Starting in the mid1980s, some Neah Bay anglers were taking kings consistently offshore, 3 to 5 miles off Makah Bay and Spike Rock in July.

Many who hunt big kings prefer to stay inside, working the shoreline all the way from Mushroom Rock in to Wadda Island—and beyond, farther east. Many small boat and charter fishermen stop well east of Neah Bay, making their home base Sekiu (pronounced "Seek-you," the Makah Indian word meaning quiet waters).

The king action begins here in June also, but is often excellent right through August. Sekiu Point, Mussolini Rock, the Coal Mine and Pillar Point are all among the areas that are fished heavily throughout the summer. Here, too,

Neah Bay and Sekiu have historically been among the top spots on the Northwest coast for trophy kings. This 40-pounder was taken on the charter Hardway VI.

Author holding up a big Chinook taken on a Krocodile spoon.

mooching is popular. Most of that is near shore with 2 to 5 ounces of lead to keep plugcut herring working near bottom in 40 to 90 feet. However, long stretches of dropoffs along shore lend themselves to downrigger trolling. Jigging is less popular than in the eastern strait, but can be just as effective for those who do it.

Often, particularly early in the morning, the best action inside the strait is just off the kelpline. There is no reason for much of an offshore run if you're after chinook. In general, tide changes are also prime periods to expect a bite.

Swiftsure Bank—Western Strait's Offshore Halibut Heaven

Too far and too rough; too deep and too tough. That was the conventional wisdom for decades about the possibility of fishing Swiftsure Bank for halibut or anything else.

It *is* far: this enormous subterranean rocky-gravelly seamount (about 20 square miles) rises from the depths of

Salmon Tips From Two Experts

Mooching plugcut herring remains one of the most popular methods for taking big chinook salmon in the western strait. Some experts, like charter skipper Pete Hanson, have found ultrasharp black hooks outfish traditional silver hooks like these.

When it comes to catching fish, guys like Pete Hanson and John Truex *have* to be good; their livelihood depends on it. Hanson, longtime Neah Bay resort owner and charter skipper, offers a few suggestions for the many anglers who come to Neah Bay to catch salmon each summer.

Despite the popularity of trolling, Hanson insists that "mooching plugcut herring is always devastating." But for mooching to be most effective, "I cannot emphasize too much to use the very lightest leaders." And Hanson offers another trick: black hooks, rather than silver. Specifically, he's had best success on black Gamakatsu hooks. Finally, moochers may want to keep this in mind: "I'm a firm believer in using a single hook on a plugcut if the bait is small enough."

Surface-trolling flies is a great way to tangle with silvers, particularly when seas are calm. "I prefer a green/mylar or orange/white fly," Hanson says. "They should be trolled with a very small belly strip at 4 to 5 mph at the minimum." Hanson points out that good light tackle or even "trout gear" offer optimal fun from these silvers.

When the coho are not at the surface and require getting deeper, most people troll flashers and hardware with downriggers. But Hanson prefers to mooch when salmon are deeper and notes that with good electronics he can be sure his drift is over fish.

John Truex has been fishing Sekiu as a charter skipper since 1982. The Sekiu area may be somewhat calmer than Neah Bay but the waters may also be more crowded with small boats. Truex offers small boat fishermen several suggestions.

"*Don't* fish way out (in the Sekiu area) for kings. Particularly in June, the big ones offer excellent fishing just off the kelp in about 40 feet of water because they're in there feeding on candlefish."

And when the chinook are schooling, drift-jigging does pay off; Truex is one of those who enjoys that approach. His favorite for Sekiu salmon: a 2 1/2-inch Pt. Wilson Dart or 4-inch Buzz Bomb. Early morning is almost always a hot time, but any slack tide can be just as productive.

When you get out on the water, look around and "ask around. See what's happening. If I'm not marking fish or bait with fish under it, I move on." Ironically, with so much feed so often available, Truex says it can be better to find fish where there is *not* much bait around.

"If you're fishing herring, motor-mooch *with* the current so you can cover ground and get the bait deep enough, then pick up and run back for another drift. When cutting herring, I do best getting as fast and tight a spin out of the bait as I can get—and at the slowest possible speed. I almost block my herring," he says, rather than cut a more obtuse angle on the bevel which produces big spirals rather than tight spins. It is, of course, always best to check your bait and readjust to make it do what you want it to.

Truex's final thought seems inevitable, considering the wall-to-wall boats that gather in favorite areas around Sekiu. "Use common sense in these crowds out here, especially when trolling. Avoid crossing paths. Keep your lines short; use more weight (if you are trolling without downriggers), not more line to get deeper."

the vast, yawning mouth of the west Strait of Juan de Fuca, beginning about 15 miles from Neah Bay. It *is* rough at times, hardly surprising given its location. It *is* deep, rising here and there to 40-some fathoms, but most of it (especially on the U.S. side) is in 300 to 400 or more feet. And it *is* tough, fishing not only such depths, but contending with heavy currents much of the time.

But despite all that, Swiftsure has proven to be eminently fishable and loaded with halibut (and other big bottomfish). In fact, its halibut fishery could be reasonably labeled as the single most exciting new development in the Northwest marine sport fishing scene during the 1980s.

That's when it all began. I still recall early in the decade a weather-perfect June weekend when I fished Swiftsure with charter skipper Ed Euken on the *Blue Chip*. He'd already done a bit of experimenting. His success was so astonishing that some folks at Neah Bay sponsored a junket for outdoor writers, who filled the boat hoping for fodder to feed their typewriters. By day's end we were all believers, with everyone aboard having a limit (at that time) of two halibut averaging 20 to 50 pounds and at least a couple lings all around averaging 15 to 40. It didn't take long for word about such fishing to get out.

Since then thousands of people have fished Swiftsure for halibut each year, the majority of them returning consistently with fish. In response to such demand, the charter fleet grew considerably, until by 1990 some 20 halibut boats were operating out of Neah Bay. (Patrons are well-advised to make reservations in advance, especially with shorter seasons these days.) During the same period, numbers of bigger, more seaworthy trailerable 17- to 25-foot boats increased dramatically as well.

But two conditions cooled this hot fishery a bit. First, in the mid1980s, the Canadian government decided to enforce a restriction on any sportfishing of Swiftsure on the B.C. side (which includes about 75% of the bank, particularly some of the higher, more easi!y fished spots) to anglers lacking Canadian sport licenses—available only in B.C. Of course, that shut off the charters from much of the bank. It also shut off private anglers who were smart enough to avoid risking a fine unless they had brought Canadian licenses with them.

But so productive is the bank that fishermen still managed to limit consistently drifting the U.S. side only. But near the end of the '80s, the North Pacific Halibut Commission went to a quota system, tightening the screws so by 1990 the long-standing limit of two halibut per day was reduced to but a single fish in order to stretch out the fishery before a rather meager quota was filled. Even so, seasons were also shortened and fishing was limited to but a few days of the week.

Wire spreaders with whole herring have become widely popular for fishing the deep waters of the western Strait.

WESTERN STRAIT / Sport Fish and Seasons

Species	J	F	M	A	M	J	J	A	S	O	N	D
	BEST MONTHS											
Blackmouth[1]	poor	best	best	best	best	poor	poor	poor	poor	poor	poor	poor
King salmon[2]	poor	poor	poor	poor	fair	fair/best	best	best	fair	poor	poor	poor
Silver, pinks[3]	poor	poor	poor	poor	poor	poor	poor	best	best	poor	poor	poor
Halibut[4]	poor	poor	poor/fair	best	best	best	best/fair	fair	fair/poor	poor	poor	poor
Lingcod[5], rockfish	best	best	best	best	best	best	best	best	best	best	best	best
Smelt[6]	poor	poor	fair	fair	poor	poor	poor	poor	poor	poor	poor	poor

[1]Check regulations carefully before fishing; ocean fishing closed, strait remains open; size and gear restrictions vary by area. Blackmouth are immature Chinook, not returning from sea. Begins February at Sekiu, April at Neah Bay.
[2]Check regulations carefully, as above. Kings are considered to be mature Chinook, returning from sea to spawn–and are considerably larger than blackmouth. Season may open as late as July.
[3]Pinks present only in odd-numbered years.
[4]Season opening and closing dates vary year to year; may end by early summer.
[5]Lingcod usually closed Dec-mid April.
[6]For an unpredictable two-week period around Twin Rivers and Deep Creek near Pillar Point.

LEGEND: best fair poor

After decades of regulations which remained the same, year-in, year-out, the quota system now means that limits, seasons and fishing days are bound to change annually. So anglers need to keep on top of regulations. If you're unsure, any local resort is bound to know.

Even the chance for one halibut per day is enough to keep lots of anglers coming to fish Swiftsure. For one thing, halibut are esteemed as food. Many people rank them as the number one delicacy among all white-meated fish of the world (and having fished the oceans around much of this hemisphere, I'm inclined to agree). For another, their average size is reasonable at 20 to 35 pounds, but there is always the very real chance for a monster—such as the 288-pounder that was boated in 1989. In fact, most years at least some halibut over 200 pounds come in.

The best chance for such barndoors seems to be later in the summer; in fact, September tends to have the largest size fish. However, dogfish can also be numerous at this time of year. And remember: quotas may close fishing long before this. May and June offer the greatest numbers of halibut on the bank. May is also the roughest halibut month. Most days *are* fishable for charters and larger private boats, but are not necessarily all comfortable.

Seaworthy private boat joins charters over Swiftsure Bank; glad to get a typical 30-pounder but hoping for a 130-pounder like this one.

Gear for fishing Swiftsure halibut has become fairly standard: a medium to heavy, fairly short "stand-up" type rod with a 4/0 sized reel (preferably fast-retrieve) to hold 700 to 1,000 feet of 50- to 80-pound Dacron line. Dacron is almost universal among regular Swiftsure anglers, its thin diameter and reduced stretch giving it the nod over monofilament.

Terminal gear has tended increasingly to favor stiff wire spreaders (in an L-shape, up to 8" by 20") with a 2- to 3-pound weight attached to the short end of the L and a steel or heavy monofilament leader tied to the long end, with the main (Dacron) line of course tied to the middle. Large herring are the bait preferred by most anglers, but octopus and squid are popular as well.

Although the use of jigs declined somewhat as spreader-and-bait tactics increased, many anglers still fish homemade pipe jigs (essentially steel tubes filled with molten lead) and big leadheads with huge twin-tailed plastic bodies. It is nice to have such lures along when dogfish move in.

Besides the right tackle, private boaters really ought to have Loran. This helps locate not only the bank but locate and relocate specific areas (''beds'') on it that produced consistently. Loran also helps keep you in U.S. waters if you lack a Canadian license.

Swiftsure halibut anglers should also carry a flying harpoon and a good gaff or two, along with plenty of rope. (For more specifics on the boating of halibut, see the box in Eastern Strait section.) And if not experienced at halibut fishing here, a day aboard a charter can teach plenty, not only about catching halibut but about hanging onto terminal gear.

Advising an angler to fish light gear on Swiftsure may seem like equipping Jack with a BB gun en route up the beanstalk. Still, I have found it fishable with monofilament lines testing 12 to 20 pounds (that's actual strength; stated spool strength is 8 to 14 pounds) but *only when currents are very light* and the drift is not too fast. One day on a busy charter, I ended up with the day's biggest halibut—a 65-pounder—on my spinning outfit loaded with 12-pound line. I fished a seven-ounce Krocodile spoon in about 280 feet of water.

There is a host of other bottomfish as well to be taken over Swiftsure. It is unusual to spend any time halibut fishing and not also hook lingcod. Even where the bottom is more a hard bed of rock or gravel than of jagged rock, lingcod can be abundant. Some impressively large, bright yelloweye rockfish are usually taken, as well. I've seen quite a few big bocaccio—including some in a bright red shade I've seen nowhere else.

Nor is all this to suggest that halibut can be taken only over Swiftsure Bank. That is far from true. After all, the

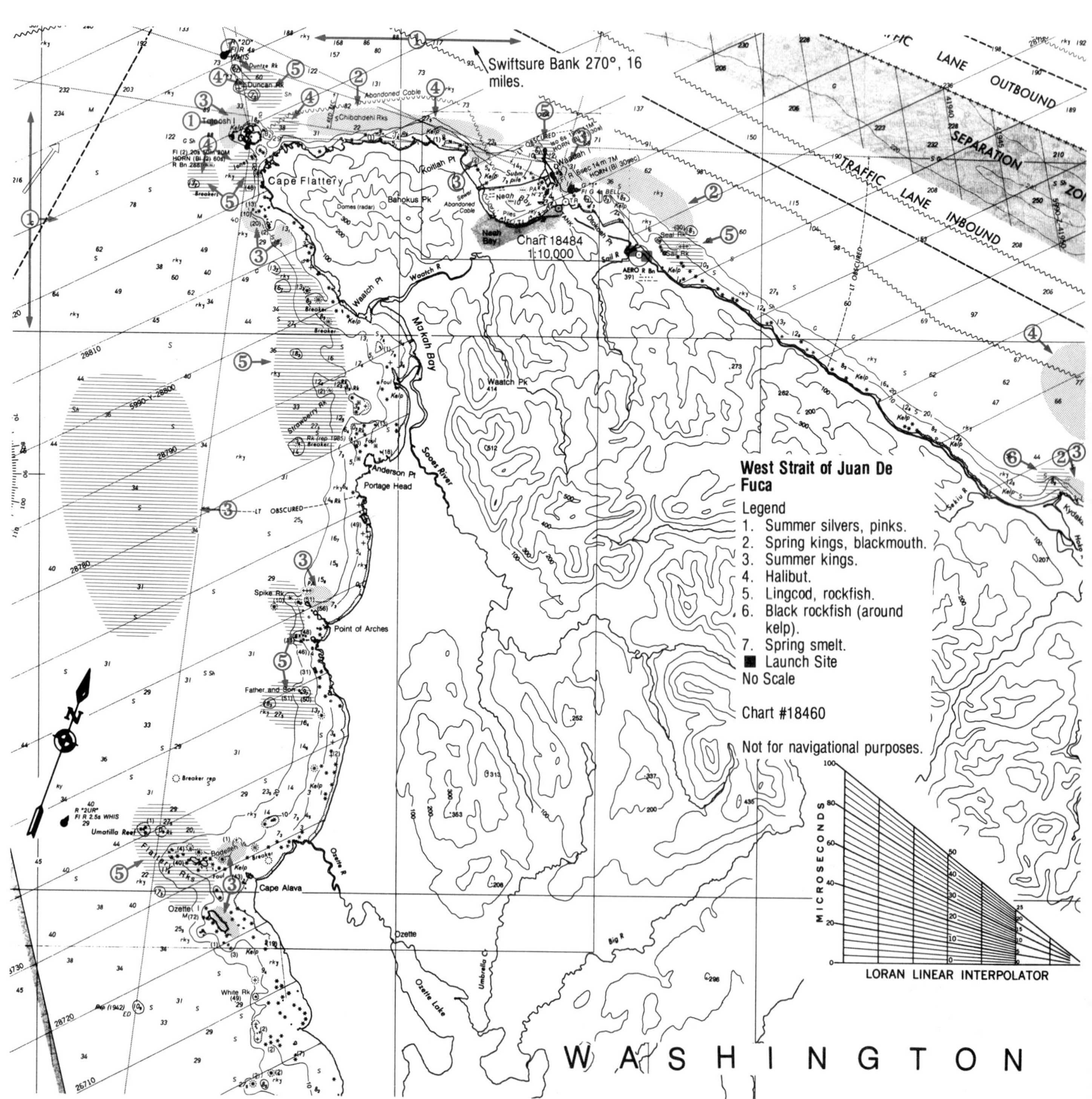

western strait has long been prime halibut country years before anyone ever thought of seriously sportfishing the bank. A great many halibut are taken each season "inside"—in waters within a few miles of Neah Bay or Sekiu, near the shore, as well as over gravel areas west and south of Cape Flattery. Some are taken incidentally by salmon anglers. Sekiu fishermen who do target on halibut tend to work the waters off the Sekiu and Hoko rivers in April, May and June (where open for halibut sport fishing).

Trolling For Silvers And Pinks

By July, trollers are beginning to find significant concentrations of feeding silvers offshore. At this time of year they tend to run 5 to 8 pounds, but by late August the same fish will be running 8 to 12 pounds and up.

Silvers are schooling fish that offer particularly fast sport, feeding actively in offshore rips in July and later closer in. It is not unheard of for anglers to limit out on coho in a half-hour when they're thick. Some fishermen then head in for the day; others go bottomfishing. Perhaps the smartest are those who pack ultralight gear and small metal jigs, to drift and enjoy some of the wildest sport the north coast has to offer. Coho are naturally wild fish. Couple that with light lines and they'll put on acrobatic displays not easily forgotten. Often pinks will be mixed in with silvers; they, too, will jump and sizzle across the surface on light lines.

Spinning reels with 250+ yards of 4- to 8-pound line or flyrods and flyreels are ideal for some tremendous catch-and-release sport. Any private boater who travels to Neah

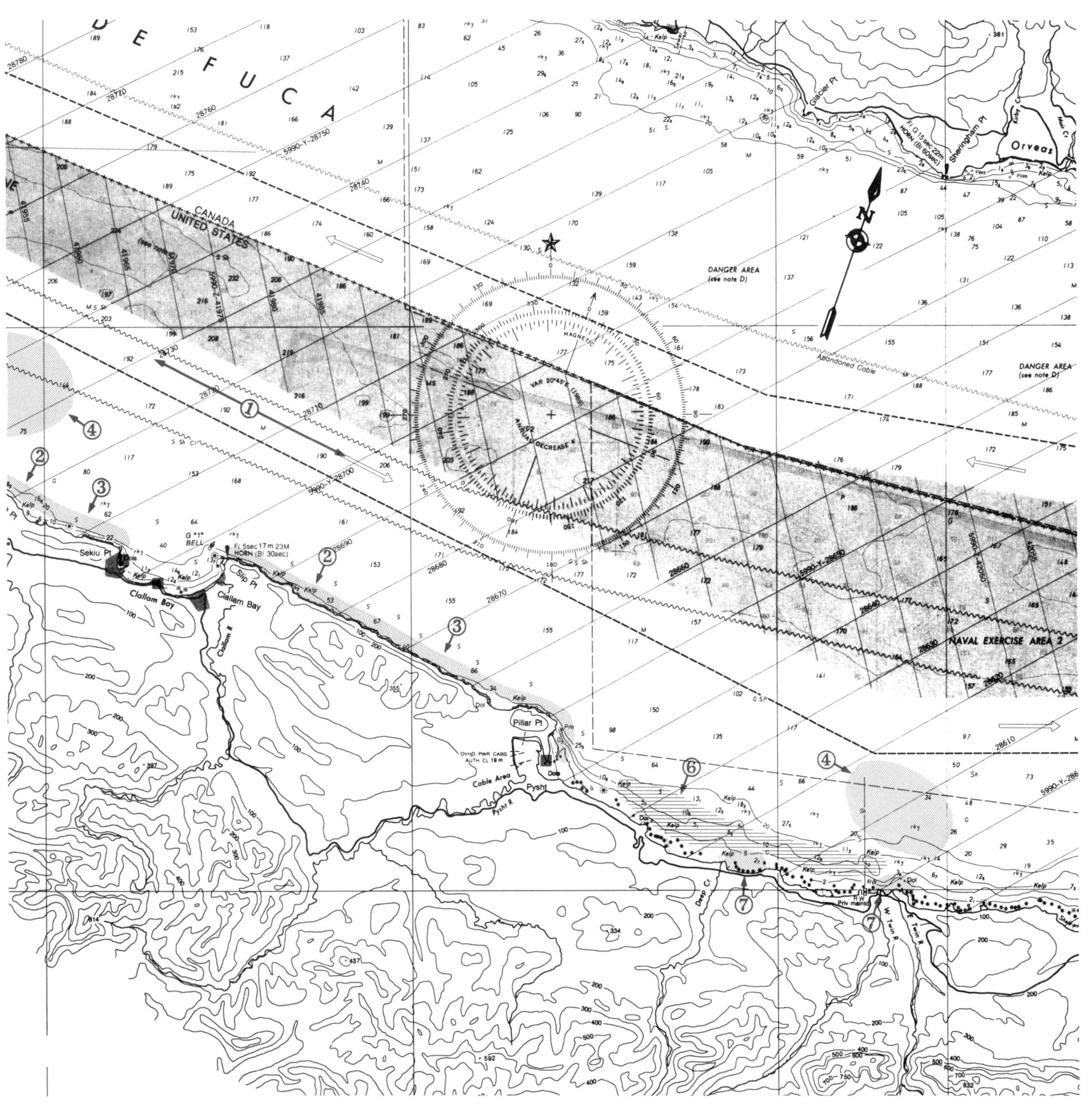

Bay or Sekiu in July or August without such gear is missing a great bet.

The method for catching silvers most often employed involves considerably heavier line and trolling without weight, especially around riplines. Plastic squid (Hoochys) remain the single most popular offering, typically with a herring strip. When the coho aren't on the surface this is fished behind a flasher and combined with a diving plane or clipped to a downrigger to get the rig deep enough (which may be 20 to 50 feet). Most charters traditionally trolled for silvers (with heavy gear and 1-pound cannonball weights) but charter skipper Pete Hanson has proven to Neah Bay skeptics in recent years that driftmooching takes just as many coho—and offers anglers much lighter gear and active, exciting fishing—so more coho charters may be using the same approach. Check at the docks before you book a trip, depending upon your preference.

Against All Odds:

Two Tenderfeet, a 13-Foot Skiff—and a 90-pound halibut

One very happy halibut tenderfoot, the author, back at the docks of Neah Bay Resort, displays the halibut that bottomed out the resort's scales at 90 pounds, taken in a 13-foot skiff.

Honestly, the last thing I expected that sunny June morning many years ago, fishing from a 13-foot skiff with 15-pound line on a spinning outfit, was that I'd hook a fish bigger than the hood of my Toyota.

I was a few miles west of Neah Bay with a longtime fishing partner, but neither of us had ever hooked a halibut back then. We were working 3-ounce leadhead jigs not far east of Tatoosh Island. I had lingcod, rockfish or perhaps a good cabezon in mind as I set the hooks. But as the line began melting, nonstop, from my screaming spool, I yelled, "Crank up the engine and follow it—it's gotta be a halibut."

During the ensuing battle, we drifted by a commercial boat, one fellow hollering advice: "Give it up—you'll never land a big halibut on that!" After over an hour with little line gained, slowly following it farther and farther out to sea in increasing swells, I began to wonder if he wasn't right.

Finally, we were able to see the huge white/brown diamond near the boat. But after all that work, the halibut dove straight back to the bottom in a flash. We were definitely not equipped with a gun or anything else we really needed to boat a halibut. But fortunately, we knew enough not to simply gaff it and haul it aboard.

We decided upon trying to slash its gills while it was in the water. Only after raising the fish three more times were we able to do so. Over two hours after I'd hooked the fish and after drifting a good two miles offshore we hauled the drained halibut into the skiff. It filled the floorboards. We hightailed it back to port where, even after the loss of all its blood, the big flatfish bottomed out Neah Bay Resort's scales at 90 pounds. Not a record by any means, but not bad for a first halibut, particularly under the circumstances.

By August, silvers are pouring into the strait and the rips off Sekiu and Pillar Point should be loaded. Many people plan their trips for later in the month, particularly for the big hooknose silvers (whose "hooking" snouts are evidence of a readiness to spawn typical at this time of larger mature fish) which can top the scales at 15 to 20 pounds. Hatchery silvers tend to move in earlier than wild fish and weigh less.

For some western strait anglers, the general rule of thumb is to head north (into the strait) until you find coho. And often private boaters will spend much of their time trolling far out in the main shipping lanes.

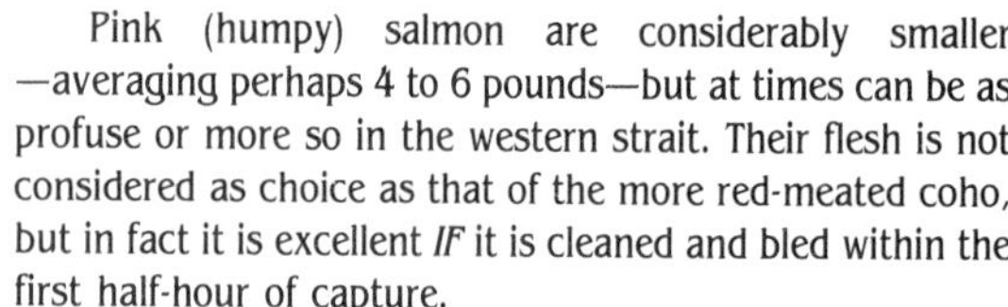

Pink (humpy) salmon are considerably smaller—averaging perhaps 4 to 6 pounds—but at times can be as profuse or more so in the western strait. Their flesh is not considered as choice as that of the more red-meated coho, but in fact it is excellent *IF* it is cleaned and bled within the first half-hour of capture.

After only two years at sea, pinks return to rivers to spawn—mostly to the Fraser in Canada and to the Skagit in Puget Sound. These fish pass through the strait en route home, but they do so only on odd-numbered years. Even knowing that the fisherman's crystal ball foretells little more: size of runs may vary wildly from one odd-year to the next. Some years the run has been so great that the Department of Fisheries has offered an emergency bonus limit allowing up to six pinks per day. Other years, the runs have been meager—or weeks later than expected.

Although the timing can vary, pinks are expected to show up around late July and through the end of August. Pinks are often picked up right along with silvers, since they form large, shallow schools in similar areas.

Bottomfish Alternatives—Light Tackle Challenge

Most fishermen who travel to the western strait are primarily after either salmon or halibut. But one way or another, many end up devoting some time to fishing for bottomfish. One thing that drifting rocky areas for species other than salmon or halibut does offer is *variety.* While jigging western strait reefs, I've boated six fish in succession, each a different species.

Any rocky reef will offer up bottomfish; those down along the open coast may hold more fish. But along the edge of the strait, just beyond the kelp beds, the bottom is mostly hard and rocky. For a few hours of very simple, fishing which is as rewarding as it is simple, try making long drifts, starting just off the kelp line (where the depth will be only 20-30 or so feet) into gradually deepening water, returning for another drift when the bottom is too far below to fish easily.

The downside to this fishing is that, admittedly, it's not a particularly good bet for anyone targeting on trophy-sized fish. You're most likely to catch several species of rockfish, cabezon, greenling, perhaps true cod, lingcod, flounder/sole (over smooth areas) and another species or two I can't even think of right now, mostly in the 2- to 6-pound range.

But the upside is, first of all, *action.* As a rule, it's reasonable to expect plenty since you're covering various habitats at various depths where fishing competition may be minimal. Secondly, there's no need for fancy electronics. Anglers in cartoppers or rental skiffs lacking depth-sounders can simply motor past the kelp, cut the engine and drift. Third, on a windy day when, for example, a southwesterly is whipping up the ocean and strait just offshore, it is likely to be calm enough to fish close in.

But to really enjoy this, light tackle is mandatory. This guide has already given reason to bring light rods, for fishing silvers offshore. Here's another reason. Light, medium-stiff rods with a long, fairly thick butt and a thin, sensitive tip of about 6 feet are ideal when paired with a spinning or baitcasting reel filled with at least 300 feet of 6-to 12-pound line. This thin line allows you to better feel what's happening below and helps the lure work more effectively, while also making it much easier to get a lure to the bottom. Moreover, it is easier to cast lighter gear.

Terminal gear can vary. Certainly whole or cut herring, squid or other natural baits should get plenty of results.

Pink salmon provide very fast action and are a great light tackle target when they move in off Neah Bay and Sekiu in odd-numbered summers.

Frozen herring will work well, often rigged on a short leader of, say, a foot in length to avoid twisting around the main line.

But for me, the real joy of light-tackle, nearshore fishing is working artificials. Three good bets: leadhead bucktail or skirted jigs (white or yellow are often most reliable) with a plastic tail—straight worm, curly-cue or twin-tail—Krocodile spoons or metal salmon-type jigs. (The latter also offer the advantage of appealing to chinook, and picking one up while jigging is always a real possiblity, even if you're targeting bottomfish.) A range of weights from an ounce or so to 3-4 ounces is advisable to allow you to respond to increasing depth as you drift as well as changing conditions in drift from wind and current.

As you start each drift, don't simply drop the jig over the side and work it up and down. Try casting far out and letting it sink for a moment (which shouldn't take long in such shallow water), then working it back toward the boat, over the bottom, in sweeps or hops. Be alert as it's falling since very often species such as copper rockfish will see it falling and pounce on it the first time you move it. As the depth increases, make these long casts into (toward) the boat's drift so before the jig is back under the boat you've had time to fish it on the bottom. By casting this way, it's often possible with light lines to get a jig of only a couple ounces to the bottom in 150 or more feet.

Copper rockfish will prove one of the gamest opponents for light lines in shallow water—unless you happen to hook a cabezon which will really test your skills, especially if you tie into a 15-pounder. The China rockfish is common and lovely to look at, but too small to generate much excitement. At times, you may drift over areas of hard (but not jagged) bottom to find it teeming with bright orange canary rockfish of 2 to 4 pounds. The bottom line on this bottom fishing is: You never know what you may hook jigging in such long drifts, including a halibut (see "Against All Odds" in this section) or even skate which seem to be around in fair numbers over sandy areas and can run to over 100 pounds.

Sometimes, good-sized lings will be found over near-shore reefs. In fact, more and more fishermen are targeting lings by jigging live herring, as more and more well-equipped private boats have live wells.

Black rockfish ("sea bass") is one species you may want to target with light gear or, even better, ultralight gear or flyfishing tackle. Anglers used to fishing inside waters such as Puget Sound may be surprised—and enticed—to see huge schools of blacks feeding at the surface.

On my first visit to Neah Bay, the sound and sight of splashing made by fish feeding in the long, lush kelp beds off which I was (fruitlessly) trolling attracted my attention. I immediately pulled up the lines and headed over in the skiff. For the next couple hours I caught black rockfish, first by casting a 1/2-ounce bucktail jig and white plastic worm with my tiny ultralight spinner using 4-pound line. If a black didn't grab it when it hit the surface, I'd begin reeling in steadily with slight twitches and usually have several strikes and misses before hooking another. Then I switched to surface plugs and enjoyed the greatest sport—watching rockfish rush up to grab the Rebel minnow. Soon, to avoid limiting out, I was releasing everything under 5 pounds.

Small Boat Safety

These are big waters. Their protected shorelines are easily fished even by small cartoppers much of the time. But it doesn't take much of a run to be in ocean swells and big riptides.

For any small boater who is planning to venture far to the west (anywhere near Cape Flattery) or offshore: (1) use the buddy system if at all possible—find another boat to travel/fish with; (2) let the resort where you're staying know of your tentative itinerary; (3) don't go without a good VHF radio—even if just a handheld—and a safety kit with flares and a long, stout tow rope; (4) watch the weather and when in doubt, head home. If you'll be traveling any distance offshore, or heading into foggy conditions, add to the above at least a good chart and a compass. And of course Loran-C is invaluable not only in getting you to the fishing holes but getting you home the most direct way possible.

In addition to the above, private boaters headed out to Swiftsure Bank should keep their VHFs on and tuned in to the frequency used by charters. Most skippers will put out the word to everyone on the bank when they feel the weather is getting too rough to remain out—and won't mind in the least small boaters following them back.

One of the trickiest areas for small boaters navigating the western strait must be the waters around the cape itself. Particularly treacherous is "the slot" betwen Tatoosh Island and Cape Flattery; through this narrow passage are swift currents with unpredictable rips and rocks awash or barely submerged around the center. For those heading out to rocky outcroppings such as Duncan or Skagway rocks, avoid fishing or navigating too close, even on calm days: sudden surging swells have been known to lift unwary boaters up to deposit them rudely against the rocks. Also use caution along the unprotected coastline from the cape eastward to Koitlah Point ("the garbage dump") whenever strong west or northwest winds prevail.

Sekiu and Pillar Point are far enough west to be relatively free from the hazards of the open Pacific and are especially popular with with small boat fishermen. But watch out for strong afternoon winds in the summer that normally whip up the strait. Mornings are likely to be calm, but may also bring fogs as thick as pea soup and hang in for hours.

U.S. Coast Guard Station—Neah Bay

Weather information (24-hour recording) . . . 645-2301
Station phone (24-hours) 645-2237

Feeding schools of black rockfish are often around the kelp, but that's hardly the only habitat where you'll encounter them. They may be almost anywhere they find small fish or invertebrates—suspended above deepwater reefs or pinnacles or even offshore in the rips. (And can, at such times, be the bane of trollers bent on catching salmon.) Of course, I've been to Neah Bay at other times and not encountered a single such school.

Still, the odds are good you'll find them. Once again, the key to really enjoying the great sport they have the potential to offer is ultralight tackle—spinning or fly gear. With more and more emphasis these days on sport vs. meat, smart anglers don't trailer up a small boat without including such gear in their arsenal of rods and reels.

Winter-spring Blackmouth: When Fish Outnumber Fishermen

Few anglers venture out to fish the western strait during the cold, wet months of winter and early spring. But those who do may be well rewarded. Summer tends to offer favorable weather but runs that come and go. But winter blackmouth are here pretty much all the time, and the weather becomes the critical factor. Winter storms often shut fishing down for days at a time. The steep shorelines well inside the strait offer protection from southwesterliers, but not from the strong northeasterly winds common at this time of year. Nevertheless, blissfully calm spells do prevail at times; the trick, then, is to plan to fish during such times.

Most midwinter fishing occurs around Pillar Point, with November through January all top months. Things get underway for blackmouth at Sekiu about the time that some resorts begin to reopen—at least enough to put a float or two back in the water.

At Neah Bay, signficant effort doesn't get underway until April. A few big, early chinook may join the blackmouth at that time. Wadda Island, blessedly close to the harbor, and Sail Rock, a few miles west, are popular spots for spring blackmouth.

Interestingly, mooching plugcut herring is *not* generally popular at this time, even though it is the method popular for winter blackmouth in Puget Sound and for summer kings in the western strait. This is the realm of deep trollers—mostly with downriggers used to replace the wire lines and heavy weights of years ago.

Standard gear for these winter blackmouth is a flasher and herring or plastic squid trolled in at least 60 to 125 feet of water and at times much deeper.

Neah Bay Area Nearshore/offshore Loran-c Numbers Coastal Lingcod, Rockfish

"**The Bass Hole**" (broad area west of Skagway, south of Tatoosh)

Rocky peaks, reefs at following spots: 28786.2 + 41864.3, 28814.9 + 41852.4, 28815.0 + 41850.8, 28808.4 + 41855.0, 28806.4 + 41855.0, 28806.1 + 41854.1.

Spike Rock to Father-and-Son

Spike Rock: 28761.0 + 41860.0, 28756.0 + 41860.010-Fathom Rock, Father-and-Son: 28748.5 + 41856.5 Father-and-Son Rocks: 28747.5 + 41860.0

Flattery Rocks

Rocky peaks at following spots: 28741.0 + 41860.0, 28740 + 41842.0, 28744.0 + 41846.0

Coastal Halibut

"The Bass Hole"

Flat, smooth/gravelly at following spots: 28822.0 + 41849.0, 28820.9 + 41849.9, 28819.3 + 41849.9, 28818.0 + 41848.9, 28817.0 + 41849.9, 28879.5 + 41860.0, 28819.6 + 41840.4, 28807.3 + 41855.0

Umatilla Reef

28750.0 + 41810.0, 28760.0 + 41815.0, 28742.0 + 41812.0

Strait 28812.3 + 41896.6

Coastal Salmon

Strait

Green Buoy: 28800.4 + 41897.2 (best pre-dawn)

N. tip Wadda Island: 28808.4 + 41894.0

E. end Duncan Rock: 28837.2 + 41861.3 (mooch/troll)

N. entrance to "the slot": 28828.6 + 41863.9 (20-80')

West of Cape Flattery

Whistle Buoy: 28842.0 + 41859.5

W. end Tatoosh: 28829.9 + 41859.4 (deep troll—kings)

2 miles south of Skagway Rock: 21810.0 + 41862.0

"Hole-in-the-Wall": 28827.2 + 41862.6 (mooch)

South of Cape Flattery (4 corners of troll quadrant)

N. of Anderson Point: 28784.0 + 41862.6, 28789.0 + 41852.0

S. of Father-and-Son: 28750.0 + 41851.5, 28747.0 + 41856.0

Swiftsure Halibut

West End 28836.1 + 41874.1

East End 28833.4 + 41875.8

52-Fathom Hole 28837.6 + 41876.5

48-Fathom Hole 28833.0 + 41880.9

Southwest

28895.0 + 41806.9, 28808.0 + 41808.0, 28807.2 + 41808.3, 28893.0 + 41805.0

Southeast

28892.4 + 41815.6, 28890.0 + 41816.9, 28891.9 + 41815.9, 28819.0 + 41814.9, 28891.5 + 41816.6, 28890.4 + 41816.3

Northeast

28891.7 + 41817.3, 28895.4 + 41813.8

Northwest

28905.6 + 41806.0, 28910.3 + 41803.6, 28908.0 + 41803.0, 28911.2 + 41803.4

Mid-Bank

28896.0 + 41816.0, 28895.5 + 41813.5, 28898.0 + 41808.0

(Note: Loran numbers courtesy Paul Jones and Far West Resort charter skippers. Anglers are encouraged to explore these areas and discover additional hotspots for their own Loran logbooks. Avoid always returning to fish the same spot; spread out your effort.)

Facilities

Area code for all listings is 206.

Resorts—Neah Bay

(**Note:** In this recreational fishing village, in addition to lodging/RV space, most resorts are full-service, offering complete *moorage/marina facilities* and *charters*, which mostly book through resorts.)

Rates vary but generally at Neah Bay, daily charters at press time were running in the vicinity of $65 for salmon and $85 for halibut. Overnight moorage rates were about 40 to 50 cents per foot. Boat rentals were running $25 or so per day without power, but at least three times that with outboard. Limited engine repair service may be available for boaters in Neah Bay, but for major work, Clallam Bay is the closest point. RV hookups rates were running $11-14.

Big Salmon Fishing Resort, P.O. Box 204, Neah Bay 98357, 645-2374. Operated by Mike and Linda Jablinske. April 1-October 15, 5 a.m. to 10 p.m., daily. Marina offers boat launching via concrete ramp good for any trailerable boat on all tides, moorage with 110 slips and fuel. Minor boat repair available. Fleet of 10 charters from 24 feet to 50 feet operates out of Big Salmon. Rents 16- to 20-foot kickerboats with or without power. Complete bait and tackle shop. In business since 1965. Does not offer lodging.

Far West Fishing Resort, P.O. Box 131, Neah Bay 98357, 645-2270. Operated by Pete and Joan Hanson. April 1-midSeptember, 4:30 am to 10 pm daily. 65 RV sites, many with full hookups. Marina offers boat launching via paved ramp, good for most trailerable boats on all tides, moorage with 78 slips. Reservations recommended. Fuel available. Fleet of 6 charters from 28 to 52 feet available (6-to 18-person). Rents 16- to 18-foot Pacific Mariner boats with or without power. Complete bait and tackle shop. Resort in business since 1936.

Neah Bay Resort, P.O. Box 97, Neah Bay 98357, 645-2288. Operated by Don and Jean Anderson. May 1-Sept. 30, open "all the time" in season. 18 "fishermen's cabins," with and without facilities; 40 RV sites, half with hookups and space for a few tents. Hoist launch for boats up to 22 feet. Moorage for 30 boats and mooring buoys for boats up to 34 feet. Reservations recommended. Fuel available. Rents 16-foot Pacific Mariner skiffs with or without power. Limited selection of bait and tackle available. Offers small cafe. Site is east of (before) town along highway—some find it quieter, more relaxed than "downtown" Neah Bay. In business since 1949.

Silver Salmon Resort, P.O. Box 156, Neah Bay 98357, 645-2388. Operated by Pete and Joyce Hirst. All year, open anytime, daily. 9 rooms and 25 RV spaces with full hookups. Not on water; just across the street in Neah Bay.

Snow Creek Resort, P.O. Box 248, Neah Bay 98357, 645-2284. Operated by Howard and Shirley Larson. April 15-midSeptember, 5 a.m. to 10 p.m., daily. 4 trailers set up with complete hook ups. Hoist launch for boats to 27 feet. Moorage for 40 boats, reservations recommended. Rents 14-foot kickerboats without power. Bait and tackle available. Located east of Neah Bay Resort off the highway. Run is longer to ocean, but waters here are more protected, area quiet. Snow Creek resort in business since 1950.

Westwind Resort, P.O. Box 918, Neah Bay 98357, 645-2751. Operated by Anthony Rodriguez. May 1-Sept. 30, open anytime every day. 4 cabins and 26 RV spaces with hookups. Good paved ramp. Moorage for 86 boats, reservations recommended at least 2 weeks ahead. 4 charters, 6-person to 14-person. Bait and tackle available. In business since 1986.

Resorts—Sekiu

Rates for cabins or rooms in Sekiu at press time were running the range of $25 to 55 per night. RV sites were running $10-13/night with hookups. Rates for salmon charters were $55 to 60.

Coho Motel and Charters, HCR 61, Box 10, Sekiu 98381, 963-2233. Operated by Buzz and Jamie Wisecup. MidFebruary-midOctober, open anytime every day. 17 motel units. Paved launch ramp across the street. Moorage available across the street—reservations recommended—months in advance for peak season. Operates 1 6-person salmon charter. In business since about 1965, half that under present owners.

Coho Resort, HCR 61, Box 15, Sekiu 98381, 963-2333. Larry Wilson, manager. Limited operation (floats in) early March; full operation May-midOctober, 4 am-10 pm (later on weekends), 7 days/week. 108 RV spaces with full hookups, 44 with sewers; 40 acres "primitive camping," restaurant nearby. 2-lane paved launch ramp with floats, good for any trailerable boat at all tides. 100 moorage slips, reservations not available. Fuel. Rents 16-foot kickerboats without power. Complete bait and tackle shop. In business since 1960.

Curley's Motel, P.O. Box 265, Sekiu 98381, 963-2281. Operated by Jerry and Holli Scott. April 1-October 15, anytime every day. 4 cabins, 18-unit motel, 13 RV spaces with full hookups. Launch ramp 1 block away. 24 moorage slips, reservations needed in season. Fuel available and some engine repair. Rents 14- to 16-foot fiberglass kickerboats with or without power. Some bait and tackle available. Curley's prides itself on getting fresh bait daily. In business since 1955.

Herb's Motel and Charters, P.O. Box 175, Sekiu 98381, 963-2346. Operated by Herb and Sandra Balch. All year. 12 motel units. Boat launch, fuel, moorage at Olson's, next door. 1 6-person salmon charter. In business since 1960, half of that time under present ownership.

Olson's Resort, P.O. Box 216, Sekiu 98381, 963-2311. Operated by Arlen and Donalynn Olson. February-midOctober, daylight to dark, daily. 14 "fishermen's cabins" and 14 motel units, as well as a house that sleeps 12; 60 RV sites with hookups, 200 without. 6-lane paved launch ramp good in all tides. Moorage, fuel. Four 6-person charters for salmon or bottomfish, 38 to 42 feet. Rents 16-to 19-foot boats with or without power. Complete bait and tackle shop. Plenty of freezer space for fish storage. In business since 1934.

Rice's Resort, P.O. Box 180, Sekiu 98381, 963-2300. Operated by Chris and Valerie Mohr. May-Sept, 4 am to 11 pm daily. 3 cabins, 50 RV sites, most with hookups. Paved launch ramp good on all but very low tides. 150 moorage slips, no reservations. 3 charters for salmon and bottomfish. Rents kickerboats with or without power. Bait and tackle shop.

Van Riper's Resort, P.O. Box 246, Sekiu 98381, 963-2334. Operated by Chris and Valerie Mohr. MidFebruary-midOctober (RV area open and docks in the water beginning in April), 4 am-10 pm daily. 2 cabins, 11 motel rooms and 80 RV sites both with and without hookups Paved launch ramp good on all but very low tides. 200 moorage slips. No fuel available on site. 3 6-person salmon charters. Rents kickers with or without power. Bait and tackle shop. In business since 1973.

Resorts—Pillar Point

Silver King Resort, HCR 61, Box 10-A, Clallam Bay, WA 98236, 963-2800. Operated by John Haller. Open year-round, daylight to dark, daily. 175 RV sites, 29 with full hookups, 36 without (tent sites). Paved launch ramp good except low tides. 154 moorage slips, reservations recommended. Fuel, bait and tackle available. Resort in business since 1970, most of that time under present ownership.

RV Parks

Hobuck Beach Park (Neah Bay—645-2422), Village Cabins/Camping (Neah Bay—645-2659), Bayview Mobile & RV Park (Sekiu—963-2750), Trettevik's RV Park (Sekiu—963-2688), Muralt's Trailer Court & Cabins (Sekiu—963, 2394), Thomas's Trailer Court (Sekiu—963-2396), Hinkle's Trailer Park (Clallam Bay—963-2394), Sam's Trailer & RV Park (Clallam Bay—963-2402).

Campgrounds

Pillar Point County Park (on Highway 112, 40 miles west of Port Angeles), Clallam Bay Spit County Park (in Clallam Bay), Clallam River Park, Dept. of Natural Resources (1 1/2 miles south of Clallam Bay).

For More Information

Clallam Bay/Sekiu Chamber of Commerce, P.O. Box 355, Clallam Bay, WA 98236, 963-2339.

Fat blackmouth are picked up within minutes of the harbor. This catch was taken just off Neah Bay Resort.

La Push

La push differs from other Washington coastal sportfishing centers in several ways. For one thing, most of the sport effort here is from private, rather than charter boats. Resorts cater to this trade, providing ample moorage. And instead of crossing a river bar, access to the Pacific is a matter of slipping around the protected side of James Island. Much smaller than either Ilwaco or Westport, La Push is entirely within the Quileute Indian Reservation, at the mouth of the Quileute River.

Salmon—Trolling For A Mixed Catch

Silvers predominate here in late July and, increasingly, in August. Most fishing takes place around riplines well offshore, where chinook are often mixed with coho. Larger chinook are taken closer to the area's dramatic coastline.

On odd years, a run of pink salmon swings by La Push before heading into the Strait of Juan de Fuca. Some years this run of 3- to 6-pounders may prove inconsequential, but other years it adds substantially to summer catches.

Most sport fishermen out of La Push troll, using downriggers or diving planes to pull flashers and plastic squid with or without herring.

Bottomfish On "The Rockpile" And Nearshore Pinnacles

La Push + "The Rockpile" = bottomfish. That's an equation not lost on fishing boats that have over the years returned from trips to this prolific spot with fish boxes filled with lings, yelloweye, other red rockfishes and many other species of bottomfish. And from the northeast corner in about 26 fathoms and deeper, over a sandy/gravelly bottom, some halibut are taken.

Some 9 miles west of La Push, the rockpile is not a small reef as its name may suggest, but an extensive area of rocky reefs roughly 1 1/2 miles by 3/4 mile and rising to within about 21 fathoms of the surface.

Fairly heavy commercial fishing during most of the year and, to a much lesser extent, an increasingly intensive sport fishery have taken their toll. But good catches still come from its rugged slopes. And there are many fine bottomfishing areas much closer to LaPush. On calm days, small boaters can get into some of these areas, in the rocky, shallow waters off the shoreline pinnacles and headlands.

Surf Fishing: More Potential Than Pressure

There is very little surf fishing along the coastline at La Push, perhaps because access is somewhat limited. However, just north, Rialto Beach at the Olympic National Seashore campground attracts fair numbers of surfcasters who fish the sandy surf for redtail perch and often do quite well during incoming tides.

Otherwise, wherever a shore fishermen can get to a rocky stretch of shoreline he or she should find perch, greenling, rockfish, cabezon and small lings willing to take baits or strike jigs and worms.

A surf fishery overlooked by many is that for smelt which move in to spawn on sandy beaches of the Olympic coast during the summer. They can be dipped near high tide at most sandy beaches, such as that at Ruby Beach and just north of Kalaloch.

When silvers are reported to be massing offshore, La Push anglers start to point their bows west and head out.

Small Boat Safety

There being no real bar to cross at La Push, one enters the Pacific and returns to this small harbor by passing south of James Island and north of the small rock breakwater. Areas to beware of: the end of the breakwater and the water close to James Island, where submerged rocks pose an immediate hazard. The Coast Guard station here can provide more information.

U.S. Coast Guard Station—Quileute River

Station phone (24-hour) 374-6469
Emergency . 374-5112

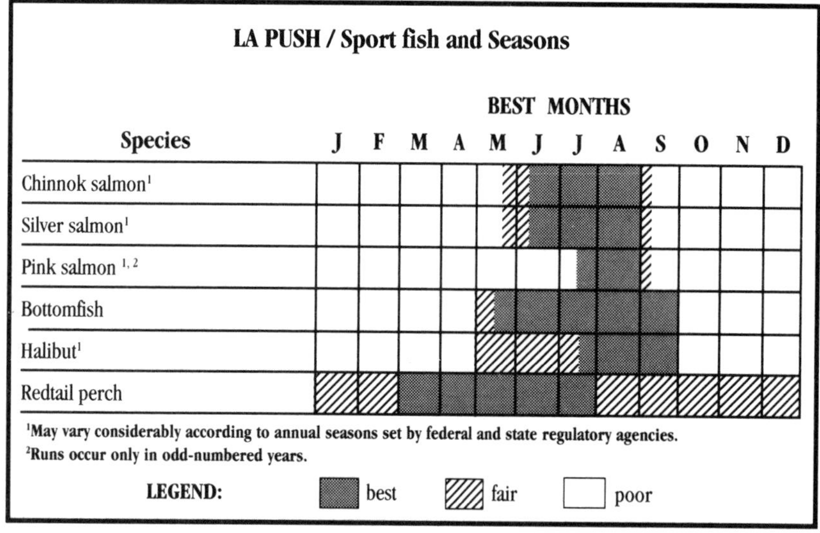

LA PUSH / Sport fish and Seasons

Species	J	F	M	A	M	J	J	A	S	O	N	D
						BEST MONTHS						
Chinook salmon[1]					fair	best	best	best	fair			
Silver salmon[1]					fair	best	best	best	fair			
Pink salmon[1, 2]							best	best	fair			
Bottomfish					fair/best	best	best	best	best			
Halibut[1]					fair	fair	fair	best	best			
Redtail perch	fair	fair	best	best	best	best	best	fair	fair	fair	fair	fair

[1]May vary considerably according to annual seasons set by federal and state regulatory agencies.
[2]Runs occur only in odd-numbered years.

LEGEND: best / fair / poor

FACILITIES

All phone numbers listed are within the 206 area code unless otherwise noted.

Ocean Park Motel and Cottages, P.O. Box 67, La Push 98350, 374-5267. Open all year, 8 am-9 pm every day. Motel rooms, cabins, RV sites, tentsites.

Shoreline Resort, P.O. Box 26, La Push 98350, 374-6488. Open all year, 7 days/week. Ocean view cabins.

La Push Marine, P.O. Box 249, La Push 98350, 374-5392. Open every day, year-round. 72 moorage slips; reservations recommended during summer. Fuel; bait and tackle nearby. Nearest engine repair in Forks (15 miles). Launch ramp okay except at low tides, moderate fee.

Olympic Sporting Goods, P.O. Box 538, Forks 98331, 374-6330, is closest major tackle outlet. Open Monday-Saturday, all year. Some saltwater gear though more emphasis in fishing peninsula's fresh waters.

Rialto Beach Campground, Olympic National Park, 442-0181 (Seattle). Located at Mora—watch for turn to west approximately 6 miles north of La Push. 95 tent/RV sites. Adjacent to beach just north of Quileute River.

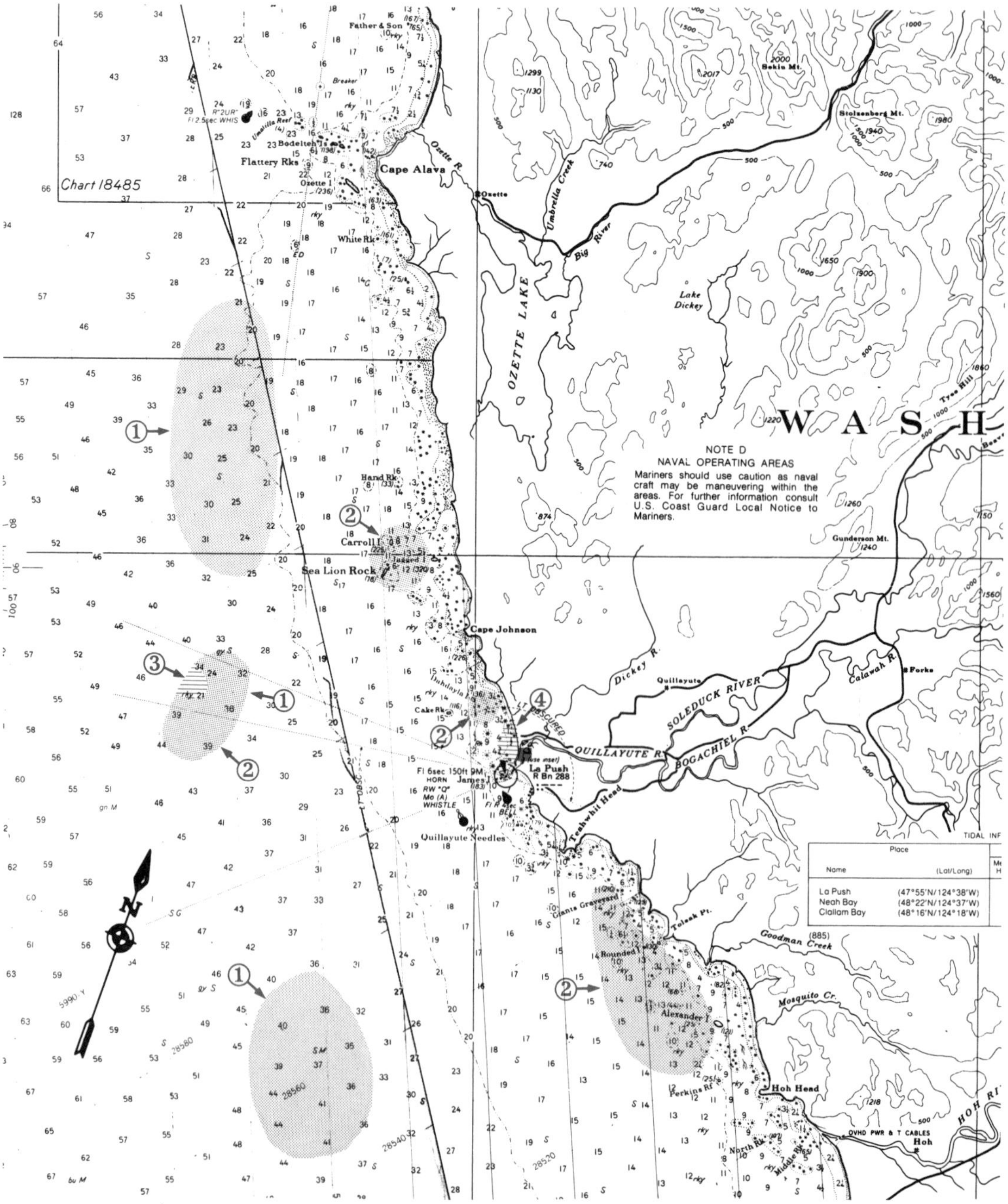

La Push

Legend
1. Chinook, silver salmon.
2. Bottomfish.
3. Halibut.
4. Surfperch.
■ Launch Site
No Scale

Chart #18480

Not for navigational purposes.

WESTPORT

"SALMON FISHING IS US" COULD WELL BE Westport's motto, since the community has largely developed around its salmon sport fisheries over several decades.

In fact, Westport bills itself as the "Salmon Capital of the World." In the mid1970s, well over 200 salmon charters were operating here. By the mid 1980s less than 100 remained and by 1990 only about 55 charter boats remained (still a sizeable fleet).

The salmon haven't disappeared, as one might suspect after looking at these figures. Westport's charter industry was stricken by years of drastically shortened seasons beginning in the early 1980s and reduced bag limits. But the smaller fleet that still operates has been rewarded in recent years with somewhat longer seasons and some of the hottest salmon fishing in decades. In fact, it has been unusual for charters (and many private boats) to return *without* limits.

At the same time, there is more variety here now than in years past. Forced into offering bottomfishing in the face of declining salmon fisheries during the '80s, Westport charters found they could provide a sport that just about guaranteed customers 15- to 18-fish limits and full filet bags. And no port north of central California has a fleet with so many well-equipped modern charters for pursuing albacore (on day trips).

Westport's charter season runs spring through early fall. In recent years, bottomfish charters have operated May and at least part of June, until ocean salmon fishing opened.

Fishing from a charter boat is the way the majority of anglers enjoy Westport fishing, but it's not the only way. Launch and moorage facilities cater to private boaters. And nonboaters can fish from the south jetty and from several finger jetties well inside the harbor and away from crashing swells where there are usually some fish to be caught. Redtail perch, particularly in the spring, can be great fun in the surf.

THE MAKING OF A "WORLD SALMON CAPITAL"

Offshore salmon fishing at Westport is a unique experience that starts when an angler first arrives. Unless he's towing a boat he'll be looking to reserve space on a charter. Even pared down from its earlier glory days, the Westport fleet is big, sleek and well-equipped with a harbor full of modern boats. The cost of a day of salmon fishing reflects both the modern boats and the short season, at $55-65.

The initial consideration confronting a charter fishermen, then, is selecting a boat. The waterfront is lined with charter offices (often with adjoining restaurants or small motels) which beckon with bright lights and photos of charter boats and fish.

By 4 a.m. next morning, fishermen (using the term to describe plenty of both sexes) will be filling cafes for breakfast, as the harbor comes alive. Bait is cut aboard charters and diesel engines are humming as anglers climb aboard. Soon, the red, green and white lights of charter after charter can be seen churning out the harbor toward the jetties in the predawn murkiness, often dipping and bouncing more as they go. On calm days, they are accompanied by swarms of smaller private boats like little pilot fish shadowing sharks.

Crossing the bar can be so smooth its unnoticeable—but more often it is decidedly noticeable, often serving up a quarter hour or so of plunging and lurching until things smooth out on the other side.

The run to the salmon grounds may last only a few minutes past the bar, or it may last an hour or more, depending upon where the fish have been. Sophisticated electronics and inter-boat cooperation on the VHF help find salmon.

Once the fish are found, plugcut herring on standard mooching leaders behind 4- to 6-ounce mooching (kidney) sinkers are lowered to the right depth according to the number of pulls of line off the reel suggested by the crew.

If the bite isn't immediately hot, some anglers may choose to set their rods in the rail holder and head into the cabin for a cup of coffee. As is often the case, though, fishing is likely to be fast enough to encourage fishermen to hang onto their rods and mooch baits actively.

In this way, Westport is a departure—for most anglers, a pleasant one—from the more prevalent coastal charter technique of trolling with heavy lines and heavy weights. I've been on trolling boats where the only time fishermen touched a rod was after a crew member pulled it from a holder with a hooked salmon and handed to the eager angler to crank in. One of the pleasures of fishing salmon at Westport is that nearly all boats drift-mooch: this is definitely hands-on fishing.

In a typical year, the season catch here may average about 80% silvers, with the rest mostly larger kings. Some years, chinook may prove much more numerous than this, as in 1987 when some estimates put catch at about 50:50 chinook to coho.

BOTTOMFISH—BY THE BOATLOAD

Tired, rubbing salty skin, men and women sit on benches inside the boat's cabin or stand around the deck, talking and drinking coffee or beer as the charter steams south toward port. Flocks of seagulls wheel, screaming overhead, fighting for scraps as deckhands in yellow slickers rush to clean and bag black rockfish and lingcod numerous enough to cover the entire back deck.

It's a scene that almost anyone who's been out on a Westport bottomfishing trip knows well. Not that many years ago, it would have been fiction. When salmon fishing

"Bottomfish by the boatload" is literally evident by the pile of black rockfish covering the deck of this Westport charter—a typical day's catch.

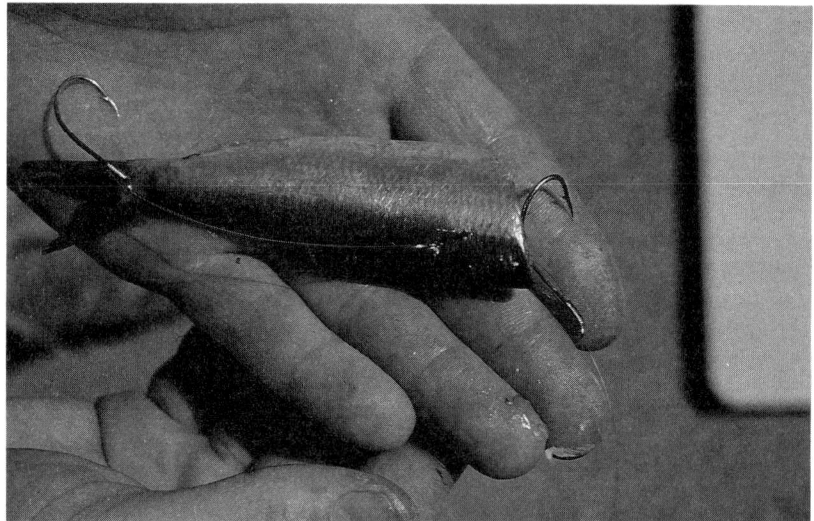

The huge majority of salmon taken off Westport are caught by mooching plugcut herring.

was in its heyday, bottomfish were little more than pests. But as salmon fishing grew increasingly restricted, bottomfish gained an audience. In fact, few bottomfish charters fail to find arm-wearying action and loads of fish—limits of up to 18 fish are the rule.

Black rockfish ("sea bass") generally account for 15 of those fish. They are the bread-and-butter of Westport bottomfish trips. Enormous schools can usually be found in relatively shallow water (50 to 130 feet), hovering around small pinnacles that rise slightly from a smooth bottom.

The area fished most often for blacks is a considerable run north of the harbor, often off Copalis Rocks. But schools of blacks may sometimes be found much closer, not always around pinnacles but in open water, below aggregations of baitfish.

Daily Bag Minimum Size Regulations For The Ocean Sport Salmon Fishery, 1921-1989.

(Wash. Dept. of Fisheries)

Year	Minimum Total Length	Daily Bag Limit
1921 (7/15)	6 inches	Three salmon over 15 inches in length and 25 between 6 and 15 inches in length, provided the aggregate weight of those between 6 and 15 inches in length does not exceed 20 pounds.
1922 (2/20)	18 inches	Three salmon.
1922 (3/30)	10 inches	Twenty-five salmon, provided the aggregate weight of the catch does not exceed 20 pounds and one additional salmon.
1935	12 inches	Fifteen salmon, provided the aggregate weight of the catch does not exceed 20 pounds and one additional salmon.
1941	12 inches	Ten salmon, provided the aggregate weight of the catch does not exceed 20 pounds and one addtional salmon.
1944	12 inches	Six salmon provided no more than three exceed 24 inches in length.
1958 (7/10)	20 inches	Three salmon.
1976	24 inches—chinook 16 inches—coho	Three salmon.
1982-1989	24 inches—chinook 20 inches—coho	Two salmon

Quotas And Regulations—Living With The Albatross

The Northwest coastal charter business in the past couple decades has had more ups and downs than a salmon boat drifting in a 10-foot sea. Nowhere has that been felt more than in communities such as Westport which rely on salmon sportfishing.

After decades of long and consistent seasons, salmon sportfishing regulations have become complex and unpredictable from year to year since the imposition of varying annual catch quotas years ago. These quotas are determined by a matrix of variables including a weak-stock management strategy that limits catches in the ocean of all stocks—however healthy most may be—if one or two north coast river stocks are in trouble (since of course stocks mix in the ocean). That has often meant shutting down seasons when the ocean seemed absolutely alive with salmon. No one knows until sometime in the spring just when ocean salmon seasons set by the Pacific Fishery Management Council (PFMC) will begin.

And even as the summer starts, there is often little idea how long salmon fishing will last—perhaps only through midAugust as it has many seasons but hopefully sometime into September. As one means to extend seasons despite stingy quotas, there has been a trend recently to close part of the coast to salmon fishing one or two days per week (when bottomfishing is still permitted, typically Friday-Saturday).

The many people who directly or indirectly make their living from the sport fishing business here acknowledge the need for regulation. But they tend to be skeptical of the need for so stringently regulating recreational use and have long been unhappy about the confusion this management approach causes the public.

A combination of factors here enhances fishing for black rockfish. They generally run a fair size, often 3 to 6 pounds, occasionally to 8. They school in shallow water, and often there are no swift currents to contend with. And they frequently feed at or near the surface, where they attack any flashing, moving object (at times even bare hooks). These favorable conditions account for catches of doubles on two-hook rigs—typically plastic worms and shrimp flies.

But at least a few anglers have begun to realize the fabulously fast sport these fish can offer on light tackle—light spinning or baitcasting gear with 6- to 12-pound line. I've even fished 4-pound test on tiny ultralights and watched others cast streamers on fly rods. Spoons, leadhead jigs, even surface plugs all draw strikes when cast and worked with light gear. It will take a bit longer to get fish to the boat, but that is all time spent in a more honest fight which can challenge your skills.

Obviously, there is no problem fishing such tackle from a private boat. What about from a charter? It's absolutely feasible; I've done so successfully for years. Plan to fish the bow: it's less crowded as a rule and you'll have close to a 180-degree radius in which to cast and work jigs. As long as you stay on top of things it is surprisingly easy to keep your line well away from others. The more gentle the drift, the easier time you'll have.

Still, before bringing light gear onto a boat, check with the skipper. Years ago, most would have frowned at the sight of such tackle. But then years ago most were still throwing rockfish back as "trash fish." Necessity is the mother of flexibility; I've found that almost any skipper these days is glad to accomodate light-tackle enthusiasts as long as they can catch most of the fish they hook and keep out of the way while doing it.

Black rockfish are the major catch of Westport bottomfishermen, but lingcod remain a major target. The daily limit, at least at press time, was still three per day (which can be added on top of 15 rockfish—if anyone actually wants that much fish). Experienced anglers know that below the schools of blacks, larger lingcod often lurk. In fact, surprising numbers of lings may be caught from very small pinnacles or little rockpiles.

At least a few lings of 5 to 20 pounds are caught on most bottomfish charters, but many trips also see a ling or two topping 35-40 pounds swung over the rails. Frequently, as a startled fisherman reels in a black rockfish, a lingcod will engulf it and keep its jaws clamped tightly shut around its prey until in the net or thrashing wildly on deck. Many anglers have learned that its hard to beat a small, live rockfish dropped back to bottom specifically to entice any big lings that may be around.

Some days the lingcod will be thick and feeding actively, so they'll take just about anything thrown at them, whether herring, jigs or live bait. I've been out on days when black rockfish action was slow—but everyone aboard had a three-lingcod limit in the boat by noon.

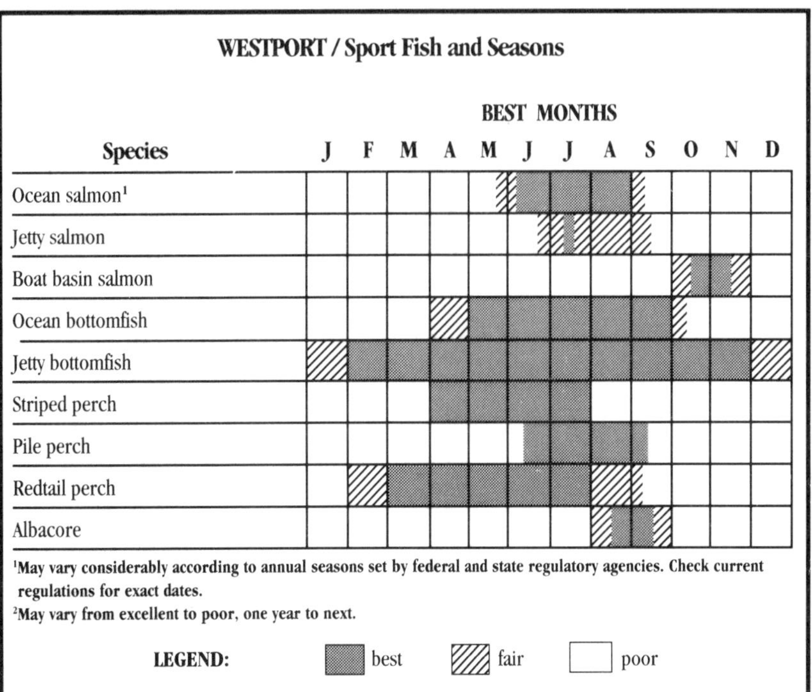

WESTPORT / Sport Fish and Seasons

Species	J	F	M	A	M	J	J	A	S	O	N	D
	BEST MONTHS											
Ocean salmon[1]	poor	poor	poor	poor	poor/fair	fair/best	best	best	fair/poor	poor	poor	poor
Jetty salmon	poor	poor	poor	poor	poor	poor/fair	fair/best/fair	fair	fair/poor	poor	poor	poor
Boat basin salmon	poor	poor	poor	poor	poor	poor	poor	poor	poor	fair/best	best/fair	poor
Ocean bottomfish	poor	poor	poor	fair	best	best	best	best	best	fair/poor	poor	poor
Jetty bottomfish	fair	best	best	best	best	best	best	best	best	best	best	fair
Striped perch	poor	poor	poor	best	best	best	best	poor	poor	poor	poor	poor
Pile perch	poor	poor	poor	poor	poor	poor/best	best	best	best/poor	poor	poor	poor
Redtail perch	poor	fair	best	best	best	best	best	fair	fair/poor	poor	poor	poor
Albacore	poor	poor	poor	poor	poor	poor	poor	fair/best	best/fair	poor	poor	poor

[1]May vary considerably according to annual seasons set by federal and state regulatory agencies. Check current regulations for exact dates.

[2]May vary from excellent to poor, one year to next.

LEGEND: best; fair; poor

In the protection of lower Grays Harbor, the "finger jetties" offer easy access and a good shot at catching something, year-round.

While black rockfish and lingcod offer reliable fishing, there may be some bottomfish alternatives at Westport. It may be worth checking around to see if any boats are working deeper reefs—running farther offshore than north.

I was part of such a trip a few years back on a bouncy May day aboard expert skipper Phil Westrick's *Gold Rush.* Fellow outdoor writer Terry Rudnick and I fished the bow with 8-pound (6-kg class) monofilament, dropping our 5-ounce Krocodile spoons and Pt. Wilson Darts to the bottom over which we were anchored—270 feet below. That's a whole different scene than the usual 80 or 90 feet Westport bottomfish trips are usually fishing.

Everyone aboard had action all morning—lots of various red-colored rockfish dominated the catch. The real surprise on this trip proved to be canary rockfish: I'd never seen so many that were so large. They averaged nearly 8 or 9 pounds and several larger were boated. Anyone who's spent much time fishing Northwest coast bottomfish knows that those are *big* canary rockfish.

Many doubles (that's 15 to 20 pounds at a crack) came over the rails for anglers using the boat's conventional, heavier gear. We didn't boat two at once, but we did take some of the biggest canaries on our light lines. And we had one *hell* of a time doing it. No cranking right up for us; rather, each fish made sustained runs and fought nearly all the way. In the end, I boated some nearly 10 pounds, but it was Rudnick who took the biggest canary (on the lightest line). That officially weighed 10 pounds back at the dock at day's end and has been a long-standing IGFA all-tackle world record for the species.

In recent years, halibut have become increasingly common in the Westport sportcatch. Incidental barndoors are not unusual, but few boats target on them since halibut catch quotas for this part of the coast are adequate for the season-long incidental catches, but would be quickly used up in a directed fishery.

Jetty Fishing, Inside And Out

Westport is an unusual spot for coastal rock hoppers since it offers good jetty fishing from a long, outer jetty and from a series of protected short finger jetties just outside the boat basin (see maps).

The finger jetties are fished fairly heavily; they provide protection from crashing swells, people can park right at their bases, and fishing is varied and often rewarding. Lingcod, rockfish (mostly blacks), sculpins, greenling and surfperch are all pulled onto the rocks.

Some fishermen on the finger jetties target on lingcod, especially in the late winter. Try catching small live baits with little, baited hooked hooks on a light rod. Then rig one with little or no weight on a heavier rod and cast out. Lings, particularly the smaller ones, will also readily hit leadhead jigs and plastic worms. Lings over 30 pounds have been landed from these jetties, particularly during the winter and spring. But of course a few pounds is a more typical size. At times, jetty fishermen will return with limits.

In the summer, hordes of anchovies often park themselves inside the harbor where they can be caught readily by anglers jigging tiny gold hooks from the docks. They offer excellent live baits for jetty fishermen.

Black rockfish are most numerous around daybreak and sunset and through the night. At such times, unweighted plastic worms may produce well when fished slowly. Surface lures and flies may also draw strikes, though many anglers fish bait. During the day, blacks are generally more elusive, though they may move in to feed around the rocks during slack tides.

Perch fishermen find striped perch around the finger jetties from April through midJuly and pile perch midJune through midSeptember. Sand shrimp are the bait of choice.

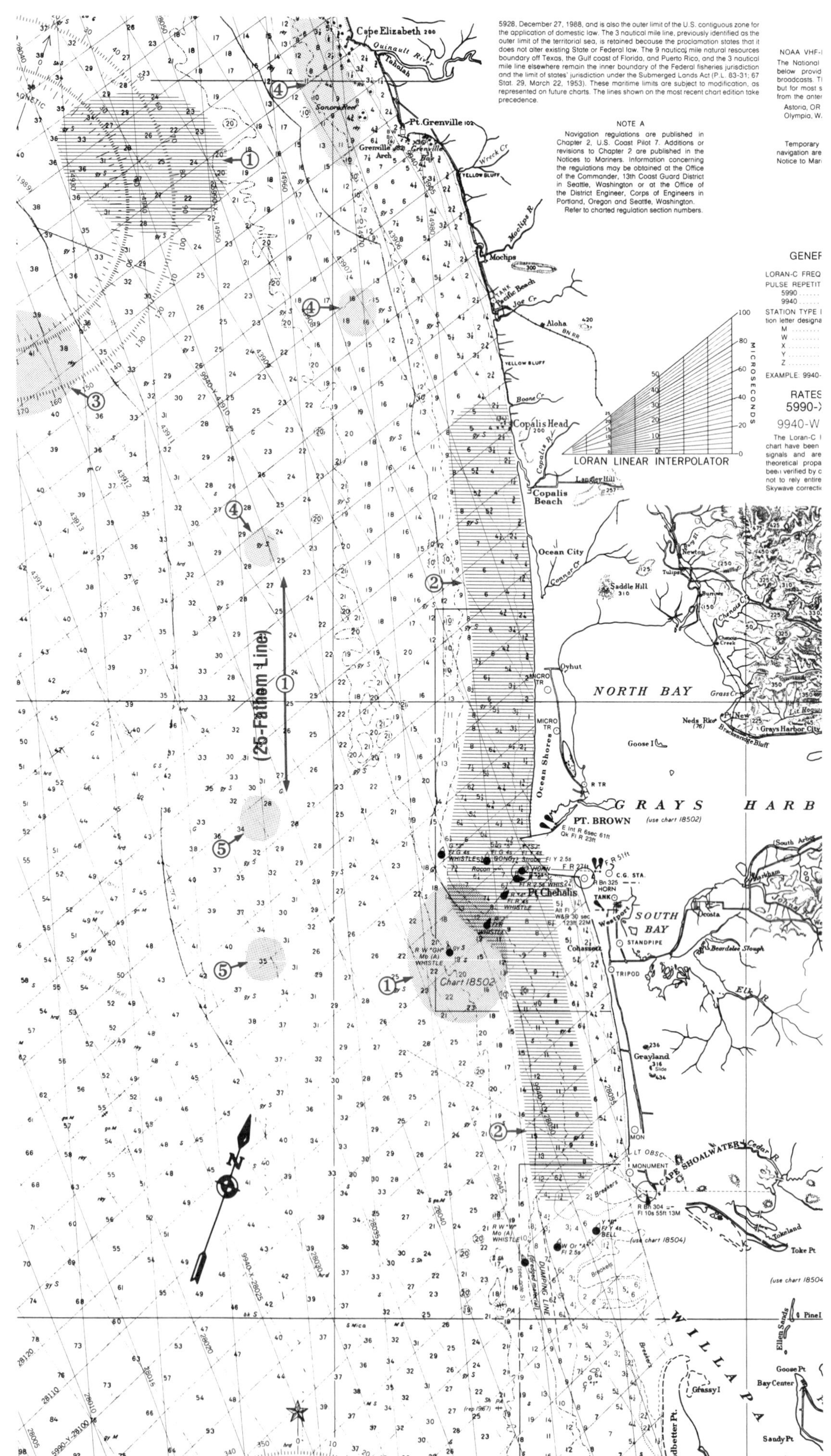

Westport Entrance & Harbor

Legend

1. Chinook outside the bar (late June-July 15)
2. Flounder.
3. Bottomfish on south jetty, training jetty.
4. Skate.
5. Redtail surfperch, south beach (March-June).
6. Redtail surfperch, inside the harbor (summer).
7. Sea-run cutthroat.

■ Launch Site

No Scale

Chart #18502

Not for navigational purposes.

Redtails to 4 pounds are most available February through August. In the spring they are abundant in the surf south of the jetty. Fish an incoming tide. If the surf is not too rough, a light or medium spinning rod will work at least as well as a big, traditional surf stick. Later in the summer, Halfmoon Bay often comes alive with redtails which, in clear, calm waters may hit tiny spoons or spinners as readily as sand shrimp or clam necks.

Some salmon fishermen are consistently successful casting from the south jetty, especially around midJuly. Most use a standard moooching rig with plugcut herring and at least a 2-ounce sinker. Above this they'll attach a large Styrofoam float with a bobber stop set up the line about 30 feet. Not so many Buzz Bombs, Darts or other metal jigs are used here, but should work well. Slack tides are periods of peak activity.

Other species occasionally caught from the south and finger jetties include cabezon, flounder and even big skates. Some years surprises such as big schools of juvenile (2-pound) bocaccio rockfish move in. The latter produced some spectacular night fishing for the few who knew about it.

Of course, jetty anglers put in their time for their fish—moreso than boat anglers. But with persistence, some good catches are made.

Bluewater Fishing: Albacore And Sharks

Albacore are notoriously unpredictable, all along the Pacific coast. There are two separate stocks, one which generally summers off central and southern California and another which summers off northern California, Oregon and Washington (even at times off southern British Columbia).

The question mark for sportfishermen is not whether they'll show up off the Northwest coast, but whether they'll

Westport Offshore

Legend

1. Chinook, coho (late summer).
2. Chinook (late summer).
3. Halibut.
4. Black rockfish, lingcod.
5. Yelloweye, canary, black and other rockfish, lingcod.

No Scale

Chart #18500

Not for navigational purposes

Not an albacore, but still a tuna: this bonito suprised the author when he cast a jig into an offshore feeding frenzy. It was one of many surprises during a warmwater "El Nino" year.

move within range of sportfishing boats. They usually do "show up" sometime in late July or August and may remain through September, but many years they stay 150 to 200 or more miles offshore—within the domain of large commercial vessels, but not smaller charters. (Only the southern California sportfishing fleet is set up with big, fast multi-crew offshore albacore charters to run 2-, 3- or even 4-day trips.)

During the late 1970s, albacore did show up within 30 to 80 miles of the Washington coast for several years in a row and the result was some fabulous fishing for these long-finned, exquisite tuna averaging 15 to 25 pounds. Catches on some trips ran as high as five or more tuna per angler.

Small Boat Safety—Crossing The Bar

Sloppy seas, even running against an ebb tide, don't usually keep sleek Westport charters in port. But under such rather common conditions, the ride over the bar, through high, cresting waves, may be exhilarating for those charter passengers not knowing what to expect.

At such times, small boaters should have sufficient sanity to remain in port but, fortunately, there are many days in summer and early fall (especially August and September) when the bar is so calm that one can hardly detect the crossing.

Of course as with any bar, crossings should be timed to tidal conditions. That is likely to mean that a strong ebb around daybreak will keep small boaters in port for a few hours *unless* the ocean is truly flat. In general, flood and slack tides are crossable.

Even when calm, though, small boaters should avoid the area between the end of the south jetty and buoy 8. Submerged, the jetty runs out a considerable distance toward the buoy. Coast Guard personnel at Westport say this is easily the most dangerous area, since breakers may occur over the rocks in even the calmest weather. Most boats cross in the deep water just north of the south jetty. A prominent rough bar warning sign is located in the harbor on the point of land northeast of the Islander Motel.

U.S. Coast Guard Station—Grays Harbor

Station phone (24-hour)................ 268-0121
Weather/bar conditions (recording)....... 268-2622

Then during most of the 1980s, to the disappointment of many anglers and skippers—who were desperately trying to make ends meet, faced suddenly with some of the shortest salmon seasons on record—the albcore fishery dried up. They simply never moved in. (At the same time, record years were registered in southern California.)

But every year brought new hope and as southern California fish disappeared in the late 1980s, albacore came back to within range of sport boats off Washington. Again, fishermen enjoyed several good years in a row.

But no one has ever been able to predict the movements of albacore, tied so closely with currents and water temperatures offshore. So each summer is a question mark. Those interested in this exciting bluewater sport should contact a charter office that runs tuna trips long before the fish normally show. They'll put you on a list and call if/when the albies are in. Then, be ready to go on short notice.

These 12- to 18-hour trips are *not* for the weak of stomach. But for many who are not prone to *mal-de-mer*, a day on the open ocean is a tonic for the soul and albacore are icing on the cake. You'll start trolling feathers on heavy gear but may be able to switch to lighter, more sporting tackle. More boats these days carry live anchovies so you can driftfish and with very little weight flyline the bait out to hungry tuna around the boat. This is done with lighter gear (typically 20- to 30-pound line), which maximizes the sport for albacore, like all tuna an incredibly powerful, relentless fighter. There can't be any Northwest coast sportfishing experience more exciting than multiple hookups of big albacore.

But that experience doesn't come free. Boats normally do a lot of running to find the tuna, reflected in the cost of $150 to $180 at press time.

Shark fishing, for years big business on the Atlantic coast, has never really taken off here. Nor has it been widely pushed, though sharks can offer as much as any angler would like in a game fish: large size, hard fight and fair-to-excellent food value. And they can be numerous.

The pelagic, ghoulish-eyed blue shark is by far the most common species in the waters off Westport. It attains at least 12 feet though averages less. Other quarry would probably include salmon sharks, soupfins, threshers (as fine eating and as hard fighting as any fish in the North Pacific—see "Encounter With a Thresher Shark" in the chapter on Fishing Northwest Salt Waters) and even great whites—rare but always possible—which can weigh thousands of pounds.

Boat Basin Salmon

A unique little salmon sportfishery at Westport offers anglers a shot at salmon long after coastal seasons have closed. No real cost or long run to fishing grounds is needed. In fact, you need only be at the harbor at the right time.

In the early 1980s, the Westport Charter Association began releasing 10,000 to 20,000 coho smolts annually from the boat basin. Soon the program was putting 200,000 coho into the harbor each year, since it was paying off.

Now a special season offers anglers the opportunity to fish for these silvers through the fall and winter—through January of the next year, though in fact peak fishing occurs during October and November. At press time, once again any fish of at least 12 inches could be legally kept and a generous six per day were allowed.

Anglers cast from the docks between charters tied up for the winter, fishing Buzz Bombs or other metal jigs or herring. Others row out in tiny skiffs and troll for the small coho.

Facilities

Unless noted otherwise, area code for all listings is 206; postal zip code in Westport is 98595.

Charters

Over 50 charterboats operate in season here. All offices run salmon trips, most offer bottomfishing and many pursue albacore when they're within range.

At press time, you could expect to pay $50 to 70 for an all-day salmon trip. Price varies depending upon individual office, size of boat (smaller boats with fewer anglers cost more), day of week (Sundays are a bit more than weekdays) and whether you bring your own gear or rent the boat's. Some smaller charters are limited to 6 anglers; larger boats can carry 25 or so. Twelve to 18 anglers are a typical boatload. Advance reservations for Sunday fishing are necessary. (For example, by midJune many offices are completely booked for Sunday walk-ons into August.) That situation is exacerbated with Sunday-Thursday-only salmon fishing, so all weekend salmon fishing is concentrated on one day. Most boats leave between 5:30 and 7:00 a.m. and return by 2:00 to 4:00 p.m.—or much earlier when fast fishing fills limits.

Bottomfish trips at press time run $45 to $60 depending upon many of the variables mentioned above. Times are similar, though boats may leave a half-hour later. Most of these trips make an effort to mix catches of black rockfish and lingcod. Some offices offer rockfish-only trips for a bit less money. They usually return earlier, as soon as 15-rockfish limits are caught, which is often within a few hours. Also, a few offices (such as Westport, Washington and Ocean charters among others—call around) offer deep-water trips upon occasion or specific demand. (See text for comments about deepwater fishing.)

If and when albacore show up (to within 60-80 miles of the coast, usually August-September), figure on paying $150 to 200 for a trip of 20 or so hours. Most boats leave about midnight (to reach the fishing grounds by daybreak, a critical period) and return about dusk the next day.

Many of the charter offices listed here own or are affiliated with specific waterfront motels and/or restaurants. Also, note that the toll-free numbers listed are in-state only and most are seasonally operative. The number of passengers shown is a maximum; most bottomfish trips and weekday salmon trips carry fewer.

With few exceptions, fishing starts in May and ends in September (limited operation for bottomfish before and after salmon fishing). Many offices offer boats for very popular whale watching trips in the winter.

Baywest (Blanchard) Charters, P.O. Box 1245, Westport, 268-0111. 2 boats, 56' (28-passengers) and 50' (20 passengers).

Bran Lee Charters, 2467 Westhaven Drive, Westport, 268-9177 (800-562-0163). 3 boats, 55 to 65' (up to 30-45 anglers).

Cachalot Charters, P. O. Box 348, Westport, 268-0323. 1 boat, 54' (to 20 anglers).

Coho Charters, P.O. Box 1087, Westport, 268-0111. 1 boat, 40' (15 anglers).

Deep Sea Charters, P.O. Box 1115, Westport, 268-9300 (800-562-0151). 9 boats, 36-53' (6 to 24 anglers).

Islander Resort, P.O. Box 488, Westport, 268-9166. 1 boat, 42' (16 anglers)—expects to add more charters.

Lady Dee Charters, P.O. Box 723, Westport, 268-0218. 1 boat, 45 feet.

Neptune Charters, P.O. Box 426, Westport, 268-0124 (800-422-0425). 3 boats, 40 to 65 feet (18 to 30 anglers). Also offers one boat during winter months, available for bottomfishing trips.

Ocean Charters, P.O. Box 458, Westport, 268-9144 (800-562-0105). 5 boats, 31' to 56' (6 to 28 anglers).

Olympic Sportfishing, P.O. Box 170, Westport, 268-9593. 1 boat, 56' (23 anglers).

Rainbow Charters, P.O. Box 585, Westport, 268-9182. 2 boats, 43' and 50' (20 to 25 anglers).

Rocky's Charters, P.O. Box 1688, Westport, 268-0881 (800-562-0167). 3 boats, 50 to 54 feet (18 to 24).

Salmon Charters, P.O. Box 545, Westport, 268-9150 (800-562-0145). 8 boats, 32 to 55' (6 to 24 anglers).

Sea Horse Charters, P.O. Box 327, Westport, 268-9100 (800-562-0171). 2 boats, 40 and 43' (12 and 18 anglers).

Travis Charters, P.O. Box 542, Westport, 268-9140. 2 boats, 40 and 50' (14 and 20 anglers).

Washington Charters, P.O. Box 466, Westport, 268-0900 (800-562-0173). 5 boats, 38 to 54' (6 to 22 anglers).

Westport Charters, P.O. Box 546, Westport, 268-9120 (800-562-0157). 8 boats, 40 to 50' (12 to 20 anglers).

Bait, Tackle

In addition to shops listed below, many charter offices sell at least a limited amount of bait and tackle.

Hungry Whale, Montesano and Wilson, Westport, 268-0136. One of best selections of tackle in Westport. Open year-round, 7 days/week. Fresh herring daily in season.

Grays Harbor Bait, 609 Neddie Rose Drive (in boat basin by the Islander), Westport, 268-0317. Open year-round, 7 days/week. Bait only: fresh herring and live anchovies in season.

Harbor Resort/RV Park, 871 Neddie Rose Drive (at farthest end of boat basin), Westport, 268-0169. Open year-round, 7 days/week. Bait and tackle. Located at foot of jetty; a particularly good source of supplies and information for jetty fishermen.

Englund Marine Supply, Box 387, Westport, 268-9311 (corner of Wilson and Nyhus), Monday-Saturday, year-round. Oriented to commercial and charter boat owners, but carries lots of sport tackle, some at near-wholesale price—can be a fun place for anglers. Also, nautical charts, marine supplies.

Motels, RV Parks

The list below includes most motels in and around the harbor but contact the Chamber of Commerce for additional listings.

Albatross Motel, 22 East Dock Street, Westport, 268-9233.

Chateau Westport, 170 Hancock Avenue, Westport, 268-9101.

Chinook Motel, 707 N. Montesano, Westport, 268-9623.

Coho Motel & RV Park, P.O. Box 1087, Westport, 268-0111.

Harbor Resort & RV Park, 871 Neddie Rose Drive, Westport, 268-0169.

Holiday Motel & RV Park, East Dock Street, Westport, 268-9356.

Islander Motel & RV Park, Westhaven and Neddie Rose Drive, Westport, 268-9166.

Ocean Gate Resort, 1939 Highway 105 South, Westport, 267-1956.

Pacific Motel & RV Park, 330 S. Forrest, Westport, 268-9325.

Sand & Surf Trailer Park, 655 Highway 105 South, Westport, 268-9746.

Shipwreck Motel, 2653 N. Nyhus, Westport, 268-9151.

Skipper's Motel, 300 Wilson (next to public boat launch), Westport, 268-9178.

Westport Waterfront RV Park, 609 Neddie Rose Drive, Westport, 268-0133.

Camping Areas

Twin Harbors State Park (Recreation Area), 3 miles south of Westport on Highway 105, 268-9565. 272 standard tent sites and 49 RV hook-up sites, plus handicapped facilities. Lots of campsites here, but they're small, close to each other and close to the road.

Westport City Park, 300 Washington (west end of Westport, near the drugstore), 268-0214. Open all year. Space for about 40 tents/RVs. Restrooms, but no hookups or showers. Early and late in season can be quiet, pleasant place to stay but much of summer, especially weekends, light sleepers may have a tough time in this busy place.

Hammond's Trailer Park, 1845 Roberts Road, Westport, 268-9645. About a mile NE of Westport, just far enough off main drag to offer a bit more seclusion than parks closer to boat basin.

Marinas, Launch Sites

Port of Grays Harbor, Westport Marina, P.O. Box 1601, Westport, 268-9665. Open year-round. 800 slips, all available for transient moorage at a modest fee. Fuel (gas and diesel) at two docks, engine repair. Excellent 4-lane launch ramp with new concrete floats at south end of boat basin. Restrooms and showers. Harbormaster monitors VHF channels 16 and 12.

For More Information

Westport-Grayland Chamber of Commerce, 1200 North Montesano Street, Westport, 268-9422 or 800-345-6223 anywhere in U.S.

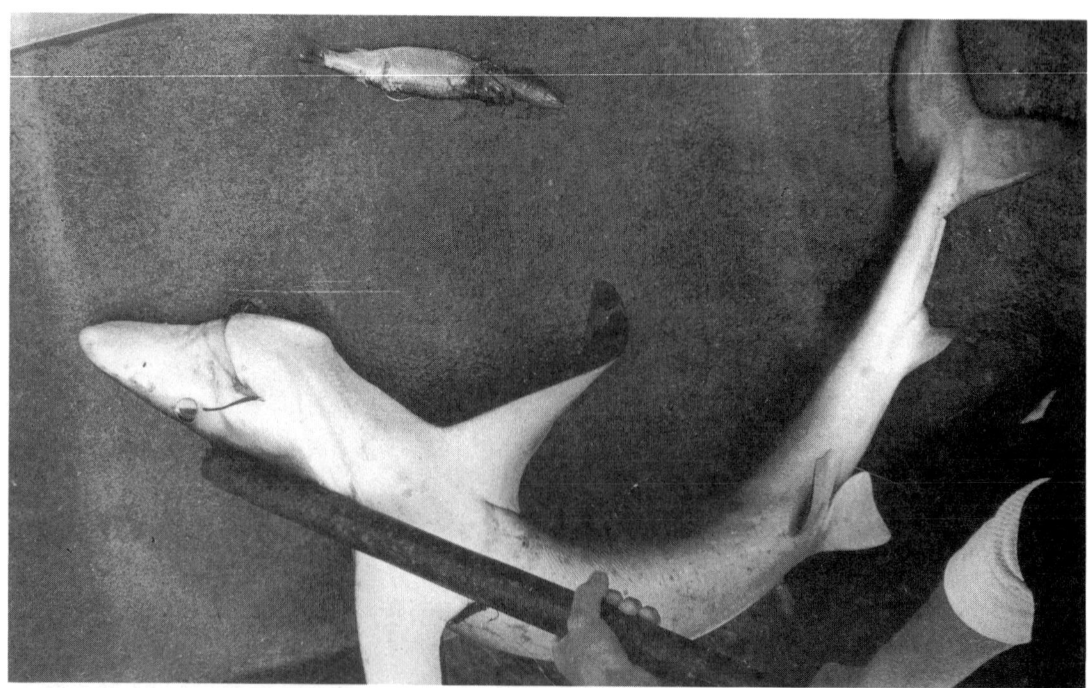

Although this small blue shark was more nuisance than prize, six-footers can be impressive and increasing numbers of anglers have them immediately gutted and iced for later consumption.

courtesy Portland District U.S. Army Corps of Engineers

ILWACO

THIS BUSY HARBOR SITS AT THE NORTHERN EDGE of the mighty Columbia River. Ilwaco has historically produced limits of salmon for sport fishermen pretty reliably over the years, most of those silvers. Nor has that changed much during the recent years of widely varying, generally shortened seasons (some less than two months).

What has changed here, just as at Westport, is the scope of the charter fleet. Of about 135 boats in the mid1970s, many succumbed to such greatly reduced seasons so now only about 45 charters remain.

Yet those that have been able to stick it out have enjoyed the development of the chaotic, productive famous/infamous "Buoy 10" fishery on the lower Columbia when ocean salmon fishing is closed and many good years of sturgeon fishing also in the lower Columbia. Some noteworthy catches of albacore have also come in to Ilwaco docks several years since the late 1980s. Nonboaters find the rugged north jetty great fishing for perch and other bottomfish, as well as salmon in the summer.

OFFSHORE—HARD TO GO WRONG FOR SILVERS

Ilwaco mushroomed as a fishing community when fishermen discovered that it is one of the most consistent salmon producers in the Northwest. There have been seasons in the past decade where charter offices have literally limited every single fisherman from opening day through the end of the season—a remarkable but actual record.

Silvers predominate in the Ilwaco sportcatch, outnumbering chinook most seasons by almost 10 to 1. As elsewhere, coho average only a few pounds early in the season but, fattening each week, by late August have begun coming in more regularly at 10 to 12 pounds and up. Many of these are Cowlitz River fish which stay around (off) the Columbia River mouth all summer.

None of that, of course, is to suggest that big chinook aren't taken off Ilwaco. Indeed, several runs of very big Columbia River kings return each year.

The approach used to catch salmon here is entirely different from that at Westport, immediately north. While Westport boats almost all driftmooch plugcut herring, Ilwaco charters troll. Most use whole herring for bait, usually rigged on a 2- to 3-foot leader behind a diving plane (without flasher), though some boats are using downriggers. Anchovies are also a popular bait and in late summer are likely to be available live from a bait receiver en route to the fishing grounds each morning.

BUOY 10—SALMON INSANITY ON THE LOWER COLUMBIA

Take a small stretch of water in the middle of one of the trickiest areas around for boaters. Add: hundreds of private boats from yachts to tiny cartoppers; swirling, rushing currents; and sometimes hordes of hungry salmon.

If that's not a surefire recipe for mayhem, the annual "Buoy 10" fishery at the Columbia River mouth between Oregon and Washington must be the figment of many imaginations.

But this often surrealistic scene is no dream. It is a situation created by the complex and in recent years highly restrictive labyrinth of salmon sport fishing regulations that dictate the actions of Northwest salmon enthusiasts.

As recently as a decade ago, there was no such tight concentration of sportfishing boats in an area called "buoy 10." This phenomenon can be attributed to two factors: (1) good salmon fishing, especially during huge returns of recent years and (2) the simultaneous late summer closure of virtually the entire ocean in this area to sport fishing for salmon.

Buoy 10 is a sentinel at the river entrance. The legal fishing line stretches directly across the river mouth from Washington to Oregon through buoy 10. Frustrated private and charter boat anglers alike have looked toward this area to wet their lines in droves starting in early August when the fishery is opened. And despite crowds and hassles, a lot of folks drive a lot of miles to fish the river mouth because salmon fishing can be outstanding.

Chinook have been plentiful and large of late. A surprising number of kings recently have been in the 50-pound range. In the late 1980s, returns of chinooks were among the highest in half a century. Coho returns have been highly variable, but again, some enormous runs have filled the river. (1986 was particularly noteworthy at 1.6 million fish, but following years were dismal.)

Even if Buoy 10 catches declined somewhat since the incredibly hot years of the late 1980s, it seems likely that the Buoy 10 fishery will remain popular, at least as long as the balmy days of August and September here offer little or no fishing in the ocean and plenty of good fishing in the lower Columbia.

Most anglers troll bait, herring or, when they're available, fresh anchovies. Downriggers can help avoid some of the inevitable interboat tangles, but many small boaters pull plastic planers to get a bit of depth—which in this relatively shallow stretch of river mouth is all that's needed. Trolling is strictly upcurrent—which means downriver since anglers work the flood tide (the only *safe* tide to fish the river mouth), so every boat's nose is looking west as the fleet trolls along at a snail's pace.

This is a fishery popular with small boaters from both the Washington and Oregon sides. There are many launch and moorage facilities along the lower Columbia. (See facilities listings at the end of this section.)

But remember that everything is going to be crowded during the Buoy 10 fishery from early August through Labor Day (unless shut down to fishing within that period). Expect some difficulty finding moorage at such periods,

Trophy-sized chinook are a prize that lures anglers to the lower Columbia, as fisheries biologists struggle to maintain or enhance runs. This 40-pounder struck a trolled J-Plug. (Photo courtesy Luhr-Jensen)

long lines at launch ramps and a shortage of fresh or frozen herring or anchovies at times.

Often, the crowds have a definite impact on fishing. The best fishing may be where the boats are fewest; some charter skippers insist that both kings and coho avoid the noise made by crowds of boats. If you wait until September, after Labor Day, you'll find considerably less competition for facilities, bait and tackle. Yet coho fishing can continue to be good on into October.

Besides watching out for fog, each other, heavy currents and windchop, small boaters in the crowded "Buoy 10" fishery must keep an eye out for busy freighter traffic.

Bottomfish—A Long Run To Good Fishing

The sea floor off Ilwaco is mostly sand, which means serious bottomfishing must occur outside of the immediate area. Most bottomfish charters head south to the nearest rocky reefs off Tillamook Head and Cannon Beach, Oregon.

Black, yellowtail and widow rockfish ("sea bass" and "brownies") compose most of this catch, but yelloweye and canary rockfish are common at times. It's rare for anglers to fail to limit, particularly during cooperative weather. Lingcod may be numerous some days but scarce other days. Best bet for lings is September and October. Halibut are rare, but less so in recent years.

Both bait (anchovies or herring) and plastic worms are used on Ilwaco bottomfish charters, typically with two hooks above a sinker. Some bottomfish charters are not only permitting lighter gear for these rockfish, but *providing* it. They're finding that spinning gear with 15-pound line enhances the experience of catching rockfish for most anglers. Rather than the double hook rigs, they simply use a 1-ounce leadhead jig-and-worm. Typically, that ounce will be plenty to get to the fish which are generally not deep. In fact, schools of rockfish are often boiling right at the surface, eager to hit whatever's thrown their way—including small surface plugs on ultralight tackle or poppers and streamers on fly gear.

Many charter offices here will book bottomfish trips anytime in their operating season, but certainly it is whenever the short salmon season closes that promotion of and interest in bottomfishing really pick up.

Columbia River's Many Salmon Runs

Lower River Spring Chinook

These provide good river fishing, returning each year to the Willamette River hatcheries. Runs in recent years have been very strong, well over 100,000 fish. Over 5 million smolts are released in the Willamette Basin each November and March. These kings head north, contributing heavily to Alaska and B.C. fisheries before returning to the Columbia as 3-, 4- and 5-year old fish.

Upriver Spring Chinook

Upriver springers travel great distances in fresh water, which in part accounts for their particularly dense, oily flesh. Historically, annual harvests of these runs numbered 2 million. But by the early 1970s, only 250,000 were returning and, following dam construction on the Columbia and Snake rivers, the count was down to a mere 50,000 by 1984. But since then, the run has been generally improving and is over the 100,000 mark. However the future remains very much a question mark for upriver chinook.

Summer Chinook

Summer chinook once numbered literally in the millions each year. One of the races of these giant salmon has faded into history after Grand Coulee dam was built in 1941. The other race has been supported by intensive hatchery operations but many dams along the migration route have not made this an overwhelming success.

Fall Chinook

"Upriver brights" are highly-prized among Columbia river anglers, but populations have been historically erratic. Their once enormous numbers declined by two-thirds in the 1940s and remained stable until the mid 1980s when populations began to increase dramatically but by the end of the decade were again declining, down from 500,000 in 1987 to an estimated 200,000 in 1990.

Another strain of fall chinook spawns in the lower river. These are less vulnerable to predation as juveniles than are upriver fish, and are very important to sport and commercial ocean fishermen. River fishermen, however, prefer the upriver fish because the lower river strains turn dark quickly after entering the river. These "Tules" are easy to raise and have historically high returns. However, survival of juveniles after leaving hatcheries in recent years has decreased markedly and mysteriously. The result: a record low return of 65,000 in 1990, about half that of just a year earlier.

The Oregon Department of Fish and Wildlife has been releasing into the lower Columbia hundreds of thousands of young chinook from the Rogue River in southern Oregon. Unlike the tules, Rogue stocks migrate south (tules go north to be intercepted in Alaska and British Columbia, not by Oregonians) and return to the river earlier, in much better physical condition.

Coho

Most lower river coho are hatchery fish. Some idea of the relative abundance of wild fish can be determined from counts of coho per mile on spawning beds. In the 1960s, 30-40 spawning coho per mile were counted on the Oregon side. In recent years, that count has averaged fewer than two fish. Less than 10% of Columbia River coho are now wild, thanks to habitat degradation and loss.

Sockeye

Although sockeye are not a major Columbia River sport fish, their decline as a prime commercial species is particularly extraordinary. Once numbering 3 million, by 1989 fewer than 50,000 sockeye passed the Bonneville Dam.

(Note: This information prepared with the help of the Oregon Dept. of Fish and Wildlife)

Albacore—Boom Or Bust Every Summer

Some of the Northwest's most productive albacore action has been off the Columbia River mouth. Some years, the fish have been within 30 or so miles. Whenever they move to within 60 or so miles, charters find it feasible to make the run out for them. These are usually 12-hour trips, which offer roughly six hours of fishing time. (Longer trips would require a second full crew.)

After some fantastic fishing in the late 1970s, opportunities to tangle with tuna were minimal until the late 1980s when they began showing again.

The general availability here of live anchovies at a bait receiver is a big plus for albacore anglers since anchovies can be used as chum and live bait offshore.

As suggested for the Westport section, anglers genuinely interested in booking an albacore trip would be wise to contact a charter office and request their names be put on a call list, when/if the tuna show. Trips will run about $150.

Boats face the same direction—heading west—as they troll into the current.

Sturgeon—Monsters Of The River Bottom

Interest in catching lower Columbia River sturgeon has steadily increased over the past couple decades. Effort and catches have both surged, prompting concern for sturgeon populations among Washington and Oregon fisheries biologists. So it is probably not surprising that this is yet another sportfishery which has been subject to increasingly tight regulation in recent years.

This means sturgeon enthusiasts have had to get used to yet another "catch record card" as well as an annual limit of 15 fish and another barbless hook fishery. (The latter may be a partial blessing, since the mouth of a sturgeon is very tough and a barbless hooks will penetrate more easily.) The daily limit is two fish but with rather specific size restrictions within a "legal window."

That "window" is the size between the legal minimum and maximum limit (40 and 72 inches, respectively, at press time) for the first fish. A second sturgeon could be kept only if within a 48-72 inch range.

But even a single sturgeon is a prize for most anglers. For one thing, legal sturgeon are respectable-sized fish. For another, white sturgeon are delectable eating. Green sturgeon are much less common—and much less valued for their flesh.

Many sturgeon caught in the lower Columbia are "shakers," less than the legal minimum length. But at the same time, it is not unusual for anglers to catch sturgeon too *large*—fish over six feet long. In fact, they can exceed 10 feet and hundreds of pounds.

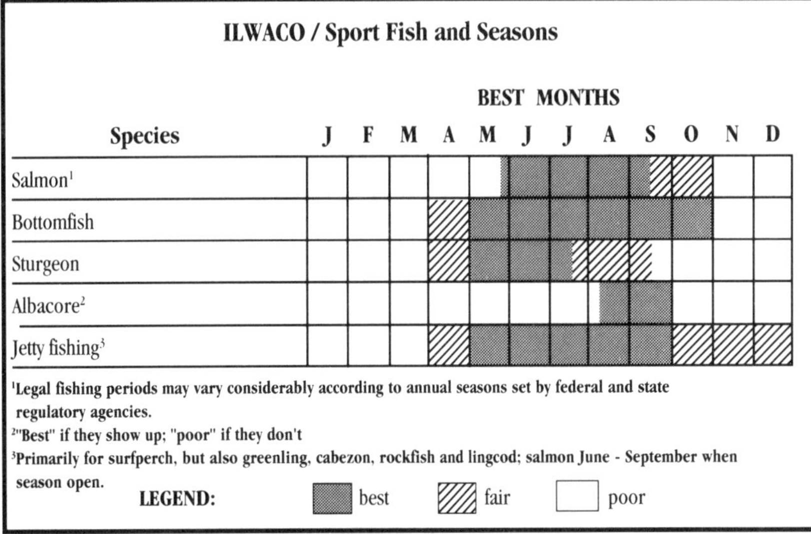

ILWACO / Sport Fish and Seasons

Species	J	F	M	A	M	J	J	A	S	O	N	D
						BEST MONTHS						
Salmon[1]	poor	poor	poor	poor	poor	best	best	best	best/fair	fair	poor	poor
Bottomfish	poor	poor	poor	fair	best	best	best	best	best	best	poor	poor
Sturgeon	poor	poor	poor	fair	best	best	best/fair	fair	fair	poor	poor	poor
Albacore[2]	poor	poor	poor	poor	poor	poor	poor	best	best	poor	poor	poor
Jetty fishing[3]	poor	poor	poor	fair	best	best	best	best	best	fair	fair	fair

[1]Legal fishing periods may vary considerably according to annual seasons set by federal and state regulatory agencies.
[2]"Best" if they show up; "poor" if they don't
[3]Primarily for surfperch, but also greenling, cabezon, rockfish and lingcod; salmon June - September when season open.

LEGEND: best · fair · poor

Some anglers traditionally fish deep holes, anchoring above them and rigging a fresh smelt, herring or anchovy with a double-hook, mooching rig to flutter tailfirst, lowered to the bottom with 8 to 20 ounces. Many anglers use Dacron leader, since it is much softer and less unnatural feeling to the sturgeon's sensitive mouth. Sinkers are rigged (generally on plastic sliders with clips) to slide freely above the leader to reduce the sort of weight that is likely to make a spooky sturgeon drop the bait. A single 4/0 beak hook is usually sufficient, with the leader often tied around the anchovy's tail with a couple half-hitches. The hook is run through the anus and out the mouth so the point faces back towards the tail.

Winter fishing is occasionally productive, particularly when sturgeon move upriver, following spawning smelt on which they feed. But late spring is the hot time—May and June in particular—when the best fishing is not over deep holes but around very shallow sandbars on days when heavy tidal runoffs ("clam tides" of - 1/2-foot or lower) create torrents. Then, fish in 15 to 25 feet of water across the river as far south as Desdemona Sands. On lighter tides (that go no lower than +1.0 foot) generally deeper holes, in 30 to 50 feet will produce best.

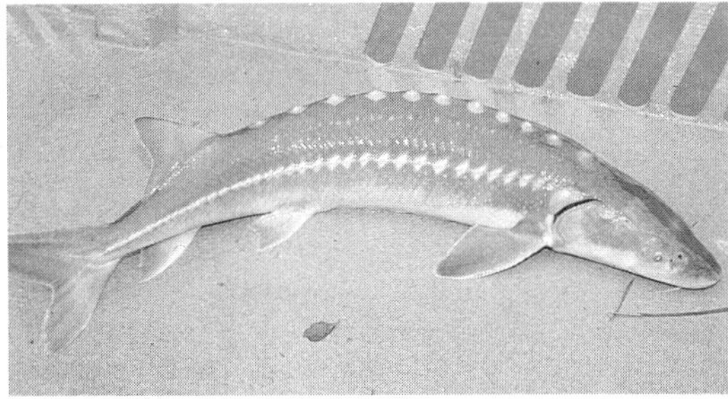

As interest in catching Columbia River sturgeon has increased over the years, regulations have become increasingly restrictive.

Stalking sturgeon in shallow water is a particularly exciting way to fish for them. These sturgeon often fight in ways that may surprise anglers who've caught them only from deep water. They make long runs and often *jump* more than once, frequently clearing the water. Most fishermen use 30-pound line, though I've found 20-pound line is still plenty heavy.

Charters such as Pacific Salmon Charter's *Ghost Rider* helped pioneer this shallow-water spring fishery. They anchor around the edge of sandbars, roughly midriver, in water from 5 to 15 feet deep. Fresh bait is essential; whenever available, live anchovies are picked up on the way out of the harbor.

Holman
Ilwaco
Wallacut R
CAPE DISAPPOINTMENT
North Head
BAKER BAY
SAND ISLAND
McKenzie Head
Fort Canby
Peacock Spit
SAND ISLAND RANGE (see tabulation)
ENTRANCE RANGE (see tabulation)
LOWER DESDEMONA SHOAL
South Jetty
CLATSOP SPIT
Jetty Lagoon
DUMP SITE
MAGNETIC
VAR 19°45'E (1989)
ANNUAL DECREASE
Mileage distar
Statute Miles
indicated thus:
Tables for con
Nautical miles

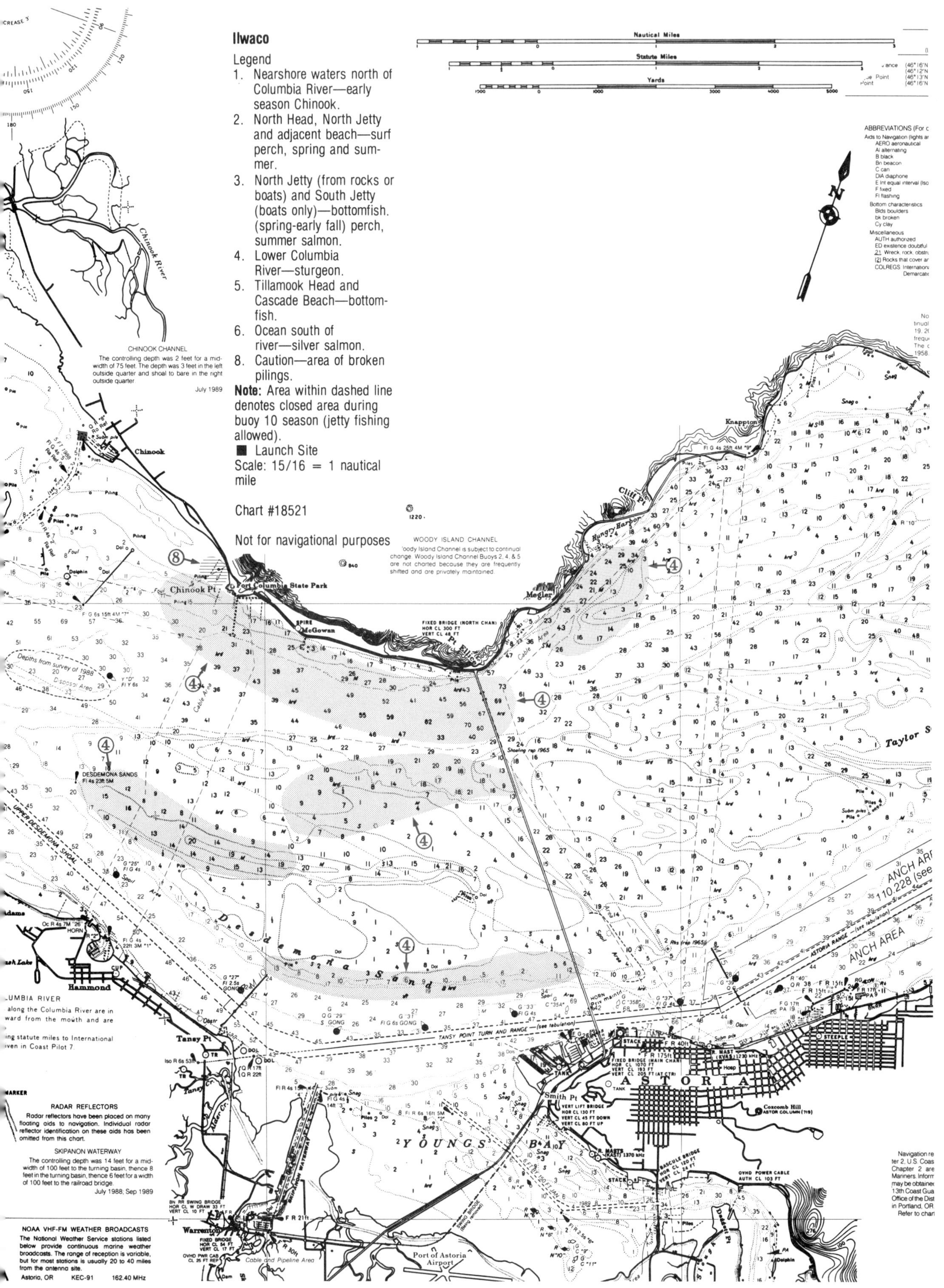
Ilwaco
Legend
1. Nearshore waters north of Columbia River—early season Chinook.
2. North Head, North Jetty and adjacent beach—surf perch, spring and summer.
3. North Jetty (from rocks or boats) and South Jetty (boats only)—bottomfish. (spring-early fall) perch, summer salmon.
4. Lower Columbia River—sturgeon.
5. Tillamook Head and Cascade Beach—bottomfish.
6. Ocean south of river—silver salmon.
8. Caution—area of broken pilings.
Note: Area within dashed line denotes closed area during buoy 10 season (jetty fishing allowed).
Launch Site
Scale: 15/16 = 1 nautical mile
Chart #18521
Not for navigational purposes
Nautical Miles
Statute Miles
Yards
CHINOOK CHANNEL
The controlling depth was 2 feet for a mid-width of 75 feet. The depth was 3 feet in the left outside quarter and shoal to bare in the right outside quarter.
July 1989
WOODY ISLAND CHANNEL
Woody Island Channel is subject to continual change. Woody Island Channel Buoys 2, 4, & 5 are not charted because they are frequently shifted and are privately maintained.
Chinook River
Chinook
Chinook Pt
Fort Columbia State Park
SPIRE McGowan
FIXED BRIDGE (NORTH CHAN) HOR CL 300 FT VERT CL 48 FT
Megler
Hungry Harbor
Cliff Pt
Knappton
DESDEMONA SANDS
UPPER DESDEMONA SHOAL
Desdemona Sands
Taylor
ANCH AREA
TANSY POINT TURN AND RANGE
ASTORIA RANGE
Hammond
Tansy Pt
Smith Pt
ASTORIA
Coxcomb Hill
YOUNGS BAY
Warrenton
Port of Astoria Airport
Cable and Pipeline Area
RADAR REFLECTORS
Radar reflectors have been placed on many floating aids to navigation. Individual radar reflector identification on these aids has been omitted from this chart.
SKIPANON WATERWAY
The controlling depth was 14 feet for a mid-width of 100 feet to the turning basin, thence 8 feet in the turning basin, thence 6 feet for a width of 100 feet to the railroad bridge.
July 1988; Sep 1989
NOAA VHF-FM WEATHER BROADCASTS
The National Weather Service stations listed below provide continuous marine weather broadcasts. The range of reception is variable, but for most stations is usually 20 to 40 miles from the antenna site.
Astoria, OR KEC-91 162.40 MHz

Teamwork on the south jetty helps this group of fishermen land a good chinook. (Photo courtesy Oregon Dept. of Fish and Wildlife)

Small Boat Safety—Crossing The Bar

Given the expanse of the Columbia River mouth and the vast amounts of water that surge in and out with the tides, logically, navigating across it can be tricky and even treacherous. Combine currents of up to 8 knots meeting head-on lines of crashing breakers and it's easy to understand the words of the Coast Guard's Columbia River Bar Guide: (The area off Clatsop Spit) may be calm with only a gentle swell breaking far in on the spit. Yet 5 to 10 minutes later, when the current has started to ebb, it can become a roaring monster...." And: "Peacock (just around the corner from Ilwaco) and Clatsop spits are called the graveyard of the Pacific for good reason."

This is not to suggest private boaters should not or cannot cross the Columbia River bar. Thousands do so safely every year—but often at least a few do so tragically.

Basic suggestions for safely traversing any bar crossing apply here (see "Crossing the Bar" section in the chapter on "Fishing Northwest Salt Waters"). Most of those suggestions and a few more as well apply to the crowded Buoy 10 fishery when great numbers of people are fishing just inside the bar.

At such times, even in docile waters wall-to-wall boats can make boating tricky. But here, vicious currents, roaring riplines, pea-soup fogs, floating gillnets and huge ships all combine to make things particularly lively.

Plan to reach the fishing grounds at low slack tide in order to fish the flood. On a good day the river mouth becomes dangerous during an ebb; on many days it is worse than that.

The current's inevitably powerful, so trolling needs to be upcurrent and directly into it. This demands someone who can be running the boat full time and not worrying about fishing.

That is even more essential when August weekend crowds back up against the buoy 10 line and a small boat can find itself caught in the middle of a floating tangle of other boats.

Nor are these the only hazards to keep an eye out for. Others include gillnets that are laid in the same sportfishing grounds when that season is also open, and huge transoceanic tankers and freighters that ply the river mouth.

Despite the inevitable close encounters, most people remain surprisingly calm and courteous. Make an effort to do the same.

Ultimately, before leaving Ilwaco for the river mouth, any boater not really familiar with the area would be wise to stop at the Coast Guard station for information—those few minutes may be among the most wisely-spent of your fishing trip.

U.S. Coast Guard Station—Cape Disappointment

Station phone: (information) . . . . . . (206) 642-3565
Weather/bar conditions (recording) . . . (206) 642-2382

Even with a sliding sinker rig like that described, sturgeon will generally mouth the bait for some time before really taking it. Give it at least a bit of time by pointing the rod directly at the fish and waiting for the line to come tight. Then set hooks *hard* (there isn't much inside a sturgeon's mouth that is soft).

This is a good fishery for small boats, a bit farther upriver than the Buoy 10 action. There's a good launch ramp at Chinook, only 10 or 15 minutes from the action. Take care when anchoring in these heavy currents. Use a few feet of chain between anchor and rope to help the flukes hold in the soft, sandy bottom. Also a good idea: a buoy, ready to attach to the anchor line in a hurry in case you need to slip the anchor in a hurry and follow a big fish.

When live anchovies are available at Ilwaco, fishing for many species improves.

North Jetty—Outstanding Action From The Rocks

The north jetty at the entrance to the mighty Columbia is easily reached by driving through Fort Canby State Park. Although the enormous rocks on this broad jetty make for some rugged rock hopping, there's some fine perch fishing in the offing. One very popular area for redtail and silver surfperch lies just off the north (ocean) side, behind the breaker line.

Generally on the Northwest Coast the fastest fishing for redtails seems to occur in the spring, but I've been on this jetty in the late summer and watched rows of weekend fishermen enjoy hits almost as fast as they could cast out a bait. In fact, this "slow period" off the jetty—November through April—is mostly a function of the large and dangerous winter swells. Similarly, perch are taken all day during any tide, though incoming tide is best, particularly from the low slack end.

The sandy beaches that seem to go on forever just north of the jetty also provide perch in abundance, spring through early fall, again when the swells do not loom prohibitively.

Another spot for some first-class perch fishing is off the rocks at North Head, the westernmost point of Cape Disappointment. Access isn't quite so easy, though, and a steep climb is necessary to reach the best fishing areas.

Black rockfish provide good jetty sport at times, and lingcod can be surprisingly numerous, occasionally quite a few 5- to 10-pounders striking the plastic worms fished for "bass."

Bait also takes a good share of rockfish and lingcod as well as greenling, tomcod some years, and cabezon. Many fish anchovies or herring rigged with only a light sinker. Often fish will dart up to swallow the bait as it flutters downward. If not, it is often picked up as it rolls in the current atop rocks.

Salmon fishing can be a truly rewarding sport from the jetty, depending upon regulations. The jetties are open to salmon fishing as long as either the ocean or the Buoy 10 season is open.

The action begins pretty much when salmon fishing starts, with good catches made during the latter part of June and through July. August and September offer peak numbers of fish cruising along the rocks. It isn't uncommon to see limits caught from the rocks at times.

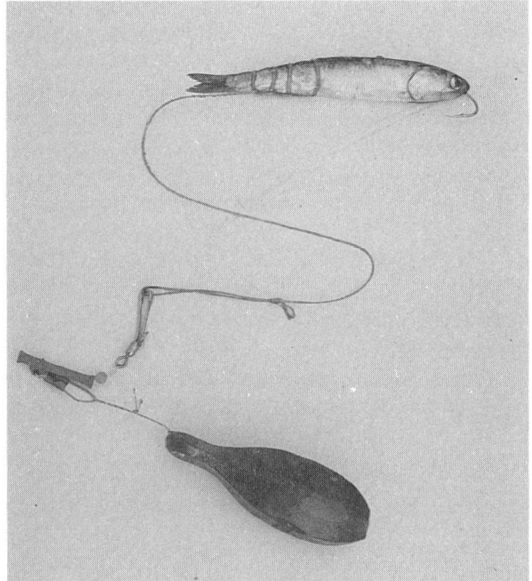

Many sturgeon fishermen use Dacron leaders when rigging anchovies, because it is softer than monofilament and less unnatural to the fishes' sensitive mouths.

Miles of beach start at the base of the north jetty and offer fine surfperch fishing. Those who take their sport serious are equipped like this fellow with insulated waders, belt bag for fish and box for bait and takle.

Most of the salmon taken from the north jetty are silvers. Though many anglers walk toward the end of the jetty, it isn't really necessary, with fish taken all along the jetties.

The silvers can be taken during any tide, though the incoming tide seems best when the fish chase anchovies in along the rocks during the rising water. Though the coho are generally feeding on anchovies, herring is the bait of choice. It seems to produce well, it's available and it stays on the hook better than anchovies. Typical rigging calls for a mooching rig with the bait set 6 or 8 feet below a float. Only a few anglers cast jigs such as Buzz Bombs, but they've proven that Columbia River mouth coho will take such lures.

Facilities

All phone numbers listed are in the 206 area code.
All Ilwaco addresses use the postal zip code 98624.

Charters

About 45 charterboats operate out of Ilwaco. Salmon are of course the main draw in the summer, but sturgeon trips gained popularity in the 1980s. Sturgeon charters begin in spring, though not all offices offer them. Check around. Bottomfish trips begin in May and run into October, depending upon weather and demand. Many offices will head offshore for albacore if they show.

Ilwaco rates for a salmon or sturgeon charter trip at press time were running $45 to $55. Bottomfish rates were $60-70 (the higher price reflects a longer run to the rocky waters off northern Oregon). Figure roughly $150 for an albacore trip. All these rates are inclusive—tackle, bait, tax.

Boats leave shortly after daybreak but often return with limits of silvers before noon. Advance reservations are always a good idea for anyone planning to fish on a summer weekend.

Coho Charters, P.O. Box 268, Ilwaco, 642-333. 3 boats, all 42′ (14 anlgers).

Beacon Charters, P.O. Box 74, Ilwaco, 642-2138. 1 50′ boat (16 anglers, maximum).

Hobo Charters, P.O. Box 303, Ilwaco, 642-2300. 3 boats from 24 feet (6 anglers) to 50 feet (20 anglers).

Ilwaco Charters, P.O. Box 323, Ilwaco, 642-3232. 9 boats from 32′ (6 anglers) to 50′ (25 anglers)

Pacific Salmon Charters, P.O. Box 519, Ilwaco, 642-3466. 12 boats from 28′ (6 anglers) to 56 feet (20 anglers).

Reel 'Em In Charters, P.O. Box 489, Ilwaco, 642-3511. 2 boats, 45′ (17 anglers) and 55′ (21 anglers).

Tidewind Charters, P.O. Box 206, Ilwaco, 642-2111. 5 boats from 32′ (6 anglers) to 42′ (up to 25 anglers).

Bait, Tackle

Chinook Bait and Tackle Shop, P.O. Box 44, Chinook 98614, 777-8475. This shop has been here for over 3 decades. It's open seasonally, perhaps as early as sturgeon fishing in May (call ahead) and into late September. Carries fresh anchovies when available, frozen herring and a complete line of salmon and sturgeon gear. Located on Main Street just across from the cannery.

Dave's Shell, Box 709, Ilwaco, 642-2320. Located in downtown Ilwaco, open 7 days/week in-season, this is more of a bait-and-tackle shop than a service station. Caters to private boaters and carries a wide selection of gear.

Fort Canby Concession, Box 709, Ilwaco, 642-3030. Open May-September, 7 days/week. Modest bait and tackle selection but excellent location, right at state park en route to north jetty.

Ed's Bait and Tackle, Box 251, Ilwaco, 642-3243. Behind Red's Restaurant (big red building). Open 7 days/week in season, but irregularly during slow winter months. Ed Johnston's small shop carries all the necessities and he's always willing to share his jetty-fishing expertise. Lots of tackle, including bins of plastic tails at great prices.

Motels, RV Parks

This list is by no means inclusive, but does offer a few places, most close in, where fishermen can stay. For a complete listing, contact the Peninsula Visitors Bureau, Box 562, Long Beach, WA 98361.

Beacon Charters and RV Park, P.O. Box 74, Ilwaco, 642-2138. About 60 RV spaces with hookups, May-September.

Chautauqua Lodge, 304 14th NW, Long Beach 98631, 642-4401.

The Cove RV Park, 411 2nd Avenue South, Ilwaco, 642-3689, 43 RV sites with hookups.

Heidi's Inn, P.O. Box 776, Ilwaco, 642-2387. Located on Highway 101 near Ilwaco, Heidi's is recommended by charter offices as reasonable, clean and close.

Our Place at the Beach, 1309 South Boulevard, Long Beach 98631 642-3793.

Super-8 Motel, 500 Ocean Beach Boulvevard, Long Beach 98361, 642-8988.

Marinas, Launch Areas

Fort Canby State Park public ramp, southeast of camping area. 2 lanes, paved, with float in fair condition. No charge.

Chinook Ramp, owned by Port of Chinook, 777-8797 (leased by Willapa Seafoods). Except at minus tides, good 3-lane ramp will accomodate large boats—and at a very minimal charge.

Port of Ilwaco, P.O. Box 307, Ilwaco, 642-3143. No ramp, but a sling launch. Plenty of moorage in the boat basin at reasonable rates.

Public Camping Areas

Fort Canby State Park, 2 1/2 miles southwest of Ilwaco on Highway 101, 642-3078. 190 tentsites, 60 spaces with hookups for RVs to 45 feet, 4 primitive tentsites. The largest of the state's coastal parks, Canby is at the foot of the morth jetty and a 5-minute drive to the boat basin. Free public launch ramp.

For More Information

Peninsula Visitors Bureau, P.O. Box 562, Long Beach 98361, 642-2400.

At midsummer, coho are normally abundant off Ilwaco but seldom exceed 8 to 10 pounds.

Oregon

Photo courtesy Oregon Dept. of Fish and Wildlife.

Bays, bars and big water. Those are key words in any description of angling along Oregon's vast, magnificently endowed coast. Much of the 400-mile Oregon coastline is a combination of rocky headlands and sandy beaches. From Coos Bay south, steep, rugged headlands are nearly continuous.

Most of the state's marine angling opportunities are centered in and around its bays, each described in depth in this guide. These bays vary greatly in size and configuration, from Coos Bay—large, sprawling, shallow—to tiny Depoe Bay—barely more than a big tidal pool.

The bars that front each bay vary, as well. (This reference is not to the bars along Highway 101 where fishermen are wont to put down a few on a windy day, though those vary too. Rather, these bars are the areas where the ocean meets rivers' outflow.) Some have eminently crossable bars and support large charter and private fishing fleets. Others have no boat access to the ocean, but do provide popular tidewater fisheries. A number of bays offer both ocean and tidewater fishing.

Offshore fishing effort of course concentrates on salmon when open season permits fishing them. And, unlike the comparatively beleaguered Washington coast, salmon sport seasons have in recent years enjoyed a trend of increasing length. One factor is that the weak stocks of the northern Washington coast are not a major concern this far south except along northernmost Oregon. But for most of the state's coast, chinook stocks have been in good enough shape to avoid imposition of quotas at all and coho quotas have often been generous enough to allow fishing 7 days per week from May into September. In fact, since the late 1980s, a rather striking success story in many rivers from the Columbia to the Chetco has been that of *fall chinook* for which cooperative state, local and private enhancement programs have really been paying off.

Ports offering ocean sport salmon fishing for charter and private boaters include these bays: Tillamook, Depoe, Yaquina (Newport), Winchester, Coos, Rogue (Gold Beach) and Chetco (Harbor). Although somewhat more limited, salmon fishermen also utilize the Nehalem and Siuslaw river entrances. In years past, special dories have launched on the beach through the surf at Cape Kiwanda, near Nestucca Bay.

Bottomfishing is somewhat more a year-round sport than along the Washington coast, probably because there are more coastal centers of population and more winter tourism on the coast. During the winter, those trips that do sneak out are generally half-day runs to fish nearshore reefs. During warmer months, many longer all-day trips head out to deepwater offshore banks. Certainly, the three most prized species are halibut, lingcod and yelloweye rockfish—all taken in greatest number on offshore trips.

Halibut sportfishing has also seen a considerable reduction in season length in recent years, most noticeably felt by the major fishery to target on halibut, that out of Newport. The imposition of quotas in the late 1980s began a new trend that at press time meant only one halibut could be kept per day and meant an indefinite season length, depending upon how quickly quotas filled.

Most nearshore trips take considerable numbers of rockfish, particularly blacks and yellowtail, but also greenling and cabezon.

The most consistent, varied bottomfish catches come from the reef-laden waters off Tillamook, Depoe, Yaquina, Coos, Rogue and Chetco bays. All are home to bottomfish charter operations; reefs outside Coos Bay and the lower Chetco are particularly accessible to private boaters on calm summer days. In general, the southernmost stretch of wild coastline is studded with rocky nearshore reefs.

All of Oregon's major bays and rivers as listed in this chapter except Depoe Bay support major tidewater salmon fisheries and all offer fall runs. Several also have spring chinook runs as well. Most of these tidewater fish are taken from small private or rented boats Some areas offer productive tidewater fishing from shore, though most of that occurs farther upriver. Sea-run cutthroat (in tidewater) and steelhead (mostly above tidewater) also are popular targets in lower rivers and bays.

Two major river systems also offer year-round tidewater fishing for striped bass: the Umpqua-Smith and, to a lesser extent these days, the Coos-Millicoma. Sturgeon inhabit most of the state's coastal estuaries. A decade ago, few anglers directed much effort toward them except in the lower Columbia and Umpqua rivers. In the past few years, fishermen have begun to enjoy regular sportfisheries for sturgeon in many others estuaries, such as the lower Nehalem River, Tillamook Bay, the lower Siuslaw River and

Wearing down a huge Umpqua River white sturgeon is a long, slow, muscle-straining process.

Anglers sort through a limit catch of Heceta Bank halibut (and other bottomfish) back at the docks in Newport.

Coos Bay. Yet another anadromous game fish is the shad, which is a popular spring target in the Siuslaw, Umpqua, Coos, Rogue and other rivers.

All these bays except Depoe support major perch fisheries around rocks, pilings, eelgrass beds and the like. Starry flounder may be caught in bays. Many species of nearshore bottomfish are available to fishermen who clamber onto rocky outcropping of coastal headlands during calm seas. Fishing for starry flounder, a great sport in the quiet, shallow flats of Oregon bays in the 1960s and 1970s, dried up in the 1980s, though in recent years the species has shown surprising strength. Starries remain, however, largely an incidental catch so far.

The jetties that protect these bays offer many more miles of rocky habitat, along which fishermen catch several species of perch, greenling, rockfish, lingcod, cabezon, flounder and salmon. Perch tend to dominate jetty catches in the spring and early summer, after which salmon are of increasing interest through early fall. Bottomfish of many species can be taken whenever seas are calm.

Finally, along mile after mile of surfpounded sandy beaches, redtail surfperch feed in the breakers. Fishing pressure is light, but those who know how to harvest these marine panfish in Oregon often enjoy consistent success.

For More Information

All phone numbers listed are within the 503 area code unless otherwise note.

Oregon Department of Fish and Wildlife, main (Portland) offices, 2501 SW 1st, P.O. Box 59, Portland, OR 97207, 229-5400. Write for current state sportfishing regulations pamphlet or call for specific information.

Oregon Department of Fish and Wildlife, marine regional offices, Marine Science Drive, Building 3, Newport, OR 97365, 867-4741.

Oregon State Marine Board, 3000 Market Street NE, #505, Salem, OR 97310, 378-8587. Write or call for several free and extremely useful publications, which are updated regularly: *Boating in Oregon Coastal Waters* is a 48-page book loaded with essential information about all of Oregon's bays, bars and river mouths, including aerial photos. *A Guide to Oregon Boating Facilities* is a 48-page comprehensive listing of public and private boating facilities in the entire state, including locations and types of moorage and launch facilities, fuel, marine supplies and more. *Oregon Boaters Handbook* is a 44-page book, also valuable for those who fish from boats.

Pacific Marine Center, 1801 Fairview Avenue East, Seattle, WA 98102, (206) 442-7657. Free index to Pacific Coast nautical charts, including list of authorized agents around the state.

Oregon Coast Association, P.O. Box 670, Oregon Coast, OR 97365, 336-5107. Write for free, annual "Oregon Coast Travel Guide" or call for specific information on any subject having to do with Oregon's coast.

Oregon Coast Charter Boat Association, P.O. Box 211, Waldport, OR 97394.

Oregon Guides and Packers Association, P.O. Box 3797, Portland, OR 97208, 234-3268. *Oregon Guides and Packers Association Directory*, a statewide annual listing of all professional guides.

Oregon Parks and Recreation Division, 525 Trade Street SE, Salem, OR 97310, 378-6305. Request free "State Parks Guide" pamphlet and campsite reservations applications. Campsite Information Center, in-state toll-free (800) 452-5687 or in Portland or out-of-state, 238-7488, early March through Labor Day weekend.

Oregon Tourism Division, Economic Development Department, 595 Cottage Street NE, Salem, OR 97310, 378-3451, or in-state toll-free (800) 547-7842.

Most of Oregon's larger river entrances have been made navigable by Corps of Engineers jetty construction and dredging. The Alsea River at Waldport is one that is not developed and remains impassable. (Photo courtesy Portland District U.S. Army Corps of Engineers.)

courtesy Portland District U.S. Army Corps of Engineers

NEHALEM BAY

NEHALEM IS THE NORTHERNMOST BAY ON THE Oregon Coast. Although it has a bar crossing protected by jetties, it is one of the least user-friendly for private boaters. In November of 1982, the U.S. Army Corps of Engineers rebuilt and extended the south jetty (which dates all the way back to 1916). That made it more passable but not easily passable.

Still, on calm days of summer and early fall during flood tides, small boaters can make the crossing successfully. Many, however, are happy to let salmon come to them, inside the jetties and lower river. When runs are solid, good numbers are taken by casting from the south jetty. Of course more are boated. About a half-dozen private and public launch ramps around the lower bay as well as several well-equipped marinas make it easy for boaters to fish the lower river.

Salmon, of course, dominate the interests of fishermen in this long, narrow, winding bay. Their efforts are directed at runs of summer and fall chinook, as well as silver runs that have improved to impressive levels.

NEHALEM'S ANADROMOUS TRIUMVIRATE—CHINOOK, COHO AND CUTTS

Ed Lyster, who has guided fishermen over waters here and at Tillamook Bay for over 40 years and owned tackle shops in both areas, believes the waters of Nehalem Bay are often better for salmon than the more renown Tillamook, immediately south. He observed a resurgence in the natural, wild run of trophy-size kings during the 1980s.

The south jetty extension may not do wonders for boaters, but may help encourage baitfish to enter the bay, without having to traverse surf-pounded sandy shallows. Jetty anglers also have a greater area to fish, which they do starting in early June and the action picks up as the summer continues. More and more cast Buzz Bombs, but many still toss out herring or anchovies for bait.

Some boaters still wander outside the bar on nice days, particularly early in the summer since salmon then are more inclined to be outside than inside. They'll generally pull herring or anchovies behind a diving planer. But this is a risky business, requiring good timing, skill and luck.

Fortunately, especially from about midsummer on, salmon move into the lower bay and fishermen can work "the jaws" well inside the bar. Large runs of anchovies may linger in the lower bay, further enticing salmon in. As the salmon move up the bay, trollers use large spinners as well as anchovies to take them. One of many good spots in upper tidewater is Deer Island (at Nehalem). The catch rate is not always high, but with kings over 50 pounds taken most years, fishermen are willing to put in the time.

Shore fishing opportunities are pretty limited in the lower Nehalem until the fish move up around the head of tidewater, just below Roy Creek Park. Then, fishing shrimp or salmon eggs below a bobber is the best bet. This is usually effective only during an ebb tide; there isn't enough drift to keep the bait moving during an incoming tide.

The Nehalem also features a good run of tidewater cutthroat in the summer. From June on, they can be taken throughout the bay above Wheeler. These fish, caught mainly by trollers, favor Ford Fenders, Doc Sheltons or other trolling spinner rigs with worms or crawdad tails. Although some sea-run fishermen insist that the incoming tide is the only period worth fishing, others report success here during any tide when the trout are in and hungry.

Another method with its own special challenges is fly-casting for sea-runs. Lyster and other Nehalem veterans like to work the river from the head-of-tidewater on up, starting about midJuly.

Northern Oregon rivers produce trophy-size kings for experts like renown flyfishing expert Jim Teeny. (Photo courtesy Jim Teeny)

PERCH IN ABUNDANCE

Nehalem Bay's main claim to angling fame lies in its runs of large fall salmon. But there are folks interested less in fame than in fun and fast fishing, spring through fall, and they target their efforts on perch. Nehalem offers all three species of large, marine perch—redtails (pinkfins), striped and pile perch.

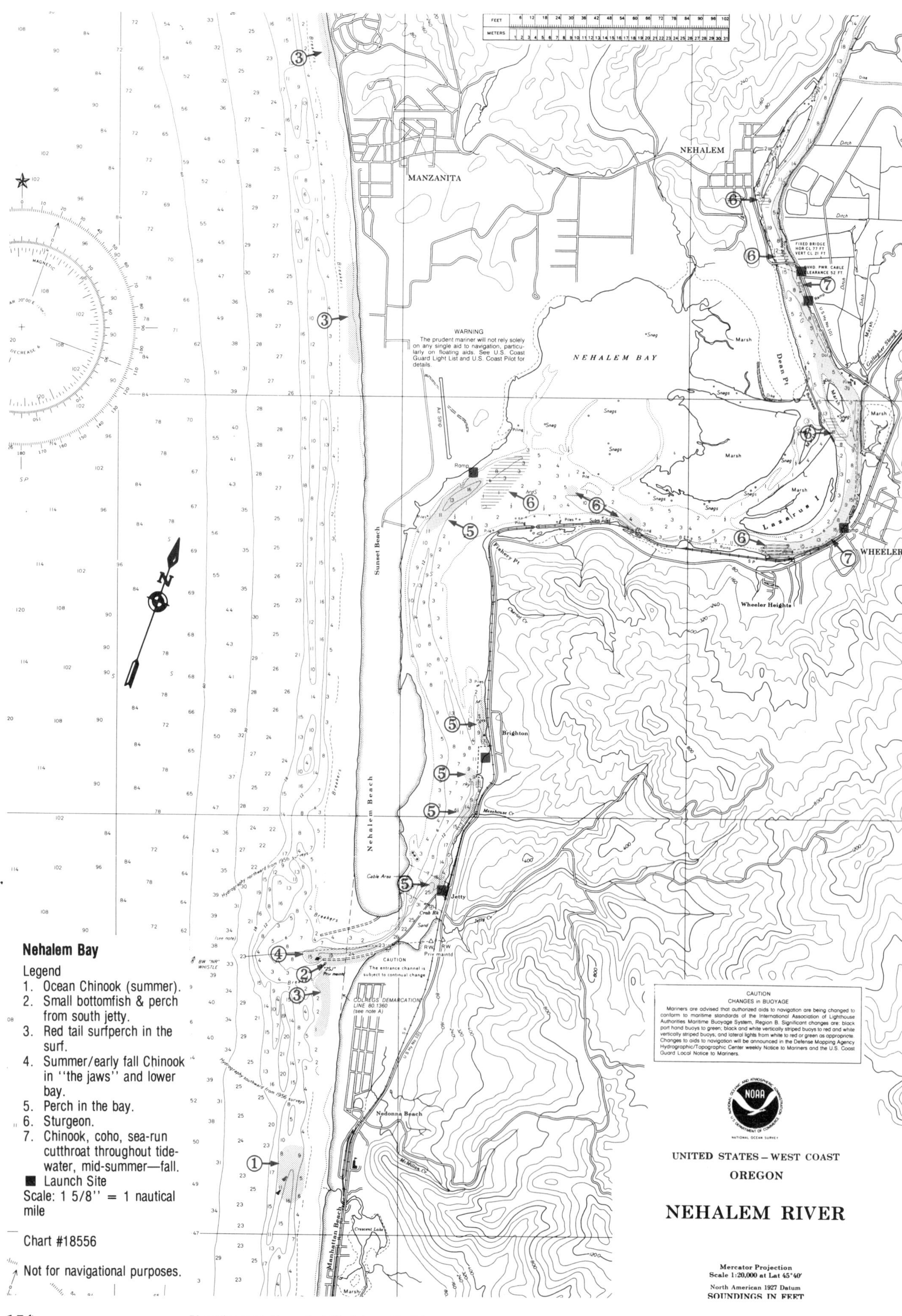

Nehalem Bay
Legend
1. Ocean Chinook (summer).
2. Small bottomfish & perch from south jetty.
3. Red tail surfperch in the surf.
4. Summer/early fall Chinook in "the jaws" and lower bay.
5. Perch in the bay.
6. Sturgeon.
7. Chinook, coho, sea-run cutthroat throughout tidewater, mid-summer—fall.
■ Launch Site
Scale: 1 5/8" = 1 nautical mile
Chart #18556
Not for navigational purposes.
FEET
METERS
MANZANITA
NEHALEM
NEHALEM BAY
WHEELER
Wheeler Heights
Brighton
Nedonna Beach
Manhattan Beach
Sunset Beach
Nehalem Beach
Dean Pt
Lazarus I
Fishery Pt
Jetty
Crab Rk
Marsh
Ramp
Cable Area
Breakers
Air Strip
Crescent Lake
FIXED BRIDGE HOR CL 77 FT VERT CL 21 FT
OVHD. PWR. CABLE CLEARANCE 52 FT.
WARNING
The prudent mariner will not rely solely on any single aid to navigation, particularly on floating aids. See U.S. Coast Guard Light List and U.S. Coast Pilot for details.
CAUTION
The entrance channel is subject to continual change
COLREGS DEMARCATION LINE 80.1360 (see note A)
CAUTION
CHANGES in BUOYAGE
Mariners are advised that authorized aids to navigation are being changed to conform to maritime standards of the International Association of Lighthouse Authorities Maritime Buoyage System, Region B. Significant changes are: black port hand buoys to green; black and white vertically striped buoys to red and white vertically striped buoys; and lateral lights from white to red or green as appropriate. Changes to aids to navigation will be announced in the Defense Mapping Agency Hydrographic/Topographic Center weekly Notice to Mariners and the U.S. Coast Guard Local Notice to Mariners.
NOAA
NATIONAL OCEAN SURVEY
UNITED STATES – WEST COAST
OREGON
NEHALEM RIVER
Mercator Projection
Scale 1:20,000 at Lat 45°40'
North American 1927 Datum
SOUNDINGS IN FEET

Spring is the best time for perch fishing throughout the bay and all the way out to the jetties and beaches. In fact, some outstanding fishing for perch occurs off the jetties as early as midFebruary and through March. The best bet at this time is fishing (with due caution) the breakers along the south side of the north jetty. However, to reach that jetty requires a walk of a couple miles from the state park.

In the bay, pinkfins become abundant in several areas, such as the northwest shore around the bend (east of) Sunset Beach. Toward late summer, striped and large silver pile perch are usually plentiful, especially around the three railroad trestles north of Fisher Point. There are also several good perch areas throughout the bay, as indicated on the map.

Most perch are taken in the bay from small boats, but there are a few areas from which bank anglers connect as well. These include the beach around Brighton Moorage and

NEHALEM BAY / Sport Fish and Seasons

Species	J	F	M	A	M	J	J	A	S	O	N	D
						BEST MONTHS						
Chinook salmon[1]	poor	poor	poor	poor	poor/fair	best	best	best	best	best/fair	poor	poor
Sea-run cutthroat	poor	poor	poor	poor	poor	fair/best	best	best	best	fair	poor	poor
Perch	poor	poor	poor	fair/best	best	best	best	best/fair	fair	fair	poor	poor
Silver salmon	poor	poor	poor	poor	fair/best	best	fair	fair	best	best	poor	poor
Sturgeon[2]	poor	poor	poor	poor	fair/best	best	best/fair	poor	poor	poor	poor	poor

[1]Ocean salmon seasons vary from year to year; consult regulations. Generally June and July find salmon offshore and around jetties; thereafter they begin to move farther up into tidewater.

[2]Check regulations carefully for min./max. sizes.

LEGEND: best — fair — poor

The lower Nehalem offers small boaters fishing for salmon, perch, trout and sturgeon.

around the trestle just above Jetty Fishery. Whether fishing from a boat or from shore, you can expect to catch the most perch during low and high slack tides and throughout the flood.

Surf fishing for redtail perch can be good along the beach just south of the jetty. North of the bay there are some historically and consistently excellent "pinkfin" beaches around Manzanita.

Larger Alternatives: Bottomfish And Sturgeon

There hasn't been a great deal of interest in offshore bottomfishing. In part that may be due to the limited access, as well as the fact that much of the sea floor in the area is sandy.

Any difficulties getting to (and returning from) offshore areas aren't much less these days, but there are anglers who cross the bar and head out for bottomfish. Those who take a northerly approach on the 25-fathom mark toward Neahkahnie Mountain have found good numbers of halibut on gravel beds and lingcod on gravel/rock areas.

The lower Nehalem is one of several estuaries in the state where anglers realized in the 1980s that of course sturgeon are residents and can be taken on hook and line, mostly May through July. Several tidewater spots have produced in recent years including along the dike (just above the break) across from the island north of Wheeler Marina and along the pilings in the bend above Paradise Cove. Around the highway bridge, at Nehalem, has been a good bet. Try the west side of the island above Wheeler—seek the deep holes, at least 12 to 20 feet deep.

This is boat fishing. Some anglers put out two anchors to hold the boat still though that isn't essential. Fish a mud shrimp or sand shrimp on a 6/0 or 7/0 single barbless hook on 2 feet of braided dacron line beneath 3 feet of steel leader attached to a main line of 30-pound monofilament. A three-ounce pyramid sinker should be about right. Remember to give a sturgeon time to take the bait and, when setting the hooks, be emphatic—several times. Also, be sure you know current size/season/limit strugeon regulations.

Small Boat Safety—Crossing The Bar

Remember: cross this bar with extreme caution and only under excellent conditions. There is no Coast Guard station immediately at hand. For information on crossing the Nehalem Bar or for emergencies, the nearest station is in Tillamook Bay: 322-3531.

There have been tragic problems some years from people fishing what's known as "the horse collar," a section of the bar that is indeed shaped like a collar which—*between wave sets*—may appear deceptively tranquil.

Boaters remaining in the lower bay should have few problems, though when a salmon run is going hot and heavy traffic can be tricky. Also, keep an eye out for Crab Rock, about 150 yards southwest of Jetty Fishery since it can pose a considerable hazard when barely submerged. It may be marked by a private buoy just west of the rock. In general, remember that white buoys indicate a slow, no-wake area and buoys with black/white stripes indicate a narrow channel.

This angler is wisely fishing well inside *the Nehalem River bar on a flood tide.*

Facilities

All phone numbers listed are within the 503 area code unless noted otherwise.

Marinas

Nehalem's marinas are all full-service operations, including boat rentals which, at press time, were renting for roughly $50 per day without power or about that much for a half-day with power.

Brighton Moorage, 29200 Highway 101 North, Rockaway 97136 (on the bay, 2 miles out of Wheeler, 4 miles north of Rockaway), 368-5745. Open 7 days/week (hours may vary), year-round. Twelve moorage slips, reservations needed in season. Fuel, bait and tackle. Launch ramp good pretty much all conditions. Rents 14' fiverglass boats without power. Also offers tentsites and RV spaces. Brighton Moorage has been an institution here since about 1950.

Jetty Fishery, 27550 Highway 101 North, Rockaway 97136 (on mouth of Nehalem Bay), 368-5746. Open all year, 7 a.m.-7 p.m., 7 days/week. Twentyfive moorage slips (for boats under 18 feet). Fuel available and minor engine repair. 2 launch ramps in fair shape, at least one okay on lower tides. Rents 16' aluminum skiffs with or without power. Also 15 RV spaces with hookups.

Wheeler Marina, Wheeler 97147 (downtown Wheeler waterfront), 368-5780. Open all year, 7 days/week May-October. 50 to 60 moorage slips; reservations urged. Fuel, engine repair, bait and tackle all available here. Launch ramp nearby, free but not good on lower tides. Rents 14' kickerboats with or without power. Rents fishing gear, canoes. Reliable fishing information (Jim Neilson).

Launch Facilties

Nehalem Bay county ramp, 1/2 miles south of Nehalem on Highway 101, no charge, floats, restrooms.

Wheeler city ramp, downtown Wheeler, no charge.

Paradise Cove ramp, south of Wheeler on Highway 101, asphalt, launch fee, restrooms, supplies. (private facility)

Nehalem Bay State Park ramp, north of Nehalem off Highway 101, no charge, restrooms, camping area.

Brighton Moorage, 4 miles north of Rockaway, Highway 101, asphalt, launch fee, supplies, restrooms. (private facility)

Jetty Fishery, 3 miles north of Rockaway Beach, Highway 101, launch fee, full facility (private).

Public Campgrounds

Nehalem Bay State Park, 3 miles south of the Manzanita Junction off Highway 101, 291 RV/tent sites with electrical hookups and separate hiker/biker camp. (Also: horse camp with corrals).

For More Information

Nehalem Bay Area Chamber of Commerce, Wheeler 97147, 368-5100.

courtesy Portland District, U.S. Army Corps of Engineers

Tillamook Bay

Tillamook bay is easily the largest bay on the northern Oregon coast and one of the largest in the Northwest. It is also the bay closest to Portland, a mere two-hour drive away. Tillamook's popularity as a coastal recreation area stems in part from this proximity. But it also offers some great sportfishing.

The bay is fed by five rivers—the Miami, Kilchis, Wilson, Trask and Tillamook. Not surprisingly, it supports runs of salmon, steelhead, sea-run cutthroat and sturgeon, providing fine ocean and bay fisheries. Not only that, but some of the very best opportunities for varied nearshore and, particularly, deepwater bottomfishing take place well offshore. Probably more halibut are brought in here than any Oregon port except Yaquina Bay.

The greater Tillamook Bay area supports a wealth of facilities, and at Garibaldi there is an impressive charter fleet as well as marinas with launch and moorage facilities, bait and tackle shops, motels, resorts, RV parks and state/-county campgrounds.

Not only are salmon king here, but fishing for them reigns nearly six months of the year, thanks to good spring, summer and fall fisheries. Chinook and silvers offer both offshore and tidewater action. Bottomfish are taken year-round, when the ocean is hospitable, in various settings: offshore, nearshore, in the bay and from the jetties. Starting in the mid1980s, anglers ''discovered'' sturgeon in the bay and a relatively hot new fishery was born.

Silver salmon like this one the author caught trolling herring behind a dodger may be so numerous many seasons that seasons end early when quotas fill.

Offshore: Varying Strategies For Salmon And Bottomfish

Early in the ocean salmon season, silvers dominate the catches of Garibaldi charters and private boats. Though rather unspectacular in size, they often make up for that in numbers. During the second half of the summer, the size of these fish increases noticeably, to the 10- to 12-pound range.

The coho fishing off Tillamook has been, if anything, too good—not for anglers, but for the local sportfishing industry. Many years, the season has ended earlier than many folks would like because coho quotas filled too quickly. (That might be a good reason to plan trips to Tillamook for offshore fishing earlier in the season.) All those coho don't just go away after the quota closes the ocean to salmon fishing, either. I've been on August bottomfish trips when silvers—no longer legal to keep—were so thick on the ocean that they kept grabbing the shrimp flies on bottomfish lines coming up or going down around the boat.

Meanwhile, numbers of chinook tend to gradually increase during the summer. Some of these offshore kings will exceed 30 pounds. Some years see great numbers of the big chinook in the ocean fishery; other years it's slim pickings. The two species are often mixed together, but in general chinook tend to hang in shallower water nearer shore. Those targeting silvers usually start trolling over 40 fathoms.

Whether for silvers or kings, trolling is pretty much standard for all Tillamook offshore salmon anglers, but beyond that techniques vary somewhat. Some charter skippers still use heavy leads to keep rigs down, while many favor plastic diving planes, but increasing numbers use downriggers. Those who use a diver often favor a leader of only a couple feet with a whole herring. Some add a flasher while others eschew them. When silvers are feeding at the surface, try trolling a fly with no weight or an ounce or two ahead of it.

Bottomfish trips have been an integral part of Tillamook Bay charter operations for many years. It was during the salmon management crunch of the 1980s that this alternative sport saw its biggest surge in popularity. Now, many Tillamook fishermen seek the fairly assured quantity and variety of fish that these ocean waters offer.

Both nearshore and offshore reefs are fished. Both produce plenty of action and good catches, but that action and those catches differ markedly.

Most private boaters and many charters concentrate on fishing close in, over chains of rocky reefs north and south of the bay that extend out from rocky headlands (such as Cannon Beach, Cape Meares, Three Arch Rocks, even as far south as Cape Lookout). Dominating their catch are ''school fish'' such as 2- to 5-pound black rockfish, sometimes mixed with blues, yellowtails, widows or other

Locating schools of yellowtail rockfish off Tillamook Bay often means multiple hookups. This deckhand pulls in two anglers' tangled lines with four nice yellowtails that gobbled up shrimp flies.

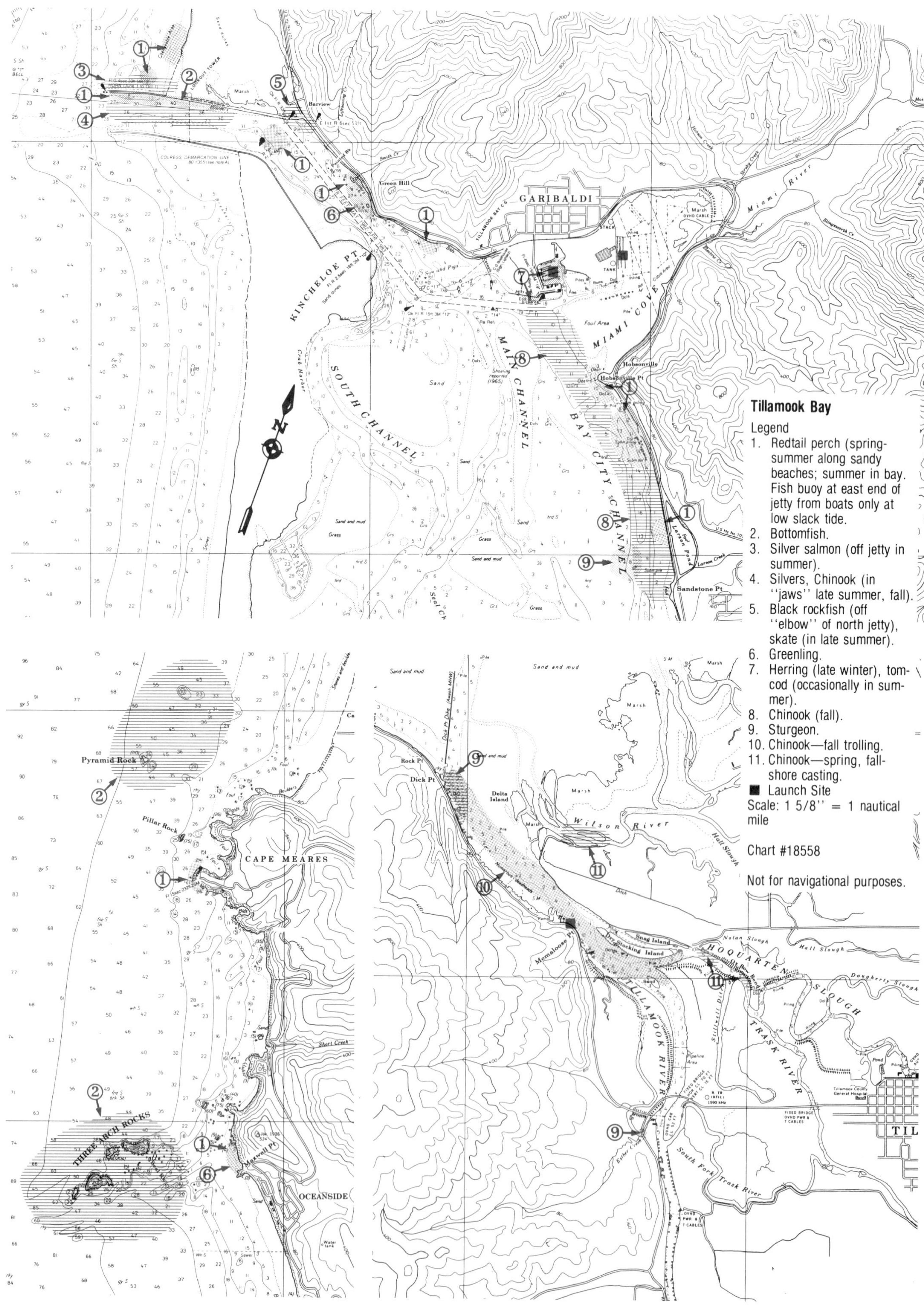

Tillamook Bay
Legend
1. Redtail perch (spring-summer along sandy beaches; summer in bay. Fish buoy at east end of jetty from boats only at low slack tide.
2. Bottomfish.
3. Silver salmon (off jetty in summer).
4. Silvers, Chinook (in "jaws" late summer, fall).
5. Black rockfish (off "elbow" of north jetty), skate (in late summer).
6. Greenling.
7. Herring (late winter), tomcod (occasionally in summer).
8. Chinook (fall).
9. Sturgeon.
10. Chinook—fall trolling.
11. Chinook—spring, fall-shore casting.
Launch Site
Scale: 1 5/8'' = 1 nautical mile
Chart #18558
Not for navigational purposes.
GARIBALDI
Barview
Green Hill
KINCHELOE PT.
MIAMI COVE
MAIN CHANNEL
SOUTH CHANNEL
BAY CITY CHANNEL
Hobsonville
Hobsonville Pt
Sandstone Pt
Miami River
Pyramid Rock
Pillar Rock
CAPE MEARES
THREE ARCH ROCKS
Maxwell Pt
OCEANSIDE
Short Creek
Rock Pt
Dick Pt
Delta Island
Wilson River
Memaloose Pt
Snag Island
Dry Stocking Island
HOQUARTEN SLOUGH
TILLAMOOK RIVER
TRASK RIVER
South Fork Trask River
Hall Slough
Dougherty Slough
Nolan Slough
Esther Creek
Tillamook County General Hospital
TIL

species, as well as some lingcod (not generally large), greenling and cabezon. Depths fished vary from 40 to 150 feet, as a rule. When the northwest wind prevails, one possibility is to run north toward Cannon Beach. A good starting point would be over the Loran-C numbers: 12255.0 + 28016.0. It's a healthy 20-mile run. From the Northwest or otherwise, if the wind doesn't blow too hard, Three-Arch Rocks is usually fishable. The run isn't so far, about 7 miles. Those with Loran-C can start at 12439.0 + 27996.9.

Charters and private boaters alike have begun to catch on to the advantages of much lighter gear for this kind of fishing. Many now fish spinning gear as described for Ilwaco, to the north. Catch rates are just as high; "fun rates" soar astronomically, however.

Some of the larger, faster charter boats regularly fish the more distant offshore reefs located west of the bay, such as Twelve-Mile Reef and beyond, generally out 15 or 20 miles to waters of 80 or so fathoms. When currents are not particularly swift, a 1-pound lead with a couple shrimp flies works well. But more often, charter skippers like Joe Gierga put on 20 ounces. Gierga has been fishing these deep reefs for decades and often takes over 12,000 pounds of fish a year—which averages out to nearly a limit for each fisherman, and not all school fish by any means. Most of these charters are equipped with heavy tackle and Dacron line.

In fact, these deep reefs offer the most consistent fishing for big female ling of 20 to 40 pounds. Many school rockfish do get into the act, of course, but so do many big deepwater prizes, notably yelloweye ("red snapper") and bocaccio of 10 to 25 pounds. (Tillamook is one of the few charter centers in the Northwest that regularly brings in the large bocaccio, probably by virtue of the deeper water fished.) I've seen quite a few canaries of 7 or 8 pounds taken here, also. The list of other species commonly encountered on these trips is long, from colorful little greenstripe rockfish to blue sharks to back-straining halibut which may exceed 100 pounds.

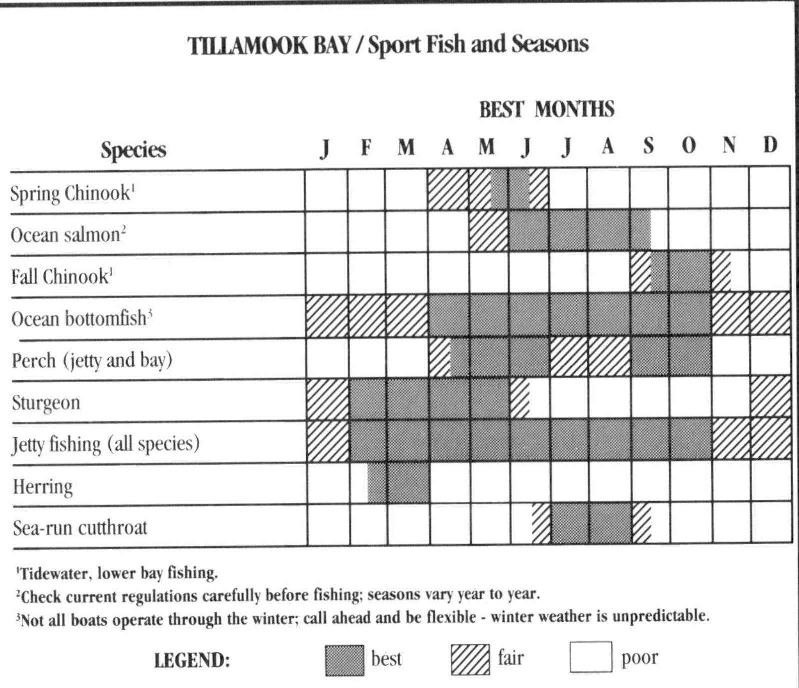

TILLAMOOK BAY / Sport Fish and Seasons

Species	J	F	M	A	M	J	J	A	S	O	N	D
	BEST MONTHS											
Spring Chinook[1]	poor	poor	poor	fair	fair/best	best/fair	poor	poor	poor	poor	poor	poor
Ocean salmon[2]	poor	poor	poor	poor	fair	best	best	best	best/poor	poor	poor	poor
Fall Chinook[1]	poor	poor	poor	poor	poor	poor	poor	poor	fair/best	best	fair/poor	poor
Ocean bottomfish[3]	fair	fair	fair	best	best	best	best	best	best	best	fair	fair
Perch (jetty and bay)	poor	poor	poor	fair/best	best	best	fair	fair	best	best	poor	poor
Sturgeon	fair	best	best	best	best	fair/poor	poor	poor	poor	poor	poor	fair
Jetty fishing (all species)	fair	best	best	best	best	best	best	best	best	best	fair	fair
Herring	poor	poor/best	best	poor	poor	poor	poor	poor	poor	poor	poor	poor
Sea-run cutthroat	poor	poor	poor	poor	poor	poor/fair	best	best	fair/poor	poor	poor	poor

[1]Tidewater, lower bay fishing.
[2]Check current regulations carefully before fishing; seasons vary year to year.
[3]Not all boats operate through the winter; call ahead and be flexible - winter weather is unpredictable.

LEGEND: best · fair · poor

Offshore, deep reefs don't suffer a great deal of pressure from many sources and populations seem to be holding well. When conditions are good, so are catches and big fish are as predominant as in past years.

Halibut fishing has always been a factor off Tillamook, with big flatfish hauled in every year. But some years recently have begun to see them caught on a more frequent basis. Some deepwater charters report taking two or three on many days and as many as four or five on occasion. Big jigs or whole herring will work well for big halibut—yet some of the biggest barndoors have been caught on little shrimp flies.

These offshore trips obviously require a somewhat longer cruising time and are likely to be pretty bumpy at times. Many anglers don't mind, given the difference in fishing quality, and in fact enjoy the ride, reveling in the boundless ocean and observing the creatures that inhabit the interface of the two worlds of air and water—sea birds, ocean sunfish, sharks, porpoises and the like.

But of course those who are easy to get queasy might be better advised to fish inner reefs. Deepwater trips are more vulnerable to weather and can get called if the seas look too ominous. Many days are flat throughout. Often the latter half of the summer becomes "lumpy" on a regular basis thanks to the usual northwesterlies.

By midsummer, warming air and water temperatures encourage some hardy souls to do their surfcasting in jeans and sneakers, and some do very well at it. This fisherman found a sandy "pocket beach" with perch near Cape Lookout.

Besides salmon and bottomfish, there is one other ocean option when conditions are right and albacore are within 50 or 60 miles of the coast in late summer. There are several large, fast Garibaldi charters equipped to pursue tuna within such distances.

Winter is hardly a busy season, with particularly inclement weather setting in November through January as a rule. But by February or so, a number of charters stand ready to sneak out on a good day for some nearshore reef fishing. And even in relatively shallow waters, at this time of year there is an excellent chance of getting some big spawning lings. Most charters will make a half-day trip if at least a half-dozen or more anglers will sign up. Call around and check if interested—then hope for a respite from winter winds.

Salmon In The Bay, Spring And Fall

Tillmook Bay anglers start their salmon fishing each year with spring-run chinook. That fishery seems to grow increasingly popular, which may have much to do with the improving status of spring runs. Springers can also be more eager to bite than fall fish.

These mint-bright kings average 30 pounds or so and move in as early as April, when they'll be found between the jetties. Every year, springers approaching 50 pounds are weighed in.

By the early June peak, some of the best fishing occurs up around the Trask and Wilson river mouths and down in the famed Ghost Hole. Fishermen know they have to get 'em when they come by, since spring fish are much less likely to linger in tidewater than are their fall-run counterparts.

Anglers fishing lower tidewater for springers usually troll herring, plugcut to spin in wide, slow loops on a stiff wire spreader, using a 6- to 8-foot leader of 20- to 40-pound monofilament and two 5/0 or 6/0 snelled beak hooks, the upper hook sliding or fixed. (There are, by the way, advocates of leaders about half this length.) Generally, springers are taken in shallow water, so a couple ounces on the spreader will suffice in the upper flats, while 4 ounces is better in the Ghost Hole. This is attached to the lower arm of the spreader with 19 inches of light (10- to 12-pound) monofilament—the idea being that it's better to lose a lead than a lunker. Troll throughout the incoming tide and especially around high slack.

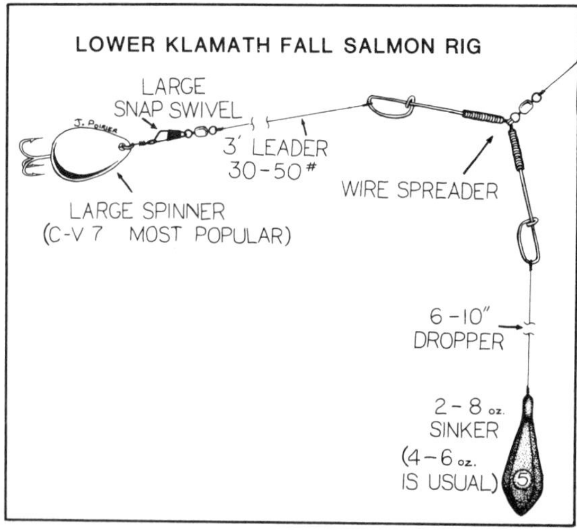

Those fishing upper tidewater drift sand shrimp or salmon eggs. These are generally rigged as shown, with a bobber stop set on the line to keep the bait about a foot above the bottom. Both the depth of the water in which the fish may be lying and the velocity of the current will determine whether the bobber is set to stop in as little as a few feet or as deep as 15. Experiment and adjust as necessary. Simple yet effective alternatives are a no. 4 spinner or a T-spoon, trolled or cast and retrieved.

From about midsummer on, chinook and to a lesser extent coho are available in and around the jetties. Much greater numbers of salmon invade the bay during the fall and hang around for a longer period of time. By August, more anglers are hooking up around and just inside the jetties. Fishing inside the bar is popular with small boaters who'd rather avoid the ocean, and popular with everyone once the ocean season has shut down.

Years back, most people thought July was too soon to start fishing the lower bay. But they've learned different. Trollers take both silvers and fall chinook, trolling plugcut herring.

This photo taken during a time of flat-calm water, shows that most boats—including one large charter—are fishing well inside the bar. But, inevitably, some boaters farther out are willing to gamble and fish right on the bar.

"It really made me think about what a fish is worth."

Paul Ingham had just seen boats tossed about and capsized like so many toys, and helped pull frightened anglers from the frigid waters off Tillamook Bay, Oregon.

Now, understand: Ingham is no stranger to salt water fishing. He keeps very busy year-round as a salmon charter skipper in Port Angeles, Washington.

So it takes plenty to shake up a seasoned salty dog like Ingham. And plenty is just what he got from a seemingly inviting Pacific on the morning of September 29, 1988.

Tragedy is no stranger to these waters. The number of sport fishermen killed each year while fishing "the bar" at Oregon's Tillamook and Nehalem bays on the north coast range from a few into double digits. There are other potentially dangerous bars up and down the Oregon coast.

Visitors to the Oregon coast and landlubbers may not know the "bar" from the tavern up the street. But if they fish the ocean from nearly any place on this coast, they'll have to cross a bar to do it. That is the area where the ocean meets a river mouth—typically between a pair of Corps of Engineers-built jetties. It's an area where the bottom suddenly grows shallow and the waves suddenly grow steep, particularly when wind-driven swells meet the outflow of a strong ebb tide.

In most cases, deaths of fishermen that occur on the bar *are* avoidable. Often they occur not when anglers are traversing the bar, as they must en route to the ocean from the harbor or vice-versa. Rather, many accidents result from anglers parked on the bar, fishing exactly where they shouldn't, even on a calm day.

"Well—salmon tend to congregate (there), in the most dangerous areas," Bob Steiner, chief warrant officer at the Tillamook Bay Coast Guard station, told me.

Lacking Paul Ingham's brush with death on the bar, many fishermen *don't* stop to think what a fish is worth. When fishing's good, caution may be thrown to the winds (and waves). That was just the situation on September 29, 1988, when Ingham and a friend headed down the lower Tillamook and out just beyond its mouth in a 17-foot deep-vee aluminum outboard.

"The day before, we'd closed the bar due to unsafe conditions," Steiner explains, "but on the 29th, about 9:30 that morning, I lifted the restriction on pleasure boats, permitting them to cross the bar." By then, the ocean and bar conditions seemed reasonable—and moderating.

There were plenty of private boats waiting for just such a go-ahead to rush out through "the jaws." That was inevitable considering "There was some of the best king fishing I've ever seen," as visiting salmon charter skipper Ingham says. He'd been out a day earlier, before the bar had closed. "It was crazy—people were fishing in 30 feet of water and catching big kings right and left!"

Ingham figures about 40 boats headed out past the jetties on this fateful morning. Many of those boats, he adds, were not exactly yachts. "You name it: there were all sorts of boats—river sleds and even little aluminum cartoppers."

He and his buddy began fishing the edge of the bar and almost immediately boated a 25-pounder.

"Then some bigger waves started to break (just inside of us). We were really hauling the fish in then and my partner wanted to stay but I insisted we move out farther."

Just after that, a much bigger wave lifted their 17-footer high in the air, but fortunately for the pair, the wall of water didn't begin to break until it had passed beyond them. That was *not* so fortunate for three other boats, two capsizing in the deluge and the other swamping.

Boats this size are advised to fish well inside the jaws and then only during slack or flood tide.

Ingham helped pull one capsizing victim from the icy waters then leapt into a nearby boat to help a fellow in the stern who had been trying in vain to lift another man from the water, over the boat's transom.

Then he remembers shouting, "We'd better get out of here! There may be more big ones coming in."

According to subsequent reports no more waves as large as that killer estimated at 15 to 18 feet in height moved in at that time—though by that afternoon swells had built quickly to over 10 feet, according to the Coast Guard, which escorted about 80 boats in over the worsening bar.

Ingham was to learn that one woman had lost her life to the wave. Looking back on the ordeal, he points out that he and his friend would have undoubtedly been among the capsized had they not moved farther out, beyond the bar, when they did.

Although Ingham was a visitor to this Oregon bar, he knew enough to stay off it. Unfortunately, says Coast Guard Commander Steiner, too many visitors are less sensible in their pursuit of salmon.

"The reason that experienced fishermen don't sit on the bar is because they know that this kind of thing can happen without warning, no matter how nice the day is.

"Aggressive salmon fishermen want to get out and get fish, but their knowledge may not be enough to keep them safe." Steiner again adds that chinook tend to gather in dangerous areas.

Tillamook Bay's most dangerous area is the shallowest spot just outside the end of "the jaws" known as "the midground."

"Locals *just don't fish there,"* he says, with emphasis. "Even when it's nice, they still run out across the bar, then fish!"

This situation describes part of fishing most of Oregon's port entrances, wherever there are bar crossings. "It seems like every area has its 'midground,'" Steiner says.

Ultimately, Steiner says, "the ocean is not the problem; it's just doing what it always does. The problem is people.

"I can't run and tell people on a calm day that they can't fish around the bar because a rogue wave might get them. I have no legal authority and would just be laughed at."

But at least a number of fishermen who were fishing the entrance to Tillamook Bay on the morning of Sept. 29, 1988 wouldn't laugh.

Three simple recommendations can help keep small boat anglers out of trouble.

1. **Do not fish or for any other reason stop on the bar.** This is simple, direct and absolute. Fish either well inside the bar (where large waves will have already broken and at least you'll have to contend only with the "suds") or well outside, beyond the bar (where large waves may begin to crest but won't yet be curling). And, as the mayhem described above should make clear, remember that nice weather and a calm bar are never guarantees of safety in this icy, unpredictable ocean.

2. **Check in with the local Coast Guard before venturing out** unless you are really experienced in fishing a particular bar. Check conditions, go over charts, ask questions. (Keep in mind that the configuration of these harbor entrances can change seasonally with shifting sands.) Find out what route to take in and out and what areas to avoid.

3. **Finally, when crossing or fishing near a bar, have life vests on**, not stowed away somewhere aboard. (The Coast Guard recommends wearing life vests at all times—sage advice, but not often heeded. But fewer lives would be lost each year along this coast if fishermen would at the very least use life vests when on or near bar crossings.)

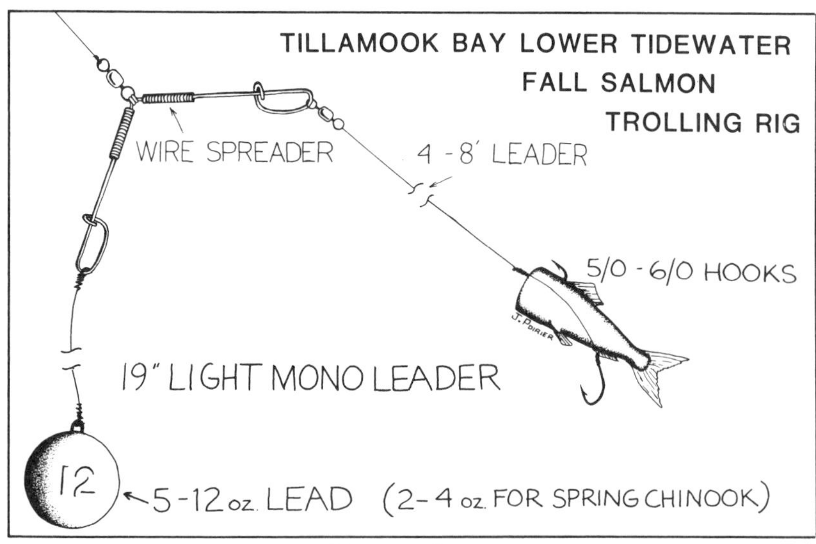

Silvers, particularly later in the month, will run 12 to 15 pounds at times. But the real monsters are fall chinook which average nearly 30 pounds and are often 40 to 60. Every year fish over 60 are landed and a few are taken over 70—weighed in to at least 74 pounds. The number of big fish in the late 1980s surprised even locals who'd fished here for many years.

Much of the hot fishing in August and early September is *just* outside, with chinook inclined to feed around the bar. Fortunately, the weather is usually good at this time of year and traversing Tillamook's so-so bar crossing on a flood tide need not be too traumatic many days. But when fishing gets hot and the fish are trophies, people here have been known to let caution lapse—occasionally with tragic results.

Besides feeding around the bar, salmon are prone to hang out around the end of the south jetty and along the north jetty from the tip to Buoy 6. Another popular trolling route goes from Buoy 11 to Buoy 14.

Whether inside or outside the jaws, anglers are generally trolling with rigs similar to those used for springers but heavier. Fall chinook are deeper than springers, usually just above the bottom, and much heavier weights—usually 5 to 12 ounces—are necessary. Of course if downriggers are used no weight on the line is needed (a much better arrangement for sportfishermen if available). Without the right gear, keeping baits near bottom is difficult with swift currents driving waters in or out of the bay. Farther up the bay, of course, less weight is needed. Large herring for fall chinook are plugcut and rigged so the lower hook swings free (is not hooked into the bait).

From a few areas, shore fishermen are able to catch Tillamook sturgeon, but most go to small boaters.

Most folks here go with pretty heavy-duty gear—lines testing at least 30 pound are the rule. The size of some of these big chinook is in part responsible for heavy lines but at least as significant are the crowds of boats, large and small, particularly on weekends that don't offer much space for the luxury of light lines.

The crowd also means that trollers should make an effort to keep lines short and near their boats. Baits should be pulled slowly. Many trollers simply kick their engines in and out of gear.

Although the chinook continue to filter in and move upbay, there can be good fishing between the jetties right through midOctober (though autumn swells may roll in some days too heavily to allow many to pursue the fish). Much of the progress of these fish, of course, is related to freshwater outflow: a period of heavy rains may send them packing upriver in a hurry.

The entire incoming tide including low and high slack water is the time to fish chinook in the lower bay. Not only does the flooding water bring salmon in with it, it is the only time that sensible fishermen in little boats between the jetties can feel safe. Troll with the current.

By midautumn, the Ghost Hole is inevitably crowded with small boats vying for big salmon. Many continue to fish herring, but here no. 5 clamshell or rainbow spinners see more use. The Ghost Hole remains one of the most consistent spots for lunker kings.

The "Ghost Hole" is much more than a single hole, as the name suggests. It's actually an extensive area along the eastern shoreline from Hobsonville Point south to Bay City. The whole stretch is fished particularly hard in September and October.

From Bay City (at the Oyster House) on up, trollers switch from herring almost exclusively to large spinners and spoons, especially around major river mouths.

Charters join private boats fishing between the jaws when a run is hot. So do jetty fishermen at times, casting herring or metal jigs. And nonboaters can move upbay to fish from shore. In both the lower Trask and Wilson rivers, shore anglers cast spinners or plunk fresh salmon eggs or shrimp below a bobber.

Shallow-water Sturgeon

As recently as the early 1980s, no one went sturgeon fishing in Tillamook Bay. But that changed in the middle years of the decade when people suddenly realized their bay was full of the prized fish.

Whether these sturgeon were always here in numbers and no one fished them is not clear. Some locals and at least one biologist have told me the surge in sturgeon populations occurred during the 1980s after Mount Saint Helens erupted. In any case, some of the tagged sturgeon taken in Tillamook Bay have traveled here from as far away as B.C.'s Fraser River and the Sacramento in California. Fortunately, the majority of these fish are whites, with only an occasional (much less desirable) green sturgeon taken.

Best success is for those who know the waters well enough to find deep holes at the end of channels. Such holes are along both east and west channels. These waters

Charter "Kerri-Lynn" as it churns out of Tillamook Bay, past a trawler.

are muddy and shallow and the going can be tricky, especially on the Cape Meares (west) side. Get a chart before heading out and check out the waters locally. (One of the best sources of information—and charts—is Sherry Lyster at Lyster's Bait and Tackle, not only a local sturgeon fishing expert but one who knows these waters like the back of her hand.) Pick your routes carefully, keep your outboard's tilt unlocked and watch the tides—or you may end up high and dry for several hours. There are productive holes that are easier to get to, as well, off Larson Pond, the Oyster House in Bay City (by the pilings) and about 3/4-mile north on the Bay Ocean Road. You'll need a good anchor in these spots and probably a fair amount of patience.

But even without a boat, fishermen catch sturgeon. For example, behind (south of) Pacific Pines Marina sturgeon are caught from shore. North, at Captain Johnson's, is another hole that can be fished from shore. Another good bet is 100 yards south of the Larson Pond culvert (at the Ghost Hole). Straight out should be 12 to 14 feet of water. One of the very best spots is reached by taking the Peninsula Road on the west side until you reach a gate. Park and walk directly east as far as you can. Start fishing the low/falling tide; the lower the tide the better—and the easier to get your bait to the fish.

In general, a good minus tide is the most popular time for sturgeon fishing. In shallow areas minus tides tend to concentrate the sturgeon in channels and holes. But sturgeon are taken at various times during tidal cycles, including high tide at the midgrounds hole.

Mud or sand shrimp are the bait of choice and in fact much of the time the only baits that seem to work. They are fished on a 6/0 or 7/0 hook beneath a sliding sinker of about 4 ounces. This is another spot where fishermen have come to favor soft Dacron leaders of about three feet beneath about the same length of wire (which helps prevent line fray when sturgeon roll and wrap themselves up).

Most sturgeon fishermen insist on pretty stout gear, typically 30- or 40-pound line. But some anglers, like Lyster, prefer 20-pound outfits with lighter graphite rods. However, Lyster also keeps anchor lines rigged to buoys for quick release so they can follow hooked fish.

Often, these fish are fought in relatively shallow water and, often, they will jump—sometimes multiple times. Lighter lines enhances that possibility.

Sturgeon are certainly in the bay year-round, but conditions for sportfishing are not always ideal. In fact, during summer months, the weed growth and bait-stealers (crabs and sculpins) make it difficult at best to keep a shrimp on the hook and available to sturgeon. Best fishing generally begins in January and lasts into midspring.

Pay close attention to regulations, since size restrictions have reduced the legal "window" (minimum-maximum sizes) in recent years.

Year-round Action From The North Jetty

Good access and good fishing make Tillamook Bay's north jetty a popular spot with anglers. Most of the effort is for rockfish, greenling and perch, but when silver salmon are feeding around the jetties in the fall, most fishermen forget those other species.

Only a few cast Buzz Bombs or other metal jigs so popular in Washington's inland marine waters for salmon. Fishermen on this jetty have been inclined to stick with a more typical bait rig, basically similar to the rig described above for upper tidewater spring chinook but with a whole herring rather than a sand shrimp and with more weight. Setting the bobber stop for about 12 feet above the bait is a good general rule. Jetty fishermen take most of their salmon during the last half of the flood tide.

Most of the year, black rockfish ("bass") are the primary target of sport fishermen on the jetties. Blacks sometimes provide good fishing during midwinter, especially in late February and March, when herring move in. Light leadhead jigs and worms worked slowly and fairly deep will yield rockfish up to 5 or 6 pounds at this time of year.

These "sea bass" run smaller in the summer but can be taken in large numbers at night when conditions are right. The trick here is to bring along a gasoline lantern or two. Placed near the water or, better, hung out from the rocks on a long pole, these lanterns help attract bait and fish. White plastic worms are cast out with little or no weight (a split shot at most) and retrieved *slowly.* Although these summer blacks will average only a pound or so, limits of them are not unheard of.

During the winter, rockfish are relatively scarce but kelp greenling ("sea trout") become a dominant part of the jetty catch. They average 1/2 to 3 pounds but can be over twice that size.

Even if the fishing's pretty quiet, many folks enjoy spending part of a warm summer day on the Tillamook Jetty rocks.

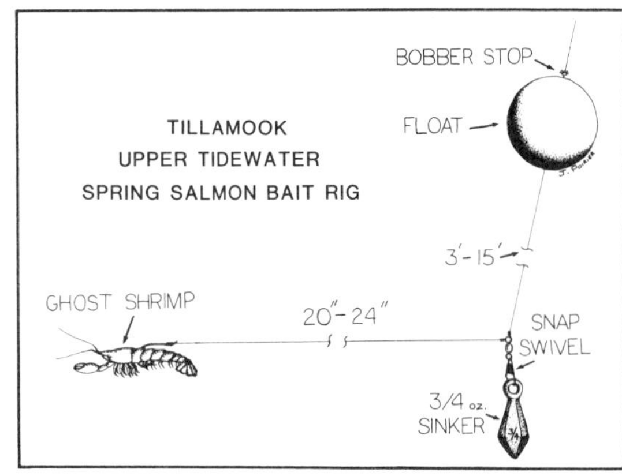

Spring signals the start of perch fishing for many jetty enthusiasts who fish sand shrimp during incoming tides for redtail ("pinkfin") and striped perch. Limits of these marine panfish are common.

The sandy beach north of the north jetty is another good bet for those who enjoy fishing the surf for redtail perch. The late incoming tide and high slack is the peak time.

Other species taken from the north jetty include lingcod. Small lings commonly strike plastic worms, especially when those are worked just over the rocks. Anglers intent on taking lingcod will rig a small, live greenling on a large hook 4 or 5 feet above a sinker, cast out and carefully retrieve it to the edge of the rocks. Then it becomes a waiting game.

Cabezon (big "bullheads") are also available, particularly in the spring, when 3- to 6-pounders are taken, most often on cut bait or shrimp.

Rocky headlands also offer good surfcasting for the agile and sure of foot. Tillamook Head and, farther south, Cape Falcon can offer good action for various smaller, inshore species.

Fishing The Bay For Panfish

Perch, greenling, rockfish, tomcod and herring are among the species caught from small boats, docks and the shore in lower Tillamook Bay. Larger surprises such as skate even turn up.

The Ghost Hole is famous for its salmon fishing, but it's also a top spot for perch. Good catches are made right at Hobsonville Point. In fact, some of the best periods for salmon fishing coincide with prime perch time—June and again in September and October. Pile perch over 3 pounds are the predominant perch species. Boaters do well fishing shrimp during low tide and throughout the incoming. The shore around the center of the Ghost Hole is a good spot for nonboaters, who cast to feeding perch that move in with the flooding tide. A wide pull-out area adjacent to the highway offers parking nearby.

Although they may not strike awe in the hearts of men, tomcod can be great fun to catch (three or four at a time) and extremely satisfying to eat. This action was photographed on a July afternoon at Garibaldi.

Most rockfish, greenling and cabezon are taken around "the bend" (at the elbow of the north jetty) and the Three Graces (large, prominent rocks along the north shore between Garibaldi and Barview). These areas are fished year-round but particularly around Christmas time when other fisheries are limited or unavailable.

Netarts Bay—Perch A-Plenty

This little bay, just south of Tillamook Bay, is very shallow, lacks a passable bar and is fed by no major rivers. It boasts little except perch (and crabs) for sport fishermen. But, particularly for anyone with a skiff, cartopper or canoe, spring and summer perch fishing can be at least as good as any other bay in the state.

Just how shallow is Netarts can be determined by looking across it during low tide, when most of the bay is exposed—a huge sand/mud flat. The main channel remains water-filled, and anglers can anchor and fish its edges, moving toward the sides of the bay as the tide—and feeding perch—move in.

On calm days, Netarts is an ideal spot for very small skiffs, even canoes, and for ultralight tackle enthusiasts. Even losing a few shouldn't hurt too badly: I've watched Netarts fishermen catch perch as quickly as they could cast out sand shrimp.

Netarts, by the way, is a top clam-producing bay in this state and is home to just about all the species of bay clams found in the Northwest.

Tomcod, miniature versions of Puget Sound's Pacific cod, average perhaps close to 1/2-pound. Highly unpredictable, some summers they move into the harbor in swarms but oftentimes not at all. If they do move in, it's likely to be late in the summer, when they can provide fun fishing from docks, mostly for kids who aren't too proud to admit an interest in such small fry. In fact, one of my favorite dishes from the Pacific has to be fresh tomcod, headed, gutted, scaled and fried.

Tomcod will strike just about any sort of bait. I've found it hard to beat small bits of tough fresh squid tentacles (available from local seafood markets) fished on no. 6 hooks above a small sinker (or any little spoon for weight—which also catches tomcod) with a trout rod. There is no bag limit on tomcod.

Herring attract more interest in the bay. They can be picked up throughout the boat basin in considerable abundance in late winter, with March a peak month. Some folks take them home to pickle; many put them up in their freezers as bait for the coming season.

Herring are but one likely target of nonboaters taking advantage of the Garibaldi Pier which in 1990 was renovated and restored in a joint project among the Department of Fish and Wildlife, the Port of Bay City and the City of Garibaldi.

If herring are too small for your taste, fish for a skate. Every summer skate from 20 or so to as much as 120 pounds are caught in the bay. One good spot lies off the elbow at the base of the north jetty, where a number of these large and very tasty creatures have been caught. Live shiner perch ("pogies") are reportedly one effective bait.

Bottomfish catches of charterboats are unloaded in a special area where they'll be sorted and cleaned for anglers before the boat returns to its slip.

Sea-run Cutthroat, All Summer

Every spring the Oregon Department of Fish and Wildlife stocks small cutthroat trout in Tillamook's estuarine rivers and adds several thousand more later in the season. Those not caught by early-season trout anglers wander to sea and return a year later, much larger and much tougher. They move up the bay rather quickly, since there is no great sudden temperature barrier in this large bay to hold them back as there is in some smaller bays.

Most effort for sea-runs takes place in the lower Tillamook River, although "bluebacks" are also taken from the lower Wilson and Trask rivers. Trolled spinners and worms take the majority of these 14- to 18-inch trout (occasionally as large as 22 inches), but a few fishermen cast and retrieve small hardware. More and more fishermen are joining Ed Lyster in flyfishing for bluebacks. He prefers to work streamers (which he ties using lots of red and white) both above tidewater and at times well down into tidewater.

Small Boat Safety—Crossing The Bar

Tillamook's reputation among small boaters eager to fish the ocean was pretty poor until the mid1970s. By then, construction of the south jetty was completed and the bar became reasonably crossable during summer and early fall months. Throughout the winter, however, this remains generally a rather tricky and inhospitable crossing. Swells run about 8 feet as a rule and may exceed 20 with offshore storms.

Even in nicer summer weather, bar conditions should be monitored before crossing—by radio or telephone contact with the Coast Guard. Tides should be noted as well, so you're not faced with trying to crash through the swells of a strong mid-ebb. And most such currents are strong, averaging 4 to 6 knots.

Best crossing slots vary from season to season, but the main channel is just south of the north jetty. The north jetty continues well out underwater; these submerged rocks can present a treacherous hazard so steer clear. Breakers seldom extend out beyond Buoy 1, just in front of the bay entrance, but "sleeper" waves can move in to surprise the unprepared. Avoid the "middle grounds," with a 6- to 8-foot swell on the ebb tide and breaks on the flood. Shoaling makes this area unpredictable.

The Coast Guard recommends outbound boats stop in the channel east of the seaward end of the breakwater and evaluate the bar. Once heading out, in any case, small boaters should not attempt to turn around if the bar is breaking. The Coast Guard also emphasizes that natural silting creates constant changes in the channel location and it's always best to inquire first. The rough bar sign is posted on the Coast Guard boathouse.

(Also see "Danger Lurks on the Bar!" elsewhere in this section.)

The Coast Guard station here is a modern facility in the boat basin and its personnel are generally very eager to help.

U.S. Coast Guard Station—Tillamook Bay
Weather/bar conditions (recording) 322-3234
General station information 322-3531

Facilities

All phone numbers listed are within the 503 area code unless otherwise noted.

There are year-round fishing opportunities here, since at least some boats pursue bottomfish during most of the winter season. Some charters and guides join troll the lower bay in the fall when chinook are in good supply. During the summer, reservations for lodging, moorage and charter fishing are wise and pretty much essential for weekend anglers.

Bottomfishermen who want to book trips with charters are urged to check around before booking a trip. The vessels that operate here vary considerably in size, age, comfort, quality/type of tackle and, as anywhere, in the skipper's experience and enthusiasm. Some trips fish strictly inner reefs (shorter ride, smaller fish); others always head far offshore to fish deep water.

Those who fish Garibaldi charters may notice an interesting, well-organized system in which most boats participate to get passengers' fish cleaned and bagged (part of trip cost here, though not at all ports). There is a central cleaning area where boats drop off the day's catch, usually winched up to the pier. Then the boat returns to its slip. Anglers then go to the cleaning station. Each has a number, issued on the boat, and in short order is issued a bag (hopefully, full) of filets.

Rates for a day of fishing are pretty uniform among charter offices. At press time, a day of salmon or bottomfishing cost $50 and "combo trips" for both ran $75. Most boats leave the docks around 5:30 a.m. and return around noon (salmon trips) or 2 or 3 p.m. (bottomfish).

Charters

Garibaldi Charters, P.O. Box 556, Garibaldi 97118, 322-0007. Runs 4 boats, 34' (6 anglers) to 44' (up to 20 anglers) from late May through September.

Joe's Deep Sea Fishing, P.O. Box 452, Garibaldi 97118, 322-3395. Fishes March through November with 8 boats from 40' to 56' which carry about 20 anglers but can take up to 30.

Siggi-G Charters, P.O. Box 536, Garibaldi 97118, 322-3285. Operates one 40' charter for up to 14 anglers from late April through October. Skipper Joe Gierga is an

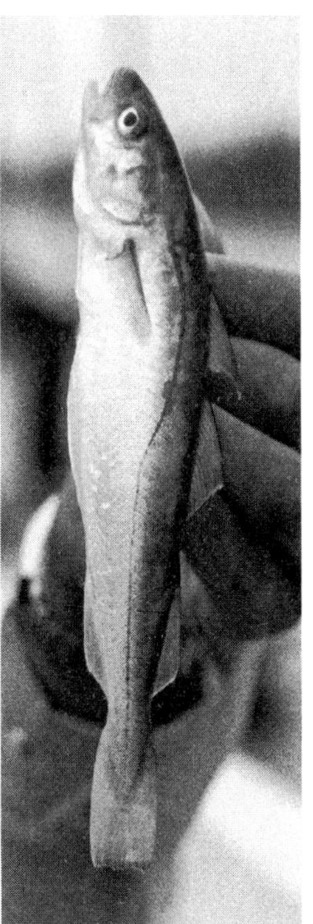

Tomcod

A man sitting on the edge of a boat looks at the perch he has just pulled in.

expert at fishing the very deep, distant, offshore reefs for the biggest bottomfish.

The Pier, P.O. Box 532, Garibaldi 97118, 322-0333. Operates several guided boats and charters to 48′ April through October.

Guides fish the lower river, some as far down as lower tidewater. For guided fishing, try *The Guide Shop*, 12140 Wilson River Highway, Tillamook 97141, 842-3474. Open daily, books for up to 25 guides in the summer. Two of the better guides who fish the lower bay—and offer sturgeon trips—are Doug Brown at 377-2669 and Ed Walder at 667-0112.

Marinas

Garibaldi Marina, 302 Mooring Basin Road, P.O. Box 841, Garibaldi 97118, 322-3312. Open year-round, 7 days/week in season. Three docks with 77 slips, reservations generally unnecessary. Fuel, fair bait and tackle selection. Port of Bay City 4-lane paved ramp with floats in great shape and good on low tides. Rents 16′ boats with or without power.

Old Mill Marina and RV Park, P.O. Box 705, Garibaldi 97118, 322-3243. Open all year but with greatly reduced schedule in winter. Guest moorage available as space permits. Fuel (gas), bait and tackle. Good paved ramp at modest cost. Rents 14′ skiffs with power at reasonable rates.

IN NETARTS BAY

Bayshore Boat Rentals and RV Park, P.O. Box 218, Netarts 97143, 842-7774. Open all year, 7 days/week. Sells fuel, bait and tackle. Gravel launch ramp, not usable on lower tides. Rents 16′ boats with or without power. Also 54 RV sites with hookups.

Happy Camp, P.O. Box 82, Netarts 97143, 842-4012. Open all year, every day. Small ramp okay for small, light boats. Rents 15′ boats with power—*including* crabbing gear. Sells some bait, no tackle. Also: 70-space RV park with hookups. Right on the beach.

Bait And Tackle

Barview Store, 15531 Highway 101, Rockaway Beach 97136, 322-3254. Open all year, daily. Lots of salmon gear.

The Guide Shop, 12140 Wilson River Highway, Tillamook 97141, 842-3474. Carries wide selection of steehead and salmon tackle.

Jetty Fishery, 27550 Highway 101 North, Rockaway 97136, 368-5746. Open all year, 7 days/week. Gear for salmon and perch fishing as well as crabbing.

Kimmel's Sporting Goods, 1812 1st Street, Tillamook 97141, 842-4281. Large, well-equipped outdoor store in downtown Tillamook with lots of tackle for fishing saltwater/tidewaters.

Lyster's Bait and Tackle, 14960 Highway 101 North, Rockaway 97136, 322-3342. Open every day all year. Carries wide selection of tackle and fresh and frozen bait. Owner Sherry Lyster Newman has been in the business all her life: like the previous owner, guide Ed Lyster, Sherry knows more about fishing these waters than almost anyone and is always ready to share what she knows. Also manufacturers of patented "Lyster's Original Crab Catcher" for crabbing with fishing tackle.

101 Sporting Goods, P.O. Box 648, Garibaldi 97118, 322-0026. Open 7 day/week, year-round. Wide selection of tackle; books for guides.

Launch Sites

Port of Bay City ramp, at the boat basin in Garibaldi. Asphalt ramp, modest charge. Restrooms, supplies, fuel.

Garibaldi Marina ramp, 1/8-mile west of Garibaldi. Asphalt ramp, free, fuel and supplies.

Memaloose Point county ramp, 2 miles northwest of Tillamook on Bay Ocean Road. Concrete ramp, fee to launch, restrooms.

Public Campgrounds

Barview Jetty County Park, at the foot of the north jetty on Highway 101 north of Garibaldi, 322-3522. 240 sites, 40 RV with hookups. A nice area in a great location for anglers. Sites are widely-spaced, many a stone's throw from jetty. Open year-round; may get crowded, especially in summer. Does not take reservations.

Cape Lookout State Park, 12 miles southwest of Tillamook off Highway 101. Very pleasant campground with 197 tentsites, 57 RV sites with hookups, hiker-biker camp area.

Cape Meares State Park, 10 miles west of Tillamook off Highway 101. Hiker-biker camp only.

For More Information

Garibaldi Chamber of Commerce, 202 Highway 101 North, Garibaldi 97118, 322-0301.

Rockaway Chamber of Commerce, P.O. Box 198, Rockaway 97136 355-8108.

Tillamook Chamber of Commerce, 3705 Highway 101 North, Tillamook 97141, 842-7525.

Photo courtesy Oregon Tourism Division.

Lower Nestucca And Siletz Rivers

NEITHER OF THESE TWO RIVERS ON THE LOWER north coast are navigable by recreational ocean fishermen. Both are strictly bay/river fishing, and fishing in both targets on three species: chinook, sea-run cutthroat and surfperch. Crabbing is also popular.

The lower Nestucca has a reputation for good spring and fall chinook fishing. It also has a reputation for crowds at times, as anglers along the shoreline jockey for position and elbow room to fish the more productive holes. From a unique fleet of special dories designed to launch from the beach through the surf at Cape Kiwanda, commercial fishermen still troll offshore waters. In years past, a few such dories took anglers on an exciting charter trip like no other.

Nestucca River fishing expert and lifelong resident Dorothy Gunness caught this 26-pound king fishing shrimp from her dock in mid-August.

Chinook salmon oblige anglers here with both spring and fall runs. Spring-run fish are mostly available May and June and into July. They move upriver fairly quickly, unlike the big fall-run fish, which linger longer and require a greater freshwater outflow before moving on up. The fall fish are available in the lower river from August through October, sometimes into November.

When the fish are still in the bay itself, trolling is in order. Whole or plug-cut herring are pulled very slowly along on a spreader rig with 4 or 5 ounces of lead (see sketch in the Tillamook Bay section). Some fishermen use a flasher as well. As fresh runs move into the bay, some action is enjoyed near the jaws, especially during a high outgoing tide. But that is not a good time to lose power, and the practice can hardly be recommended for boats without two engines. In any case, the river mouth is often rather filled in with sand and, at times, nets, so fishing can be difficult.

Surf-launch Charter Trip—Only At Cape Kiwanda

I glanced back at Zane Grey as salt spray swished against my yellow slicker. "We're not coming back in until the bottom of this scow's covered with 30-pounders, or...." The rugged novelist's words were drowned out by the roar of a huge, curling breaker which had lifted our wooden dory high and crashed just behind us.

"Pull!" cried the skipper as the oarsmen leaned back to gain distance before another—possibly devastating—breaker loomed. I stood in the bow next to Grey.

"I think you ought to sit down now."

"Huh?" I muttered.

"He said 'Sit down,'" said my fishing buddy. The command snapped me from my daydream of Pacific City, Oregon dory fishing in decades past when Zane Grey came up often from his Rogue River cabin to fish for salmon.

The charter skipper on our dory had been telling us of that history en route to the beach, as he towed his 21-foot custom dory with the outboard mounted in a well, forward of the unbroken transom. Like all surf dories, it had a high bow and flat bottom. Once at the beach, just inside Haystack Rock, we could see other trucks with empty trailers, dories already on the water.

At the entrance to the beach, a sign warned drivers to stay away unless launching a dory. This area had been set aside by the state specifically for that purpose.

Fortunately on this day the Pacific was reasonably benevolent, but negotiating the surf still offered exciting moments. Some of these dorymen are known to launch into some pretty formidable foam. Dorymen are adept at waiting for a lull between sets of breakers then quickly moving out. Returning can be even trickier in following seas—while also looking for a patch of firm sand to land on for easier trailering out.

We made it pretty easily both in and out and even caught a few fish. But more importantly, we did something few anglers have ever done, fishing the Oregon coast on a charterboat that didn't come out of a harbor but right through the surf.

Unfortunately, what was years ago a limited operation is even more limited today and dories for recreational charter are hard to come by.

As salmon proceed up tidewater, fishermen entice them with sand shrimp, eggs or large spinners. Shrimp are typically rigged as shown. (Be sure to check current regulations for any hook restrictions which, for years, have required that the hook gap between point and shank be no more than 5/8-inch when fishing from Pacific City bridge

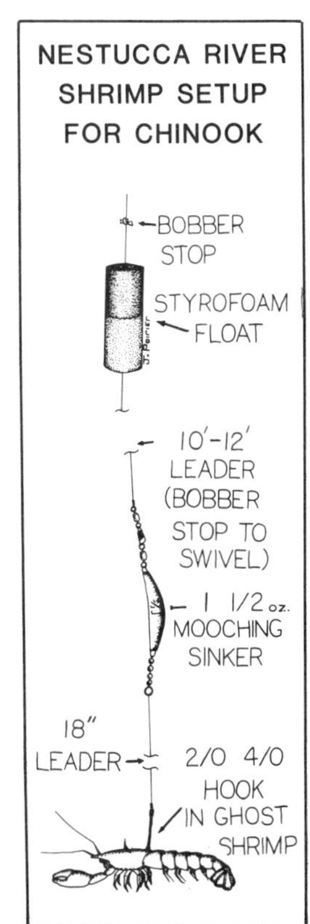

High-bowed, flat-bottomed Cape Kiwanda surf dories use a motor well inside the boat to facilitate launching through the breakers.

down to Cannery Hill at the mouth of the Little Nestucca, August 15-December 15.)

Large spinners, cast and slowly retrieved, also take many chinook. The locally-made Pacific City Rainbow spinner is popular and has been ever since, back in 1980, a 70-pounder was landed after it grabbed a Rainbow spinner near Haines Resort.

Whether you fish shrimp or spinners, keep the offering slow and deep—very near bottom. Though the general rule is that best fishing occurs at low tide, when the fish are concentrated in deeper holes the salmon in the Nestucca strike at any tide or time. Few fishermen here limit their efforts strictly to low tide.

Most salmon anglers use fairly stout gear with 20- to 25-pound line. Some go much lighter and that sporting approach is certainly the most fun. But it's also risky when the river is crowded.

Although the river may be crowded with boats, shore fishing is very popular. Unfortunately, public access is very limited and private access can be hard to come by. So of course when salmon are in, the more accessible holes are sure to be elbow-to-elbow on fall weekends.

Specific directions to reach the better-known holes should be available from resorts or tackle dealers listed at the end of this section. Some of the more popular lower river areas include the "Guard Rail Hole" near the boat ramp on Brooten Road at the south end of Pacific City (look for the white guard rail) and the "Parking Lot Hole" on the west side of the river, just below the Ezra Beachy Bridge, west of town. A stretch of river around Raines Resort (at Woods) has also gained considerable repute over the years.

Shore fishermen who find these areas too popular for their liking may seek out their own hot spots, but often it will be necessary to ask a landowner's permission to get to the water.

Seals have become something of a pestilence to many fishermen here, who watch the vast populations of the sleek mammals devour salmon in great numbers, so be mentally prepared to see just that.

"Bluebacks," as sea-run cutthroat are widely known in the state, are a popular late-summer sport fish in the

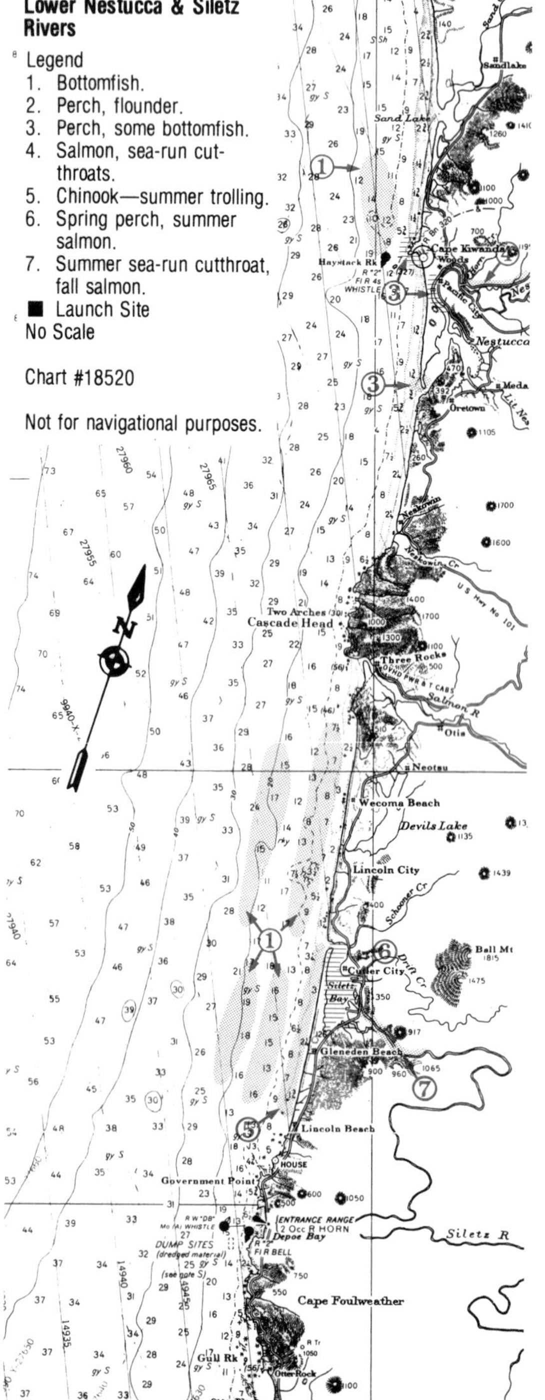

With no harbor entrance for miles, Kiwanda surf dories have this wild section of coast much to themselves.

Salmon From The Cape—Witnessing A Phenomenon

Although it's been many years, those days in late July and early August remain etched in my mind. It was a compelling scene in a dramatic setting, as perhaps a hundred fishermen crowded along steep rocky slopes and even atop high, precipitous cliffs to cast anchovies or herring into a sea boiling with birds, bait (anchovies)—and schools of chinook salmon.

It seemed that salmon were almost constantly being landed somewhere along Cape Kiwanda. One fisherman would work his way to the water with a large net to help a compatriot capture another fish. Along the bank behind the fishermen were strewn 15- to 30-pound salmon as anglers hurriedly unhooked fish and rebaited.

A few fishermen busily dipnetted anchovies with fine-meshed nets from the thick clouds of baitfish crowded in against the rocks. (Some enterprising adolescents were netting and selling the fresh bait.) Others swore as they tried to unook or untangle yet another murre, the omnipresent diving seabirds that sometimes beat the salmon to a fisherman's bait.

All in all, it was an amazing week or so in the history of this magnificent headland—but not one entirely without precedent. Locals said they had seen salmon fishing from the cape like this in the past and would expect to again, though not often.

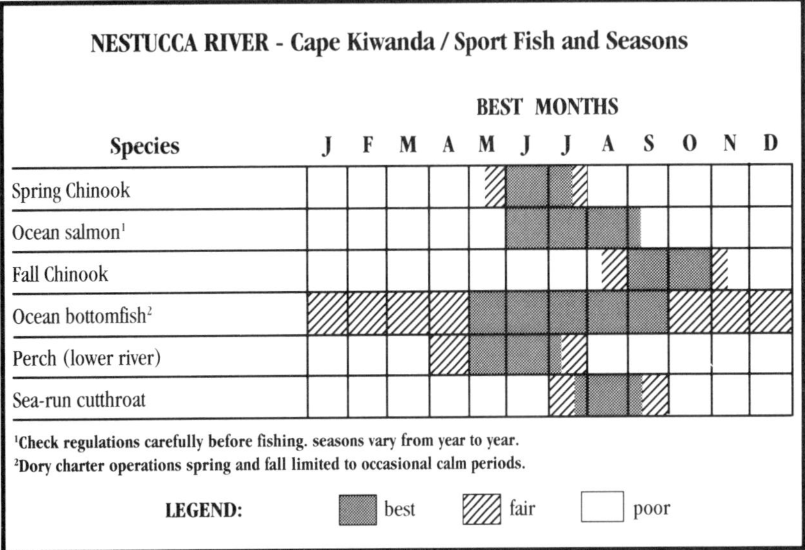

NESTUCCA RIVER - Cape Kiwanda / Sport Fish and Seasons

Species	J	F	M	A	M	J	J	A	S	O	N	D
	BEST MONTHS											
Spring Chinook	poor	poor	poor	poor	poor/fair	best	best/fair	poor	poor	poor	poor	poor
Ocean salmon[1]	poor	poor	poor	poor	poor	best	best	best	best/poor	poor	poor	poor
Fall Chinook	poor	poor	poor	poor	poor	poor	poor	poor/fair	best	best	fair/poor	poor
Ocean bottomfish[2]	fair	fair	fair	fair	best	best	best	best	best	fair	fair	fair
Perch (lower river)	poor	poor	poor	fair	best	best	best/fair	poor	poor	poor	poor	poor
Sea-run cutthroat	poor	poor	poor	poor	poor	poor	fair/best	best	best/fair	poor	poor	poor

[1]Check regulations carefully before fishing. seasons vary from year to year.
[2]Dory charter operations spring and fall limited to occasional calm periods.

LEGEND: best / fair / poor

Nestucca's upper tidewater. Most are taken from Pacific City upriver for about 3 miles on trolled Ford Fenders or Wedding Rings with a worm. A few anglers plunk eggs from shore. A cadre of flyfishermen casts streamers, working from boats to drop their offerings in, along undercut banks.

Surfperch provide fine sport from May through July, particularly for small boaters who anchor and fish shrimp just above the river mouth. Those who prefer fishing the breakers will take perch in the surf below the river mouth, especially in the spring.

In years past, it was possible to cast to salmon from the lower part of the sheer rock sides of Cape Kiwanda. But a cyclone fence has been put along the top of the cape following accidents. Still, when anchovies are in thick at the base of the cape, salmon may be right behind them.

Fishermen visiting the lower Siletz would be advised to do so between May and October. During the rest of the year, it is crabbing rather than fishing that occupies most of the interest in tidewater. But from midspring through midfall, there is usually some sort of action, whether one is seeking a 2-pound perch or a 40-pound salmon.

Spring fishing does not involve chinook, however, since the Siletz has no run of springers. But big fish do show most years.

These chinook begin to invade the bay by early August and are taken throughout tidewater well into October. Most lower river (bay) fishermen troll. Early in the season, during late summer, herring or anchovies are pulled behind a dodger, which in turn is placed 1 1/2 to 2 feet behind a 1- to 2-ounce mooching sinker. Later in the season, in early autumn, a large spinner or spoon replaces bait.

Such light weights suffice in this relatively shallow river to keep the slowly-trolled bait or lure near the bottom. While many fishermen insist on rising early out of habit, the tide here seems a more critical variable than time of day in determining peak fishing periods for salmon. Smart anglers make sure they're fishing just before, during and after any change of tide. Between tide changes, fish are still taken, but more sporadically and the current may make trolling trickier.

There are some good shore fishing spots along the lower river. One of the better areas is also one of the easier to find: it's on the north side of the river next to State Highway 229, across the river from the home locally famous as "the movie house." This distinctive building will be recognized at once by anyone who remembers the 1971 movie of the novel *Sometimes a Great Notion* by Oregon native Ken Kesey. The house only *looks* as though it was built in the '20s; it was built specifically for the movie. Most salmon taken from the bank in this part of the river go for hardware or herring. Now and then an angler will take a chinook while plunking sand shrimp, but sculpins make that an exercise in futility much of the time.

There are several other good tidewater spots for chinooks as far up as Medicine Rock, including Coyote Rock and Chinook Bend. Whether fishing lower or upper reaches of tidewater, you will profit by checking locally for the best spots at that time. Marinas listed at the end of this section can generally supply that information.

Somewhat less hard to find are perch, which in fact this bay has very generously shared with anglers over the years. Several species are taken, including pile and striped perch, plus a few smaller walleye and silver perch. But midspring through midsummer, redtail (pinkfin) perch are most abundant and easiest to catch.

Waiting for the bite: a crowd of anglers waits for another round of chinook to move in feeding along the cliffs of Cape Kiwanda in the summer of '82.

Many fish have been caught within sight of this famous landmark on the banks of the Siletz, the "movie house" of the film Sometimes a Great Notion.

Small boaters often limit on hungry pinkfins by anchoring and casting sand shrimp or other natural baits (pileworms, clam necks, etc.) on two small hooks set a foot or two apart, above an ounce or two of lead.

One of the very best spots for perch is right under the U.S. Highway 101 bridge, around the concrete supports. Many perch are also taken around the old pilings, just above and below the bridge.

Shore fishermen can find a few areas where feeding perch are also well within reach. Again, under the bridge is a best bet, particularly from the south shore.

As a rule, perch everywhere feed most heavily during the incoming and high slack tide.

For many Siletz anglers, sea-run cutts ("bluebacks") are a warm-up exercise for the mighty chinook that follow, but these scrappers are themselves worth fishing for, especially when a good run fills tidwater. As in many bays, feisty jack salmon can be numerous here in August and are taken along with trout.

The main blueback fishery occurs from the U.S. Highway 101 bridge on upriver for about 10 miles. Among the many popular stretches of river within this area, Windy Bend is one of the most productive.

Bluebacks seem likely to hit throughout the day in this upper tidewater fishery. Siletz fishermen use Doc Shelton or similar spinning rigs with nightcrawlers, trolling at a slow to moderate pace. A 6- to 8-pound-test line is plenty for these trout, which will average 13 to 15 inches (occasionally topping 17 or 18.

Facilities

All phone numbers listed are within the 503 area code unless otherwise noted.

Marinas, Launch Areas

Coyote Rock RV Park, Kernville Route, Box 299, Lincoln City 97367, 996-6824. Small concrete ramp, minimal launch charge. Guest moorage available. Bait and tackle shop. Rents aluminum skiffs. RV spaces with hookups—tends to be greener, quieter and more pleasant than many coastal RV parks. (Siletz River)

Nestucca Marina, 34560 Brooten Road, Pacific City 97135, 965-6410. Open all year, 7 days/week. 30 moorage slips, reservations recommended in summer. Fuel, bait and tackle. Single-lane launch ramp, one of better around. Rents 12′ aluminum skiffs without power.

Raines Resort, 33555 Ferry Street, Cloverdale 97112 (at the Woods Bridge), 965-6371. Open all year, every day. No moorage or fuel, but sells bait and tackle and rents 12′ skiffs. Launch ramp best for smaller boats, not at low tides. Also 4 cabins. (Nestucca River)

Riverview Lodge, 36220 Resort Drive, Cloverdale 97112 (1 miles from Highway 101 bridge), 965-6000. Open year-round, daily. 20-35 moorage slips, reservations recommended in season. No fuel or bait and tackle but rents 14′ aluminum skiffs. Also, 4 cabins. (Nestucca River)

Siletz Moorage, Kernville Route, Box 81, Lincoln City 97367 (about 2 miles south of Lincoln City, adjacent to Highway 101 bridge), 996-3671. Asphalt launch ramp (charge to launch), bait and tackle, fuel.

Sportsman's Landing, about 4 miles east of Highway 101 on State Highway 229, 996-3640. Hoist launch.

Bait And Tackle

Nestucca Country Sporting Goods, 34650 Brooten Road, Pacific City 97135, 965-6410. Open daily, year-round. Sells all sorts of bait and tackle for fishing the river. Can offer dory charter referral if any are operating.

Pacific City Sporting Goods, P.O. Box 45, Pacific City 97135, 965-6466. Open daily, year-round. Carries lots of gear for salmon, perch, trout and crabbing. Can suggest dory charters if any are operating.

Public Campgrounds

Devil's Lake State Park, near Lincoln City on Highway 101, 994-2002. 68 tent sites and 32 RV sites will hookups, hiker-biker camp.

For More Information

There is a wealth of resorts and motels on the coast in this area, ranging from small, simple, inexpensive cottages to huge, lavish resort complexes. For more lodging or other information:

Lincoln City Visitors Center, P.O. Box 787, 3939 Northwest Highway 101, Lincoln City 97367, 994-8378 or toll-free nationwide 800-452-2151.

Pacific City Chamber of Commerce, 33315 Cape Kiwanda Road, Pacific City 97135, 965-6161.

courtesy Portland Diestrict, U.S. Army Corps of Engineers

Depoe Bay

"THE WORLD'S SMALLEST HARBOR." THAT'S THE title this seashore community has given to itself, and with plenty of reason. The harbor is little more than big tidepool, roughly 6 square acres in size. Yet good things do come in small packages: this tiny port is home to a big, efficient fleet of salmon and bottomfish charters and to commercial and private vessels moored at the Port of Depoe Bay docks. It also boasts a marina and fine launch ramp which, the only one to serve many miles of coastline, is strategically located. Visitors here will find ample motels and RV parks as well as a number of specialty shops and fine little restaurants along U.S. Highway 101, just north of the bridge. (Visitors may recognize that bridge from scenes of the commandeering of a charterboat filmed here for the Academy Award winning movie of Ken Kesey's *One Flew Over the Cuckoo's Nest.*)

Depoe Bay has no tidewater and therefore no tidewater fishing. Anglers here look to the ocean for their sport. The two main fisheries outside the bay are ocean salmon and bottomfish angling. There are also opportunities to cast for perch and a variety of bottomfish from the rocky shorelines north and south of the bay.

As small as this harbor may be, offshore sport fishing is big business and has been for over a half-century. Charter offices and signs line the highway around the bridge, and private boats fill much of the port's dock space during the summer, to join charters. Depoe Bay fishermen enjoy considerable success for both salmon and bottomfish; the waters off the bay are a rich feeding grounds for salmon and the rock-strewn reefs of nearshore waters provide a home for abundant bottom dwellers. There is no time-consuming ride down a river mouth, between long jetties and over a big bar. In essence, two minutes out of the tiny harbor and you're in the Pacific.

Coho make up the bulk of the salmon sport catch off Depoe Bay, as off most of the state's central coast. And as everywhere along the coast, seasons vary from year to year according to regulations established the preceding spring and according to how quickly quotas fill. The trend in recent years has been for earlier openings, with certain area limitations, and for longer seasons.

Sport salmon boats seek feeding salmon wherever they suspect the fish might be found; there is no specific offshore area where wandering coho gather. Water temperature is a key determinant, though, and it may be necessary early in the season to travel many miles offshore into water as deep as 50 fathoms to find temperatures of at least 49 degrees where coho are inclined to feed.

Depoe Bay salmon are caught by trollers, most using a small plastic squid with a strip of herring. This is not universal, though: some charters prefer to troll whole herring, or later in the season, whole anchovies.

Year-round bottomfish trips have increasingly become a key part of the Depoe Bay charter fleet. Many anglers come seeking these "other species," and they're seldom

Small Boat Safety—Crossing The Bar

The bar here matches the bay in its meager proportions. A very short channel running under the U.S. Highway 101 bridge connects the harbor to the open Pacific. The sheer rock walls on either side of this channel are a mere 50 feet apart and the channel depth just 8 feet at low water.

On calm days, basic navigational skills will serve to make the ride quick and easy through the channel and into the ocean. Under less favorable conditions, passage should not be attempted by those unfamiliar with the area. The margin for error is as narrow as the opening in the rocks.

Those who navigate from Depoe Bay should head straight out to the red bell buoy (about a 1/2-mile run). Avoid the reefs to the north and south since seas break unpredictably in these areas. The Coast Guard urges recreational boaters never to fish between the bell buoy and the harbor entrance.

On nice summer mornings, whether heading out on a charter or on private boat, be prepared for a wait at the opening as boats queue up to slip out the narrow slot.

There is a rough bar advisory sign located 25 feet above the water, visible from the channel inside the harbor looking seaward, on a building on the north side of the entrance channel. Use it.

Fishermen are reminded by the Coast Guard to never fish between the channel entrance and the red gong buoy.

Besides the Coast Guard as an obvious source of local information, charter skippers are by and large about as friendly and hospitable here as any you'll find on the Pacific Coast. Catch one at a charter office and he'll usually gladly share his best advice with you about navigating the bay entrance—or about where the fish are.

U.S. Coast Guard Station—Depoe Bay

Bar conditions, weather (recording) 765-2122
General information (station phone) 765-2123

A charter churns out the tiny Depoe Bay harbor entrance en route to the fishing grounds.

ORANGE "OYSTERS" OF THE OPEN COAST?

A black carpet of huge coastal mussels offer both bait for perch fishing and a tender meal of bright orange, sweet morsels of meat.

I still remember the first time I had occasion to sample *Mytilus californianus*. Like vast black carpets, acre upon acre of these big mussels cover coastal rocks.

My buddy and I had fished offshore early, returned with limits and gotten in an hour nap—all before midafternoon. With the tide low and falling, we headed off to the rocky surf—not with rod and reel this time, but with bucket and small prybar.

In no time we had filled our bucket with all we figured to want—though far short of our daily limit of 72 each. Back at camp, we dropped the fresh mussels into a big pot with a bit of steaming saltwater at the bottom.

In a few minutes, the shells were steamed open to reveal inside each a bright orange mussel the size of a small oyster. We quickly discovered a genuine delicacy—every bit as flavorful and tender as the exquisite little bay mussels (*M. edulis*) served in restaurants—but much larger.

That evening's feast was the first of many since then. And every time I pop one of these orange delicacies into my mouth I never fail to wonder why so few people who frequent Oregon's rocky headlands show much interest in collecting mussels.

In any case, should this whet your interest and appetite, keep in mind you need only something to pry the mussels loose with—even a screwdriver would help—and a bucket or burlap bag to put them in. Cotton gloves can help avoid scraped hands. You can get to mussels at any reaonably low tide in most areas. Remember that there are limits and a few special closed areas, as listed in the state's sport fishing regulations pamphlet.

Larger mussels offer a chunk of meat as large (and as tender) as a small oyster.

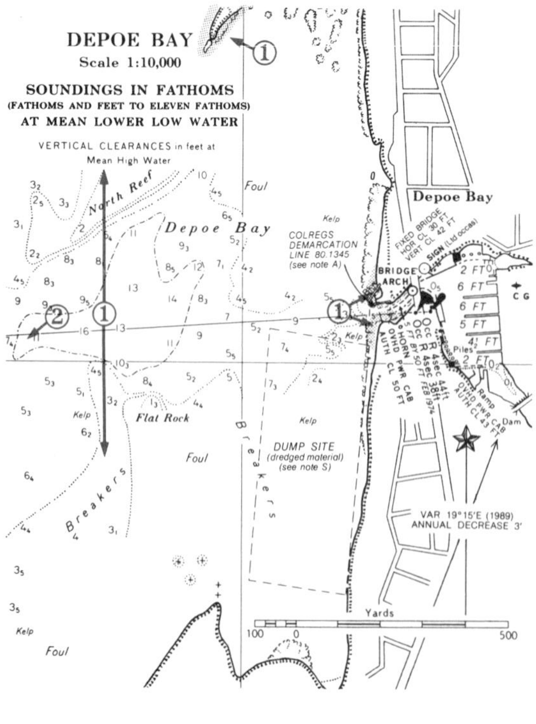

Depoe Bay

Legend
1. Bottomfish, perch—along shore.
2. Salmon offshore.
■ Launch Site

No Scale
Chart #18561

Not for navigational purposes.

disappointed. Still, the bottomfish resource near the bay is not without signs of strain. Depoe Bay skippers who've been at it for many years have seen changes, with the most prized catches of big lingcod and yelloweye rockfish (the popular "red snapper") less common these days and with smaller black rockfish ("sea bass") making up a larger percentage of most days' catches. But changes in tackle and fishing techniques have helped compensate.

Many bottomfishing boats here have joined a Northwest coastwide trend to lighter gear. Charters increasingly equip customers with spinning or conventional rods and reels holding 15-pound test line. Such gear is not only more fun but catches more fish than traditional heavy gear during late spring and summer in heavy drift conditions and for nearshore fishing. Simply working 1- to 2-ounce leadhead jigs with plastic worms catches just about anything that swims these reefs and of course the lighter line makes it much easier to get the jigs down and feel strikes.

Traditionally heavier tackle is still used, particularly for deepwater areas farther offshore and during winter trips when the big lingcod are particularly available. Line testing 40 or 50 pounds is used with lead jigs of 8 to 10 ounces, often with a smelt, herring or squid. Often a shrimp fly will be added above the jig.

Many Depoe Bay charter skippers don't mind sharing a run of salmon with private boaters, many of which are visible in the background.

DEPOE BAY / Sport Fish and Seasons

Species	J	F	M	A	M	J	J	A	S	O	N	D
	BEST MONTHS											
Bottomfish	fair	fair	fair	fair	best	best	best	best	best	best	best	fair
Salmon[1]	poor	poor	poor	poor	fair	best	best	best	fair	poor	poor	poor
Albacore[2]	poor	poor	poor	poor	poor	poor	poor	best	best	poor	poor	poor
Rocky surf bottomfish	fair	fair	fair	best	best	best	best	best	best	best	best	fair

[1]Check current regulations carefully before fishing; seasons vary year to year.
[2]Many years albacore do not show up within reach of sport boats at all; when they do, it may be for a day or for weeks.

LEGEND: best / fair / poor

Depoe Bay charters offer both 5-hour nearshore trips for salmon or bottomfish and eight-hour combination salmon and bottomfish offshore trips. Some offices offer 3-hour "sunset trips" which, on a nice summer evening, can be a lovely time to spend a few hours fishing nearshore waters—and can be very productive.

Halibut have always been a rare but occasional catch for Depoe Bay bottomfishing boats. But in recent years, charters have offered special halibut trips. The Tradewinds fleet began this option in the late 1980s, running 12-hour trips to spots 1 and 1/2 to 2 hours out, over deepwater halibut beds marked on Loran. Heavy rigs with weights up to 2 pounds are used to put large, whole herring on bottom.

Charters here are easily substantial enough to offer albacore trips any year they show within 60 or so miles of the coast, as the long-finned tuna can do anytime from late July through early October. When they show in numbers, those lucky enough to be fishing them will enjoy some of the fastest, most productive and exciting sport the northern Pacific has to offer. To participate in this unpredictable sport, get in touch with one of the offices under "Charters" at the end of this section and ask to be put on an albacore call list.

Those who don't own a boat or perhaps are more comfortable on solid ground can enjoy fishing the many areas north and south of Depoe Bay which provide good access to mile after mile of rocky shorelines. Cast into the rocky surf and, with baits or lures, you're likely to catch any of several species.

Government Point, just north, is one such spot, as is Fogarty Creek. To the south, Rocky Creek State Park and Otter Rock are worth fishing. Good catches of perch are taken even right from the rocks around the Depoe Bay channel entrance.

Surf fishing here has year-round potential, though spring is probably the most productive period. The real key is ocean conditions. When swells are light, getting to the fish is surprisingly possible. On the other hand, trying to fish while towering swells pound the rocks is not only difficult but foolhardy.

A variety of baits are effectively used in this increasingly popular fishery for greenling, small lings, cabezon and rockfish. Larger baits or small live fish are best bets for lings, while leadhead jigs and plastic worms work well for black rockfish. Small natural baits are best for perch, sometimes abundant around the rocks.

The author brought his own spinning gear aboard to catch this Oregon rockfish on a spoon. Today, some years after this photos was taken, many Depoe Bay charters offer anglers light line bottomfishing.

Loran Numbers To Good Bottomfishing

Private boaters with good electronics and a nautical chart can probably find ocean reefs that hold fish in the productive waters north of Depoe Bay. Still, those who haven't a clue can start at any of the following spots, generously provided by longtime skipper Rich Allen of the Tradewinds Fleet. And he says he'll be glad to share more spots with private boaters who want to give the office in Depoe Bay a call or stop by.

Government Point (About 2 miles north of Depoe Bay for good rockfish and lingcod fishing).

12711.4 + 27948.6 in 10 fathoms, 12751.1 + 27948.8 in 10 fathoms, 12748.8 + 27948.8 in 15 fathoms.

Siletz River (About 6 miles north of Depoe Bay for good rockfish and lingcod fishing).

12711.4 + 27955.4 in 15 fathoms (lots of lingcod), 12704.0 + 27958.6 in 10 fathoms, 12700.0 + 27958.4 in 10 fathoms.

Lincoln City (6 to 12 miles north of Depoe Bay for all reef-dwelling bottomfishes in an extensive reef area of several miles from kelp beds west into 30 fathoms).

12691.7 + 27959.7 in 12 fathoms, 12689.2 + 27960.2 in 10 fathoms, 12681.4 + 27958.1 and 12680.6 + 27958.0—both 20-fathom areas which jump to 8 fathoms in spots.

With rocky headlands up and down the coast in the Depoe Bay area, perch fishing is a readily accessible sport when seas are calm.

Facilities

All phone numbers listed are within the 503 area code unless otherwise noted.

Charters

After years of weekly telephoning up and down the coast to write stories for a major outdoor publication, I came to the conclusion that the charter people here are genuinely friendly and honest, with little competitive conflicts between charters or between charters and private boaters.

Rates are pretty much standard on all boats, typically at press time about $40 for a five-hour salmon or bottomfish trip and $65 for an eight-hour combination (salmon/bottomfish) trip. 12-hour halibut or tuna trip were running about $100—which makes Depoe Bay one of the cheapest places on the Northwest coast to fish albacore.

Depoe Bay Sportfishing, P.O. Box 388, Depoe Bay 97341, 765-2222. Operates 3 boats, from 28' to 45' during the spring and summer months.

Dockside Charters, P.O. Box 1308, Depoe Bay 97341, 765-2545. Operates 5 boats from 25' to 45' most of the year.

Tradewinds Charters, P.O. Box 123, Depoe Bay 97341, 765-2345. Operates 12 boats carrying from 6 to 16 passengers. This largest of Depoe Bay offices has been an institution here for well over a half-century.

Deep Sea Troller, P.O. Box 513, Depoe Bay 97341, 765-2248. Operates 2 boats, spring-fall. Office in the Spouting Horn restaurant.

Marinas, Bait And Tackle

Depoe Bay True Value Hardware, P.O. Box 307, 234 Southeast Highway 101, Depoe Bay 97341, 765-2534. Open daily, all year. Good spot for tackle as well as a good selection of bait, including gear for fishing rocky surf.

Imperial Marine, Box 363, Depoe Bay 97341, 765-2535. Open 7 days/week, year-round. Carries bottomfish and salmon tackle.

Port of Depoe Bay, P.O. Box 8, Depoe Bay 97341, 765-2361. Port office open Monday-Friday. Guest moorage along docks, no fuel or engine repair. Bait and tackle available, restrooms. Single-lane asphalt launch ramp at south end of the bay in great condition with tie-up floats, no charge.

Public Campgrounds

Beverly Beach State Park, about 8 miles south, is nearest state camping facilty. 152 tentsites, 127 RV site with hookups, hiker-biker camp area. (Popular and often packed in summer.)

There are also many private RV parks and motels in the area.

For More Information

Depoe Bay Chamber of Commerce, 214 Southeast Highway 101, Depoe Bay 97341, 765-2889.

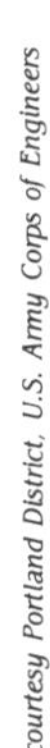

YAQUINA BAY

THIS MAJOR PORT IS WELL KNOWN TO SPORT fishermen for good fishing most of the year, tremendous offshore sport fishing with a fleet to take advantage of it and modern, well-equipped facilities for fishermen and boaters.

With its long jetties and deep channel, Yaquina Bay is home to many charter boats and an impressive commercial fleet. Tourism is a major industry, as well; there are ample motels and lodges, RV parks and full-service marinas (including a major marina-resort complex).

Also located here are the marine research laboratories of both the Oregon State University Marine Science Center and the Oregon Department of Fish and Wildlife. This facility, located on the south side of the bay, just east of the U.S. Highway 101 bridge, welcomes visitors. Charter offices are located along the downtown waterfront, which is in itself an event, crowded as it is with seafood shops, commercial fish docks and processors and small restaurants.

A fine offshore charter fleet, the state's most productive offshore halibut beds and outstanding bottomfishing banks and one of Oregon's most popular jetties for sport fishing all highlight Yaquina Bay's angling opportunities. In season, of course, salmon can be plentiful in the ocean and between the jetties, where small boaters and jetty-hoppers alike try for them. Perch and flounder are taken in the bay and herring are jigged at various times of the year.

Visiting fishermen should have no trouble pursuing their quarry, whatever it may be, here. Charters operate year-round. There is fine access to the south jetty (where a dive/bait and shop offers current jetty fishing information and tackle). Northeast of the U.S. 101 bridge is a public fishing pier. Tidewater marinas offer small boat launching, moorage and some rentals. And a modern, outstanding public port facility in the lower bay provides year-round launching and moorage on a large scale, for pleasure craft of nearly any size.

YAQUINA OFFSHORE: HALIBUT ON GRAVEL BEDS, LUNKER LINGS ON ROCKY REEFS AND COHO ON TOP

Yaquina Bay is blessed with some of the most productive and varied offshore fishing anywhere along the Oregon coast. Newport's charter fleet includes many of the largest and most sophisticated boats and fishes the ocean year-round. In calmer weather it's joined by many private boats which make use of the bay's excellent facilities and take advantage of the usually hospitable deepwater bar crossing.

The most exciting opportunities here are all-day (8-or 12-hour) trips to Stonewall Bank ("The Rockpile") for big lings and yelloweye rockfish and a host of other species or beyond to Heceta Bank for halibut and other large bottomfish.

These are vast, irregular reefs that offer countless acres of prime habitat for bottomfish. They are immediately visible on any nautical chart. Stonewall sits 12 to 16 miles offshore. It's roughly 9 miles long and 3 miles wide. Heceta is about a 28-mile run and is even larger, about 18 by 4 miles.

Although bottomfishing off Yaquina Bay has long been recognized for its excellence, only in the mid1980s did halibut fishing become a specific focus of much offshore activity. At the same time, more and more charters (and well-equipped private boats) were making the run to Heceta Bank—since that's where they found halibut, usually taking limits. In those days, the rules were pretty simple: two halibut per day, any size, all season.

Since then, the International Pacific Halibut Commission has put the clamps on somewhat, imposing quotas that limit season length and—to keep the season open longer—closures on certain days of the week. Also size limits have been imposed, limits which may mean an allowable catch of but a single halibut per day, depending upon sizes. Of course, all these regulations are subject to change year to year; take nothing for granted.

Skippers on halibut sport boats do *not* univerally use Dacron line here. Some do but many use monofilament, such as Burt Waddell at the Tradewinds Fleet. He's used Dacron but has better success with 40-pound monofilament. A large, whole herring is lowered to bottom with as much lead as it takes. Some days that may be but 12 ounces; other days up to 32 or even 40 ounces may be needed. That depends somewhat on depths fished but more on the drift. That's a critical variable, a function of the velocity and direction of both wind current. A really fast drift certainly doesn't make fishing deep water any easier. On the other hand, a calm ocean and light current make getting to bottom easier and faster.

Oregon law allows three hooks. Here, every one of those has brought up a rockfish from the depths of Stonewall Bank—and each a different species (rosethom, yellowtail and yelloweye, left to right).

Known as "longfins" for their unusually long pectoral fin, albacore usually show up off the central Oregon coast. The question every year is how far offshore they arrive.

Above the sinker and herring are tied two shrimp flies—the typical offshore rig. (These inauspicious little attractors take at least as many halibut as the big herring baits.) Some halibut fishermen use spreaders like those favored at Neah Bay, Washington; others do well with big leadhead or pipe jigs.

Halibut fishing usually begins sometime in May. Both May and June are excellent months. July can still be hot, but the catch rate may taper off.

These fish will average 15 to 25 pounds. Smaller fish really deserve to be thrown back, babies that they are, and besides that, they're too small to be legally kept. Of course, larger fish are certain to come over the rails—sometimes much larger. Many fish over 100 pounds are caught and occasionally a barndoor will top 150. The largest of recent years pulled the scale needle to 188 pounds.

Although serious halibut trips head out to Heceta Bank, quite a few flatfish are taken regularly on Stonewall Bank. And while halibut are the primary target on Heceta, all sorts of big bottomfish fill fish boxes over both banks.

Many trophy-size lingcod are taken, fish in the 30s and even 40s. Some of these grab herring or jigs, some shrimp flies. But inevitably, many of the biggest lings can't resist small rockfish—often those just being reeled in which they grab onto, as well as those hooked and lowered specifically as live bait.

Another notable feature of deepwater fishing off Yaquina Bay is how *red* things get. The many, varied and often large rockfish hauled up are, by and large, red in color. The real prizes are the big yelloweye which may exceed 20 pounds. But many other red rockfish species are pulled up, including canaries, vermilions, bocaccio and the little, stunningly-colored gold and scarlet rosethorn.

Surprise catches are rare but big sharks sometimes get into the act during summer. These are most often blue sharks of 5 to 7 feet. More anglers are keeping these to eat. They should, of course, be bled at once and kept cool. Along with unexpected catches are such unexpected sights as whales, porpoises, various sea birds and the very strange ocean sunfish.

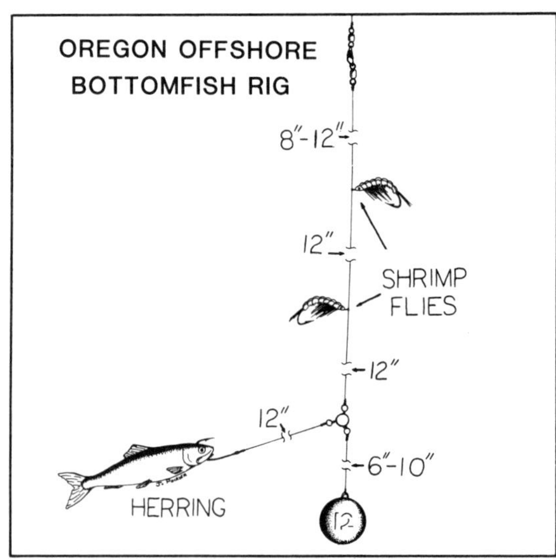

Some charter offices offer all-day "combo trips" which are a great way to fish the ocean off Newport and a great way to bring back both red- and white-meated filets since both salmon and bottomfish are targeted. Sometimes a "combo day" is easy. Coho can be swarming over Stonewall Bank so thickly that limits will be taken early in the morning—all on the shrimp flies of bottomfishermen!

Not all bottomfishing is 15 to 30 miles out, nor need it be a full-day affair. Half-day (5-hour) trips on charters fish a whole host of what are called the "inner reefs," spots on charts that show names such as Johnson and Seal rocks. From these rather well-known landmarks north to Yaquina Head the coastline is loaded with nearshore reefs and pinnacles. Private boaters make considerable use of these nearby reefs. Wise anglers on small boats join charters fishing the inner reefs in using light tackle with 12- to 15-pound line and 1- to 2-ounce leadhead jigs with plastic worms. Heavier tackle is unnecessary and takes a lot of the joy out of fishing.

In fact, in terms of numbers of fish and variety, nearshore reefs compare favorably to those offshore. The big

Eating The Bizarre Ocean Sunfish (Mola-mola)—An Experiment That Failed

One for the frying pan? This ocean sunfish became just that, as the author made a chewy discovery.

Years of fishing around the United States and elsewhere have taught me to question common wisdom about which fish taste good and which are unpalatable. I was therefore skeptical of general assumptions that ocean sunfish couldn't be good to eat when I had the deckhand aboard the *Sea Venture* off Yaquina Bay one fine sunny July afternoon gaff a small (25-pound) ocean sunfish for me.

On calm summer days these odd, truncated fish (which look as though the last half of their bodies had been cut off) can be seen flipping idly at the surface. They may grow quite large and make easy, slow-moving targets. Yet no one I've heard of ever tried taking some home for dinner.

So I elected to do just that. Our first task was to filet the critter which meant cutting through its tougher-than-leather hide and then trying to locate some meat inside.

You are what you eat, the saying goes. The ocean sunfish eats jellyfish. After a great deal of cutting and searching, we ended up with only a little more than a handful of meat (and had somewhat lost our appetite, if not our resolve).

But with high hopes that evening, my buddy and I fried the stuff up over a camp stove at South Beach State Park, along with chunks of lingcod and yelloweye rockfish. With logic that Mr. Spock would have appreciated, we agreed the texture, at once mushy and fibrous, would not prejudice our judgment of the taste. We sampled an initial, small bite. At first, as we chewed (and chewed), I commented, "Well, it's sort of bland, but not really bad," until we were simultaneously overcome by the urge to spit the stuff on the ground.

I can't say I'd die before I'd eat ocean sunfish again. But I would have to be pretty damn close to starvation.

difference has to be the average size of fish caught—they run much smaller from waters close in. On the other hand, besides costing considerably less, the much shorter run can be a blessing if the seas loom large. Understandably, winter trips pretty much stick to inner reef fishing. (But then many of the big female lings from the deeper waters farther out have moved in to lay eggs, anyway.)

Yaquina Bay—Inner Reefs And Stonewall Bank Loran-C Numbers

Inner Reefs, South

12903.4 + 27922.9 (outside, north pinnacle)

DANGEROUS AREAS to be avoided

12906.6 + 27922.7 (north pinnacle—30 feet, breaks in heavy swell), 12913-12914 (Johnson Rock—20 feet in surrounding 80 feet, breaks in moderate swell)

Inner Reefs, North

12839.8 + 27932.5 (Cricket Rock), 12811.3 + 27939.9, 12820.5 + 27938.0, 12836 to 12839 + 27913 to 27917.5 (halibut flats off light house), 12843.8 + 27932.7, 12841.2 + 27935.2

Marguerita Reef

12920.0 + 27920.0, 12917.7 + 27920.2, 12919.6 + 27921.9, 12919.0 + 27921.6, 12921.9 + 27920.1, 12936.9 + 27919.1, 12924.0 + 27919.8, 12935.4 + 27918.4

Way South

12944.0 + 27918.3, 12968.0 + 27912.9, 12968.0 + 27912.9, 12980.7 + 27910.1, 12981.6 + 27910.1, 12948.7 + 27886.9, 12975.0 + 27916.5, 12956.3 + 27884.5, 12935.8 + 27882.6

Rock Pile South, Inside

12935.1 + 27884.5, 12935.2 + 27892.0, 12940.9 + 27890.9, 12950.2 + 27890.8, 12938.0 + 27889.9, 12941.0 + 27888.1, 12939.4 + 27892.6H, 12937.0 + 27888.6H, 12945.2 + 27888.2H, 12934.0 + 27886.0. 12936.0 + 27893.2H

Rock Pile South, Outside (including halibut spots)

12938.7 + 27886.6, 12940.9 + 27886.1, 12940.0 + 27886.8, 12942.0 + 27884.5, 12950.1 + 27887.0H, 12953.0 + 27886.1, 12955.0 + 27885.3, 12958.0 + 27882.0, 12965.2 + 27882.1, 12943.5 + 27885.3

Rock Pile, Center

12920.8 + 27888.8, 12918.9 + 27886.5, 12922.8 + 27886.8, 12917.0 + 27887.3, 12914.8 + 27887.0, 12910.0 + 27891.0H, 12923.0 + 27888.0H, 12925.0 + 27887.4H, 12902.0 + 27892.0H, 12908.0 + 27897897891.0H, 12903.4 + 27893.6H, 12900.2 + 27891.4, 12909.7 + 27889.6H, 12910.7 + 27890.8H

Rock Pile, Far North

12865.0 + 27897.1, 12874.7 + 27895.4, 12876.3 + 27896.7, 12880.0 + 27895.8, 12896.7 + 27893.0H, 12880.4 + 27898.2H

Note: Loran numbers from logbooks of local charter skippers. Anglers are encouraged to explore these areas and discover additional hotspots for their own Loran logbooks. Always avoid returning to fish the same spot over and over; spread out your effort.

YAQUINA BAY / Sport Fish and Seasons

Species	J	F	M	A	M	J	J	A	S	O	N	D
	BEST MONTHS											
Bottomfish (ocean)[1]	fair	fair	fair	best	best	best	best	best	best	best	fair	fair
Salmon (ocean)[2]	poor	poor	poor	poor	fair	best	best	best	fair	poor	poor	poor
Bottomfish (jetty)	fair	fair	best	best	best	best	best	best	best	fair	fair	fair
Salmon (jetty, bay)	poor	poor	poor	poor	poor	fair	best	best	best	fair	poor	poor
Perch (jetty, bay)[3]	poor	poor	poor	best	best	best	best	best	best	fair	poor	poor
Herring (bay)[4]	best	best	best	poor	poor	poor	poor	poor	poor	poor	poor	poor
Albacore (ocean)[5]	poor	poor	poor	poor	poor	poor	fair	fair/best	best/fair	fair	poor	poor

[1]Good year-round, but conditions in winter often preclude fishing.
[2]Check regulations carefully before fishing; seasons vary year to year.
[3]Fish concentrated in lower bay April-May, and up above Coquille Point to Toledo from June on.
[4]Sporadic; concentrations come and go during this period.
[5]Unpredictable fishery; it can be red-hot for weeks or never materialize at all during this period.

LEGEND: best · fair · poor

Even with so much fine bottomfishing off the coast, here, when salmon season begins interest is intense. Coho account for most of the catch, though some good runs of kings do move through periodically. Standard trolling variations used along most of the Oregon coast are popular. Charters often use planers to get herring baits on siderail rods down a bit and use kidney sinkers for rods off the stern. Most salmon trips on charters are 5 or 6 hours in length. Private boaters sometimes return much sooner with limits.

Albacore are not particularly more or less likely to venture into Pacific waters off Yaquina Bay than off other Oregon ports. But they are more likely to be intercepted if they do because the Newport charter fleet is one of the few to offer two-day (33-hour) trips on big, fast ships with two full crews (required by law).

Catches of starry flounder like this were common in the 1970s and flatfish enthusiasts hope coming years will see a resurgence in their numbers.

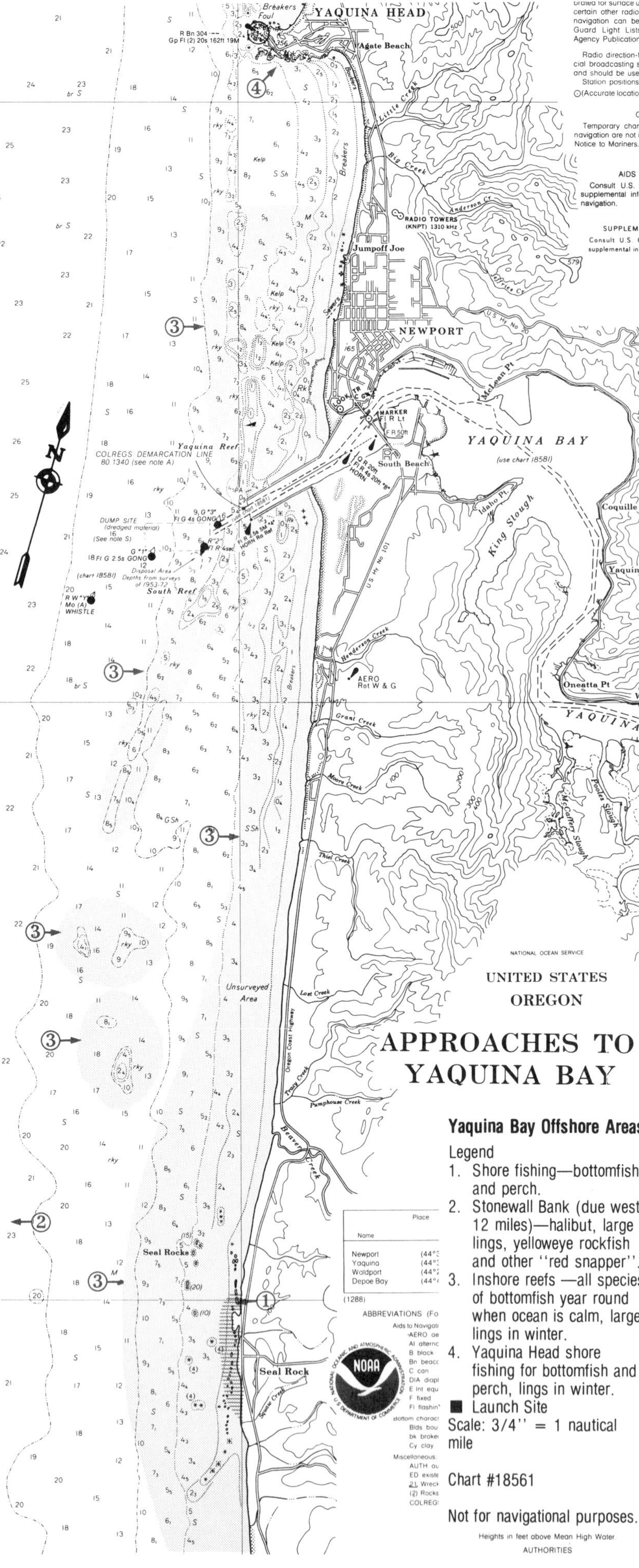

The real advantage of these trips is not so much that they may go much farther out for the albacore but that they are in a better position to be fishing during the critical early morning and late evening periods. That's when albacore feed most heavily and in greatest concentrations; they tend to be more scattered during the day. Typical all-day trips often miss some of the dawn action and are heading in long before twilight.

Presumably, no angler would consider 33 hours at sea unless he or she was unequivocally impervious to motion sickness, especially considering the price tag of these trips, at $250. Not cheap by any means, but if the fish are in, passengers get their money's worth. For example, seven fishermen on what proved to be the last 33-hour trip of the season for the Tradewinds fleet not long ago returned with 96 albacore—which works out to about 14 of the 15- to 35-pound tuna per rod. Clearly, they earned their sore arms.

Even if catches aren't so phenomenal on more conventional all-day (12-hour) albacore trips, they can be very rewarding. It's not unusual for these boats to return with three to six tuna per angler—often well over 100 pounds of superb eating.

Tuna fishing off Yaquina Bay is strictly trolling feathers. Live bait drifting has not become an option here, with a lack of a consistent source of live herring or anchovies. Many skippers use consecutive numbers given to each angler in a random drawing, so as each hookup occurs the next angler in line grabs the rod.

Fishing The South Jetty For Salmon And Bottomfish

The south jetty at Yaquina Bay remains one of the most popular in the state among jetty fishermen. There's easy access over a road extending well out onto the jetty. Most of the year, people fish from the rocks and do well.

Salmon, of course, attract a great deal of interest at any jetty whenever they come within reach. At Yaquina Bay there can be some particularly fine salmon fishing throughout the summer, mostly for those willing to be out fishing by daybreak. As the sun begins to climb, the salmon usually disappear.

This is an inconsistent fishery and varies from week to week and summer to summer. Often catching a salmon means "putting in the time." But there are periods when many fishermen indeed walk away from the rocks carrying big, mirror-bright salmon.

Most of these are taken on bait—anchovies or herring—on a double-hook mooching rig. Some anglers use a sliding float with a bobber stop (similar to that illustrated in the Nestucca River section). Others are successful simply tying up a three-foot mooching leader with a 1- to 3-ounce kidney sinker, baiting up, then casting and retrieving until a salmon picks up the bait.

Metal jigs can certainly be very effective here, though more fishermen use bait. There's little doubt that salmon will take lures cast off the jetty. One year, a surprised young fellow managed to pull in a 24-pound chinook that had taken a small Rapala lure he was casting. Occasionally a salmon is even hooked on a white plastic tail being fished for rockfish.

Salmon move in as early as July. Somewhat later, particularly when clouds of anchovies move in so thick they shade the waters around the jetty dark, more salmon are available around the jetties.

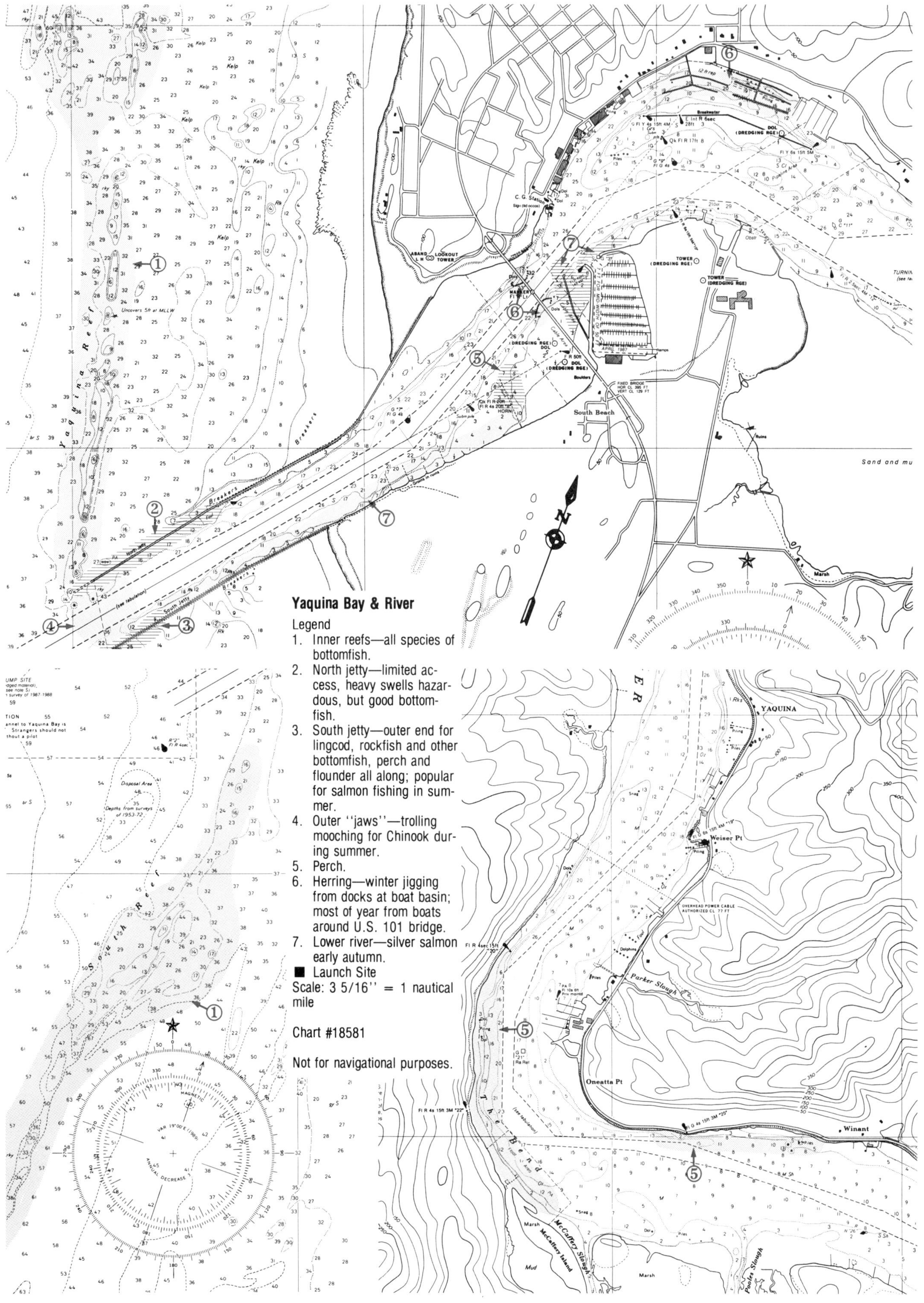

Yaquina Bay & River

Legend

1. Inner reefs—all species of bottomfish.
2. North jetty—limited access, heavy swells hazardous, but good bottomfish.
3. South jetty—outer end for lingcod, rockfish and other bottomfish, perch and flounder all along; popular for salmon fishing in summer.
4. Outer ''jaws''—trolling mooching for Chinook during summer.
5. Perch.
6. Herring—winter jigging from docks at boat basin; most of year from boats around U.S. 101 bridge.
7. Lower river—silver salmon early autumn.

■ Launch Site

Scale: 3 5/16'' = 1 nautical mile

Chart #18581

Not for navigational purposes.

Newport's south jetty offers some of the most consistent and accessible action around.

Yaquina's jetties are among several in the state where black rockfish are a predominant sport species year-round. Perhaps the most popular "sea bass" season is summer, when lanterns dot the rocks as groups of nocturnal fishermen work white plastic worms slowly with little or no weight. Often in midwinter, nice catches of blacks can be taken during cloudy, calm days, when light leadhead jigs are worked slowly well off bottom, over snags. Generally, an incoming tide is favored for these 2- to 3-pound rockfish.

Lingcod are a prize for any jetty fisherman, and Yaquina's jetties have in past years rated among the best for lings. Spring is the prime period, with the fish remaining in the rocky shallows following winter spawning and the males more aggressive than ever, guarding egg masses. Don't expect to see many lings taken from the jetties that rival in size those caught aboard offshore charters. Lings of a few pounds are common and occasionally exceed 15.

The small, pretty relative of the ling, kelp greenlings, are common, taken particularly well on sand shrimp. Many people fish shrimp specifically for perch. Pile, striped and pinkfin (redtail) perch can be taken most of the year, though winter may be slow. Spring and summer are best times, though the action can vary considerably from one week to the next. Whenever you try for perch, make sure the tide is slack or flooding.

There is a limited interest, it seems, in surfcasting from sandy beaches in the area. Some fishermen catch perch in the sandy surf along South Beach State Park. The many rocky headlands along the central coast can be productive throughout the year, when the surf is reasonably calm. Two prominent possibilities are Seal Rock, about 7 miles south of the bay, or Yaquina Head, some 5 miles north.

Starry flounder were once taken in generous numbers from the jetties during spring and summer, occasionally running as large as 5 pounds. The 1980s saw the same nosedive in flounder populations as elsewhere along the Oregon coast. However, there seems to be some reason for hope that they may be on the upswing again, since increasing numbers are being picked up here and in Alsea Bay by perch fishermen.

Calm Seas + Common Sense = Safe Jetty Fishing

Caution is advisable anytime you're planning to fish the jetties, but particularly during the winter. Even when breezes are light, you may arrive at the Yaquina south jetty to find a surprisingly heavy groundswell. Such groundswells can be quite dangerous. In fact, every year along the Oregon coast people are swept into the ocean from jetties because they are careless and stand too near the water's reach, especially with a heavy, unpredictable surf pounding the rocks. Even when seas are moderate, a sudden towering "sleeper" wave can crash over the jetty.

There's no substitute for using your head, but at the other end of things, there's also much to be said for footwear. A good pair of boots will not only keep your feet dry but can provide a skid-resistant surface.

Inside The Bay—Salmon, Perch, Herring

Although the focus of much attention at Newport is offshore fishing, successfully trolling for salmon here does not require a long run in a large boat. Many good chinook and coho have been taken from little cartoppers working the jaws in good weather.

Jerry Butler, Marine Sportfish Studies Project Leader at the Department of Fish and Wildlife's marine research facilities at Newport, recalls how worthwhile he's found trolling between the jetties.

"I remember one calm summer day when two friends and I picked up five chinook, trolling right around the bar. They weighed out at 28 pounds each, like peas in a pod. We see people catching salmon off the jetties in June and July, as well as the more popular months of August and September, and suspect there are salmon feeding in the jaws all summer. Yet most guys go screaming right by them, heading 'way offshore to look for silvers."

Butler also points out that those fishing inside the bar here for salmon have the option to do some drift-mooching with herring, a productive method that some find less monotonous than trolling. (For details on this method, see the chapter on "Fishing Northwest Salt Waters.")

Toward late summer, salmon can be picked up throughout the lower bay. (And of course before or during early September, salmon fishing is likely to be closed outside the jetties.)

Fine perch fishing is available here April through September. Redtail action, which peaks in May, is often very fast but not nearly so frenetic a spring phenomenon as one sees in a number of other Oregon bays. Pile and striped perch are equally common here and occasionally whites, silvers and walleyes are taken.

During April and May, the best perch fishing usually occurs from the jetties up to the Coquille Point area. In June, the perch are working their way well up into the upper bay, into the Toledo area. For the duration of the summer there can be good perch fishing at intervals throughout the entire bay.

Although they're not as commonly taken in Yaquina Bay as in several other Oregon bays, sturgeon do make these waters their home and good fish are taken at times.

Flounder fishing in Yaquina Bay was once outstanding. As elsewhere along the Oregon coast, however, that fishery went into a tailspin during the 1980s. Some blame that on surging seal populations, but the reasons are probably more complex. But biologist Jerry Butler has observed more flounder in bay catches, albeit incidentally, particularly in Yaquina Bay. If populations regain their former strength, look for good fishing for small boat and bank fishermen at Idaho Point, around Coquille Point and around the gas tank (the Northwest Natural Gas storage facility north of Idaho Point). There is, by the way, a fishing pier at the gas tank with wheelchair access. In past years, February and March were peak times for flounder (which provided welcome sport with most other fisheries at a lull).

Ultralight tackle and a 1/2-ounce bucktail or plastic-tailed jig can produce a nice stringer of small black rockfish from the jetties. (Photo by Terry Rudnick)

Flounder offered an interesting sport that only a few took advantage of: shallow-water flycasting. If numbers of flounder increase again, trying easing a small skiff into areas like Sally's Slough during a low incoming tide and casting any sort of small red streamer weighted with a bit of lead wire ahead of it, working it back across the bottom in 2 or 3 feet of water as the tide floods the slough. An alternate choice would be crappie jigs with ultralight gear.

Another winter fishery enjoyed by small boaters and nonboaters alike in Yaquina Bay is herring jigging. These fish are sporadically available from about midJanuary through March, as schools move in to spawn and leave, to be followed by another group. If you hit it right, you'll luck into huge concentrations of these baitfish. Unlike flounder, the fishing for herring has remained strong with some record years in the 1980s.

Even when they're in the bay, herring schools may be thick in one area and absent everywhere else. At times people will be hauling them in one after the other from boat basin docks or along the south bay docks. The herring sometimes concentrate in the small boat channel, out of reach of those without a boat. At such times, anyone with a depth sounder is way ahead in finding schools that often hover in middepths or near the bottom.

By May the herring, now running smaller, are often schooled around the massive concrete supports under the Highway 101 bridge. Small boats are usually working these schools, stopping en route out the bay to jig some fresh bait.

Once located, the herring are not hard to entice. Most anglers favor commercial herring jigging rigs, strings of four or more shiny gold or silver hooks with a bit of yarn or bright plastic on the shank.

Small Boat Safety—Crossing The Bar

Deep and well-protected by long jetties, the Yaquina Bay bar is one of the state's more crossable. The main channel follows the centerline between the jaws, and the Coast Guard advises that route—*not* hugging the jetties on either side. (They put it this way: "Boaters should remain in the channel entering and leaving the river so if their engines should fail, they will have time to anchor before the current or wind sweeps them onto the rocks.")

Stay well clear of the ends of both jetties, remaining in the main channel when inside of buoy no. 3, at the south end of Yaquina Reef. Do not head south until coming to the lighted bell buoy no. 1. And any turn to the north should be made well beyond buoy no. 3, to avoid Yaquina Reef. This shallow rocky area runs north starting at the end of the north jetty and should be avoided. Even in a light sea, a large swell can cause a tremendous breaker on this reef without warning.

Those who fish in the vicinity of the productive Johnson Rock should also be careful. The reef rises to about 20 feet at low water from 80 feet or so around it. On a heavy swell day, the waves will break on this rock and have dumped boats more than once.

Observe the rough bar advisory sign, posted on shore at the west end of the Coast Guard pier.

U.S. Coast Guard Station—Yaquina Bay
Bar/weather conditions, recording....... 265-5511
Information, station phone............. 265-5381

Facilities

All phone numbers listed are within the 503 area code unless otherwise listed.

Charters

Rates are fairly uniform around the bay and, typical of the Oregon coast, are a function of time. Most trips vary from 5 hours for salmon or nearshore bottomfish (about $45 at press time) to 7 or 8 hours for more distant bottomfishing or combination trips (about $80) to 12 hours for halibut trips ($100). For about the same or a little more, you can book a tuna trip if the albcore show within range. Just about all offices have boats operating year-round, with fine bottomfishing just a short run out of the jetties when winter weather permits.

Blue Pacific Charters, 839 Southwest Bay Boulevard, Newport 97365, 265-3028. 42' charter will carry up to 17 anglers (usually fewer and only 10 or 11 on deepwater trips), says skipper Lee Estabrook.

Fish-on Deep Sea Charters, P.O. Box 159, Newport 97365, 265-8607. 50' can carry up to 20 anglers. Fishes salmon and halibut. Skipper Scott Martin has been running charters out of Newport for many years and helped pioneer the Heceta Bank offshore halibut fishery.

Newport Sportfishing, at the Embarcadero, 1000 Southeast Bay Boulevard, Newport 97365, 265-7558. Operates 8 charters in the 40' to 50' range which carry up to 10 or 12 anglers. The office also sells tackle.

Newport Tradewinds, 653 Southwest Bay Boulevard, Newport 97365, 265-2101. 9 charters, 6 to 30 passengers, year-round for all offshore gamefish species. No one has more experience or knowledge of these offshore waters than owner/skipper Burt Waddell.

Sea Gull Charters, 343 Southwest Bay Boulevard, Newport 97365, 265-7441. Operates March 1-October 1 for all species with 6 charters from 30' to 50'.

South Beach Charters, P.O. Box 1446 (at South Beach Marina docks), Newport 97365, 867-7200, 4 charters, 36' to 50'.

Marinas

Embarcadero Resort Hotel Marina, 1000 Southeast Bay Boulevard, Newport 97365 (just east of downtown harbor), 265-8521 or toll-free nationwide 800-547-4779. Year-round, 7 days/week. 230 slips but limited guest moorage. Gas and diesel, fair bait and tackle selection. Closest launch ramp is at South Beach. Rents 14-foot fiberglass boats with 7 1/2 outboards. Beyond its marina facilities, the Embarcadero is a very elegant, first-rate resort facility with condo units, indoor pool and sauna, recreation center, restaurant/lounge and more.

Anglers clean catch at docks; Highway 101 bridge in background.

Newport Marina at South Beach, 600 Southeast Bay Boulevard, Newport 97365, 867-3321. Open daily, all year. A huge, fairly new marina complex just south of the Highway 101 bridge, with over 600 slips, 150 for guest moorage. Gas and diesel, lots of bait and tackle, groceries, restrooms, showers, laundromat, public fishing pier, charters. Recently resurfaced 4-lane launch ramp with floats, outstanding facility, with nearly unlimited parking and fish-cleaning stations. Also a sling launch. 60 RV spaces with hookups.

Other launch sites include **Idaho Point Marina**, 1 mile east of Highway 101, a private concrete ramp with a charge for launching; and **River Bend Moorage**, 5 miles east of downtown on Bay Road, a hoist.

Bait And Tackle

Bittler Brothers Sport Center, 355 Southwest Coast Highway, Newport 97365, 265-7197. Open 7 days/week. Excellent tackle selection.

Harry's Bait and Tackle, 404 Southwest Bay Boulevard, Newport 97365, 265-2407. Open 7 days/week, year-round. Small shop on downtown waterfront is loaded to the, gills with all sorts of tackle.

Lou's Tackle, 1229 North Coast Highway, Newport 97365, 265-5546. Open 7 days/week except closed Sundays December-February. Carries gear for virtually every sort of saltwater fishing. Repairs rods and reels. Free maps, tide books and information.

Newport Watersports, P.O. Box 1676, Newport 97365 (at the foot of the south jetty on South Jetty Road), 867-3742. Open daily, year-round. Carries some general salmon gear and lots of tackle for fishing jetties.

Randy's Bait and Tackle, 921 Southwest Coast Highway, Newport 97365, 265-7189. Open 7 days/week. Began operation in 1990, carries a fair supply of saltwater gear, as well as flyfishing equipment, and baits including live sand shrimp. Rents and repairs rods and reels.

South Beach Marina Grocery, at South Beach Marina, Newport 97365, 867-7404. Open every day, all year. A big selection of saltwater tackle and bait.

Public Campgrounds

Beverly Beach State Park, about 7 miles north on Highway 101. 152 tentsites, 127 RV site with hookups, hiker-biker camp area. Popular and often packed in summer with long lines waiting to register. A and C sections seem the nicest.

South Beach State Park, 2 miles south on Highway 101. 254 sites with electrical hookups and hiker-biker camp. Right on beach, flat and open, popular.

For More Information

There are a number of private RV parks and over 30 resorts and motels in and around Newport. For information on these as well as plush condominiums, bed-and-breakfasts and vacation house rentals:

Greater Newport Chamber of Commerce, 555 Southwest Coast Highway, Newport 97365, 256-8801 or toll-free nationwide 800-262-7844.

Oregon Coast Association, P.O. Box 670, 245 Olalla Lake Road, Newport 97365, 336-5107 or toll-free nationwide 800-982-6278.

courtesy Portland District U.S. Army Corps of Engineers

Siuslaw River

THE LARGEST "BLUEBACK" (SEA-RUN CUTthroat) fishery in the world is the way Department of Fish and Wildlife biologists characterize the Siuslaw. Too short and narrow to justify the label of "bay," the lower river here has many attributes that help explain its popularity with fishermen and vacationers. The fishing is good not only for "bluebacks," but for salmon summer and fall, sturgeon in late winter, pinkfin (redtail) surfperch in the spring, and shad in June. With a reasonably passable bar, ocean salmon fishermen work the ocean.

The bar here changed for the better in the 1980s with extensions of both north and south jetty. That moved the outer bar entrance in 19 or 20 fathoms of water and helps keep sand from filling in the channel so quickly as often occurred in the past. Not only was access improved for boaters, but jetty fishing has been better than ever.

The Siuslaw is one of the two major rivers (the Umpqua, at Winchester Bay, is the other) in the Oregon Dunes National Recreation Area, a coastal strip of fascinating sand formations and a series of large, fertile lakes that provide some of western Oregon's best fishing for largemouth bass, yellow perch and trout.

With so many outdoor recreation opportunities to attract visitors to the area, there are a number of motels and campgrounds in and around Florence. There are also several marinas along the lower river, where you can find moorage and launch facilities and at least one outlet for rental skiffs. Although there are no offshore charters here at press time, some guides work the lower river.

Blueback Capital Of The World?

If that title were to somehow be awarded, the strongest contender would probably be the lower Siuslaw. "I don't know of anyplace else in Oregon or Washington with so many people fishing for bluebacks," asserts Jerry MacLeod, district fishery biologist for the Department of Fish and Wildlife who has spent many years at the Siuslaw.

If you intend to sample what may indeed be some of the Northwest's best tidewater sea-run cutthroat trout fishing, August and often September are good months to be here. But the action often picks up as early as midJuly.

Shore fishing is limited; most trout are taken from small boats. Trollers account for greatest success, particularly those who go slow and stay close to shore. Most experts say the slower the troll the better, and they rely on unweighted Doc Sheltons or Ford Fenders with nightcrawlers behind an 18-inch leader. Work in along the log booms and brush.

An alternative method, of course, is flyfishing in the upper reaches of tidewater in September. Again, while drifting, cast streamers in toward the brush along the shoreline. Ultralight spin fishermen do well tossing small spinners or wobblers in along the shoreline.

A Limited Offshore And A Major River Fishery For Coho And Chinook

In recent years, Siuslaw anglers have taken both coho and chinook in fair numbers. Through the late 1960s, the coho catch here was relatively enormous. Those runs have declined but healthy numbers continue to return.

Hoping to restore these runs to the levels the Siuslaw is capable of supporting, in the early 1980s, the Department of Fish and Wildlife released millions of coho presmolts each year. Those are fish that have been at the hatchery for three months before release. They had hoped these would return without adversely competing with wild populations. Unfortunately, subsequent studies showed that the hatchery fish actually threatened to replace the wild fish. The best hope now seems to lie in a program to develop a native broodstock that will be reared by volunteers in the hatchboxes and net pens as part of the STEP (Salmon, Trout Enhancement Program).

The ocean fishery for salmon is good throughout the summer, depending upon legal seasons. Many start trolling just outside the river mouth. Coho dominate the offshore catch most of the time.

Trolling is fairly universal in the ocean with pretty much the same methods employed elsewhere along the Oregon coast, using weights, diving planes or downriggers to pull herring, anchovies, plastic squid or flies. Some trollers use a flasher ahead of bait or lure.

Bottomfishing is not a major activity offshore, with the ocean floor (like the land) here largely flat and sandy.

Neptune Beach State Park is one of many good coastal spots in the area where rocky headlands are accessible. The author found good fishing from the rocks only a few minutes' hike from the highway.

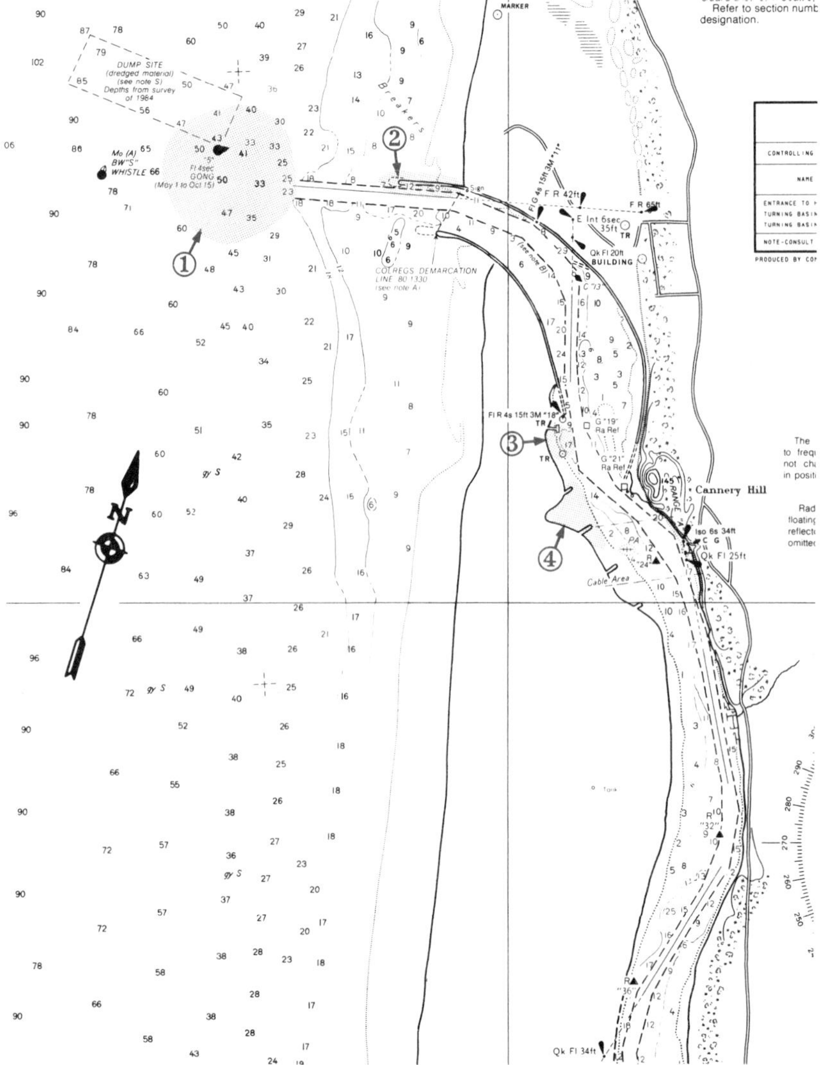

Lower Siuslaw River

Legend
1. Starry flounder.
2. Redtail perch from north jetty.
3. Fishing pier.
4. Good digging for sand shrimp on flats at low tide.
5. Redtail perch.
■ Launch Site

Scale: 1 15/16'' = 1 nautical mile

Chart #18583

Not for navigational purposes.

Note: Jetties are scheduled to undergo extension in 1984 which would lengthen them from the depiction on this chart by another 2,000 to 2,500 feet.

Although some mature salmon wander into the lower bay during the summer, jacks of a few pounds are more usual, typically mixed in with bluebacks. Tidewater action for bigger prizes really begins in September, when anglers battle coho to 15 pounds or so and chinook commonly 20 to 30 pounds and occasionally as large as 60. The salmon fishing in the lower river should remain good through October and into November, with rainfall and runoff the main determinants of salmon movements.

In the lower river, many fishermen troll herring or anchovies but large spinners are also popular. Farther upriver spinners such as a Blue Fox gain in popularity.

More salmon and lots of steelhead are taken father up still, above tidewater, mostly by anglers backtrolling Hot Shots and the like.

Pinkfins By The Pailful

It is not unusual for bays that provide good blueback-ing to also be a source of fast fishing for pinkfish (redtail) surfperch—and the lower Siuslaw is no exception. In May, when the pinkfins move into the lower river, there are likely to be two or three weeks of tremendous perch fishing, though the exact timing and extent of these spring ''runs'' vary from year to year. The 2- and sometimes 3-pound perch re usually concentrated from the boat basin up to the mouth of the Siuslaw's north fork (about a 1/2-mile stretch). Folks anchor here and fish sand shrimp during an incoming tide. When the perch are really feeding heavily, tiny lures may produce well, especially on ultralight tackle.

The jetties here must be rated among the best in the state for pinkfin fishing. That starts early in the spring and extends on and off into November when storms generally beset the coast. Some anglers gather mussels for bait from the rocks at low tide while many bring along sand shrimp. (Sand shrimp, by the way, can be dug at low tide in great numbers from the mud flats just above the south jetty.)

Starry flounder are caught occasionally along with perch, but this another Oregon estuary where locals talk of flounder fishing ''the way it used to be.''

Marine Panfish From Rocky Headlands And Jetties

Good as perch fishing from the jetties may be, black rockfish, cabezon, lingcod and greenling are also taken in considerable numbers. The fishery for such rock-loving species improved after the jetties were extended in the 1980s and has become quite popular. Also popular but with the option of having more area to yourself is fishing the surf from rocky headlands.

At Heceta Head, about 8 miles north of the bay and just north of Sea Lion Caves, are a series of rocky, mussel-covered outcroppings. These are popular with rock-scrambling surf fishermen after greenling, cabezon and perch. For perch, in particular, try fishing on fingers of rock that extend out into surrounding sandy pockets.

Successful anglers simply gather mussels and kelp worms from the rocks late in the ebb tide, then fish them rigged above a weight—which may be a sparkplug since losing a pile of lead sinkers can get expensive. Best fishing is during the last hour of the ebb tide and the first hour of the flood.

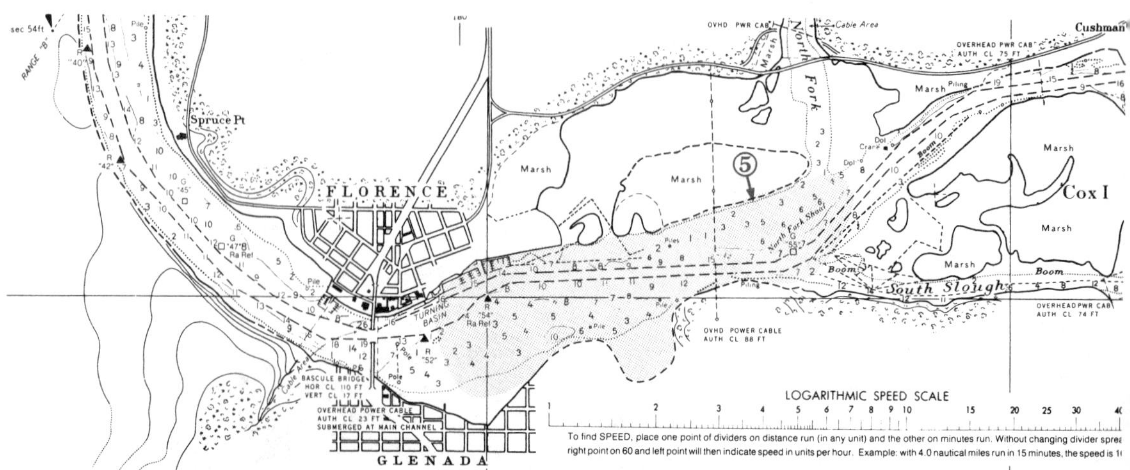

Just north of Heceta Head there are other good rocky areas, though shore access may be limited. I've enjoyed fast fishing for small pinkfin and silver perch from the rocks right in front of the parking area at Neptune State Park.

Just north of this is the town of Yachats (pronounced "Ya-hots"), noted for its annual May-July surf smelt runs. Some outstanding smelt netting is enjoyed here (check locally for details). And though not many netters try the surf around the Siuslaw, some have reported good success around local beaches.

Stripers In The Siuslaw?

Anyone who plans a trip to the lower Siuslaw to fish for stripers will almost surely go away disappointed. Most locals would probably insist there are not stripers in the Siuslaw. Yet there have been—and probably still are—striped bass in this river.

"In fact, we know there are stripers in the river," says biologist Jerry MacLeod. Nor are these necessarily lost, little "school" fish, he adds. "We weighed one in 1981 that we found floating dead in the river. It was 55 pounds." Commercial shad netters have occasionally caught them in their nets.

Tackle shop owner Warner Pinkney agrees, recalling a couple years when there were in fact striped bass runs in the Siuslaw and when they were caught by anglers. But that hasn't happened since the 1970s.

All this is not to suggest that one gather up his striped bass gear and head for the Siuslaw. But all this might be worth remembering just in case something too big to stop should happen to spool you in the lower Siuslaw.

The Siuslaw's "Other" Fisheries—Sturgeon And Shad

The Siuslaw is yet another lower river where people really began to catch on to catching sturgeon only recently. "They've been here in the river all along," says Warner Pinkney, Siuslaw River fishing expert and longtime owner of The Sportsman in Florence. "But people just recently began fishing them," with 1989 the first year sturgeon fishing really captured the attention of many.

These are almost all the desirable white sturgeon and plenty of big ones are caught, with many over the legal 6-foot maximum taken and released. The fishery begins in February and pretty well fades in May. But within that period, they are caught throughout the day; time or tide seems to make little difference.

Most of the river from the Highway 101 bridge up to the "Dairy Hole" above Cushman is fished by anglers in anchored boats. (This could be a fine shore fishery, but there is little access.) Shrimp are probably the most popular bait with smelt particularly hot when it is fresh and the smelt are moving up coastal streams. Fresh herring is also used.

Shad fishing is not something for which this river is traditionally known, yet there are shad here and—according to the Department of Fish and Wildlife—plenty of them. And increasing numbers of anglers are taking advantage of shad here, according to Pinkney. Shad of 2 to 3 pounds are most abundant from midMay through June when they'll hit shad darts during the day. This fishery begins at the head of tidewater and continues up as far as Brickerville. It is pursued from shore as well as from small boats and when the fish are in offers all-day fishing. Catching 10, 20 or more of the silver jumpers is quite possible; many sportfishermen catch and release.

LOWER SIUSLAW RIVER / Sport Fish and Seasons

BEST MONTHS

Species	J	F	M	A	M	J	J	A	S	O	N	D
Ocean salmon[1]	poor	poor	poor	poor	fair	best	best	best	fair	poor	poor	poor
Tidewater salmon[2]	poor	poor	poor	poor	poor	poor	poor/fair	best	best	best	poor	poor
Sea-run cutthroat	poor	poor	poor	poor	poor	poor	poor	best	best	poor	poor	poor
Pinkfin perch[3]	poor	poor	fair	best	best	best	fair	fair	fair	fair	fair	poor
Shad	poor	poor	poor	poor	poor/best	best	poor	poor	poor	poor	poor	poor
Rocky surf bottomfish[4]	fair	best	best	best	best	best	best	best	best	best	best/fair	fair
Surf smelt[5]	poor	poor	poor	poor/fair	best	best	fair/poor	poor	poor	poor	poor	poor
Steelhead[6]	best	best	fair	poor	poor	poor	poor	poor	poor	poor	poor	best
Sturgeon	poor	fair/best	best	best/fair	fair	poor	poor	poor	poor	poor	poor	poor

[1]Check regulations carefully before fishing; seasons vary from year to year.
[2]August fish tend to be small jacks; mature fish show up in September.
[3]Large concentrations available in lower river in May; mostly jetty fishing otherwise.
[4]February – May best from jetties.
[5]Netted at the Yachats River mouth.
[6]Taken mostly above tidewater.

LEGEND: best fair poor

Shad have long been an underutilized species in the Siuslaw though most years there are plenty of them in the lower river in late spring.

Small Boat Safety—Crossing The Bar

Jetty extensions completed in the mid1980s make the bar entrance considerably more crossable than it used to be. But that doesn't mean it's easy.

The channel itself is unusually narrow where it continues out beyond the jetties. This tends to make it impassable for small boats, particularly at ebb tide on even a moderate swell. It's essential to keep that in mind if you head offshore, since obviously you also have a substantial interest in getting back in.

The river channel lies along the northern half of the river entrance (that is, along and near the northern jetty). Water depth ranges from 6 to 20 feet. When crossing the entrance, boaters should stay near the south jetty. Ranges will mark the "preferred depth channel" but, depending upon conditions, these do *not* necessarily mark the best route to follow. That takes experience, skill and good eyes.

Avoid the outer end of the south jetty—at times (west/southwest swells) waves may break all the way out past the whistle buoy. Avoid, also, the outer end of the north jetty.

The rough bar advisory sign is located on the Coast Guard tower, facing 150 degrees (true).

Siuslaw Coast Guard Station

Bar/weather conditions (recording). 997-8303
Station phone (general info.) . . 997-2486 or 997-3631

FACILITIES

All phone numbers listed are within the 503 area code unless otherwise noted.

No charters are listed since at press time none were operating. There has been a charter or two running out of Florence over the years, but few seem to last too long at it in part because this is not one of the coast's most reliable bars. Still, there are likely to be more charters setting up shop here in the future; check with local sources listed below for information if interested.

Also, two inland guides do fish the river, though generally well above tidewater. Both run very reputable, well-established guide services: **Don Hill Whitewater Guide Service** in Springfield, 747-7430 and **Ray Baker's Whitewater Guide Service** in Eugene, 343-7514.

MARINAS

Bay Bridge Marina, 1150 Bay Street, Florence 97439 (just below Port of Siuslaw Marina), 997-2406. 90 moorage slips available; longer boats need reservations midJune through midAugust. Open all year, 7 days/week. No fuel, engine repair, bait and tackle or boat rentals. Nearest boat launch 1/2 mile upriver.

Coast Marina and RV Park, 07790 Highway 126, Florence 97439 (about 6 miles east of Florence), 997-3031. Limited guest moorage, at press time no fuel available. Some bait (no tackle) available. Sling launch for use of guests only. 45 RV spaces, about 10 available for overnight/guest use.

Cushman Store, 06750 Highway 126, Florence 97439 (3 miles east of Florence), 997-2169. Open every day, all year. 300 feet of dock space with moorage available on both sides (expansion to second dock planned at press time), space usually—but not always—available without reservations. Gas, engine repair and lots of bait and tackle for tidewater/offshore fishing. New concrete launch ramp good on all tides, modest fee. Rents 14-foot skiffs with or without power at reasonable rate. 10 RV spaces with full hookups, showers, laundromat. The Cushman store has been here since 1889.

Port of Siuslaw Marina, P.O. Box 1220, 1499 Bay Street, Florence 97439, 997-3426. Port office open Monday-Friday; RV park open 7 days/week in season. 170 total moorage slips but no more than 10 available for transient moorage. Gas and diesel. Free public launch ramp operated by port about 2 blocks east, 2 lanes, concrete with float, good at most tides. Some bait and tackle available at Pacific Seafoods at ramp. Showers, restrooms. 80-space RV park, reservations recommended May-October.

Siuslaw Marina at Cushman, 06516 Highway 126, Florence 97439 (just above the north fork), 997-3254. About 800 feet of moorage space, pretty full July-October but usually some space is available. Engine repair, lots of commercial and recreational gear packed into small store. Showers, restrooms. Paved, wide single-lane launch ramp with float at a minimal charge and lift for boats to 60 tons. Rents 14-foot aluminum skiffs with power at reasonable cost. Also RV park with 36 hook-up spaces. Marina in business since about 1940.

Siuslaw Pacific Marina and Store, 3231 Rhodendron, Florence 97439 (about 2 miles northwest of Highway 101), 997-2356. Limited guest moorage—may be tied up with commercial traffic at this commercial receiving station. Sells tackle and lots of fresh baits. 2 launch ramps, 1 paved, the other gravel for a modest charge. RV spaces planned at press time.

BAIT AND TACKLE

The Sportsman, 249 North Coast Highway, Florence 97439, 997-3336. Open 7 days/week, year-round, the area's only large outdoor store. An extensive selection of tackle for all kinds of fishing and lots of information.

The **Coast-to-Coast** hardware store also stocks quite a bit of tackle.

PUBLIC CAMPGROUNDS

Jessie M. Honeyman State Park, 3 miles south of Florence on Highway 101. 240 tentsites, 66 RV sites with full hookups, 75 with electrical, hiker-biker camp area. Store, restaurant and 500-foot-high sand dunes.

FOR MORE INFORMATION

Florence Area Chamber of Commerce, P.O. Box 26000, 270 Highway 101, Florence 97439, 997-3128.

courtesy Portland District, U.S. Army Corps of Engineers

Lower Umpqua River & Winchester Bay

Considering the variety and quality of its sport fisheries, the long, winding, lower Umpqua River and Winchester Bay at its mouth can justifiably be described as one of the premier sportfishing areas along the Northwest coast.

Facilities for recreational fishermen here are well developed, with a large charter fleet poised to intercept ocean salmon; guides for anadromous species such as striped bass, sturgeon and salmon; and motels, campgrounds and RV parks in and around Reedsport and Winchester Bay. Those who trailer boats will find moorage and several good launch facilities. Nonboaters can catch perch from the jetties and from several spots along the shore in the Gardiner-Reedsport area.

If there is any estuary in the Northwest that demands a wide selection of tackle, the Umpqua qualifies. There is fine fishing here for many species of game fish, from smelt and herring up to 8-10 inches to white sturgeon which may be well over 10 feet long.

Those who trailer seaworthy boats would have the best shot at the most species, especially during midsummer when good fishing can be found offshore, nearshore, in the bay and above tidewater.

Umpqua Stripers—Tough, Tricky And Troubled

The history of striped bass in the Umpqua River has been uneven and often controversial. They apparently found the estuary on their own, migrating up from California long ago, and liked what they found.

Of course, not everyone liked them, thanks to their propensity to eat not only (mostly) shiner perch, sculpins and herring or smelt but also small salmon.

But these intelligent and rugged game fish quickly attracted an enthusiastic following and remain one of the lower Umpqua's premier game fish. Their populations have frequently faded and occasionally flourished over the years and are likely to continue to do so. Recently they have been averaging 6 to 12 pounds, with a fair number of 20-pounders available and a few in the 30- to 40-pound range taken. Although a 51-pounder was caught near Scottsburg in 1990, there are far fewer stripers over 50 pounds than were caught in the 1960s and '70s.

Catching striped bass is possible only if you're fishing where the fish are. And that is determined by water conditions and food availability on a seasonal schedule. Beginning in the spring, through the summer and much of the fall, stripers are in the lower river. They are there because decreased rainfall and more saline conditions permit an influx of small marine forage fish to move into the river—fish such as shiner perch, sculpins and herring. Stripers are likely to be found anywhere in tidewater, up to a mile or so above the Highway 101 bridge in both the Umpqua and Smith.

Then, as fall rains flush the lower river with fresh water, many of these small marine fish leave and so do the stripers. They tend to move farther upriver from late fall into spring, feeding in upper tidewater and above, in fresh waters. Stripers can be pretty well counted on to hold upriver from January into April, feeding largely on squawfish, suckers and redside shiners. But during the early spring outmigration of wild and (particularly) hatchery salmon smolts, yes, stripers are generally waiting to intercept them at the head of tidewater.

Of course such seasonal movements are highly variable and unpredictable since they are based on weather and water conditions which in themselves vary, year to year.

Stripers feed day and night, at times in water that is shallow as well as in deep holes. They can be taken where the river is muddy or in clear shallows. And they will eat just about anything that moves. Such diverse habits account for the many different approaches anglers take in trying to outsmart them. The majority of anglers plunk bait or troll lures, but some plugcasters and flycasters do very well.

Live bait is nearly always a top bet for stripers, particularly in the lower river. That live bait can be nearly any small fish; what is most available for anglers is often what is available for stripers in the river, as well. Herring can be jigged or purchased live in Winchester Bay. Small sculpins ("bullheads") and shiner perch ("pogies") are usually easily caught on tiny baited hooks or jigs.

Anglers drift or troll these baits, using a sliding sinker rig (as illustrated in the Coos Bay section). Try around Buoy 25, in the main channel as it curves around the Big Bend, or above the U.S. Highway 101 bridge. At other times, especially early in the morning, anglers will "flyline" herring in these areas, drifting the bait with no weight, often near shore.

Shore fishermen do well in many areas, among them Otter and Hudson sloughs in the lower Smith. In the Umpqua, try the shore south of the railroad trestles below Gardiner.

Bait is effectively fished at night, with fresh often as productive as live bait. Boats anchor, cast and wait, patiently *and quietly*. Bangs on a boat's deck will send wary stripers packing. They are very spooky, cautious predators. Nonboaters can also fish bait at night from spots such as the Smith River Road bridge.

Trolling has always been one of the most popular methods for catching stripers in the lower Umpqua and, particularly, the lower Smith. Two widely used lures are large Rebels and black Jig-a-Do eels. Trollers fish during the day and often after dark. A shallow running plug is effective, trolled at a medium speed with quite a bit of line out.

Plugcasters favor the Big Bend area and the lower Smith, spring-fall and both rivers at the top of tidewater in

cooler weather. Rebels and Rapalas are traditionally the most popular lures. Some experts stick with broken-back (jointed) models. Bucktail jigs can be very effective as well.

Plugcasters take fish from shore where they can gain access, but a small boat can offer a real advantage. Some of the best plugcasting is at night. Locate the stripers by trolling but *only with an electric motor,* not a gas outboard which will spook these bass in a hurry—especially in the narrower, quieter upriver areas. Then, once fish are located, drift and cast very quietly.

Flycasters also do well for striped bass at times, tossing large streamers.

Early on calm summer mornings, stripers can be found in the small channels that snake through the expansive stretch of flats south of the Big Bend. I've fished there at such times with river guide Denny Hannah who'd work his river sled far up into these channels when the tide was ebbing off the flats and the fish would be increasingly concentrated in the channels. Then it was a matter of waiting and watching. Sight-casting is the most exciting way to fish any species.

Generally when feeding here the stripers will be visible in water shallow enough to show their wake or even expose their dorsal fins. By maintaining a quiet, low profile it is possible to cast a live herring in their path. The result is usually an immediate strike and a sizzling run across the flats that is reminiscent of a hooked bonefish or permit in the Caribbean.

In general, striper anglers use medium gear with 10- to 20-pound line, either plugcasting (levelwind) or spinning tackle.

The lower Umpqua and Smith rivers offer the only large, moderately succssful self-sustaining population of striped bass north of the San Francisco Bay area. This angler trailered his boat from Seattle to catch this pair of "schoolies."

Stripers In The Umpqua—A Troubled History

Striped bass are widely prized as one of the greatest game fish of the East Coast, a very catchable, often large fish of inshore waters and surf that embodies many qualities anglers like. Stripers are smart, tough, opportunistic and delicious eating.

Unfortunately, they take advantage of whatever food source is available. That means in the spring, a major food source is smolts—small downstream migrant chinook. That characteristic has made the striped bass an unwanted, uninvited marauder for a great many local fishermen. This is, after all, Salmon Country where the chinook is king not only in name but in all things.

As one veteran charter skipper told me, "To most salmon fishermen, the striped bass is a scourge that should be done away with. I'm one of these people. Don't get me wrong because I think they're a great fish to catch and I've caught hundreds of them. However, they do not belong in the same water with salmonids."

On the other hand, Umpqua stripers have always had a much smaller but dedicated following of fishermen who insist this river is big enough for the both of them, bass and chinook. In fact, some striper enthusiasts would dearly love to see the populations enhanced by the state.

And in fact the state has considered it now and again, but the sentiment against doing anything to enhance populations of this salmon-eater (though in fact the huge percentage of its diet is *not* salmon) would never permit that.

But the lack of any artificial enhancement of striped bass populations has meant that populations in the Umpqua hang on but have not really thrived. The problem is that this is really the very northern extremity of the species' range and, with Coos Bay fish, is the only naturally-sustaining populations of stripers north of San Francisco. Conditions for spawning must be just right for much success.

Conditions were just right for a few years, back in the 1950s and 1960s. The result was a river full of bass—some of the hottest striper fishing in the country, in fact. And some of the largest. Even into the 1970s, stripers over 50 pounds were not all that unusual—and several IGFA records were set here, including a 64 1/2-pounder taken in the lower Smith in 1973. All the fish weren't lunkers, but five-fish limits were common.

But many successive years when water conditions weren't right for spawning success, as well as commercial fishing pressure (finally ended by law in the 1970s) and an apathetic sportfishing community took their toll. Umpqua-Smith striped bass populations have been in a depressed state for years. But the species is a survivor and enough fish make it most years to keep at least fair numbers of them in the system.

In the meantime, there will be plenty of stripers to attract anglers trying to outsmart them in the Umpqua/Smith rivers, anglers hoping for more years when conditions will make for high spawning success. Such years can come frequently, or not for a decade or more. No one knows.

Of course there will also be plenty of local fishermen hoping just as much that such conditions won't happen. But even most of the striper's opponents will concede that by any standard it's one hell of a game fish.

An Ocean Of Silver

Some of the best catch averages of silver salmon on the Oregon coast are taken by the Winchester Bay fleet. Of course, the nomadic nature of these fish make predictions tenuous. But historically, the coho fishing has been consistently good off the Umpqua.

It is often a fairly short run from Salmon Harbor docks out to concentrations of coho. As a result, most charter operations offer three- or four-hour trips at a modest cost. Many private boats join them in their quest. Larger chinook are frequently mixed in with coho. Trolling herring and/or plastic squid is fairly universal.

Bottomfishing is of less interest overall, but beginning in the late 1970s with the unprecedented brevity of salmon seasons, trips for bottomfish became a regular feature. At least a couple of small but productive areas are fished, reefs within about 10 miles of the harbor in this mostly sandy ocean floor. Catches are generally high, often with a considerable percentage of red rockfishes.

Testing Patience, Skill And Strength On Monster Sturgeon

The lower Umpqua is home to both of the Northwest's species of sturgeon. The larger, more desirable whites predominate, with some influxes of greens during the summer when salinity in the river is highest.

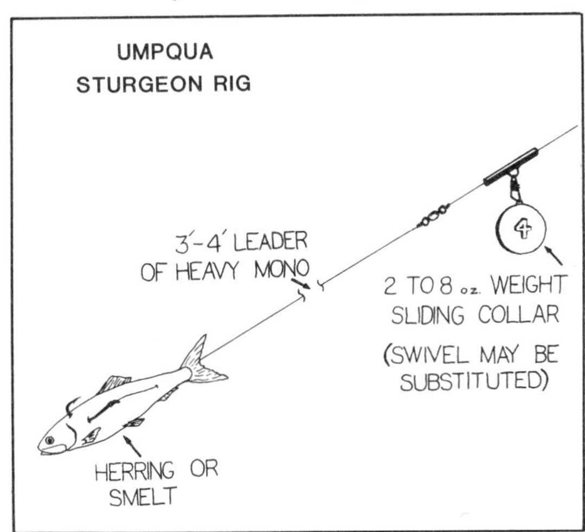

Sturgeon populations remain particularly strong in the lower Umpqua. (Department of Fish and Wildlife biologists have never found much evidence for natural spawning here, and suspect the fish migrate in.) But the river could support an even greater fishery and the DFW is looking at artificially enhancing populations in future management plans for the Umpqua—and possibly other rivers as well.

Umpqua sturgeon are noteworthy for an exceptionally large average size. More fish are released here for exceeding the 72-inch maximum than for failing to meet the minimum (at press time) of 40 inches. It is not unusual to see anglers battle a big sturgeon for an hour or more, knowing full well they'll have to release it but wanting the satisfaction of seeing just how large their catch really is and—if they're smart enough to have a camera along—to maybe snap a photo or two before releasing it.

In many respects both species of Umpqua sturgeon are similar. Both often nibble as gently as a minnow but, when hooked, move off about as subtly as a Trident submarine. But in many ways, the two species differ.

The Sturgeon Too Large For A World Record

Sturgeon fishing is a waiting game, and we had waited. All afternoon. My intrepid associate, Brock Gilman, and I were fishing with Darrel Gabel on a warm July afternoon. Gabel was certainly one of the best to ever guide anglers for sturgeon and striped bass on both the Umpqua/Smith and Coos/Millicoma river systems.

We were anchored in Gabel's river boat a few miles upriver from Reedsport. All three of us were using light tackle, reels with good drags and lots of line capacity, and rods with enough backbone to handle big fish. We were fishing 10-pound (6-kg) line and at that time it would take a sturgeon over 85 pounds to qualify for a new IGFA line-class world record. But of course it couldn't be *too* much bigger: by law any sturgeon over 6 feet in length couldn't be brought in to a certified scale for weighing. But after a few hours, it all began to seem moot.

Then suddenly Brock's levelwind rod quivered as it will when a little suckerfish or a big sturgeon is mouthing the bait. Since the whole outfit was nearly pulled over the side before he could grab it, we decided against it being a little sucker.

Brock set the hooks several times and the fight was on. It didn't end for well over an hour, and a considerable distance upriver, when we eased the fish alongside the boat. It was a huge green, beaten on the wispy 10-pound line.

Before releasing it, we measured it at almost exactly 7 feet and a brawny 37 inches in girth. We lifted it gently over the boat's bow long enough to remove from its flesh a heavy monofilament commercial salmon rig that had become wrapped around the sturgeon and was cutting deeply into its flesh.

We had no choice, of course, but to leave the existing line-class record intact at 85 pounds (though it has been broken more than once since then). But Brock had the satisfaction of knowing that with 10-pound line he had shattered that record with a fish that, judging by the textbooks, would have weighed in at 200 to 300 pounds.

Green sturgeon are bronze, with long tapering snouts, and tend to prefer fairly saline water. Whites are lighter, more grayish in color and have more blunt, abrupt snouts. Whites spend a great deal of time in fresh water while greens are largely marine, but both species are common in the lower Umpqua at times. Greens rarely exceed 7 feet, while Umpqua whites may be over 10.

White sturgeon of any size are a considered a delicacy. Greens are much less esteemed, though most people say those of only 3 or 4 feet are good and some insist even the larger greens are just fine. Both species are outstanding when smoked.

Few sturgeon fishermen are interested in light tackle. Often they use gear similar to that used for deepwater bottomfishing: big reels filled with 30- to 50-pound test line on heavy rods. In fact, though, much lighter tackle can be successfully used and offers advantages of greater sensitivity for the angler.

Fresh herring or shrimp or—especially in midwinter—smelt are among favored sturgeon baits. A sliding sinker rig, as illustrated, is best. Leads from 2 to 8 ounces are used, depending upon tidal flow. There are differing theories among sturgeon fishermen as to whether the bait should be cut or left whole and how it should be rigged, with some rigging the bait tail first but others insisting on a

First sturgeon of the day for these Umpqua anglers is right at the 6-foot maximum—too heavy to lift very high.

head first approach. In any case, the days of barbed hooks are long gone: all hooks for sturgeon must be barbless. Bait stealing sculpins and squawfish can be a real problem in summer. Take plenty of bait.

Probably the trickiest part of sturgeon fishing is determining when to set the hooks. Hundreds of pounds of fish can nibble so gently that a rod tip will barely twitch. For experienced anglers, though, even such a twitching is enough to set hearts a'beating. Occasionally, a sturgeon will grab a bait and go, but more often it will continue to play with the bait. It is usually best to set hooks as the sturgeon begins to move off. Set them hard: there isn't much soft flesh in the sturgeon's bony mouth.

It is not unusual for this scene to be played out several times in a row. The rod twitching, the tense waiting as movement is felt, the sudden and firm whipping back on the rod—all with nothing to show for it, many times. But for whenever luck and timing come together, hook points should be kept as sharp as needles.

The best fishing time is generally from late in the ebb tide through low slack and on into the early flood. As the incoming current picks up, the bite usually slows again until close to high tide.

Be prepared to pick up and follow a big fish until you can tire it. If you're not ready to move quickly, chances are you'll lose a really large sturgeon—and all of your line with it. Most sturgeon enthusiasts have a large float tied to their anchor ropes so they can quickly release the boat, returning later for float and anchor.

This protected tidewater fishery is very well-suited to even small cartop boats. Carrying along some rope would be wise, since a 6-foot sturgeon may not fit conveniently in

Fishermen can stillfish live bait for stripers from bridges or shore in several locations.

Umpqua River

Legend
1. Redtail perch in surf south to Tenmile Creek.
2. Perch bottom fish from south jetties.
4. Fall salmon.
5. Perch from the rocks.
■ Launch Site

Scale: 1 15/16'' = 1 nautical mile.

Chart #18584

Not for navigational purposes.

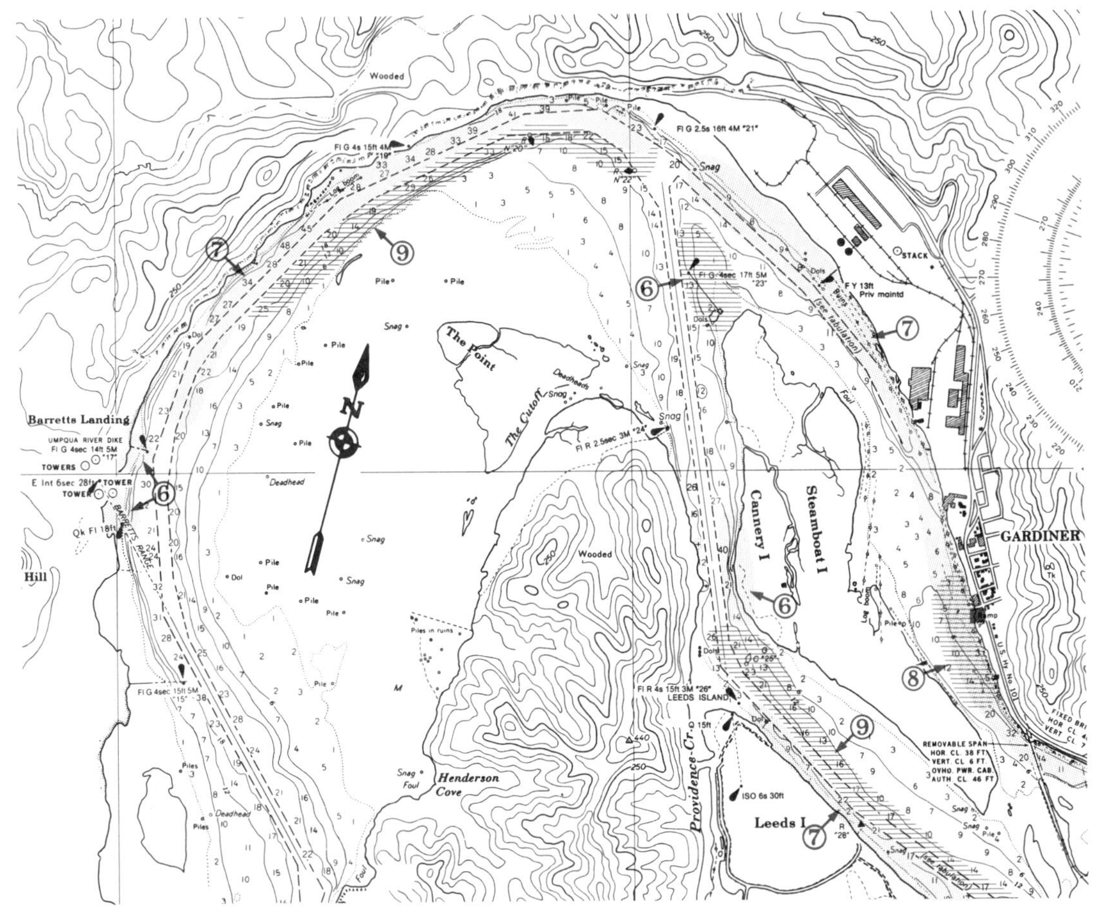

Umpqua River

Legend
6. Perch from skiffs.
7. Striped bass.
8. Sea-run cutthroat.
9. Sturgeon (spring).
■ Launch Site (also ramps at Bolon and Reedsport, not shown)

Scale: 1 15/16'' = 1 nautical mile

Chart #18584

Not for navigational purposes.

a small boat. They can generally be noosed by forming a slipnot and passing the noose over the butt and length of the rod and down the line. Ease it around the sturgeon and pull tight just before the tail. You are likely to see people fishing from small boats at anchor with keepers thus noosed tightly alongside.

Perhaps, to help the uninitiated avoid heart failure, it should be pointed out that sturgeon (especially greens) up and down the river may jump spontaneously. It can be somewhat disconcerting to be waiting anxiously and silently for a bite only to have the stillness shattered by 5 to 10 feet of fish, clearing the water near your boat and crashing loudly back into the water.

Trolling Tidewater For Fall Salmon

In September and October, fall-run salmon begin their migration into and up through tidewater where they become a very popular target for Umpqua fishermen. Fall chinook in general seem to be on the increase since the late 1980s, for whatever reason—and probably a variety of reasons. These are mostly wild fish.

In September, most of the action is centered around the jaws and on up to the Winchester Bay area. By October or, if rainfall remains light, as late as November, salmon can be widely available all the way through the Gardiner area on up to Dean Creek and into the lower Smith.

Just as in the ocean, the lower bay catch is composed of both species of salmon but silvers predominate. Some fishermen troll a flasher with herring or anchovy, but single spinners are preferred by the majority. Hot Shots also take a share of fall salmon.

After the salmon move through, steelhead move upriver, usually from midNovember through January. The Smith offers some particularly outstanding steelheading, though relatively few steelies are taken as far down as tidewater. Most Umpqua steelheading begins at the head of tidewater, above the Scottsburg Bridge.

Upper Tidewater's Spring Smorgasbord

From about the first of the year, anglers here gear up for a succession of runs through the upper reaches of tidewater, runs of species very different from one another.

The action begins with smelt. They follow their own schedule, some years arriving early in January, some years not showing until midFebruary, and most years appearing sometime in between. Numbers are equally unpredictable. Very few smelt may appear in a lean year, but during many winters runs will fill the river, especially just below the Scottsburg Bridge, the most popular dipping area. The best dipping goes on at night or during dim, overcast days, Most netters work from the bank (there's good access at Scottsburg Park) and often fill buckets with 25-pound limits in a hurry. If the smelt are sparse, small boaters will have the best shot at them.

Sturgeon are also taken at this time and logically so. They too find smelt a tasty treat and crowd up the Umpqua after the spawning fish.

The next run of fish to hit the area are spring-run chinook. The popularity of fishing for springers endures, though they have become almost exclusively hatchery fish and even at that over the past few years, numbers have been declining.

Pound for pound, shad fight as hard as tarpon on ultralight tackle.

Small Boat Safety—Crossing The Bar

The main channel in this deepwater entrance parallels and runs close to the training jetty. Stay close to it until well clear of the surf zone. Stay well away from the north jetty and the extensive north spit that runs out from it. In fact the north spit begins at the first rock spar jetty and long pier on the east side of the channel far upriver from the jetty. The north spit meets the middle ground at the outer end of the training jetty. Avoid the middle ground—the entire area from the end of the north jetty out to the black bell buoy since even slight swells can cause breakers large enough to capsize vessels. When leaving Salmon Harbor, remain in the main channel until clear of the end of the sea wall which extends out to the no. 2 fog signal/light.

The rough bar advisory sign is positioned on shore.

U.S. Coast Guard Station—Umpqua River

Bar/weather conditions, recording 271-4244
Information, station phone 271-2137

These chunky 20- to 25-pound kings (occasionally to over 40) move upriver quickly, staying brighter and livelier than fall kings. Most fishermen anchor and, using levelwind salmon reels, let weighted spinners (or herring) "walk downcurrent" along the bottom. Those who fare best let their spinners work back into deep channels that the current has cut into the basaltic rock river bottom until it drops into a deep pool. Hold the spinner there to flash back and forth in the current at "the mouth" of the channel it drifted down until a salmon hits.

The most popular fishing area for spring chinook is also around the Scottsburg Bridge, where you may luck into fish but will have less chance for any solitude.

About the time these springers are leaving the head of tidewater, American shad are beginning their spring assault on the lower Umpqua and Smith. In the Umpqua, most shad are caught between Dean's Creek and Scottsburg. These hard-fighting acrobats, resembling miniature tarpon in appearance and tactics when hooked, average 2 or 3 pounds. Ultralight tackle ensures the greatest sport yet allows skilled, persistent anglers to catch the 25 the law allows—though many catch and release for fun.

Just as the shad are disappearing, the first summer steelhead are nosing their way upriver and will continue to be taken through the summer, all well above tidewater.

About the time steelhead are showing far upriver, herring schools are moving into Salmon Harbor. On and off through early fall, herring—occasionally mixed with anchovies or smelt—may be jigged or snagged from docks. At times, these herring will run 8 to 10 or more inches, too large for silver salmon baits, but a great size for bottomfish or for pickling. These "horse herring" may far outnumber smaller herring; we've visited Salmon Harbor in midsummer when bait dealers were netting them in such great numbers they were practically giving them away. On ultralight tackle, by the way, 10-inch herring can be great fun to catch.

Spring Perch In The Lower Bay

Despite the constant influx of various game fish far up tidewater through the spring, some anglers find it most rewarding to concentrate their efforts in the lower river, where pinkfin (redtail) perch are schooling.

In the surf and from the south jetties, pinkfins begin providing good sport by April, as a rule, and are available pretty consistently through June. As elsewhere along the Oregon coast, serious anglers fish the incoming tide, using sand shrimp, clam necks or mussels.

From May through July, perch will usually swarm about the lower river. The most popular areas for pinkfins then include the Big Bend, especially at the end of Steamboat Island, and the wing dams. From anchored boats, fishermen rig one or two small hooks with sand shrimp above a light sinker. Limits—for many years and still at press time 25 perch—are often taken by those who want that many 1- to 3-pound perch.

Perch are not the only species caught from the jetties or in the bay. The variety of small bottomfish taken from most other Oregon jetties is available here, though the Umpqua jetties are not renown for outstanding mixed catches. Starry flounder are still taken occasionally.

Scenic shot of Winchester Bay harbor.

Shad—For More Than Just The Roe?

If you've chosen not to release all those shad you're having so much fun catching, you've probably discovered why all the fuss about shad roe. The tiny eggs that fill the body cavities of these spring spawners are considered a delicacy in California and all along the Atlantic Coast as well as here.

However, common knowledge among most Oregonians also says that about all you can do with the pound or two of meat remaining on a shad after you've removed the eggs is to smoke it, and many don't bother to do that. As a result, a great deal of shad meat is simply discarded each spring.

Fact is, however, many folks—especially back East—consider shad flesh excellent. In an effort to reduce waste by sport fishermen, the Oregon Department of Fish and Wildlife has printed up several pages of shad recipes, most from East Coast housewives or seaboard governmental agencies. Sample recipes: Virginia-fried shad, New Jersey planked shad, shad without bones, golden broiled shad steaks, and baked stuffed shad.

Although not common these days, good-sized starry flounder are still caught by small boaters and shore fishermen in the lower bay.

UMPQUA-WINCHESTER / Sport Fish and Seasons

Species	J	F	M	A	M	J	J	A	S	O	N	D
	BEST MONTHS											
Striped bass[1]	fair	fair	fair/best	best	best	best	fair	fair	best	best	fair	
Sturgeon[2]	fair	best	best	best	best	best	best	best	best	fair		
Ocean salmon[3]					fair	best	best	best	fair			
Ocean bottomfish					fair	best	best	best	fair			
Fall salmon									best	best	fair	
Smelt[4]	fair	best	fair									
Spring Chinook			fair/best	best	best							
Shad					best	best						
Pinkfin perch[5]			fair	best	best	best	best/fair					
"Bluebacks," jacks							fair	best	best			

[1]September-October are particularly good months to fish the lower Smith, January-April fish are in upper tide water or farther up.
[2]Whites most available January-October; greens occur mostly July-October.
[3]Check regulations carefully before fishing; seasons vary from year to year.
[4]Timing and size of run varies widely from year to year.
[5]April-June best in surf, jetties; May-July best in lower bay.

LEGEND: best fair poor

Sea-Run Cutthroat—Late Summer Warmups For Fall Salmon

"Bluebacks" are taken in tidewater of both the Umpqua and Smith rivers in August and September. They are particularly prone to prowl in and around tributary streams such as Scholfield Creek, Hudson Slough in the Smith, or Dean Creek, far up the Umpqua.

The usual gear for Oregon bluebacks is popular here—trolling blades such as Ford Fenders or Doc Sheltons with a nightcrawler. Some fishermen swear by a small filet of meat, such as a side of sculpin ("bullhead") as used so successfully for Puget Sound sea-runs. The greatest number of these 14- to 17-inch trout are likely to be caught during the last half of a flood tide by trolling slowly near shore or around sandbars (such as those in the Gardiner area).

Summer coho fishing just offshore is often so good that charters will return to Winchester Bay by midmorning with full limits.

Close-up of striped bass.

Facilities

All phone numbers listed are within the 503 area code unless otherwise noted.

Guides, Charters

Two respected guides who regularly fish the lower Umpqua are listed below. Check with local tackle dealers or the chamber of commerce for other guides. Most lower river guided trips are for striped bass, sturgeon or salmon, but most will gladly fish for any of the other species here, including perch or shad. Rates vary according to the guide, number of anglers aboard and length of trip, but figure (at press time) on spending $100 to 200 per person for a day of fishing.

Hannah Fishing Lodges, Elk River Road, Port Orford 97449, 322-8585. Takes 4 to 6 anglers in large river sled. Denny Hannah has been guiding this river for decades. He fishes stripers and sturgeon primarily April-June. Offers package trips including lodging at "Elkton Camp 5" 36 miles from Reedsport. Fishes fall chinook, October-November.

Terry Jarmain, P.O. Box 213, Reedsport 97467, 271-5583. Takes 2 or 3 anglers for any/all species on 6-, 8-or 10-hour trip. Expert striper, sturgeon guide.

Winchester Bay charter trips typically last 4 hours and, at press time, were going for $35 or so. Although bottomfishing is not a major item here, some offices will run bottomfish trips—particularly before, after or between salmon season. Most operate May-September, depending upon salmon seasons set annually by federal and state managing agencies.

Becky Lynn Charters, 596 Laskey Lane, North Bend 97459, 271-3017. One 6-passenger boat, 28′ Tollycraft.

Gee-Gee Charters, Beach Boulevard, Winchester Bay 97467, 271-3152. Operates 2 boats, 36′ (6 passenger) and 48′ (16 passenger, but usually takes 8-10). Salmon and occasionally bottomfish.

Holiday Charters, P.O. Box 93, Winchester Bay 97467, 271-3702. Fishes 2 boats, 34′ and 38′ with up to 8 and 10 anglers, respectively for salmon and bottomfish. Will fish bottomfish through October and offers bay crabbing.

The Main Charters, c/o Stockade Tackle and Marine Supply, P.O. Box 602, Winchester Bay 97467, 271-3800. Skipper Vern Knutch fishes 38′ boat with 8-10 anglers (licensed for 16) for salmon and occasionally bottomfish.

Marsadon Charters, P.O. Box 601, Winchester Bay 97467, 271-3122. 30′ boat for up to 6 anglers. Salmon only.

Shamrock Charters, P.O. Box 208, Winchester Bay 97467, 2 34′ boats. Salmon and occasionally bottomfish.

Marinas, Launch Facilities

Salmon Harbor, P.O. Box 7, Winchester Bay 97467, 241-3407. Only moorage facility on lower river. 900 slips—usually no problem finding space here. Gas and diesel, engine repair. Bait and tackle at nearby Stockade Market. 2 paved launch ramps, 1 at east basin (by Coast Guard station) with 6 lanes and 3 floats—an outstanding launch facility—and the other at the west end with four lanes and one float, also excellent. Modest fee charged for launching.

Other launch ramps in the lower river: **Reedsport City ramp** just north of the Highway 101 and railroad bridges, a free paved ramp with limited parking. The **Gardiner county ramp** in Gardiner offers one lane with float, in good condition. It's also free and provides quick access to Big Bend area and lower Smith. Just south of Gardiner is the **Bolin Island county ramp**, also free.

In the Smith River, farther up but still in good striped bass country, is the **Smith River Marina**, 271-3919.

Bait And Tackle

Reedsport Outdoor Store, 2049 Winchester Avenue, Reedsport 97467, 271-2311. Open year-round, 7 days/week. Offers the most complete tackle selection in the area, as well as rod and reel repair (also sells and repairs outboard motors and boats).

Stockade Tackle and Marine Supply, P.O. Box 602, Winchester Bay 97467 (at the head of the harbor), 271-3800. Open daily, all year. 7 days/week. Carries a complete line of sport and commercial fishing gear.

Public Campgrounds

Umpqua Lighthouse State Park, 6 miles south of Reedsport off Highway 101, 271-4118. 42 tentsites, 22 RV sites with hookups. Spaces tend to be small and somewhat crowded but campground located near ocean.

Windy Cove County Park, Beach Road across from Salmon Harbor. Area 1—271-4138, Areas 2 and 3—271-5634. Area 1 has 25 RV/tent spaces; areas 2 and 3 have 80 sites. No reservations accepted. These are lovely on-the-harbor spots and, as you might suppose, tend to be packed during the season. But September-May they are largely empty and delightful places to stay. The park is a Douglas County facility. For more information on Windy Cove and many other county parks, write for a free Douglas County Parks brochure: Douglas County Park Headquarters, 6536 Old Highway 99 North, P.O. 800, Winchester Bay 97459, 271-4631.

William M. Tugman State Park, 8 miles south of Reedsport off Highway 101. 115 sites with electrical hookups, hiker-biker camp. A little farther from the ocean than Umpqua Lighthouse, but more pleasant—sites are farther apart with more foliage and the campground is less often crowded.

For More Information

Lower Umpqua Chamber of Commerce, P.O. Box 11, Highway 101 and Highway 38, Reedsport 97467, 271-3495 or toll-free in state 800-247-2155.

courtesy Portland District U.S. Army Corps of Engineers

Coos Bay

THIS SPRAWLING BAY, VEINED WITH WARM, shallow sloughs and tributaries, is quite unlike most other bays of the Northwest coast. One long, narrow channel snakes around to the north (around the city of North Bend, appropriately) then heads far south to Coos Bay. Around the channel are great areas of shallow mud flats. Much of the shoreline of the main and connecting channels and the lower Coos River are lined with log booms and huge ships. A considerable portion of the bay's many miles of shoreline is inaccessible to shore fishing.

The contiguous communities of Coos Bay, North Bend and Charleston form the largest real metropolitan area along the Oregon coast. There is considerable interest in sport fishing among both local and visiting anglers. A well-established charter fleet goes out for salmon in season and for bottomfish on a limited year-round basis. In addition to nearshore and offshore rocky reefs, smaller bottomfish are caught in surprising numbers in the lower bay and along rocky headlands that begin in this area and continue south to Brookings.

The Port of Coos Bay offers boat launching and moorage and other launch ramps are scattered about the bay. Large state and county parks are located on the beach, just south of the bay. There is no shortage of RV parks and motels.

Coos Bay Offshore—Summer Silvers And Year-round Bottomfish

A good charter fleet, a generally crossable deepwater bar entrance and miles of offshore reefs account for a year-round ocean fishery out of Charleston.

Salmon fishermen here have enjoyed one of the higher catch averages, for many years thanks to good silver fishing. But that's been changing since the late 1980s, with the increasing strength of fall chinook runs from many Northwest rivers—including a major source of fish, the nearby Rogue.

Salmon charters generally run two five-hour trips daily, departing at 6 a.m. and 11 a.m., charging fairly uniform rates. Bottomfishing is quite popular, as it ought to be with so much fish-rich habitat nearby. Famous reefs such as Simpson's are but a short run and offer great variety. Farther out, deeper reefs produce catches loaded with yelloweye, canary and vermilion rockfish (all "red snapper" locally), along with lots of lings. During welcome calm periods between winter storms, some of the largest lingcod are taken.

This general area is so loaded with rocky reefs that Loran numbers aren't particularly necessary. Most private boaters simply head down to Simpson's Reef (immediately visible on a nautical chart; head south of "the whistler" for about four miles). From there all the way down to Bandon you'll find endless reefs and pinnacles in 15 to 40 fathoms, prime habitat loaded with bottomfish.

You may even luck into a halibut. In years past, quite a few 50- to 70-pound halibut came from flat areas here in early spring. Few charters make the 20- to 25-mile run south and offshore to get to halibut beds in up to 100 fathoms, particularly in summer when northwesterlies can be a bear to return into, but good numbers of halibut are out there. The last trip that veteran Charleston skipper Bob Pullen made out to such deepwater halibut spots, everyone aboard limited (then two-fish) easily.

Small Boat Safety—Crossing The Bar

This is one of the deeper, larger bar entrances on the Northwest coast. Its deep channel accommodates considerable traffic from huge freighters. These gargantuan vessels demand caution from small boats fishing or traveling in the lower bay and the jaws, since there is little opportunity in the channel for freighters to quickly stop or change course for obstructions—including small boats.

Areas requiring particular caution include the South Slough sand spit, on your left as you leave the Charleston Boat Basin. Avoid that area and then a submerged jetty by staying to the left of light no. 1 at all times when leaving the boat basin.

Avoid the sand spit at the south end of North Beach. Exercise extreme caution in the vicinity of Guano Rock, between the base of the south jetty and the main channel, especially on low ebb tides. The north jetty runs out a considerable distance submerged; when departing do not turn to the north until you've passed buoy 3. Also the area north of buoy 5 can be very dangerous when there are large swells on the bar or during ebb tide.

The rough bar advisory sign is located 8 feet above the water on the jetty just north of the Charleston Boat Basin.

U.S. Coast Guard—Coos Bay

Weather/bar conditions (recording) 888-3102
Information, station phone 888-3267

Small Boat Fishing In The Lower Bay: Bottomfish, Five Species Of Perch

Small boaters can do something here that many on the Oregon coast can't: fish *inside* the bay for rockfish (predominantly blacks), kelp greenling and a few cabezon, well inside the bar and away from ocean swells. True, these species run much smaller inside the bay than offshore, but they offer some fine light tackle sport on bait (herring or shrimp) or small leadhead jigs.

Probably the most popular stretch for this is "the cribs," a rocky area extending near shore from the base of the north jetty about a mile into the bay. The buoys just across the channel from the cribs, leading into the Charleston Boat Basin, mark another good area. Some anglers report consistent success in the deep water beneath the North Bend railroad trestle traversing the lower river.

Perch fishermen find their quarry in great quantity here. They also enjoy quite a variety. I've caught pile, striped, walleye, white and redtail (pinkfin) all in one area. Many spots offer perch fishing to nonboaters, especially those willing to do a bit of driving or walking. And virtually any shallow rocky area a small boater wants to fish should harbor some perch, particularly during spring and summer. I've caught them in large schools in no more than a couple feet of water on a low incoming tide near Pigeon Point.

Schools of feeding perch do move around and it may take a bit of looking to locate one, but it's worth the effort since perch generally feed in such large numbers.

The usual offerings for perch work well in Coos Bay, with fresh ghost shrimp by far the most popular bait. These can be readily dug in many places around the bay, such as the beach near the Menasha Fill just southwest of Jordan Cove and northwest of North Bend. A no. 1 or 2 hook beneath a sliding sinker rig is favored.

Perch, particularly the larger pile perch, seem particularly abundant in the bay prior to spring spawning. Fishing can be at its fastest at this time when crowds gather at the Menasha Fill to enjoy it.

Small boaters may want to drop a few crab traps or rings in lower Coos Bay, since it often produces particularly well.

Coos Bay Anadromous Tidewater Fisheries—The Struggling And The Strong

Coos Bay's extensive estuarine area is a rich feeding grounds for many species of game fish, but in recent years populations of some species have remained depressed while others are strong or rebounding.

The most discouraging story for those who love striped bass is the decline of a once-thriving sportfishery throughout Coos Bay and the lower Coos and Millicoma rivers. It has been many years since striper fishing was red-hot here. Thanks to the unusually good spawning conditions decades ago, most notably in 1958, striper fishing was red hot in the 1960s.

Then, and for many years after, stripers were available throughout the system and offered great small boat and shore fishing. Plugging in areas such as the Highway 101 bridge at night was a great way for shore fishermen to take big bass.

However, conditions for striped bass spawning are seldom right here, thanks in part to typical spring runoff

Coos Bay

Legend
7. Perch—several species (spring and summer).
8. Bottomfish from small boats.
9. Bottomfish, perch from rocks at Cape Arago.
■ Launch Site
Scale: 1 15/16'' = 1 nautical mile

Chart #18587

Not for navigational purposes.

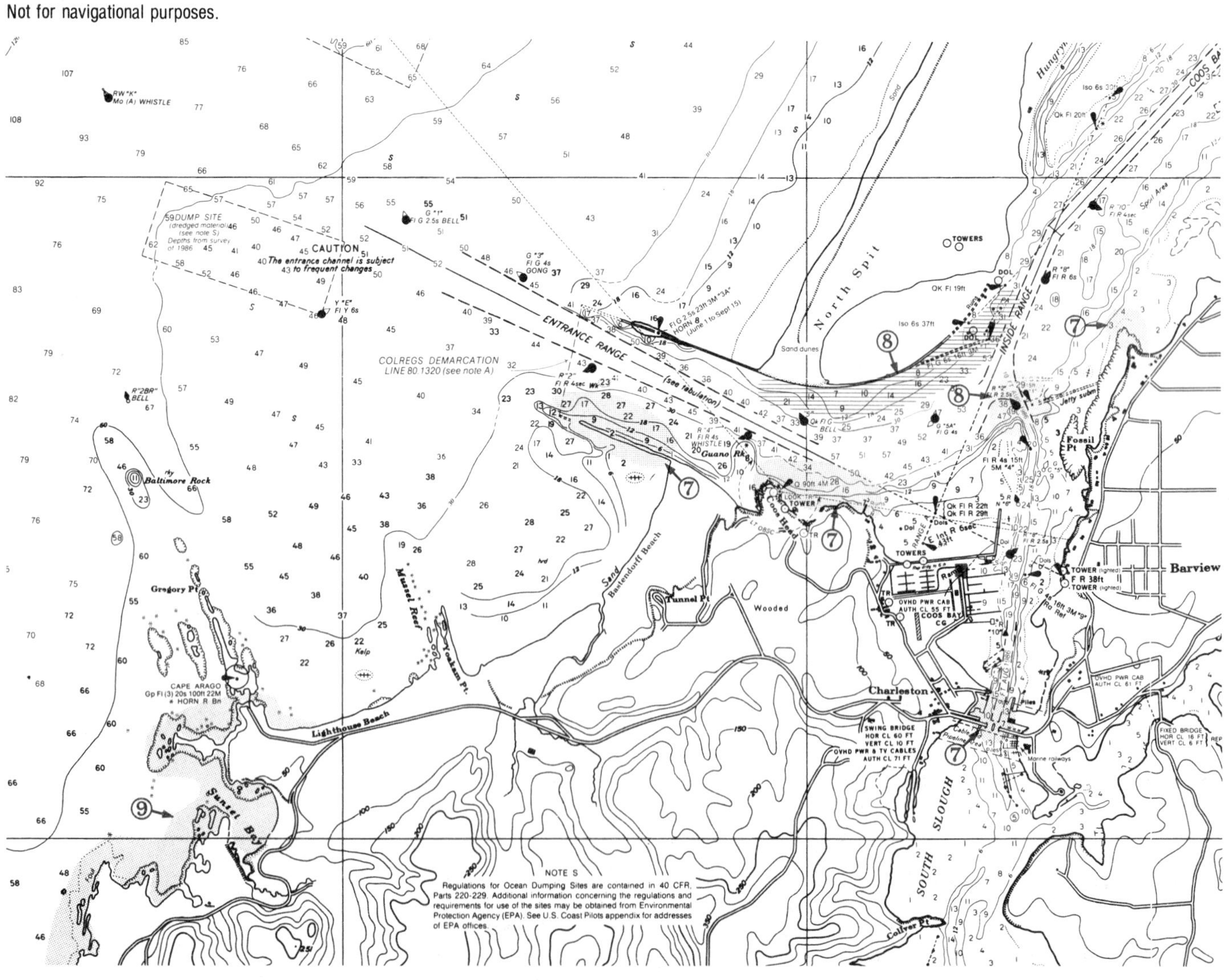

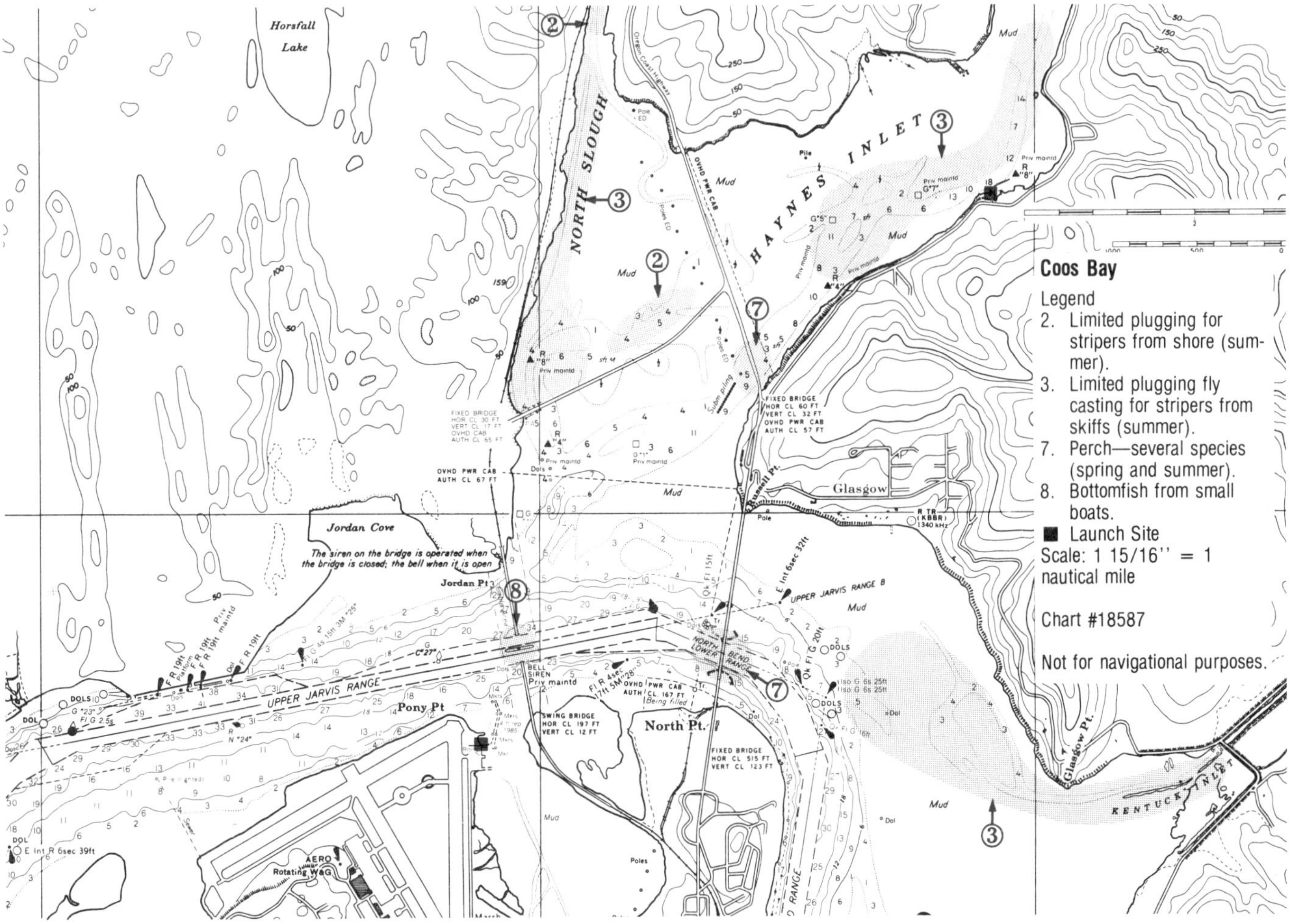

Coos Bay

Legend
2. Limited plugging for stripers from shore (summer).
3. Limited plugging fly casting for stripers from skiffs (summer).
7. Perch—several species (spring and summer).
8. Bottomfish from small boats.

■ Launch Site

Scale: 1 15/16'' = 1 nautical mile

Chart #18587

Not for navigational purposes.

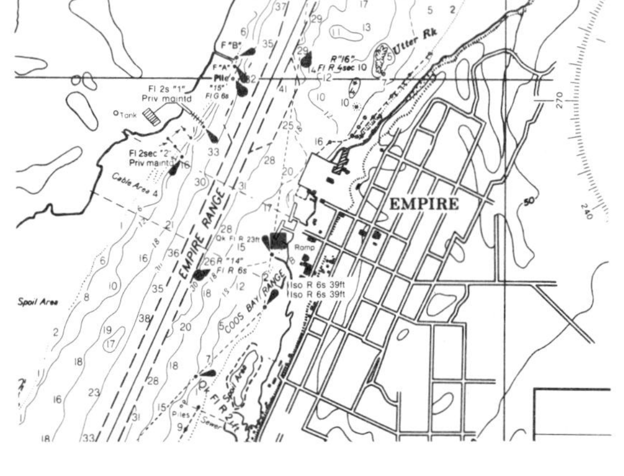

COOS BAY \Sport Fish and Seasons

Species	J	F	M	A	M	J	J	A	S	O	N	D
	BEST MONTHS											
Striped bass	poor	poor	poor	fair	fair	poor	fair	fair	fair	fair	poor	poor
Ocean salmon[1]	poor	poor	poor	poor	fair	best	best	best	fair	poor	poor	poor
Bottomfish	best	best	best	best	best	best	best	best	best	best	best	best
Perch	fair	fair	best	best	best	best	best	best	best	best	fair	fair
Shad	poor	poor	poor	poor	best	best	poor	poor	poor	poor	poor	poor
Fall Chinook	poor	poor	poor	poor	poor	poor	poor	poor	fair	fair	poor	poor
Spring Chinook	poor	poor	poor	poor	fair	fair	poor	poor	poor	poor	poor	poor
Smelt, anchovies	poor	poor	poor	poor	poor	poor	best	best	poor	poor	poor	poor
Sea-run cutthroat	poor	poor	poor	poor	poor	poor	fair	best	best	best	poor	poor
Albacore (maybe)	poor	poor	poor	poor	poor	poor	poor	fair	fair	poor	poor	poor

[1]May vary considerably according to annual seasons set by federal and state regulatory agencies.

LEGEND: best fair poor

that flushes eggs downriver and to heavy siltation from big boat traffic. Annual failure of stripers to spawn effectively meant that numbers of fish gradually decreased while average size (of older fish) went up—as high as a 64-pounder taken in 1983.

Today, the once-great Coos Bay striped bass fishing is minimal. There are, of course, many who are delighted at the decline of these predators that do eat some salmon smolts. There are others who feel that the Coos System could benefit from bringing back this distinctive fishery and the Department of Fish and Wildlife has gradually begun an enhancement program. But critics say it is so limited in scope that unless expanded the program won't do much to restore stripers.

In the meantime, there are still a few stripers in the estuary, including some trophy-sized fish. A few anglers still fish for them using live bait (traditionally on rigs like that shown). Fly-fishermen may still encounter a few fish feeding in shallow sloughs. If they can make casts with 6-inch streamers long enough to avoid spooking the fish, especially late in the spring, they may connect.

Using light tackle, Darrel Gabel took this fair-sized striper. Gabel was for years one of the few and certainly one of the best guides on both Umpqua and Coos bays for striped bass, but he gave up the business in the 1980s when decreases in populations left him unable to consistently offer clients success.

Be advised that parts of the upper estuary are now closed to protect spring spawning. And those who do fish for and luck into stripers are encouraged to enjoy the battle and release the fish, at least until/unless the resource can be re-established.

The Coos is yet another of Oregon's bays where sturgeon have become a viable target for sport fishermen only recently, and another bay where fishermen are saying that the sturgeon were always around, but no one really knew or tried.

These days more and more fishermen *are* trying and succeeding. At least one or two guides have been booking sturgeon trips. They do most of their fishing in the winter in tidewater and some in early spring farther upriver. The tidewater fishing is limited to winter because of the problems that sturgeon fishermen have in many coastal rivers. They seem amplified in this wide, shallow bay. That is, without good freshets the bay becomes so filled with crabs that it's nearly impossible to keep a shrimp on the hook long enough for sturgeon to find it.

Best fishing is around the North Bend bridge and below on an ebb tide. Most of the sturgeon can be taken in 5 to 10 feet of water using 3 to 5 ounces of weight. Although some anglers insist on heavier lines, 30-pound test is adequate. Guides favor 80-pound Dacron leader.

Tidewater salmon fishing has not been outstanding in the Coos system. During the reign of salmon aquaculturing in the 1980s, two private firms dumped hundreds of thousands of silver smolts into the bay each year and provided anglers with a renewed sportfishery that, for a couple years, was super. But the apparent demise of those firms ended that source of salmon.

Anglers do troll for fall chinook from the forks on up to the head of tidewater, usually pulling spinners. Some drift salmon eggs. Either way, those who fare best develop the knack of keeping baits or lures near bottom without hanging up in the boundless snags.

Big jacks (mostly two-year-old chinook of 3 to 6 pounds) may be abundant at times. Jacks can be great fun on light tackle. Try salmon eggs fished 5 or 6 feet below a bobber.

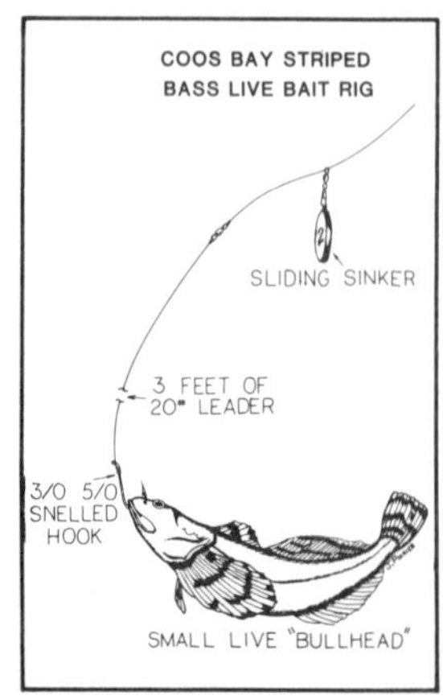

Shad mean spring chaos for many anglers who are overtly enthusiastic about them. For about six weeks, usually midMay through June, shad fill the Coos and Millicoma rivers above the forks, though the size of runs can vary considerably from year to year.

Even when they're thick, shad are not always biting readily. As a rule, the hottest bite seems to occur during the hottest part of the day on sunny afternoons. As elsewhere, shad darts or small spinners are popular, generally trolled right along the bottom. There are some stretches from which shore anglers cast and retrieve with success.

Ultralight gear is ideal for shad, offering more strikes and more sport from these acrobatic 2- to 6-pounders. Many anglers release most of the shad they catch. Others keep them for the tasty roe or to smoke. Those who are keeping their shad should also keep count; at times, they may reach their 25-fish limit suprisingly quickly.

Some spring chinook may be taken in the upper reaches of tidewater (above the forks) during May and June. Biologists contend that these are actually Rogue River fish.

Sea-run cutthroat receive scant attention here but can provide good late-summer sport in upper tidewater. Those who fish for them generally troll spinners, drift eggs or flyfish.

Although not always known as a steelheader's paradise, the Coos/Millicoma may be somewhat closer to that in the future, thanks to the STEP (Salmon Trout Enhancement Program) begun in the 1980s. Steelhead populations are on the rise.

Fishing piers in the lower bay, such as that near the Charleston Bridge, can be very productive for jigging herring and smelt. Small gold hooks above a light sinker draw strikes.

Fishing The South Jetty And The Sandy Surf

Access to the south jetty is via a small road that winds down past the Coast Guard lookout station. There is a small, sandy parking lot at the jetty's base. Though inaccessible to those without four-wheel drive vehicles, the north jetty also provides good fishing.

Pinkfin perch are a prime target, spring through midautumn; at times, striped and pile perch are equally abundant. April is often a particularly hot time for fishing pinkfins from the jetties.

Just about all nearshore species of bottomfish are taken from the rocks, mostly on incoming tides. Bait and jigs with plastic worms take several species of rockfish, greenling and cabezon. Lingcod populations remains substantial enough for anglers to fish live sculpins or greenling specifically for them.

Salmon fever hits hard among jetty fishermen, traditionally starting July Fourth and persisting through about midSeptember. But Rogue springers linger between the jetties as early as May some years. Many jetty fishermen cast whole herring from the rocks, with typical coastal rigs that use large floats to keep baits up and out of the rocks. Long-handled nets are part of gear carried by serious Coos Bay jetty anglers.

Rather than climb out on the rocks to try for perch, some fishermen prefer to wade into the surf. In early spring, pinkfins are attracted to a stretch of beach west of north Coos Bay known as Horsfall Beach. This is one of the most popular surf-fishing beaches along the southern Oregon coast. Surf anglers cast sand shrimp or sand crabs rigged above 2- to 4-ounce pyramid sinkers when breakers aren't too intimidating.

Facilities

All phone numbers listed are within the 503 area code unless otherwise noted.

Big ship traffic is a common sight in lower Coos Bay. In foreground, a man on the flats digs marine worms for bait.

Charters

As in many other Oregon ports, rates tend to be uniform. Most charters operate year-round, weather permitting, taking advantage of the very fine bottomfishing over widespread, rocky habitat, though December and January are pretty slow months for fishing. (Whale watching trips are also part of the winter schedule for Charleston charters.) Typically, either salmon or bottomfish trips last 5 hours and, at press time, cost $40. Most offer light-tackle fishing for bottomfish, with spinning tackle to cast leadhead jigs and worms. If albacore show in late summer, tuna trips are available (for $100 at press time).

Betty Kay Charters, P.O. Box 5020, Charleston 97420, 888-9021. Runs two 36′ boats which usually carry 5 to 10 anglers (though licensed for 13).

Bob's Sportfishing, P.O. Box 5018, Charleston 97420, 888-4241. 36′ boat carries 5-10 anglers as a rule.

Charleston Charters, P.O. Box 5032, Charleston 97420, 888-4846. One 44′ foot charter.

Guides who regularly fish the lower river are hard to come by. One is **Bob Hughes' Millicoma Guide Service**, 269-0957. Hughes, a Bureau of Land Management fire fighter when not guiding, fishes the lower bay and rivers for sturgeon and other species as available.

Marinas, Launch Areas

Charleston Marina, Port of Coos Bay, P.O. Box 5409, Charleston 97420, 888-2548. 565 moorage slips, total. All of B-dock is reserved for guest/overnight moorage. Gas and diesel available at adjacent Fletcher Marine. Engine repair also available nearby, and bait and tackle at nearby Basin Tackle. Restrooms, showers, laundromat. Free boat launching via a fine 3-lane paved ramp with floats on either side, lots of parking. Hoist available at Charleston Shipyard. RV spaces with hookups.

Other launch ramps—both free—include the **Empire city ramp** in Coos Bay, Newmark Street and Empire Boulevard and the **Pony Point North Bend city ramp** at Virginia and Marion streets.

Bait And Tackle

Basin Tackle Shop, 4565 Kingfisher, Charleston 97420 (in the boat basin), 888-3811. Open 7 days/week May-October and irregularly "depending on the weather" November-April. Stocks all sorts of baits and saltwater gear.

Disco Sporting Goods, 790 South 2nd, Coos Bay 97420, 267-6097. Open Monday-Saturday year-round. Carries saltwater basics but most emphasis on steelhead and trout.

Empire Sport Shop, 270 South Empire Boulevard, Coos Bay 97420, 888-2316. Open year-round, 7 days/week. En route to boat basin and jetties with essential tackle and lots of bait plus information on jetty and small boat fishing.

Englund Marine, 5080 Cape Arago Highway, Charleston 97420, 888-6723. Open Monday-Saturday. Great supply of bottomfish and salmon rods, reels, terminal gear.

Fishin' Shack, 818 South Broadway, Coos Bay 97420, 267-3474. Open Monday-Saturday, year-round. Fair selection of saltwater gear, lots of jetty stuff.

Stuff-n-Things, 658 South Empire Boulevard, Charleston 97420, 888-9787. Open daily, carries salmon gear, extensive selection of jigs and plastic worms and just about everything for saltwater fishing (plus steelhead gear in season). Good information source.

Surplus Corner, 310 South Broadway, Coos Bay 97420, 267-6711. Open daily, wide selection of tackle.

Public Campgrounds

Bastendorff Beach County Park, 2 miles west of Charleston, 888-5353. 55 sites. Fine location and very pleasant, with sites surrounded with trees and hedges. Expect competition for space on nice summer weekends. Open year-round.

Bluebill Campground (U.S. Forest Service), 4 miles northwest of North Bend near Horsfall Beach (surfperch fishing spot). 19 sites (no hookups).

Sunset Bay State Park, 12 miles southwest of Coos Bay off Highway 101, 888-4902. 109 tentsites, 29 RV sites with hookups, hiker-biker camp. Large area in a nice location, but fills quickly during summer and is often very busy and very noisy. Space between sites and from the perimeter road is minimal.

For More Information

Charleston Information Center, P.O. Box 7535, Boat Basin Drive and Cape Arago Highway, Charleston 97420, 888-2311.

Coos Bay Area Chamber of Commerce, 50 East Central, Coos Bay 97420, 269-0215.

North Bend Information Center, 1380 Sherman, North Bend 97459, 756-4613.

Lower Rogue River

courtesy Portland Distict U.S. Army Corps of Engineers

Unlike the meandering, laid-back waters of Coos Bay, the Rogue lives up to its name, roaring down from coastal mountains (actually part of the Siskiyous) to the sea. This big, swift, steep river empties almost directly into the Pacific. In fact, there is no real bay as such here, just a few miles of tidewater extending a mile or so above Elephant Rock to the "Ferry Hole."

Few areas around the Northwest coast are more dramatically scenic than the southern Oregon coast from Port Orford south to Brookings, with Gold Beach right in the center. There is much here to attract visitors beyond the good fishing—the dramatic beauty of the river and rugged coastline, the tranquility of the town and the history of the famous Rogue (one of 10 federally-designated wild rivers), which jet boats ascend daily on tours.

There are RV parks, several motels and one enormous, first-rate resort-condo complex north of the bridge and plenty of shopping in Gold Beach. Fishermen will find charters, guides, excellent launch and moorage facilities and a couple of large tackle shops.

In the relatively short stretch of Rogue tidewater, around the jetties and offshore there are ample opportunities to catch fish. Several charters and many smaller private boats make the trip over the short bar crossing, finnicky but polite on calm summer days. They seek feeding chinook, silvers and some tremendous bottomfish populations on steep, jagged nearshore pinnacles. From the jetties, fishermen catch salmon in the summer and pinkfin perch spring through fall. In tidewater, you can troll or anchor to catch salmon, sea-run cutthroat, steelhead, smelt or shad.

A simple diving plane-and-herring rig accounts for many of the salmon taken off the Rogue, as this skipper on a charter out of Jot's Resort shows.

Rogue River Salmon—Spring, Summer And Fall

The Rogue is blessed with several runs of salmon, including at least one major run for each of three seasons. In recent years, Rogue chinook in particular have shown tremendous resurgence, making the river one of the truly bright spots on the Oregon coast. The strength of south coast chinook stocks is reflected at least in part from the absence of quotas south of Humbug Mountain (at least at press time) as a determining factor in ocean salmon fishing closures.

At least part of that success may be due to a more controlled commercial impact thanks to an international salmon ocean interception treaty, but much of it stems from STEP, the state's cooperative Salmon Trout Enhancement Program. Early efforts from the program in the mid1980s brought great results. What began as STEP releases from Indian Creek have now given way to full hatchery production there, bringing even greater numbers of salmon upriver.

A very strong spring chinook run moves in about April, making the Rogue one of the finest estuaries in the Northwest for spring salmon fishing. "Springers" tend to move quickly to destinations far upriver to spawn, pausing long enough in the upper reaches of tidewater to be taken by fishermen in boats anchored around the Elephant Rock area. These fishermen use spreader rigs with 2 to 4 ounces of weight and a no. 5 spinner (or in clear water a no. 3 or 4 spinner). Anglers who want to try their luck from shore can try the Ferry Hole.

Summer-run fish begin showing up offshore by June and in the lower bay during July and August. Ocean salmon catches, once dominated by silvers, are now increasingly chinook. Most are taken by trollers who fish anchovies or herring behind a planer or mooching sinker (unless they have downriggers). Charters generally offer four-hour trips, with fishing grounds a quick ride out past the short jetties.

By midsummer, many small boaters need not be concerned with crossing the bar since summer-run kings are coming to them. Chinook move into the bay with the flood tide to feed on baitfish, often moving back out on the ebb. But during the flood tide, anglers troll bait or large spinners between the jetties. (Not only is fishing best then but it is also the safest time, since engine trouble won't mean being swept out over the bar.) It may get quite crowded here at times.

The area between the jaws and on upriver beyond the Coast Guard station to the mailboat dock is popular. It is also fairly shallow, so less weight is needed to keep rigs similar to those used offshore near bottom. Also, within this area, keep an eye out for diving pelicans which may signal schools of baitfish.

Kings may stack up in the lower bay in considerable numbers, hanging around and feeding until the first heavy rains. Then a large portion of fish will push on upriver. And as more rains move in, the pattern continues.

In the fall, inmigrations of chinook are joined by silvers. Although the Rogue's enormous run of wild silvers was decimated years ago, possibly from intensive logging upstream, there has been at least some success in restoring coho here.

From midsummer through early fall, jetty fishermen often target efforts on salmon. The relatively small distance between jetties and the great numbers of salmon that pass between them allow rockhoppers a pretty good shot at success. Some jetty enthusiasts travel to the Rogue specifically to fish for salmon.

Many use a weighted, baited wire spreader below a Styrofoam or plastic float. As much as 2 ounces of weight may be used to keep either an anchovy or a herring down. Others cast spoons (crystal Dardevles have been popular here for some years) or metal jigs such as Buzz Bombs or Darts. Incoming tide is almost inevitably prime time. Serious salmon enthusiasts who fish the jetties have a long-handled net with them.

I have heard reports of anglers who drift cluster eggs inside the south jetty for steelhead. Although never substantiated, catching steelhead this way doesn't seem impossible considering charter skippers report that fall steelhead are occasionally picked up while trolling for salmon in the lower bay.

Once chinook have begun pouring into the lower river, the focus for some anglers shifts from the river mouth to upper tidewater. Boaters run up to the Clay Bank and beyond to anchor and fish either bait or spinners.

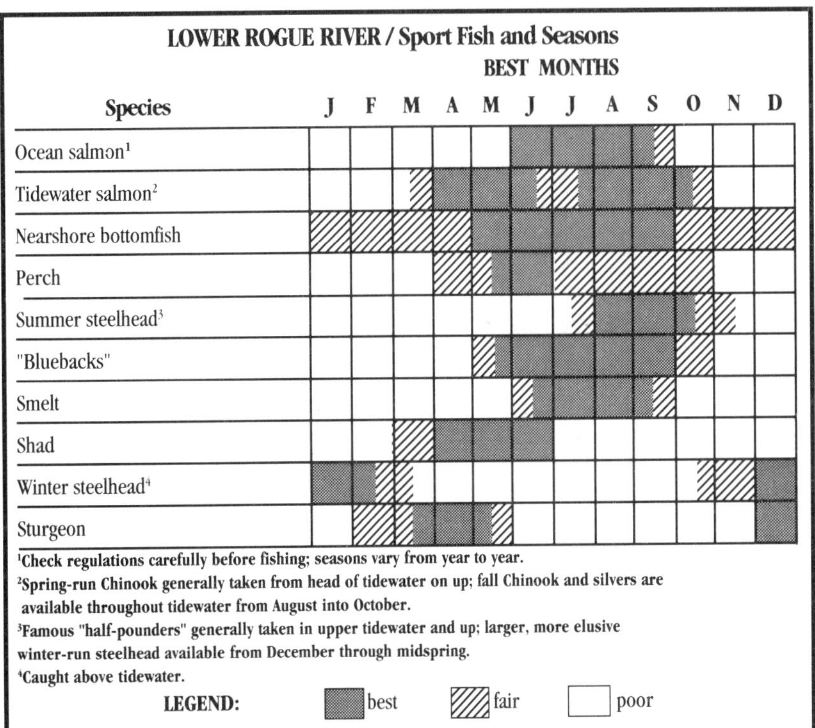

LOWER ROGUE RIVER / Sport Fish and Seasons

BEST MONTHS

Species	J	F	M	A	M	J	J	A	S	O	N	D
Ocean salmon[1]	poor	poor	poor	poor	poor	best	best	best	best/fair	poor	poor	poor
Tidewater salmon[2]	poor	poor	poor/fair	best	best	best/fair	fair/best	best	best	best/fair	poor	poor
Nearshore bottomfish	fair	fair	fair	fair	best	best	best	best	best	fair	fair	fair
Perch	poor	poor	poor	fair	fair/best	best	fair	fair	fair	fair	poor	poor
Summer steelhead[3]	poor	poor	poor	poor	poor	poor	poor/fair	best	best	best/fair	fair/poor	poor
"Bluebacks"	poor	poor	poor	poor	fair/best	best	best	best	best	fair	poor	poor
Smelt	poor	poor	poor	poor	poor	fair/best	best	best	best/fair	poor	poor	poor
Shad	poor	poor	fair	best	best	best	poor	poor	poor	poor	poor	poor
Winter steelhead[4]	best	best/fair	fair/poor	poor	poor	poor	poor	poor	poor	poor/fair	fair	best
Sturgeon	poor	fair	fair/best	best	best/fair	poor	poor	poor	poor	poor	poor	best

[1]Check regulations carefully before fishing; seasons vary from year to year.
[2]Spring-run Chinook generally taken from head of tidewater on up; fall Chinook and silvers are available throughout tidewater from August into October.
[3]Famous "half-pounders" generally taken in upper tidewater and up; larger, more elusive winter-run steelhead available from December through midspring.
[4]Caught above tidewater.

LEGEND: best fair poor

Nearby Offshore Reefs: Labyrinths Of Pinnacles, Loads Of Bottomfish

Just a few minutes outside the river mouth is an expanse of reefs, collectively (on NOAA nautical chart #18601) known as Rogue Reef. Here and there rocks jut from the surf-washed waters; in other spots they don't quite make it and lush kelp beds mark their presence near the surface.

Running along the reef while graphing the bottom on a chart recorder will reveal endless summits and chasms, with very little flat or smooth area between. If that isn't heaven for lingcod and rockfish, there isn't any. Despite its proximity to the harbor, bottomfishing pressure on this area has not been overwhelming.

Another topnotch series of reefs is located a bit farther south, south of the river mouth and a little farther out, in waters 20 to 40 fathoms. Personal experience makes for fond remembrances of these reefs.

The currents around the reefs—especially the shallower, jagged peaks of Rogue Reef—can be swift enough to make fishing tough and the loss of tackle high. Try to pick a day when currents aren't too bad and the wind drift is minimal. On such days, try light gear for plenty of fish and considerably more fun, especially when fishing metal or leadhead jigs with plastic tails. With lines of 8-to 14-pound test, jigs of no more than 2 or 3 ounces will suffice.

Two-pound Bluebacks And "Half-pound" Steelhead

Most years, very substantial populations of sea-run cutthroat are feeding in the lower Rogue. They are particularly numerous from late spring through early summer, when bank fishermen find them feeding around gravel bars just above the U.S. Highway 101 bridge. They plunk a chunk of meat such as a sculpin or anchovy filet on an incoming tide. Sea-runs well over 18-20 inches are taken this way, though the more usual coastal average of 14 to 18 inches prevails. The small cadre of trollers that actually expends much serious effort on cutts in the Rogue pull small spinners or Flatfish. The rig so popular in coastal estuaries of northern Oregon—trolling blades and nightcrawlers—is less popular here, though it may be equally effective.

The lower Rogue River produces some of the state's largest chinook. (Photo courtesy Jot's Resort)

Lower Rogue River

Legend

1. Rogue River reef—bottomfish.
2. North & South jetties—perch & smelt, (spring & summer).
3. Lower tidewater—trolling & bank fishing (summer-fall).
4. Creek mouths—sea-run cutthroat, shad (late spring-summer).
5. Upper tidewater—salmon (spring-fall), steelhead (winter).

■ Launch Site

Scale: 15/16'' = 1 nautical mile

Chart #18601

Not for navigational purposes.

Small Boat Safety— Crossing The Bar

The Rogue River bar has not been widely known as a friendly crossing. In fact, its channel is very narrow and tricky much of the time. On the other hand, when the ocean is calm the crossing may be fast and effortless.

The jetties are short and end in shallow water. So even when calm seas prevail (the only time small boats should even consider crossing), consideration should be given to tides for the return trip since a strong ebb can set up large breakers with even a modest swell. Plan to come back during flood or dead slack water.

The channel lies along the north jetty. Shoal water lies along the south side—and prevailing northwesterlies have been known to set boats without power into breakers over these dangerous shallows. Run straight out toward the bell buoy far past the ends of the jetties, since breakers may occur as far as 1,000 feet out.

Good salmon fishing between the jaws creates additional concerns. Don't try it without a good anchor and plenty of rope, all quickly accessible. With so many trollers in a small area, line occasionally ends up spinning around a propellor. The result, if a strong ebb tide is running or a strong northwesterly is blowing, can be disastrous. A disabled boat should anchor immediately and call for help.

From the highest reaches of tidewater and on upriver, the Rogue offers one of the most productive runs of summer steelhead anywhere.

This particular run is unusual in many respects. It is long in duration, beginning in July and continuing through October. These summer steelhead generally do *not* grow large. They are known as "half-pounders" though in fact they usually run at least a couple pounds and up to six or so. Half-pounders are characterized by their great numbers, aggressive feeding and wild fight when hooked.

"Plunkers" take them from the bank, casting out bait and waiting, while others cast plugs, hardware or flies. But more are taken from river boats, anchored or drifting. I have done well with small Hot Shots. Visitors to the area will, of course, have their best chance to enjoy fast steelheading from a guide boat. Several guides are available in and around Gold Beach and through Jot's Resort.

Swarms Of Spring Perch Around The Jetties

Late spring perch fishing off the Rogue jetties is often very fast and productive. Pinkfins and some striped perch can be taken year-round, but the fastest fishing occurs in May and June. Those who fish the south jetty might try the sandbar.

Sand shrimp are always popular as bait, but when pinkfins are feeding along the Rogue jetties they'll take mussel meat, clam necks, marine worms and other natural baits. Probably no one knows the river's fisheries from all angles better than longtime resident and charter skipper John Briggs, who told me he does well for perch using a tiny F4 Flatfish with a bit of weight. Perch can be caught just about anywhere along both jetties, though some favor the north jetty.

Although often the perch offer fishing just about as fast as it gets, it would be a mistake to expect hot action automatically. There are plenty of off-periods when hardly a perch can be found. No one's ever been able to predict the movements of perch from day to day.

Rogue River Bottomfishing: A Fast, Full Four Hours

One August afternoon I hopped aboard the charter *Shamrock*, skippered by veteran Gold Beach charter captain Dennis Anderson. Salmon fishing that morning had been dead slow, and at least one group of anglers had the good sense to try a four-hour trip for bottomfish.

They never regretted that decision. Anderson quickly found fish and in several long gentle drifts over these reefs (on what also happened to be an ideal day: the merest of breezes and a light current) everyone aboard had caught lingcod. In fact, we ended up limiting (which at that time meant three lings per person) with lings averaging about 20 pounds and running to nearly 40, and added lots of rockfish—bright orange canaries, dusky red vermilions and shiny blacks to five pounds, primarily.

As on any bottomfishing trip, there was no lack of excitement, especially aboard a boat of inland anglers unaware of the ling's habit of following up a hooked fish and engulfing it before it could be cranked to the surface. So seemingly little fish grew suddenly very heavy, offering a particular flurry of commotion when the toothy brown fish the length of man's leg appeared next to the boat.

In no time, the trip was over, all too soon. But the full fishbox showed a day's worth of bottomfish, all taken in four fast, memorable hours, all within a short hop of the Rogue River jetties.

Rogue Benchwarmers: Sturgeon, Smelt, Shad

How times change. "There *are* sturgeon in the lower Rogue River....This is never likely to be a signficant fishery, however." Those words appeared in the first edition of this book, written in the early 1980s when the best evidence from decades of fishing and from all local experts and biologists all pointed to that conclusion.

But as they've done in other Oregon estuaries, fishermen have discovered lower Rogue sturgeon and the effort seems to increase each year. Much of it is in the Clay Bank area in upper tidewater just below the ferry hole, particularly through the spring months. The fish at this time of year lay in deep eddies where they'll suck in sand shrimp fairly willingly for both boat and bank fishermen. Many oversize fish (over 72 inches) are released. A somewhat higher portion of greens to whites has been showing in the Rogue.

Shad are less appreciated here than in many other estuaries where they occur. They move into the lower Rogue, often in considerable numbers, each spring and offer fast fishing. Probably most here are caught incidentally on the little jigs to catch herring for bait, though a few anglers do take advantage of them and fish riffles with shad darts.

Anglers motor in among the shelter of towering cliffs at Port Orford on a windy day to cast for rockfish and other species.

Jigging with strings of tiny gold hooks with nylon or yarn is a popular pastime for anglers fishing from the north jetty during the summer when schools of smelt move in. Anchovies may be mixed with them. Those who prefer snagging to jigging use three trebles hooks. As with most estuarial fisheries, incoming tide is the best bet when seeking smelt along the rocks. When they are thick, small boaters occasionally pull in near the north jetty to fish for them.

Several runs of salmon move up the Rogue in spring, summer and fall.

Although not a primary target for many anglers fishing the Rogue, shad can offer some action on light gear.

Just under 30 miles north of the Rogue is the tiny coastal community of Port Orford, popular in the summer for the fact that its harbor is tucked away from the then-predominant northwest winds. Port Orford offers another attraction: boaters here can reach the ocean without worrying about crossing a bar. (In fact, it's the only port in Oregon located on the open ocean. On the other hand, if a southwesterly blows up, there is no protection.)

Most of the limited fleet of vessels moored here in summer are commercial boats. There are no regular charters, no major marinas for recreational boaters and no paved launch ramp. There is, however, a sling hoist at the harbor.

On calm days even cartoppers fish here. (Some make use of an old, rough, one-lane ramp—but no boat should be launched here if it can't be carried to and from the water.) And even though this is in fact part of the "windbelt" that keeps the south coast very breezy much of the time, August and September days are often very calm. Loaded with rocky reefs, the offshore waters here offer bottom-fishing as good as anyplace to be found on the Oregon coast—including a shot at some of the state's biggest lingcod. Fishing for chinook can be excellent, also.

Even visitors without boats can take advantage of the habitat. Wherever they can gain access to the water, beneath or around towering and jagged cliffs, shore fishermen casting bait or jigs catch rockfish, small lings, greenling, cabezon and perch.

There is a small tackle shop called "The Dock" at the harbor, open in season. Much of its tackle is oriented to commercial fishing, but some sportfishing supplies and information may be available.

There are two excellent state campgrounds nearby, Humbug Mountain State Park (6 miles south) and Cape Blanco State Park (9 miles north). The latter, atop high cliffs overlooking the austere lighthouse, may be one of the nicest campgrounds on the Oregon coast. Tall, thick hedges between the spacious, grassy campsites provide an unusual degree of seclusion.

North and south of Cape Blanco are the Sixes and Elk rivers, respectively. The lower reaches of these rivers are worth checking out if you're going to be in the area from mid- to late fall. Some very impressive fall salmon runs crowd into these rivers. With them come crowds of anglers. The popularity of these rather isolated rivers skyrocketed in the 1970s. Drifters and plunkers now pack the river when kings are in.

For more general information about this area, write the Port Orford Chamber of Commerce, P.O. Box 637, Port Orford, OR 97465 or call 332-8055.

The configuration of the coastline and an extended jetty offer protection from northwest swells during summer months at the Port Orford harbor.

Facilities

All phone numbers listed are within the 503 area code unless otherwise noted.

Charters, Guides

While the two charters below are not fancy, they are adequate for the job—and both skippers Dennis Anderson (Shamrock) and John Briggs have been doing that job for many, many years. The rate for a standard 4-hour trip salmon or bottomfish trip at press time was $40. These charters typically offer 4 such trips per day, leaving at 6 a.m., 10 a.m. and 2 p.m.

Briggs Charter, 95691 Jerry's Flat Road, Gold Beach 97444, 247-7150.

Shamrock Charters, P.O. Box J, Gold Beach 97444, 247-6676. Operates out of Jot's Resort.

There are a wealth of guides operating on the lower Rogue River. Figure on roughly $100 to 150/day per person, at least at press time. Guides can be booked through most resorts and/or tackle dealers. In particular, **Jot's Resort** can supply guides at any time. Farther upriver, the **Rogue Fly and Tackle Company** in Medford at 779-6445, books for many river guides. One independent guide is Mike Hoefer at **Rogue Sportfishing Unlimited** who fishes tidewater and up (as well as the Elk, Sixes, Chetco and California's Smith rivers). He can be reached at P.O. Box 872 in Gold Beach 97444, 247-6358. **Greg Eide** fishes the Rogue for salmon and steelhead: P.O. Box 1248, Gold Beach 97444, 247-2608.

Resorts, Marinas

Four Seasons Trailer Resort, 96526 North Bank Road, Gold Beach 97444, 247-7959. Open all year, all day. 45 RV spaces, also some tentsites. 15 moorage slips, fuel, paved single-lane launch ramp in good shape. Bait and tackle, recreational hall, laundry facilities, guide service. Located about 7 miles above Gold Beach: the head-of-tidewater stretch here is excellent for salmon and steelhead. Nonboaters do very well at times right form the dock (free for guests' use; slight charge for nonguests). Sturgeon are also taken here, occasionally.

Indian Creek Recreational Park, 94680 Jerry's Flat Road, Gold Beach 97444. Open year-round, daily. 100 RV/tent sites—tent area is separate, in back of RV area, more quiet and wooded for a bit of seclusion. Lodge offers all guests free coffee and tea, plus a recreation area with pool and ping-pong and more. Laundry facilites, restaurant, store, large grassy play area.

Jot's Resort, P.O. Box J, Gold Beach 97444 (on north side of river, just below Highway 101 bridge), 247-6676. Open year-round, daily. 140 waterfront condo, motel units (many elegant two-story condo units with high-beamed ceilings, loft bedrooms and wood-burning fireplaces). Single-lane paved launch ramp generally adequate. 30 moorage slips, fuel (straight gas and premix), huge tackle shop, charter.

Oceanside RV Park, Route 2, Box 1514, Gold Beach 97444, 247-2301. May-October. 36 spaces with hookups, 50 tentsites. Location is great for anglers, right at base of south jetty, though esthetically unrewarding—an open, gravel lot. Office sells some bait and tackle; caters especially to jetty fishermen.

Port of Gold Beach, P.O. Box 1126, Gold Beach 97444, 247-6269. Office open Monday-Friday, year-round. Dock space available for guest moorage. Gas and diesel, engine repair, some bait and tackle. Launch ramp good at low tides, modest launch fee. RV park.

Bait And Tackle

Jot's Resort, P.O. Box J, Gold Beach 97444, 247-6676 (ask for tackle store). Open 6 a.m.-10 p.m. daily, year-round. Very large, exceedingly well-stocked shop for just about any fishing-related need. Also books guides.

Rogue Outdoor Store, P.O. Box 726, 560 North Ellensburg, Gold Beach 97444, 247-7142. Open daily, year-round. Carries lots of steelhead gear as well as tackle for salmon and bottomfishing.

Public Campgrounds

Cape Blanco State Park, 9 miles north of Port Orford off Highway 101, 332-6774. 58 sites with electrical hookup, hiker-biker camp. Awesome view from high cliffs at lighthouse and secluded campsites separated by tall hedges.

Humbug Mountain State Park, 6 miles south of Port Orford off Highway 101, 332-6774. 78 tentsites, 30 RV spaces with hookups, hiker-biker camp.

For More Information

Gold Beach-Wedderburn Chamber of Commerce, 510 South Ellensburg, Gold Beach 97444, 247-7526, toll-free in-state at 800-452-2334 or toll-free nationwide at 800-542-2334. (Ask for brochure "Where to Stay and Play at the Beach.")

Lower Chetco River

It's a long way to just about anywhere from the mouth of the Chetco River, but no matter where you live, it's probably worth the drive if you enjoy fishing the ocean from a private boat.

What you'll find here, about 4 miles from the California border, are 3 essential ingredients for a successful coastal trip for small boaters: great fishing, a benevolent bar and ample facilities.

These words could be lifted from a local promotional pamphlet, but in fact they're honest impressions based upon experience. The harbor here provides acres of fine small-boat moorage, a super multilane launch area with floats and well-equipped fish-cleaning stations nearby, a tackle shop as complete and wellstocked as any on the coast (with adjacent restaurant), a large beachside RV area, charter and guide boats, and excellent Coast Guard facilities (including an 80-foot tower looking out over the very busy bar to monitor small boat traffic). The bar here is one of the safest and, much of the time, most readily crossed by small boaters.

With the ocean so accessible, so full of chinook (many headed north to the Rogue) and so full of bottomfish-laden rocky reefs, it is logical that most interest among fishermen here is directed toward fishing "outside." That's not to say that tidewater fishing is not very productive in the fall, when many relatively monstrous chinook—some 50 to 60 pounds—are taken in the lower river. Flyfishermen take a share of those big kings in the Chetco, below the Highway 101 bridge. Cutthroat are also commonly taken in this area.

Some of the best nearshore bottomfishing along the Northwest coast awaits, north and south, once out of the jetties. It's a small-boat, light-tackle angler's paradise. The rocky coastline also offers nonboaters a chance to try for bottomfish and perch.

Ocean Salmon: Nearshore And Offshore, Action All Summer

Chinook have become increasingly numerous in ocean catches off the Chetco, based in part on the strength of healthy south coast runs. Many kings are caught within a mile or two of shore and often by surprisingly small boats. If the chinook fishing is slow, many seaworthy boats will head farther offshore in search of coho.

Traditional trolling is popular, most often with medium diving planes pulling whole anchovies. But downriggers have become much more prevalent in recent years, not only allowing anglers to use lighter lines and fight fish unencumbered with gear on the line, but to get baits deeper when chinook are targeted. Some anglers in these waters have found drift-or motor-mooching effective.

During the 1980s, the ocean around the Chetco River mouth was particularly popular with small boaters in the fall since it offered a special late-season nearshore fishery for chinook that remained open most of the fall months. More recently, south coast chinook fishing has ended in early September outside of the river mouth, so fishing will be limited to the lower river.

The Chetco's fall run does enter the river late: often October and November are a prime months.

Tidewater Salmon: Trolling And Flyfishing

Fall tidewater fishing for salmon many be shortlived, depending upon rainfall. Lots of rain will send most of the salmon that are hanging around the lower river shooting upriver past tidewater in a rush. But until those rains set in, there can be some hot tidewater fishing for some very big kings. (Fish topping the 60-pound mark have been occasionally taken.)

Many anglers fish from the jaws on up to the Highway 101 bridge, trolling whole anchovies on wire spreaders with 1 to 3 ounces of weight. But locally popular is a specialized fishery among flycasting enthusiasts. They work the river below the 101 bridge from small prams and the like, casting Comets or shrimp patterns and take some impressive salmon.

Sea-run cutthroat (bluebacks) to around 20 inches are available in tidewater, late spring and, particularly, late summer. Much as in the Rogue, small bright spoons and spinners are popular, but plunkers do well using filets of sculpin ("bullhead") or anchovies. The two main difficulties you may find fishing Chetco cutthroat, especially as a nonboater, are limited bank access and omnipresent moss growth in the river.

The Chetco offers fine winter steelheading—above tidewater, of course. Some will run to 15 or 20 pounds. The Winchuck, a few miles south (immediately above the Oregon-California border) is also a good bet for steelhead from about Thanksgiving through March. Some late fall chinook and summer sea-run cutthroat are also taken in Winchuck tidewaters.

Bottomfishing Nirvana For Small Boaters

Just about any direction you want to go once you clear the Chetco River bar, you'll find rocky reefs loaded with bottomfish. Rocky headlands dominate the southern Oregon coastline for mile upon mile. Just offshore, the bottom drops away steeply and is as rocky beneath the surface as the visible coast.

Lingcod are a major feature and prize of this fishery. All species of rockfish are taken, including fair numbers of red vermilions and larger yelloweye. Many of these larger bottomfish are taken in relatively shallow water, often 50 to 100 feet.

I've enjoyed some spectacular light-tackle bottomfish action over reefs here; no one who recognizes the sporting potential of bottomfish should plan a trip here without taking light gear with 8- to 12-pound line and jigs.

Even ultralight tackle can be used for the greatest thrill and in fact line testing 4 pounds is perfect for big schools of abundant black rockfish ("black snapper" or "sea bass") from 2 or 3 pounds to 7 or 8. These are often at or near the surface and on light line may make runs to rival a salmon of similar size. I found that to be the case, drifting in calm seas off submerged boulders in 20 to 40 feet of water and casting small leadheads or lures such as Mirrolures and diving Rebels much as one might in a northern lake. (Generally, stick with brighter colors for this shallow fishing—yellows, pinks, silver, gold, white). And when large black rockfish are schooling at the surface, flyfishermen will enjoy action they won't soon forget—or find almost anywhere else on the Northwest coast.

Local anglers can enjoy the bottomfishing here year-round. The real determinant of fishing activity from November through April or so is, of course, the ocean. Between Pacific storms, a calm winter day or two can make for some fast bottomfishing, particularly for large female lings moving in to spawn.

Small Boat Safety—Crossing The Bar

"The safest bar on the Oregon coast" is the local tag hung on this river entrance. It is a label not easily disputed. After all, the Chetco bar doesn't face west, into the Pacific, as do most other Oregon bars. Rather, it looks south-southwest. Incoming westerly breakers crash into the outside of the west jetty, so small boaters needn't face oncoming swells. Some years, only the Columbia River registers more bar crossings by small boaters than the Chetco.

There are dangerous areas, nevertheless. As with all jetties, avoid crossing over or near the submerged ends of these jetties. One tricky area lies well inside the jetties. Inside (east) of the west jetty, about two-thirds of the way up from the end, is a large shoal area, between the jetty and the main channel. This may appear navigable at higher tides, but is in fact shallow and rock-strewn and should be avoided.

The entrance channel is always shifting slightly: stay within the red and white range markers when entering or leaving.

The rough bar advisory sign is located on the Coast Guard fuel dock, facing north-northwest. When pleasure boat traffic is high, the Coast Guard monitors the bar from an 80-foot tower at the base of the east jetty.

The gentle bar and calm ocean lure even cartoppers outside into the Pacific to try for chinook. These smaller boats should be particularly alert for changing conditions and be ready to head in quickly. Many anglers fish the rocky reefs nearshore. Many of these reefs ascend to just under the surface or even above, with rocks sticking well out of the water. Often excellent light-tackle casting can be enjoyed right around such pinnacles, but beware: fish close only on truly calm days, for even slight breakers can thrust the unaware boater into the rocks in a hurry or drop him on those barely submerged.

U.S. Coast GUARD—CHETCO River

Weather/bar conditions (recording) 469-4571
Information, station phone 469-3885

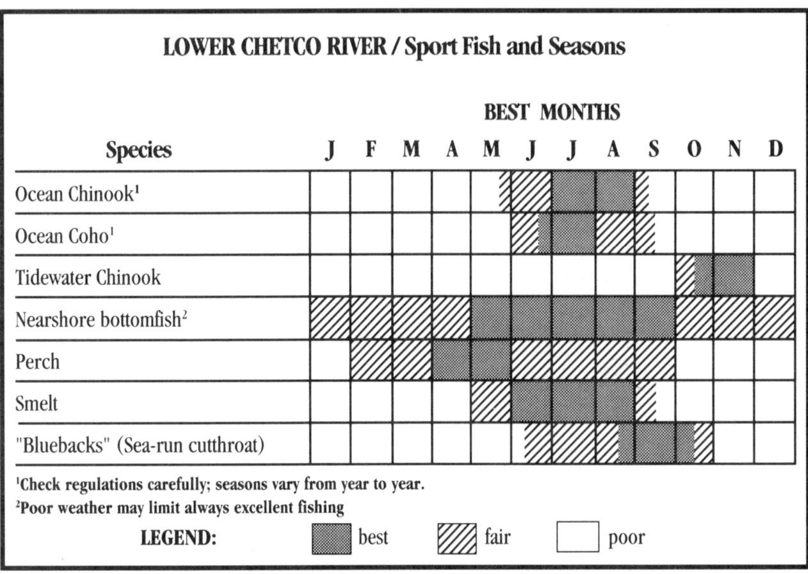

LOWER CHETCO RIVER / Sport Fish and Seasons

Species	J	F	M	A	M	J	J	A	S	O	N	D
	BEST MONTHS											
Ocean Chinook[1]	poor	poor	poor	poor	poor/fair	fair	best	best	fair/poor	poor	poor	poor
Ocean Coho[1]	poor	poor	poor	poor	poor	fair/best	best	fair	fair/poor	poor	poor	poor
Tidewater Chinook	poor	poor	poor	poor	poor	poor	poor	poor	poor	fair/best	best	poor
Nearshore bottomfish[2]	fair	fair	fair	fair	best	best	best	best	best	fair	fair	fair
Perch	poor	fair	fair	best	best	fair	fair	fair	fair	poor	poor	poor
Smelt	poor	poor	poor	poor	fair	best	best	best	fair/poor	poor	poor	poor
"Bluebacks" (Sea-run cutthroat)	poor	poor	poor	poor	poor	poor/fair	fair	fair/best	best	best/fair	poor	poor

[1]Check regulations carefully; seasons vary from year to year.
[2]Poor weather may limit always excellent fishing

LEGEND: best / fair / poor

Fishing The Jetties And Rocky Surf

Good access and good fishing make jetty fishing popular at the Chetco River mouth. There is particularly easy access to the east jetty, where redtail and striped or rainbow perch and some flounder are taken much of the year, probably in greatest numbers during April and May. The west jetty seems more productive for lingcod and rockfish, spring through fall. (Winter action slows when turbid freshwater runoff fills the jaws.) Most fishermen use bait on one or two dropper hooks above a 1- to 4-ounce sinker.

There is also a jetty fishery for salmon at the Chetco, in the late summer and early fall. A bait rig successfully used here is a slight variation on jetty tackle used elsewhere along the coast. A leader of 4 or 5 feet separates an anchovy on a 2-hook mooching rig from a 1 1/2- to 4-ounce mooching sinker. No float is used above the leader. Rather, a cork float is attached to the leader about two-thirds down its length. This keeps the bait above the rocks, rather than snagged in them, and fluttering in the current. Some anglers cast shiny, heavy spoons such as Kastmaster and Krocodiles.

As one might surmise, there is a great deal of rocky surf fishing along this southernmost Oregon coast. State parks such as Harris Beach and Lone Ranch to the north are among the good access points. Just about anywhere

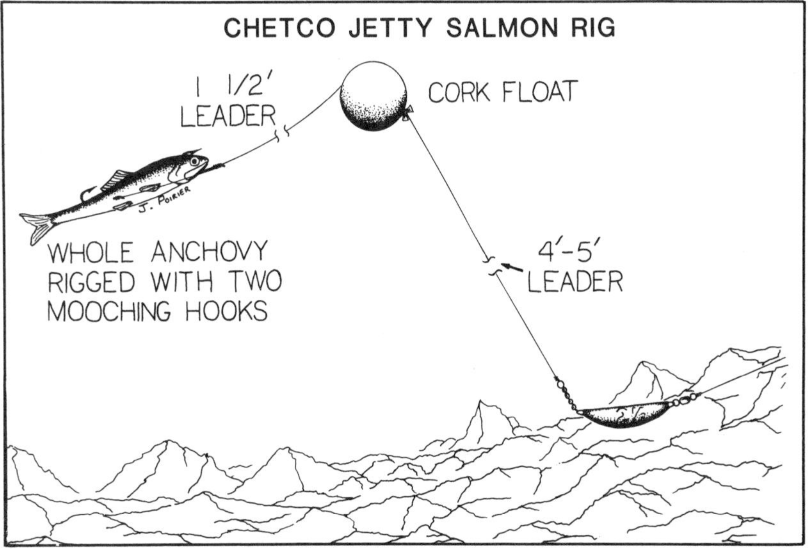

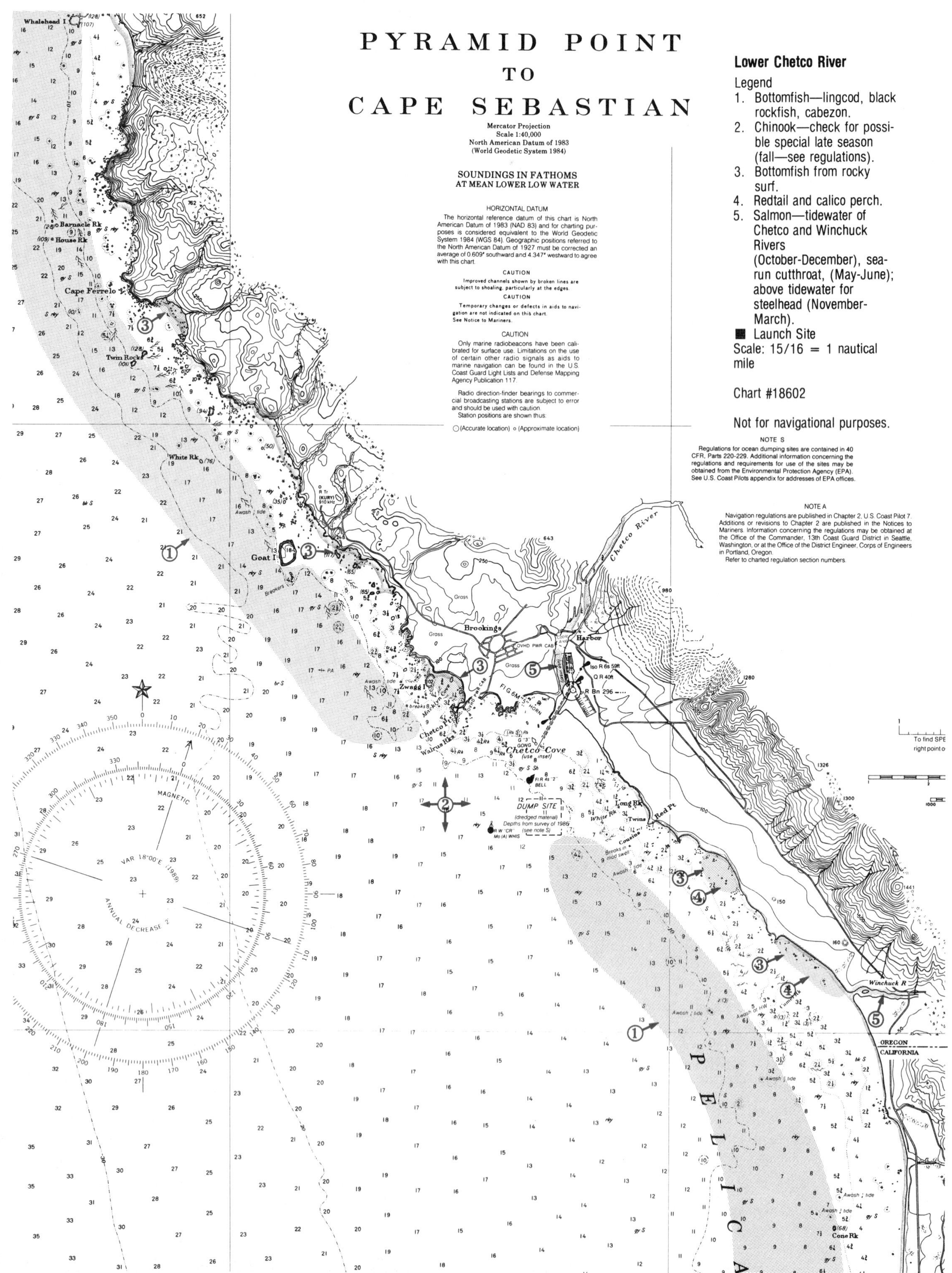
PYRAMID POINT
TO
CAPE SEBASTIAN
Mercator Projection
Scale 1:40,000
North American Datum of 1983
(World Geodetic System 1984)
SOUNDINGS IN FATHOMS
AT MEAN LOWER LOW WATER
HORIZONTAL DATUM
The horizontal reference datum of this chart is North American Datum of 1983 (NAD 83) and for charting purposes is considered equivalent to the World Geodetic System 1984 (WGS 84). Geographic positions referred to the North American Datum of 1927 must be corrected an average of 0.609" southward and 4.347" westward to agree with this chart.
CAUTION
Improved channels shown by broken lines are subject to shoaling, particularly at the edges.
CAUTION
Temporary changes or defects in aids to navigation are not indicated on this chart. See Notice to Mariners.
CAUTION
Only marine radiobeacons have been calibrated for surface use. Limitations on the use of certain other radio signals as aids to marine navigation can be found in the U.S. Coast Guard Light Lists and Defense Mapping Agency Publication 117.
Radio direction-finder bearings to commercial broadcasting stations are subject to error and should be used with caution.
Station positions are shown thus:
(Accurate location) (Approximate location)
Lower Chetco River
Legend
1. Bottomfish—lingcod, black rockfish, cabezon.
2. Chinook—check for possible special late season (fall—see regulations).
3. Bottomfish from rocky surf.
4. Redtail and calico perch.
5. Salmon—tidewater of Chetco and Winchuck Rivers (October-December), sea-run cutthroat, (May-June); above tidewater for steelhead (November-March).
Launch Site
Scale: 15/16 = 1 nautical mile
Chart #18602
Not for navigational purposes.
NOTE S
Regulations for ocean dumping sites are contained in 40 CFR, Parts 220-229. Additional information concerning the regulations and requirements for use of the sites may be obtained from the Environmental Protection Agency (EPA). See U.S. Coast Pilots appendix for addresses of EPA offices.
NOTE A
Navigation regulations are published in Chapter 2, U.S. Coast Pilot 7. Additions or revisions to Chapter 2 are published in the Notices to Mariners. Information concerning the regulations may be obtained at the Office of the Commander, 13th Coast Guard District in Seattle, Washington, or at the Office of the District Engineer, Corps of Engineers in Portland, Oregon.
Refer to charted regulation section numbers.
Whalehead I
Barnacle Rk
House Rk
Cape Ferrelo
Twin Rocks
White Rk
Goat I
Brookings
Harbor
Chetco River
Zwagg I
Chetco Pt
Walrus Rk
Chetco Cove
DUMP SITE
(dredged material)
Depths from survey of 1986
(see note S)
Long Rk
Twins
Red Pt
Cousins
Winchuck R
Cone Rk
OREGON
CALIFORNIA
MAGNETIC
VAR 18°00'E (1989)
ANNUAL DECREASE 2'
PELICA

Angler rigs up while kneeling among rocks of jetty. Photo by Terry Rudnick.

one can find access, one can find fish—typically smaller rockfish and lings, greenling and cabezon. During those occasional winter periods of calm season, this fishing can be especially rewarding.

Whenever the surf is high, remember that fishing will be not only tough but potentially dangerous on this rugged coast. Also, watch the tides. Surfcasters have been stranded on rocks as the flooding tide cuts off their route back to the shore. Children are particularly vulnerable and small kids are likely to require too much watching to do much serious fishing.

Plenty of surfperch are taken in the area, also. Spring is a fine time to fish for them around Winchuck River mouth. After the April-May spawning period, just about the entire coastline along U.S. Highway 101 from the Winchuck south to the Smith River (California) can be good for redtails. Perch are also among the species taken from Harris Beach. Often any sandy "pocket beach" between rocky points will yield plenty of perch to fishermen casting either out from the beach or parallel to shore from out on the rocks.

The Chetco jetties themselves can offer some fabulous perch fishing in the spring and can be very productive on and off from midwinter through late fall. Methods and baits used are similar to those of other jetties—small hooks baited with shrimp or other natural baits set above the sinker.

Bait (and food) fish are also taken at times from the jetties—often smelt and in the summer anchovies and occasionally herring. At times schools of baitfish can be thick right in the harbor around the docks. Some anglers snag them with treble hooks, but many prefer jigging with strings of tiny, bright hooks.

Facilities

All phone numbers listed are within the 503 area code unless otherwise noted.

Charters, Guides

Six to 8 different charters were operating out of this harbor at press time, of which 4 booked through the Sporthaven. Rates are similar to those elsewhere along the northern Oregon coast, with $50 an average rate at press time for a 5-hour salmon or bottomfish trip. Some boats offer special 8-hour light tackle trips for an additional $35 to 40. With so much good, rocky habitat all around and one of the state's better bar crossings, it isn't surprising that many charters operate year-round, weather and interest permitting. Salmon of course take precedence May into September (according to seasons).

Dick's Sporthaven Marina, P.O. Box 2215, Harbor 97415, 469-3301. 4 independent boats charter through the Sporthaven, from 28' to 40' (6 to 15 passengers, respectively).

Marty K Charters, P.O. Box 985, Brookings 97415, 469-2551. two 6-passenger boats, 28' and 36'.

Leta J Charters, 97748 North Bank, Brookings 97415, 469-6964. One 40' boat for up to 15 people.

With several productive salmon/steelhead rivers along this general stretch of coast, most river guides who fish the Chetco also fish other streams such as the Rogue, Elk, Sixes and Smith. At press time you could figure on spending $100 to 150 for a day of guided fishing.

A few of the many guides here: **Ray Benner** in Brookings at 469-5965, **Ken Mountain** in Brookings at 469-3043, **Six Rivers Guide Service** in Crescent City, California at 707-458-3577.

The multi-lane launch ramp at the Chetco harbor is one of the nicest, largest ramps on the Northwest Coast. Behind it is a huge harbor with small-boat transient moorage at a very reasonable rate.

Marinas, Bait And Tackle

Brookings Sports Unlimited, P.O. Box C, Brookings 97415, 469-4012. Open 7 days/week and carries pretty much everything for salmon.

Dick's Sporthaven Marina, P.O. Box 2215, Harbor 97415 (at head of boat basin), 469-3301. Open 7 days/week, year-round. Adjacent to Port of Brookings moorage and outstanding public launch ramp. Gas and diesel fuel. Engine repair nearby. Charter boats, restaurant and bar. Huge tackle shop with a great selection of just about everything.

Loring's Lighthouse Sporting Goods, P.O. Box L, Brookings 97415, 469-2148. Open Monday-Saturday. Fair selection of salmon and steelhead gear.

Port of Brookings, P.O. Box 848, Brookings 97415, 469-2218. Open 7 days/week. 900 slips—lot of transient moorage in very well-protected harbor. Gas and diesel fuel. One of best launch ramps on the northwest coast, with 8 paved lanes in great shape separated by four floats; launch at any tide. Moderate launch fee. Adjacent fish-cleaning stations. Also a travel lift for larger boats (28′ or so and up).

Also, upriver about 3 miles from Brookings is the "**Social Security Bar" ramp**, managed by the city and the State Department of Fish and Wildlife. There's no charge to launch at this paved ramp.

As small boaters return from the ocean on summer mornings, fish cleaning tables at the Chetco harbor docks become increasingly busy.

Public Campgrounds

Harris Beach State Park, 2 miles north of Brookings on Highway 101, 469-2021. 86 RV sites with hookups, 66 tentsites, hiker-biker camp. An exceptionally nice coastal campground, with large spaces. Coastline is replete with places for anglers of rocky and sandy surf to explore.

There are a number of private RV parks and motels in the area. For specific information on these, inquire with the chamber of commerce.

For More Information

Brookings-Harbor Chamber of Commerce, P.O. Box 940, Highway 101 South-Harbor, Brookings 97415, 469-3181.

Northern California

The northern coast of California is much more like Oregon and Washington than it is like the rest of California, to the south. The coastal topography is generally a continuation of southern Oregon but with longer stretches of dark sandy beaches between rocky headlands and with awesome redwoods towering over the coast. Anglers are presented with a north Pacific mixed bag of fisheries, including tidewater, open ocean and sandy/rocky surf.

In all five areas covered in this guide, salmon reign supreme, whether people are fishing the ocean or rivers. One distinction that northern California shares with a bit of southern Oregon but unfortunately not with most of Oregon nor any of Washington is a long salmon season. So far, at least, that has usually been opening early May and lasting through September. A barbless hook required *is* shared among salmon anglers with states to the north.

Over the years, both the Smith and Klamath rivers earned their famous reputations for tremendous runs of chinook (as well as steelhead above tidewater). In both rivers, particularly the Klamath, salmon runs have been reduced in recent years by habitat degradation and overharvesting from the high seas to the river itself. But in both, tidewater fisheries remain popular in late summer and fall. These fall-run chinook are large, with 30- to 40-pounders taken regularly from skiffs trolling or "hoglining" anchovies or spinners. Ample small boat facilities and guides are available in both the Smith and Klamath.

Off Crescent City, Trinidad Harbor and Humboldt Bay, salmon are taken in the ocean through September from charter boats and smaller private craft. The salmon (more coho but some years nearly as many chinook) are no more than a few miles from port. The only port with a bar crossing, such as those along the Oregon coast, is Humboldt and it can be tricky. Trinidad and Crescent City offer immediate access to the ocean without traversing a bar crossing. Small charter fleets operate out of all these ocean ports. In addition to the coast's rocky surf fishing, both of Humboldt Bay's long jetties offer nonboaters action for small, mixed bags of bottomfish.

Ocean bottomfishing is somewhat limited by habitat and access. Two major reefs, one near and heavily fished, one far and less harvested, await out of Crescent City. Trinidad is blessed with many reefs jutting from the bottom along its coast. Although 75 miles down the coast from the southernmost area in this guide, Humboldt Bay, the Shelter Cove area offers the most wide-open bottomfishing for all sorts of small boats.

The sandy beaches so prevalent along the northern California coast provide many miles of good surf fishing for redtail perch and netting for surf smelt, spring and summer. The 1- to 4-pound perch are ubiquitous around most beaches. In particular, some of the Northwest's best redtail fishing takes place in May and June right at the mouth of both the Smith and Klamath rivers. Two species of smelt known in this state as "day fish" (surf smelt) and "night fish" (night smelt) spawn spring and summer right in the surf.

In fact, they are found along most Northwest beaches, but are only actively pursued in a big way on northern California beaches. Smelters walk the beaches carrying A-frame nets (as shown in the chapter on "Fishing Northwest Salt Waters") or nylon throw nets during high incoming tides, watching the breakers for telltale flocks of gulls diving or hopping along the beach to devour smelt.

Northern California fishermen can try for species not available in bays and rivers to the north. In Humboldt Bay, there are large populations of leopard and cow sharks (to over 10 feet) and bat rays (to over 100 pounds). These large fish offer an exciting, very accessible skiff fishery that only a few fishermen really take advantage of.

Weather patterns of concern to coastal anglers are much the same as Oregon's, with frequent foggy periods and a prevailing northwesterly wind/swell much of the offshore sportfishing season.

For More Information

California Department of Fish and Game, main office, 1416 Ninth Street, Sacramento, CA 95814, (916) 445-3531. Write or call for free *Sport Fishing Regulations* pamphlet—a necessarily elaborate but very well-organized summary of regulations for this huge and diverse coast. Also available: a publications price list for ordering some of the department's excellent publications (such as booklets on California offshore, inshore and anadromous fishes; marine baits; fishing maps of the Klamath River and of Del Norte, Humboldt and Mendocino counties; and a salmon and steelhead guide map.

California Department of Fish and Game, Region 1 office, north coast, 619 Second Street, Eureka, CA 95501, (707) 445-6493.

Toll-free in-state poaching hotline (800) 952-5400 (7 days/week).

Pacific Marine Center, 1801 Fairview Avenue East, Seattle, WA 98102, (206) 442-7657. Free index to Pacific Coast nautical charts, including list of authorized agents around the state.

California Department of Parks and Recreation, P.O. Box 2390, Sacramento, CA 95811, (916) 445-6477. For reservations: Mistix, 1-800-444-7275. Call or write for campsite reservation request forms.

California Chamber of Commerce, P.O. Box 1736, Sacramento, CA 95808, (916) 444-6670.

Lower Smith River

The Smith, California's northernmost coastal river, is short, steep and renowned among tidewater fishermen for fall runs of large chinook. Facilities along the lower river are limited to a few motels and RV parks. Most fish are caught from private boats trailered to the river or those of guides.

Famed Fall Chinook

Although a very small run of chinook enters the Smith in the spring, it is around the end of August that fishermen get the fever here, for that is the start of the Smith's major claim to fame: its run of big, bright chinook. It is around the end of August that the lower Smith, quiet nearly to the point of desertion much of the summer—becomes quickly overrun with crowds of fishermen.

They're after kings that average 20 to 25 pounds and can be at least twice that size. (Probably 10 or so fish over 50 pounds are taken every year from the Smith.)

Old timers still talk of a 102-pounder taken in nets here back in '39. Paul Saxton, who spent a long lifetime fishing the Smith, told me of seeing two fishermen fight a chinook for over 7 hours. "The salmon had to be over 100 pounds," Saxton said. "We could *see* him!" But in the end the huge king proved too large to subdue and gained its freedom.

All fall-run fish aren't monsters. Good numbers of jacks (precocious young early-returners) fill the river in early September. Although small, these chinook are aggressive and can be great early sport. The big fish are starting in at the same time, and hit a real peak around midNovember as a rule. Timing can vary considerably from year to year since influx and upriver movements of the runs are so dependent upon freshets from fall rains.

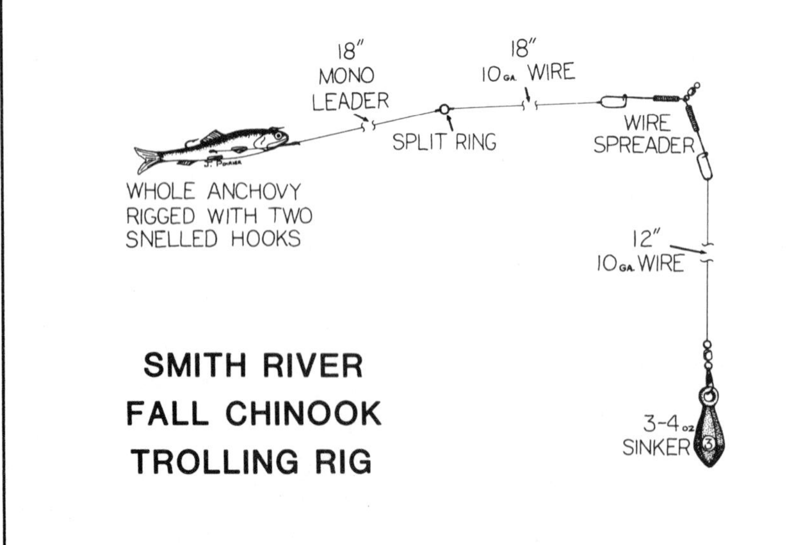

When the main run is in, fishermen will be working the river from the very mouth on up. When the seas are calm some anglers work as far down as the bar, but it isn't particularly advisable. Generally, in lower tidewater, trolling anchovies with a weighted spreader rig (like that shown) is popular. Some, more simply, tie an 18- to 30-inch leader with rigged anchovy directly to a 3- to 4-ounce kidney sinker. (In swift currents, as much as 6 or 7 ounces could be required.) In either case, a sliding upper hook helps ensure a curve in the anchovy so it will spin in the current. Spinners are often used in place of bait and occasionally a lure such as a Flatfish or Hot Shot does the trick. Many anglers choose to row for slow speed and maximum control.

Those who anchor use the simple rig described above, adding a cork float onto the leader to keep the bait off the bottom. (See illustration of this rig as described for jetty angling in the Chetco River, Oregon section.)

Some stillfishing occurs just inside the river mouth but seldom anymore in a gunnel-to-gunnel line that used be known as "anchor row." Large spinning and levelwind reels are both popular.

With light lines, some anglers are successful "flylining"—fishing fresh bait on a single hook with little or no weight. This method is particularly effective when large schools of bait are balled up near the river mouth. On the other hand, up around the head of tidewater (and on upriver), roe and sand shrimp are both used by boaters who "back-bounce" or "side-troll." (Side trolling is simply tossing a bait without much weight off the side of the boat as it drifts down through deeper holes.)

The Smith's fall chinook run also provides flyfishermen great opportunities to tangle with a bright slab. Nearly any deep hole may produce, such as the Bailey or Piling holes. Gold or Silver Comets and shrimp or egg sac patterns regularly account for salmon over 30 pounds.

Neither tide nor time of day are critical determinants of when to fish the lower Smith. Water conditions, of course, *are* important. Fortunately, the Smith is one of the fastest-clearing rivers on the north coast, requiring but a day or two to clear (unlike long, large rivers which can take a week or more).

There is no good access to offshore reefs from the river, but not far south is Crescent City which offers not only good salmon trolling but some fabulous bottomfishing on the immense, rugged St. George Reef.

Big Winter Steelhead And A Modest Cutthroat Fishery

Some of the biggest steelhead in the state come from the Smith River—including some past state records. Steelies here average about 12 pounds, and quite a few over 20 pounds are taken every year. Most steelheading occurs above tidewater, December through March; fishermen plunk roe from shore on a three-way swivel using a dropper line to hold some weight. Boaters backtroll Hot Shots through the holes. The upper river, above the forks, produces most steelhead.

The few anglers who really pursue Smith River sea-run cutthroat do so by trolling nightcrawlers or small spinners or they cast from shore. Summer moss in the river can be a real problem, however. Try the sloughs behind the dikes (south and west of Tillas Island) and the main river below the Piling Hole. Cutts and fall-run silvers are taken in greatest numbers in Lake Earl, south of here, and in the narrows between Lake Earl and Lake Talawa.

Lake Earl is actually a brackish-water estuary and it offers what many consider to be one of the top fisheries on the west coast for cutthroat. Ten-pounders have been taken here and every year quite a few cutthroat well over 5 pounds are taken. This fishery peaks from April through early July. Most anglers troll hardware such as Little Cleos but flyfishermen can enjoy great action simply drifting with the wind and casting out a shrimp pattern fly with 50 feet of a sinktip line.

This is a boaters show (small cartoppers are ideal), since shore access is difficult at best in high grasses and soggy ground. But be advised: no outboard motors are permitted. There are two launch ramps on Lake Earl, one just west of Teal Point and one at the end of Lakeview Road, on the southest side of the lake.

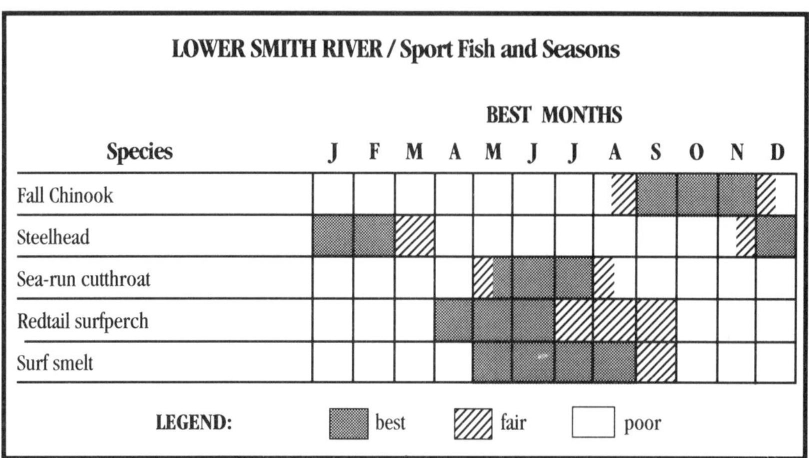

LOWER SMITH RIVER / Sport Fish and Seasons

Species	J	F	M	A	M	J	J	A	S	O	N	D
Fall Chinook	poor	poor	poor	poor	poor	poor	poor	fair/poor	best	best	best	fair/poor
Steelhead	best	best	fair	poor	poor	poor	poor	poor	poor	poor	poor/fair	best
Sea-run cutthroat	poor	poor	poor	poor	fair/best	best	best	fair/poor	poor	poor	poor	poor
Redtail surfperch	poor	poor	poor	best	best	best	fair	fair	fair	poor	poor	poor
Surf smelt	poor	poor	poor	poor	best	best	best	best	fair	poor	poor	poor

LEGEND: best / fair / poor

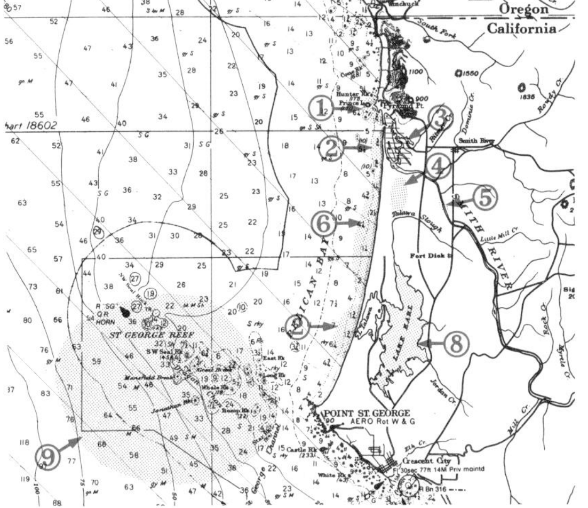

Not for navigational purposes.

Lower Smith River
Legend

1. Rocky surf fishing from shore north of river mouth (anytime ocean is calm).
2. Redtail perch.
3. Lower tidewater—troll for Chinook, fish tributaries for cutthroat.
4. Upper tidewater—backtroll plunk for steelhead, cutthroat.
5. "Balley Hole" (head of tidewater)—excellent for all species including Chinook.
6. Serf netting for smelt.
7. "The Narrows" for cutthroat.
8. Lake Earl for cutthroat silver salmon.
9. St. George Reef—fabulous bottomfish for charters or seaworthy private boats out of Crescent City.

■ Launch Site
No Scale
Chart #18600

Fishing The Surf: Perch And Smelt From The Sand, Bottomfish From The Rocks

Redtail perch invade the lower river in great numbers in April and May. For the rest of the summer they provide more sporadic—but at times quite fast—fishing from the surf. A popular spot is the south spit at or near the river mouth. This can be reached by motoring or rowing the few hundred feet across the river from the Ship Ashore boat ramp (nonboaters may be able to find someone with a boat to shuttle them across).

When the surf is light, traditional surf sticks are hardly necessary. I've done well here with medium spinning reels, enough to handle a 3-ounce pyramid sinker. Bait up with a sand crab (as the little burrowing intertidal animal—not a true crab—is known) when you can get them. Tube worms, shrimp, even nightcrawlers are also effective when redtails are feeding actively. On calm days, small lures such as spinners will also work. Perch are caught here on either tide, but they do come and go in schools, so have some patience in between.

One word of caution: when fishing gets hot, remember that the California bag limit is 10 perch. Along the Oregon coast, just a few miles north, the daily limit is 25.

There is some opportunity to take a more mixed bag of bottomfish from the rocks north of the river mouth. An incoming tide is likely to be the best time to do it. Most anglers are likely to fish whole or cut anchovies, but sand crabs and other natural baits are sure to take fish.

Smelt dipping, described in more detail in the Klamath River section, is a delightful pastime for those with a pair of waders (or old jeans and a thick skin) and an A-frame scoop net. Both the bite-sized "night fish" and the slightly larger "day fish" (surf smelt) are taken from beaches in the area. At the state park access at the end of Kellogg Road, north of Lake Talawa, both commercial and sport netters often work the breakers toward high tide.

It takes a fall Chinook even larger than this trophy to really raise eyebrows of veteran Smith River fishermen.

When big wolf eels like these grab a "poke-polers" offering, he's in for one hell of a tussle.

"Poke-poling"—A Lost Art For Tasty "Eels"

A traditional but largely forgotten northern California fishery, as simple as it is specialized, is known as "poke-poling."

It is just what its name implies: poking in and around rocks and tidal surge channels exposed by very low (minus 1- to 2-foot) tides with a stout pole (such as an old fiberglass bottomfish "meat stick"). Tied to the end of the pole with a short wire leader is a single baited hook with a strip of tough squid.

This is then worked in holes and crevices. The aggressive intertidal "eels" that grab on are really elongate species of fish: pricklebacks, gunnels, monkey face eels, wolf eels and others). Although most of these fish are no longer than 1 to 1 and 1/2 feet in length, they can powerfully entwine their bodies among the rocks. When one strikes be ready to pull hard and do it quickly.

Though poke-poling is seldom practiced anymore, and even at that is limited to a few days a year when tides are low enough, it is different, fun and worthwhile. One old river guide and veteran poke-poler told me, "You fry those eels up and they taste just like chicken!"

Facilities

All phone numbers listed are in the 707 area code unless otherwise noted.

Guides

Rivers West Outfitters, P.O. Box 947, Klamath 95548, 482-5822. Open 7 days/week; also sell tackle.

Six Rivers Guide Service, 5625 South Bank Road, Crescent City 95531, 458-3577. Many guides available to fish a number of southern Oregon/northern California, certainly including the Smith.

Smith River Outfitters, 487-0935.

Resort, Public Campgrounds

Salmon Harbor Resort, 200 Salmon Harbor Road (off Highway 101 North, just inside the north spit at the river mouth), Smith River 95567, 487-3341. Large popular RV area (not much silence or seclusion though).

Ship Ashore Resort, P.O. Box 75, Smith River, 95567 (right at the river mouth), 487-3141. Open year-round, 7 days/week. Motel rooms, 200 RV sites. Restaurant. Moorage available on floating dock, July-October; reservations recommended. Launch ramp in good shape, usable most tides. Rents 12' rowboats.

Jedediah Smith Redwoods State Park on the Smith River at U.S. Highway 199. Actually located about 10 miles from tidewater, this is a very pleasant park, amidst the giant redwoods. It is also popular, and reservations are wise. (However, I've found a spot or two despite the "campground full" sign posted!)

For More Information

Crescent City/Del Norte Chamber of Commerce, 1001 Front Street, Crescent City 95531, 464-3174.

courtesy Portland District U.S. Army Corps of Engineers

Crescent City

Several populations around Crescent City swell during the summer—those of baitfish, seabirds, salmon and fishermen. Without a bar to cross, anglers generally find it easy to reach salmon which apparently find it easy to reach the Crescent City area (judging by the numbers of salmon taken here in recent years).

Many fishermen trailer up their own boats and take advantage of a four-lane launch ramp and full-service marina with many transient slips—though in July and August it may be difficult to find a spot. Nonboaters will find at least a couple charterboats making regular trips offshore.

An Ocean Full Of Salmon

Typical of the northern California coast, chinook are most prevalent early in the season, but silvers tend to dominate catches from midsummer on, most years. Salmon fishing begins in May, generally, when many fishermen concentrate on kings—at least some of which are probably Rogue River springers.

Fishing in recent years has lasted into September, though annual quotas may vary considerably. Some seasons, in order to stretch out those quotas and guarantee fishing through most of the summer, the state may close salmon sportfishing on certain days of the week or may reduce limits. Clearly, it is essential to check regulations carefully before planning a trip.

The majority of Crescent City salmon fishermen troll. Those who fare best will often use a line or two on a downrigger and a put a shallower-running rig or two out with plastic planers. But an increasing number of salmon enthusiasts mooch these offshore waters, fishing bait from a drifting boat. Recent summers of abundant salmon have also encouraged the intelligent use of lighter tackle, some anglers simply switching to their steelhead rods. In fact, such gear is well-suited to silvers in particular, which average 6 to 10 pounds.

Bottomfishing: A Tale Of Two Reefs

A long and generally productive salmon sportfishing season notwithstanding, bottomfishing is very popular here, with most of the action on two extensive reefs, one near and one far.

South Reef is a mere 3 miles from Crescent City and easy to locate: once out of the harbor, run south on a 210 degree heading until the bottom rises sharply after dropping to about 30 fathoms. This reef extends for about 2 miles, offering a mixed bag with the emphasis on blue and black rockfishes.

Point St. George Reef, to the north, is about a 13-mile run, enough to discourage many small boaters. But of course less pressure also means larger fish. The average size of lings taken here tends to be noticeably larger than those from South Reef. Expect many in the 15- to 25-pound range, with some to 50 pounds very possible. Anglers are also likely to bring home good catches of "reds"—vermilion and canary rockfish running 4 to 8 pounds. Point St. George Reef is a good 2 to 3 miles of rocky reef, with many "high spots" rising to 15-25 fathoms. Occasionally, most likely when anglers drift off the rocks and onto sandy-gravelly stretches between, some good halibut are picked up here.

In general, bottomfish here are caught on shrimp flies and the big leadhead jigs with plastic twin-tail bodies that carry down the shrimp flies. But local tackle dealers report brisk sales of metal jigs to bottomfishermen, jigs such as Pt. Wilson Darts (actually designed for drift-jigging for salmon, but very effective for other species as well).

A run to Point St. George or even to South Reef is hardly necessary to catch fish, however. Even anglers in very small boats can enjoy consistent action by simply drifting along just off the kelp and casting light leadhead bucktail jigs with plastic worms or pork rind strips. Fair-sized shallow-water rockfish, cabezon and small lings are a sure bet anytime the ocean is calm enough to be accessible.

Fishing ultralight tackle along the Pacific coast on a warm, still, foggy summer morning yielded this heavy cabezon for the author.

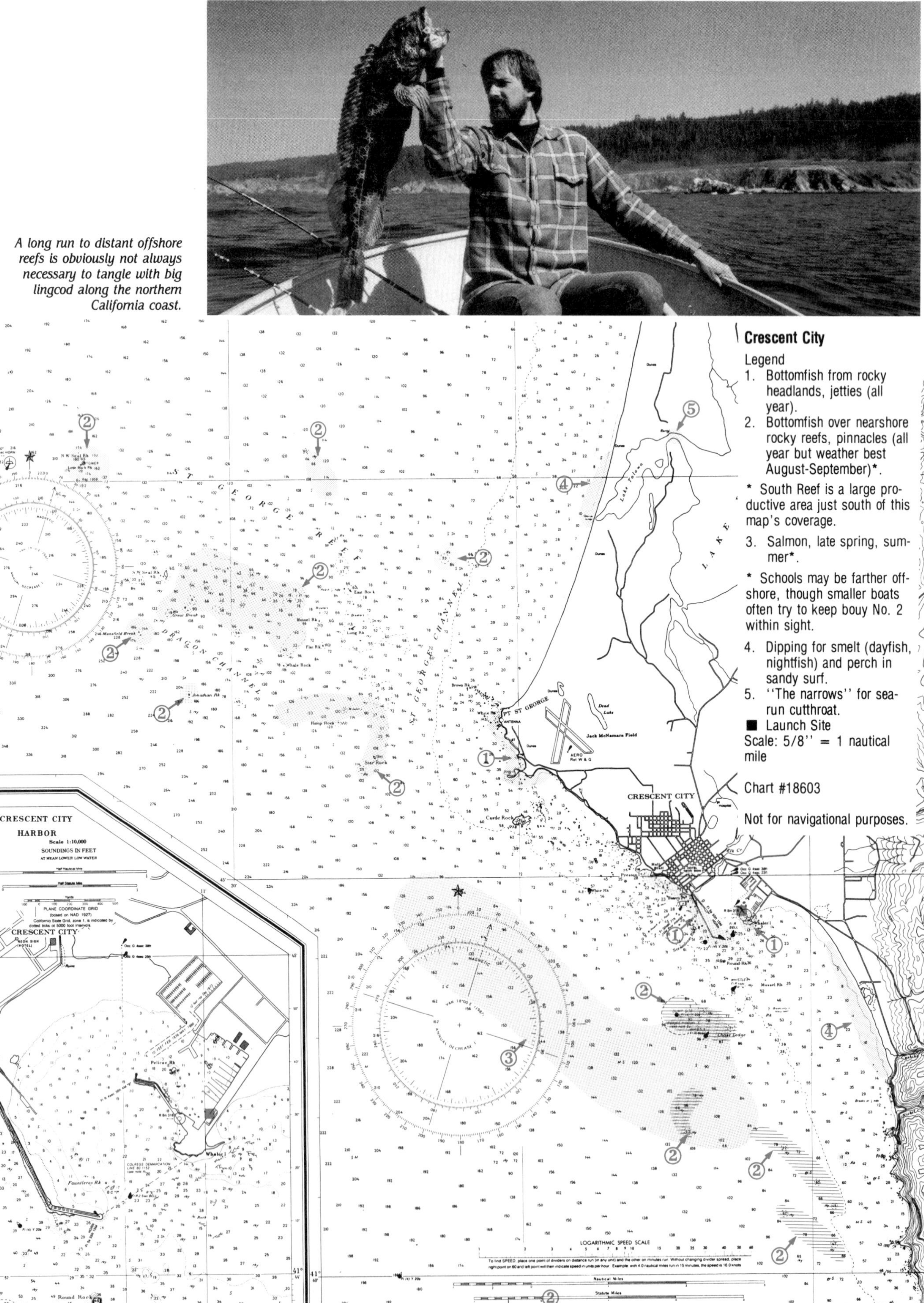

A long run to distant offshore reefs is obviously not always necessary to tangle with big lingcod along the northern California coast.

Casting From Sandy And Rocky Beaches

There is generally something to be caught from beaches in this area. Most often, surfcasters are after redtail perch, casting from any sandy beach up and down the coast where they can find access. Many fish locally at South Beach, below the bluff. Others drive north 8 or 9 miles to Kellogg Beach just south of the Smith River.

Wherever an angler can gain access to steep rocks along the coast here, he should be able to take small lings, black rockfish and the like. The Pebble Beach area offers many such places from which to fish. One good spot is near the ''Brothers Johnathon'' memorial, from which good rocky beach fishing extends northward.

Most beaches offer good smelt dipping. Many dippers go no farther than South Beach to dip smelt, both day and night.

Winter offers few angling opportunities, other than some bottomfishing when the ocean is calm enough. One opportunity for fast action most years in January and February is right in the harbor. A run of herring fills the boat basin, where the 7- to 8-inch herring can be taken on herring jig rigs or simply snagged with treble hooks. Filling a bucket can be surprisingly easy.

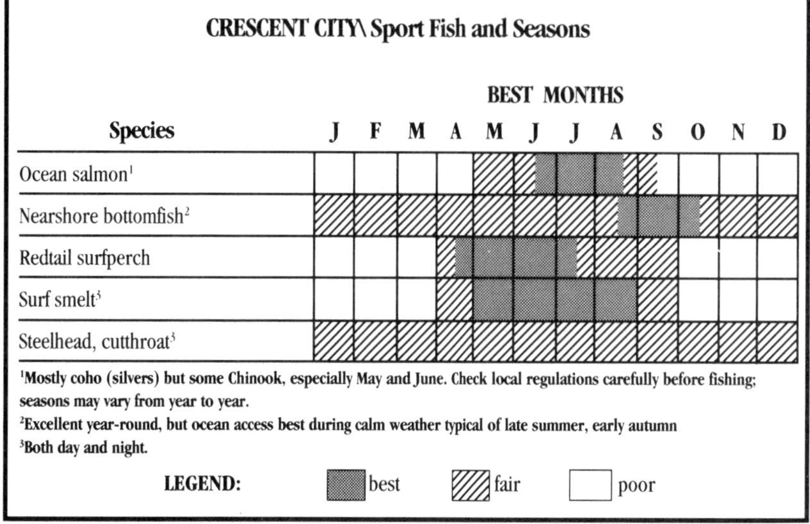

CRESCENT CITY\ Sport Fish and Seasons

Species	J	F	M	A	M	J	J	A	S	O	N	D
Ocean salmon[1]	poor	poor	poor	poor	fair	fair/best	best	best/fair	fair/poor	poor	poor	poor
Nearshore bottomfish[2]	fair	fair	fair	fair	fair	fair	fair	fair/best	best	best/fair	fair	fair
Redtail surfperch	poor	poor	poor	fair/best	best	best	best/fair	fair	fair	poor	poor	poor
Surf smelt[3]	poor	poor	poor	fair	best	best	best	best	fair	poor	poor	poor
Steelhead, cutthroat[3]	fair	fair	fair	fair	fair	fair	fair	fair	fair	fair	fair	fair

[1]Mostly coho (silvers) but some Chinook, especially May and June. Check local regulations carefully before fishing; seasons may vary from year to year.

[2]Excellent year-round, but ocean access best during calm weather typical of late summer, early autumn

[3]Both day and night.

LEGEND: best fair poor

Facilities

All phone numbers listed are within the 707 area code unless otherwise noted.

Charters

At press time two charter offices were running trips out of Crescent City. Rates and sizes of boats do vary, so call. At press time you could expect to pay $35 to 40 for a 5- to 7-hour trip. But add another $5 to that for tackle (unlike Oregon charters, it is not necessarily included in the cost of the trip). These charters troll heavy gear for salmon using planers or dropoff leads.

Lindbrook Sportfishing, 101 Starfish Way, Crescent City 95531, 464-7687. Skipper Mike Price's 65′ boat carries up to 30 anglers (though licensed for 53). Fishes salmon in season, bottomfish year-round.

Harbor Charters, 128 Anchor Way, Crescent City 95531, 464-2420. 2 boats, 38′ (6 anglers) and 42′ (12 anglers on salmon trips, 16 anglers on bottomfish trips). Fishes salmon May-September or so. Offers special rates for groups chartering boat.

A number of guides fish rivers north and south of Crescent City. See the guides listed in the Smith River and Klamath River sections. In Crescent City, there's **Tracy's Guide Service**, 2051 Northcrest Drive, #10, Crescent City 95531, 464-5108.

Marinas

Chart Room Marina, 130 Anchor, Crescent City 95531, 464-5993. Open year-round, 7 days/week. 500 moorage slips but can be hard to find a spot in July and August (in other words during salmon season), gas and diesel, engine repair nearby. Bait and tackle. Paved 4-lane launch ramp with flaots. (At press time there were plans to add 4 more lanes.)

Crescent City Harbor, 101 Citizen Dock Road, Crescent City 95531, 464-6174. Open all year, Monday-Friday. 500 moorage slips, gas and diesel, engine repair on site, bait and tackle. Excellent launch ramp and hoist.

Bait And Tackle

Englund Marine, 201 Citizens Dock Road, Crescent City 95531, 464-3230. Great selection of gear for all saltwater fishing and expert information from Mark Fleck.

Campgrounds, Lodging

There are many motels and private RV parks in the area. A few right around the harbor include: **American Best Motel**—464-4111, **Northwoods Inn**—464-9771, **Bayside RV Park**—464-9482, and **Sunset Harbor RV Park**—464-3423. There are also a number of state camping areas.

For More Information

Crescent City/Del Norte Chamber of Commerce, 1001 Front Street, Crescent City 95531, 464-3174.

This surf fisherman is wisely equipped with chest waders. However, on warm summer days, the northern California surf is fished by many clad in shorts and sneakers.

Lower Klamath River

Photo by Buzz Ramsey

There isn't a river on the U.S. Pacific Coast more traditionally synonymous with wild fall salmon runs than northern California's Klamath River. Unfortunately, these runs have been kept reeling by problems for decades, affected by tribal netting, degradation of spawning habitat and sport fishing pressure. A special management zone closing salmon fishing well offshore for a considerable amount of time as been in effect each summer for many years.

Yet the runs remain strong enough to endure and to attract many late-summer anglers to tidewater where a number of fishing camps still offer camping, cabins, boat launching and moorage, boat rentals, bait and tackle sales and the like.

And, fishing aside, the area remains breathtaking in its natural beauty, surrounded by steep foothills which are covered with awesome redwoods overlooking the Pacific.

The Klamath shares much in common with the Smith, to the north. Fall salmon account for by far the greatest share of interest in tidewater fishing. As in the Smith, steelhead are a major reason many people come to fish this river. And similarly lacking a navigable bar, the Klamath offers no ocean fishery for boaters. Sport fisheries other than those for salmon and steelhead lack the glamour but not the productivity. And there is, of course, much less competition for other species such as redtail perch, smelt and cutthroat trout.

Still-Sensational Sport For Klamath River Salmon

The Klamath has always had a tremendous tidewater fishery. The 1980s saw some poor years but also some seasons that were exceptionally fast, according to professional guides. They attribute improvements in part to increased state regulation of commercial and tribal fisheries.

Fall chinook begin making their way across the shallow river entrance in early August. For the next couple months or so, trollers and still-fishermen (the latter fishing from shore) vie for these kings which average 15 to 18 pounds but may tip the scales at 50 or more pounds. How long the kings remain around in tidewater is a function of fall rains, since when these really set in the kings move up quickly.

Silvers move in somewhat later, typically about midSeptember, to remain in tidewater—like kings—until about midOctober, depending upon rainfall.

Spreader rigs are overwhelmingly popular in the estuary with trollers. Some bait up with an anchovy, much like that illustrated in the Smith River section. But even more popular than bait are large, bright spinners as illustrated.

Trolling should be very slow, allowing the current to work the lure or bait after the sinker has been lowered to bottom and cranked up a turn or two. Most people favor fairly short rods and levelwind or ocean reels with at least 30-pound test. (Some fish with line as heavy as 50-pound test.) With crowds of anglers on and along the lower Klamath, this is *not* the place for light tackle. Besides the many lines all around, big Klamath fish are tough customers that head straight for the bottom before tearing off line.

Nor is this the place to neglect the caution necessary with such crowds. Fishing from anchored boats inside the river mouth can be productive but also dangerous. "Anchor row" also became known as "suicide row" and the Coast Guard years ago outlawed anchoring too near the bar. (It is said they grew weary of dragging in the bodies of fishermen from the surf after their motors failed and they were swept into the breakers.)

Shore fishermen use a setup like that favored by trollers. They cast it upcurrent and retrieve slowly. Among the fishermen lining the banks of the more popular spots are some who spend most of their time unraveling tangled lines and swearing. More than one longtime Klamath guide told me that things can get ugly and advise, only half-jokingly, wearing hard-hats as insurance against flying leads and hooks.

Most Klamath fishermen pay little attention to time of day, though a change of tide is by far the best period to fish. In general, it can pay to fish the river anytime after a good summer rain sends in a fresh influx of salmon from the ocean.

When the salmon ascend beyond tidewater, jetboaters "sidetroll," queuing up to take turns drifting through runs that hold fish. Most of this is bait fishing; relatively few pull plugs.

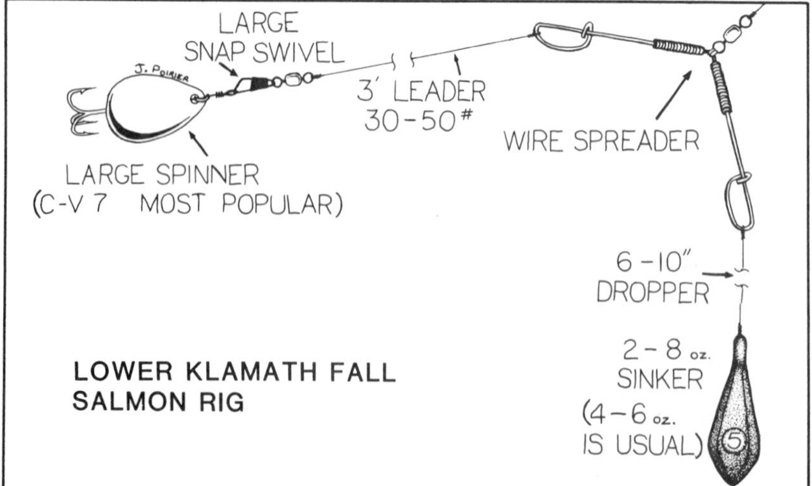

Sizzling Surfperch Fishing At The River Mouth

Redtail surfperch lack the size and status of salmon. But there are lots and lots of them here, and I've enjoyed some of the Northwest coast's fastest fishing in the surf at the Klamath River mouth for some of the largest perch.

There is a definite season for the hot perch action, usually beginning in late May and lasting through July. Unless the surf is flat (there are usually at least modest breakers), you'll need nothing lighter than medium spinning or baitcasting tackle to heave out 3- to 5-ounce pyramid sinkers, rigged 1 to 2 feet below one or two no. 1 or 1/0 hooks. Sand (mole) crabs are the favored bait locally. They may be purchased or gathered from the sand between breakers during low tide. Marine worms (sandworms, tube worms, pileworms) and mussels are also very popular perch baits.

A pair of waders is most helpful, but some anglers fish in shorts, with sneakers or even bare feet. One needn't stand in the surf while awaiting a bite, but unless the perch are feeding unusually close to shore, it's best to dash out into knee-deep water between breakers to cast as far as possible.

Fish the south spit at or near the river mouth. To reach it, follow Klamath Beach Road to its westernmost point and take a narrow, winding private road to Dad's Camp (you can't miss the sign). After paying a modest day-use fee (for road upkeep, say the folks at Dad's), park and hike out to the spit or, with a 4X4, drive right out to the end.

This smelt dipper's last attempt earned him but a few of the delectable silver fish. Other dips yielded two and three dozen. It's all a matter of timing and, of course, luck.

Around many Northwest bays, redtails seem to feed mostly during incoming tide. But 10-fish limits are commonly taken here on any tide. Perhaps more important than timing is patience. I have seen rows of anglers along the beach south of the spit draw nary a strike for some time, then suddenly start bringing in redtails right and left. Schools of perch are on the move, so things can go from bust to boom in a hurry.

Rocky stretches intermittently separate sandy beaches along this stretch of the California coast, and on calm days the rocks are good bets for a mixed bag of bottomfish. Most fishermen prefer an incoming tide when they fish anchovies. Those who are fairly serious about the sport come armed with lots of old spark plugs for weights (rigged on a dropper off the main line) which they can afford to lose to the rocks.

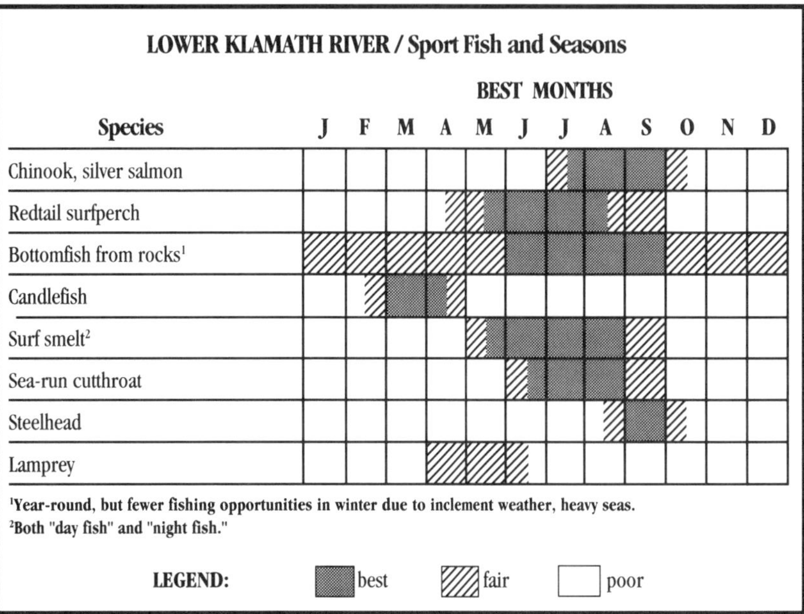

LOWER KLAMATH RIVER / Sport Fish and Seasons

Species	BEST MONTHS J	F	M	A	M	J	J	A	S	O	N	D
Chinook, silver salmon	poor	poor	poor	poor	poor	poor	fair/best	best	best	fair/poor	poor	poor
Redtail surfperch	poor	poor	poor	poor/fair	fair/best	best	best	best/fair	fair	poor	poor	poor
Bottomfish from rocks[1]	fair	fair	fair	fair	fair	best	best	best	best	fair	fair	fair
Candlefish	poor	poor/fair	best	best/fair	poor	poor	poor	poor	poor	poor	poor	poor
Surf smelt[2]	poor	poor	poor	poor	fair/best	best	best	best	fair	poor	poor	poor
Sea-run cutthroat	poor	poor	poor	poor	poor	fair/best	best	best	fair	poor	poor	poor
Steelhead	poor	poor	poor	poor	poor	poor	poor	poor/fair	best	fair/poor	poor	poor
Lamprey	poor	poor	poor	fair	fair	fair/poor	poor	poor	poor	poor	poor	poor

[1]Year-round, but fewer fishing opportunities in winter due to inclement weather, heavy seas.
[2]Both "day fish" and "night fish."

LEGEND: best / fair / poor

Tidewater Trout (Cutthroat And Steelhead)

The lower Klamath enjoys a good summer run of cutthroat, and there are more than the usual opportunities to catch them from docks and shore, here. Trout are most popular among anglers in June and early July, when salmon are not yet in, but they can be caught right through September.

The best areas are around Requa Resort, the mouth of Hunter Creek, Panther Creek and Dad's Camp. Simply stillfishing salmon eggs (and occasionally nightcrawlers) or casting small lures takes most of the 1- to 2-pound trout and a few up to 4 pounds.

The Klamath's famed "half-pounder" run of steelhead (which are actually pretty similar in size to sea-run cutts) provide a rare opportunity for good steelheading in

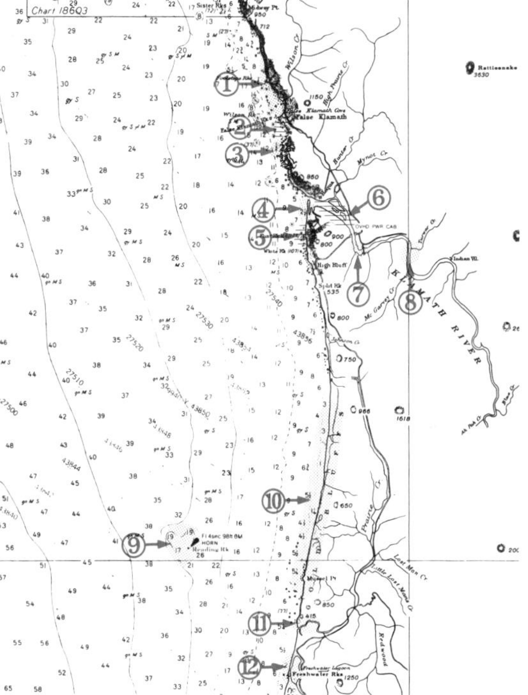

Lower Klamath River

Legend

1. Footstep Rock to False Klamath Cover—rocky surf for bottomfish.
2. DeMartin's Beach—retail perch, bottomfish (south end).
3. Hidden Cove—redtail perch in sandy surf.
4. Sand spit south of river mouth—redtail perch in sandy surf.
5. Beach south of river—day and night smelt in sandy surf.
6. Lower River—trolling and shore casting for Chinook, silvers, cutthroat.
7. Upper tidewater around U.S. 101 bridge—Chinook, silvers, cutthroat.
8. Terwer Riffle—steelhead.
9. Reading Rock—large, abundant bottomfish (a long run from Trinidad Harbor to the south).
10. Gold Bluffs, Fern Canyon—redtail perch and smelt in sandy surf.
11. Redwood Creek—mixed salmon/steelhead (fall).
12. Freshwater Lagoon Beach—smelt inside, planted rainbow in lagoon.

■ Launch Site
No Scale
Chart #18600

Not for navigational purposes.

tidewater (as well as on upriver for many miles beyond the estuary) during late August, September and early October.

These fish have been subjected to less stress than chinook stocks and they continue to provide very fast fishing. It is not unusual for anglers who know the river well or fish with a good guide to catch and release 10 or 20 in a day. They aren't as finnicky as winter steelhead, taking nightcrawlers, single salmon eggs, Mepps spinners, Glo-Bugs, Spin-n-Glos, Kastmasters and the like. Such offerings are usually fished at the end of a light leader behind about 1/4-ounce of pencil lead in a surgical tubing snubber. Flyfishermen can enjoy grand sport for half-pounders.

One fish found in the lower river but not much sought by sport anglers is the sturgeon. These fish sometimes show up in nets and some very large ones prowl the deep holes of the Klamath. While there is no directed fishery, the potential is there. They do occasionally show up as an incidental catch for those fishing for salmon.

Smelt In The Surf: Fun To Catch, Fine To Eat

Candlefish, ''night fish,'' ''day fish''—all are various species of smelt and all are taken in or around the river mouth, often in great numbers.

Candlefish (eulachons) run upriver in great schools. Sea lions and diving birds in the lower river around March usually provide a tip off of candlefish runs to the locals, a few of whom use long-handled, fine-meshed nets to dip them. These oily little fish make fine bait and they are also very tasty.

''Day fish'' (surf smelt) are most available late spring through summer. Watch for gulls hopping along the beach and for cormorants diving just behind the breakers—sure signs of smelt in the surf—especially along the beach south of the south spit and at False Klamath Cove, north of the river.

At times these 6-inch smelt will be so thick that each receding breaker will leave many of them flopping on the sand, where they can be gathered by quick hands. More often, you will need a simple A-frame net, which can be purchased or rented from area tackle shops. (See illustration in the chapter ''Fishing Northwest Salt Waters.'') Hold the wide end down against the gravel in knee-deep water between waves. Just before an incoming breaker hits, lift the net up and out in one sharp motion.

An alternative, not yet as prevalent but increasingly popular, is the cast- or throw-net, a weighed nylon net which when thrown correctly forms a wide circle as it drops over the smelt.

''Night fish'' (night smelt) are similar to ''day fish,'' but smaller averaging 3 to 4 inches. To many, they are the greatest delicacy of all. They tend to show up along beaches in the same areas as day fish, but, living up to their name, mostly at night.

Facilities: Guides

Guides can be booked through most lower river resorts/fish camps listed below. Most guided trips fish above tidewater. At times, guides find action in the estuary. But often the lower river is fished by anglers from shore or from small (private or rented) boats. In any case, a guide is likely to cost a person $100 (at press time) for a day of fishing the Klamath.

Damm Drifter Guide Service, 380 Terwer Riffle Road, Klamath, CA 95548, 464-7192 or 464-6635. Darol Damm and 14 other guides drift the Klamath and all regional rivers from the Rogue south to the Eel and Mad beginning in July and continuing for salmon into December and for steelhead into March.

Rivers West Outfitters, P.O. Box 947, Klamath 95548, 482-5822. Books for several guides. Minimum of 2 anglers per trip. Season runs from August through December for salmon and through March for steelhead. Fish several southern Oregon/northern California rivers. This is also one of the few tackle shops anywhere around.

Six Rivers Guide Service, 5625 South Bank Road, Crescent City 95531, 458-3577. Many guides available to fish a number of southern Oregon/northern California, in addition to the Klamath.

Fish Camps, Rv Parks

Chinook RV Resort, P.O. Box 7, Klamath 95548, 482-3511. Open 7 days/week all year. 73 RV spaces with hookups. 83 moorage slips. Fuel, bait and tackle in well-stocked shop, rents 14- to 16-foot boats with or without power. Paved launch ramp in good condition.

Dad's Camp, P.O. Box 557, Klamath 95548, 482-3415. Open May-October, 7 days/week. About 100 RV/tent sites on 235 acres adjacent to the beach. Store with bait and tackle. Modest day-use fee for use of (read that: access to) the south spit to fish the surf for pinkfin perch (and smelt)—a real hot spot.

Klamath Beach Camp, P.O. Box 589, Klamath 95548 (just upriver from Dad's), 482-5591. Open April through October, 7 days/week. 28 RV sites with hookups in quiet, secluded area with showers and restrooms; rents trailers.

Terwer Park Resort, 641 Terwer Riffle Road, Klamath 95548 (3 miles up from Klamath), 482-3855. Open all year, 7 days/week. Cabins, 100 RV sites with hookups. 50 moorage slips. Fuel and oil available. Bait and tackle. Paved launch ramp in good shape at all tides. Books for river guides.

There are other RV parks and motels in the general area. For a complete listing, consult the Klamath Chamber of Commerce.

Bait And Tackle

Damm Drifter Tackle Shop, 380 Terwer Riffle Road, Klamath 95548, 482-6635. Open midJuly through November. Stocks complete line of river tackle including wide selection of top rods.

For More Information

Klamath Chamber of Commerce, 16400 Highway 101, Klamath 95548, 482-7165.

Crescent City/Del Norte Chamber of Commerce, 1001 Front Street, Crescent City 95531, 464-3174.

Trinidad

The 80-mile stretch of U.S. highway from Eureka north to Crescent City is punctuated by craggy headlands, steep cliffs and magnificent redwood forests in the hills beyond. In the midst of this spendor are several small coastal villages, among them Trinidad Harbor.

This tiny coastal community, one of California's oldest and once a major whaling center, offers fishermen a naturally protected harbor (with no bar to cross) amidst excellent salmon and bottomfish grounds. Facilities are minimal but sufficient; at least a charter operation or two are available during the summer and a rail launch in the harbor will accommodate small boats. Dock space is limited; most boats tie up to floats and travel to the dock by skiff. There are ample campgrounds and RV parks in the area.

Unlike most of the other sportfishing centers described in this guide, there is neither tidewater nor bay to fish at Trinidad. There is the ocean and it sits at the harbor's doorstep. Although not completely protected, the harbor is pretty well tucked in behind the immense, austere rock known as Trinidad Head.

Fishermen find redtail perch and smelt in the breakers of sandy beaches up and down this coast. Small coastal rivers, to the north and south, offer limited salmon and steelhead angling and in two brackish-water lagoons steelhead, sea-run cutthroat and some flounder are taken throughout the year.

Nearshore Salmon And Bottomfish

Salmon fishermen begin taking fish here in May (unless the season should open later), both chinook and coho. Often, their fishing begins only minutes past the harbor.

Most fishermen still troll, with many using downriggers these days. Those may not be set very deep, but at times depths of 100 to 125 feet will be a best bet for kings. Many anglers still troll more traditionally, with diving planes or heavy weights.

For many years, a common practice here has been to rig a 1- to 2-pound lead ball on a dropper hooked to the swivel with a release to free the weight when a fish is hooked. The benefit, obviously, is not having to fight a good fish with so much weight on the line. The drawback is lost lead, which can get costly.

Many trollers still rely on plastic squid (Hoochys) and anchovies, separately or in combination.

A recent trend among salmon fishermen locally has been drift-mooching anchovies. The basic pattern is much as in Washington, finding bait and fish with electronics (or often just looking for birds and boats), then working anchovies on a leader behind a 2- to 4-ounce kidney sinker. But here 3 rather than 2 (barbless) hooks are typically tied on a leader. The forward hook, a slider, is hooked into the anchovy's head, the middle hook is run through the body and the third hook is left to trail free.

Although early morning may be the best time to fish salmon, they are taken throughout the day. That's a good thing, since getting out at dawn may be difficult for many small boaters who rely on the only launch in the harbor, a single rail system. The wait can be long. On the other hand, much of the summer it can be disadvantageous to wait too long: typically the Northwest wind will come up by early afternoon and set up a substantial swell.

Less initial wait is involved by hopping aboard a charter. At press time that could be one large boat that has been around for many years or a newer, fast four-person operation.

A glance at the nautical charts (no. 18605, 18600 and 18620) should reveal immediately why bottomfishermen are so successful. Nearshore pinnacles rise abruptly just beneath the surface or just above it, rugged reef tips that bear names such as Cap Rock, Double Rock, Flat Rock, Prisoner Rock, Pilot Rock, Blank Rock and Flatiron rock. The particularly rugged area west and north of Flatiron makes this ideal bottomfish habitat.

Species taken in these areas include, of course, lingcod, as well as several types of rockfish including blacks ("black snapper"), yellowtail, vermilion ("red snapper") and others. In shallow water, near rocky headlands, cabezon, greenling and copper rockfish join these species in catches.

Baited shrimp flies remain very popular for all species of bottomfish, as they have for decades. Heavy (8- to 16-ounce) jigs with treble hooks are used for large lings. Big leadheads and plastic (twin) tails are also in common use.

But at least some regulars who fish these reefs are getting into lighter lines with spinning gear, casting a light jig. Many realize that this is a great way to take "black snapper" but may find that they can also handle larger lings and vermilions from deeper water, and have a great time doing it.

The catching often starts within a mile or two of the Trinidad harbor.

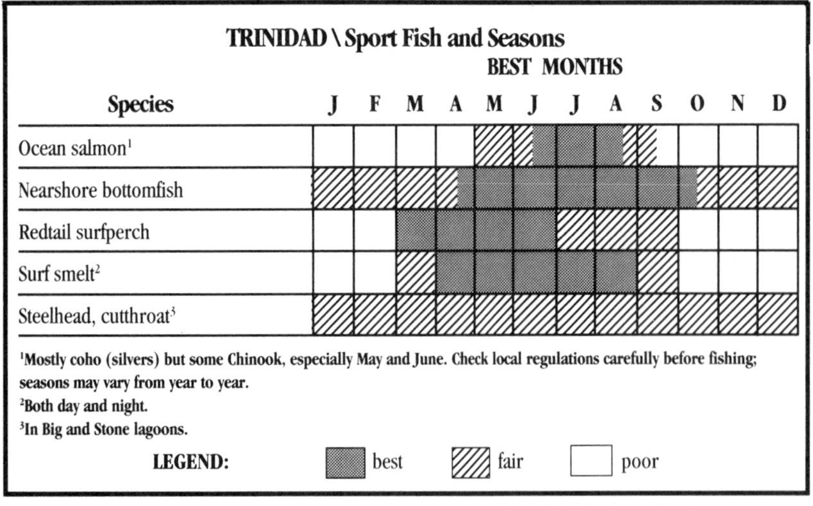

TRINIDAD \ Sport Fish and Seasons

Species	J	F	M	A	M	J	J	A	S	O	N	D
	BEST MONTHS											
Ocean salmon[1]	poor	poor	poor	poor	fair	fair/best	best	best/fair	fair	poor	poor	poor
Nearshore bottomfish	fair	fair	fair	fair/best	best	best	best	best	best	best/fair	fair	fair
Redtail surfperch	poor	poor	best	best	best	best	fair	fair	fair	poor	poor	poor
Surf smelt[2]	poor	poor	fair	best	best	best	best	best	fair	poor	poor	poor
Steelhead, cutthroat[3]	fair	fair	fair	fair	fair	fair	fair	fair	fair	fair	fair	fair

[1]Mostly coho (silvers) but some Chinook, especially May and June. Check local regulations carefully before fishing; seasons may vary from year to year.
[2]Both day and night.
[3]In Big and Stone lagoons.

LEGEND: best / fair / poor

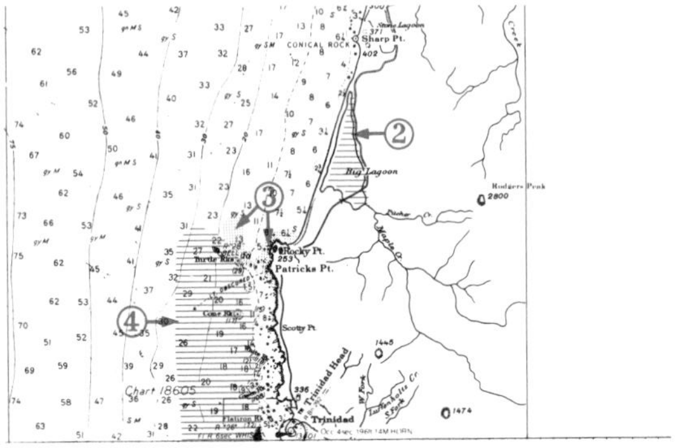

Some private boats and Salty's Charters do make the run occasionally to Reading Rock. It's 18 miles from the harbor and not a trip to be made in a boat that can't be trusted in heavy seas. But from all reports the bottomfishing remains nothing short of sensational for some of California's biggest lingcod and many, many other species.

Sampling The Surf—Casting For Perch And Dipping For Smelt

Either direction from Trinidad are good beaches for surf-lovers after perch or smelt. These beaches stretch from the northern tip of Big Lagoon up to upper Stone Lagoon and below Gold Bluff (along Fern Canyon Road). Beaches all along the Mad River mouth are similarly popular. Any of the little "pocket beaches" of sand between rocky headlands or points are typically productive.

Standard surf fishing techniques are employed—a 2- to 6-ounce sinker fished at the end of the line or leader (below the bait) on a dropper. On a no. 2 hook, sand crabs, tube worms, shrimp or nightcrawlers are fished. The most consistent catches are usually made during incoming tide. Redtails can be taken from the surf just about year-round, but the main fishery occurs spring and summer.

Just about everywhere people can cast for perch, they can also net smelt—both "day fish" (surf smelt) and "night fish" (night smelt)—using A-frame nets as described in the Klamath River section. Around the entrances to Big and

Trinidad Area

Legend
2. Stone and Big Lagoons—steelhead, sea-run cutthroat, flounder.
3. Patrick's Point State Park—rocky surf for bottomfish.
4. Bottomfish.

■ Launch Site
No Scale
Chart #18600

Not for navigational purposes.

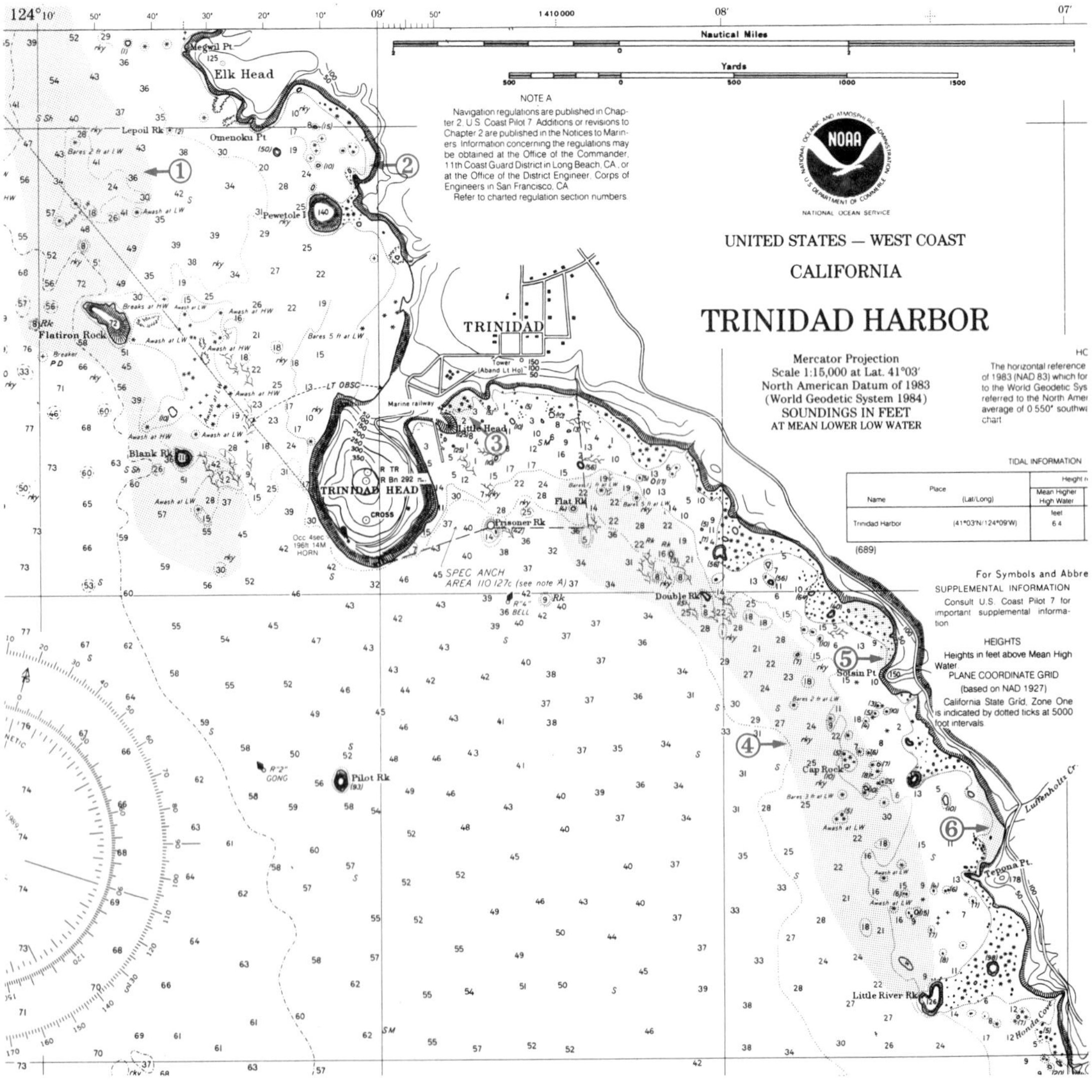

Trinidad Harbor

Legend
1. Excellent bottomfishing.
2. College Cove—rocky surf fishing for bottomfish.
3. Trinidad Harbor launch.
4. Fair Bottomfishing.
5. Baker Beach—rocky surf fishing for bottomfish.
6. Luffenholtz Beach (County Park)—rocky surf fishing and smelt in sandy pockets.

■ Launch Site
No Scale
Chart #18605

Not for navigational purposes.

Stone lagoons, smelters often find fish. A high incoming tide is considered ideal. Some smelters have taken up using cast (throw) nets, as described in the Klamath River section.

Fishing From The Rocks

The intermittent rocky headlands and projections along the shore offer good opportunities for catching various shallow-water bottomfish. Near Trinidad, in fact, some good catches are made from Luffenholz Creek and Baker Beach (about a mile southeast of the harbor), and just north of Trinidad Head at College Cove. Patrick's Point has ample opportunities for rock hoppers and the state park there offers access to the entire headland.

Because this popular fishing method does consume quite a bit of gear, most fishermen use medium to heavy spinning tackle and take plenty of bait (squid or anchovies most often), hooks and, for use as cheap sinkers, spark plugs or tobacco sacks. Sold in local tackle outlets, these sacks are filled with sand or small rocks and tied to the line below one or two baited hooks.

Year-round Steelhead And Flounder In Seaside Lagoons

Big Lagoon and Stone Lagoon, both north of Patrick Point, are separated from the Pacific by only a narrow strip of sand. High tides with heavy seas frequently open a channel to the ocean, keeping the lagoons high in salinity and accessible to steelhead, sea-run cutthroat and starry flounder.

Although the steelhead fishing is inconsistent, it *can* be good anytime during the year for 2- to 5-pound "half-pounders" and smaller sea-run cutthroat. The steelhead can be much larger, though. Reliable reports suggest some steelhead of 15 pound have been taken here. Many are taken, along with the cutthroat, by anglers in cartop boats trolling blades or stillfishing with nightcrawlers and marshmallows. There are special daily limits in these lagoons, recently two fish per day, so check regulations carefully.

The Mad River, south of Trinidad, offers a limited river-fishery for salmon, starting about midAugust and, in the fall, for steelhead as well. When it is possible to fish the river, fishermen cast lures such as Kastmasters or fish salmon roe and nightcrawlers from the bank. But it is more often than not impossible to fish because of high, muddy water. Also be aware of regulations that permit fishing within a 200-yard radius of the river mouth only from Jan. 1 through July 31.

During summer mornings, this rail launch tucked into the rocks at Trinidad Harbor is going nonstop.

Facilities: Charters

Size and condition of boats and cost of trips vary considerably. At press time, rates for a half-day of fishing varied from $45 to 65.

New Corregidor, P.O. Box 123, Trinidad 95570, 677-3625. Operates during salmon season only. Leaves 7 am and 1 pm for 1/2-day trips (bottomfishing by arrangement). George Collins has been skippering charters since just after World War II and enjoys it. "I don't keep doing this because I need the money," he says. The boat is neither new nor fancy, but it gets people out to the fish. Books through Bob's Boat Basin.

Salty's Charters, P.O. Box 3050, Trinidad 95570, 677-3874. Operates 22-foot Whaler "O-Six" for up to four anglers. Versatility is emphasis, offering ocean salmon trolling (with downriggers), mooching, light tackle trips or bottomfishing. For hefty additional charge, Skipper Jim Shrum will make the long run up to Reading Rock for trophy-size lingcod and rockfish.

Marina

Bob's Boat Basin, P.O. Box 123, Trinidad 95570, 677-3625. Open May-September, 7 days/week. Moorage space on floats, gas and diesel, engine repair, bait available. Rents 16-foot skiffs. Restaurant. Rail launch—busy summer weekend mornings.

Perch

Tackle

Salty's Sporting Goods, P.O. Box 3050, Trinidad 95570, 677-3874. Open 7 days/week, April-December. Complete line of tackle for salmon, bottomfish, surf and flyfishing.

Public Campgrounds

Big Lagoon County Park, about 9 miles north of Trinidad on Highway 101. Good surf fishing and steelheading.

Patrick's Point State Park, 6 miles north of Trinidad off Highway 101. 462 acres. Tends to fill quickly on summer weekends; when not crowded, it's quiet and pleasant. Good bottomfishing from rocky headlands.

For More Information

Trinidad Chamber of Commerce, P.O. Box 356, Trinidad 95570, 707-677-0591 or 677-3448.

Humboldt Bay

THIS SHIPPING, LUMBER AND COMMERCIAL FISHING center is the only major California bay north of Bodega (near San Francisco). Salmon are a major interest to sport as well as commercial fishermen here. Anglers pursue them offshore from several seasonal charter operations, and from private boats (with excellent launching and moorage facilities in the bay), as well as from very accessible jetties. Visitors find ample lodging and restaurants: fast-growing Eureka and Arcata derive a good share of their economic well-being from tourism.

The greatest effort among recreational anglers is directed toward salmon between May and August or September. These are primarily coho but can include a good percentage of kings as well, not headed into the bay but lingering just offshore to feed. At times, concentrations of salmon will be found chasing schools of anchovies around the jetties where rockhoppers and small boaters have a good shot at them.

Even when salmon aren't in, jetty fishing retains a popular following among those after bottomfish: greenling, rockfish, lingcod, cabezon and perch.

The large, shallow bay supports a fine redtail perch fishery, popular among bank and skiff anglers. It also offers some exciting fishing for species not generally available elsewhere along the Northwest coastal areas covered in this guide—leopard and cow sharks and bat rays.

The Eel River, just to the south, can be a good spot for steelhead and salmon in the late summer and early fall.

A big Chinook in the net for outdoor photographer Doug Wilson—he caught this one off Humboldt Bay in 1962, but it is a scene repeated thousands of times each year, decades later.

Summer Salmon, Offshore And Inside

The first salmon typically start showing offshore in May and offer hit-and-miss fishing for a while. By June, catches become more consistent, as a rule. There can, of course, be considerable differences in run strength from year to year. Recent summers have been very generous.

July is a peak month, and August can be nearly as good. Remember that this is a quota-directed season and while it usually lasts as long as there are fish around in September, it is best to check locally for any seasonal or daily closures. Salmon tend to swing in close to the coast here, so sportfishing most days is within a few miles of the jetties. At times, the salmon are plentiful in the lower bay, and jetty fishermen cast along both sides and from the ends of the jetties, while skiff fishermen work the jaws. The presence of salmon is normally tied closely to movement of anchovies; when the baitfish move in, so do salmon.

Trolling still accounts for nearly all the effort here, with anchovies and/or plastic squid accounting for most salmon. Downrigger use continues to gain in popularity over more traditional use of sinkers and/or planers to keep gear down. It would seem that well over half the private boat anglers out of Humboldt Bay are using downriggers.

Small Boat Safety—Crossing The Bar

Humboldt Bay's bar is well-traveled, with considerable commercial ship traffic, but it is hardly one of the coast's most civilized crossings. In fact, the California Department of Navigation and Ocean Development has pointed out that the Humboldt Bar is "considered to be very dangerous, and indeed, many disasters have occurred in this area."

Small boaters should avoid the bar and outer area of the jetty entrance during rough weather and, during a strong ebb tide, even when fairly light seas prevail. This bar often builds into steep breakers during the outgoing tide.

But on calm summer days skiff fishermen have little trouble traversing the bar during flood or slack tides.

Small boaters are advised to follow the channel (dredged to maintain a depth of 40 feet) along the south jetty. Use caution in the general area west and north of the north jetty since breakers may occur up to 1/2-mile west of the jetty end.

U.S. Coast Guard, Humboldt Bay

Bar/weather conditions, recording....... 443-7062
Samoa Station phone.................. 443-2212

Mooching for salmon has also seen some increased levels of interest, especially when anglers find themselves over substantial concentrations of salmon. That technique, driftfishing bait, long a tradition among Washington salmon fishermen, spread south in the late 1980s to the Monterey Bay area. Since then it has been working its way northward on the California coast. Effort with metal salmon jigs has yet to catch on, but salmon are salmon: that such jigs would work from jetties or drifting boats is certain.

Offshore bottomfishing out of Humboldt Bay is not a particularly popular option. That's because the ocean floor in this area tends to be shallow and muddy, not rocky. Some fair catches are made by small boaters fishing bait along the jetties. But the nearest major reef is south, off Cape Mendocino, a run too far for most private sportfishing boats. Shelter Cove, just over halfway south to Fort Bragg, offers small boaters who launch or rent locally excellent bottomfishing near Cape Mendocino.

North And South Jetties—Year-round Fun Fishing

Rarely are the catches taken from Humboldt's jetties so hefty that they can't be easily carried from the rocks. But even if fast-paced action is rare, both jetties remain very popular with fishermen who enjoy fair mixed-bag fishing at very little cost or inconvenience.

A primary target is the "black snapper," as black rockfish are known locally. Leadhead jigs of 1/2 to 1 ounce with plastic tails are most effective, especially from the north jetty. Blacks are also picked up from the rocks at the southeast end of the North Spit. As with nearly all jetty fishing, incoming tide is the most productive period. Lings, generally not over 10 pounds, also strike leadheads readily. A few anglers will fish small, live greenling to entice larger lings from their rocky lairs.

Shelter Cove—Fishing Big Waters From Small Boats

Though about 75 miles south of Eureka, Shelter Cove warrants mention. While the Humboldt area boasts no significant bottomfishery, Shelter Cove has gained a reputation as one of the very best areas along the entire California coastline for small boaters to tangle with big bottomfish.

There are no moorage facilities or launch ramps, yet there is a marina that provides launching of most trailerable craft via a tractor lift over the sand and offers reasonably-priced rental skiffs and outboards. (Mario's Marina and Lost Coast Landing, 707-986-7432, open 7 days a week in season.) At press time a charter service was also operating out of the landing.

While there can be excellent salmon fishing here, much of the effort is directed at plentiful populations of big bottomfish along the upper edges of the remarkably deep oceanic canyons that lie just offshore. Most of that effort is within 3 miles, an easy run, and within the shadow of Cape Mendocino, that helps keep fishermen out of summer's northwesterly swells and in calm waters.

Baits—tube worms, anchovies, shrimp—are fished on a no. 4 to a no. 1/0 hook. Sinkers are often the inexpensive little tobacco sacks filled with sand or gravel, popular with much of the north coast jetty fishing crowd. These are attached to the main line with a small piece of monofilament lighter than the main line. Quite a few "sea trout" (kelp greenling) and cabezon to 3 or 4 pounds, along with some redtail perch, are primary targets of jetty fishermen, particularly from the south jetty.

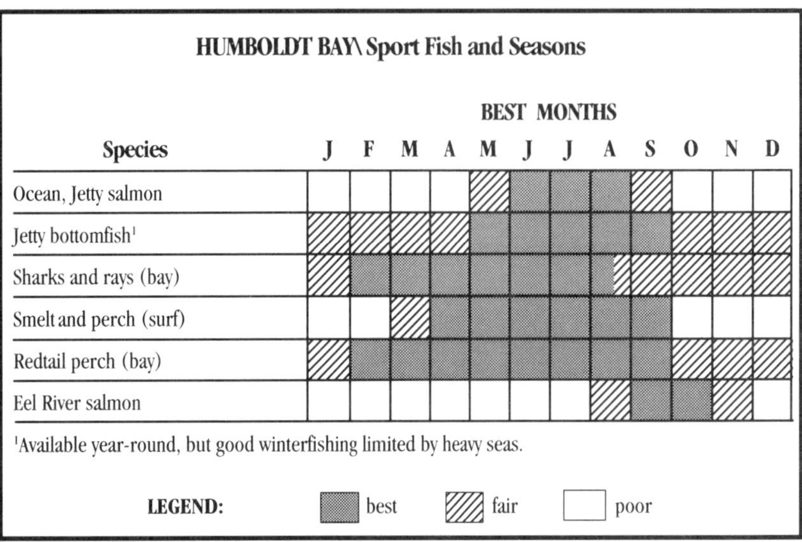

HUMBOLDT BAY\ Sport Fish and Seasons

Species	J	F	M	A	M	J	J	A	S	O	N	D
	BEST MONTHS											
Ocean, Jetty salmon	poor	poor	poor	poor	fair	best	best	best	fair	poor	poor	poor
Jetty bottomfish[1]	fair	fair	fair	fair	best	best	best	best	best	fair	fair	fair
Sharks and rays (bay)	fair	best	best	best	best	best	best	best/fair	fair	fair	fair	fair
Smelt and perch (surf)	poor	poor	fair	best	best	best	best	best	best	poor	poor	poor
Redtail perch (bay)	fair	best	best	best	best	best	best	best	best	fair	fair	fair
Eel River salmon	poor	poor	poor	poor	poor	poor	poor	fair	best	best	fair	poor

[1]Available year-round, but good winterfishing limited by heavy seas.

LEGEND: best — fair — poor

Jetty fishing for salmon can be an exciting prospect during the summer—or, some summers, it can be no prospect at all. When the salmon are in *en masse,* I've seen them taken even on leadhead jigs cast out for rockfish. Normally, anchovies are the bait of choice of those fishing for salmon. Spoons and metal jigs will also produce.

In The Bay: Redtails, Sharks, Rays

On a year-round basis, probably the most popular local fishery is that for redtail perch in the bay. Unlike most northern California and Oregon estuaries, where redtail fishing is predominantly a spring phenomenon, folks fish Humboldt Bay for perch throughout the year (not only recreationally but commercially as well). Spring does tend to be the hottest period for perch sportfishing (and when the bay closes to commecial perch fishing). But you are likely to see see limit catches of 10 fish taken just about anytime when winds are light and the bay smooth.

Leopard sharks that frequent Humboldt Bay are not only one of the most strikingly-colored sharks, they are fine eating if properly cared for (cleaned and iced immediately). Photo by Abe Cuanang.

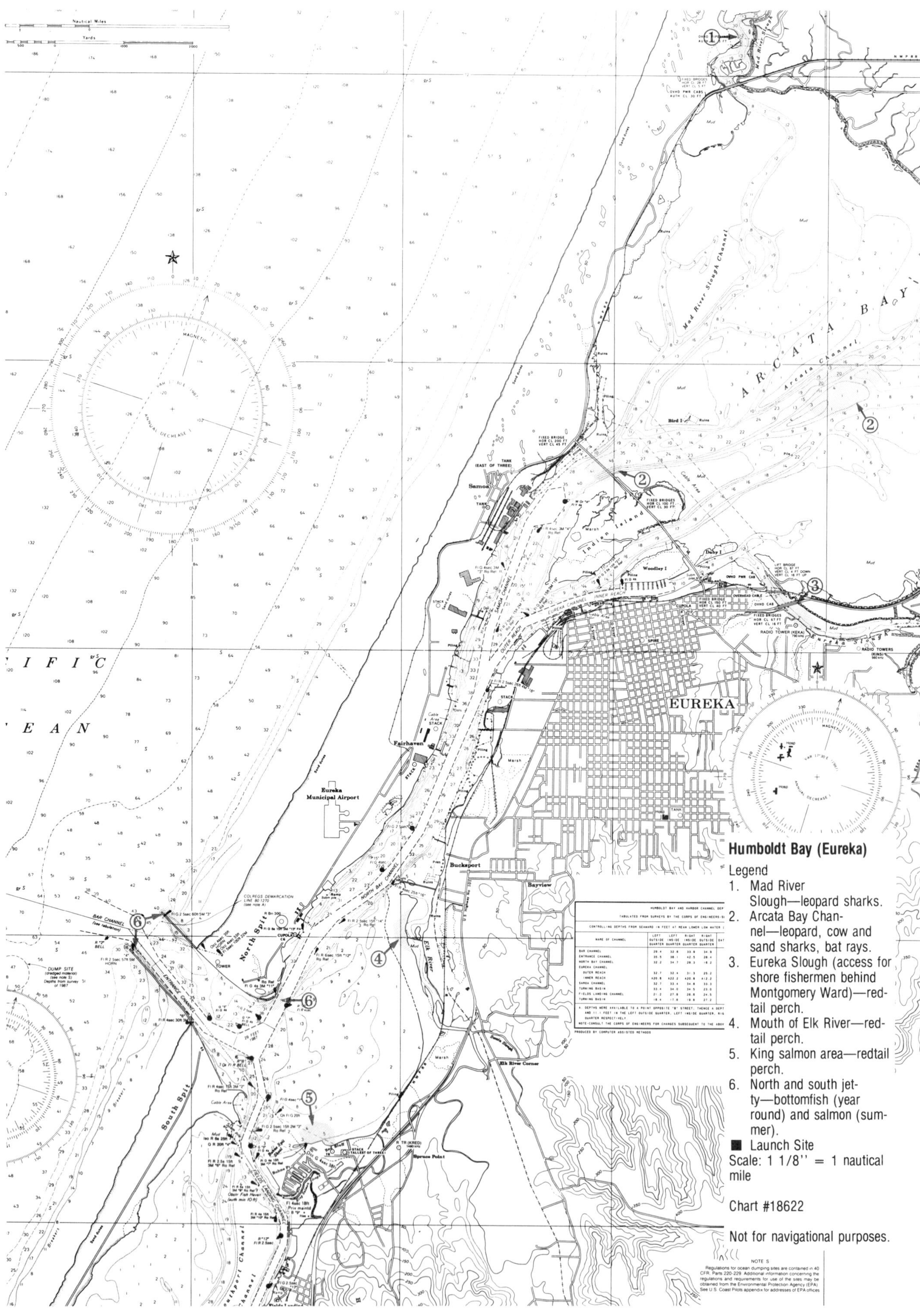
Humboldt Bay (Eureka)
Legend
1. Mad River Slough—leopard sharks.
2. Arcata Bay Channel—leopard, cow and sand sharks, bat rays.
3. Eureka Slough (access for shore fishermen behind Montgomery Ward)—redtail perch.
4. Mouth of Elk River—redtail perch.
5. King salmon area—redtail perch.
6. North and south jetty—bottomfish (year round) and salmon (summer).
Launch Site
Scale: 1 1/8'' = 1 nautical mile
Chart #18622
Not for navigational purposes.
ARCATA BAY
EUREKA
Samoa
Fairhaven
Eureka Municipal Airport
Bucksport
Bayview
North Spit
South Spit
Indian Island
Woodley I
Bird I
Elk River
Elk River Corner
Spruce Point
Mad River Slough Channel
Arcata Channel
Eureka Slough

Most serious perch fishermen favor the last half of the flood tide in any of several favorite spots, including Eureka Slough (around the bridge, behind Montgomery Ward), the point west of the Elk River mouth (at Buckport), above Buhne Point at the power plant's warmwater outfall, and around Fields Landing. Most go with a simple double-hook setup (no. 1 to a no. 4 hook) above an ounce or two of lead, baited with sand crabs or worms (sandworms, bloodworms or tubeworms).

Leopards, cows, bats—all are found in the channels and at times the flats of Arcata Bay. Leopard sharks to 5 feet, cow sharks to at least 10 feet and bay rays well over 100 pounds are very much available to sportfishermen here. Sportfishermen have long ignored them, but in recent years interest in these fish has picked up. All are great sport and can be very good eating.

The opportunity to take these large bay dwellers awaits anyone with a small boat. Sharks and rays can be caught nearly anywhere in the long deepwater channel that passes under the Samoa Bridge into Arcata Bay. In fact, right around the bridge itself is a particularly popular spot. Mad River Slough in the northernmost end of the bay is also popular for summer leopard shark fishing. Incoming tide is the time of greatest feeding activity, and night fishing is generally faster than that during the day.

Whole squid are fished on large hooks at the end of long, wire leaders kept right on the bottom with at least 3 or 4 ounces of weight. Unfortunately, heavy tackle is customary. In fact, though, these fish make ideal targets to challenge the skills of real sport fishermen using light tackle. The use of a pram or small boat to follow fish, good equipment, finesse and patience all help to wear down a large shark or ray on light line.

There are also sturgeon in the bay, though they are caught only rarely and there is no sport fishery directed at them.

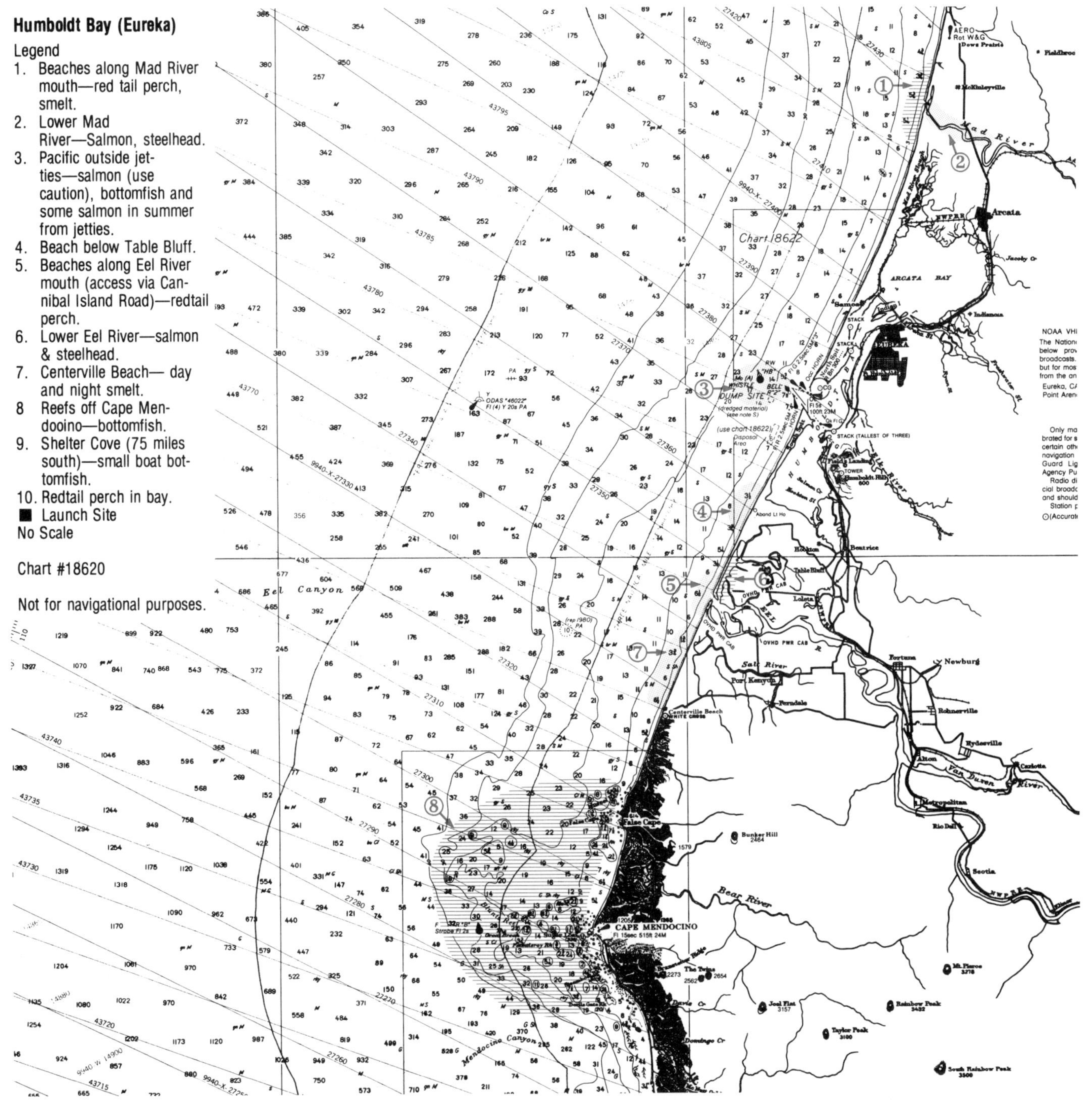

Like most Humboldt Bay jetty anglers, this young enthusiast was after black "snapper" (rockfish) with a leadhead jig and white plastic tail when surprised by this salmon.

Miles Of Sandy Beaches Offer Perch, Smelt

When the surf is quiescent—most often late spring through midautumn—redtails can be caught from beaches north and south of the jetties. Most fishermen use medium surf tackle and sand crabs or marine worms for bait.

Along these same areas and around the Eel River mouth are surf smelt (both "day fish" and "night fish"). As elsewhere, netters watch for birds working the breakers on an incoming tide. A-frame nets are commonly used to scoop up these 3- to 7-inch smelt, nylon cast nets are being more frequently thrown here than along many north coast beaches.

Tidewater Salmon In The Lower Eel River

The Eel River, south of Humboldt Bay, attracts a modest run of chinook and coho salmon, enough to support a skiff fishery in the lower river each fall. When a good fall rain invites up another batch of salmon, they are taken on trolled lures—Kastmasters, Flatfish, Li'l Cleos and the like—or on anchovies. Above tidewater, shore anglers catch some fall salmon and summer steelhead by plunking salmon eggs. Remember that extensive special regulations govern Eel River sportfishing; scrutinize a current Department of Fish and Game regs pamphlet if you're not positive what's what, before fishing.

Facilities: Charters

Most Humboldt Bay charters vary in size and at press time $50 for a 6-hour trip was standard. All fish both salmon and bottomfish, May through September/October.

Trinidad Bay Charter, Captain Tom Lesher, 839-4743. Salmon and Bottom fishing and light tackle expert.

Celtic Charter Service, 5105 Woodland Way, Eureka 95501, 442-7580. 50' boat carries up to 18 anglers.

King Salmon Charters, 5333 Herrick Road, Eureka 95501, 442-3474. 36' *Moku* takes up to 12 anglers (though certified for more). Skipper Denny Pecaut has been fishing these waters for many years.

Sailfish, 1821 Buhne Drive, Eureka 95501, 442-6682. 50' boat carries up to 17 anglers. Operates out of Johnny's Marina.

Bait And Tackle

Bucksport Sporting Goods, 3650 South Broadway Eureka 95501, 442-1832. Open 7 days/week. For many years, one of the best equipped outdoor stores on the Northwest Coast; plenty of local fishing knowledge, too.

Times Flies Takle Shop and Guide Service, 815 J St., Arcata, 95521, 822-8331. Owner David Schachter and Staff are saltwater fly fishing and light tackle experts.

Pro Sport Center, 508 Myrtle Avenue, Eureka 95501, 443-6328. Open 7 days/week all year.

Marinas, Launch Areas

Johnny's Marina and RV Park, 1821 Buhne Drive, Eureka 95501, 442-2284. Open May-September, daily. Limited moorage; reservations recommended. Sling launch for boats up to 22 feet, hoist for larger craft. Fuel available, bait and tackle. 53 RV spaces with hookups. Johnny's has been in business since about 1950.

E-Z Landing RV Park and Marina, 1875 Buhne Drive, Eureka 95501, 442-1118. 63 moorage spaces, sling launch, gas, 41 RV spaces, some tackle. Laundry facilities and restrooms.

Woodley's Island Marina, P.O. Box 1030, Eureka 95502, 443-0801. Open year-round, daily. At least some guest moorage available at this large complex with space for commercial pleasure craft. Bait and tackle, cafe, laundry facilities, showers. Nearest launch is across the bay, 1 1/2 miles.

Samoa public access ramp, excellent two-lane facility with lots of parking, no charge. Also RV overnight parking with water and restrooms for a very modest charge.

Field's Landing Boat Launch (west side of Humboldt Bay, just off Highway 101). Fine two-lane concrete ramp with parking.

The Humboldt Bay area is loaded with private RV parks and motels. For specifics, request a free Visitor's Guide from the chamber of commerce.

For More Information

Arcata Chamber of Commerce, 1062 "G" Street, Arcata 95521, 822-23619.

Greater Eureka Chamber of Commerce, 2112 Broadway, Eureka 95501, 443-5057 or toll-free 800-223-0663.

How's fishin'? Find out anytime (in season) by calling the "fishphone" recording at 707-444-8041.

Southwest Vancouver Island, B.C.

The west coast of Vancouver Island is but a quick hop from the northwestern U.S. But the island's rugged Pacific side offers abundant salmon, halibut and rocky bottomfish angling amidst coastal wilderness more akin to Alaska than to the lower 48.

Yet until the past decade or two, this exciting area has been largely overlooked and remained generally unvisited. The only major exception even now is sprawling Barkley Sound, the most southerly of the five major sounds which cut deeply into this island's long open ocean coast. Only at Barkley Sound has a proliferation of sportfishing resorts and charters sprung up to host throngs of fly-in/drive-in fishermen from all over the U.S. and Canada. Easily reached, with similar facilities but on a much more limited scale due to geographical realities, is Clayoquot (''Kla'-quaht'') Sound just to the north. Still farther north, near the center of Vancouver Island's Pacific side is Nootka Sound, fished largely by anglers who fly in to the lone fishing resort in this almost completely undeveloped area.

Both Barkley and Clayoquot sounds are popular with those who trailer small boats. There are no bar entrances to contend with to reach the ocean. And there can be great fishing inside the protected waters of these sounds. Often fishing farther up in the sounds seems to be a different world than the waters just a few miles offshore—the former sunny and bright, the latter foggy and cold. However, many times the fastest fishing is available to those who can make the run offshore.

Visitors reach western Vancouver Island in one of three ways: flying, driving or boating in. Relatively few take the latter route, but larger, seaworthy boats have little trouble in decent weather crossing the Strait of Juan de Fuca from Washington to the southern shore of the island.

Many fly in, with landing strips for small planes and quiet bays—facilitating commercial and private floatplane flights from many populations centers including Vancouver, B.C. (Port Alberni Air) and Seattle (Lake Union Air).

The majority drive to the island, thanks to the extensive, efficient B.C. ferry system. Huge multilevel ferries on several routes take cars (and trailered boats) from the mainland across the Georgia Strait to the island, including those out of Tsawwassen to Swartz Bay (just north of Victoria) and the 30-mile crossing out of Horseshoe Bay (northern Vancouver) to Nanaimo (almost due east of southern Barkley Sound—and the most direct route by ferry for those headed to the island's western sounds). There is also a short run from Powell River to Comox.

In addition, Washington State Ferries offer runs from Anacortes to Victoria (but these take relatively few vehicles and waits in line at the terminal can be hours). And a Blackball ferry line crosses the Strait of Juan de Fuca from Port Angeles north to Victoria.

The drive from Nanaimo to Ucluelet (northern Barkley Sound) or Tofino (southern Clayoquot Sound) is typically three hours or a bit more on good paved road. The distance to Bamfield (southern Barkley Sound) is not more, but much of the road is gravel and slower. By road, it is possible to reach the head of Nootka sound at Gold River, four or so hours or more from Nanaimo.

Among the reasons for western Vancouver Island's increasing popularity among fishermen from the U.S. is the fact that not only are fish out there, but you can go out and fish for them most of the time. Seasons are long, often wide-open and limits are generous—some of the most generous left on the whole Pacific coast for salmon. While these limits are subject to change, at press time and for many years before, a daily limit of four salmon (any species) remained in effect. Similarly, halibut season at press time remained open nearly all year (except for the month of January—hardly a blow to most sportfishermen) for a two-fish-per-day limit.

Despite the availability of many of the same fish along the northern Washington coast, sportfisheries there struggle with much shorter seasons and stingier limits (to meet quotas). The real difference: generous B.C. limits reflect the fact the provincial coast is long, wild, unpopulated and lightly fished; its salmon and bottomfish populations have not undergone the same sorts of habitat and harvesting stress as in the U.S.

Another way of putting all this is that an area like Vancouver Island offers fishing today ''the way it used to be'' in the U.S. Northwest. Unfortunately, the inevitable increase in fishermen and fishing pressure, both sport and commercial has already begun to be felt. But it seems likely that for the near future, at least, Vancouver Island will continue to offer reliably high-quality coastal fishing opportunities.

Chinook Salmon: Prize With Many Names

(A Quick Reference Guide)

Most of the fish encountered off the B.C. coast are known by the same labels that U.S. fishermen use: halibut are halibut, lingcod are lingcod (though often you'll hear Canadian's simply say ''cod''), and rockfish are... well, like in the U.S., they're sometimes rockfish but more often ''rockcod,'' ''bass,'' or ''snapper.'' Furthermore coho are coho or silvers and pinks, chum and sockeye are all the same. But it's another matter when it comes to the most prized sportfish, the chinook.

For handy reference, these are the names you'll hear, generally with varying connotations about size:

Spring—Similar to the ''blackmouth'' of Washington anglers, this is generally any chinook under 30 pounds, most often taken in the winter and spring.

Feeder—Often used synonymously with ''spring.''

Tyee—Widely used now to mean any trophy-size chinook of at least 30 pounds.

Slab—A more general term for trophy-size chinook, often connoting larger tyee (i.e. 40 to 60+ pounds).

British Columbia offers great light tackle fishing for salmon and bottomfish. The author caught this 36 pound, B.C. tyee (Chinook) on 8-pound test after it hit a big Krocodile spoon near bottom.

All species of salmon are caught along the island's Pacific coast. There is limited fishing during winter and spring months for "springs," generally in the sounds and the ocean, near shore. Generally June and July mark months of increasingly numerous tyee, both offshore and near shore, with the prized slabs generally most available in August and into September. Silvers move in offshore in July and August, and in September and October are taken near shore and up in the sounds.

Halibut may be caught from midspring through midautumn, but May and June seem to be peak months, most years. They are quite abundant, little effort is targeted specifically on halibut. Still, incidental catches and those taken during casual efforts produce consistent results. Other bottomfish are available year-round. In fact, some of the best light-tackle bottomfishing for big lings, rockfishes of many species and cabezon is available to those drifting ocean pinnacles and reefs near shore. The variety of species can be startling with some species more available here than in most Northwest waters.

Fishermen who tote their own tackle are likely to use whatever they're used to, typically levelwinds on mooching-type rods. But those who fish out of a resort or buy tackle locally will note that traditional Canadian gear, used up and down this coast, is considerably different than U.S. gear. Reels are large, single-action "knucklebusters" which are in some respects more limiting to anglers using them but also more demanding and, many would say, more responsive than conventional levelwinds. They are usually filled with at least 300 yards of 25-pound monofilament. (It is unusual to see significantly lighter gear used except in Georgia Strait waters from Campbell River south.) Rods are typically very long (10 feet or so) and very limber graphites.

Herring, plugged, whole or stripped, and Hoochys (plastic squid) are among the particularly popular offerings for Vancouver Island salmon for decades. As in the U.S. they are traditionally tied to the main line with a long leader slightly lighter in strength than the main line (e.g. 20-pound test).

British Columbia tidal water sportfishing licenses are required for taking all species of fish from the ocean. In addition, stamps are needed for salmon. Although regulations for western Vancouver Island have been generous, relatively uncomplicated and stable for years, that may well change. It is always essential to carry and be familiar with regulations before fishing.

For More Information

All telephone numbers are in the 604 area code except as noted.

British Columbia Ferries, 1112 Fort Street, Victoria, B.C. V8V 4V9. For information, vehicle reservations or to receive a complete route description/fare schedule pamphlet: 669-1211 in Vancouver, 386-3431 in Victoria, (206) 441-6865 in Seattle. For 24-hour recorded schedule information: 685-1021 in Vancouver or 656-0757 in Victoria.

Washington State Ferries, Colman Dock, Seattle, WA 98104, (206) 464-6400.

Lake Union Air, 1100 Westlake Avenue North, Seattle, WA 98109, (206) 284-0300, toll-free in-state at (800) 692-9223, toll-free elsewhere in U.S. at (800) 692-9224, toll-free in B.C. at (800) 826-1890. Flights to all Vancouver Island west coast destinations, some charter only, others via regularly-scheduled service.

Harbour Air Limited, South Terminal, Vancouver International Airport, 278-3478. Offers charter air service to all areas of Vancouver Island (and beyond).

Canada Department of Fisheries and Oceans, Main Offices, 555 West Hastings Street, Vancouver, B.C. V6B 5G2, 666-0383 or 666-0583. 24-hour recording 666-2268 or toll-free in-province at (800) 663-9333. Recreational Fisheries Division, 666-0419. For fish/wildlife violations, toll-free in-province hotline is (800) 663-9453.

Canada Department of Fisheries and Oceans, District Offices. Port Alberni: 724-0195. Tofino: 725-3468.

B.C. Parks, 4000 Seymour Place, Victoria, B.C. V8V 1X5. For information on provincial parks.

Ministry of Environment and Parks, Parks and Outdoor Recreation Division, 2930 Trans Canada Highway, RR #6, Victoria, B.C. V8X 3X2. For information about southern Vancouver Island Marine Parks. Request a free copy of the "Coastal Marine Parks of British Columbia" map.

Ministry of Environment and Parks, Parks and Outdoor Recreation Division, P.O. Box 1479, Parksville, B.C. V0R 2S0. For information about northern Vancouver Island Marine Parks.

Canadian Hydrographic Service, Department of Fisheries and Oceans, Institute of Ocean Sciences, Patricia Bay, 9860 West Saanich Road, P.O. Box 6000, Sidney, B.C. V8L 4B2. Request a copy of the free "Pacific Coast Catalog of Nautical Charts and Related Publications."

Tourism British Columbia, Parliament Buildings, Victoria, B.C. V8J 1X4, 660-2300 or (800) 663-6000. In Seattle: Tourism B.C., P.O. Box C-34971, Seattle, WA 98124. Request free booklet: *Saltwater Fishing Guide.* Also available: free "Road Maps and Park Guide" and a voluminous book of accomodations.

Tourism Association of Vancouver Island, Suite 302, 45 Bastion Square, Victoria, B.C. V8W 1J1, 382-3551.

British Columbia Sport Fishing magazine, 909 Jackson Crescent, New Westminster, B.C. V3L 4S1. This bimonthly magazine offers a wealth of generally informative where-to how-to articles on B.C. coastal fishing and its ads are a colorful compendium of resorts.

Photo courtesy Province of British Columbia

Barkley Sound

It would be impossible to describe Barkley Sound as a destination for Northwest saltwater anglers without using superlatives. In terms of its accessibility, scope, beauty, variety and quality of fishing there's no place quite like it.

Visitors arrive at this largest sound on Vancouver Island's west coast by sea, land or air. You can sail in by private boat, drive in after ferrying to the island or fly in via small plane. For those who drive, it's a mere two hours on the ferry from Horseshoe Bay to Nanaimo and another three or so hours from there. (Add three or so more hours from Seattle.) The highway is an excellent paved road (occasionally scenic) all the way to Ucluelet; expect gravel much of the way in to Bamfield, however, on the south side.

Since the late 1970s, Barkley has been "discovered" by more and more visitors, many of them fishermen. With that surge in popularity, facilities have mushroomed in Ucluelet ("You-clue-let") on the north side of the sound and in and around Bamfield on the south side. That means an abundance of resorts and motels, campgrounds and RV parks, public and private moorage areas, launch ramps, marinas, shops and restaurants, and guides and charters. There are similar facilities at the head of the sound around Port Alberni.

Visitors find much to attract them here. Although the beauty of the area is marred by clearcuts on many surrounding slopes, the sound itself remains pristine. In the center of the lower sound are the lovely, undeveloped Broken Islands, part of the vast Pacific Rim Provincial Park. On some are developed camping areas, and the island group is popular with kayakers as well as powerboaters. Just to the north of Uculelet are unspoiled, uninterrupted miles of beach on the renown Long Beach peninsula, more of the provincial park. Whales move into the sound during the winter and remain, often into summer, attracting crowds onto whale-watching boats.

But of course fishing is still the main draw. The Barkley Sound sportfishing community has not yet had to suffer the uncertainties of tight catch quotas on salmon and halibut imposed on the U.S. coast (only 60 miles or so south). For salmon fishermen, this has meant relatively unlimited seasons which can begin in spring when the mature salmon show up and remain into fall when they have headed upriver; daily limits of salmon remain much more generous; and gear restrictions are minimal (with barbed hooks still permitted at press time). Salmon and bottomfish offer fast fishing for small boaters fishing inside the sound's protected areas as well as those fishing farther out from private boats or charters.

Salmon, Inside And Out—hard To Go Wrong

Even as interest and sportfishing effort here have grown consistently, there has been no shortage of salmon. They are here much of the year, though the major fishing season begins in April or May and runs through September. Many salmon caught in the vicinity of lower Barkley Sound are passing by, bound for other areas such as Port Renfrew, Georgia Strait sites and the Fraser River and, in the U.S., Puget Sound, the Columbia River, Tillamook Bay and beyond. And particularly later in the season many—well over 150,000 some years in fact—are bound for the sound itself, up the inlet toward Port Alberni. The formidable Robertson Creek Hatchery produces enormous numbers of salmon smolts to be released each year—as many as 9 million silvers alone.

During the winter months, springs (immature, resident chinook—blackmouth in Washington) are prevalent. Fishing pressure is minimal, however. The servings of winter weather dished out by the Pacific don't encourage large numbers of folks to plan fishing vacations here in the winter months. But locals can slip onto the lower sound on calm days and catch some good 10- to 15-pound springs.

These same fish are of growing interest in April when they are mixed with increasing numbers of larger springs and a few tyee (chinook of 30 or more pounds). During the summer, catches are truly a mixture of springs, tyee and silvers. Tyee become particularly numerous in late May and June and, if somewhat less abundant later, are largest in late July, August and September when some of the largest "slabs" are caught. Silvers of 5 to 15 pounds make up the biggest percentage of salmon caught each season, moving into offshore waters in late June and caught in large numbers offshore and increasingly in the sound during July, August and September. Often anglers will be boating fish with great success from the mouth of the sound all the way nearly up to Port Alberni.

The Broken Island Group in the lower center of Barkley Sound are filled with quiet coves and beaches that beckon small boaters. photo by Terry Rudnick.

The larger yelloweye rockfish generally await along the deeper slopes of pinnacles.

Trying to predict the timing or prevalence of one group or another is pretty difficult. There are nearly always salmon to be caught in and outside of Barkley Sound, but it is often hard to say what will be moving in at any given time since it varies so widely from year to year.

You'll see different anglers catching salmon by all methods here—trolling, mooching or jigging. All work well and fishermen tend to fish their preference. But what you *won't* see in the "Lower 48" are so many choosing to jig. That is the method long in vogue here, particularly among B.C. fishermen. And you certainly won't see packed charterboats driftjigging in the U.S. as you'll see them doing off Ucluelet.

Of course wherever offshore the fish may be, the charters are well-equipped to find them. That is not always true of anglers in small private or rented boats, many of which may not be suited to go far offshore but can easily fish the lower sound. They should be able to find salmon without venturing far out. Many who don't jig choose to troll anchovies or Tomic plugs on downriggers in front of Cree Island, off Cape Beale, at the entrance to Beale Harbor or—near Ucluelet—around Chrow Island, just to name a few of many areas anglers find fish.

The locally popular rig among trollers calls for an anchovy on a double-hook rig at the end of a 6-foot leader behind an Okie flasher. That doesn't give the anchovy a great deal of action, but it seems to work.

Of course many "inside" fishermen do well casting jigs. When silvers are around, casting and retrieving Buzz Bombs may prove more effective than vertical drift-jigging. I recall spotting some suspicious targets on a chart recorder while cruising slowly through a quiet bay north of Wouwer Island in the Broken group on a dead-calm July afternoon. We cut the engine and both my buddy and I cast our Buzz Bombs and immediately began working them back. We both hooked salmon; mine jumped and threw the hook but he landed a long, bright 11-pounder after a memorably exciting battle in those quiet waters on his 4-pound test line.

"The real key to finding salmon in Barkley Sound is finding the feed," says veteran Barkley angler Bill Otway. He's also the Sportfisheries Ombudsman for the Canada Department of Fisheries and Oceans in Vancouver. The salmon move into and out of the sound according to movements of baitfish, Otway points out.

Often, finding that "feed" is easy. Huge, thick balls of herring or "needlefish" (eulachon or candlefish) or anchovies can be spotted at the surface by diving birds. Clearly, the private boater with an LCD, chart or video sounder will be way ahead in finding big clouds of baitfish when they're deeper.

Unfortunately, there are times when salmon won't be nearly as much in evidence around big schools of bait as dogfish may be. I've seen schools of big doggies in these quiet inside waters so thick that people were free-gaffing them for "sport." Any effort to fish for salmon in such spots are sure to be frustrated, at least with bait. And even then, the dogfish may be so numerous that they'll be caught repeatedly on metal jigs.

Even if fishing is slow, the waters around Barkley's islands, rocks and kelp beds are often alive with marine wildlife—eagles, seals and sea lions and grey whales. Although by summer, major whale migrations are long past, a few greys often stick around and can be seen almost daily feeding just off the kelp along the reefs that line the mouth of the sound southeast of Ucluelet Harbor. Watching them from small boats, from a reasonable distance of course, is an breathtaking, fascinating experience.

Barkley's Bountiful Bottomfish Bonanaza

With so many salmon to be caught here and with daily limits generous enough (still four at press time) to keep fishermen busy chasing salmon to fill those limits, bottomfishing—though increasingly popular every year—still tends to remain an incidental or secondary sport for many.

But the fact is that it offers what may be the very finest light-tackle sport for nonsalmonid gamefish to be found anywhere on the Pacific Coast. That is attributable to three factors: extensive and ideal habitat, large and varied populations of game fish, and the availability of most of these fish in relatively shallow water.

I have enjoyed some of my fastest fishing ever here. One summer I was among a group of light-line enthusiasts

Join The Jigging Fleet—Fly-in Trips And Charterboat Fishing At Barkley Sound

Much of the growing familiarity with and enthusiasm for Barkley Sound fishing can be attributed to the the Canadian Princess. That's a resort—in fact, an old restored cruise ship permanently moored next to the Ucluelet government docks and rooms in an adjacent land-based lodge complex—run by the Oak Bay Marine Group in Victoria. Part of this success has to do with a very high-profile, aggressive marketing of reasonably-priced "quickie" fly-in packages that squeeze in two full days of fishing and two nights with all amenities, as well as longer trips.

Visitors who do fly (or drive) in to stay at the Princess to fish Barkley Sound will take advantage of its very large, busy charter fleet (at a very affordable rate for a day of fishing). Many who aren't staying at the resort also fish from these charters (at a slightly higher daily rate).

It is surprising to see 10 43- to 50-foot charters keeping so busy here. But even more surprising is *how* it fishes. Canadian Princess charters do nothing but driftjig, generally offshore, and are wonderfully successful for both salmon and halibut.

These boats supply anglers with long (9-foot) graphite jigging rods and hefty levelwind reels filled with 25-pound main line. To that, a 20-pound leader is tied and at the end, simply, a typical metal salmon jig, usually green, of 70 grams, which is about 2 1/2 ounces, or for days when the drift is fast, a jig not quite twice that size.

The charters most often fish offshore at least several miles, at times over the 40-fathom bank there. The crew instruct anglers to lower their jigs to approximately the depth where salmon are showing and simply work them vertically. More extensive instruction than that is seldom necessary. Both chinook and silvers are taken this way and limits are hardly unusual. When the springs are close in, the charters will drift just off the rocks sometimes no farther from the harbor than Carolina Channel.

Halibut, often scattered on the bottom in considerable numbers, are also caught consistently on jigs. Often, an angler intentionally (or perhaps inadvertantly) will lower his jig to the bottom and battle up a big flatfish—whereupon most other fishermen immediately begin prospecting similarly. Other times, the crew will specificlly instruct passengers to let their jigs hit the bottom for halibut.

These charters also offer bottomfish trips, usually in the afternoon. They work the reefs and pinnacles off the Broken Islands and seldom return without lots of variety and lots of fish.

fishing from small boats. We averaged 100 to nearly 300 pounds of fish *per person per day* on lines testing only 4 to 12 pounds! (Of course we released most of these though there were no limits at that time; we were after sport, not meat, though we got plenty of both.)

Just a glance at a nautical chart that shows the waters out front (to the south) of the Broken Islands should explain quickly such productivity. The rocky, ragged, rugged, vermicular pinnacles, ledges and channels that make up these reefs provide unlimited places to hide and feed. Often, a drift over higher pinnacles with a video or chart recorder is a show in itself, with clouds of bait and fish continually on the screen.

We fished artificials strictly—leadhead jigs and worms or pork rind, metal "salmon" jigs or Krocodile spoons. Keep at least a couple rods rigged and ready at the start of each drift—starting with, say, a levelwind or spinner holding 6-pound test. Begin your drift atop a pinnacle or high spot, in 30 to 60 feet of water. Cast out a white leadhead jig of an ounce or two with a plastic tail. *IF* it can fall through massive schools of black, yellowtail or blue rockfish, you'll probably pick up a cabezon.

I've caught more cabezon here than in any other one area on the Pacific Coast. These big "bullheads" of 5 to 15 pounds (and up) are distinguished less by their relatively ugly appearance (much like a shorter, stubbier lingcod) than by their extra-firm, tasty flesh and their surprisingly dogged fight. No bottomfish fights harder, pound for pound, than the "cab." Hook a good one on 6-pound line and you'll be in for a long battle with plenty of reel-screeching runs.

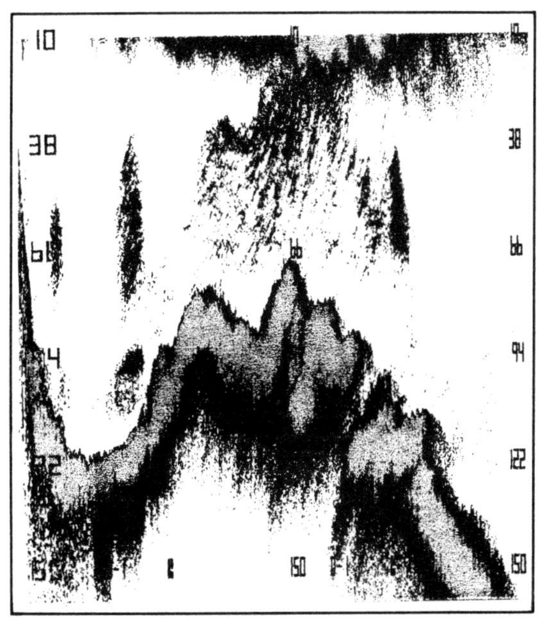

This transcript from a chart recorder shows a typical series of pinnacles off (west of) the Broken Islands, jutting from 180 feet to 66 feet. Clouds of fish and bait hover around and over the top.

On the other hand, it is not unusual for schools of rockfish to be so abundant right at the surface that you may want to cast out a shallow-running plug such as Mirrolure. Sometimes they'll be feeding and boiling right at the surface and you can watch them hit the lure. Flyfishing enthusiasts can enjoy action they'll remember for a long time. Incidentally, blue rockfish (very similar to the black to the average eye, yet very distinguishable) are not often common north of northern California except at Barkley Sound.

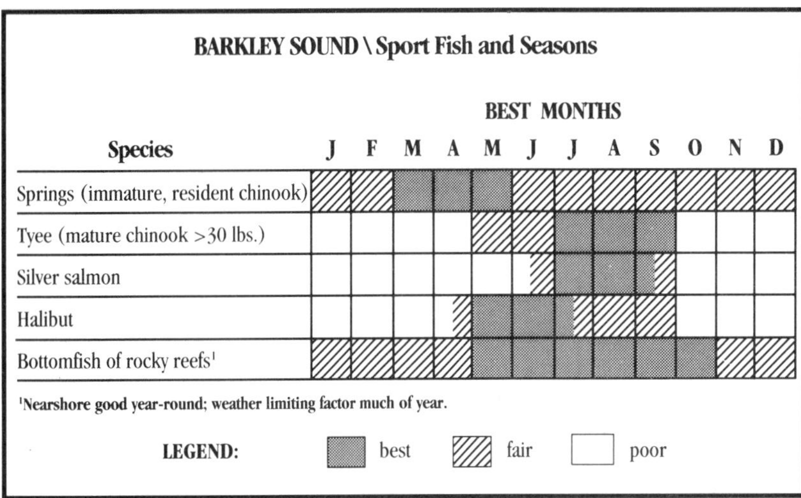

BARKLEY SOUND \ Sport Fish and Seasons

Species	J	F	M	A	M	J	J	A	S	O	N	D
	BEST MONTHS											
Springs (immature, resident chinook)	fair	fair	best	best	best	fair	fair	fair	fair	fair	fair	fair
Tyee (mature chinook >30 lbs.)	poor	poor	poor	poor	fair	fair	best	best	best	poor	poor	poor
Silver salmon	poor	poor	poor	poor	poor	poor/fair	best	best	best/fair	poor	poor	poor
Halibut	poor	poor	poor	poor/fair	best	best	best/fair	fair	fair	poor	poor	poor
Bottomfish of rocky reefs[1]	fair	fair	fair	fair	best	best	best	best	best	best	fair	fair

[1]Nearshore good year-round; weather limiting factor much of year.

LEGEND: best fair poor

You'll pick up other species atop the pinnacles, including other rockfish—the hard-fighting copper, the colorful little China, quillbacks. You may run into schools of Pacific mackerel as well. Tiger rockfish are always beautifully-marked and always rare—but, again, I've seen more from western Vancouver Island than elsewhere.

As the drift continues and the bottom drops away to 60 to 120 feet, look for other species including canary and vermilion rockfish. Vermilion rockfish are distinguishable by the dusky black tint over the brick red body and the red eye. Most sport-caught vermilions come from very deep waters off central and southern California. Yet we've caught a great many just in front of Barkley Sound, averaging 5 to 10 pounds. They tend to fight noticeably harder than other rockfish taken from the same depths (and are somewhat more easily released unaffected).

With increasing depth, set down one rod and pick up another—perhaps rigged with 10-pound line and a three-ounce spoon. Lingcod may latch onto a spoon or jig (or, of course, onto another fish already hooked) at any depth, but bigger ones are more frequent during the summer in deeper waters. The deep slopes of these pinnacles and reefs, in 150 to 300+ feet, produce some 20- to 40-pound

Casting a metal jig toward fish marked just below the surface in the Broken Islands produced this long silver after a tough battle on 4-pound line.

Terry Rudnick, an outdoor writer who has spent many days fishing Barkley Sound, puts the gaff through the jaw of a big lingcod which had attempted to make lunch of a small yellowtail rockfish bait.

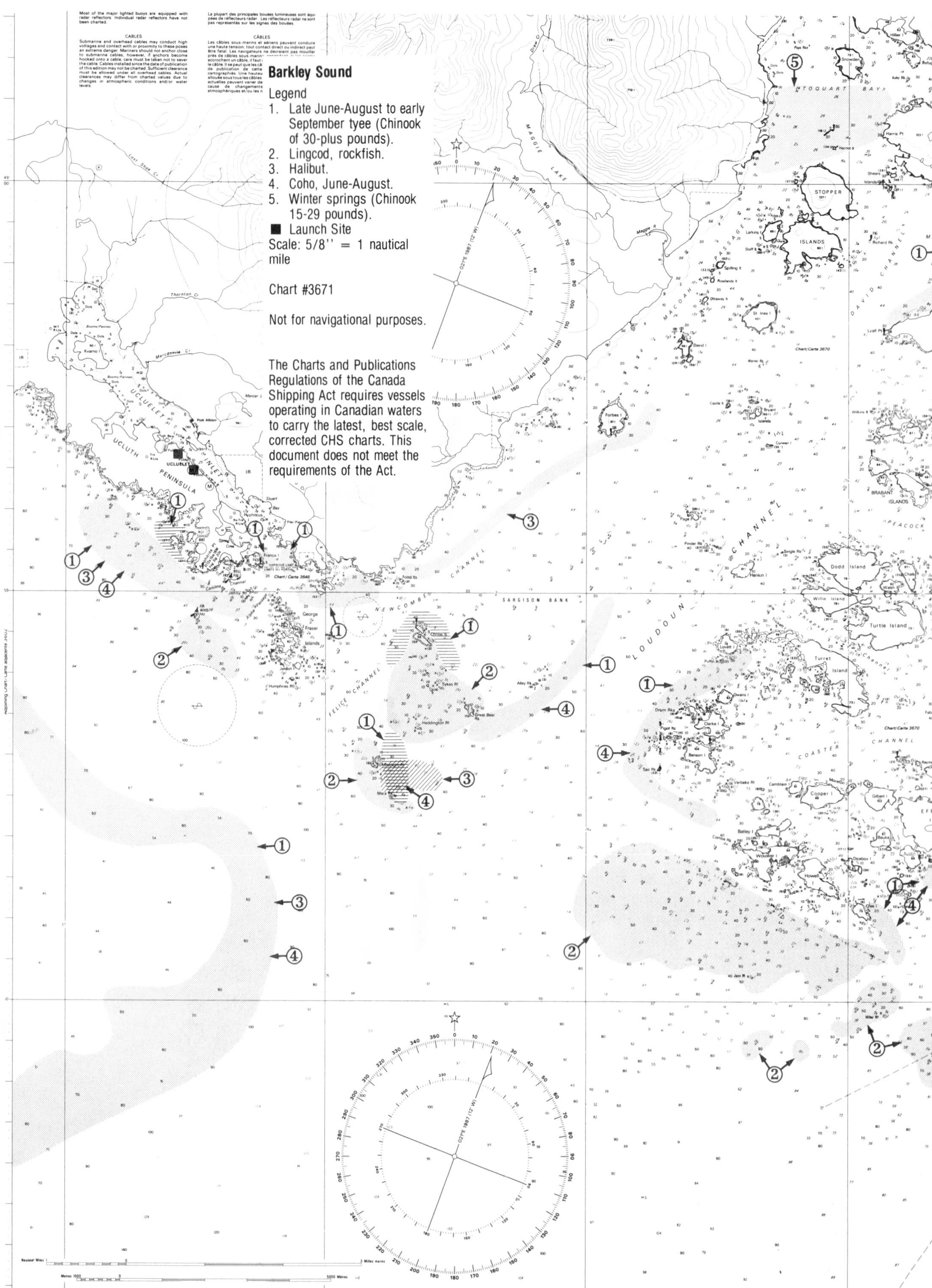

Barkley Sound
Legend
1. Late June-August to early September tyee (Chinook of 30-plus pounds).
2. Lingcod, rockfish.
3. Halibut.
4. Coho, June-August.
5. Winter springs (Chinook 15-29 pounds).
■ Launch Site
Scale: 5/8'' = 1 nautical mile
Chart #3671
Not for navigational purposes.
The Charts and Publications Regulations of the Canada Shipping Act requires vessels operating in Canadian waters to carry the latest, best scale, corrected CHS charts. This document does not meet the requirements of the Act.
UCLUELET
UCLUTH PENINSULA
NEWCOMBE CHANNEL
LOUDOUN CHANNEL
SARGISON BANK
FELICE CHANNEL
TOQUART BAY
STOPPER ISLANDS
MAGGIE LAKE
MACOAH PASSAGE
DAVID CHANNEL
BRABANT ISLANDS
PEACOCK CHANNEL
Dodd Island
Turtle Island
Turret Island
COASTER CHANNEL
Cooper I
Batley I
Howell I

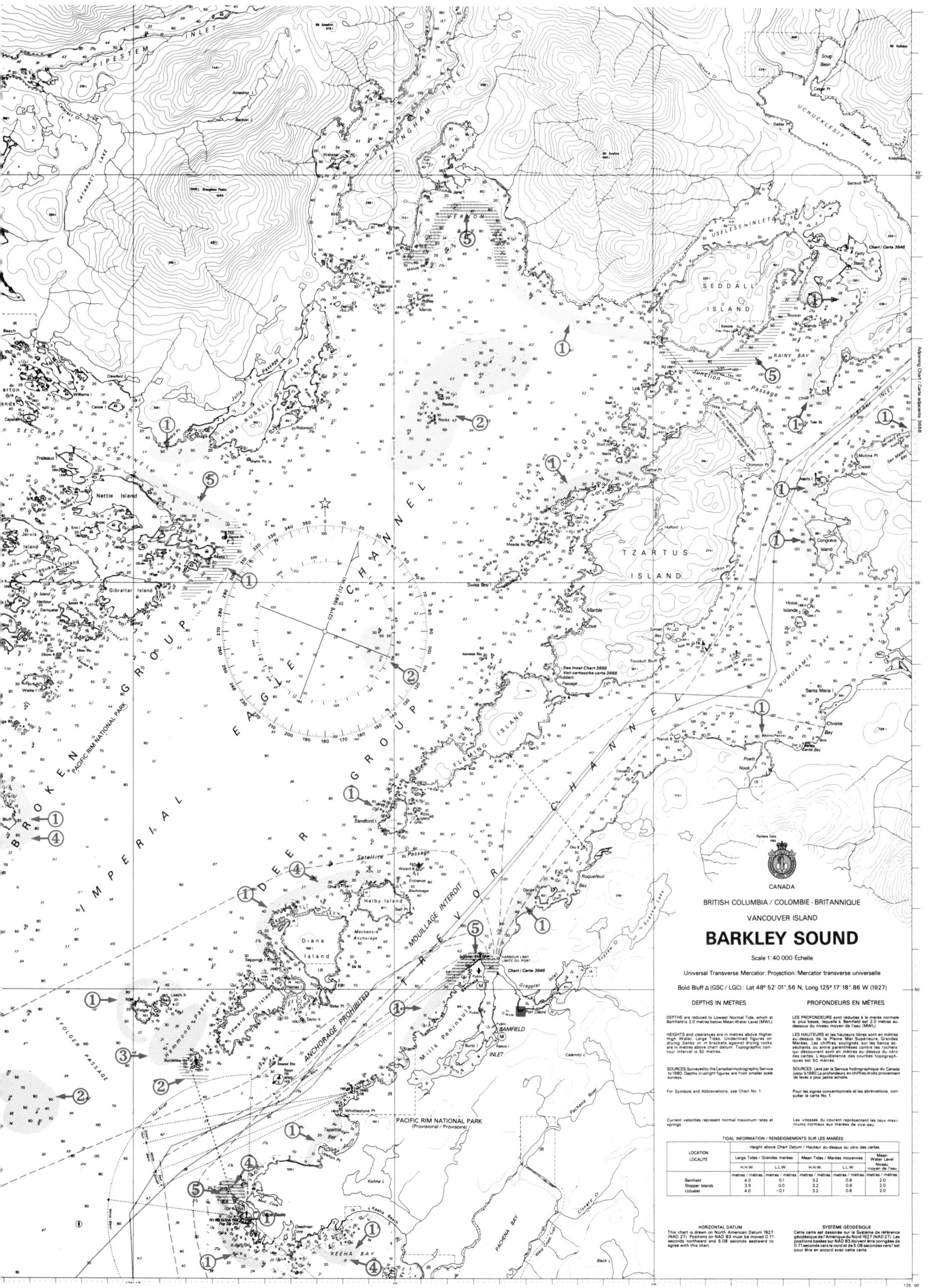

LOCATION / LOCALITÉ	Height above Chart Datum / Hauteur au-dessus du zéro des cartes				
	Large Tides / Grandes marées		Mean Tides / Marées moyennes		Mean Water Level / Niveau moyen de l'eau
	H.H.W.	L.L.W.	H.H.W.	L.L.W.	
	metres / mètres	metres / mètres	metres / mètres	metres / mètres	metres / mètres
Bamfield	4.0	0.1	3.2	0.6	2.0
Stopper Islands	3.9	0.0	3.2	0.6	2.0
Ucluelet	4.0	−0.1	3.2	0.6	2.0

lings (though lingcod over 60 are taken here) and good numbers of big yelloweye rockfish, often 15 to over 20 pounds.

If an angler is here only for meat, he can drop over a chunk of bait on heavy salmon gear, crank in a few fish in no time, fire up and run back to the docks. But any small boat angler who enjoys real sport fishing at its fastest and most varied would be making a major mistake to come to Barkley without light tackle and light lures as described above. It is also advisable to be ready to *catch and release* since on a calm day you'll have more fish than you want in no time—even on light gear.

This area of fabulous habitat does have one drawback. Although very close to the Broken Islands, it is nevertheless very *exposed*, on the edge of the open Pacific. These waters can get plenty nasty any time and more so on a strong ebb tide. Only foolish small boaters remain on "the outside" when seas kick up, as they can do in a hurry. But there are almost always protected waters up inside the sound with so many islands and reefs. If salmon fishing is slow on the inside, light-tackle bottomfish can be fun. There won't be the variety or numbers of fish, but there should still be enough action to keep things interesting. Just drift around the edges (slopes) of any exposed rocks or, better, submerged reefs. Expect many smaller lings and copper rockfish, as well as smaller black rockfish. (But don't be surprised with larger fish, including some lunker lings.)

There is much less rocky habitat once offshore. But there are big gravelly banks and often these can be loaded with halibut. Knowing exactly where on these banks halibut are located is a matter of gaining access to some skippers' secret logbooks, probably in their safety deposit boxes, or lucking into your own hotspots. Actually, with so many taken incidentally, "lucking into" halibut beds offshore is not unlikely. Then, Loran-C is invaluable in permitting you to return to that spot again. The movements and abundance of halibut are annual variables here, but a somewhat more consistent factor is timing: halibut tend to be most prevalent in May and June and, often, into July.

Bottomfish regulations remain generous at press time, with 8 bottomfish and/or cabezon per day and 3 lings per day allowed at press time. But more anglers fishing the sound and more interest in bottomfish have meant a decided increase in fishing pressure, and Ocean and Fisheries biologists will be scrutinizing the situation in coming years. Tighter regulations are at least a possibility, so check each year before making assumptions based on a previous season's regulations.

The launch ramp at Uclulet is free but limited to boats of modest size.

Small Boat Safety

A major hazard and, often in the summer, a plague to Barkley Sound recreational boaters are Pacific fogs. They roll in frequently, thick and enduring and often with little warning.

Ironically, the nicest (warmest, sunniest) summer weather is usually a harbinger of the thickest fogs. These are likely to enshroud the coast overnight, so the darkness greeting anglers who awaken before dawn to head out for the salmon bite never really brightens until the fogs lifts, much later in the morning as a rule.

It is not unsual for the fog to remain offshore, at least for a while. Anglers may run out in their small boats to join the charter fleet only to see, off on the horizon, a dark bank of fog resembling a distant line of cliffs on a shoreline. Yet that "distant" fog bank can, at some point in the morning, roll in almost without warning and quickly white-out everything more than 50 feet away.

Most fishermen without radar—which of course the great majority of small boaters lack—won't run offshore (or attempt to navigate the rock-studded sound) in a fog. But anyone who fishes offshore may end up in fog. Cautious anglers may run back in when an offshore fog bank appears to be rolling toward them. I must confess that I have remained out, fishing right among the radar-equipped charters, knowing I could steam back into the inlet behind them. A good plan—unless one has engine trouble!

Still, fogs are a part of summer life here. They are frequent and may be pea-soup thick for hours. Charter anglers needn't worry and can, in fact, enjoy the smooth ocean a fog usually brings and the unique, eerie feeling of fishing "lost" in a world without horizons or reference points. Small boaters who fish here much are likely to end up at some point in the same "world." Yet, according to local Coast Guard officials, amazingly many of the boats they check or assist have neither a good working compass or a radio (CB or, preferably, VHF)! Those two items, plus a nautical chart, are indispensible for safe navigation. **Don't** venture offshore or even far into the lower sound without them!

Another fact of oceanic life here in the summer are afternoon westerly winds. More often than not, you can count on these kicking up mid- to late morning and blowing at a steady 15 to 20 knots or so right on through to about suppertime, when they usually settle right down. The Pacific can get pretty rough pretty quickly; many small boaters fish the early-morning bite (when the fog will let them) and the evening bite, choosing to catch up on some sleep during the sunny, breezy afternoons.

Ironically, some days the fog remains thick through late morning and almost as soon as it lifts the day's wind has blown up. (But at least at such times, small boaters can fish up inside the sound. And unlike the open ocean, the sound has many protected bays into which one can duck and a fair amount of traffic leaving a broken-down boat a bit less alone.)

Canadian Coast Guard—Tofino

(There is no search-and-rescue station in Barkley Sound. Tofino, just to the north, covers this area.)

Search and Rescue Station.............. 725-3231

Facilities

Area code for all listings is 604 except as noted.

(Charters vary from office to office, year to year. Generally, these 4- to 6-person boats are chartered by the hour. At press time, a rate of $50/hour for boat, bait and tackle was typical—often with a minimum of six hours or so.)

Resorts, Marinas And Charters

Canadian Princess, Oak Bay Marine Group, 1327 Beach Drive, Victoria, B.C. V8S 2N4, 598-3366 or (800) 663-7090, 7 days/week. Lodging aboard restored ship in Uclulet Harbor or in adjacent shoreside chalets, with fishing aboard 10-ship fleet of 43- to 50-foot charter boats. Walk-on anglers welcome as well as guests at very reasonable rates for a day of fishing offshore. Offers daily rates and complete packages including fly-in trips from Vancouver.

Island West Resort, P.O. Box 32, Ucluelet V0R 3A0, 726-7515. On central Ucluelet Harbor with full facilities for all anglers, year-round: charters, boat rentals, tackle and bait, RV spaces with hookups, campground, showers, boat launching and moorage.

Bamfield Inn, Reservations and information—P.O. Box 8056, Blaine, WA 98230, (206) 272-2221. Lodge—P.O. Box 111, Bamfield, V0R 1B0, 728-3354. Resort for fly-in or drive-in clientele, offers package trips that include unlimited use of 17-foot whaler-type fiberglass skiffs with 30-hp outboards, May-September.

Seabeam Fishing Resort/Bamfield Kingfisher Marina, P.O. Box 38, Bamfield, V0R 1B0, 728-3228 or 728-3286. Offers lodging in main lodge, cottages and "wilderness camping," boat rentals, guided fishing trips, moorage, fuel, and package fishing trips

Port Alberni Sportfishing Centre and Marina (Clutesi Haven), 5104 River Road, Port Alberni V9Y 6Z1, 723-8022. Salmon and bottomfish charters, boat rentals, moorage, fuel, tackle shop, food; many accomodations nearby. Also works with river steelheaders. Open year-round. The Murphy family has been running the marina here for 27 years; they're friendly helpful and no one knows the waters of Port Alberni and Barkley Sound better.

Poett Nook Marina and Charters, 2178 Cameron Drive, Port Alberni V9Y 1B2, 723-7930 or 724-6651. Campsites, moorage, boat launch, fuel, tackle and bait, store and guided fishing in 18- to 20-foot boats, March-September.

Action Fishing Charters, 3894 Morton Street, Port Alberni, V9Y 3V3. 723-3056. Several boats out of Port Alberni, May through October.

Alberni Pacific Charters, 5440 Argyle Street, Port Alberni V9Y 1T7, 724-3112. Year-round salmon and steelhead angling, complete packages.

Imperial Eagle Charters, Bamfield, V0R 1B0, 728-3375. Three boats (21-foot Campion Fishing Machines), March through September.

Bob Welsh West Coast Outfitting, P.O. Box 1219, Port Alberni V9Y 7M1, 723-1009.

Breaker's Marine, P.O. Box 99, Bamfield V0R 1B0, 728-3281. Inboard, outboard engine service.

P.Y. Marine, Bamfield, V0R 1B0, 724-2322. Inboard, outboard engine service (Johnson/OMC).

Tyee Lodge, P.O. Box 32, Bamfield, V0R 1V0, 728-3296. Exclusive salmon fishing lodge for 12 people whose main market is corporations in Canada, United States, Europe and Kuwait.

Motels

Seaside Motel, 160 Hemock Street, Ucluelet V0R 3A0, 726-4624.

West Coast Motel, P.O. Box 275, Ucluelet V0R 3A0, 726-7732.

Bamfield Trails Motel, P.O. Box 7, Bamfield V0R 1B0, 728-3231.

Tyee Village Motel, 4151 Redford Street, Port Alberni V9Y 3R6, 723-8133.

Timberlodge, Suite 210, C-12, Port Alberni V9Y 7L6, 723-9415.

Moorage, Boat Launching

Public moorage is available at the government docks behind the Canadian Princess. Five separate floats can accomodate 100 or so small boats and, according to harbormaster Arnie Dugan, there is usually space all summer except during times of offshore storms when commercial and larger private yachts come in seeking shelter. Charges are minimal—at press time, a bit over a buck per meter (yard, approximately). For more information, call the harbormaster's office at 726-4241.

Small boats put in at the shallow ramp at the end of Seaplane Base Road. It is free, but rough and not much good for larger boats.

A better, private ramp, charging a moderate fee in and out, is located at the Island West Resort (described above).

Public Campgrounds

Pacific Rim National Park, Box 280, Ucluelet V0R 3A0.

Broken Islands wilderness campgrounds are reached by boat only. Camping is permitted in areas displaying a campground symbol on Gilbert, Hand, Willis, Clarke, Benson, Turret and Gibraltar islands. Some freshwater may be available but it is best to bring a supply.

For More Information

Bamfield Chamber of Commerce, Box 5, Bamfield V0R 1B0.

Ucluelet Chamber of Commerce, Box 428, Ucluelet V0R 3A0, 726-4641

Alberni Valley Tourist Info Centre, Site 215, C-10, R.R. 2, Port Alberni V9Y 7L6, 724-6535.

Clayoquot Sound

While Barkley and Nootka sounds are largely wide-open inlets with islands and reefs scattered through the open water, Clayoquot (pronounced "Kla-kwot") Sound—located between the two—is more a series of large islands with narrow inlets and channels snaking their way between.

Nearly all sportfishing effort here comes from one spot: Tofino. This little commercial fishing/tourist village at the southeastern edge of Clayoquot Sound (and at the northern tip of Pacific Rim National Park) is the only population center on the sound. It is reached easily by paved highway from Nanaimo. (The 140-mile route is the same as to Tofino, except for the last 15 or so miles.) Land-based or float planes arrive reguarly, as do private yachts.

In general, development of the sound for tourists and anglers is minimal, particularly compared to the rapid growth of such facilities around Barkley Sound. Tofino retains the flavor of a small coastal community with traditions in sportfishing and an interest in the sea, its history and fauna. Small hotels, resorts, shop and galleries and a number of restaurants make this an appealing tourist destination increasingly "discovered."

Although much of the sportfishing effort here is from private boats trailered up, small charters do operate from one or two resorts in Tofino oriented to sportfishing. Just about all fishing occurs in one of three settings: in channels on the inside, off rocks and reefs out front or over 20-fathom waters offshore.

Salmon Inside And At The Mouth Of The Sound: Rocks, Reefs And Points

One needn't travel far from the harbor at Tofino to find fishing for salmon. Many of the largest kings here are caught just off the kelp in the surge of swells rolling in to batter exposed rocks, around areas such as Lennard Island, Nob Rock, Surprise Reef, McKay Reef, Wilf Rock and Cleland Island, to name a few. (Wilf Rock is, by the way, the premier hotspot for big tyee.)

Author holds up chinook, while anglers in "Orca Lodge" boat fish in background.

The action can be nearly year-round in this nearshore fishery for chinook. Springs (resident chinook to over 20 pounds) are taken during the winter and at least through early summer, with catches peaking in the spring.

Many anglers pursue springs in the area of Russell Channel to fish such areas as Tibbs island the shallow water around Kutcous ("cut-cuss") Island.

Larger, mature tyee (chinook over 30 pounds) move in during June and increase in number and size until they peak in August. Then, the rocks and points mentioned above that jut out of the water from Lennard Island (south of Esowista Peninsula) all the way northwest fronting the mouth of the sound to Sea Otter Rock.

The majority of anglers prefer drift- or motor-mooching herring here. You'll also see trollers pulling bait and drift-fishermen working metal salmon jigs.

Perhaps the pace of action is at its fastest in September and October when the big silvers have moved inside. Although all the methods used for chinook work for silvers, "bucktailing" is an exciting sport: fast-trolling large flies or plastic squid right on the surface.

For silvers, popular spots include Russell Channel, Monks Island and, particularly, the huge sandbar in the channel west of the Catface Range (between the western edge of that peninsula and Yates Point on the southeast corner of huge Flores Island).

That same "sandbar area" also attracts populations of chinook, springs early in the year and tyee beginning in June. It offers a shot at big salmon in water shallower than usual. That is just one of the areas where flyfishermen could score a good-sized spring or tyee. That thought prompted Weigh West Marina/Resort to begin a "challenge" for flyfishermen—during its first year, 1990, worth $2,000—to the first fisherman registering and paying a modest fee who can boat a tyee (30+ pounds) by casting a fly with a tippet no heavier than 12-pound line.

Nearshore And Offshore Waters For Salmon, Halibut (And Other Stuff)

Many boats head offshore in May or June for combined catches of springs, a few tyee and some of the season's best halibut fishing. There is no "magic spot" that requires a top-secret book of Loran-C numbers. Fishermen are successful who simply head out from Portland Point to 20-25 fathoms. There, most troll lines set on downriggers, generally near bottom for springs and halibut, or shallower for silvers later in the summer.

While monster halibut are not particularly common, most years there seem to be no shortage of 10- to

30-pounders. Driftjigging is always an effective method, particularly when a productive "bed" is located. But a surprising number of these "bottomfish" are caught on gear trolled for salmon.

By July, along with some larger tyee, silvers move in. At this time of year they'll average 4 to 9 pounds, but that size increases considerably later in the summer. Timing and size of silver runs vary from year to year and are seldom predictable. Often silvers move along the coast in great numbers, sometime so thick that commercial chinook trollers have to freespool their gear down to get past the coho quickly. I have seen them three or so miles out, southwest of Portland Point, thick enough to watch them striking lures or bait alongside a drifting boat.

When large concentrations of feeding silvers are located, there is no more fun way to fish them than driftjigging with light tackle. Coho are wild and unpredictable anytime but particularly on light lines. Often a strike on one side of a boat will be followed seemingly simultaneously with that hooked coho leaping on the opposite side. Small (1- to 2-ounce) white or brightly-colored metal jigs fished on small spinning outfits with 4- to 8-pound line offer the most action and excitement, simply worked gently just 10 to 30 or 40 feet below the boat, as a rule. I've enjoyed mornings of catching and releasing many coho beyond a daily limit just this way.

Some years, particularly large runs of sockeye pass by. Although these deep-red-meated salmon tend to feed on very small fish and invertebrates, they can be taken on hook and line. Dick Close, manager at Weigh West Resort, suggests following the lead of commercial trollers who have learned how to take sockeye consistently. He says trolling a long string of dodgers end-to-end (a dozen wouldn't be too many) seems to attract sockeye and they end up following behind ready to strike "anything red." The idea of red (or in some areas bright pink) as a preferred color for sockeye has been around for some time. For trollers, this could mean small Hoochys, spoons, U-20 Flatfish or perhaps flies. Driftfishermen might do well with small, pink, white or chrome Buzz Bombs or Dart jigs.

Certainly most anglers are after salmon or halibut offshore, but there are other species to be caught. In fact, drop a jig in the summer to the bottom and there's no telling what you might come up with.

We did just that one summer day and beyond catching a limit of coho (and a 20-pound spring that grabbed a Buzz Bomb I lowered to bottom with six-pound line), three of us came up with a small halibut, several rockfish (including tigers, coppers, quillbacks), Pacific cod, big skate, squid and Pacific mackerel.

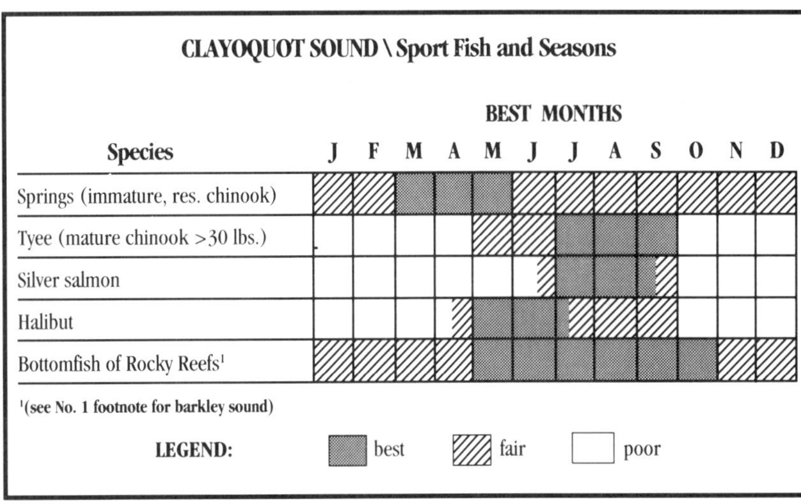

CLAYOQUOT SOUND \ Sport Fish and Seasons

Species	J	F	M	A	M	J	J	A	S	O	N	D
	BEST MONTHS											
Springs (immature, res. chinook)	fair	fair	best	best	best	fair	fair	fair	fair	fair	fair	fair
Tyee (mature chinook >30 lbs.)	poor	poor	poor	poor	fair	fair	best	best	best	poor	poor	poor
Silver salmon	poor	poor	poor	poor	poor	poor/fair	best	best	best/fair	poor	poor	poor
Halibut	poor	poor	poor	poor/fair	best	best	best/fair	fair	fair	poor	poor	poor
Bottomfish of Rocky Reefs[1]	fair	fair	fair	fair	best	best	best	best	best	best	fair	fair

[1](see No. 1 footnote for barkley sound)

LEGEND: best — fair — poor

At times immense schools of mackerel may be encountered in these offshore waters, typically during July and August. Although only a couple pounds, they are amazingly strong fighter for their size (as are all members of the tuna family). The meat is dark and probably strong for many tastes, though they can make an excellent smoked or canned product. And it is very possible that a live mackerel lowered to bottom could entice a big halibut or lingcod in short order.

Lingcod are occasionally taken offshore, when baits or lures are drifted or trolled near small rockpiles. However, much more consistent catches or rock-loving bottomfishes such as lings and yelloweye rockfish are taken around more pronounced rocky areas where the waters drop off from 15 or 16 fathoms to 20+. A glance at a nautical chart (no. 3640) will show this line running along the front of the sound. Bottomfish populations here receive less pressure then those close to Ucluelet and seem to be holding up well. In good conditions (not too much current or wind), a drift almost anywhere there are rocks should produce fish. (See Barkley Sound section for suggestions about light tackle bottomfishing sport.)

Small Boat Safety

The trickiest area for boaters not famililar with Clayoquot Sound is probably the area around Tofino itself, rife with rocks and shallow areas. Watch marker signs carefully and use a nautical chart (no. 3685 offers a detailed chart of the harbor and all approaches).

The sound is swept by significant currents, often to 3 knots, which can make the going tricky also, around Tofino itself as well as areas like Tibbs Island in Russell Channel. Many shallow shoals can leave the unwary foundering; the Coast Guard receives many such calls from sailboats.

Another problem the Coast Guard has with recreational boaters here involves the buoys marking the channel in to the harbor from areas such as Russell Channel. Naturally boaters will keep red buoys to their right as they're returning—heading up the channel toward Tofino. However, upon coming past Dunlap Island down the top of Father Charles Channel, the red buoys should be to the boater's *left:* Although still "heading in" toward Tofino, the route has now changed to south and heading back out eventually to the ocean. Coast Guard officials say that surprisingly often boaters end up aground because they're on the wrong side of the channel markers having failed to recognize the point at which they're no longer headed up the sound but out toward the ocean—even though still toward the harbor.

Fogs of course are a common summer problem anywhere along the Northwest coast. No place seems to have more than this area, though. Again, the Coast Guard offers advice: don't venture far out without at least a *good* working compass. Seems pretty obvious, yet every year many boaters here run into problems because they have no compass (or at least no reliable, working compass). Similarly, some boaters go forth with no sort of working radio.

Those heading offshore should, of course, keep in mind the usual—though not inevitable—westerlies that come up by late morning and blow through early evening.

Canadian Coast Guard—Tofino

Search and Rescue Station. 725-3231

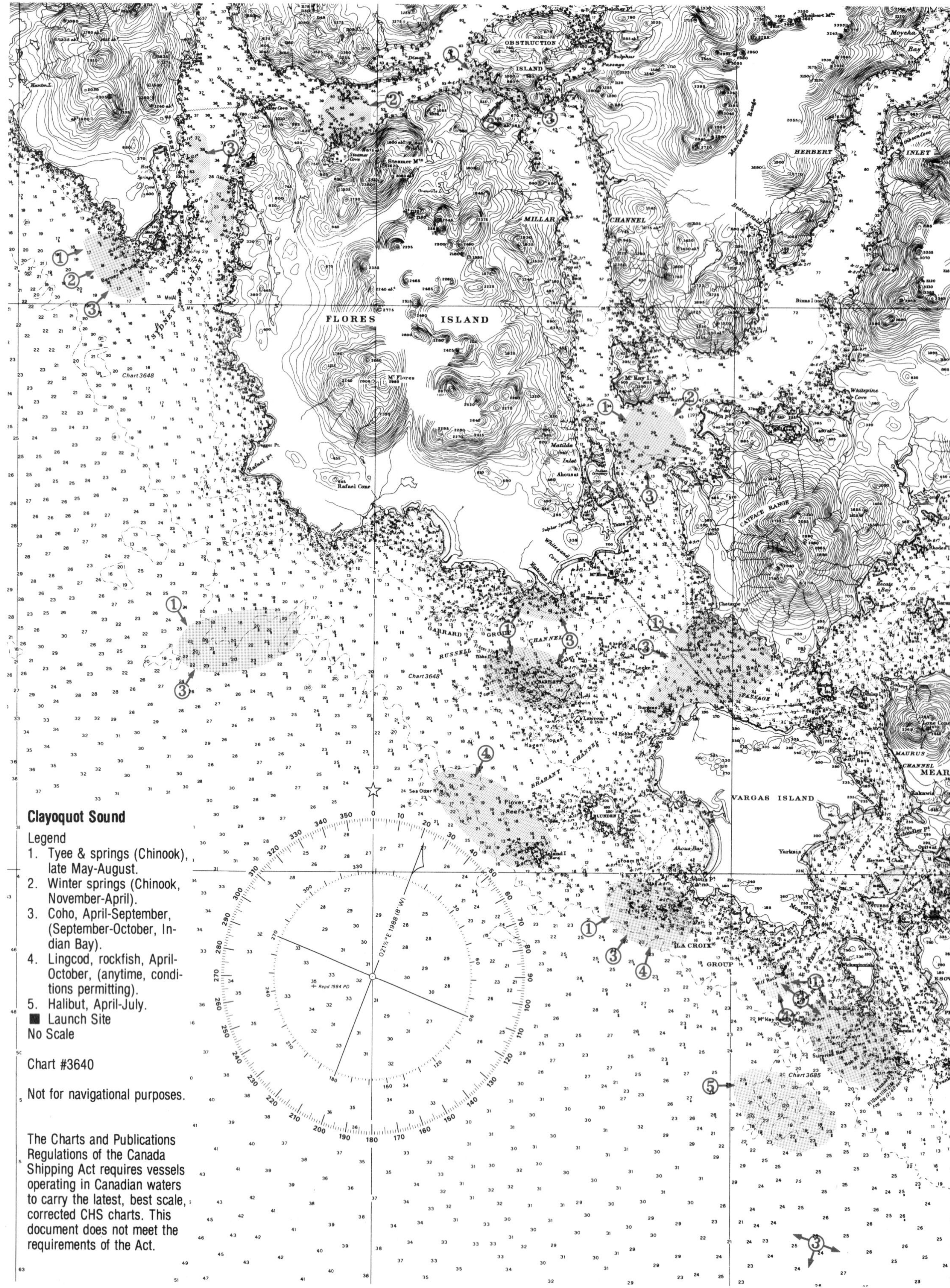

Clayoquot Sound
Legend
1. Tyee & springs (Chinook), late May-August.
2. Winter springs (Chinook, November-April).
3. Coho, April-September, (September-October, Indian Bay).
4. Lingcod, rockfish, April-October, (anytime, conditions permitting).
5. Halibut, April-July.
■ Launch Site
No Scale
Chart #3640
Not for navigational purposes.
The Charts and Publications Regulations of the Canada Shipping Act requires vessels operating in Canadian waters to carry the latest, best scale, corrected CHS charts. This document does not meet the requirements of the Act.
FLORES ISLAND
VARGAS ISLAND
OBSTRUCTION ISLAND
MILLAR CHANNEL
HERBERT INLET
CATFACE RANGE
GARRARD GROUP
RUSSELL CHANNEL
BRABANT CHANNEL
Plover Reefs
LA CROIX GROUP
MAURUS CHANNEL
Chart 3648
Chart 3685
021½°E 1988 (8°W)

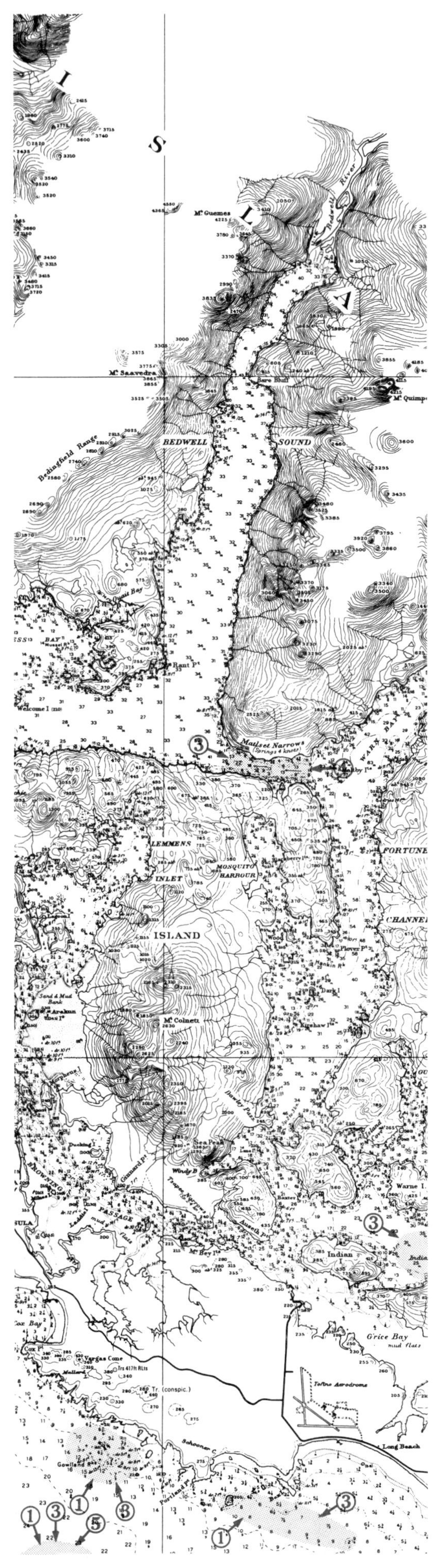

Facilities

Area code for all listings is 604; postal code is V0R 2Z0. Prices vary from place to place and year to year; call to check At press time, small-boat charters were generally on a per-boat basis, hourly or daily, with eight-hour daily rates—for three to four anglers—running about $500 Canadian.)

Resorts, Marinas And Charters

Weigh West Resort, Box 533, Tofino, 725-3277. This year-round resort offers lodging and moorage with 50 slips (in season these are pretty much reserved for guests only), and bait and tackle. The marina rents boats (16′ fiberglass with 9.9-hp outboards). Charter trips are offered aboard 17-and 19-foot Whalers for guests or nonguests (same rate). Charters troll, mooch or jig depending upon decisions made by guests and guides. Light tackle/flyfishing encouraged.

Orca Lodge, Box 479, Tofino, 725-3344. Located off highway a few miles east of Tofino, not on the water. Basically a relatively new motel in a quiet setting with fine lounge and restaurant that also offers charter fishing aboard a four-person Bayliner.

Ocean Village Beach Resort, Box 490, Hellesen Drive, Tofino, 725-3755, rustic quansit-type huts located southeast of town on McKenzie Beach.

Pacific Sands Beach Resort, Box 237, Tofino, 725-3322.

MacKenzie Beach Resort, Box 12, Tofino, 725-3439.

Bella Pacifica Resort & Campground, 725-3400

Moorage, Boat Launching

Public moorage is available at two government docks. Those in town are largely used by commercial vessels, but harbormaster Art Clark will put up recreational boats when space permits. The other government dock is located at Olson Road (about three blocks east of Weigh West Resort) and can fit in 15 or so sportfishing boats. Space runs out quickly in season and its first-come first-served (no reservations). Charges are minimal—at press time, a bit over a buck per meter (yard). For more information call the harbormaster's office at 725-4441.

The main launch ramp in town is a municipal ramp, free of charge, located at the foot of Fourth Street. It is a wide single lane, newly repaved and usable by most boats at most tides.

A smaller, less well-known ramp is located in Grice Bay, east of town, on Grice Bay Road past the golf course.

For More Information

Tofino-Long Beach Chamnber of Commerce, Box 476, Tofino, 725-3414.

Long Beach Information Center, 726-4212 or 726-7721.

Nootka Sound

THE FARTHER NORTH ONE GOES ALONG VANCOUVER Island's rugged Pacific (west) coast, the less development is evident. Resorts, visitors and traffic are all much in evidence in the southernmost major sound, Barkley.

But at Nootka Sound, on the central Vancouver Island coast, there is practically no development. Except for one resort near the mouth on the northern shore, lower Nootka Sound remains essentially as it has for centuries.

From several hundred feet up in a floatplane, this feeling of unspoiled coastal wilderness is strikingly evident. About all the development one can see along the northern shore below, as you near Friendly Cove and Yuquot Point, is the lighthouse at the point, a cabin at Friendly Bay and the small resort, Nootka Island Fishing Camp.

A few decades earlier you could have seen much *more* development, since the resort sits at the site of what was then the huge Nootka Cannery that at one time employed nearly 2,000 people. Yet as the floatplane motors up to the dock, few visible reminders are evident.

In fact, the area is rich in history which is generally invisible. One visible reminder is the distinctive stone monument at Yuquot Point to Captain James Cook, commemorating his historic landing here in 1778.

The small, quiet fishing resort tucked into a tiny bay just up from Yuquot Point today fits the sound. Nootka Fish Camp is neither fancy nor posh, but is laid-back and personal.

Guests from this fish camp account for most of the very minimal sportfishing effort in lower Nootka Sound. They fly in from Seattle most often, with regular service via Lake Union Air offered at a reasonable price. But a few fly in from Gold River at the head of the sound, a flight of a little over 10 minutes.

It is also quite possible to trailer to Gold River, put in a boat and cruise down to the lower sound. A few folks do just that. However, it takes a good-sized boat with a good cruising capacity since there are *no* facilities at this time for independent boaters in the sound below Gold River.

Fat tyee and the standard Nootka Sound tackle that took it—a white plug and single-action "knucklebuster" reel on a long, limber graphite rod.

Certainly the majority of anglers who experience Nootka Sound are most likely to do so via the Nootka Fish Camp. That being the case, some description of that facility here is justified, particularly since compared to costs of many coastal fly-in fishing packages, Nootka's rates have long been a real bargain.

The camp opened in 1983 and is still run by the same family, the Cyrs. Days are planned to take advantage of best salmon fishing and weather periods (which are fortunately much the same). So guests are out about daybreak, usually two to a guest with a guide in a 15-foot twin-hull fiberglass. These boats are very stable and do a good job for the area. The boats will fish until about noon, run in for a big lunch and several hours of nap time. After an early dinner, they're back out for 2-4 hours of fishing the evening bite. (Remember that during early summer it is light enough to fish until well after 10 p.m.)

Almost all fishing is trolling using downriggers. The fish camp has found it unnecessary to bother with bait, instead relying mostly on large white plugs but also hoochys (plastic squid) behind flashers or spoons. Often downriggers are set deep for chinook, 50 to 100 feet.

The resort equips guests with traditional Canadian salmon tackle: 10-foot whippy graphite rods with big single-action reels filled with 25-pound line. However, levelwinds and spinning gear with lighter line work just fine, also.

Much of the fishing is in the area from San Rafael Island (site of the lighthouse) west to Maquinna Point, along the southeastern shore of Nootka Island. Occasionally boats will run over to fish the mainland shore across the mouth of the sound (Burwood and Discovery points) or up Zuciarte Channel to Anderson Point.

Much of the effort is for chinook—springs in May (though available all year) and tyee in July and August. But the sheer abundance of silvers starting in July means the kind of fast action that makes many visitors forget the chance for a big chinook and troll shallower for silvers.

Halibut can be quite abundant in 20 to 30 fathoms. Some guides know by simple triangulation a few specific "beds" just offshore where they can do well consistently. But often just drifting "blind" or deep-trolling baits will put halibut in the boat. Don't look for many over 50 pounds or so; most will be 15 to 30 pounds. They'll certainly strike baits or lures set on downriggers: guides often use their downriggers to put an offering just over bottom (where they occasionally pick up feeding salmon as well). But for fishermen who enjoy driftfishing, working metal jigs or spoons is effective (and, again, also takes chinook occasionally). I have caught a number of halibut this way, fishing 12-pound line in 80 to 140 feet of water.

At times over these areas of sandy/muddy bottoms, dogfish can move in to plague fishermen. I have encountered them so thick here, especially when tides were light, that they would be fighting over a metal jig and almost every cast would bring another dogfish. That's unusual and not particularly desirable, and about all you can do is pick up and move to a different area.

The nearshore bottom tends to be largely smooth. Incidental catches of lingcod and large rockfish are somewhat less common than in the other sounds, though small lings are hardly unusual. There *are* some very rocky, very fishy reefs and pinnacles, particularly down toward Escalante Point, though that is a fair run from the safety of Friendly Cove.

There are always surprises, as well. For example, one day Ray Williams showed me his secret "longjaw" (Bocaccio) spot. William is a Nootka native of the Mochat ("people of the deer") tribe who, with his family, lives year-round in their home at Friendly cove to care for tribal lands. Besides offering fascinating glimpses of native Indian lore and language and more details on the rich history of Nootka Sound,

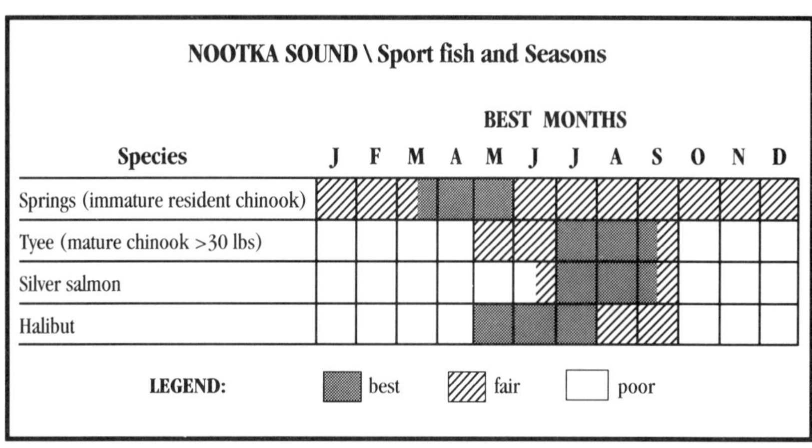

NOOTKA SOUND \ Sport fish and Seasons

Species	J	F	M	A	M	J	J	A	S	O	N	D
	BEST MONTHS											
Springs (immature resident chinook)	fair	fair	fair/best	best	best	fair	fair	fair	fair	fair	fair	fair
Tyee (mature chinook >30 lbs)	poor	poor	poor	poor	fair	fair	best	best	best/fair	poor	poor	poor
Silver salmon	poor	poor	poor	poor	poor	poor/fair	best	best	best/fair	poor	poor	poor
Halibut	poor	poor	poor	poor	best	best	best	fair	fair	poor	poor	poor

LEGEND: best, fair, poor

Nootka Sound

Legend
1. Springs.
2. Coho.
3. Tyee.
4. Bottomfish.
■ Launch Site

No Scale

Chart #3664

Not for navigational purposes.

The Charts and Publications Regulations of the Canada Shipping Act requires vessels operating in Canadian waters to carry the latest, best scale, corrected CHS charts. This document does not meet the requirements of the Act.

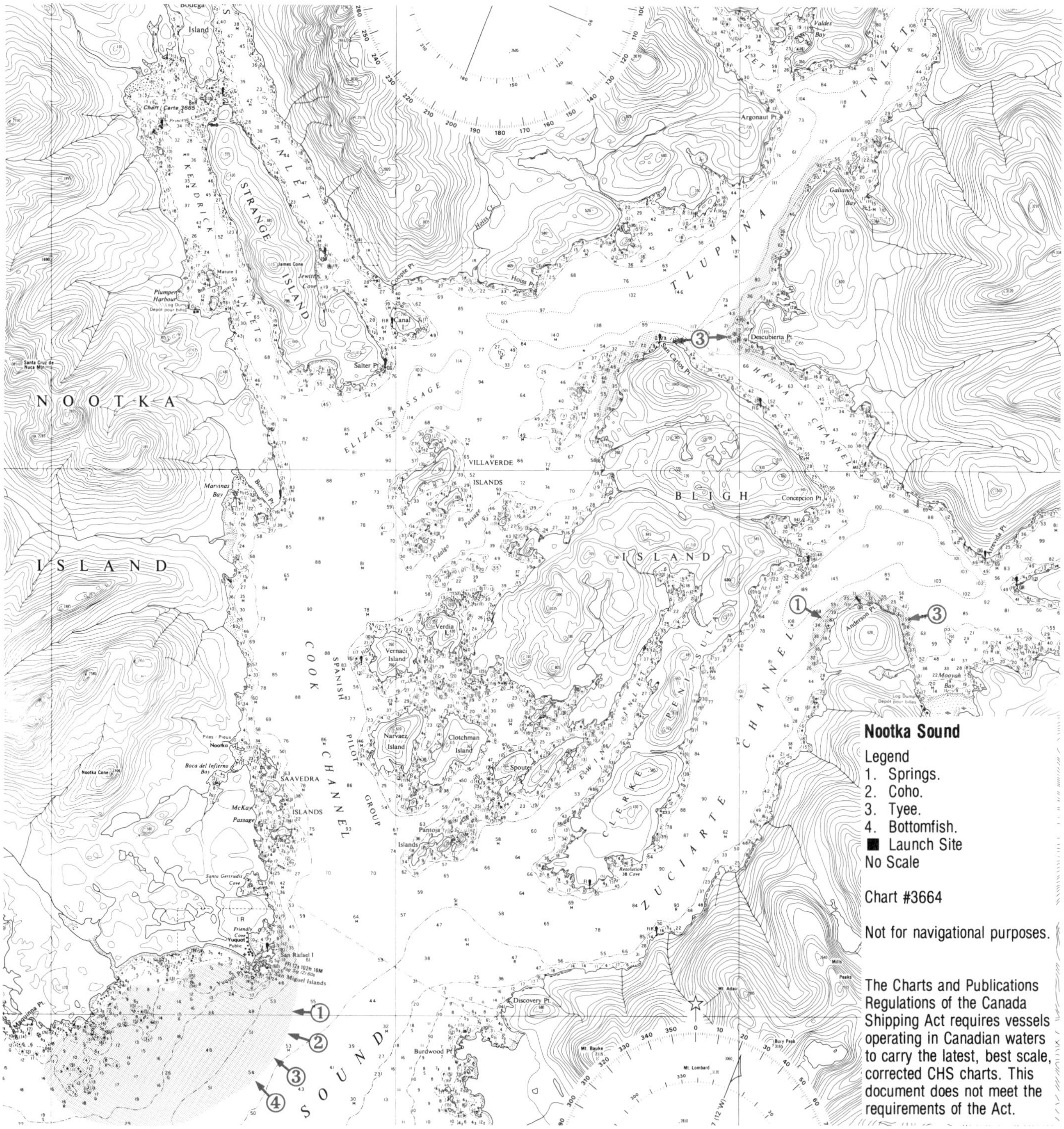

This 30-pound halibut was one of several the author and a partner took on a sunny July morning, though all but this one were released. It hit a Pt. Wilson jig fished with 12-pound line.

Williams knows the waters. Apparently schools of bocaccio rockfish nicknamed "longjaw"—a new one on me but very appropriate to the fish's appearance—move into the sound in very specific spots. I dropped a 1 1/2-ounce metal jig on six-pound line just where Williams said and, sure enough, before it could approach bottom a 3-pound rockfish had picked it up. We caught only a few, but could have caught and released many more.

Weather follows the typical coastal patterns here, with southeast winds prevailing winter and spring. That gives way to an increasingly regular pattern of calm evenings and mornings and afternoon westerlies. Although mornings may be foggy, that seems to be a decidedly less frequent problem than just to the south in Clayoquot and Barkley sounds. Often, thick, dark fog banks will hold just offshore.

Afternoons are typically brisk but sunny and surprisingly warm in the summer—the ideal time to leave the whitecaps to the murres and return to port to find a warm spot on a dock or a patch of grass and catch up on some sleep under the sun, before the evening bite. (A wonderful system, as I recall from fond memories of doing just that.)

Fortunately, the sound is situated in such a way that Pacific swells, at least most of the summer and early fall, don't generally intrude directly into Nootka Sound. A glance at a map shows why: the sound faces southwest, not directly west into incoming swells. So the heavy ocean "lump" tends to remain a bit offshore.

As recommended for any coastal waters, though, private boaters venturing far should have a nautical chart (no. 3664) and working compass as a minimum. A fixed or hand-held VHF radio is also advisable. The nearest Coast Guard facility is the search-and-rescue station in Tofino (725-3231).

Facilities

Area code for all listings is 604; postal code is V0P 1G0.

Prices vary from year to year; call to check. At press time, fly-in package trips to Nootka Fish Camp were running about $500 to $700 (U.S.) for 3 to 5 days and round-trip air fair from Seattle another $250, but of course these are likely to increase so check.

Resorts

Nootka Island Fish Camp, Box 820, Gold River, 283-7474. As described in text of this section, a small resort run by the Cyr family offering 3- to 5-day package fly-in trips.

For More Information

Gold River Tourist Cooperative, P.O. Box 610, Gold River, 283-2202.

Uchuck III, P.O. Box 57, Gold River, 283-2515. (This passenger/freight ship offers regular service from Gold River to points up and down Nootka Sound and Esperanza Inlet.)

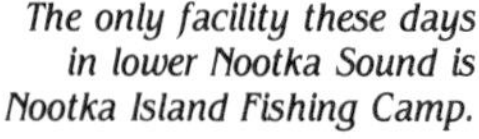

The only facility these days in lower Nootka Sound is Nootka Island Fishing Camp.

List Of Nautical Charts

Washington

Oregon

Northern California

Vancouver Island

(Canada Department of Fisheries and Oceans nautical charts)

List Of Illustrations

Ocean salmon fishing can be a waiting game. On this Coos Bay charter, anglers sit and watch lines down with planers or heavy weights for the telltale bounding of a hooked fish.

INDEX

A

B

C

D

E

F

G

M

N

O

P

Q

R

S

T

U

V

W

Y

Z